History

Option B: the 20th century
for Cambridge IGCSE™ and O Level

COURSEBOOK

Paul Grey, Rosemarie Little, Robin Macpherson & John Etty

CAMBRIDGE
UNIVERSITY PRESS

Shaftesbury Road, Cambridge CB2 8EA, United Kingdom

One Liberty Plaza, 20th Floor, New York, NY 10006, USA

477 Williamstown Road, Port Melbourne, VIC 3207, Australia

314–321, 3rd Floor, Plot 3, Splendor Forum, Jasola District Centre, New Delhi – 110025, India

103 Penang Road, #05–06/07, Visioncrest Commercial, Singapore 238467

Cambridge University Press is part of the University of Cambridge.

It furthers the University's mission by disseminating knowledge in the pursuit of education, learning and research at the highest international levels of excellence.

www.cambridge.org
Information on this title: www.cambridge.org/9781009289597

© Cambridge University Press & Assessment 2023

This publication is in copyright. Subject to statutory exception and to the provisions of relevant collective licensing agreements, no reproduction of any part may take place without the written permission of Cambridge University Press.

First published 2002
Second edition 2017
Third edition 2023

20 19 18 17 16 15 14 13 12 11 10 9 8 7 6 5 4 3

Printed in Poland by Opolgraf

ISBN 978-1-009-28959-7 Coursebook with Digital Access (2 Years)
ISBN 978-1-009-28958-0 Digital Coursebook (2 Years)
ISBN 978-1-009-28962-7 eBook

Additional resources for this publication at www.cambridge.org/9781009289597

Cambridge University Press has no responsibility for the persistence or accuracy of URLs for external or third-party internet websites referred to in this publication, and does not guarantee that any content on such websites is, or will remain, accurate or appropriate. Information regarding prices, travel timetables, and other factual information given in this work is correct at the time of first printing but Cambridge University Press does not guarantee the accuracy of such information thereafter.

All exam-style questions and sample answers have been written by the authors.

Cambridge International copyright material in this publication is reproduced under licence and remains the intellectual property of Cambridge Assessment International Education.

Third party websites and resources referred to in this publication have not been endorsed by Cambridge Assessment International Education.

....

NOTICE TO TEACHERS IN THE UK
It is illegal to reproduce any part of this work in material form (including photocopying and electronic storage) except under the following circumstances:
(i) where you are abiding by a licence granted to your school or institution by the Copyright Licensing Agency;
(ii) where no such licence exists, or where you wish to exceed the terms of a licence, and you have gained the written permission of Cambridge University Press;
(iii) where you are allowed to reproduce without permission under the provisions of Chapter 3 of the Copyright, Designs and Patents Act 1988, which covers, for example, the reproduction of short passages within certain types of educational anthology and reproduction for the purposes of setting examination questions.

....

NOTICE TO TEACHERS
The photocopy masters in this publication may be photocopied or distributed [electronically] free of charge for classroom use within the school or institution that purchased the publication. Worksheets and copies of them remain in the copyright of Cambridge University Press, and such copies may not be distributed or used in any way outside the purchasing institution.

Endorsement statement

Endorsement indicates that a resource has passed Cambridge International's rigorous quality-assurance process and is suitable to support the delivery of a Cambridge International syllabus. However, endorsed resources are not the only suitable materials available to support teaching and learning, and are not essential to be used to achieve the qualification. Resource lists found on the Cambridge International website will include this resource and other endorsed resources.

Any example answers to questions taken from past question papers, practice questions, accompanying marks and mark schemes included in this resource have been written by the authors and are for guidance only. They do not replicate examination papers. In examinations the way marks are awarded may be different. Any references to assessment and/or assessment preparation are the publisher's interpretation of the syllabus requirements. Examiners will not use endorsed resources as a source of material for any assessment set by Cambridge International.

While the publishers have made every attempt to ensure that advice on the qualification and its assessment is accurate, the official syllabus, specimen assessment materials and any associated assessment guidance materials produced by the awarding body are the only authoritative source of information and should always be referred to for definitive guidance. Cambridge International recommends that teachers consider using a range of teaching and learning resources based on their own professional judgement of their students' needs.

Cambridge International has not paid for the production of this resource, nor does Cambridge International receive any royalties from its sale. For more information about the endorsement process, please visit www.cambridgeinternational.org/endorsed-resources.

2022 CAMBRIDGE DEDICATED TEACHER AWARDS

Teachers play an important part in shaping futures. Our Dedicated Teacher Awards recognise the hard work that teachers put in every day.

Thank you to everyone who nominated this year; we have been inspired and moved by all of your stories. Well done to all of our nominees for your dedication to learning and for inspiring the next generation of thinkers, leaders and innovators.

Congratulations to our incredible winners!

WINNER

Regional Winner
Australia, New Zealand & South-East Asia

Mohd Al Khalifa Bin Mohd Affnan
Keningau Vocational College, Malaysia

Regional Winner
Europe

Dr. Mary Shiny Ponparambil Paul
Little Flower English School, Italy

Regional Winner
North & South America

Noemi Falcon
Zora Neale Hurston Elementary School, United States

Regional Winner
Central & Southern Africa

Temitope Adewuyi
Fountain Heights Secondary School, Nigeria

Regional Winner
Middle East & North Africa

Uroosa Imran
Beaconhouse School System KG-1 branch, Pakistan

Regional Winner
East & South Asia

Jeenath Akther
Chittagong Grammar School, Bangladesh

For more information about our dedicated teachers and their stories, go to
dedicatedteacher.cambridge.org

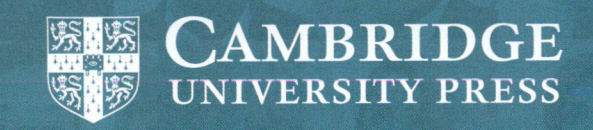

CAMBRIDGE UNIVERSITY PRESS

Brighter Thinking
Better Learning

Building Brighter Futures Together

> Contents

Items with this icon ⬇ are available on Cambridge GO and can be accessed using the scratch code inside the book.

How to use this book	vi
Introduction to command words	viii
How to use this series	ix
Introduction	x

Introductory chapters

Introduction Part 1:	What is the big picture of the 20th century?	1
Introduction Part 2:	The First World War	9

Section A: Core content

1	**Key Question 1:**	Was the Treaty of Versailles fair?	27
2	**Key Question 2:**	To what extent was the League of Nations a success?	67
3	**Key Question 3:**	How far was Hitler's foreign policy to blame for the outbreak of war in Europe in 1939?	103
4	**Key Question 4:**	Who was to blame for the Cold War?	144
5	**Key Question 5:**	How effectively did the United States contain the spread of communism?	184
6	**Key Question 6:**	How secure was the USSR's control over Eastern Europe, 1948–c.1989?	221

Section B: Depth studies

7	Germany, 1918–45	258
8	Russia, 1905–41	301
9	The United States, 1919–41	351
⬇ 10	The First World War, 1914–18	
⬇ 11	The Second World War in Europe and the Asia-Pacific, 1939–c.1945	

Preparing for assessment	397
Glossary	409
Acknowledgements	417
Index	419

> How to use this book

Throughout this book, you will notice lots of different features that will help your learning. These are explained below.

FOCUS POINTS

Focus points set out the important learning points to help you navigate through the coursebook. They can be found at the start of each core content chapter and at various points in the Depth study chapters.

FOCUS TASK

These are activities for you to complete which are linked closely to the focus points you will be learning in each chapter or topic. They are designed to help you practise and apply the skills you are developing as you study History.

KEY SKILLS EXERCISES

These activities will help you to develop important historical skills, such as chronological thinking, research skills, analysis and evaluation.

THINKING SKILLS

After learning about a key historical event or period, thinking skills exercises encourage you to think hard about how you would have felt or acted in a particular situation. This is a reflective activity, and you won't usually need to write down your answers, but you might discuss your thoughts as a class.

SOURCE

Throughout the book you will find a range of primary and secondary sources. You may be asked to analyse, evaluate and compare them in order to help you form conclusions about the events of the past.

THINK LIKE A HISTORIAN

This feature helps you to draw links between the world as we know it now and key historical events. You will be encouraged to apply your knowledge and experience of life today and apply it to past historical situations.

KEY TERMS

Key vocabulary is highlighted in the text when it is first introduced, and definitions are given in boxes near to their first mention in the text. You can also find definitions of these words in the Glossary at the back of the book.

KEY FIGURE

This feature offers a brief profile of a key historical person. You will find out a bit about them, what they contributed to the historical era you are studying and why they remain significant today.

ACTIVITY

Each chapter contains a mixture of group and individual tasks to help you develop your skills and practise applying your knowledge of a topic.

SOURCE ANALYSIS

Evaluating and analysing sources is an important skill you will need to develop to study history. This feature will encourage you to investigate different types of sources in detail and think about the intended message, audience, purpose and reliability.

IMPROVE THIS ANSWER

This is your opportunity to evaluate a sample answer written by the authors and then challenge yourself to write a better one based on the annotated guidance given.

REFLECTION

Reflection questions encourage you to think about the approach that you take to your work, and how you might improve this in the future.

REVISION TIPS

Revision tips are provided throughout the book to help you with your learning. Tips might remind you to avoid common mistakes, advice on essay-writing, evaluation and analysis skills or guidance to help you remember important dates and events.

PROJECT

Towards the end of a chapter, you will have the opportunity to review and apply what you have learnt and put together a project. This might be a poster, a presentation or a performance in pairs or groups where you can demonstrate your understanding.

SUMMARY

This feature contains a series of statements which summarise the key learning points you will have covered in the chapter.

PRACTICE QUESTIONS

At the end of each chapter, you will find a set of more challenging questions. To answer some of these, you may need to apply what you have learned in previous chapters as well as the current chapter you are studying. The answers to these can be found in the Digital version of the Coursebook.

SELF-EVALUATION CHECKLIST

At the end of each chapter, you will find a series of statements outlining the content that you should now understand. You might find it helpful to rate how confident you are for each of these statements when you are revising. You should revisit any topics that you rated 'Needs more work' or 'Almost there'.

You should be able to:	Needs more work	Almost there	Ready to move on

CAMBRIDGE IGCSE™ AND O LEVEL HISTORY OPTION B: COURSEBOOK

> Introduction to command words

The command words and meanings in the following table are taken from the Cambridge IGCSE™ and O Level History syllabuses (0470, 0977, 2147) for examination from 2024. You should always refer to the appropriate syllabus document for the year of your examination to confirm the details and for more information. The syllabus document is available on the Cambridge International website at www.cambridgeinternational.org. The guidance and the suggested approach that appears in this table have been written by the authors.

Questions will often start with one of the command words in the table below. It is important that you understand what each command word is asking you to do.

These are the command words used in the Cambridge IGCSE™ History syllabus (0470), and in the practice questions and many of the activities in this book. In time, and with experience at answering questions, you will find it easy to understand what skills you need to demonstrate in your answers to each question.

Command word	Meaning	Guidance	How to approach these questions
Explain	Set out purposes or reasons / make the relationships between things clear / say why and/or how and support with relevant evidence.	You should give one or more explanations for how or why, and provide evidence to support what you are explaining.	Make sure that in your explanations you present evidence to support your judgment and that you clarify the relationship between the points you are making in your response.
Discuss	Write about issue(s) or topic(s) in depth in a structured way.	You should write in detail, drawing from your background knowledge of the event or situation as well as any sources that accompany the question.	Make sure your answer follows a clear structure and that you make clear how your background knowledge relates to your discussion of any sources.
Describe	State the points of a topic / give characteristics and main features.	You should outline the main points, features or characteristics of the event or topic in the question. This should include either four facts or two facts with supporting evidence.	Make sure the main points are specific to the question you are being asked.

The following guidance and suggested approach have been written by the authors.

The following phrases may also be seen in the assessment for the syllabus:

How far do you agree...? Consider the key message of the source or question and discuss how far you agree or disagree. It is important to consider BOTH sides of the argument and then include a judgment about the extent of your agreement/disagreement using evidence to support your answer.

Write an account... Write a clear and structured account of events, including the causes for those events and the consequences that arose from them. Make sure your answer follows a logical structure and that you explain how the causes are connected to the outcome.

How to use this series

This suite of resources supports learners and teachers following the Cambridge IGCSE™, IGCSE and O Level History syllabuses (0470, 0977, 2147) for examination from 2024. The components in the series are designed to work together and help learners to develop the necessary knowledge and skills for studying History.

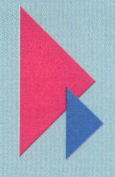

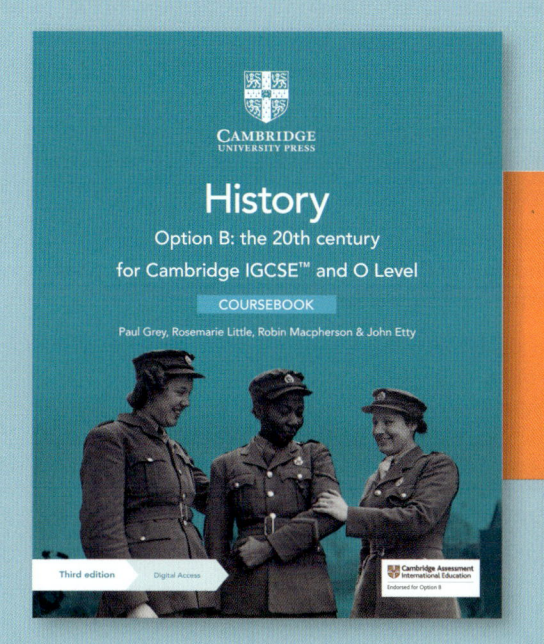

The Coursebook is designed for learners to use in class with guidance from the teacher. It offers coverage of Option B: the 20th century of the Cambridge IGCSE™ and O Level History syllabuses. Each chapter contains in-depth explanations, definitions and a variety of activities and questions to engage learners and help them to develop their historical skills.

The Teacher's Resource is the foundation of this series because it offers inspiring ideas about how to teach this course. It contains teaching notes, how to avoid common misconceptions, suggestions for differentiation, formative assessment and language support, answers and extra materials including worksheets and PowerPoint slides for every chapter.

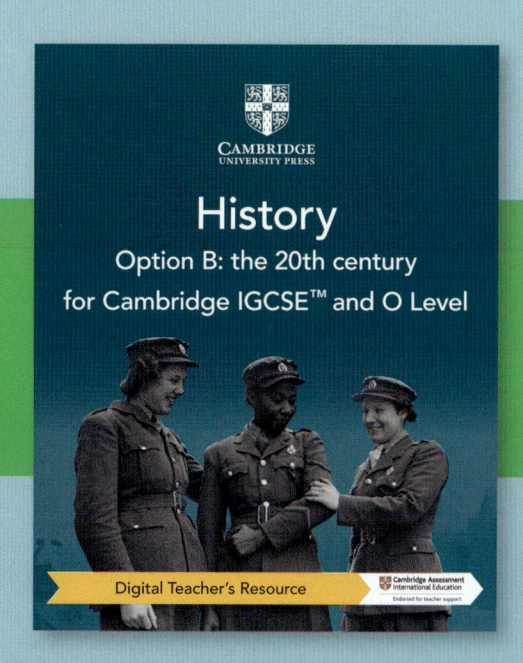

> Introduction

History is the study of events, people, places and ideas in the past. Historians gather evidence, evaluating the quality of it as they do so, and ask questions about causation, consequence, changes and continuities, and similarities and differences. They investigate what happened, tell stories about the past, and explain using different perspectives. This Cambridge IGCSE™ and O Level History resource encourages you to delve beyond simply asking 'what?', 'where?' and 'when?' to explore 'why' and even 'what else might have happened?'.

This book provides you with an overview of some of the major events of the 20th century, and it goes into depth on events in some of the regions and periods where extremely significant changes occurred. The first two chapters in this book are an introduction to the course, providing an overview of the 20th century and the First World War. The rest of the book is divided into two sections: Core content and Depth studies. You won't necessarily be studying all of the content in this book, but your teacher will be able to tell you which Key Questions and Depth studies your school will be covering.

Reading beyond the textbook, especially for the depth studies, will enrich your knowledge and understanding of the topics. Historians always use more than one source of evidence! This book also contains a chapter about preparing for assessment. The chapter explains the structure of the assessment and the skills that are being tested.

Sensitive content warning: please be aware that this book contains some historical images which are sensitive or graphic in nature, so viewer discretion is advised. Further advice for teachers can be found in the Teacher's Resource.

Note on maps: The boundaries and names shown, the designations used and the presentation of material on any maps contained in this resource do not imply official endorsement or acceptance by Cambridge University Press concerning the legal status of any country, territory, or area or any of its authorities, or of the delimitation of its frontiers or boundaries.

> Introduction Part 1:

What is the big picture of the 20th century?

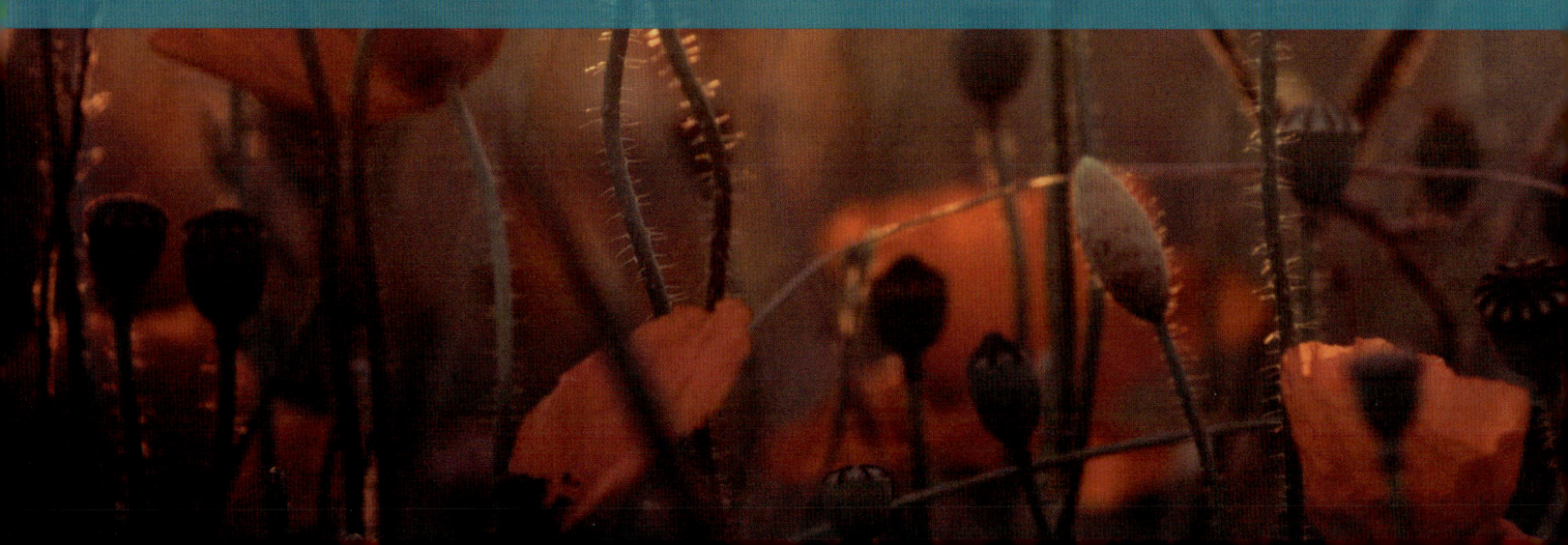

People and history

Harry Patch and Leonid Brezhnev never met. Their lives stretched across much of the 20th century and both became famous during their lifetimes.

Patch was not a king, politician, business leader, film star or great scientist. He was the son of a stonemason who worked as a plumber, an ordinary person who took part in extraordinary events. He was born in the UK in 1898 and lived for 111 years, 1 month, 1 week and 1 day. When he died in 2009, Patch was the last of the soldiers who had fought in the trenches during the First World War (1914–18).

Brezhnev was born in 1906. His home was Russia, which was ruled by a **tsar**. While he was a boy, several members of the royal family were executed during a period of political violence and the survivors fled from the country. The huge country changed from being a **monarchy** to being a **communist state**. Brezhnev, the son of a metal worker, went into politics. By the time of his death in 1982, he was the leader of the country, one of the most powerful in the world during the years of the Cold War (1945–89). In the years after his death, that country changed again. It broke apart into different, separate countries, something he could almost certainly never have expected.

Figure 0.1: Harry Patch, during a ceremony to mark the 90th anniversary of the end of the First World War, 11 November 2008

Figure 0.2: Leonid Breznev, giving a speech to world leaders in 1976

KEY TERMS

tsar: a Russian emperor

monarchy: a country that is ruled by a king, queen, emperor or tsar

communist state: in theory, a society that is based on the principles of equality and common ownership of property

In this book, you will learn about the key developments and events that Leonid Brezhnev and Harry Patch both lived through during the 20th century. Most of the people you meet in this story will be like Brezhnev – decision makers. You will see Brezhnev's name again (in Chapter 6), but not Patch's. As you read, remember that in the background there are always a lot of people who, like Patch, had to live with the consequences of other, more powerful people's decisions.

Introduction Part 1: What is the big picture of the 20th century?

Life and death

Between 1901 and 2000 people lived longer, healthier lives than they ever did before (see Figures 0.3 and 0.4). For all but the richest few in the **Global North** in 1900, life expectancy was low. Since then, improvements in life expectancy have been dramatic all over the world. However, as historians, you should think about what caused these developments and the effects that they had in turn. Improvements were largely the result of the development of cures for common diseases and lower infant mortality rates. Despite this, at the end of the 20th century the gap between the Global North and the **Global South** remained wide.

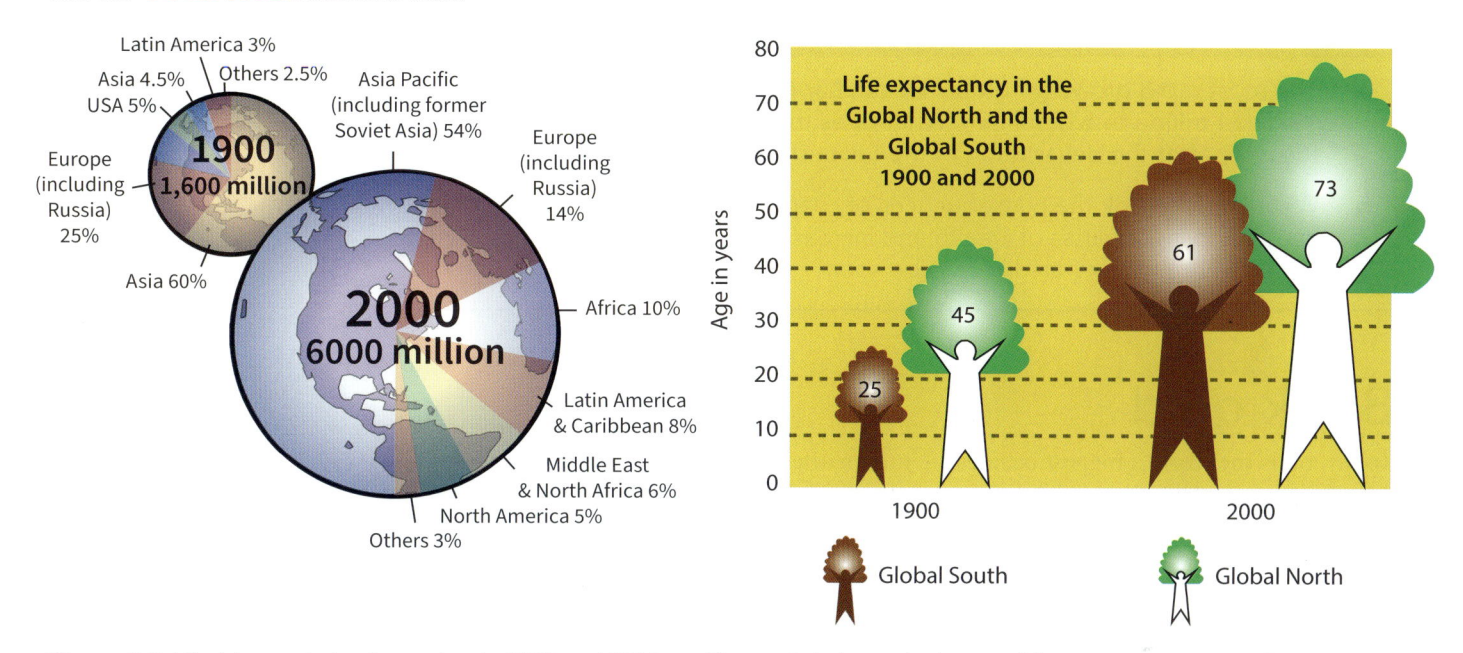

1900 — 1,600 million
- Latin America 3%
- Asia 4.5%
- Others 2.5%
- USA 5%
- Europe (including Russia) 25%
- Asia 60%

2000 — 6000 million
- Asia Pacific (including former Soviet Asia) 54%
- Europe (including Russia) 14%
- Africa 10%
- Latin America & Caribbean 8%
- Middle East & North Africa 6%
- North America 5%
- Others 3%

Figure 0.3: World population by region in 1900 and 2000

Life expectancy in the Global North and the Global South 1900 and 2000:
- 1900: Global South 25, Global North 45
- 2000: Global South 61, Global North 73

Figure 0.4: A graph showing life expectancy across the 20th century

ACTIVITY 0.1

Look at Figures 0.3 and 0.4.

a What would you expect the consequences of the changes in population to have been? Would the increase put pressure on resources and drive an increase in technology?

b How would the political structures, which had been in place since the 18th and 19th centuries, cope? Would more people lead to more wars, more extreme politics and more revolutions? Write down a few predictions.

c When you have worked through the book, come back to this activity and see how many of your predictions were right. You might decide that the important causes of major events are the things going on in the background, not the decisions made by individuals.

KEY TERMS

Global North: includes the wealthiest and most industrialised countries mostly located in the northern hemisphere

Global South: includes the areas of Latin America, Asia, Africa and Oceania; most of them are less economically developed

Wealth

World consumption rose from $1.5 trillion in 1900 to $4 trillion in 1950. It then grew rapidly to $12 trillion in 1975 and $24 trillion in 1998. However, the benefits were not fairly distributed. Poorer countries had a much smaller share than they did in 1950. As we move further into the 21st century, this has been combined with the increasing access to mass media, which has allowed more people to see more of the world. Even where standards of living have risen, such differences in prosperity between different groups are now more visible than ever before.

> **ACTIVITY 0.2**
>
> a   The most rapid growth of global wealth happened between 1950 and 1975 ($4 trillion to $12 trillion). What does this suggest about global recovery after the devastation of the Second World War (1939–45)?
>
> b   What do you think the consequences of changing levels of wealth, continuing inequalities of wealth and increasing media coverage have been or are now – or are likely to be soon?

Black gold

Today, oil is the world's biggest business. Until an alternative source of energy is found in sufficient quantity, the availability and price of oil will have far-reaching effects on the global economy and on people's lives.

The battlefields of the First World War, where Harry Patch fought, established the importance of oil when the internal combustion engine began to be used more than the horse and the coal-powered train. In the first years of the 20th century, the oil business provided the industrialising world with a product called kerosene, which was used in oil lamps. Gasoline (petrol) was then only a by-product and of little value. However, just when the invention of the light bulb seemed to mark the end of the oil lamp and the oil industry, a new era for oil began with the development of the internal combustion engine and petrol-powered cars. The oil industry had a new market.

In the 20th century, oil, together with natural gas, took the place of coal as the most important power source for the industrial world. Oil-powered ships, trucks and tanks, and military planes in the First World War showed that oil was a strategic energy source and critical military asset. The Middle East became a key place of interest for industrial powers like France, Britain, Germany and the USA when oil was discovered in Persia (Iran) in 1908 and in Saudi Arabia in 1938. Since then, powerful countries have tried to protect the oil from rival nations.

Introduction Part 1: What is the big picture of the 20th century?

Germany's desire to have access to oil was a factor in the outbreak of the Second World War. Oil was also vital to all sides throughout the war. After it ended in 1945, there was a contest for control of oil between international companies and countries in the Global South that were struggling to gain independence after decades, even centuries, of European rule. Today, the USA is the world's largest oil producer and its largest consumer. Even so, it has to **import** 37% of its oil supply.

> **KEY TERM**
>
> **import:** to buy or bring in goods from another country

Oil (and natural gas) are the essential ingredients in fertiliser, on which world agriculture depends. Oil makes it possible to transport food to the dependent megacities of the world. Oil provides the plastics and chemicals that are the very foundations of our way of life.

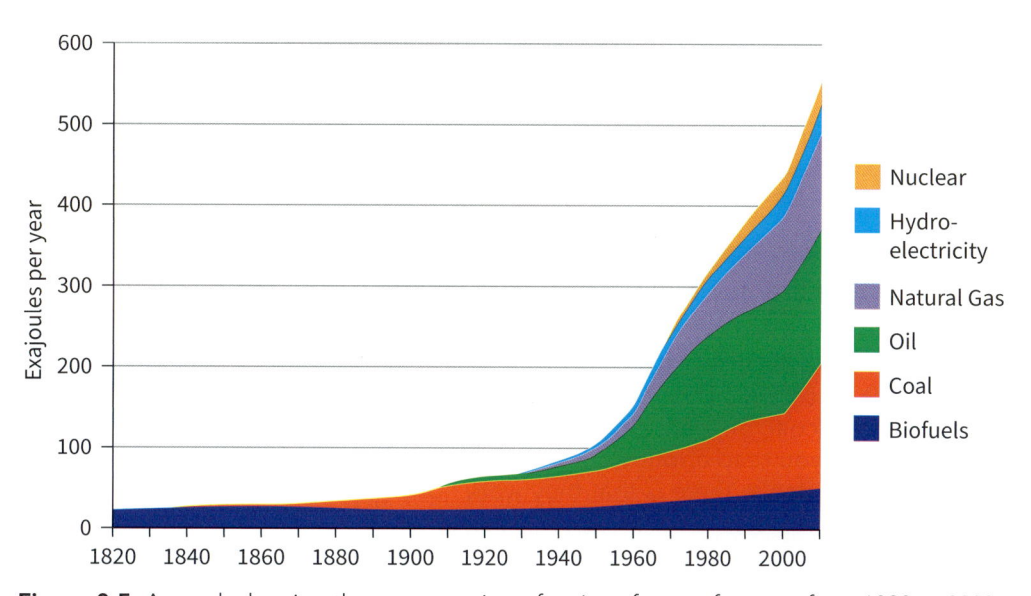

Figure 0.5: A graph showing the consumption of various forms of energy from 1820 to 2000

> **ACTIVITY 0.3**
>
> a   Look at Figure 0.5 and the information on wealth above. What links might there be between energy and global wealth?
>
> b   Why do you think that oil consumption has increased at a faster rate than other forms of energy?
>
> c   Why do you think nuclear energy has such a small portion of world energy consumption?
>
> d   Why did nuclear energy only start to be consumed in the late 1960s and early 1970s?

The impact of industrialisation and growth

People had a far more destructive effect on the global environment in the 20th century than in all the thousands of years that preceded it.

- The release of chlorofluorocarbons (CFCs) into the atmosphere from the 1930s onwards caused holes in the ozone layer that protects the Earth from the Sun's ultraviolet radiation.
- About two-thirds of the effect of global warming comes from the emission of carbon dioxide from the burning of fossil fuels. Over half the total increase in carbon dioxide levels between 1750 and 1990 occurred after 1950.
- About half the world's tropical forests (which help slow climate change by absorbing carbon dioxide) were destroyed after 1950. About 75% of the clearance provided land for agriculture.

> ### ACTIVITY 0.4
>
> How many of the conflicts covered in this book were due to competition for energy or mineral resources? Draw an outline graph. The horizontal axis should be divided into decades from 1900 to 1980. The vertical axis should be divided in equal parts, too: energy sources (coal, oil, etc.) and mineral sources (iron ore, metals, sands and gravels). When you read about wars breaking out or peace treaties being signed, see what evidence there is that they were not just military and political affairs, but economic ones. Mark these on the graph in the appropriate decade.

The fall and rise of empires

In 1901, the peoples of Western Europe and North America seemed to have every reason to greet the 20th century as the start of a new and happier era in the history of humankind. Science and technology were already improving their standard of living and they dominated the world with their trade, their finance and their military power. Most of the continent of Africa, the Indian subcontinent and much of Asia outside China had been either directly colonised by Europeans or deeply influenced by European culture. However, by the end of the century, much of this had changed.

European countries had lost their **empires** and Europe itself had become less important. One of the factors that caused this was the immense cost involved in fighting two world wars. Europe and several other parts of the world saw periods of savage fighting during the 20th century. Europe's economic power meant that relationships between individual European countries affected the rest of the world, either directly or indirectly. The existence of their empires turned European wars into world wars. Because European countries built up their industries, towns and empires at different speeds, the balance of power changed within the continent. Britain was the first to industrialise, and during the 19th century it was the most powerful of the group. By 1900, Germany was also industrialising at a great rate, and its population was growing. Britain started to view Germany not just as a competitor, but as a direct threat.

> **KEY TERM**
>
> **empire:** an area of territory usually comprising more than one country, ruled by a single monarch or government

Introduction Part 1: What is the big picture of the 20th century?

In the period 1900–50, the European countries exhausted themselves in the destruction and huge cost of wars. Many empires started to fall as nationalist movements grew, putting pressure on the colonising country to grant independence. As Europe's power and influence waned, new empire builders such as Japan and the USA came forward. The economic might of the USA was vital in winning the two world wars.

As the European empires broke up in the second half of the century, the world's diplomatic and military picture also changed. There were now new powers to consider. With the decline of old imperial powers such as Germany, Britain and France, the **USSR** (formerly Russia) and the USA became even more important. These 'superpowers' developed huge numbers of new, deadly weapons: atomic bombs. Now, every action by these two countries had consequences for everyone else.

> **KEY TERM**
>
> **USSR:** Union of Soviet Socialist Republics (also known as the Soviet Union), a communist state that spanned parts of Europe and Asia from 1922 to 1991

Figure 0.6: The atomic bomb explodes over the Japanese city of Nagasaki, August 1945

War and peace

We often take for granted the idea that countries and nations are the same thing, and also that there is something natural and permanent about them. For example, during the Second World War, one popular song declared that 'there'll always be an England'. In fact, all countries have come about through a process, and there is nothing inevitable about their make-up or their borders. For example, one key disputed area over many centuries was the border between France and Germany. Although few historians would want to say that this was what the First World War and the Second World War were fought over, the fact is that countless wars had been fought over this area, pushing the border one way and then the other, depending on who won. In addition, countries tend to be collections of groups, not of individuals. In any population there are likely to be different religious groups, different social classes, different languages and dialects, and different genders. Inside each country the most powerful force holding together these diverse groups as they entered the 20th century was that of **nationalism**.

For a century the power of the state increased. Improved communications (telephone, newspapers, radio, railways, roads and finally television) enabled governments to increase their control over the administration, welfare and education of their citizens, and allowed governments to force citizens to serve in their armies. As the power of the state increased, so did the sense of being a 'nation'. This could be seen in military parades and ceremonies, in anthems and flags, and patriotic symbols. Pride in one's country created a sense of common dignity and purpose. As the new century developed, appealing to nationalist feelings was the most powerful way any government could mobilise its citizens in a cause, perhaps, most importantly, in war.

During the 20th century, other political **ideologies** emerged. People could identify with others like them and form groups. The group they chose might indeed be a nation (for example, German nationalism), but it might instead be a social class (for example, the Marxist ideology of the Soviet Union), an ethnicity (decolonisation disputes and movements) or a religious faith. As you will see, any of these forces, and indeed others, might speed up or slow down major political developments and wars.

To people in 1900, the prospect of war was terrible due to all the destructive weapons that technology had made possible. The 19th century had seen a long period of peace in Europe and the idea of a new war using new weapons was viewed with concern. So much so that the leaders of European countries met in The Hague in 1899 to see what could be done to reduce the chances of war occurring. Another conference followed in 1907. A third such conference, scheduled for 1914, never took place. Talking and reaching agreement about weapons were overtaken by the start of the First World War in 1914. There was still the widespread belief that even if war was terrible, it remained the ultimate test of the fitness of a nation to survive.

Another important aspect of wars in the 20th century was not just who won and who lost but what happened next. In Chapters 1 and 2, you will find out about the situation at the end of the First World War. Chapter 3 explores the longer-term consequences of the war. But the aftermath of war is an important element in later chapters as well. You may well conclude that however important winning a war might seem, 'winning the peace' is at least as important – and just as hard.

> ### KEY TERMS
>
> **nationalism:** a great love for and pride in your own country and a desire for its political independence (if it does not already have it) as well as a belief that the interests of that nation and its people should be promoted above all others
>
> **ideology:** a particular set of ideas and beliefs, especially ones on which a political system, party or organisation are based

ACTIVITY 0.5

a What do you think the differences are between 'winning the war' and 'winning the peace'?

b As you study conflicts in this book, make notes on which seems to have been more difficult to achieve.

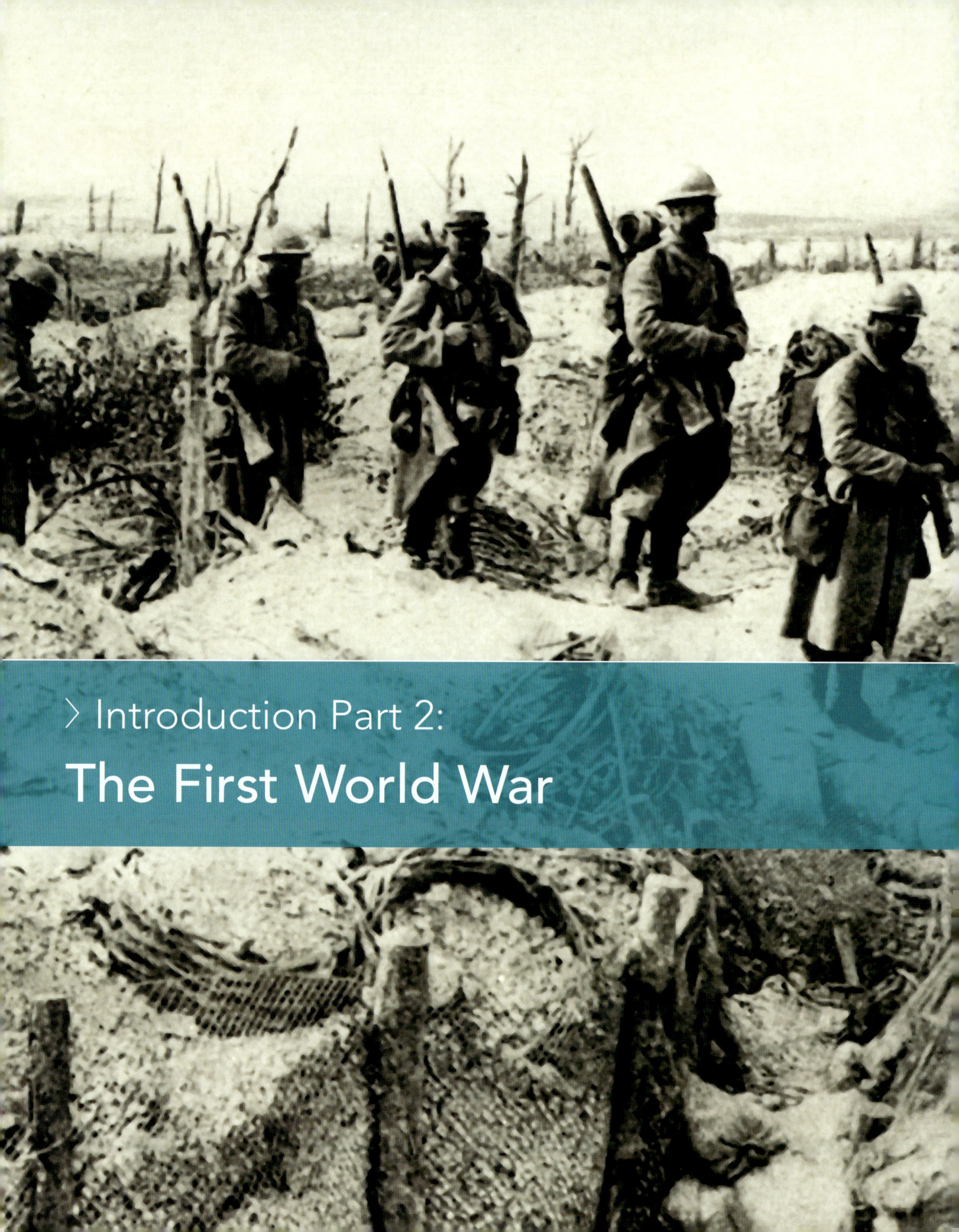

> Introduction Part 2:
The First World War

The Great War

The First World War, or the 'Great War' as it was known at the time, lasted from 1914 to 1918. By the time the **armistice** was signed on 11 November 1918, 10 million people had been killed and 20 million had been wounded. Empires and royal **dynasties** had been destroyed, including the Hohenzollerns in Germany, the Habsburgs in Austria and the Romanovs in Russia.

A young man named Adolf Hitler fought for Germany during the war. He was wounded twice, and was honoured for his bravery. He later recalled the night of 13 October 1918. The British were firing **gas grenades** on the German **trenches** and Hitler could hear them hissing their deadly gas as they landed nearby. By morning, Hitler's eyes were 'red-hot coals', but he groped his way out. He was sent to a hospital further east where, four weeks later, he was told that a revolution in Germany had forced the **kaiser** to **abdicate**. The leaders of the new German **republic** had asked for peace terms. Hitler was devastated, believing this was a betrayal of the German army and the German people. 'It had all been in vain,' he later wrote. 'In vain all the sacrifices and starvation, in vain the hunger and thirst often of months without end [. . .] in vain the death of [. . .] millions [. . .].' Soon after, he decided to become a politician.

Figure 0.7: Adolf Hitler (right) as a soldier in the First World War

How and why did the First World War break out?

Historians still debate the key causes of the First World War and who to blame for the catastrophe. Figure 0.8 is a map showing the system of **alliances** between different countries in 1914. Many historians suggest that this system was to blame for dragging the **Great Powers** into war. Each government felt it had to honour its agreement to support other members of the alliance if they were attacked.

Other historians blame Germany for encouraging Austria-Hungary to declare war on Serbia, despite knowing that the Russian Empire would come to Serbia's aid. In fact, Austria-Hungary and then Russia were the first countries to order the **mobilisation** of their armies. Austria-Hungary did so because the challenge from Serbia already existed. Russia began mobilising because it was a large country and would need time to be fully prepared.

KEY TERMS

armistice: a formal agreement between countries at war to stop fighting for a period of time to allow peace talks to take place

dynasty: a series of rulers who are all from the same family

gas grenade: a small, handheld weapon, designed to be thrown at an enemy, which releases a poisonous gas

trench: a narrow, deep hole or ditch dug into the ground where soldiers hide while attacking an enemy

kaiser: the German name for an emperor or king

abdicate: to give up the throne or the responsibility of leading a country

republic: a country that does not have a king or queen but which is usually governed by a president along with officials elected by the people

alliance: a group of two or more countries that agree to support each other if they are attacked by another country

Great Powers: countries that have considerable military, diplomatic and economic power, and influence

Introduction Part 2: The First World War

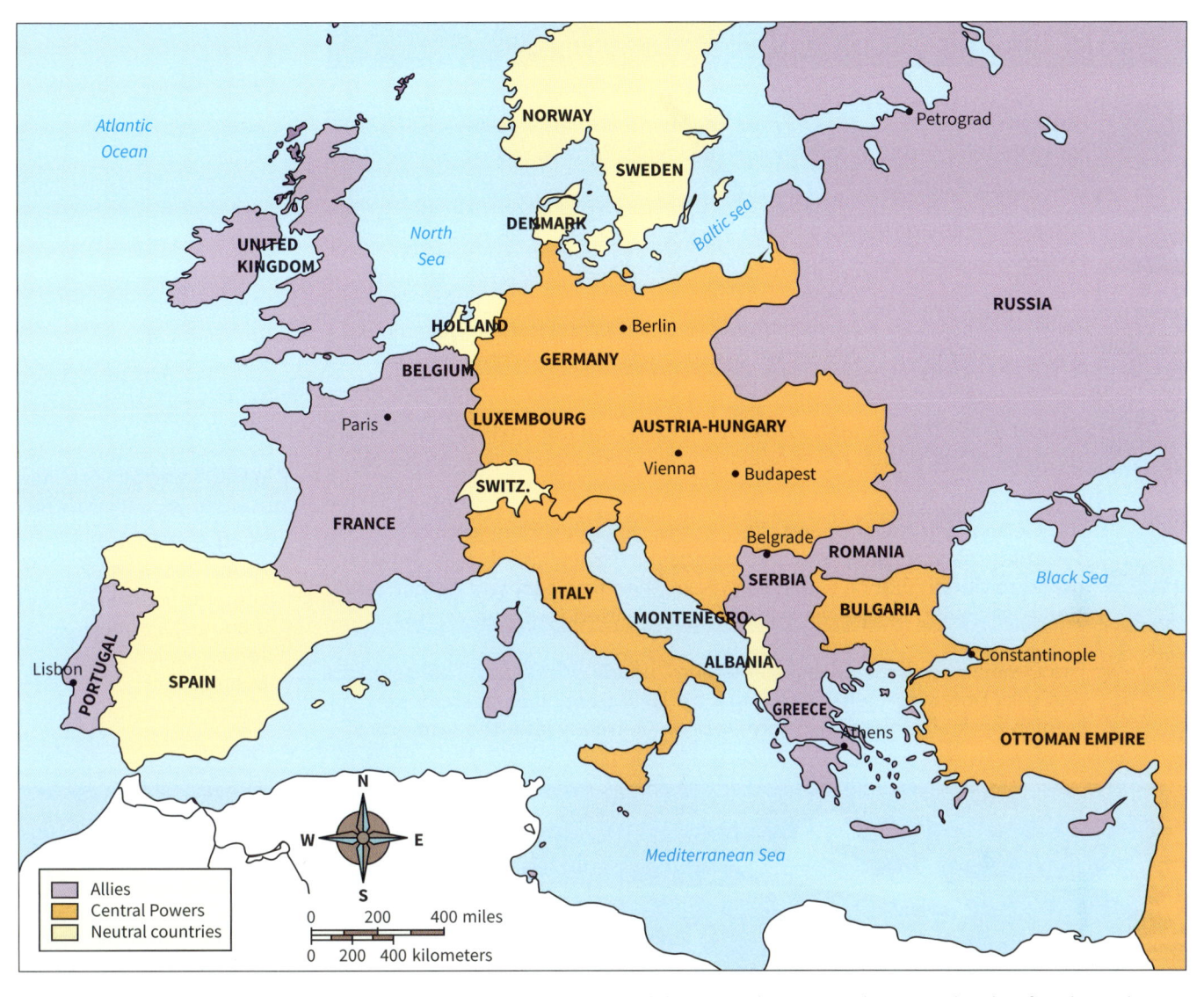

Figure 0.8: A map of Europe in 1914 showing the Allied Powers and the Central Powers – the two sides that fought each other in the First World War

There were other causes too. Several European countries had developed large empires in Africa and Asia, while Germany had not. Nationalism encouraged competition with neighbouring countries. One example of this was the naval arms race between Germany and Britain, which increased tension and distrust. Ordinary citizens, military leaders and politicians expected war at some point. This encouraged the German and Austro-Hungarian governments to take risks in 1914, which increased the threat to the fragile European peace. There had not been a major European war for a hundred years, but in 1914 the tensions developed into live conflict.

KEY TERM

mobilisation: all the actions taken by governments and their military services (army, navy, etc.), including gathering weapons, equipment, and human resources, to prepare for war

EVENTS IN 1914 THAT LED TO THE WAR IN EUROPE

28 Jun — Austro-Hungarian Archduke Franz Ferdinand and his wife are assassinated by a Serbian nationalist, Gavrilo Princip.

28 Jul — The Austrian government blames the Serbs and declares war on Serbia, seeing this as an opportunity to put an end to Serbian nationalism.

30 Jul — Because of an alliance between Russia and Serbia, the Russian government announces a general mobilisation of its army to defend Serbia.

1 Aug — Germany, allied by treaty to Austria-Hungary, regards Russian mobilisation as an act of war against its ally and declares war on Russia.

3 Aug — The German **High Command** triggers the Schlieffen Plan, a strategy designed to avoid war on two fronts against France and Russia. They intend to defeat France within six weeks, then turn east and defeat Russia, believing Russia will not be fully mobilised for some weeks.

4 Aug — The German army marches into Belgium, heading for Paris. The Belgian king asks Britain for help. Standing by a 1839 treaty that guaranteed Belgian neutrality, Britain declares war on Germany later the same day.

> **KEY TERM**
>
> **High Command:** a group of the most senior officers in a country's armed forces, which oversees all military decisions

Figure 0.9: Austrian Archduke Franz Ferdinand and his wife Sophie, duchess of Hohenberg, just a few minutes before they were shot and killed by Gavrilo Princip

Introduction Part 2: The First World War

> **ACTIVITY 0.6**
>
> a   Research the Serbian Gavrilo Princip. What were his motives for killing the Austrian archduke? If Gavrilo Princip had failed in his assassination attempt, do you think the war would still have happened? Discuss your ideas in pairs.
>
> b   Would you say that the 1914 system of alliances caused the war to break out, or did it just mean that once a war had started it was bound to get bigger and bigger? Talk about this in your pairs, giving reasons for your ideas.
>
> c   On a large sheet of paper, sketch a diagram that shows the links between the events, decisions and actions that led to the outbreak of war in 1914. Share your diagrams with another pair and give each other feedback.

Did Europeans welcome war in 1914?

When the conflict began, many people believed it would be over by Christmas. Large crowds welcomed the declarations of war in London, Paris, Berlin and St Petersburg. Across Europe, people welcomed the opportunity to fight. Some did so out of a sense of duty, some out of **patriotism**, and others because they believed it was the only way to make things right. Europeans had been prepared for war by the first mass newspapers and by years of intense nationalism that set country against country in bitter rivalry.

A 'short war'?

Another reason for the public enthusiasm for the war in 1914 was that very few people understood what it was really going to be like. It was impossible at this time for anyone to fully realise how much modern weapons could lengthen a war beyond a quick battle. The belief in a short war was based on previous conflicts. The most recent conflict between major European powers, the Franco-Prussian War of 1870, had only lasted six months.

So, before the outbreak of the First World War in 1914, the Great Powers all believed this would be a brief conflict, whose outcome would be decided by one or two decisive battles. The truth is that this might have happened. If the German army had won the Battle of the Marne, which it came very close to doing, the war would have been more or less over on the Western Front in 1914. It would not have taken long for it to end on the Eastern Front as well.

Despite the widespread acceptance of the war, there were also many people who were anxious about it. British politician Sir Edward Grey famously said: 'The lamps are going out all over Europe, we shall not see them lit again in our lifetime.' Members of **socialist** and **pacifist** organisations in Europe were horrified at the prospect of war. Some groups began planning **strikes** to slow down or stop the mobilisation of troops. However, governments won popular support for the war by claiming it was a defensive action.

> **KEY TERMS**
>
> **patriotism:** loving your own country more than any other, and having a great pride in it
>
> **socialist:** a believer in socialism, a social and economic system in which wealth and the means of producing and distributing goods are shared and cooperatively managed
>
> **pacifist:** someone who believes that war is wrong and that conflicts should be resolved peacefully
>
> **strike:** a sudden military attack

Reactions in Germany

The idea that a war was inevitable was also widespread in Germany. Many German people believed that France and Britain were preventing Germany from expanding its own empire. There were also fears at the prospect of an alliance between France, Britain and Russia. This would mean that Germany was effectively surrounded by enemies. Many members of the German middle classes were enthusiastic about the war as a result of this.

Not all Germans wanted war, though. The working classes organised a series of major demonstrations in German cities. These mobilised hundreds of thousands of workers to oppose Germany going to war. However, the German government did not waver in its pro-war attitude.

Figure 0.10: German crowds in the capital Berlin at the start of war in August 1914; the photos show the German kaiser Wilhelm II and Otto von Bismarck, another German leader

Reactions in France

In France, opinion was mixed. There were pro-war demonstrations in Paris and several other cities and large towns. However, anti-war protests were more common. In rural France, people were hardly aware of the shadow of war. Focused on the harvest, few people in the countryside had time to read newspapers. When news of war reached them, many people were shocked and surprised.

Reactions in Britain

In Britain, too, opinion varied. Patriotic pro-war crowds gathered outside Buckingham Palace in London and many young men signed up to join the army. The British government had presented the conflict as a defensive war, as if they had no choice. Many people believed this. However, others were horrified at the prospect of war, and thousands declared themselves to be **conscientious objectors**. The government made sure that they were not given a platform to broadcast their views.

> **KEY TERM**
>
> **conscientious objector:** someone who refuses to serve in the armed forces for moral or religious reasons

Female pacifists

A few months into the war, it became clear that this would not be the quick victory everyone had expected. Some women took it upon themselves to try to stop it. In April 1915, more than a thousand women from both warring and neutral countries travelled to the Hague in Holland. At this conference, organised by the German feminist and pacifist Anita Augspurg, women argued against the war and discussed how to stop future wars. The conference drew up a list of principles for a future peace settlement, including the right to vote in local and national elections, called 'female suffrage'. The men in power took little notice. Eight months after the start of the war, the conflict was gathering momentum and could not be stopped.

Figure 0.11: American members of the Women's Peace Party arriving at the International Congress of Women, April 1915

Fighting the war

In its scale and the way it was fought, the First World War was different from any conflict that had gone before. The slaughter was more terrible than anyone expected. No one has ever exactly calculated the numbers killed and wounded, but for 4 years about 5000 men died on average every day. The intense warfare was not confined to land. From the start, the struggle at sea was fierce as each side tried to starve the other by **blockade**. Air space became a combat zone for the first time. In 1914, the Great Powers had just over 100 planes each. By the end of the war, air forces had grown enormously. The Royal Air Force had over 20 000 machines in 1918, but this was only one sign of the new importance of technology in war.

> **KEY TERM**
>
> **blockade:** a form of economic warfare where one country attempts to prevent goods being imported to its rival. The Royal Navy's blockade in the First World War also ensured that German ships could not get out of port

Country	Dead	Wounded	Missing	Total
Australia	58 150	152 170	–	210 320
Austria-Hungary	922 000	3 600 000	855 283	5 377 283
Britain	658 700	2 032 150	359 150	3 050 000
Canada	56 500	149 700	–	206 200
Caribbean	1 000	3 000	–	4 000
France	1 359 000	4 200 000	361 650	5 920 650
Germany	1 600 000	4 065 000	103 000	5 768 000
Greece	5 000	21 000	1 000	27 000
India	43 200	65 175	5 875	114 250
Italy	689 000	959 100	–	1 424 660
Japan	300	907	3	1 210
New Zealand	16 130	40 750	–	56 880
Russia	1 700 000	5 000 000	–	6 700 000
South Africa	7 000	12 000	–	19 000
Turkey	250 000	400 000	–	650 000
USA	58 480	189 955	14 290	262 725

Figure 0.12: A table showing some of the countries involved in the First World War with the estimated numbers of their dead, wounded and missing

ACTIVITY 0.7

In your analyses, always remember that numbers do not tell their own story. They need to be put in context, and historians may interpret them differently. The numbers in Figure 0.12 are raw data, which means they are without much context. In pairs, do some research to find out more and answer these questions.

a   Which countries suffered most during the First World War in terms of loss of life and injured survivors? Create a list of five in rank order and identify which alliance system each country belonged to, **Allied Powers** or **Central Powers**.

b   Find out what the total population of some of the different countries was at the time of the First World War. Create a simple table to record your findings.

c   Calculate what percentage of the populations the numbers of dead and wounded add up to. Add a column to your table to record the percentages.

d   Look back at your ranking from part a. How different is your opinion of which countries suffered most now? Discuss your findings in your pairs.

KEY TERMS

Allied Powers: the name given to the alliance of France, Britain and Russia at the start of the First World War. Japan (1914), Italy (1915), and the USA (1917) later joined the Allied Powers

Central Powers: the name given to the German and Austro-Hungarian empires at the beginning of the First World War. The Ottoman Empire joined the Central Powers later in 1914 and the Kingdom of Bulgaria joined in 1915

Technology of death

On 22 April 1915, German forces shocked the Allies along the Western Front by firing more than 150 tonnes of deadly gas at two French divisions at Ypres in Belgium. This was the first major gas attack by the Germans, and it devastated the Allied line. In time, both sides would make use of gas. This new weapon blinded, injured or killed thousands.

Weapons became even deadlier. Soldiers were maimed or killed by gas, flame-throwers and tanks. Machine guns were developed that were capable of firing 600 rounds a minute. New field guns could fire three or four times a minute at a range of 9 kilometres, and heavier guns could hit enemy targets up to 11 kilometres away. The scale of the battlefield, like the scale of dead and wounded, was much bigger than ever before.

Who died?

In all the countries involved, military officers were more likely to be killed than the men they led out of the trenches and into machine-gun fire. About 12% of all British soldiers who took part in the war were killed, but for the upper class, the figure was 19%. Of all those who had graduated from Oxford University in 1913, 31% were killed. The chancellor of Germany and the British prime minister both lost their eldest sons.

Soldiers on both sides were captured and made prisoners of war. In general, because they were treated well, prisoners tended to be better off than those still on the front lines.

Figure 0.13: German prisoners of war captured in France, being taken to a prisoner of war camp, 1915

European war to global war

The First World War may have started as a European war but it spread quickly. However, the two alliance systems in 1914 did not mean that all countries were on one side or the other. Some countries delayed their decisions until the war had started.

Japan joined the Allied Powers once Britain agreed that it could take Germany's territories in the Pacific – the Mariana, Caroline and Marshall Islands. The Ottoman Empire joined the Central Powers because Germany wanted this powerful empire as an ally. The Berlin–Bagdad Railway had been a joint German–Ottoman project and Germany wanted to extend it further to gain easy access to its African colonies and to trade markets in India. To keep the Ottoman Empire from joining the Allied Powers, Germany encouraged Bulgaria to join the Central Powers too.

In 1914, Italy had an existing alliance with Germany and Austria-Hungary. However, Italy refused to join the Central Powers, arguing that the alliance was defensive and that Austria-Hungary had been the aggressor in its attack on Serbia. Italy also wanted the regions of Trentino, Fiume and Dalmatia, which were all part of the Austro-Hungarian Empire. So, in April 1915 it joined the Allied Powers and by the Treaty of London was promised parts of South Tyrol and Dalmatia.

Throughout 1915 and 1916, as **stalemate** developed, the search was on for new allies. Romania joined the Allied Powers in 1916 because the government wanted to take Transylvania – which had a largely Romanian population – from Austria-Hungary. Greece followed in 1917. In Europe only Spain, Switzerland, Holland, Norway and Sweden remained neutral throughout the four-year struggle.

The war was not one struggle between only two sides. You could see it as a collection of different wars, larger and smaller, all being fought at the same time. In the Middle East, the British, French, Russians and Arabs all fought in a war against the Ottoman Empire. In East Asia, Japan took the opportunity to strengthen its position in China. In Africa, fighting broke out between different countries' **colonies**. Finally, in April 1917, the USA became an Associated Power of the Allies. The conflict had truly become a world war.

Stalemate on the battlefield

On the battlefield, the quick war that was expected never happened. Instead, both sides settled down to **siege warfare** on an unprecedented scale. Military operations were dominated by the huge killing power of new weapons. When human targets were not visible, the explosive force of **artillery** could destroy the unseen enemy.

Another reason for the stalemate was that the land in France and Belgium is mostly very flat, and it was easy for machine gunners to fire a stream of bullets across the landscape to deadly effect; the best way to take cover when facing this was to dig a trench. Both sides had machine guns, so both developed trench systems.

> **KEY TERMS**
>
> **stalemate:** a situation in which neither side in a war can take decisive action to break the deadlock
>
> **colony:** a country or region under the political rule of a more powerful country that is often far away
>
> **siege warfare:** a tactic in which an armed force surrounds and blockades a town or fortified area in the hope of capturing it
>
> **artillery:** large guns that fire shells great distances that, upon landing, explode causing death and destruction

Figure 0.14: A photo of part of the Western Front in France in October 1917. Big field guns fired shells scarred the landscape and turned the surface to mud during the winter months, making it impossible to advance any distance against the enemy.

Conscription and conscientious objectors

To begin with, men flocked to join the military as volunteers. Many felt that war would be an adventure. However, by 1916 the high numbers of casualties on the Western Front forced the British government to introduce **conscription**. Now, opposing the war as a conscientious objector was not just an attitude, it was illegal. Men between the ages of 18 and 41 were made to join up, but pacifists in Britain refused to be conscripted. Some did so for religious reasons, believing that killing was a sin whatever the circumstances. Others felt that the government had no right to interfere in people's private lives.

The government knew it could not force everyone to fight. It set up **tribunals** to hear the cases of those who believed they should not have to fight. About 10 000 gained **exemption**. Of these, 7000 worked as **non-combatants**. The remaining 3000 were sent to government labour camps. Being a 'conchie' (conscientious objector) was not an easy option.

> **KEY TERMS**
>
> **conscription:** the act of forcing people by law to join the armed forces
>
> **tribunal:** a special court or group of people chosen to examine a particular type of problem
>
> **exemption:** special permission not to do something
>
> **non-combatant:** someone, especially in the armed forces, who does not fight, such as doctors or religious ministers

> CAMBRIDGE IGCSE™ AND O LEVEL HISTORY OPTION B: COURSEBOOK

SOURCE 0A

We were placed in handcuffs and locked in cells and tied up for two hours in the afternoon. Sometimes we were confined to our cells for three days on a punishment diet – four biscuits a day and water. Some objectors were tortured to make them obey army orders. They tried to break a [soldier's] will by throwing a live bomb at his feet after removing the pin and demanding that he throw it when ordered. [The soldier] stood perfectly still and calm when the bomb was hissing at his feet and the officer who threw it ran for cover.

[The same soldier] was stripped naked, a rope fastened around his abdomen and he was pushed into a filthy pond and held under the water eight or nine times in succession. The pond contained sewage. [The soldier] gave in and obeyed army orders after that.

Source 0A: Howard Marten, a conscientious objector, describes his experiences

SOURCE ANALYSIS 0.1

Read Source 0A.

a   Are you surprised by any of the treatment that was handed out by the British army?

b   Some conscientious objectors were very brave, yet they did not fight for their country. Explain this contradiction.

c   Source 0A was written by a pacifist. What value does it have for a historian investigating attitudes to war in 1916?

d   Thousands of men signed up for the army when conscription started in Britain in 1916. Why do you think so many did so instead of becoming conscientious objectors?

Total war

The First World War was the first total war, which means that whole societies were engaged in warfare. The mills, factories, mines and furnaces of Europe worked as never before. So did those of the USA and Japan. Everywhere, governments attempted to control materials, production and conscript labour. Thousands of women filled the gaps in both industry and farming that men had left when they joined the military (see 'The female workforce' section). Much of this work was vital and dangerous. Both civilians and soldiers were vulnerable in the First World War.

What happened on the Home Front?

On the Home Front, poorer diets and the spread of disease became more common as the war went on and each side tried to starve the other into surrender by naval blockade. Undernourishment and sickness hit children and older people more than the soldiers. For the first time in warfare, death also came by air. German airships called Zeppelins made about 50 bombing raids on Britain during the First World War. These killed 557 and injured another 1358 people. Aeroplanes carried out 27 raids, resulting in 835 deaths.

Introduction Part 2: The First World War

Figure 0.15: A photograph of the morning after a Zeppelin raid on Surrey in the south of England, 19 January 1915

The female workforce

Although women's working roles were historically rather limited, women had been working in factories since the Industrial Revolution. In 1914, many women were also teachers, nurses or governesses looking after the children of those rich enough to pay for their services. At the outbreak of war, with so many men leaving for the battle fronts, there was a huge demand for women to take over some of their jobs, especially in the **munitions** factories. Some women paid with their lives while handling explosives.

> **KEY TERM**
>
> **munitions:** this includes both ammunition such as bullets and shells, as well as weapons like guns, revolvers and rifles

Figure 0.16: Women working in a British munitions factory during the First World War

Propaganda

Governments in many countries used images of children as part of their war **propaganda** on posters and postcards. The images presented the idea of the innocent child or the heroic child. The innocent child represented the reason why the nation was fighting – the future of the country. For example, postcards showed soldiers and patriotic women watering gardens where children were the plants. The innocent child was also often cast as a victim of war, to encourage patriotism and show citizens that it was worth fighting to protect children from the enemy. Children who had been orphaned took part in ceremonies honouring soldiers who had been killed.

Heroic children were shown in pictures as patriots, often in uniform or waving the national flag. Their youthful patriotism was designed to inspire a deeper sense of patriotism and duty in adults. For example, children were given pride of place in marches in parades by the Boy Scouts that encouraged men to enlist.

Figure 0.17: A British poster from 1915 designed to encourage men to join up and fight in the war. How does it communicate its message?

Why did the Allies win and the Central Powers lose?

At the end of 1916, the German High Command concluded that Germany would lose the war because of the impact of the British blockade. It was preventing supplies getting to Germany. Something had to be done quickly. In German cities people were suffering, and food riots and strikes were becoming more frequent. To turn the direction of the war, German submarines had to be used differently. If submarines could operate without restrictions and torpedo both Allied shipping and the shipping of neutral countries, like the USA, then Britain could be starved out of the war. Of course, if German submarines happened to sink any US (neutral) ships then this might bring the USA into the war on the Allied side.

On 31 January 1917, Germany gambled. The US government was informed that the following day unrestricted submarine warfare would begin. The German decision was a direct threat to US interests and the safety of its citizens. Germany believed that if Britain could be defeated by starvation, France would give in before US soldiers could arrive in large numbers from across the Atlantic.

For a while it looked like the gamble might be successful, but on 6 April 1917 the USA declared war on Germany. The Allies could now be sure of eventual victory if they could hold on long enough for US armies to reach France. That year did not go well for the Allies. The new strategy followed by German submarines sank many supply ships. The Battle of Passchendaele cost another 300 000 dead and wounded. Exhausted, the French army was shaken by a series of **mutinies**. Then military and political discipline in the Russian Empire collapsed. A **Bolshevik** government seized power in Russia and sued for peace with the Germans.

> **KEY TERMS**
>
> **propaganda:** information, ideas, opinions or images that show one side of an argument and which are designed to influence public opinion on a matter
>
> **mutiny:** an occasion when a group of people, especially sailors or soldiers, refuses to obey orders or attempts to seize control from senior officers
>
> **Bolshevik:** another word for communist – someone who believes in creating a classless society where everyone is equal

The Treaty of Brest-Litovsk

German hopes were raised by the news that Russia had pulled out of the war on the Eastern Front. The new Russian government led by the Bolshevik leader Lenin wanted an immediate peace treaty with Germany. In March 1918, the Treaty of Brest-Litovsk was signed. You can see from Figure 0.18 that the terms were very harsh on Russia. The country lost 2.6 million square kilometres of territory to Germany. With it went one-third of Russia's population and significant resources such as oil, coal and iron. Finally, the Germany demanded 6 billion German gold marks in **reparations**. Lenin and the Bolsheviks had to sign the treaty because the German and Austrian armies were making further advances into Russian territory. Following the peace in the East, Germany transferred thousands of soldiers to the Western Front. The Allies were afraid that the arrival of these troops would change the military situation there.

> **KEY TERM**
>
> **reparations:** payment for harm, loss or damage caused, often made by countries defeated in war to the countries that won

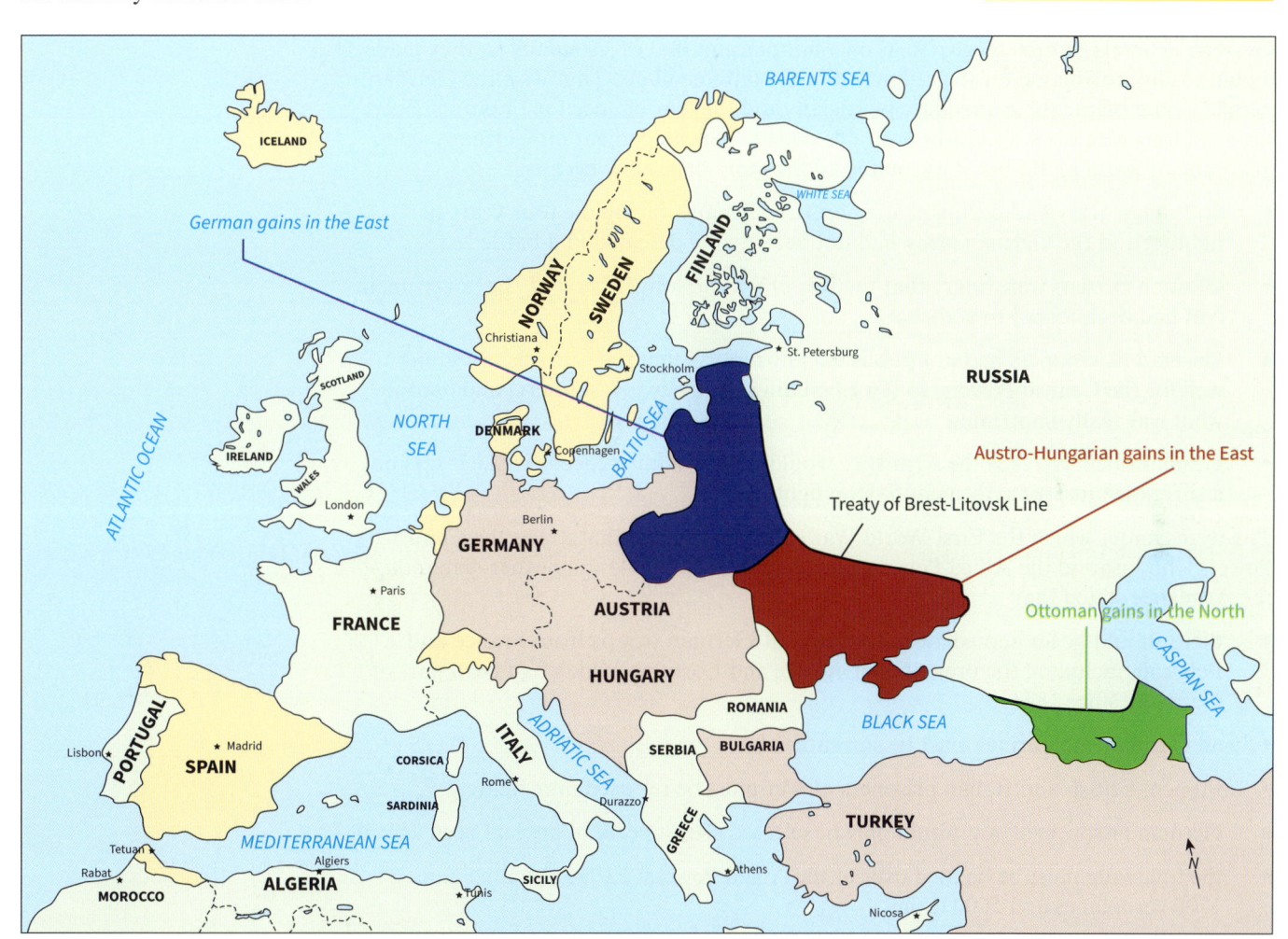

Figure 0.18: A map showing the territory that Russia was forced to give up to the Central Powers in March 1918

What happened to Germany?

However, with US resources crossing the Atlantic to support the Allied Powers, the end for the German war effort was getting closer. A German Spring Offensive in 1918 led to a breakthrough and it looked as though they might seize victory. But the cost of the operation, in deaths, injuries and materials, exhausted the resources of the German army. More and more soldiers **deserted**. Sailors mutinied and refused to go to sea. The British blockade was hurting German civilians as well as soldiers by creating severe shortages of food, fuel and other essentials.

The German High Command knew that defeat was not far away. On 29 September 1918, it told Kaiser Wilhelm II that the military situation was hopeless. Some believed that if he abdicated, the Allies could be persuaded to negotiate a peace settlement. The Kaiser did so on 9 November, and political power fell to German democratic politicians. Two days later, on 11 November, the Armistice was signed.

German generals wanted to save their own honour and that of Germany so they made a plan to shift the blame for the military disaster onto civilians. That way, the German people would blame the democratic politicians and the new chancellor Friedrich Ebert for what they would see as a dishonourable defeat. This judgement on Germany's new government was a myth, but it was made all the more believable because:

- no foreign army had occupied any part of Germany during the four years of fighting and the German army had not been finally defeated in a battle
- German citizens were angry that the Kaiser was no longer head of the government and had been forced to abdicate
- German newspapers had not published any reports that the war was not going well for the Central Powers, so few (including relatively few soldiers) understood what was really happening
- Germans believed that the Armistice would lead to a fair peace because it was not a surrender, just an agreement to stop fighting.

The terms under which the First World War ended emphasise that it was the Central Powers who lost and the Allied Powers who were the victors. Among other demands, the Armistice stated that:

- there should be an immediate withdrawal of German troops from France and Belgium, including the provinces of Alsace and Lorraine, which had been part of Germany since 1871
- all German submarines must be surrendered
- French, British and Italian prisoners of war must be released immediately
- German prisoners of war would only be released after a peace treaty had been agreed
- the following must be handed over to the Allied Powers: 25 000 machine guns, 1700 aeroplanes and 5000 trains.

So, as the guns fell silent on 11 November, what happened next? At 11 a.m. there were a few examples of greetings exchanged between the two sides, but in general, reactions were muted. A British corporal reported: 'The Germans came from their trenches, bowed to us and then went away. That was it.' Unsurprisingly, the dominant feeling was one of silence and emptiness after 52 exhausting months of war. The Allied Powers had won the war, now could they win the peace?

> **KEY TERM**
>
> **desertion:** leaving the armed forces without permission

The situation in France

Of all the countries involved in the fighting on the Western Front, France suffered huge losses and devastation. The data on French casualties sums up the impact of the First World War on this one country:

- Around 1.4 million soldiers were killed, an average of 893 deaths per day.
- More than 4.3 million men were wounded, an average of 2745 per day, including 1.1 million disabled, 300 000 mutilated, 42 000 blinded and 15 000 with broken faces.
- The deaths of soldiers created 700 000 widows and more than 1 million orphans.
- Between 81 000 and 97 000 men from the French colonies were killed, including 26 000 Algerians. These numbers are counted in the 1.4 million French deaths.
- Of France's total population, 1 out of 20 were killed.

As a result of the First World War, France's entire north-east was devastated. More than 1600 kilometres of canals, 7 million acres of land, half the roads in the region, nearly 5000 kilometres of railroads and an estimated 220 000 houses were destroyed. The estimated cost of the destruction was 34 billion francs. This was later revised to 55 billion francs.

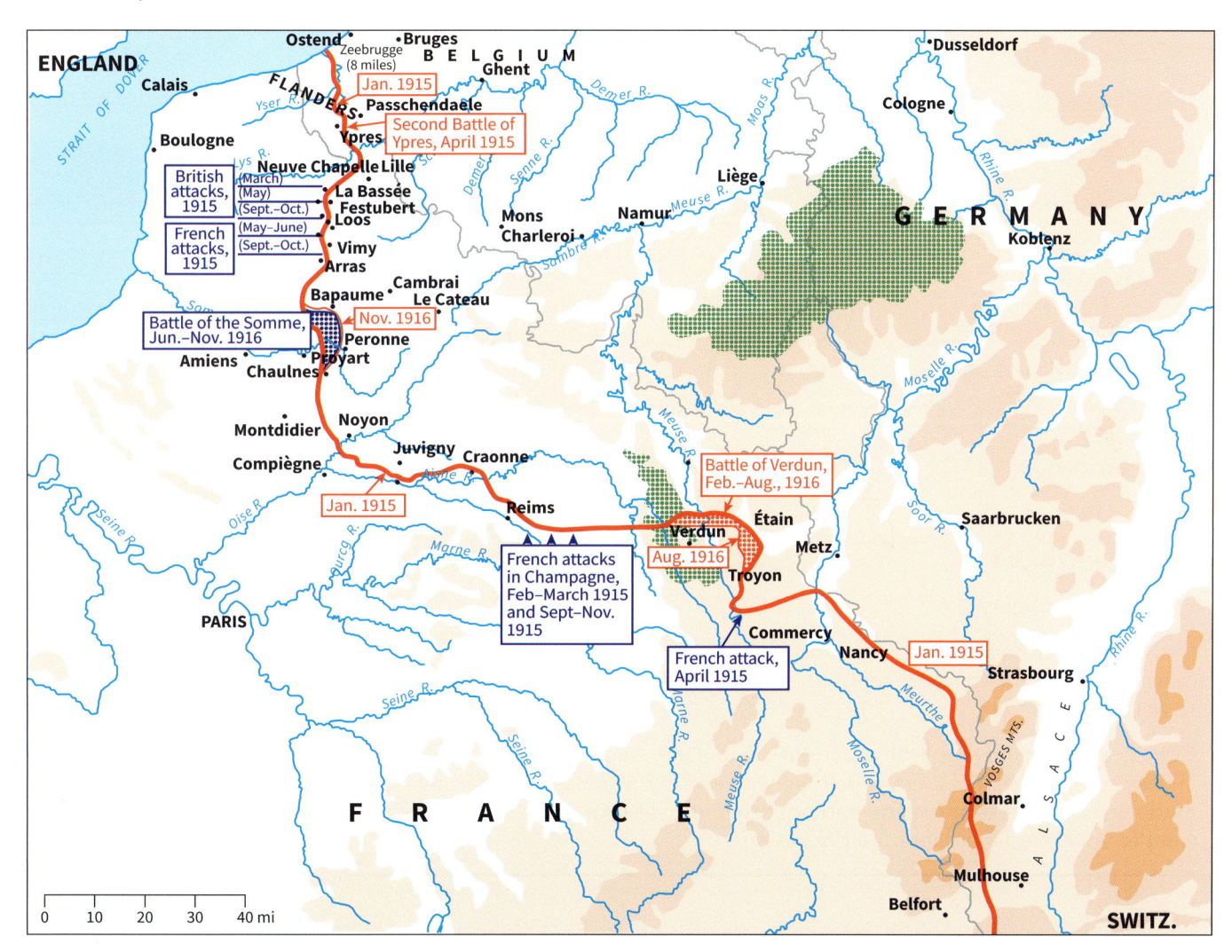

Figure 0.19: A map showing the Western Front 1915–16 (in red), with major offensives (in blue) and the main battlefield locations; note how much of the fighting took place on French soil

ACTIVITY 0.8

a Write a paragraph describing four key tasks that the French government would need to do once the war ended.

b Why was Britain less affected than France by the impact of the First World War? Discuss your ideas in pairs.

c In your pairs, talk about what you think French people would have wanted most from the peace conference when the fighting stopped.

FOCUS TASK 0.1

You are going to create a mind map. Write the following words and phrases on a large sheet of paper, leaving plenty of space between each one.

- assassination
- alliances
- nationalism
- Archduke Franz Ferdinand
- Gavrilo Princip
- European empires
- total war
- women and children
- munition factories
- new war technology
- propaganda
- European to world war
- Kaiser Wilhelm
- death and injury

Draw lines to connect different factors. You can connected each one to as many others as you think are relevant, but every factor should be connected to at least one other.

Compare your mind map with a partner's. Explain to each other why you have chosen to make the links. Do you agree with each other? Has your partner made any connections that you had not thought of? Make any changes you want to your mind map after the discussion.

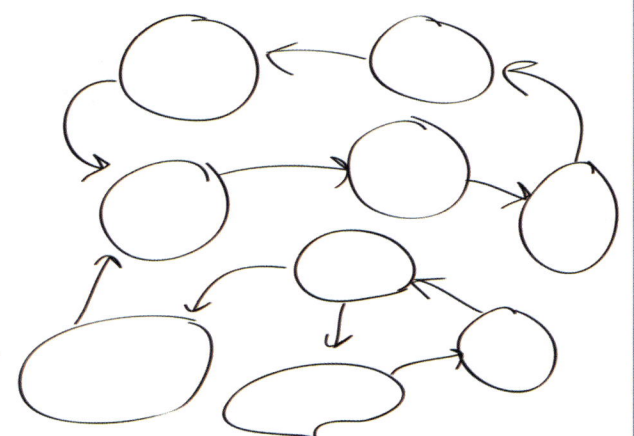

Chapter 1, Key Question 1:
Was the Treaty of Versailles fair?

FOCUS POINTS

This chapter will help you to answer these questions:
- What were the motives and aims of the Big Three at Versailles?
- Why did the victors not get everything they wanted?
- What was the impact of the Treaty on Germany up to the end of 1923?
- Could the Treaty be justified at the time?

1.0 What is this enquiry about?

When wars come to an end, countries send their leaders to discuss and agree **peace treaties**. At the end of the Great War in November 1918, the leaders of the Allied Powers quickly prepared for the peace conference. It was to begin in Paris in January 1919.

The situation that faced the peacemakers in Paris in 1919 was difficult. Even though the Allied Powers had won the war, they were not totally free to dictate the terms of peace. Many different factors shaped the decisions that were made.

The cost of war

The huge loss of life and destruction of property made many countries unwilling to compromise. When the fighting stopped, 30 million were dead, wounded or missing. In France alone, 20 000 industrial sites had been damaged or destroyed, 2.5 million hectares of agricultural land were ruined, nearly 20 000 kilometres of canals and 2000 bridges were destroyed, as well as damage to 60 000 kilometres of road and more than 5000 kilometres of railway lines.

A new world order

The war had created unstable conditions in which revolution and violence could break out at any time, just as they had in Russia in 1917, when the Bolsheviks took power. In July 1918, the Russian tsar and his family had been murdered. The Central Powers collapsed under the pressure of fighting a losing war. By November 1918, the monarchs of Germany, Austria-Hungary and Bulgaria were all in **exile**, afraid of how the people of their countries would accept news of defeat. Millions of soldiers and civilians were dying from the **epidemic** of Spanish flu that was sweeping across Europe.

Wartime treaties

The peacemakers had to take account of the commitments and treaties that had been made, often in secret, to ensure support for the Allied cause. For example, the Treaty of London had brought Italy into the war on the side of the Allied Powers in exchange for promises of territory once the war was over (see Figure 1.1). The Allies now had to honour that agreement.

Public expectation

Public opinion was a worry for the negotiators. The prime ministers and presidents of the world's **democracies** had been elected to serve the people of their countries. Hundreds of journalists were in Paris to cover the peace conference, so the public would know what was going on and would hold their leaders accountable for every decision they made.

KEY TERMS

peace treaties: documents signed by the countries involved in a war, formally ending the conflict and agreeing on the terms of peace. This might include changing national boundaries, the payment of reparations (resources such as money or coal), and actions to avoid a future conflict

exile: when an individual, group or government is forced out of their own country and lives in or operates from a different country

epidemic: an infectious disease that has spread over a wide area, affecting thousands of people

democracy: a country in which people vote freely for the political party they want to govern them

Chapter 1, Key Question 1: Was the Treaty of Versailles fair?

Figure 1.1: A map showing the territory promised to Italy by the Treaty of London, 1915

Map legend:
- Italy pre-1914
- Territory promised under 1915 Treaty of London
- Disputed City of Fiume (ceded to Italy, 1924)

REVISION TIP

It is useful to practise remembering maps. On your own, focus on Figure 1.2 for 30 seconds, then cover it up. On a piece of paper, draw your own version of the map from memory. Colour any parts of the map you cannot remember clearly. Look at Figure 1.2 again for 10 seconds, focusing on the areas you had coloured. Cover the map and repeat the process until the map is complete. Practise this with other maps in this book as you come across them. When you have drawn a draft map, ask a partner to check and correct or change it from their own memory.

REFLECTION

How successful was the Revision tip? How would you change the instructions to help you learn more? Share your experience with a partner. Do you end up with a more accurate map if you work together?

Figure 1.2: A map showing the four European empires in 1914 that had broken up by the end of the war in 1918: the German Empire, the Austro-Hungarian Empire, the Russian Empire and the Ottoman (Turkish) Empire

Chapter 1, Key Question 1: Was the Treaty of Versailles fair?

1.1 What were the motives and aims of the Big Three at Versailles?

'You hold in your hands the future of the world.' With these words, the president of France, Raymond Poincaré, opened the Paris Peace Conference on 18 January 1919.

Who attended the peace conference?

Leaders and their **delegations** from 32 countries came to France to decide what should happen now that the war was over. Together, they represented three-quarters of the world's population, all with different aims and viewpoints.

Germany and Russia were noticeably absent from the peace conference. Russia was not invited because the Bolshevik government had stopped fighting the war in December 1917, having made public several secret Allied agreements and having refused to pay back large loans from the Allies. Germany was widely seen as having caused the conflict, with no right to define the peace terms, so Germany had no representatives in Paris either.

Of the countries on the winning side, the leaders of the USA, France and Britain were the most important decision-makers at the peace conference. They were:

- Woodrow Wilson, president of the USA
- Georges Clemenceau, prime minister of France
- David Lloyd George, prime minister of Britain.

Known as the 'Big Three' (see Figure 1.3), each of these leaders arrived with different motives and aims. They were also under different types of pressure to achieve certain outcomes.

> **KEY TERM**
>
> **delegation:** a group of people who officially represent a country or organisation at meetings or conferences

Figure 1.3: A photograph of the 'Big Three' in Paris, 1919: Clemenceau (left), Wilson (middle) and Lloyd George (right)

> CAMBRIDGE IGCSE™ AND O LEVEL HISTORY OPTION B: COURSEBOOK

> KEY FIGURE
>
> **Woodrow Wilson (1856–1934)**
>
> Wilson served two terms as US president, from 1913 to 1921. He had a strong moral sense and believed in doing what he thought was right. He brought the USA into the war in 1917, believing this was a campaign against Germany for justice and a new, more civilised world. Wilson was also a reformer with a reputation for being stubborn. As a **Democrat**, he refused to include any leading **Republicans** from the US Congress in the Paris delegation, which in the end meant he had less authority with the legislative branch of government back home.

What did Woodrow Wilson want from the peace treaties?

The USA declared war on Germany in April 1917. Immediately, Wilson announced that he was joining France, Britain and Russia not as one of the Allied Powers but as an 'Associated Power', stressing that that the USA's motives were different from those of the European countries it was joining. He believed that Britain, France, Russia and Italy were only interested in securing their empires and increasing their influence in Europe. In contrast, Wilson claimed that the USA was fighting for world peace, wanting 'no conquest, no dominion. We seek no indemnities for ourselves, no material compensation for the sacrifices we shall freely make.'

The US president arrived in Paris believing that Germany had to accept some punishment, because it was the German decision to permit unrestricted submarine warfare that had brought the USA into the war. However, Wilson was an idealist and believed it was possible to achieve long-lasting peace if all nations worked together to remove the causes of war.

The Fourteen Points

Wilson had published his aims for the post-war world as early as January 1918. These became known as the 'Fourteen Points'. In summary, they were as follows.

1. There should be no more secret treaties. These had become problematic when the Bolsheviks seized power in Russia in 1917 and published the previous regime's secret treaties.
2. There should be no restrictions on ships sailing the seas during peace or wartime.
3. Barriers to free trade (such as **quotas** and **tariffs**) should be removed as they reflected and created an economic power struggle between countries.
4. **Armaments** must be reduced in all countries to the level needed only for defence, so that countries would not have enough military force for aggression.
5. Disputes about colonies must be decided by taking account of the interests of the people in the colony and the governing country.
6. German troops must leave Russia.
7. Belgium's independence must be restored from German occupation.
8. The provinces of Alsace and Lorraine, which had been seized by Germany, must be returned to France.

> KEY TERMS
>
> **Democrat and Republican:** members of the two main opposing political parties in the USA
>
> **quota:** a strict quantity of goods that may be exported or imported under government control
>
> **tariff:** a tax imposed by a government that has to be paid on imports or exports
>
> **armaments:** military equipment and weapons

9   The borders around Italy must be adjusted to match the nationality of the people who lived in them.
10 The different ethnic groups living in the Austro-Hungarian Empire must be granted **self-determination**.
11 Romania, Serbia and Montenegro should be created, and Serbia should have free and secure access to the sea.
12 The Turkish parts of the Ottoman Empire should form one country. Other nationalities within the empire should be allowed to form their own countries.
13 An independent Poland should be created with access to the sea.
14 A League of Nations should be formed that would guarantee the independence of all member countries and secure borders.

These points were the basis of the Armistice signed on 11 November 1918. They gave the people of Germany the impression that the USA might stand between them and the **punitive** demands of France and Britain in the final peace treaty. In fact, Wilson's peace proposals were very popular with the European public at large, and he was seen as something of a saviour.

However, Wilson's authority had been undermined by the November 1918 midterm elections in the USA, when the Republicans won control of both Houses of Congress. Congress would have to **ratify** any peace treaty. This put Wilson in a difficult situation because US politicians, and the public, would consider his Fourteen Point plan for a peaceful world to be too idealistic (aiming for future change that is too ambitious and not rooted in reality). Knowing this also gave Clemenceau and Lloyd George an advantage in negotiations.

> **KEY TERMS**
>
> **self-determination:** the right of an ethnic group to their own independent country instead of living in a country dominated by a different ethnic group
>
> **punitive:** intended as a punishment
>
> **ratify:** to officially vote on and accept a treaty

FOCUS TASK 1.1

Create a table like the one below. Fill in the row for Woodrow Wilson based on what you have learnt so far. Update the table with information about Wilson, Clemenceau and Lloyd George as you work through the rest of this chapter.

Leader	Motives	Aims
Wilson		
Clemenceau		
Lloyd George		

ACTIVITY 1.1

Study Wilson's Fourteen Points. In pairs, discuss the following questions. Afterwards join up with another pair and compare your answers and reasons.

a   Which of the points do you think were aimed at preventing major wars involving the Great Powers (those that had significant global influence, resources and military power)?

b   Which points do you think were aimed at preventing local wars involving smaller powers (those that had limited political influence, few resources and little military strength)?

Self-determination and the League of Nations

Wilson felt that the principle of national self-determination was vital to the long-term stability of Europe. The announcement of this principle in January 1918, and its emphasis in points 9, 10, 12 and 13 of Wilson's ideals, meant that many different ethnic groups wanted to be represented at the Paris conference.

The establishment of a League of Nations was the last of Wilson's Fourteen Points, but for him it was the most important. He wanted to create an organisation that included every country in the world, large and small. It would use negotiation to prevent disputes between countries developing into wars, ensuring global peace in the future.

> **ACTIVITY 1.2**
>
> a   In small groups, discuss which of the Fourteen Points might have been welcomed by people living in Britain, France and the USA at the end of the First World War. Give reasons for your choices.
>
> b   Do any of the Fourteen Points contradict one another? In what ways? In your groups, draw a spider diagram or other graphic organiser to highlight any connections and contradictions.

What did Georges Clemenceau want from the peace treaties?

Clemenceau took a tough approach towards Germany in Paris because he remembered Germany's invasions of France in 1870 and 1914. In 1870, France had lost the areas of Alsace and Lorraine to Germany. Regaining them was important for restoring national pride.

Clemenceau's key aim was to ensure that Germany would never again threaten France. The only way to do this was to weaken Germany so much that it was no longer a threat. In addition, Clemenceau wanted Germany to pay for the reconstruction that Europe, and France in particular, needed because of the war. Reparations must be paid – and on time. With strong support from the French public, Clemenceau demanded:

- the **disarmament** of Germany's army, navy and air force
- high reparations to cover the cost of the widespread damage to France
- the return of the provinces of Alsace and Lorraine
- the German region of Saarland to be given to France
- the Rhineland (an area around the river Rhine, bordering France) to be made an independent state so that there was a security 'buffer', or safe area, between the two countries
- some of Germany's overseas colonies to be given to France.

KEY FIGURE

Georges Clemenceau (1841–1929)

Before entering politics Clemenceau was a journalist, nicknamed 'The Tiger' for constantly criticising those in government (see Source 1A). In 1917, he became prime minister of France and was preoccupied with French defence and security. He held France together until the end of the war, for which he earned the nickname 'Father of Victory'.

KEY TERM

disarmament: the process of destroying some or all weapons and armed forces that could be used in fighting a war

Chapter 1, Key Question 1: Was the Treaty of Versailles fair?

SOURCES 1A & 1B

Source 1A: A cartoon from a French newspaper, published in 1919

Source 1B: A cartoon of Georges Clemenceau published in a German newspaper in 1919. Clemenceau is shown as a vampire and Germany is the female figure in the bed.

SOURCE ANALYSIS 1.1

Study Sources 1A and 1B.

a   Explain how these sources show Clemenceau's aims at the Paris Peace Conference.

b   What tells you that Source 1A was published in a French newspaper and Source 1B was drawn by a German artist?

c   Which of the sources is more critical of Clemenceau's approach to making peace with Germany?

d   Why do you think Wilson and Lloyd George do not appear in either of these sources?

> KEY FIGURE

David Lloyd George (1863–1945)

British politician David Lloyd George loved the excitement of politics. During the early years of the war he was a very successful government minister with responsibility for munitions and the war. He became prime minister at the end of 1916 and was popularly known as the man who led Britain to victory in 1918. Optimistic by nature, Lloyd George believed that even the most difficult problems had solutions. He was a pragmatist (someone who aims to make changes that are practicable and not overambitious) – not an idealist like Wilson.

What did David Lloyd George want from the peace treaties?

In the general election of December 1918, the British public returned the wartime government to power. Lloyd George went to Paris knowing that the British people were in no mood for a moderate peace. They wanted to prevent such a war happening again.

Making Germany pay

In both Britain and France, most ordinary people blamed Germany for the war. They wanted Germany to be punished for this. Newspapers called for the kaiser to be tried in court for his crimes. 'Squeeze the German lemon until the pips squeak,' wrote the First Lord of the Admiralty, Eric Geddes. Such emotional responses to the bloody four-year war were understandable. Many of those who had died were from Britain and the British Empire. In addition, the war had cost the Allied Powers the huge sum of $147 billion. The economies of European countries had switched from making goods to making military materials. This meant they lost valuable overseas markets to their non-European competitors, such as Japan and the USA.

During the election campaign of 1918, Lloyd George had promised that he would ensure that Germany paid the full cost of the war. However, when he got to Paris in January 1919, he aimed to be more moderate. He was motivated not by revenge but by national self-interest, wanting to ensure the growth and success of the British Empire. His key aims were to:

- re-establish a balance of power in Europe so that no single power could dominate the continent
- return to the trading patterns with Europe and the Empire that had made Britain so wealthy before the First World War
- preserve British **naval supremacy** to guard the British Empire and its shipping lanes.

Ensuring economic recovery

All these aims were focused on ensuring economic recovery for both Britain and Europe. To guarantee this, Germany must be allowed to recover some of its pre-war economic strength. If the reparations bill was too high, it would take money out of the German economy that would be needed for rebuilding and recovery.

The First World War had transformed Britain's economic position. It had lost its place as the world's financial centre to the USA. It had huge debts from fighting the war,

> KEY TERM
>
> **naval supremacy:** having a greater number of battleships than other countries

most of them owed to the USA. Despite this, Lloyd George went to Paris with some things in his favour. The German fleet was in British hands, some of the German colonies had been seized and Germany, Britain's biggest trade competitor, had been held back.

> ### SOURCE 1C
>
> *Our terms may be severe, they may be stern and even ruthless, but at the same time they can be so just that [Germany] will feel in its heart that it has no right to complain. But injustice, arrogance displayed [by the Allied Powers] will never be forgotten.*
>
> *For these reasons I am strongly [against] transferring more Germans from German rule to the rule of some other nation than can possibly be helped.*
>
> **Source 1C:** An extract from a memorandum written by David Lloyd George during the peace-making process, 25 March 1919

SOURCE ANALYSIS 1.2

Read Source 1C.

a   Does this source suggest that Lloyd George shared the opinion of the British public?

b   Which parts of the source do you think Wilson and Clemenceau would agree with?

c   This source is a note written by Lloyd George and his advisers, not a public document. Does this limit its value when considering Lloyd George's real aims at the Paris Peace Conference? Give reasons for your answer.

d   If Lloyd George wanted to make this memorandum public, what changes do you think he would make to it?

FOCUS TASK 1.2

a   Write a paragraph in response to each of these questions:
   - Why was Lloyd George in such a difficult position in January 1919, even after winning the election in December 1918?
   - Why were Wilson's ideals so different from the aims of Clemenceau and Lloyd George?

   Swap your paragraphs with a partner. Compare your ideas and give each other feedback.

b   Which of the Fourteen Points would Clemenceau and Lloyd George have agreed with? Which would they have disagreed with and why? Discuss your ideas, giving reasons.

c   Work in small groups. Look at your completed table from Focus task 1.1. Which of the Big Three's aims do you think the German public would have thought would be most favourable towards them? Explain why.

Key points

The Paris Peace Conference

- The peace talks involved 32 countries but excluded Russia and Germany.
- The main leaders were Wilson (USA), Clemenceau (France) and Lloyd George (Britain), known as the 'Big Three'.
- At the start of the Conference there were no agreed goals, although Wilson had made his aims clear in the Fourteen Points.
- One of Wilson's key aims was to create a League of Nations to keep peace in the future.
- Clemenceau wanted security and a weakened Germany to stop any future invasion.
- Lloyd George wanted to keep Britain's empire, maintain its naval strength and avoid any expensive commitments on the continent of Europe. He recognised that a weakened Germany would never allow Britain to return to pre-war trading patterns.

1.2 Why did the victors not get everything they wanted?

From the start, the number of countries that attended and the complex issues to be addressed at the Paris Peace Conference caused problems. There were too many delegations for everyone to take part in the discussions, even though President Wilson was keen for all countries to be involved. The six **plenary sessions** that did take place focused on the creation of the new international organisation, the League of Nations. Other decisions were made by Britain, France, Italy, Japan and the USA – the Great Powers that won the war.

How were decisions made?

The Great Powers set up the Council of Four (Britain, France, Italy and the USA) (see Figure 1.4). Japan decided to focus on issues concerning Asia rather than getting involved in discussions relating to Europe. To begin with, the Council of Four was not very efficient, and meetings took place without any agenda or record-keeping. However, the system became more organised. Some of the detailed work was handed to special **commissions**, which countries other than the Great Powers were involved in.

None of the Great Powers was entirely satisfied with the terms of the treaty that was presented to Germany. For a start, they disagreed on what should happen to two important regions of Germany.

> ### KEY TERMS
>
> **plenary session:** a part of a meeting or conference that everyone attends
>
> **commission:** a committee made up of officials who investigate an issue or dispute and then produce a report that reaches conclusions and makes recommendations

> ### THINK LIKE A HISTORIAN
>
> All Big Three leaders went to Paris with advisers, experts and secretaries. Lloyd George brought 1200 people from across Britain and its empire. If you were helping the British prime minister in the selection process, what skills and knowledge would you want successful applicants to have to be part of the Paris delegation? On your own, draft a list with two columns: 'Essential characteristics' and 'Desirable characteristics.
>
> Compare your list with a partner and make any changes needed to improve your list.
>
> In your pairs, identify three key differences between the list for the British delegation and the skills and knowledge that might be needed for the French and US delegations.

Chapter 1, Key Question 1: Was the Treaty of Versailles fair?

Figure 1.4: The Council of Four (seated): Italian prime minister Vittorio Orlando, along with Lloyd George, Clemenceau and Wilson; the men standing are secretaries to the leaders

The Rhineland

The future of the Rhineland was a cause of much argument amongst the Big Three. The French wanted to control this region because it would give France a natural border to protect against future invasion. However, the population of the Rhineland was German, so according to Wilson's principle of self-determination, it could not be handed over to France. The British government was also against the move, believing that controlling the Rhineland would give France too much power in Europe.

In the end, the Rhineland remained part of Germany but was **demilitarised**. Fortifications were destroyed and no German soldiers could be stationed there. Britain and the USA guaranteed that if Germany attacked France in the future, both countries would come to France's aid. That seemed to settle French nerves in the short term, but when the US Congress refused to ratify the Treaty of Versailles, the USA's guarantee to defend France ended.

KEY TERMS

demilitarised: describing an area of land in which no soldiers and no weapons are permitted

The Saarland

Clemenceau claimed the coal-rich Saarland because the French wanted compensation for the mines they said had been deliberately flooded by the Germans as they retreated in the last year of the war. Lloyd George supported Clemenceau in this, but Wilson was strongly opposed to it. He pointed out that the Saar region was entirely German, so it could not be handed to France. As a compromise, Germany was forced to give the League of Nations **sovereignty** of the area and ownership of its mines for 15 years. After that time, the people of the Saarland would be allowed to vote on the future of the region. In 1935, a **plebiscite** was held and the population decided to return to Germany.

What were the key terms of the treaty?

After months of negotiation, bargaining and compromise, the final treaty was signed in the Hall of Mirrors at the Palace of Versailles on 28 June 1919. It was a **diktat** – a treaty over which the defeated country had no control or input.

'War Guilt'

Article 231 of the Treaty of Versailles said that Germany and the other Central Powers had to accept full responsibility for causing the war. This became known as the 'War Guilt' clause, and for many Germans it was the worst part of the treaty. From this important clause, all the punitive clauses followed, including reparations.

Reparations

Germany would have to pay money and goods as reparations to France Britain, and the other Allied Powers. The amount was not agreed at the Paris Peace Conference. Instead, a Reparations Commission was set up to work out an appropriate figure. In May 1921, the total was set at $33 billion. Reparations were paid in money and resources, including railway equipment, livestock, coal, timber, bricks, glass, steel, lime and cement. Germany had to borrow money to pay the reparations, and the final loan was not paid off until October 2010.

Reduction of military power

To ensure it could not cause another war, the Treaty of Versailles stated that Germany:

- had to limit its military forces to 100 000 soldiers; restrictions were also placed on the numbers of rifles, machine guns and rounds of ammunition it could maintain
- must dismantle all defences in the West
- was excluded from the arms trade
- was limited in the type and quantity of weapons it could hold
- could not make or **stockpile** chemical weapons such as poison gas, armoured cars and tanks
- had to give up its air force
- was limited to six battleships.

> **KEY TERMS**
>
> **sovereignty:** the power of a country to control its own government
>
> **plebiscite:** a popular vote open to the entire electorate of a country or region on a specific issue
>
> **diktat:** a treaty or other agreement that has not been negotiated with a defeated country but imposed without any discussion with it
>
> **stockpile:** the gathering and storing of a large collection of weapons, including nuclear weapons after 1945

Territorial changes

Germany kept the Rhineland, but the area was demilitarised. However, it lost other territories.

- All its overseas colonies were divided between the Allied Powers.
- Alsace and Lorraine were given to France.
- Union with Austria (*Anschluss*) was forbidden.
- The Treaty of Brest-Litovsk with Russia was cancelled. Part of the territory Germany had gained from that treaty was made into three new independent states: Estonia, Latvia and Lithuania.
- East Prussia's 2 million Germans were cut off from their fellow Germans in what became known as the Polish Corridor, which gave Poland access to the sea.

Most territories were transferred because of the Treaty of Versailles. However, other changes came about as result of plebiscites. For example, North Schleswig was awarded to Denmark after a plebiscite in 1920. A plebiscite in 1921 awarded one-third of Silesia to Poland and the rest to Germany. Two parts of East Prussia, Allenstein and Marienwerder, were awarded to Germany after a plebiscite. Following the French occupation of the Saarland, a plebiscite was held in 1935 and it was returned to Germany (see Chapter 3).

As Germany's borders were redrawn in the years after the war, millions of Germans found that they were no longer living in Germany.

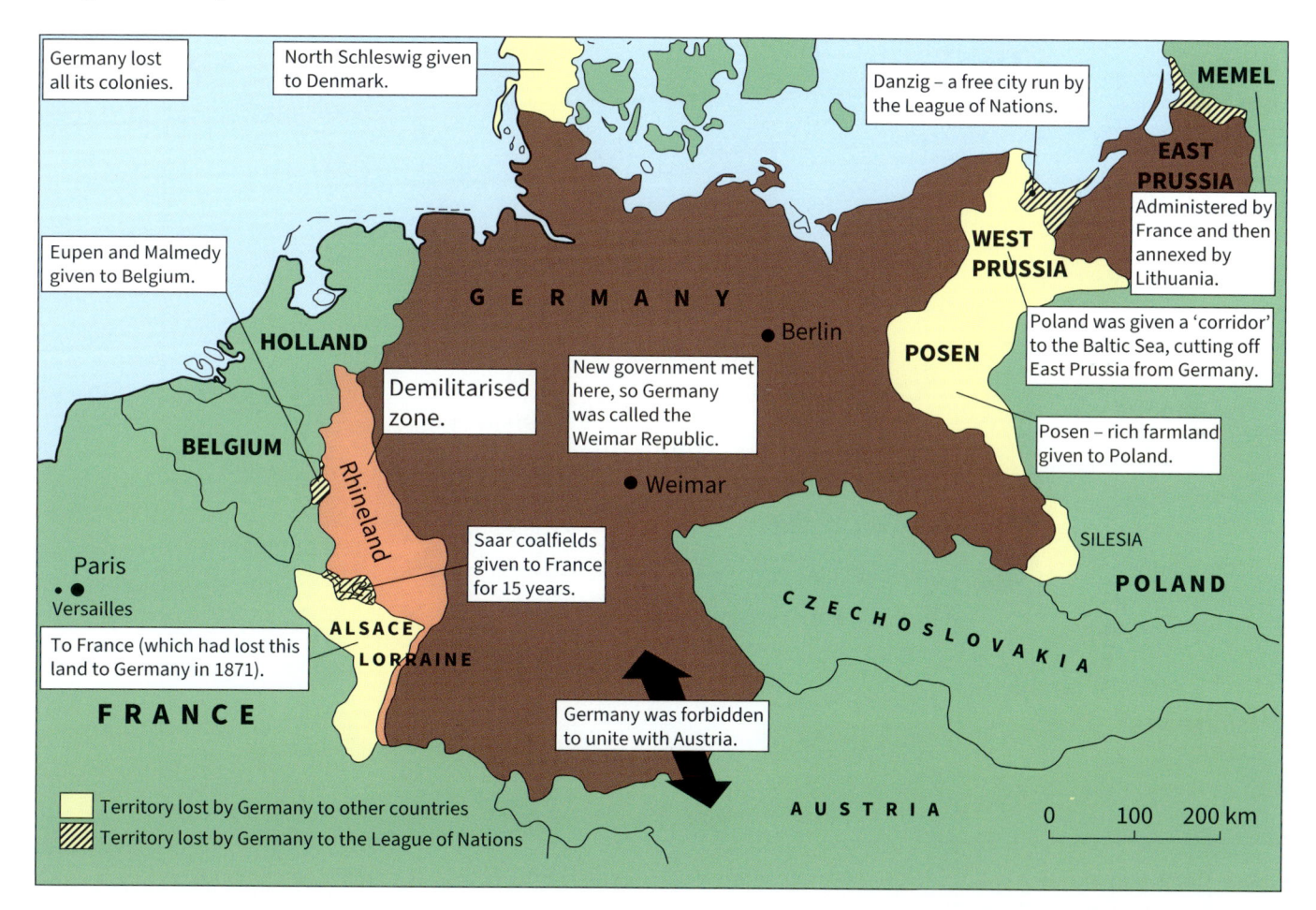

Figure 1.5: A map showing the territorial changes that resulted from the Treaty of Versailles

What happened to Germany's colonies?

During the war, the Allied Powers had agreed to share some of Germany's colonies between them when it was over. Wilson was strongly against this, but the leaders reached a compromise in Paris. All German colonies would pass to the League of Nations and be administered by one of the League's members as a **mandate** (see Figure 1.6). Countries would report to the League of Nations on their management of the former colony each year.

Britain received the mandate for German East Africa (Tanganyika). Belgium took control of Ruanda-Urundi. South Africa was given German South West Africa (now Namibia). In the Pacific, Japan gained Germany's islands north of the equator (the Marshall Islands, the Caroline Islands and the Marianas) and the German concession on mainland China, Shantung. France and Britain were given a shared mandate for the Cameroons and Togoland.

> **KEY TERM**
>
> **mandate:** a legal responsibility for the development of an area or country following the dissolution of the German Empire

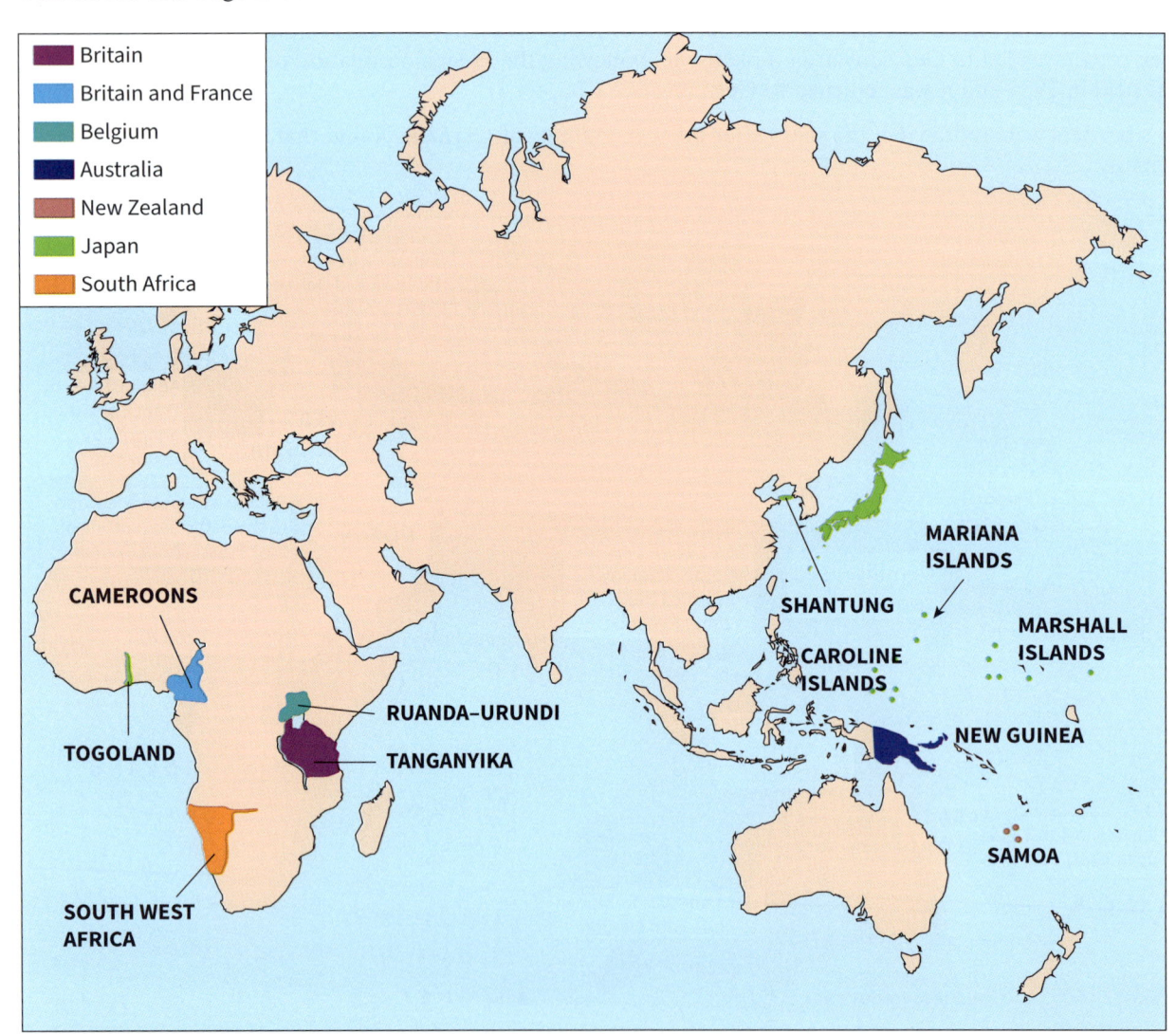

Figure 1.6: A map showing which countries were granted which former German colonies to manage as mandates in the years after the First World War

Chapter 1, Key Question 1: Was the Treaty of Versailles fair?

> **THINKING SKILLS**
>
> How would you have reacted to the end of the German Empire if you were:
> - a German government official living in one of the former colonies
> - a businessperson who was involved in exploiting mineral deposits in one of the former colonies
> - a politician who wanted Germany to expand its empire to match that of Britain or France
> - a person living in a former colony whose farm had been exploited by German officials?

> **REVISION TIP**
>
> Try using acronyms to remember the terms of the Treaty of Versailles. Think of an acronym and make notes on the key information relating to each aspect. For example, **DRAWL**:
>
> **D**iktat: Treaty was not negotiated; no discussions; dictated to the Germans.
>
> **R**eparations: Payment in money or goods for damage one during the Great War. Total set in April 1921: $33 billion.
>
> **A**rmaments: No air force or submarines; army restricted to 100 000 and navy to six ships; Rhineland demilitarised.
>
> **W**ar guilt: Germany blamed for the war.
>
> **L**oss of territory: Reduced Germany's size, population and economic resources; colonies given to the Allied Powers as mandates.

SOURCE 1D

Country (total population)	Ethnic minorities
Poland (27 million)	3–5 million Ukrainians 1 million Russians 1 million Germans
Czechoslovakia (14.5 million)	3.25 million Germans 0.75 million Magyars 0.5 million Ruthenes
Romania (18 million)	0.5 million Germans 0.5 million Ukrainians 0.25 million Slovaks
Yugoslavia (12 million)	0.5 million Germans 0.5 million Magyars 0.5 million Albanians 0.25 million Romanians

Source 1D: A table showing some of the new countries created by the post-war peace treaties and the estimated minorities that lived in them

SOURCE 1E

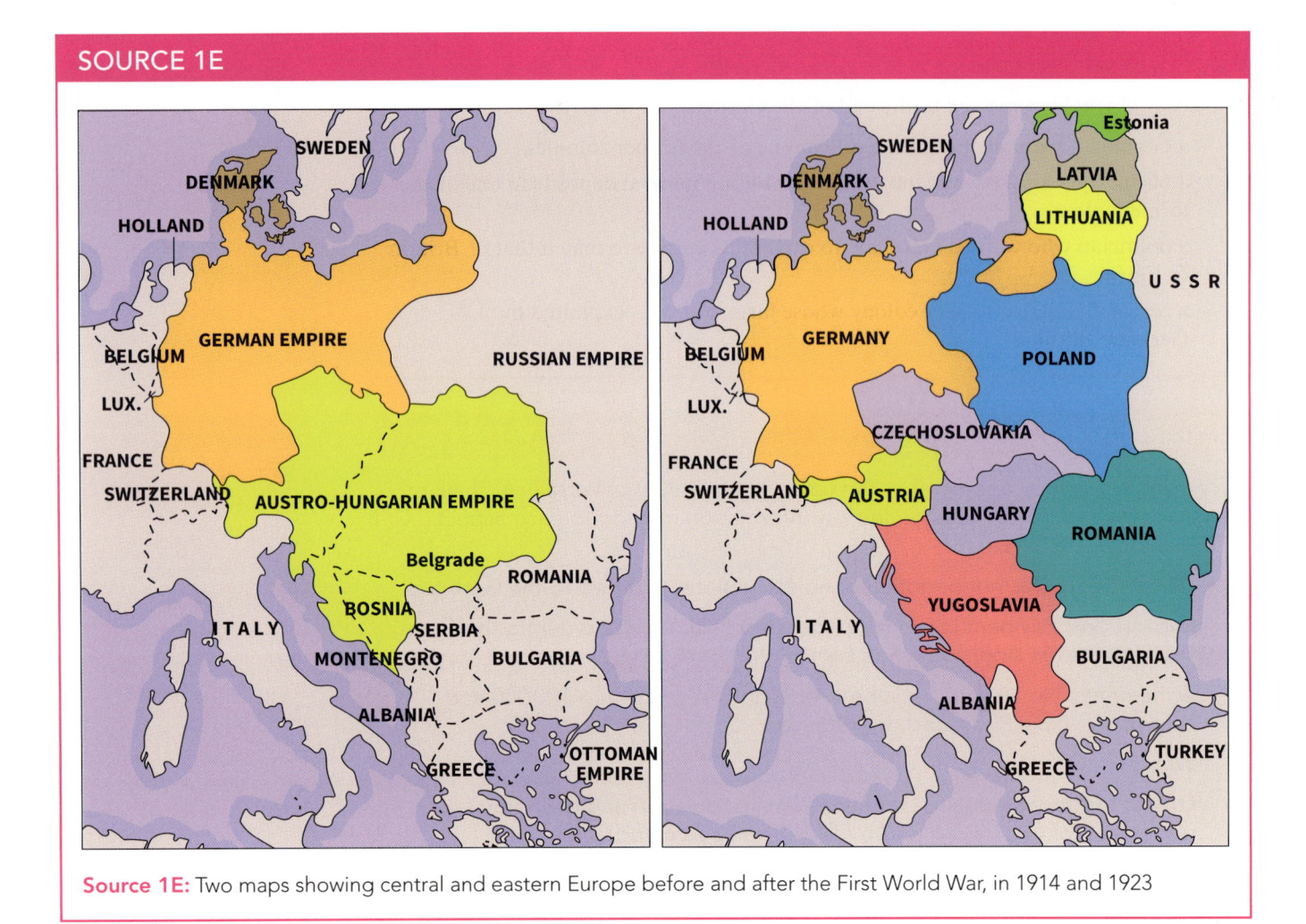

Source 1E: Two maps showing central and eastern Europe before and after the First World War, in 1914 and 1923

SOURCE ANALYSIS 1.3

Study Sources 1D and 1E.

a   Which countries existed in 1923 that did not exist in 1914?

b   Which of these sources provides evidence of issues that were not solved by the Paris Peace Conference? Explain your thinking.

c   Why was it not practical for every ethnic minority group to have its own country?

d   Germans became a minority group in several of the new countries of Central and Eastern Europe. Why might this weaken the defence of these new countries?

The United States

Wilson left Paris immediately after the Treaty of Versailles had been signed. What parts of the settlement had met his own aims and desires? Firstly, he had laid the groundwork for establishing the League of Nations. All parties had agreed that the covenant of the League should be included in all five peace treaties. In addition, Wilson had got his wish for disarmament of the Central Powers.

In line with Wilson's principle of national self-determination, the Rhineland was to be demilitarised but would remain part of Germany. This also meant that Germany could eventually become an important trading partner with the USA. The collapse of the Austro-Hungarian, Russian and German empires in 1918 allowed **successor states** to be created in Europe. Poland, which had not been an independent country for a century, was restored. Hungary was separated from Austria. Czechoslovakia and Yugoslavia were created. Wilson could view these as successes.

However, in other ways, Wilson was disappointed. Point 2 of the Fourteen Points (no restrictions on shipping) was never going to be acceptable to Britain because the British navy was vital for protecting the country's empire. The British and French empires had increased in size because the Allied Powers were now running some of Germany's former colonies as mandates. This did not apply Wilson's principle of national self-determination.

Things got worse for Wilson. When he presented the Treaty of Versailles to the US Congress, he did not win the majority of votes needed to approve it. Wilson's dream of a new world order with the USA leading the League of Nations was shattered. He died a disappointed man in 1924.

> **KEY TERMS**
>
> **successor states:** a new, smaller country created after a larger country has been broken up, usually after a conflict
>
> **buffer zone:** a neutral area that separates two other areas that might come into conflict

> **FOCUS TASK 1.3**
>
> **a** Make brief notes to summarise why Wilson could not implement all of his Fourteen Points during the Paris Peace Conference. Then swap notes with a partner and discuss your ideas.
>
> **b** Was it ever likely that Wilson would win approval for all the points from other nations during the peace talks? Write a short paragraph to explain your ideas.

France

Clemenceau was reasonably satisfied with the outcomes of the Paris Peace Conference. To begin with, Alsace and Lorraine, which had been lost to Germany in 1871, were restored to France. In addition, most of the reparations would go to France to allow it to rebuild the areas destroyed in the First World War and to pay off debts it owed to Britain and the USA.

With the Rhineland established as a **buffer zone** between France and Germany, guarded by Allied troops, French security was stronger. The articles of the Versailles Treaty would ensure that Germany would never be strong enough to start another war. A separate Anglo-American treaty committed Britain and the USA to support France if Germany invaded again. Unfortunately, this guarantee lapsed when the US Congress refused to ratify the treaty, as Britain would not help France without US support.

The French people did not believe that the League of Nations would stop Germany attacking their country again.

On balance, France was still not secure. This was Clemenceau's biggest disappointment. During the 1920s and 1930s, French actions were mostly driven by the need to secure the country's border with Germany and to avoid another war.

Britain

Lloyd George was pleased with the results at Paris. He had wanted to ensure that British interests were not damaged by a peace that would slow Germany's economic recovery, which would hurt Britain as well as Europe. With the reparations total to be fixed at some point in the future, Lloyd George hoped that the fierce emotions he witnessed in Paris would cool and that the reparations demands would be reasonable.

Britain's empire grew, thanks to the system of mandates that allowed Britain to control some of Germany's former colonies. Britain's naval strength also increased when the Germans **scuttled** their fleet at Scapa Flow in Scotland on 21 June 1919, to avoid the ships ending up in Britain's hands.

In 1918, the press had already given Lloyd George the unofficial title of the 'man who won the war'. In 1919, he returned to London to an enthusiastic reception.

> **KEY TERM**
>
> **scuttle:** to deliberately sink a ship. In wartime, navies may do this so that the enemy cannot capture a vessel and begin to use it themselves

FOCUS TASK 1.4

Write short answers to the following questions.

a   Why did the Big Three have to take account of public opinion when negotiating the Treaty of Versailles? In which countries might public opinion welcome or oppose the treaty?

b   At the end of the Paris Peace Conference, Clemenceau said: 'America is far away, protected by the ocean. Not even Napoleon himself could touch England. You are both sheltered; we are not.' Napoleon was a famous French leader who controlled most of Europe 100 years before the First World War. What did Clemenceau mean by this? How secure was France as a result of the Treaty of Versailles?

c   Why would the German government and public want to see the Allies disarm? When Britain and France did *not* disarm, what effect might this have had on the German people's view of the Treaty of Versailles?

Swap answers with a partner and assess their responses. Give them feedback in the form of three 'what went well' (WWW) points and two 'even better if' (EBI) suggestions. Then swap back and improve your own responses based on your partner's feedback. Finally, get your partner to check the improvements you have made.

Chapter 1, Key Question 1: Was the Treaty of Versailles fair?

> **REFLECTION**
>
> How did you find the process of assessing and improving in Focus task 1.4? Did you agree with your partner's feedback? If not, why not? What criteria did you use to assess your partner's writing? Did you make sure your suggestions for improvements were helpful? In your pairs, discuss the processes each of you used and what you could do to improve next time you are assessing your own or each other's work.

Who else lost out?

Russia was excluded from the peace talks because it had signed a separate peace with Germany and withdrawn from the war in March 1918. The new Bolshevik government in Russia was not officially recognised by the Allies. After the war, Russia and Germany felt they had shared interests. Diplomatically and militarily, they started to work together.

Despite being one of the Allied Powers, Italian leaders felt they had been betrayed because they had not received all the territories promised by the Treaty of London. This anger remained throughout the 1920s and 1930s, as Italy resisted forming a close relationship with Britain and France.

China lost out, too. In the early stages of the war, Japan occupied the German colony of Shantung, a peninsula on mainland China. At the peace conference, the Chinese delegation argued that Shantung should be returned to China, but Japan was allowed to keep the region. This meant that Japan controlled an area with a population of 30 million Chinese people and could exploit the coal and other resources there. As a result, the Chinese delegation in Paris refused to sign the Treaty of Versailles.

Even though the Japanese delegation left Paris with some territorial gains, they were not entirely happy. Japan had wanted to include a 'race equality' clause in the League of Nations **covenant**. This would ensure it and other countries would be treated equally with the Western Allies. Wilson rejected the clause because he knew that the idea of equal treatment for different ethnic groups would never be approved by the US Congress.

> **KEY TERM**
>
> **covenant:** a formal and binding set of rules for an organisation

> **ACTIVITY 1.3**
>
> In pairs, draw a table like this, with a row for each of Wilson's Fourteen Points. Discuss each of the points and then, using three colours, underline those that were *fully met* in green, *partly met* in orange and *not met at all* in red. Note down the reason for your choice in the second column.
>
> | Wilson's Fourteen Points | Explanation |
> |---|---|
> | | |

47

1.3 What was the impact of the Treaty on Germany up to the end of 1923?

Germany was in turmoil when the Treaty of Versailles was signed. The kaiser had fled to Holland and a new German state, known as the Weimar Republic, had been established, with new political leaders. The British naval blockade was still in place, causing severe shortages of fuel and food. Uprisings, demonstrations and mutinies took place across the country. In January 1919, the government had to leave the capital, Berlin, because it had been seized by communists. The terms of the treaty were met with a hostile response from the press and public.

SOURCES 1F & 1G

Source 1F: A photograph of one of many demonstrations by German citizens once the details of the treaty had been made public in May 1919. The placard reads: 'We Germans, living outside Germany, are protesting against the peace forced upon us and against the theft of our private property.'

The immediate effect of the signing was a blaze of indignation in the German press and depression among the people. In Berlin an atmosphere of gloom settled on the city. Several newspapers appeared with black borders on their Versailles articles with headings like 'Peace with Annihilation'. The churches set aside 6 July as a day of mourning. On 24 June a number of German officers seized fifteen flags that had been captured from the French in 1870 and publicly burned them. There was mob violence in Berlin and Hamburg throughout the week of the signing of the peace.

Source 1G: An extract from a report in the *New York Times*, July 1919

> **SOURCE ANALYSIS 1.4**
>
> **a** Look at Source 1F. Identify the age range of those who took part in the demonstrations. What does this suggest about the impact of the treaty?
>
> **b** Read the translation of the placard in Source 1F. In which areas of post-1919 Europe could this demonstration have taken place?
>
> **c** Read Source 1G. To what extent does this text support the photograph in Source 1F in relation to the impact of the treaty on Germany? What does it add to your understanding of the impact of the treaty?

The social impact of the treaty in Germany

To fully understand reactions to the treaty in Germany, it is important to remember several facts about how the German people viewed the war. No enemy soldier had set foot on German land during the entire four years of war and the German army had not been defeated in any major battle. Throughout the war, German newspapers had not informed the public about Germany military setbacks. Instead, readers were fed a diet of propaganda victories.

Four main features of the Treaty of Versailles caused the most anger in Germany. To start with, it was a dictated peace. There had been no negotiations, but German politicians had to sign it otherwise the naval blockade would have continued. The German people also felt bitter about being held responsible for causing the war. They thought the 'War Guilt' clause shamed the whole nation. Many Germans had been convinced by wartime propaganda suggesting that the Allied Powers were responsible for the war. The fact that Germany had been encircled by Russia and France in 1914 supported this idea.

The demand for reparations also caused resentment and concern. The exact sum had not been fixed at Versailles, but reports made it clear that reparations would have to be made. Having lost the Saar region, with its valuable coal mines, how could Germany afford to pay?

Finally, the tiny army of just 100 000 soldiers that Germany was permitted to keep meant that it was not able to defend itself against its now much stronger neighbours, France and Poland. This caused fear and anger.

Resentment was particularly bitter in those parts of the country that had been awarded to new countries. The new boundaries caused major social problems as different ethnic groups were forced to live alongside each other. For example, in Silesia, Allied troops were called in to keep the peace between groups of Poles and Germans before a plebiscite could be held on the future of the region.

The German public did not respect the **constitution** of the new Weimar Republic, nor its democratic processes. They did not believe the government would do anything to right the wrongs forced on Germany by the treaty. When the government accepted the reparations bill of $33 billion in May 1921, the humiliation was complete. This sense of powerlessness and desperation pervaded German society during the 1920s. The people began to look for a political party that offered a way out of the shame of Versailles.

> **KEY TERM**
>
> **constitution:** the main set of laws by which a country is governed; the constitution sets out the powers of the government and the rights and freedom of the individual

CAMBRIDGE IGCSE™ AND O LEVEL HISTORY OPTION B: COURSEBOOK

SOURCE 1H

Source 1H: A cartoon published in a German newspaper in 1919. The caption reads: 'When we have paid 100 billion marks then I can give you something to eat.'

SOURCE ANALYSIS 1.5

Study Source 1H.

a What is the message of this cartoon? Sum it up in one sentence.

b The final reparations bill was not agreed until May 1921. Why do you think this cartoon appeared in 1919?

c Why has the cartoonist decided to show a mother and two children?

THINKING SKILLS

Consider the impact the terms of the Treaty of Versailles would have had on the German people. Which parts of the treaty would have most upset you if you were:

- a German living in the newly created Poland
- a German mother whose son had died fighting in France
- a German politician who strongly supported Kaiser Wilhelm II and the old political system
- a German soldier who had to leave the army?

SOURCES 1I & 1J

Source 1I: A photograph of German soldiers marching back to Berlin from the front line in late 1918

It is easy to understand the harsh reaction in Germany to the Treaty of Versailles. Most Germans had little idea of the size of the German defeat and believed that because Germany had requested an armistice, a lenient settlement would follow [. . .] All Germans considered the treaty to be harsh and blamed it for the social, economic and political [problems] of the Weimar Republic.

Source 1J: An extract from a book by historian Frank McDonough, published in 2013

SOURCE ANALYSIS 1.6

Look at Source 1I.

a   There are crowds on both sides of the road. Why do you think the German public came out to welcome home soldiers although they had lost the war?

b   Why did the German president, Friedrich Ebert, tell these returning soldiers that 'you return undefeated from the battlefield' when he knew that Germany had lost the war?

c   Why did the soldiers in these pictures not know the truth about the German army's defeat?

CAMBRIDGE IGCSE™ AND O LEVEL HISTORY OPTION B: COURSEBOOK

> **ACTIVITY 1.4**
>
> a In pairs, use Sources 1I and 1J, and your own knowledge, to write an alternative outcome to the Paris Peace Conference. Consider the following.
>
>   - What could the Allied Powers have done differently to avoid the hostile German reaction to the Treaty of Versailles?
>   - What could have been done differently to ensure that the German people fully understood that their country had been defeated?
>   - What changes to the Treaty of Versailles might have reduced German hostility towards it?
>
> b Join up with another pair and read each other's accounts. Then have a group discussion about whether or not reactions in Germany were inevitable and whether the peacemakers in Paris should have done things differently.

The political impact of the treaty

The impact of the treaty on Germany was significant and long-lasting. Many soldiers found themselves out of work because the Treaty of Versailles had dramatically reduced the size of the German army. Many joined the Freikorps – groups of ex-servicemen that effectively worked as small private armies. These unofficial militia groups hated the Weimar politicians and attempted several **coups**. The famous Kapp **Putsch** took place in Berlin in March 1920, under the command of Wolfgang Kapp. It aimed to overthrow the Weimar authorities and install a **right-wing** government that would overturn the Treaty of Versailles. Berlin workers went on strike and public services were stopped. The coup collapsed and the Weimar Republic survived this putsch.

Other attempts to weaken the government in this period included a right-wing takeover in the Bavarian Republic in May 1919 and an event known as the Munich Putsch (or Beer Hall Putsch) in November 1923.

> **THINK LIKE A HISTORIAN**
>
> Today, about two-thirds of the world's countries are governed by some form of democracy. Apart from having features of a democratic system, such as free elections, voting rights and an independent judiciary, what other factors make a country democratic? Discuss your ideas in small groups. Think about:
>
> - voter trust in politicians
> - a culture of acceptance of election results
> - limited time scale before the next election.
>
> What examples can you think of where democratic principles have been challenged in democratic countries? Why do you think this happens? What effect does it have on the country?

KEY TERMS

coup: an attempt to seize political power by force rather than through democratic means

putsch: an attempt to take power from the government, usually by a small number of armed citizens or soldiers

right-wing: describing people or groups, often strong nationalists, whose political beliefs are based on an ordered society that values tradition and discipline. They usually oppose socialism and communism, believing that social inequality is natural and desirable, and because both pose a threat to private property

Political murders

In addition to these organised attempts to weaken the government, hundreds of politicians and political activists were murdered. Even high-ranking members of the Weimar government were not safe. In 1921, a right-wing gang called Organisation Consul murdered the finance minister, Matthias Erzberger. The reaction to this murder is revealing, as it was not just extremists who approved. One newspaper wrote that: '*Erzberger, the man who is alone responsible for the humiliating armistice; Erzberger, the man who is responsible for the Versailles Treaty of Shame. Erzberger [. . .] has at last secured the punishment suitable for a traitor.*'

In June 1922, the same group that killed Erzberger assassinated the foreign minister, Walther Rathenau, because he had been involved in arranging the Armistice and in trying to improve the Treaty of Versailles.

Figure 1.7: Matthias Erzberger, the German finance minister who was murdered in 1921

Figure 1.8: Walther Rathenau, the German foreign minister who was assassinated in June 1922

Dolchstoss

The Weimar politicians who signed the Treaty of Versailles in June 1919 had also signed the Armistice in November 1918. Mistakenly, the German public now began to believe a powerful myth – that the politicians and not the army generals were to blame for the country's humiliation and downfall at the end of the war. Many people believed that the Weimar government was made up of cowards who had betrayed the German army by signing the Armistice and had let the country down further by signing, instead of resisting, the Treaty of Versailles. This legend of the *Dolchstoss* ('stab in the back') was widespread. Many returning soldiers also believed it, and it had a significant effect on German politics in the following years. It showed the armed forces as honourable and trustworthy, and politicians as unpatriotic liars who could not be trusted.

Political structures in the Weimar Republic

In the years after the war, some politicians and many German citizens would have been glad to see the return of the kaiser. Many felt that the new constitution and political structures had been imposed on the country by the same people who had betrayed it at the end of the war.

The new constitution established a voting system that did not produce clear winners. Instead, Weimar governments were **coalitions**, formed from two or more political parties. In these coalitions there was often in-fighting, and decision-making was slow. These had not been problems under the kaiser's rule.

> **KEY TERM**
>
> **coalition:** a government made up of two or more different parties, often established when no single party wins a majority of votes

ACTIVITY 1.5

a As a class discuss the following questions.

- In your opinion, what was the impact on public trust in the Weimar system of so much political violence in the early years of the Weimar Republic?
- What steps could the Weimar government have taken to build the public's trust and belief in the Weimar system?

b To what extent was the Treaty of Versailles to blame for the instability of the Weimar government? Were there other factors? Split into groups depending on the extent to which you believe the treaty was to blame: totally, somewhat or hardly at all. Discuss your reasons as a group, then present them to the class. Afterwards, you can move to another group if you have been persuaded by their arguments. Do a final count of how many people are in each group.

FOCUS TASK 1.5

In a democracy, if an individual does not like the government's policies, they can vote for another party or leader. Why do you think some groups in Germany in this period chose violence rather than the democratic process to make changes?

a First, discuss your ideas in pairs and record your points in note form. Then go through your points, numbering them in order of importance.

b Join up with another pair and compare your lists. Tick any points that you have both written down and discuss any points that are different. If, after discussion, all four of you consider them to be significant, add them to your original list.

> **REFLECTION**
>
> How well did you learn as a group of four? Did you find working in pairs more or less effective than in small groups? Discuss with your group of four what makes group work effective. Share your ideas with the class and take a vote on the five most important factors for working effectively as a group.

The economic impact of the treaty on Germany

When Germany signed the Treaty of Versailles, the exact figure for reparations had not yet been decided, but Germany started to make some payments immediately. In May 1921, the Reparations Commission announced its decision: Germany would have to pay $33 billion. However, the country had lost all its colonies, 13% of its land, and with it 26% of its coal deposits and 75% of iron ore deposits. Without these resources, the German authorities said that they could not pay the reparations bill.

The German economy was struggling. Government expenditure was high but income from taxes was low. The rising **budget deficit** was resolved by borrowing or by printing money, which caused **inflation**. The reparations bill made the situation worse, but it is important to remember that prices in Germany were already increasing (see Figure 1.9).

Date	German Marks needed to buy one ounce of gold
Jan 1919	170
Sep 1919	499
Jan 1920	1 340
Sep 1920	1 201
Jan 1921	1 349
Sep 1921	2 175
Jan 1922	3 976
Sep 1922	30 381
Jan 1923	372 477
Sep 1923	269 439 000
2 Oct 1923	6 631 749 000
9 Oct 1923	24 868 950 000
16 Oct 1923	84 969 072 000
23 Oct 1923	1 160 552 882 000
30 Oct 1923	1 347 070 000 000
5 Nov 1923	8 700 000 000 000
30 Nov 1923	87 000 000 000 000

Figure 1.9: A table showing how inflation turned into **hyperinflation** in Germany, 1919–23

> **KEY TERMS**
>
> **budget deficit:** when a country's expenditure is more than its income; the deficit is the difference between the two amounts
>
> **inflation:** an increase in prices and an accompanying drop in the purchasing value of money
>
> **hyperinflation:** inflation that occurs at a very rapid rate without control

The invasion of the Ruhr

In December 1922, Germany failed to deliver its quota of timber. In January 1923, it was unable to deliver its quota of coal. The prime minister of France, Raymond Poincaré, sent troops into the Ruhr region to make sure that the deliveries were made on time. He saw this as a test case for the enforcement of the whole of the Versailles Treaty.

The Ruhr region was rich in coal and iron, making it the heart of Germany's industrial strength. In January 1923, 60 000 French and Belgian troops were sent into the Ruhr (see Figure 1.10). They took control of all industries and railways, and seized resources instead of reparations payments that were now overdue.

The Weimar government called for non-violent opposition across the region, and Germans united behind this campaign. In late March, French soldiers killed 13 German workers in an event known as the 'Bloody Easter on the Ruhr'. In total, more than 140 Germans were killed in fights with French troops.

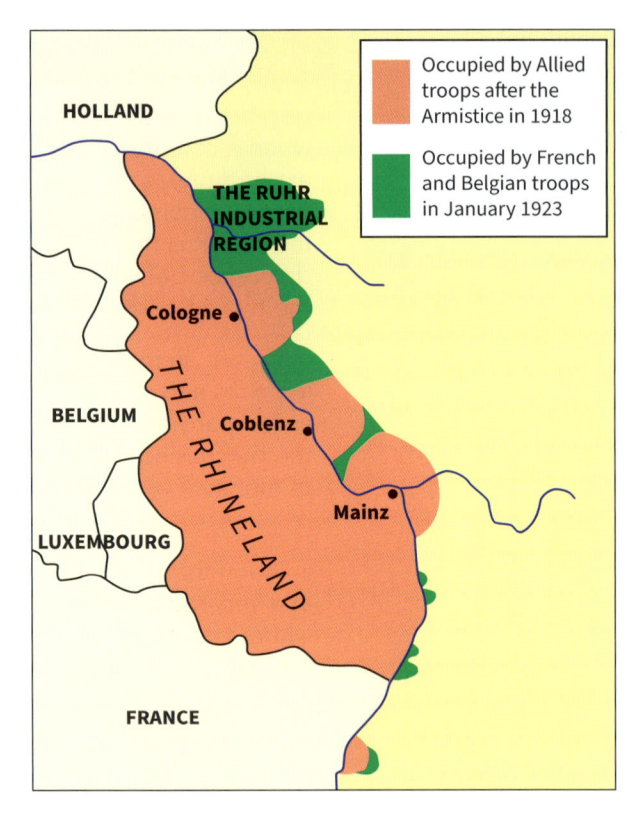

Figure 1.10: A map showing the different areas that French and Belgian troops entered in force

Figure 1.11: A German woman lighting her kitchen stove using money made worthless by hyperinflation in 1923

Hyperinflation

Government income fell as Germany's industry stopped in the Ruhr region. Civil servants, miners and others went on strike. During this period, the government continued to print money, and people were paid using paper money that was fast losing its value. Hyperinflation took hold, and people's savings became worthless. In cafés and restaurants, menus did not list prices because they would have increased while customers were sitting at their tables!

The Ruhr occupation not only prevented coal, iron and steel from reaching the rest of Germany, it also reduced government income from valuable foreign exports to the world. To make matters worse, the German government tried to keep the **passive resistance** going by giving money to the strikers, again by simply printing more money.

By 1923, 300 paper mills and 2000 printing businesses were working all day, every day to keep up with demand for paper money. The value of the German currency dropped dramatically. In the face of economic collapse, the strikes were eventually called off in September 1923 by a new coalition government led by Gustav Stresemann. Despite this, civil unrest turned into attempts to overthrow the Weimar Republic. Adolf Hitler (see Chapter 3) tried to seize power in the Beer Hall Putsch of November 1923 and a separatist Rhenish Republic was announced at Aachen in October 1923. Both coups were stopped by forces loyal to Stresemann's government.

> **KEY TERM**
>
> **passive resistance:** showing in a peaceful way that you oppose something, rather than using violence

At this point, Chancellor Stresemann and his Commissioner for National Currency, Dr Schacht, began trying to restore confidence in a new currency. All the old currency was collected and destroyed. In its place the Rentenmark was issued in November.

Reducing reparations

The French succeeded in taking German resources for reparations during their occupation of the Ruhr. However, many people in Europe and the USA felt sympathy towards the Germans because of the problems caused by hyperinflation. This led to a major revision to the reparations schedule. Following pressure from the USA, the French agreed to the Dawes Plan in April 1924. This substantially lowered German reparations payments. It also allowed US banks to make loans of $200 million to the German government. Finally, in August 1925, France withdrew from the Ruhr region and industrial production restarted.

FOCUS TASK 1.6

Discuss these questions in pairs.

a Was the economic impact of the Treaty of Versailles greater than the political impact? Justify your reasons.

b Which do you think lasted longer in the minds of German people: the political impact, the economic impact or the social impact of the Treaty of Versailles? Why?

REVISION TIP

Use the following concepts to help you revise this topic.

- Armistice
- Big Three
- blame
- diktat
- dolchstoss
- fair
- harsh
- humiliation
- justice
- national self-determination
- negotiations
- plebiscites
- reparations
- revenge
- shame
- treaty
- 'War Guilt' clause

Working in pairs and using a large piece of plain paper, write down all the concepts, spacing them out roughly equally. In a different colour underneath each one, write a brief definition. Draw lines to link any concepts/ideas that are related to one another. There is no limit on the number of lines (links) you can draw and lines from one concept could connect with several others.

Key points
The impact of the Treaty of Versailles in Germany

- Germans felt humiliated by the 'War Guilt' clause, believing that Germany was not to blame for the war.
- The reparations payments were a regular reminder of the punishments that were included in the treaty.
- The Weimar Republic was not respected by many German citizens because the politicians had signed the Treaty of Versailles. Weimar politicians were blamed for the unstable coalition governments that were elected under the new democratic system.
- The German minorities now left in countries like Poland were very unhappy at being cut off from Germany.
- Inflation that had started during the war was made worse by the actions of the Weimar government and led to hyperinflation. This became much worse when the French invaded the Ruhr in 1923 and stayed until 1925.

1.4 Could the Treaty be justified at the time?

Politicians, leaders, soldiers and ordinary citizens around the world held different views about the Treaty of Versailles. Most debate focused on whether the terms were fair or harsh.

FOCUS TASK 1.7

In pairs, look at this list of some features of the Treaty of Versailles:

- blame for the war and reparations
- disarmament
- territorial losses
- colonial losses
- population losses
- dictated peace
- no union with Austria.

a   Which features do you think were justified or necessary at the time? Draw a line to represent the range, with 'Very justified' at one end and 'Not justified' at the other.

b   Discuss each feature and mark where you think it goes on the line. For each one, ask yourself: Is this more or less justified than the one before? The answer will help you to gauge the degree of fairness. Start with any feature you like.

c   Present your findings to the class or in groups. Remember to justify your decisions.

REFLECTION

How well do you think you and your partner performed Focus task 1.7? Was the discussion and decision rushed or well considered? Did it make a difference if you started with the first feature on the list or the last in the list? How could you change your approach to improve your learning with a similar task in the future?

Chapter 1, Key Question 1: Was the Treaty of Versailles fair?

Contemporary views on the Treaty of Versailles

Naturally, the countries that suffered by the terms of the Treaty of Versailles and the treaties with the other Central Powers felt the terms were too harsh. People in the victorious nations might have felt the terms were fair. However, many people and politicians realised that extremely harsh terms that caused a great deal of suffering and hardship were not justified.

SOURCES 1K, 1L, 1M, 1N & 1O

Do not think of this treaty as merely a settlement with Germany. It is a very severe settlement with Germany, but there is nothing in it that she did not earn. Indeed, she earned more than she can ever be able to pay for, and the punishment exacted of her is not a punishment greater than she can bear, and it is absolutely necessary in order that no other nation may ever plot such a thing against humanity and civilization.

Source 1K: Part of a speech by President Wilson delivered on his tour of the USA in September 1919

PEACE AND FUTURE CANNON FODDER

The Tiger: "Curious! I seem to hear a child weeping!"

Source 1L: This cartoon was published in the British newspaper, the *Daily Herald*, 13 May 1919. The child to the left has just read the Treaty of Versailles.

CONTINUED

This is not a peace treaty, it is an armistice for twenty years.

Source 1M: A comment by the French military leader Marshall Foch at the ceremony to sign the Treaty of Versailles.

PUNCH, OR THE LONDON CHARIVARI.—April 23, 1919.

THE RECKONING.

Pan-German. "MONSTROUS, I CALL IT. WHY, IT'S FULLY A QUARTER OF WHAT *WE* SHOULD HAVE MADE *THEM* PAY, IF *WE'D* WON."

Source 1N: A British cartoon published in *Punch* magazine shortly after the Reparations Commission had announced the bill for Germany to pay: $33 billion.

The criminal madness of this peace will drain Germany's national life-blood. It is a shameless blow in the face of common-sense. It is inflicting the deepest wounds on us Germans as our world lies in wreckage about us.

Source 1O: Part of a speech made by a German Member of Parliament in the **Reichstag** in 1919

KEY TERM

Reichstag: The German parliament during the first half of the 20th century

SOURCE ANALYSIS 1.7

a Compare Sources 1N and 1O. Write down in one sentence the message of each source.

b What is the attitude of the cartoonist towards Germany in Source 1N?

c Summarise the German reaction to the Treaty of Versailles in your own words, using the evidence in these sources.

d To what extent is the German reaction in the sources supported by the sources from other countries?

FOCUS TASK 1.8

Sources 1K, 1L, 1M, 1N and 1O are about the Treaty of Versailles. In pairs, draw a table like the one below, with a row for each source. Decide whether each one is commenting that the treaty is too harsh, fair or not harsh enough. Note down your evidence and anything you know about the treaty that supports the source's conclusion.

Source	Too harsh? Fair? Not harsh enough?	Evidence	Is this source supported by your knowledge of the Versailles Treaty?
K			
L			

Historians' views on the Treaty of Versailles

Historians disagree about the treaties that ended the First World War. Not many think they were a triumph of **diplomacy**. However, while some criticise their faults and failures, others think they were the best that could have been achieved by those people in those circumstances. Here are two examples of these views.

> Margaret Macmillan, 2001:
>
> *The peacemakers of 1919 made mistakes, of course. [...] If they could have done better, they certainly could have done much worse. They tried to build a better order. They could not foresee the future and they certainly could not control it. When war came in 1939, it was the result of twenty years of decisions taken or not taken, not of arrangements made in 1919.* (Source: M. Macmillan, *Paris 1919* (John Murry, 2001), p. 500)

> Eric Hobsbawn, 1996:
>
> *[...] the Versailles settlement could not possibly be the basis of a stable peace. It was doomed from the start, and another war was therefore practically certain [...]*
>
> (Source: E. Hobsbawm, *The Age of Extremes* (New York: Vintage Books, 1996), p. 34)

KEY TERM

diplomacy: the management of relationships between countries

Historians' views have changed over time. The treaty is now over 100 years old. Several writers have considered what different decisions *might* have been made. They make the following points.

- Germany only accepted the Fourteen Points when it was clear they were losing the war in the autumn of 1918.
- In the Treaty of Brest-Litovsk made between Russia and Germany in March 1918, the Germans took 34% of Russia's population and 50% of its industry. The reparations bill was 300 million gold roubles (Russian currency).
- Clemenceau wanted the treaty to be harsher and Germany to be broken up into smaller states. Wilson and Lloyd George stopped this from happening.
- The reparations payments introduced in May 1921 cost Germany only 2% of its annual production.
- Germany's main economic problem in the 1920s was not reparations but war debt, which it had planned to pay by winning the war and making other countries pay reparations.
- In 1924, Germany received huge loans from the USA to help its economy recover.
- The years 1924–29 were fairly successful for Germany. For example, Germany produced twice as much steel as Britain in 1925.

FOCUS TASK 1.9

a   What does 'fair' mean? Write down your own definition of the word.

b   Now use your table from Focus task 1.8 to plan for a piece of extended writing answering the question 'Was the Treaty of Versailles fair?' using the following structure:

- introduction, to include your overall judgement
- arguments that support the judgement that the Treaty of Versailles was fair
- arguments that support the judgement that the treaty of Versailles was not fair
- a conclusion that evaluates the strengths and weaknesses of each side of the debate and explains your view.

c   Now consider the process of essay planning and writing. What is your strategy for planning so that you do not miss out important factors?

d   Swap plans with a partner before you write. What can you learn from your partner's plan? Could you write their essay using their plan?

e   Now write your essay. Afterwards, first assess your own approach. Was time for planning and time for writing on schedule? If not, why not? Then swap writing with your partner. Have they followed their own plan?

Chapter 1, Key Question 1: Was the Treaty of Versailles fair?

SUMMARY

- When the Great War ended in November 1918, there were strong feelings among both the winners and losers.

- Without Germany and Russia, 32 countries met in Paris to draw up the peace treaties that would shape the post-war world.

- The Treaty of Versailles was the peace treaty drawn up for Germany. Most of its terms were compromises worked out by three very different leaders: President Wilson of the USA, Prime Minister Georges Clemenceau of France and Prime Minister David Lloyd George of Britain.

- When it was signed by the German delegates, it caused uproar in Germany. The clauses that blamed Germany for starting the war, reduced the size of its armed forces, took away its colonies and left millions of Germans living in alien countries were not forgotten quickly by politicians and people living in the new Weimar Germany.

- The German politicians who had signed the treaty were regarded as traitors. Some were murdered.

- When Germany was unable to make reparations payments, France and Belgium invaded the Ruhr region and took over German industry, causing greater economic difficulties.

- The German economy suffered hyperinflation until November 1923. Paper money became almost worthless and the German people suffered severe hardship.

- At the time and in the 100 years since the Treaty was created, people have had different opinions on how fair it was, and whether the terms could be justified.

KEY SKILLS EXERCISES

Knowledge and understanding

1. Which countries formed the Allied Powers in 1914?
2. Which countries were the Central Powers in 1914?
3. Give **one** way in which the victors in the war were influenced by public opinion.
4. Give **two** ways in which the USA did not agree with Britain and France during the Paris peace talks.
5. What was **one** purpose of the League of Nations?

Application

6. How did the methods of working in Paris change over the course of the conference?
7. Why do you think it would have been difficult to reach decisions in a plenary session?
8. In a large conference, what should be the role of plenary sessions?
9. Suggest **two** methods of involving small powers in a meaningful way between plenary sessions.

Analysis

10. Analyse **two** benefits of making decisions in small groups at the peace talks.
11. Analyse **two** disadvantages of stating before the conference what the objectives were, as President Wilson did with his Fourteen Points.
12. Analyse **three** reasons why compromises had to be made in decision-making processes in Paris. Would any peace treaty have been possible if sides did not compromise?

CAMBRIDGE IGCSE™ AND O LEVEL HISTORY OPTION B: COURSEBOOK

CONTINUED

Evaluation

13 Discuss the reasons for the lack of representation at the highest levels of women and people of different backgrounds in Paris.

14 Evaluate the importance of the 'War Guilt' clause in the peace conference. If the clause had not been agreed, what do you think would have happened at the peace conference?

15 Evaluate the importance of the fact that Germany and Russia did not attend the peace talks. What would have been easier and what would have been harder for the peacemakers due to their absence?

IMPROVE THIS ANSWER

What was the impact on Germany of the Treaty of Versailles?

Sample answer: The treaty had a major impact on German politics, the economy and society. **1** The new Weimar political system was regularly criticised and lacked public support because many of its politicians were called traitors for signing the Armistice in November 1918 and then signing the Treaty of Versailles in June 1919. **2** During the 1920s, the Weimar governments could not shake off the public's lack of faith and its yearning for the old system headed by Kaiser Wilhelm. **3** Worse still, signing the treaty strengthened the myth of Dolchstoss. Hundreds of political murders, like those of Erzberger and Rathenau, summed up the political instability caused by the treaty. **4**

Most Germans demonstrated their hatred of the treaty through attempted coups such as the Kapp Putsch of 1921 and the Beer Hall Putsch of 1923. **5** These failed to topple the government, but the resistance to the French invasion of the Ruhr in 1923 united Germans against their recent enemy. The invaders could take coal from Germany's industrial heartland, but the spirit of the Germans who went on strike could not be broken, especially because the government printed money to pay the strikers. **6**

7 The hyperinflation that resulted was linked to the $33 billion reparations bill demanded by its enemies: Britain and France. The impact of both was ruinous on those who had savings, particularly the German middle classes. The treaty was blamed once again for harming ordinary German men and women. **8** Many of them were already bitter because the terms of the treaty had meant that millions of Germans now lived under foreign rule: 1 million were in Poland, 3.25 million in Czechoslovakia. Now, these Germans were minorities instead of being the majority. Families and friends were split up, separated and ruled by different governments.

---

1 This starter sentence sets up the structure for the answer.

2 Always try to answer the question directly early in your answer.

3 The impact of the treaty on Weimar Germany's politicians is contrasted with the previous political system to highlight the effect it had.

4 The paragraph ends with carefully selected evidence to highlight the impact of the treaty.

5 This opening statement uses the powerful word 'hatred' and links it to attempts to take political power from the Weimar government.

6 The invasion of the Ruhr was an event that brought all Germans together in their opposition to the treaty. All the examples are linked directly to the question: the impact of the treaty.

7 This paragraph links the political impact of the treaty with the economic impact of the treaty as anticipated by the very first sentence of the answer.

8 Here the student revisits the focus of the answer. This time, the impact is on ordinary Germans and those Germans who were separated from Germany by redrawn frontiers.

Chapter 1, Key Question 1: Was the Treaty of Versailles fair?

9 This opening sentence again reflects the third aspect of the impact of the treaty: society.

10 This paragraph is not as strong as the previous three. It needs to be improved with more precise evidence: mention could be made of Germany being refused membership of the League of Nations or the occupation of the demilitarised Rhineland with Allied troops.

CONTINUED

The Germans could not forget about the treaty. **9** It blamed them for starting the war in Article 231; it said they were defeated when no foreign soldier had stood on German territory and Germany had not lost a major battle. German society was scarred by the treaty. Germany's great power status was questioned with much reduced military power and its empire was gone. All this was achieved with huge loss of life as well. **10**

Now write an improved response using this guidance.

PRACTICE QUESTIONS

1 The Big Three made all the major decisions about the terms of the Treaty of Versailles.
   a What was the 'War Guilt' clause in the treaty of Versailles? [4]
   b Why did Clemenceau want Germany to be punished in the Treaty of Versailles? [6]
   c To what extent was the Treaty of Versailles a fair peace for Germany? [10]
   [Total: 20]

PROJECT

In pairs, reflect upon what you have learnt in this chapter. Prepare a presentation for your class either using software or a large sheet of paper. Divide it in two, with headings *Expectations at Paris in 1919* and *Reality at Paris in 1919*.

- Identify six expectations (two for each of the Big Three) and put them on the left. On the right describe what happened to those expectations during negotiations. On a separate sheet note down all the reasons why expectations were not fully met.
- Deliver your presentations to the class.
- Germany was not invited to the peace conference at Paris. After everyone has given their presentation, have a class discussion on the following question:

  What sort of peace would have been acceptable to Germany?
- Make sure you consider why any proposals that Germany might have made would not have been acceptable to the Big Three.

SELF-EVALUATION CHECKLIST

After studying this chapter, complete this table:

You should be able to:	Needs more work	Almost there	Ready to move on
understand the terms of the Armistice in November 1918, why Germany could no longer fight and the peacemaking process in Paris in 1919			
explain why the defeated powers were not invited to Paris for peacemaking			
explain who the 'Big Three' were and why they made all the major decisions			
describe the different aims and motives of the Big Three and explain where major compromises had to be made in the final treaty			
understand the terms of the Treaty of Versailles			
explain why the Treaty of Versailles was forced on the Germans and how they reacted			
explain why the Germans who signed the peace treaty immediately became traitors in the eyes of the military and the German public			
describe the social, political and economic impact of the treaty on Germany			
show knowledge and understanding of a range of views about the Treaty of Versailles.			

Chapter 2, Key Question 2:
To what extent was the League of Nations a success?

FOCUS POINTS

This chapter will help you to answer these questions:

- How far did weaknesses in the League's organisation and membership make failure inevitable?
- How successful were the League's attempts at peacekeeping in the 1920s?
- How important was the League's humanitarian work?
- How far did the Depression make the work of the League more difficult in the 1930s?

2.0 What is this enquiry about?

In all the treaties that resulted from the Paris Peace Conference after the end of the First World War, US President Woodrow Wilson had insisted on including a reference to the League of Nations. This was to be the organisation that ensured the 1914–18 conflict really had been a 'war to end all wars'.

Your challenge in this chapter is to decide *to what extent* the League of Nations was a success. Questions that ask 'To what extent . . . ?' or 'How far . . . ?' are asking you for an opinion, and you should present evidence that shows how you reached that opinion. This diagram shows a range of options for expressing *extent*. Where will your judgement lie on this spectrum?

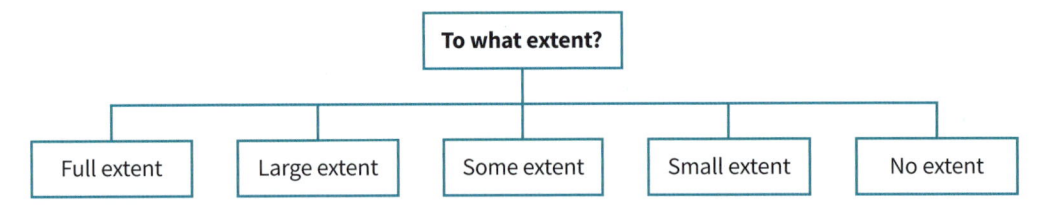

To what extent?

Full extent | Large extent | Some extent | Small extent | No extent

FOCUS TASK 2.1

Your judgement is the final part of the enquiry. Before you get there, you need to collect evidence. Copy this table and fill it in as you work through this chapter.

Focus question	Judgement: to what extent?	Evidence
How far did weaknesses in the League's organisation and membership make failure inevitable?		
How successful were the League's attempts at peacekeeping in the 1920s?		
How important was the League's humanitarian work?		
How far did the Depression make the work of the League more difficult in the 1930s?		
Overall judgement on the success of the League of Nations		

What were the aims of the League of Nations?

The two main aims of the League of Nations were:

- to maintain world peace through collective security by dealing with disputes among nations
- to encourage international cooperation to solve economic and social problems, thus improving living and working conditions for all people.

Figure 2.1: Forty-two nations were represented at the first session of the League of Nations in 1920

The Covenant of the League of Nations

One factor to consider when judging the League's effectiveness is its Covenant, the rules that set out how members should behave. As you look at each of the issues the League addressed, decide which articles of the Covenant were triggered. If the League was successful then the articles were followed and the action resolved the dispute.

Article of the Covenant	Action
Articles 8 and 9	Members must promote disarmament so that countries will only have enough military strength to maintain national security.
Article 10	Any member that is attacked will have the support of all League members.
Article 11	Any member can ask the League for help if it fears attack.
Articles 12–15	Disputes will be settled by a process: investigation of the issue, discussion in the League, then putting the issue before an international court, or going to **arbitration**. Members pledge not to go to war until three months have passed from the date at which the dispute was brought to the League's attention.
Article 16	Members agree to take prompt action against anyone going to war. Such an attack will be seen as an act of war against all other members. It could lead to economic **sanctions** such as the cutting of trade links and, possibly, military action of some kind.

KEY TERMS

arbitration: a method of resolving a dispute peacefully using an independent, neutral authority that listens to evidence like a judge and then issues a ruling

sanctions: penalties or punishments imposed by an official body such as a court of law, intended to affect the country's decision-makers so they change their policies. A typical sanction in international relations is a ban on trade

ACTIVITY 2.1

a   What difficulties would you expect the League to face in trying to use these articles to prevent conflict or stop it once it started? In pairs, role play a dialogue between a representative of the League of Nations and a representative of a country that has broken one of the articles of the League Covenant.

b   Join up with another pair. Take it in turns to read the dialogue again while the listening pair assesses how well you have understood the articles and sanctions of the Covenant. Give feedback in the form of three 'what went well' (WWW) points and two 'even better if' (EBI) points.

The crises and conflicts where the League of Nations intervened or attempted to intervene that you will examine in this chapter are:
- Vilna, 1920
- Åland Islands, 1920–21
- Corfu, 1923
- Greece versus Bulgaria, 1925
- Japanese invasion of Manchuria, 1931
- Italian invasion of Abyssinia, 1935.

REFLECTION

In which part of Activity 2.1 did you feel you learnt most effectively? When creating the dialogue, or when listening to and assessing someone else's? When working in pairs or in groups of four? Why? How was your initial response improved when you formed groups and gave feedback?

Chapter 2, Key Question 2: To what extent was the League of Nations a success?

> **FOCUS TASK 2.2**
>
> To meet the challenge of this enquiry you will need to keep a record of what the League tried to do, its successes, and its failures. Copy and complete this table as you learn about each of the crises the League dealt with.
>
> | Where was the crisis? | When was the crisis? | What was the result: success / failure / mixed? | Why was that the outcome? |
> |---|---|---|---|
> | | | | |

2.1 How far did weaknesses in the League's organisation and membership make failure inevitable?

The new international organisation had three main parts: the Secretariat, the Assembly and the Council. These are the functions of each one.

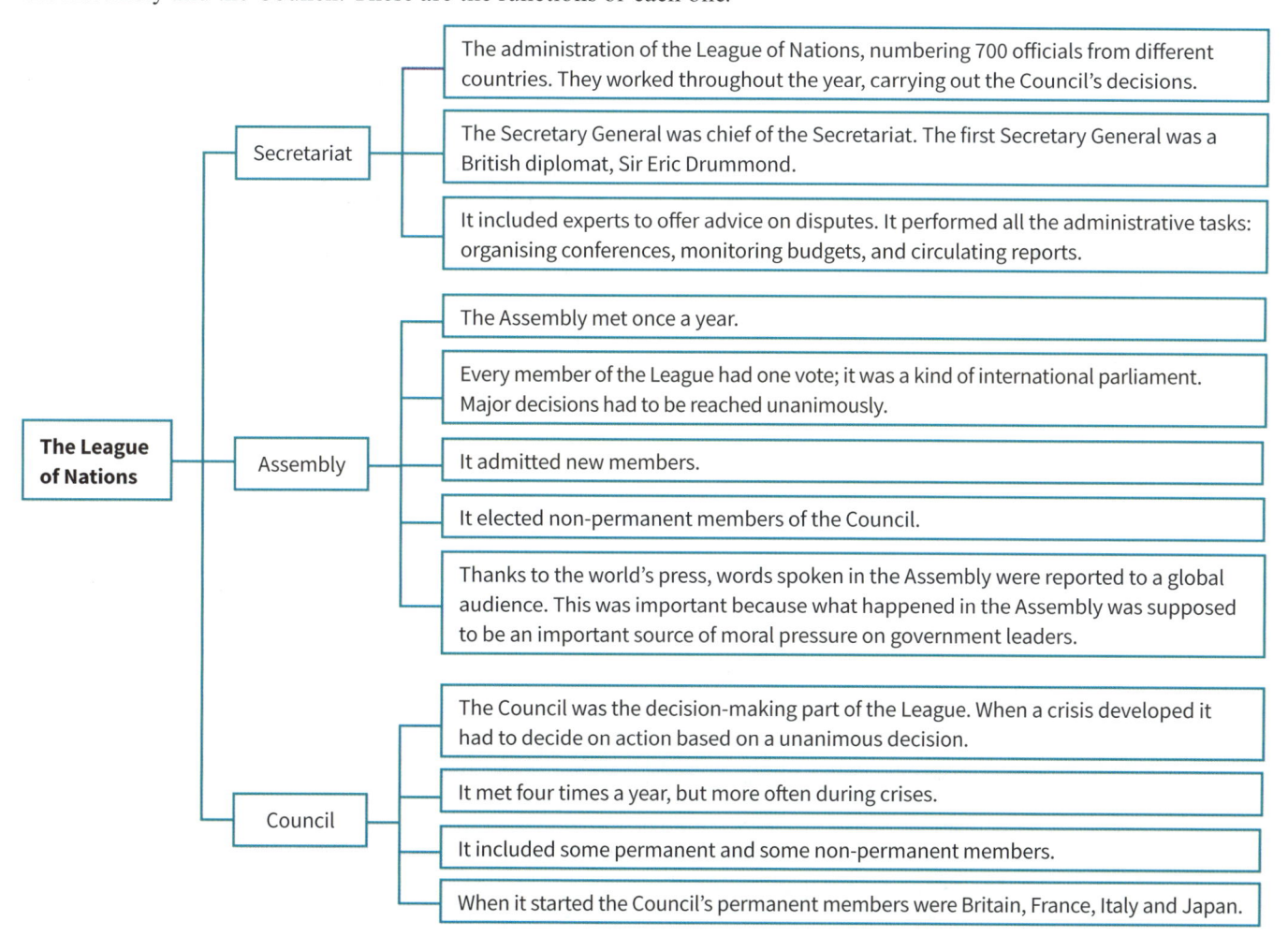

The League of Nations

Secretariat
- The administration of the League of Nations, numbering 700 officials from different countries. They worked throughout the year, carrying out the Council's decisions.
- The Secretary General was chief of the Secretariat. The first Secretary General was a British diplomat, Sir Eric Drummond.
- It included experts to offer advice on disputes. It performed all the administrative tasks: organising conferences, monitoring budgets, and circulating reports.

Assembly
- The Assembly met once a year.
- Every member of the League had one vote; it was a kind of international parliament. Major decisions had to be reached unanimously.
- It admitted new members.
- It elected non-permanent members of the Council.
- Thanks to the world's press, words spoken in the Assembly were reported to a global audience. This was important because what happened in the Assembly was supposed to be an important source of moral pressure on government leaders.

Council
- The Council was the decision-making part of the League. When a crisis developed it had to decide on action based on a unanimous decision.
- It met four times a year, but more often during crises.
- It included some permanent and some non-permanent members.
- When it started the Council's permanent members were Britain, France, Italy and Japan.

71

> CAMBRIDGE IGCSE™ AND O LEVEL HISTORY OPTION B: COURSEBOOK

> ### ACTIVITY 2.2
>
> **a** Look at the structure of the League of Nations. In pairs, discuss these questions.
>
> - In which part of the League were all the members represented?
> - Did smaller powers have equal status with the Great Powers?
> - Why could all members not be part of the League Council?
>
> **b** Create a poster summarising the organisation of the League and annotate it to identify any potential areas of weakness.
>
> **c** Research the structure and organisation of the **United Nations** that exists today. How does it compare to the structure and organisation of the League of Nations? What are the differences and similarities? Create a short slide presentation for the class.

> ### KEY TERMS
>
> **United Nations:** an international organisation founded in 1945 to promote development, peace and human rights, replacing the League of Nations
>
> **boycott:** to refuse to take part in something as a way of expressing disapproval
>
> **credit:** the ability to buy goods but to defer payment until an agreed date in the future
>
> **veto:** an official power or right or refuse to allow something

What were the League's weaknesses?

The failure of collective security

The idea of collective security was essential for the League to maintain peace. Acting together, members could place economic and/or military pressure on aggressors. There were three processes by which the League could try to stop wars:

- **Moral disapproval:** The Council would meet to condemn any act of aggression. The aggressor would cease its military actions knowing that the world was watching.

- **Economic sanctions:** If moral disapproval failed, then the Council could exert pressure using economic sanctions. This could mean a trade **boycott** and refusing **credit**.

- **Military sanctions:** If economic sanctions did not work, the Council could use military sanctions. This might involve sending military help to the victim of the attack.

Collective security sounds like a sensible way to stop war, but its potential for success was limited by the fact that the USA was not a member of the League of Nations. Two other problems restricted the collective security approach:

- All decisions taken by the Council or the Assembly had to be unanimous (agreed by everyone). It took only one **veto** to ensure nothing got done. Approval by even a majority of members was not enough to act.

- The League did not have its own army, so imposing military sanctions would be difficult. Member states would have to send soldiers and resources. This would take time, and there was no guarantee that members would do so.

Collective action requires that countries are willing to go to war over issues that might otherwise not affect them directly. It demands that all countries maintain significant military forces and it has the potential to turn local conflicts into global affairs. This was of particular importance when the League faced serious challenges in the 1930s from Italy (in Abyssinia) and from Japan (in Manchuria).

Chapter 2, Key Question 2: To what extent was the League of Nations a success?

Organisational issues

The Treaty of Versailles had many flaws, but in spite of these the League was supposed to enforce it. Germany hated the treaty and Italy and Japan disliked parts of it, so the League was not fully supported in its efforts to implement the terms of the treaty. Another issue was that even when decisions were made, the League had no army to enforce them. Its main 'weapons' were moral condemnation and economic sanctions – and these were not effective punishments for aggression. In addition, the League's membership did not include all countries that had the economic and military potential to cause trouble.

Despite these weaknesses, the League could have been a stronger force for peace if the Great Powers had wished. The articles of the League Covenant provided for economic and military sanctions against aggressors, but the Great Powers were often not willing to give up national self-interests for the sake of peace. The French and British governments were not inclined to use their military strength against aggressors because it went against popular opinion. Once it became clear that the USA would not be part of the League, Britain and France were much less interested in its role as peace-keeper.

Financial issues

The League of Nations was always run on very little money and this restricted what it could achieve. Between 1921 and 1927, it cost just $4 million per year. Britain was the biggest contributor ($550,000 per year), while others contributed what they could. With so little funding, when crises arose the League had to ask members for extra money. Sometimes it took a long time for governments to respond, so the League often turned to charities like the American Red Cross or Save the Children to react quickly to **humanitarian** disasters.

> **KEY TERM**
>
> **humanitarian:** relating to actions aimed at improving peoples' lives and reducing suffering

SOURCE 2A

An Expected Arrival.
Will the stork make good as to this infant?

Source 2A: 'Birth of Hope', a cartoon published in the USA in 1919. It shows the formation of the League of Nations after the First World War. The caption reads, 'Will the stork make good as to this infant?'

> **SOURCE ANALYSIS 2.1**
>
> Study Source 2A.
>
> a What does the phrase 'make good' mean?
>
> b Why were the stork and the baby 'expected'?
>
> c What suggests that the League of Nations had not yet started?
>
> d What is the message of the cartoon?
>
> e Can you tell from the source if the cartoonist was in favour of the US joining the League of Nations or not? Explain your answer.

SOURCE 2B

Source 2B: 'Ready to Start', a British cartoon published in 1919. The plane represents the League of Nations and the signpost says 'To disarmament and the abolition of war'. The figure in the plane is Uncle Sam, representing the USA.

SOURCE ANALYSIS 2.2

Study Source 2B.

a   What does 'The old order of things' mean?

b   Why do you think the cartoon shows the plane on the edge of a cliff?

Compare Sources 2A and 2B.

c   Which one is more optimistic about the future of the League of Nations? Explain your answer.

d   How far do the cartoonists agree about the future of the League?

e   To what extent do these sources provide evidence that the League was doomed from the start?

Chapter 2, Key Question 2: To what extent was the League of Nations a success?

Who joined and who left the League?

Was the League seriously weakened as a peacekeeping organisation by its membership? Both the Assembly and the Council were weakened because not all of the Great Powers were members.

The USA

Although President Wilson was a key supporter of the League, the US Congress voted three times between November 1919 and March 1920 not to join. Many Congressmen were worried that US involvement in the League would lead to its involvement in future wars. 116 516 US soldiers had died fighting in the First World War and there was no enthusiasm for more blood to be shed. So, despite Wilson's ambition for the USA to play a major part in the League, it did not join at all.

Germany

The Allied Powers at the Paris Peace Conference refused to allow Germany to join the League when it started. They wanted Germany to prove that it took a peaceful approach to international relations before it could be granted membership. Germany joined the League in 1926 and became a permanent member of the Council. Adolf Hitler (see Chapter 3) saw the League as a club for 'winners' in the First World War and in 1933 he decided to take Germany out of the League.

The USSR

This USSR was not invited to join the League because it was a communist country. **Communism** stood against **capitalism**, which frightened the other, capitalist, League members. The USSR was not interested in joining what looked like a capitalist club run by the very powers – Britain, France, the USA and Japan – that had invaded the Soviet Union during its **civil war** (1918–20) in a failed attempt to destroy the new communist government. By 1934, the USSR was no longer a threat to capitalist countries and it was admitted to the League. It was thrown out again in 1939 for invading Finland at the start of the Second World War.

Japan

Japan was one of the original members of the League and had a permanent seat on the Council. However, it left in 1933 following a highly critical report from the Lytton Commission over its invasion of Manchuria (part of China).

Italy

Italy was one the Great Powers, and an original member of the League of Nations. However, it left in 1937 after the League imposed economic sanctions after Italy invaded Abyssinia in East Africa.

Britain and France

These were the only two Great Powers who remained members during the League's entire existence. Reluctantly, Britain and France carried most of the responsibility for making the League work. Britain was anxious about its empire, and France was most worried about the border with Germany. In the official circles of these Great Powers, however, the League of Nations was an afterthought. Instead of using the new mechanism for resolving disputes, Britain and France relied on the traditional methods of **bilateral** talks.

KEY TERMS

communism: an economic and social system in which property and economic activity are controlled by the state. In communist countries, religion is banned and the media is censored, and everyone works for the state

capitalism: an economic and social system in which property is privately owned, the role of the state is small and people enjoy freedom of expression and religion, and have a choice of political parties to elect as the government

civil war: a war in one country between two or more sides from within that country

KEY TERM

bilateral: involving two countries or sides

Figure 2.2: A photograph of the Council of the League of Nations meeting in 1936

> ### FOCUS TASK 2.3
>
> How weak do you think the League was because of its organisation and membership?
>
> **a** In pairs, reach a judgement through a strategy of 'supposing'. First, think about the League's membership. Go through each of the countries that were not members of the League at the start (the USA, the USSR, Germany) and ask: *Suppose . . . (the USA, for example) had joined the League – would its membership have made much difference to its success?* Create a chart noting your judgement and your explanation against the country name. Then think about the League's structure and organisation and repeat the task.
>
> **b** Team up with another pair to discuss your findings. Do you agree with each other? If not, try to convince the other pair of your viewpoint to reach a shared conclusion.
>
> **c** Present your ideas to the class and invite questions and feedback.
>
> **d** At the end, use your notes and the consensus of the class to write a paragraph in response to the question.

2.2 How successful were the League's attempts at peacekeeping in the 1920s?

In its first ten years, the League dealt with 30 disputes between states. This topic explores some of these issues.

Vilna, 1920

The population of the city of Vilna included Poles, Jews and Lithuanians. After the First World War, the city was recognised as part of Lithuania. However, the Treaty of Versailles had left Lithuania's border with Poland unclear, so Poland brought the issue to the League Council. The League sent a commission to investigate. It drew up a provisional border, confirming that Vilna was part of Lithuania, and both states signed the agreement on 30 September 1920.

Shortly after this, Polish General Lucjan Żeligowski and his soldiers marched into Vilna. He may have been secretly supported by the Polish government, but there is no firm evidence for this. Lithuania was not a member of the League but it was still able to raise the matter with the Assembly. Initially, the League ordered Poland to withdraw from the city. The Polish government said it would do so, but actually sent more troops.

The League announced it would hold a plebiscite in Vilna policed by an international force organised by the League. Both Poland and Lithuania opposed the League's proposal. In March 1921, the League abandoned its plebiscite plan and instead asked a Belgian representative, Paul Hymans, to investigate the situation in Vilna and report to the League.

The Hymans Report was published in September 1921. It recommended that both Lithuanian and Polish languages were granted official status. It also suggested that all **minority groups** in Lithuania should have equal rights to education, religion, language and association. Finally, it recommended that steps be taken to align the two countries' economic and foreign policies.

The Hymans Plan was a delicate balancing act, but both sides rejected it. In January 1922, the League issued a public statement saying that it had exhausted all possibilities. So the occupation of Vilna was allowed to continue. In March 1923, the Conference of Ambassadors recognised Vilna as part of Poland.

Results for the League of Nations:

Successes	Concerns
Left with a difficult issue by the Paris peacemakers, the League responded with an innovative proposal – even if it was rejected.	Some contemporaries were outraged at the Polish takeover of Vilna. The Polish government must have known about the general's actions and the League should have invoked Article 16. The first time the League was asked to deal with an invasion, they failed to do so.
The Vilna issue made headlines around the world, but in the event, there was no war.	Poland had a strong relationship with France, based on a historical alliance, so a country was allowed to benefit from aggression.

KEY TERM

minority group: a recognisable group of people whose religion, language, culture or ethnicity is different from that of most people (the majority) in a country or region

FOCUS TASK 2.4

Write brief answers to the following questions.

a Why did the dispute over Vilna not turn into a war?

b Which of the articles of the League's Covenant were activated by this dispute?

c Was the League's reputation enhanced or weakened by this dispute?

Swap your answers with a partner and give each other feedback. If you have given different responses, justify your answers to your partner.

The Åland Islands, 1920–21

The Åland Islands are located between Sweden and Finland (see Figure 2.2), and both countries claimed them. Although 95% of the population were ethnic Swedes, the islands belonged to Finland. In June 1920, the dispute between Sweden and Finland over the Islands was referred to the Council of the League of Nations. The League ordered an investigation of the issue. It concluded that the island should remain under Finland's rule. The Council felt that awarding the Åland Islands to Sweden would set a dangerous **precedent**, encouraging other Swedish communities living in Finland to make similar claims. Outside the area, other minority groups in Europe might want to do the same.

Alongside the decision to leave the Islands in Finnish hands, the League's report recommended that the Swedes should have more **autonomy** to preserve their traditions and customs. For example, the Swedish language should be taught in schools.

These decisions meant that Finland maintained its borders but that the Swedes who lived on the Islands could keep their Swedish customs. It was the first European international agreement concluded directly through the League of Nations. In the short term, the settlement was a success, but in the 1930s the League's judgement on the Åland Islands was used by the Japanese government to justify expanding its empire to islands in the Pacific.

> **KEY TERMS**
>
> **precedent:** an action or situation that has already happened that can be used as a reason why a similar action or decision can be taken or made
>
> **autonomy:** the right of a country or region to be independent and to govern itself

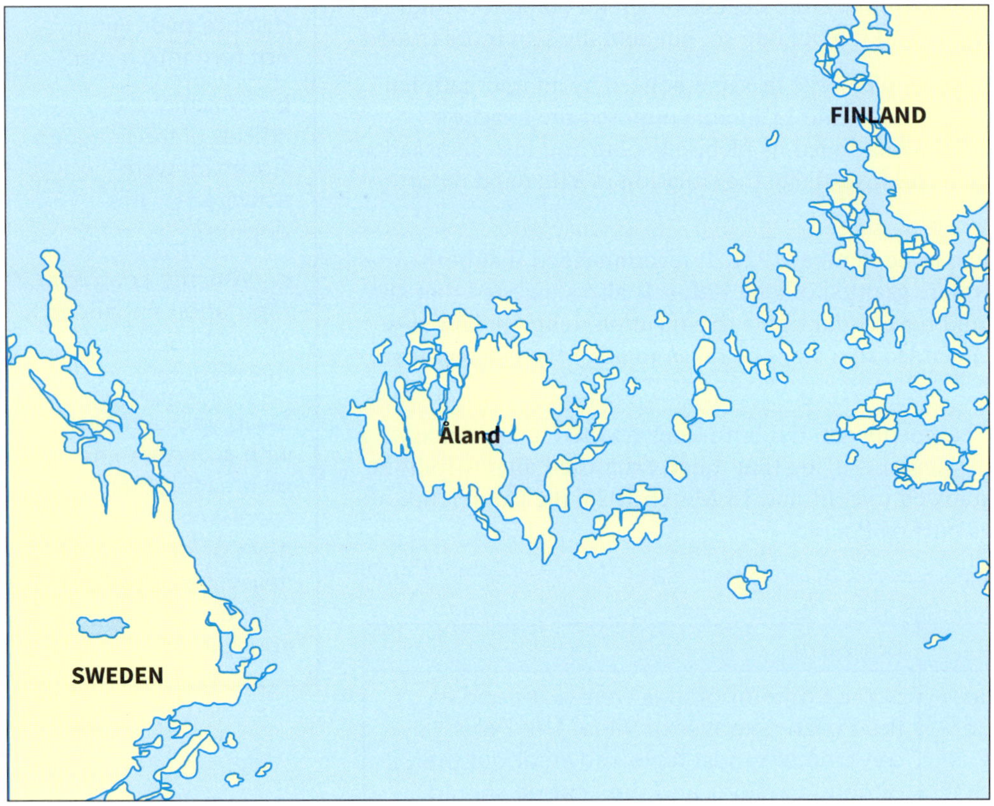

Figure 2.3: A map showing the location of the Åland Islands

Chapter 2, Key Question 2: To what extent was the League of Nations a success?

Results for the League of Nations:

Successes	Concerns
The development of autonomy was important and Swedish customs were preserved. It was only a formality that the people of the Åland Islands were Finnish citizens.	This dispute raised an important question in relation to President Wilson's principle of national self-determination. How far should the principle be applied?
Finland had preserved its borders to avoid setting a precedent that might lead to other ethic claims, thus destroying the Paris Peace Settlement.	The way to resolve disputes over island ownership was now established: the island belongs to the country of which it was once a part. This principle was used by Japan in the 1930s to justify its expansion in the Pacific Ocean.

FOCUS TASK 2.5

Write brief answers to the following questions.

a Why didn't the Åland Islands dispute turn into a war?

b Which articles of the League Covenant were used in this dispute?

c Was the League's reputation enhanced or weakened by this dispute?

Swap your answers with a partner and give each other feedback. If you have given different responses, justify your answers to your partner.

The Corfu Incident, 1923

The map in Figure 2.4 shows Greece and its neighbours in the 1920s. In August 1923, an Italian general, Enrico Tellini, was murdered in Greece along with four of his assistants. The men had been working for the **Conference of Ambassadors**, reporting on a border dispute between Greece and Albania. The Greek authorities failed to arrest anyone for the murder so the Italian leader, Benito Mussolini, ordered Italian troops to occupy the Greek island of Corfu. He hoped to force the Greek government to compensate Italy for Tellini's death.

KEY TERM

Conference of Ambassadors: a diplomatic organisation established at the Paris Peace Conference, and based in Paris, to supervise the completion of issues that were resolved by the peace treaties

KEY FIGURE

Lord Robert Cecil (1864–1958)

British politician Lord Robert Cecil was one of the men who helped to plan and create the League of Nations. He believed that it should be compulsory for peaceful discussions to take place before any conflict and that there should be a three-month gap between these procedures and any armed conflict. He also argued that Germany should be a member of the League right from the start. Throughout his life, Cecil highlighted the importance of the League for peace in international affairs. He was awarded the Nobel Peace Prize in 1937.

Greece appealed to the Council of the League of Nations. Italy argued that its occupation was not an act of war. The British representative on the Council, Robert Cecil, disagreed. He wanted the League to impose sanctions on Italy and to send some ships from the British navy to the coast of Corfu as a warning. However, the British government did not want to risk damaging trade relations with Italy. Instead, the Council decided to send a commission to the Albanian–Greek border to investigate Tellini's death. The commission reported that it could find no evidence that Greece had failed to investigate the murder properly. On 25 September, the Conference of Ambassadors met to consider the report. As a result of Italian pressure, Greece was made to pay 50 million lire as compensation. Two days later, the Italians began evacuating Corfu.

Results for the League of Nations:

Successes	Concerns
Greece was able to appeal to the Council when it felt it was not being fairly treated by the Conference of Ambassadors.	Italy committed an act of war, but this injustice was not punished by the other Great Powers. The League failed to stop Italy from invading the Greek Island of Corfu even though Greece asked for help.
Italy and Greece did not go to war and Italian forces did not stay in Greek territory for long.	The League of Nations had little involvement in the final settlement of the crisis. It appeared that the Conference of Ambassadors was more important.
–	The Corfu Incident was seen as a serious failure for the League. It showed that powerful nations could still bully a less powerful neighbour (Greece was a small, weak country with no powerful friends on the Council).

Figure 2.4: A map showing south-eastern Europe in 1925, including Greece, Corfu, Albania and Bulgaria

Chapter 2, Key Question 2: To what extent was the League of Nations a success?

> **FOCUS TASK 2.6**
>
> Write brief answers to the following questions.
>
> a   Why didn't the Corfu incident turn into a war?
>
> b   Which of the League's articles were used to resolve the dispute?
>
> c   Do you think the League's reputation was enhanced or weakened by this dispute?
>
> Swap your answers with a partner and give each other feedback. If you have given different responses, justify your answers to your partner.

Greek-Bulgarian confrontation, 1925

It is unclear exactly what started the confrontation between Greece and Bulgaria in 1923. Whatever the facts, fighting broke out between the two countries and the Bulgarian government appealed to the League to intervene.

The League ordered an end to the fighting and said that troops from both sides should withdraw to their own country. The Greek government was ordered to pay $218,250 in compensation. Both countries accepted this decision. British, French and Italian officials travelled to the area to confirm that the Council's instructions had been obeyed. The confrontation was over.

Results for the League of Nations:

Successes	Concerns
The Council's demand to end military action as a first step was obeyed.	Greece thought that the League's involvement in the Corfu Incident two years earlier resulted in a different outcome for Italy than the one on the Greek-Bulgarian border. It felt like there was one rule for powers like Italy and another for smaller countries like Greece, so the League was not treating nations fairly.
The Council then investigated the reasons for the incident and reported them. In the past, small border incidents like this had started wars.	–

On this occasion, the only major concern to weigh against the successes was the unequal treatment of smaller powers like Greece. However, the League's action in 1925 should be considered in context. It may have looked for a time as though Greece and Bulgaria were about to go to war, but in fact neither country was in a position to conduct a serious military campaign. Both had domestic difficulties: Greece was struggling with a million refugees from Turkey, and Bulgaria had been mostly demilitarised. Furthermore, neither Greece nor Bulgaria was allied to a Great Power that could have acted to support them. This alone was likely to have prevented the war from growing in importance and involving neighbours. This prospect was always the great fear of any diplomat who remembered the assassination of Archduke Franz Ferdinand in 1914 (see Introduction Part 2).

FOCUS TASK 2.7

Write brief answers to the following questions.

a   Why didn't the Greek-Bulgarian dispute turn into a war?

b   Which of the articles of the League's Covenant were activated by this dispute?

c   Was the League's reputation enhanced or weakened by this dispute?

Swap your answers with a partner and give each other feedback. If you have given different responses, justify your answers to your partner.

THINKING SKILLS

The year is 1929. You have been invited to Geneva, where the League of Nations has its headquarters, to a **summit** on how the League has operated so far and to address its weaknesses. Write answers to the following questions.

- What is the League's greatest weakness, in your opinion?
- Is the organisation fit for purpose? If not, why not?
- Does the Covenant need to be changed? If so, how?
- How well is the relationship between the major powers and smaller ones working?
- Overall, what recommendations would you give to ensure greater success in the future?

KEY TERM

summit: a formal meeting between government leaders from two or more countries

ACTIVITY 2.3

You should now have partially completed the table you created in Focus task 2.2. Look back over this table and at the tables in this section showing the results for the League of Nations of each dispute. Compare the different disputes. Write two paragraphs in response to the following questions.

a   What patterns do you see in terms of differences in the nature of the disputes?

b   How far do you think these explain why they led to different results?

2.3 How important was the League's humanitarian work?

The League had agencies and commissions to address humanitarian issues such as disease, poverty, **exploitation**, prisoners of war and refugees. Through its actions, the League showed the world how international cooperation could encourage peace by successfully managing these issues. As you read about each commission, consider how successful it was and how important the League's work in this area was. Record your judgement in the table you began in Focus task 2.1.

The Commission for Refugees

Led by the Norwegian explorer Fridtjof Nansen, the Commission for Refugees was established in 1921 to look after the interests of refugees. This included overseeing their return to their home country and, when necessary, **resettlement**. At the end of the First World War, there were between 2 million and 3 million ex-prisoners of war from various nations in Russia. Within two years, the Commission had helped 425 000 of them return home. It established camps in Turkey in 1922 to support the country in dealing with a refugee crisis, helping to prevent disease and hunger. Working in difficult circumstances and with little money, Nansen and his staff used imaginative methods to look after these people. They set up camps and taught new skills to refugees. They provided them with identity papers, such as the Nansen passport, which allowed displaced people to move around more easily.

The League's work with refugees was not always successful. During the 1930s, it made only limited attempts to help Jewish people fleeing Nazi Germany. However, the initial work of the Commission for Refugees showed the world that it was possible to take collective action to help those who had been forced to leave their homes and countries. The League's work was also important in beginning to organise international relief efforts. Its legacy was an agreed set of international rules about the care and protection of refugees that still exists today.

> **KEY TERMS**
>
> **exploitation:** the act of using someone unfairly to your own advantage, e.g. people may be exploited in the workplace by being overworked and underpaid
>
> **resettlement:** the process of helping someone to move to another place to live

Figure 2.5: A sample Nansen passport

Figure 2.6: Fridtjof Nansen (second from the right) with Greek refugees in Thrace, Greece

The Health Organization

Under the leadership of Ludwig Rajchman, the League's Health Organization became one of its most successful bodies. It established links with countries outside the League, such as the USA, Germany and the USSR to provide an information service, technical assistance and advice on public health matters. For example, it supported the USSR in trying to prevent a typhus epidemic in the early 1920s by organising a public information campaign on health and **sanitation**. By 1923, the worst of the epidemic was over.

The Health Organization reduced cases of **leprosy** and began an international campaign to eliminate mosquitoes, which reduced the spread of malaria and yellow fever. For example, the death rate among workers building the Tanganyika railway in East Africa fell from 50% to 4% as a result of the efforts of the Health Organization. Research institutes based in London, Copenhagen and Singapore developed internationally accepted vaccines for diphtheria, tetanus and tuberculosis.

After the Second World War, the League's Health Organization became the World Health Organization, which is still part of the United Nations.

> **KEY TERMS**
>
> **sanitation:** the systems for taking dirty water and other waste products away from buildings in order to protect people's health
>
> **leprosy:** a contagious disease that affects the skin and the nervous system
>
> **trafficking:** buying or selling goods or people illegally
>
> **convention:** an informal agreement between leaders and politicans on a matter than involves them all
>
> **regulation:** a rule or a set of rules for organisations that affect parts of the economy

KEY FIGURE

Rachel Crowdy (1884–1964)

Rachel Crowdy worked as a nurse during the First World War. After the war, she began working at the League of Nations. She became the only woman to head a department, Opium Traffic and Social Issues. She became famous for her thorough investigations into the **trafficking** of women and children, and the drug trade in opium. In 1920, Crowdy went to Poland to help contain a typhus epidemic there. When she retired from the League in 1931, she was guest of honour at the Café Royal in London, where 600 women saluted her achievements.

The International Labour Organization

The International Labour Organization (ILO) was created in 1919. It fought for social justice in the form of safe, healthy and fair working conditions. The ILO could make recommendations to national governments about labour matters. These would appear in the form of **conventions** agreed by the ILO's annual conference. If accepted there, the conventions were presented to national parliaments within one year by League members. The ILO adopted the first six International Labour Conventions, which focused on hours of work in industry, unemployment, maternity protection, night work for women, minimum age and night work for young persons in industry. By itself, the League could not force countries to change their laws and practice, but it did hold countries to account for not making progress in these areas.

Little by little, an international network of labour laws and **regulation** started to develop. By 1939 the work of the ILO had agreed 67 conventions. For example, the ILO's efforts to regulate child labour resulted in children only working an eight-hour day in the Persian carpet industry and their rooms being properly ventilated. The ILO successfully restricted the addition of lead to paint. It also convinced several countries to adopt an eight-hour working day and 48-hour working week. Hours of work

Chapter 2, Key Question 2: To what extent was the League of Nations a success?

remained on the ILO agenda throughout the 1920s and 1930s, and the organisation was the main forum for international debate and the adoption of international labour standards. This was one of the League's most important achievements.

In August 1934, the USA became a member of the ILO, which widened its impact. During the worldwide Depression in the 1930s, the organisation worked to address the widespread social distress caused by the economic collapse. In 1932, it called for major international action on finance, trade and public works policies to try to overcome the Depression. When the League ended, the ILO became an **agency** of the United Nations in 1946.

Figure 2.7: Child labourers

ACTIVITY 2.4

Look at the photograph of child labourers in Figure 2.7. It was taken before the ILO was formed. Discuss the following questions in small groups.

a What issues can you see that the ILO would be concerned about?

b The ILO's conventions did not have the force of law. Does this mean that the efforts of ILO staff were wasted?

c Child labour still exists today. What does this tell you about the difficulties of the ILO's work? How might this affect your judgement about the importance and effectiveness of the League's agencies?

KEY TERM

agency: an organisation that acts on behalf of other organisations. In the League of Nations, different agencies focused on specific issues under the authority of the Council

85

The Slavery Commission

The Slavery Commission aimed to end enslavement and the trade in enslaved people across the world. Its work included supporting people forced to become sex workers. Its main success was ending enslavement in the mandates that had been established by the Treaty of Versailles (see Chapter 1). The League secured a commitment from Abyssinia to end slavery as a condition of membership in 1923, and worked with Liberia to abolish forced labour and the enslavement of people between tribes. Records were kept to control enslavement, sex work and the trafficking of women and children.

Partly because of pressure from the League of Nations, Afghanistan abolished slavery in 1923, Iraq in 1924, Nepal in 1926, Transjordan and Persia in 1929, Bahrain in 1937 and Abyssinia in 1942. Overall, efforts by the League of Nations freed around 200 000 enslaved people. The League's humanitarian work was very important in making the issue a priority for many member and non-member states. By itself, the League could not abolish slavery, but its reports, photographs and observations kept the issue in the public eye.

Figure 2.8: A photograph showing child labour in Cameroon, 1919

> ### FOCUS TASK 2.8
>
> In pairs, discuss the following questions. You can use the judgements: very important / important / little importance.
>
> a   What did the League do to improve the social and economic conditions in which people worked around the world?
>
> b   What did the League do to improve the health of people around the world?
>
> c   If the League had not acted to bring together international resources, how would individuals and groups have been affected?
>
> Create a poster that highlights the importance of the League's humanitarian work. Include the different commissions and agencies and highlight some of their achievements.

Chapter 2, Key Question 2: To what extent was the League of Nations a success?

> **THINK LIKE A HISTORIAN**
>
> Working for the League of Nations in the 1920s required specific skills and knowledge. In pairs, choose one part of the League, such as the Secretariat and the General Assembly, and remind yourselves of its role. Under two headings, 'Essential' and 'Desirable', write a list of skills and knowledge that you would want candidates to have if they applied for a post in your division.
>
> Today, the United Nations tries to achieve similar aims to the League. In what ways would your two lists be different from the ones you drew up for the 1920s if you were recruiting for a similar role today?

Key points

The League of Nations' humanitarian work

- The League of Nations did a variety of humanitarian work. Some tackled immediate problems such as the prisoners of war in Russia; others improved situations for people over the longer term, such as working to eliminate diseases.

- The Commission for Refugees helped people who had been displaced by the war and paved the way for international relief efforts during times of conflict.

- International Labour Organization (ILO) gave guidance on working conditions that ultimately helped both children and adults to live longer and healthier lives.

- The Health Organization contributed significantly to preventing and treating diseases including malaria, typhus and leprosy around the world.

- The Slavery Commission worked with both member and non-member states to secure commitments to end enslavement and the trade in enslaved people.

2.4 How far did the Depression make the work of the League more difficult in the 1930s?

What was the Great Depression?

The Great Depression was a series of connected economic developments that affected countries around the world in 1929 and lasted well into the 1930s. Where order books for cars and household products had once been full, the 1930s saw a downturn in demand, and cuts in production and trade soon followed. Factories closed, farmers went bankrupt, and millions lost their jobs and joined long lines of the unemployed. To make matters worse, the banking system failed and people lost their money. Although it began in the USA, countries in Europe and Asia, particularly Germany, Italy and Japan, all faced similar problems.

Figure 2.9: Unemployed men wait in line to get free food at a soup kitchen in the USA during the Great Depression

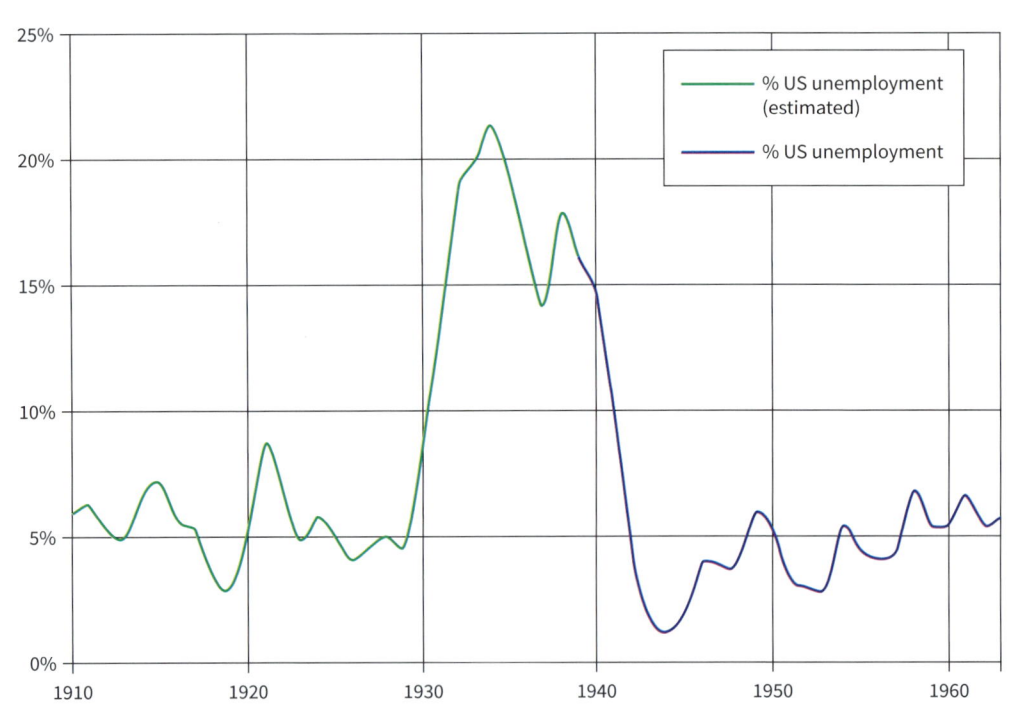

Figure 2.10: A graph showing the sudden and huge rise in unemployment in the USA during the Great Depression

Chapter 2, Key Question 2: To what extent was the League of Nations a success?

The League of Nations was supposed to maintain world peace by organising collective action to prevent war. Working collectively to keep the peace was hard enough in the 1920s. What difference did the Great Depression make?

Whether League members or not, all countries, large and small, were tested by the impact of the Great Depression. Politicians now prioritised dealing with unemployment, suffering and poverty. Foreign affairs came second. This attitude and policy is known as 'economic nationalism'.

The two member countries that were most affected by the Great Depression were Japan and Germany. They were also the two countries that were most disruptive to international relations in the 1930s.

The work of the League in the 1930s

Much of the humanitarian work by the League's agencies continued to be effective in the 1930s. However, the Great Depression created new problems to solve in relation to peacekeeping. By the end of the 1930s, the League could not prevent a second world war from starting. In this sense it failed in its primary purpose. After Germany invaded Poland in 1939, the League did not meet again until April 1946. It closed its door and its assets were transferred to the newly formed United Nations organisation, based in New York City.

Two key events made it obvious to the world that the League was ineffective when faced with countries that pursued national rather than international interests as a result of the Depression:

- the Japanese invasion of Manchuria
- the Italian invasion of Abyssinia.

Across the world, the Depression meant that countries were far less concerned with peace and justice. When called upon, the League could not gather enough support to uphold collective security. Eventually, it was powerless to keep the peace.

The Manchurian crisis, 1931

The Japanese invasion of Manchuria in 1931 was the first time the League of Nations had faced a challenge from one of the Great Powers. If the League had met the challenge and stopped the invasion, it might have stopped other countries, such as Italy and Germany, trying to extend their power. The League's failure showed not only Japan, but also leaders such as Hitler and Mussolini, that it could not prevent an aggressive country from making territorial gains (see Chapter 3).

What caused the crisis in Manchuria?

The population of Japan was increasing rapidly. With almost no natural resources to sell abroad, Japan was hit especially hard by the Great Depression. It had to import oil, iron, steel and other goods to support its industry and military. To do so, Japan had to export its own products. This became harder to do in the Depression as countries increased tariffs to protect their own struggling industries.

> **REVISION TIP**
>
> When revising the League's humanitarian work, think about the key question: *To what extent was the League a success?* To answer this question, you need to focus on the impact it had on the humanitarian problems it tried to solve as well as how successful it was in peacekeeping. This will help you reach an overall judgement. Do not simply describe the League's *actions*; always consider its *impact*, and support your ideas with evidence.

The weaknesses of the Japanese economy could only be addressed by distracting public opinion through a more aggressive foreign policy. Japan looked to China, a country with a population of 450 million, as an ideal market to exploit. China was vulnerable to both economic and military invasion in the 1930s, mainly because it lacked a strong central government. Three groups were competing for power in China at the time: the Nationalists led by Chiang Kai-Shek, the Communists led by Mao Zedong, and provincial warlords.

The Chinese region of Manchuria seemed perfect for exploitation. It was bordered by Korea, which had already been occupied by Japan in 1910, to the south. To the north and east, it bordered the USSR (see Figure 2.11). It was also rich in resources such as lumber, rubber and oil.

Figure 2.11: A map showing the Japanese invasion of Manchuria

Short-term causes of the crisis in Manchuria

On 18 September 1931, an explosion damaged a small section of railway track near the city of Mukden in Manchuria. Japan owned the railway, and blamed Chinese Nationalists for the incident. In fact, the bomb was planted by officers in the Japanese army to give Japan an excuse to invade Manchuria – which it did. The Japanese government was shocked by the Mukden Incident, because it was unaware of this plot by the military. However, as the Japanese army started winning victories in Manchuria, the government was powerless to stop it. Under the Japanese constitution, the government had to include representatives from the army and the navy. Without these military personnel, the government would collapse.

Within a few months, the Japanese army had taken over a region more than 300 kilometres around Mukden. The Chinese army was mostly untrained and offered little resistance. In February 1932, Japan declared the resource-rich area to be the new autonomous state of Manchukuo, although in reality it was under the control of the local Japanese Army. The Japanese installed Puyi, the nephew of the Chinese Emperor, as the **puppet ruler**.

> **KEY TERM**
>
> **puppet ruler:** someone given the title of a ruler but who has no real power and is actually controlled by another person or group, such as the military

Chapter 2, Key Question 2: To what extent was the League of Nations a success?

The Nationalist leader Chiang Kai-Shek reported the invasion to the League of Nations. Would it be able to keep the peace between Japan and China?

The Lytton Report

The League of Nations sent a commission led by Lord Lytton to China to investigate. It was months before the Lytton Report was issued in October 1932. This gave the Japanese plenty of time to secure their control over Manchuria. However, the report concluded that Japan was the aggressor and that it had no right to invade Manchuria. The report advised that the region should be returned to China and that the puppet state should not be officially recognised by other countries.

The League voted to accept the report's findings. In response, Japan left the League. It continued with its nationalist policies, kept Manchukuo and launched a full-scale attack on China in 1937. Only defeat in the Second World War in 1945 ended Japan's rule in the region.

SOURCE 2C & 2D

Source 2C: An American cartoon from 1931, commenting on the Manchurian crisis

Source 2D: A British cartoon, published 24 November 1932, called 'Trial by Geneva' about the League of Nations' reaction to the Lytton Report

SOURCE ANALYSIS 2.3

Study Sources 2C and 2D.

a What is the purpose of drawing the big artillery blasting through a number of international agreements?

b What does Source 2C tell you about US attitudes towards Japan?

c Explain the message of the cartoon in Source 2D.

d What is the difference in attitude towards Japan between Sources 2C and 2D? Explain the difference.

e What do the cartoons focus on: the causes of the Manchurian crisis, what happened or the consequences of it? Explain.

f Which of the cartoons is an example of propaganda? Explain.

The consequences of the invasion

The Manchurian crisis damaged the moral strength and influence of the League of Nations. The League was powerless if a strong nation decided to pursue an aggressive policy against another nation. By 1932, the League had shown the world it was incapable of enforcing world peace. The stability of international relations had reached a turning point. It was tipping towards conflict, in favour of those **dictators** who wanted to build their own empires and had the military strength to do so.

The Abyssinian crisis, 1935–36

Like Japan, Italy was a member of the League Council, and just like Japan, Italy had ambitions to increase its territory. The Italian leader, Benito Mussolini, was a **fascist** who wanted to create a new Roman Empire and make Italy 'great, respected, and feared'.

Causes of the Abyssinian crisis

Italy had been interested in Abyssinia for a long time. In 1896, Italy had attempted an invasion, but failed. Once Benito Mussolini took power in the 1920s, the dream of conquering Abyssinia was high on his agenda. The Italian colony of Somaliland was very close to Abyssinia (see Figure 2.13). By 1932, Mussolini had completed his invasion plans. The crisis began early in December 1934 at Wal-Wal, in a border region between Abyssinia and Somaliland. During a **skirmish**, about 30 Italians and three times as many Abyssinians died.

Mussolini demanded compensation for the loss of life. With tension increasing, other Great Powers got involved, including Britain and France. They did so without following any procedures set by the League of Nations, or even consulting it. Selfish motives drove the leaders of these countries, as they were anxious to maintain positive relations with Mussolini. They wanted his friendship to isolate Hitler's Germany, which had by now left the League of Nations and begun rearming (see Chapter 3).

Figure 2.12: Mussolini giving a stirring speech to the Italian people, inspiring them with dreams of a new Roman Empire

> **KEY TERMS**
>
> **dictatorship:** a system of government in which one person controls a country without holding elections and without being restrained by a parliament, maintaining power using the army and police
>
> **fascist:** someone who follows fascism, an extreme right-wing political system based on a single powerful leader with no political opposition, state control and extreme pride in country and race
>
> **skirmish:** a short, unplanned period of fighting

What happened?

The Italian invasion was unprovoked aggression. The League immediately condemned it and imposed economic sanctions. One delegate told the Assembly that 'great or small, strong or weak, near or far, white or coloured, let us never forget that one day we may be somebody's Abyssinia'. Sanctions included banning the sale of armaments and other war supplies, and ending credit to the Italian government and Italian firms.

The sanctions failed to hurt Italy's economy. This was mainly because oil and coal, essential for running the war, were not on the list of banned trade. Furthermore, Britain kept open the Suez Canal, which was the main supply route for the Italian army, fearing possible attacks by the Italian navy on British colonies such as Malta and Gibraltar.

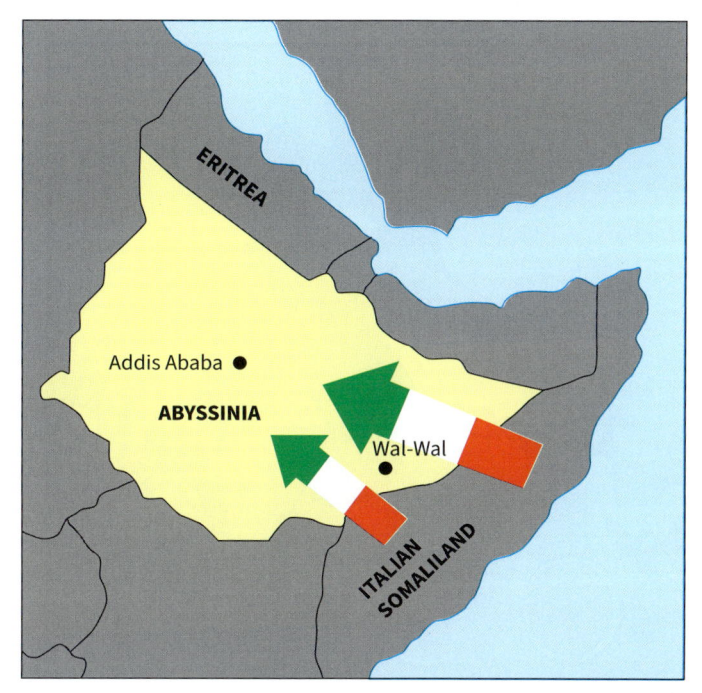

Figure 2.13: A map showing the Italian invasion of Abyssinia, October 1935

Britain and France made a secret deal with Mussolini, without the League's knowledge. The Hoare-Laval **Pact** promised that Italy would receive two-thirds of Abyssinia in return for ending the war. This amounted to more than 155 000 square kilometres of Abyssinian territory. In exchange, nearly 8000 square kilometres of Somaliland would be given to Abyssinia to provide access to the sea. When news of the pact leaked, Hoare – who was involved in drafting the pact – was forced to resign as British foreign secretary and Laval resigned as the French prime minister.

In January 1936, Mussolini appointed a new commander, who launched a fresh attack. This time, Italian troops made greater progress, partly because they used **mustard gas**. The League considered imposing an **embargo** on oil again, but France rejected the idea. By this time, Europe was becoming more concerned about Hitler's actions. In March 1936, he violated the Treaty of Versailles by remilitarising the Rhineland (see Chapter 3). The Italians were left alone and overran Abyssinia. The capital was taken on 5 May.

The Emperor of Abyssinia, Haile Selassie, travelled to Geneva to give an emotional speech to the Assembly on 30 June. His outrage was heard around the world. But with the war nearly over, League members had little reason to maintain sanctions. They were abandoned in July, and in December 1937 Italy withdrew from the League of Nations. No one believed that the League had the power to prevent war any more.

KEY TERMS

pact: a written agreement between two or more countries to act together in a particular way

mustard gas: a weapon used during the First World War, which causes large blisters on exposed skin and lungs

embargo: a partial or complete end to trade with a country (an example of a trade sanction)

SOURCES 2E & 2F

Source 2E: An Italian postcard from 1935–36, during the Abyssinian War. The text says: 'Armaments. Here is the best weapon'.

I [. . .] am here today to claim that justice which is due to my people, and the assistance promised to it eight months ago, when fifty nations asserted that aggression had been committed in violation of international treaties.

There is no precedent for a Head of State himself speaking in this assembly. But there is also no precedent for a people being victim of such injustice and being at present threatened by abandonment to its aggressor. Also, there has never before been an example of any Government proceeding to the systematic extermination of a nation by barbarous means, in violation of the most solemn promises made by the nations of the earth that there should not be used against innocent human beings the terrible poison of harmful gases.

Special sprayers were installed on board aircraft so that they could vapourise, over vast areas of territory, a fine, death-dealing rain. Groups of nine, fifteen, eighteen aircraft followed one another so that the fog issuing from them formed a continuous sheet [. . .] Soldiers, women, children, cattle, rivers, lakes and pastures were drenched continually with this deadly rain. In order to kill off systematically all living creatures, in order to [. . .] poison waters and pastures, the Italian command made its aircraft pass over and over again. That was its chief method of warfare.

Source 2F: An extract from an appeal by Haile Selassie, Emperor of Abyssinia, to the League of Nations, June 1936

SOURCE ANALYSIS 2.4

Study Sources 2E and 2F.

a Is the postcard in Source 2E in favour of the war or against it? Select details to support your judgement.

b Is this an example of propaganda? Explain your thinking.

c What similarities can you see in Italian attitudes and behaviour in the two sources?

d How does Haile Selassie seek to influence the audience he is addressing?

Chapter 2, Key Question 2: To what extent was the League of Nations a success?

> **THINKING SKILLS**
>
> When Haile Selassie gave the speech in Source 2F, Italian journalists in the audience booed him. Imagine you are a journalist working for a newspaper also listening to the emperor's speech. How would you have reacted? Would you feel embarrassed, humiliated, thoughtful, pleased, angry? Write two paragraphs explaining what happened, how you felt, and why.
>
> In the article you are writing for your newspaper, the editor has asked you to include some of the options available to the League in dealing with the issue. List any ideas you have. You could begin with:
>
> - extend the economic sanctions
> - kick Italy out of the League.

The consequences

This was the only occasion when the League launched a full-scale security action. It went beyond negotiations and imposed economic sanctions. The problem for Britain and France was that their increasing concern about Germany meant they had to keep a working relationship with Mussolini. Unfortunately, France and Britain did not pursue a consistent policy. They wavered between working within the League and taking action outside it. This made them look weak and confused to Mussolini.

As time went on, it became harder for Britain and France to keep Italy on their side, detached from Hitler's Germany. Italy withdrew from the League in 1937. In September 1937, Mussolini visited Berlin. In November of the same year, Italy signed the Anti-**Comintern** Pact with Germany and Japan to present a united front against Soviet communism – an ideology all three countries hated (see Chapter 3).

Other League members realised that its procedures had not saved a League member from complete destruction. The League could no longer be trusted to protect them against aggression. After Abyssinia, the League and collective security were abandoned. Instead, most countries acted in their own interests.

Key points

The League in the 1930s

- The Depression was a worldwide economic collapse that made peacekeeping much harder throughout the 1930s because **domestic** problems overcame **foreign** ones.
- The governments of the Great Powers focused on finding solutions to unemployment and the decline of trade. Economic nationalism made it far less likely that the Great Powers would prioritise the League of Nations.
- Three countries suffered more than most during the Depression: Japan, Italy and Germany. All three countries were led by dictators or groups whose policies were fascist, nationalistic and militaristic.
- Britain and France let the League down by not supporting its work in dealing with the Manchurian Crisis or the war in Abyssinia.
- By the mid-1930s the League's reputation was in ruin.

> **KEY TERMS**
>
> **Comintern:** a Soviet-led organisation designed to promote communist ideology in countries outside the Soviet Union
>
> **Domestic policy:** matters that relate to the home country
>
> **Foreign policy:** government attitudes and action towards countries that lie outside the borders of the home country

FOCUS TASK 2.9

To help you remember the various causes for why the League failed, use this mnemonic, **'WAS DUMB'**:

Weak

Abyssinia

Structure

Depression/Disarmament

Unsuccessful

Manchuria

Bullies

a   In pairs, develop each letter in 'WAS DUMB' to explain the reason more fully. Make sure you include evidence to support each point.

b   Afterwards, rank the different reasons in order of significance and justify your decisions.

SOURCES 2G & 2H

Source 2G: A British cartoon published in 1935. Mussolini, the Italian leader, is the larger figure. The female figure to the right represents Western Civilisation. The cartoonist is commenting on the fact that Italy was a member of the League of Nations

The League did not really fail in the 1930s, rather it was sidelined, as politicians chose increasingly to work beyond its corridors. The Covenant was not applied, its spirit was not honoured and the principles of universality were not taken seriously.

Source 2H: Historian Martyn Housden, commenting on the League's performance in the 1930s

SOURCE ANALYSIS 2.5

Study Sources 2G and 2H.

a   To what extent does Source 2G confirm the mnemonic in Focus task 2.9, explaining the reasons for the League's failure?

b   To what extent does Source 2H agree with the cartoonist in Source 2G and the mnemonic?

ACTIVITY 2.5

Work in small groups.

a   Discuss and compare the two crises, Manchuria and Abyssinia. Consider what were the main differences and similarities between them. Did the League perform better in one crisis than the other? Make notes of your ideas.

b   'Great Powers always act in their own interests.' To what extent do Manchuria and Abyssinia illustrate this statement? Debate this idea in your groups. Reach a judgement on *the extent to which* the Great Powers were working in their own interests using the scale you explored at the start of this chapter: full extent, large extent, some extent, small extent, no extent. Present your decision to the class and give each other feedback.

FOCUS TASK 2.10

Peacekeeping was not easy for the League of Nations in the 1930s. What judgement will you make in answering the question: *How far did the Depression make the work of the League more difficult?* Keep in mind these points.

- The phrase 'work of the League' does not mean just peacekeeping. It includes humanitarian activities too.
- In general, small and great powers behave in ways that serve their own interests.
- The League's various agencies were only funded by its members, principally the Great Powers.

Now write a paragraph in response to the question.

When you have finished, swap with a partner and assess each other's work using the following checklist.

Has your partner:

- included both the League's peacekeeping role as well as its humanitarian work
- explained how 'economic nationalism' made countries far less likely to work cooperatively with the League
- explained how the Depression made some governments look to aggressive foreign policies to distract public opinion from domestic problems
- used the examples of the Manchurian Crisis and the invasion of Abyssinia as evidence to support their points?

> CAMBRIDGE IGCSE™ AND O LEVEL HISTORY OPTION B: COURSEBOOK

THINK LIKE A HISTORIAN

Peacekeeping was a central aim of the League of Nations and it is one of the key aims of today's United Nations (UN). However, there have been at least 285 armed conflicts since the UN was formed.

Research one of the conflicts that interests you. Find out the causes of the conflict, how the UN tried to stop it and whether it succeeded. Share your research with the class and explain whether or not the conflict could have been averted. If so, how?

How do conflicts around the world today directly affect the lives of people in different countries? Do you feel that any conflict directly affects you? How do you know about events going on in different countries? Do you trust the sources you use? Discuss your ideas as a class.

REFLECTION

How easy did you find Focus task 2.10? How well did you complete it, based on your partner's feedback? Would you have preferred to have time to discuss the question first before writing? What does discussion enable you to do before writing?

SUMMARY

- The League of Nations was established on a tide of high hopes after the First World War.
- The 1920s saw mixed success for the League of Nations. Its humanitarian work was well-organised and effective for the most part, but it could not impose its decisions on other countries.
- Disputes about territories were resolved peacefully where the League's decision was accepted and where the Great Powers did not see their national interests compromised.
- The Depression made peacekeeping much harder for the League because disputes involved some of the Great Powers, notably Japan, Italy and Germany. They did not like or accept the League's decisions.
- Britain and France eventually started working in their own interests, ignoring the League's processes and making secret agreements.
- The work of the League was increasingly undermined in the 1930s, as the Great Powers looked to protect themselves.

KEY SKILLS EXERCISES

Knowledge and understanding

1. What aspects of the League Covenant were intended to prevent war?
2. Explain the relationship between the Great Powers and the Council of the League of Nations.
3. Name the only two Great Powers that joined the League at the start and remained members until it ended.
4. Name two of the League's humanitarian commissions or agencies.

Application

5. Why was Germany not allowed to join until 1926?
6. Why was the League only partly successful in the 1920s?
7. Why did the Depression have such a negative impact on the League?
8. Why was humanitarian work easier to achieve than peacekeeping?

Chapter 2, Key Question 2: To what extent was the League of Nations a success?

> **CONTINUED**
>
> ### Analysis
> 9 Analyse three reasons why the League was not supported by France and Britain.
> 10 Analyse why the League was weakened by the aggression of Italy, Germany and Japan.
> 11 Analyse how the way the League was funded limited its success.
> 12 Analyse the key differences between the disputes of the 1920s and those of the 1930s.
>
> ### Evaluation
> 13 Evaluate the importance of the absence of the USA in bringing about the failure of the League.
> 14 Would the active support of Britain and France have ensured a successful League?
> 15 Did the Great Depression make the League's failure inevitable?
> 16 Evaluate why public opinion did not have more of an impact on political leaders and governments when it came to supporting the League.

> **1** This opening sentence is not helpful because the question is not about the organisation of the League, but about the causes of its failure to stop aggression. It would be better if this writer started to address the question directly; for example, 'There are several reasons why the League failed to stop aggression, one of which is that the USA was not a member and could not shape the League's decisions. This absence was important because ….'

IMPROVE THIS ANSWER

> 'The League of Nations failed to stop Italian and Japanese aggression in the 1930s because the United States was not a member.' How far do you agree with this statement?

Sample answer: The League of Nations was formed in 1920 and based in Geneva. It had a Council, an Assembly and a Secretariat. **1** The League tried to address the Italian invasion of Abyssinia and the Japanese aggression in Asia-Pacific but could not do so without the USA and the support of other great powers. The USA never was a member of the League because both the American public and the American Congress did not want to get involved in it. Instead, the USA adopted an 'isolationist' attitude. **2**

> **2** Again, the writer has not focused on the question and instead is trying to explain why the USA was not a League member. This is not the question. The answer needs to weigh up the main factors for the League's failure to confront aggression. One strategy to use when evaluating the importance of different factors is to ask 'What if … factor X or Y was not present? How much difference would that have made to the failure of the League?' If you did this for the US membership of the League, you would likely draw the conclusion that the League would still have failed to stop Japanese and Italian aggression because military intervention was really the only action that would have halted the tide of aggression. No country wanted to do this in case a local conflict became another world war.

CONTINUED

The Great Depression was a more important factor than the absence of the United States. **3** Across the world, great and small powers were caught in an economic blizzard that forced their governments to focus on solving the problems of unemployment, shrinking trade and lower investment. Attending to the aggression of Japan in Manchuria and Italy in Abyssinia was not a priority, even though it meant that the League was without support and unable to confront these two great powers and make them back down. **4** So, in the case of Japan, the League sent Lord Lytton to investigate the invasion of Manchuria. His report was read to the League; the Japanese were to blame and should withdraw from China. But the Japanese walked out in protest. The League was powerless to stop it. The Great Depression had reduced the political will of the great powers, and this resulted in aggression going unpunished. **5**

The absence of the United States also weakened the League. **6** To enforce sanctions against aggressors, all the great powers would need to agree. If the United States had been a member of the League, such economic sanctions could well have been tighter, but would this have stopped Italy and Japan? **7** It is likely that the aggression would not stop because the United States was badly affected by the Great Depression and needed to boost trade rather than restrict it.

Now write an improved response using this guidance.

---

3 In this sentence, the writer is targeting the question precisely and comparing the USA with a second factor and has compared the two ('more important than') but has not yet provided analysis to back up this judgement. How has the writer reached this judgement?

4 The answer has now focused correctly on the question in focusing on the Great Depression as a factor, but what is missing here is a comparison with absence of the United States from the League.

5 In this section, the writer has analysed clearly why the Great Depression was a factor in the failure of the League. The writing is analytical and not complicated with too much evidence. The Lytton Report is cited but not in unnecessary detail. The point is made: the Great Depression did contribute to the League's inability to confront aggression from Japan.

6 This is an encouraging start to the paragraph, but it would have been better to start the answer with this sentence. This could then have been followed by paragraphs devoted to other factors such as nationalist aggression, rearmament, and the role of great powers like France and Britain. This structure would have helped the writer to evaluate the importance of factors against the one in the question – the US membership of the League.

7 This shows good quality thinking about the USA and its possible role. Economic nationalism was a key factor in explaining why the League suffered from lack of support.

Chapter 2, Key Question 2: To what extent was the League of Nations a success?

PRACTICE QUESTIONS

1 The League of Nations was the hope of humankind after the devastation of the First World War. However, it had mixed success and could not stop the world war that broke out in 1939.

   a What were the aims of the League of Nations? [4]

   b Why did the League have mixed success in the 1920s? [6]

   c Which contributed most to the failure of the League in the 1930s: the Great Depression or the Great Powers? Explain your answer. [10]

   [Total: 20]

PROJECT

You are going to work in pairs to research and deliver a presentation about how the League of Nations could have been more effective.

First, look back at the information on the structure and organisation of the League, and the features of its Covenant, in this book. Use any resources available to do more research about these things. Make notes as you go.

Review your notes and start thinking about what features made the League ineffective. How would you improve its effectiveness? Consider the following points.

- Would you change the League's membership? If so, how?
- Which articles in the Covenant would you change / delete / amend? Why?
- Do you want to change the structure of the League? How?
- Does it need better funding? How would you achieve this?
- How would you deal with the League's weaknesses in the 1920s?

Remember, you would not have to change everything; of the work of the League's humanitarian work was important and successful.

When you have a list of around ten suggested improvements, present your findings to a small group of your classmates. They should award you marks out of 5 for each suggestion: 5 for an idea that might have changed outcomes in the 1920s and 1930s, and 1 mark for an idea that would have made very little difference.

From this feedback, narrow your list of suggestions down to six ideas. Make your final presentation to the class. Use evidence, examples and images to support your ideas. End your presentation with a judgement about whether the League was doomed to fail from the start or whether it was undermined by later events. Take questions and be prepared to justify your decision.

SELF-EVALUATION CHECKLIST

After studying this chapter, complete this table:

You should be able to:	Needs more work	Almost there	Ready to move on
describe the membership of the League, when it started work and how it changed over time			
describe the structure and organisation of the League: its weaknesses and strengths			
give examples of the League's peacekeeping successes and failures in the 1920s			
give examples of the humanitarian activities of the League's agencies, and explain their impact			
explain how the Great Depression affected the work of the League			
understand how the Great Depression affected policies in countries such as Italy, Germany and Japan, and their attitude towards the League			
explain the lack of support from Britain and France that undermined the reputation of the League in the 1930s			
understand the League of Nations' role in the Manchurian Crisis and the Abyssinian war in the 1930s			
explain how the League's failures contributed to the rise of leaders such as Hitler and Mussolini.			

Chapter 3, Key Question 3:
How far was Hitler's foreign policy to blame for the outbreak of war in Europe in 1939?

FOCUS POINTS

This chapter will help you to answer these questions:

- What were the long-term consequences of the Treaty of Versailles?
- What were the consequences of the failures of the League of Nations in the 1930s?
- Was the policy of appeasement justified?
- How important was the Nazi–Soviet Pact?
- Why did Britain and France declare war on Germany in September 1939?

3.0 What is this enquiry about?

In this chapter, you will investigate the foreign policy introduced by Nazi leader Adolf Hitler in the 1930s. What were his aims? What was his strategy for achieving those aims? You will learn about **militarism** and nationalism in Germany, and the responses of other countries to German aggression. You will find out why those responses could not prevent war breaking out in Europe by 1939.

Hitler turned his government into a dictatorship and Germany into a **totalitarian** society. Hitler pursued an aggressive foreign policy after 1935. The two main European countries opposing Germany were Britain and France – both democracies. Leaders in democracies must take account of popular opinion otherwise they are likely to be removed from power at the next election. So, it is important to understand events in the 1930s from the perspective of the decision-makers at the time.

It is also important to understand Germany's relationship with other countries, especially Italy. During the late 1930s, Germany and Italy gradually drew closer together and the Rome–Berlin Axis was agreed in 1936. The nationalistic and militaristic nature of both governments gave them a common cause, building empires in Europe (Germany), and in Africa and south-east Europe (Italy). The fact that each country had imperial ambitions in different parts of the world was key to their growing friendship because it meant they were not in competition with each other.

> **KEY TERMS**
>
> **militarism:** the belief that a country should maintain a strong army, navy and air force and be prepared to use them aggressively to defend or promote national interests. Militarism also suggests the glorification of military ideals such as duty, order, loyalty and obedience
>
> **totalitarianism:** a political system in which those in power have complete control and allow no opposition

Figure 3.1: A map showing German aggression in the late 1930s

Chapter 3, Key Question 3: How far was Hitler's foreign policy to blame for the outbreak of war in Europe in 1939?

SOURCES 3A & 3B

Source 3A: A propaganda poster from the Nazi Party, which governed Germany after 1933. The caption reads: 'Long Live Germany!'

Source 3B: A photograph of the Italian leader, Benito Mussolini, surrounded by officers from the Italian army

SOURCE ANALYSIS 3.1

Use the map in Figure 3.1 and Sources 3A and 3B to answer the following questions.

a   What features of nationalism and militarism can you see in the map and the two photographs?

b   What evidence can you find on the map and from your own knowledge that nationalism and militarism led to 'successes' for Germany in the 1930s?

c   What can you learn from the map and sources about how the growth of nationalism and militarism might threaten the international peace in Europe during the 1930s?

FOCUS TASK 3.1

Create a table like this. As you work through this chapter, use the table to record Hitler's aims, actions and policies and how various other countries and the League of Nations reacted to them. This will help you to answer the key question: *How far was Hitler's foreign policy to blame for the outbreak of war in Europe in 1939?*

Date	Hitler's aims, actions and policies	Reactions and actions of the League of Nations, Britain, France, Italy and the USSR

3.1 What were the long-term consequences of the Treaty of Versailles?

In Chapter 1, you learnt about the Paris Peace Conference. After the decisions had been made, it was time to apply the terms of the Treaty of Versailles. However, this was difficult, as Germany, which had not been part of the negotiations, was deeply unhappy with the settlement. The treaty had several significant long-term consequences that affected Germany directly or indirectly.

German minorities in other countries

The redrawn borders in Europe left significant numbers of German minorities in new countries, including one million German people in Poland. The newly created states to the east of Germany were weak and had few defence forces. The successor states of Poland, Hungary, Austria and Czechoslovakia were now positioned between two strong 'friends' – Germany and the USSR. In the years after 1919, these minority groups campaigned to be allowed to return to Germany.

This campaigning grew stronger and louder after the Nazis came to power in 1933. The Treaty of Versailles and the bitterness it generated in Germany was a useful tool for nationalist politicians. They aimed to unify all Germans behind one message: that the peace was unfair and must be changed – or destroyed.

Relationship between Germany and the USSR

The two outcasts from Europe after 1919, Germany and the USSR, signed the Treaty of Rapallo in 1922. They gave up all territorial and financial claims on each other and opened up diplomatic relations. Both countries claimed territory in the newly created Poland because Germany lay to the west of it and the Soviet Union to the east. They were also moving closer economically. The USSR needed Germany's skilled industrial workers, its engineers and its knowledge of advanced industrial methods. The USSR provided a market for German products and a source of raw materials.

Relationship between France and Britain

Disagreement about implementing the Treaty of Versailles worsened relations between France and Britain. France wanted every feature of the treaty to be fully implemented, believing this was the only way to secure itself against future German aggression. However, Britain saw the need for flexibility, especially to allow trade with Germany, which was essential for a healthy British economy. This was to cause serious difficulties in the 1930s as the two countries tried to keep the peace in Europe against the aggression and nationalism of Hitler's Germany.

> **REFLECTION**
>
> In pairs, discuss why peace is often hard to establish after war. Write down four reasons. Join with another pair to share your thoughts. Reduce your group's list of reasons to just three.
>
> Now reflect on how you approached this activity and how successful it was. Did one pair dominate the discussions? If so, what could be done to prevent this from happening next time? If you were teaching this activity to your class, what could you say that would help two pairs work well as a group? Put these ideas into practice in the next activity that has a similar structure.

Chapter 3, Key Question 3: How far was Hitler's foreign policy to blame for the outbreak of war in Europe in 1939?

SOURCE 3C

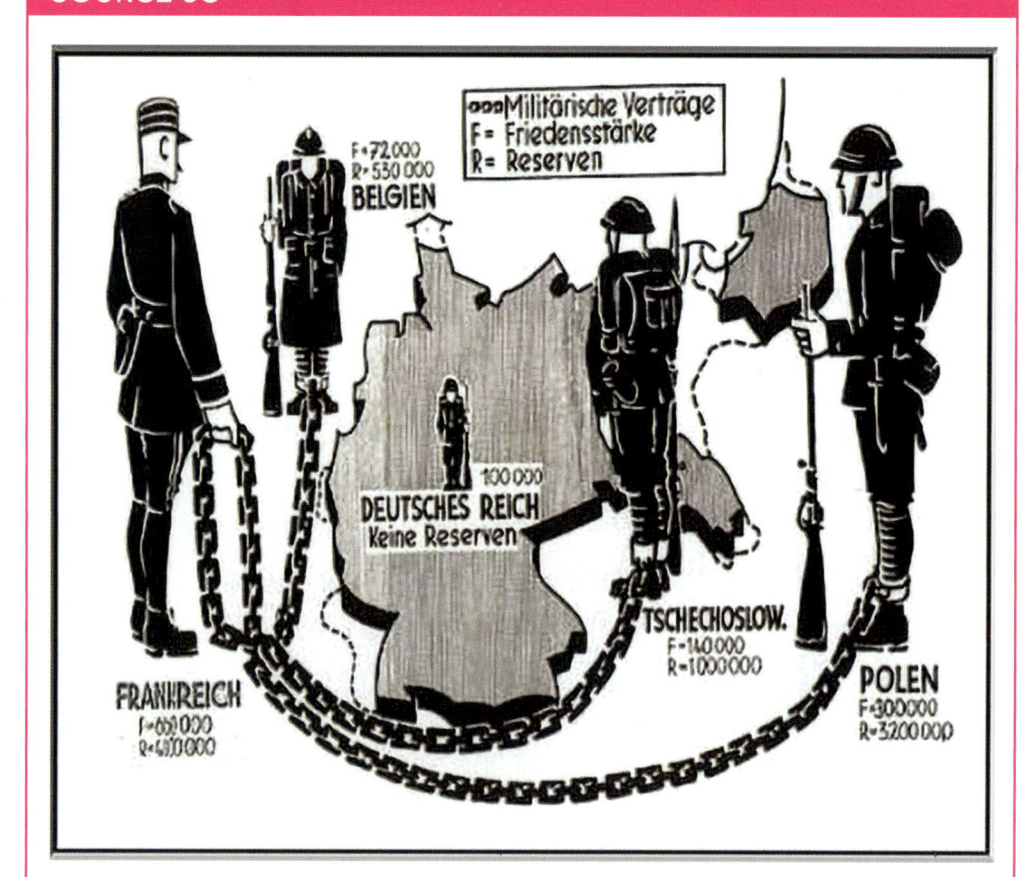

Source 3C: A poster showing a German view of the Treaty of Versailles. The countries shown are: Belgium (*Belgien*); Poland (*Polen*); French Empire (*Frankreich*); German Empire (*Deutsches Reich*); and Czechoslovakia (*Tschechoslow*). *Militärische Friedensstärke* are peacetime military forces. *Reserven* means reserve military forces

SOURCE ANALYSIS 3.2

Study Source 3C.

a What aspect of the treaty does the poster focus on?

b Why are there chains linking countries?

c Why have the figures been drawn in different sizes?

d Based on this poster, write down three words that sum up the German view of the Treaty of Versailles.

e Is the poster an example of propaganda or not? Give reasons for your answers.

KEY TERM

anti-Semitism: hostility towards or prejudice against Jewish people

KEY FIGURE

Adolf Hitler (1889–1945)

Hitler was born in Austria but fought for Germany in the First World War. Afterwards, he joined the German Workers' Party, later the National Socialist Workers (Nazi) Party. He soon became its leader. He was sent to prison after an attempt to overthrow the state government in Munich in 1923 and spent some of his time there writing a book called *Mein Kampf* ('My Struggle'). In it, he explained his **anti-Semitism** and the need for Germany to have more *Lebensraum* ('living space'). Hitler became chancellor of Germany in 1933. His actions to overturn the Treaty of Versailles, including rearming, proved popular. However, his racist policies had a terrible effect on the lives of minority groups, particularly Jewish people. Hitler enjoyed some initial successes in the Second World War, but when the USA and the USSR allied against him, the tide of war turned, and Germany was defeated. In the ruins of Berlin, Hitler took his own life.

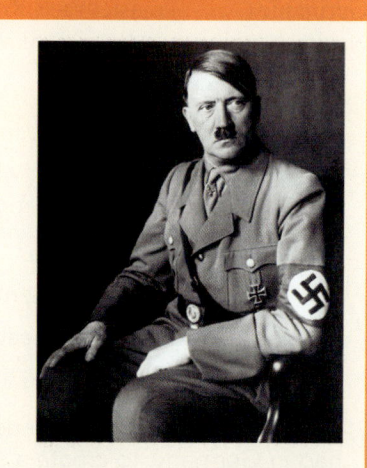

Hitler's foreign policy aims

Historians are divided on whether Hitler had a long-standing plan to go to war, or whether he saw opportunities when they arose and used them to his advantage. However, he had several clear foreign policy aims throughout the 1930s.

Tearing up the Treaty of Versailles

In Germany, resentment at the Treaty of Versailles lasted long after it was signed. Reversing the terms of the treaty was one of Hitler's main aims in the 1930s. His demands, his actions and his motives mostly came from the dictated peace. The steps he took between 1935 and 1939 in defiance of the treaty included:

- rearmament
- remilitarising the Rhineland
- *Anschluss* ('union') with Austria
- the transfer of the Sudetenland from Czechoslovakia
- the invasion of Prague
- the seizure of Memel
- claims over Danzig and the Polish Corridor.

Creating *Lebensraum* ('living space')

The search for *Lebensraum* was driven by the limited German resources of food and raw materials. This convinced Hitler that Germans required 'living space' to survive. He believed that this could only be found to the east, from Russia. The search for *Lebensraum* partly shaped Hitler's foreign policy after he became chancellor in 1933.

Establishing a new *Reich* ('empire')

Hitler's third foreign policy aim was to unite all German-speaking people into one *Reich*, or empire. Hitler believed that history was all about the struggle between 'races'. 'Superior races' flourished or they died. To grow and develop, the German people had to maintain their biological purity and take over more *Lebensraum*. To expand abroad, Germany must have a pure German population at home. The Nazis believed that having all Germans in one *Reich* meant that anyone who was not German had no right to live in Germany. According to Nazi ideology, the Jews were a parasitic 'race' that plotted to enslave the Germanic (**Aryan**) master race. Russians were **Slavs**, who were considered inferior by the Nazis, so taking over Russian/Slavic lands for *Lebensraum* perfectly fitted Hitler's plans.

> **KEY TERMS**
>
> **Lebensraum:** the idea that a successful country needs extra land in which to settle its people. In Hitler's thinking this was the area east of Germany in Poland and the Soviet Union
>
> **Aryan:** belonging to a group of white people with pale hair and blue eyes, believed by the Nazis to be better than other groups
>
> **Slavs:** a number of ethnic groups of people in eastern and south-eastern Europe. Slavs and their languages (Russian, Polish, Czech, Serbian) are related, and many (though not all) of them belong historically to the Orthodox Christian churches

> **REVISION TIP**
>
> It is important to remember why there was such widespread resentment of the treaty in Germany. You can record and revise this information using key headings:
>
> - **Guilt** for War
> - **Land** lost for punishment
> - **Reparations** for the destruction caused
> - **Military** cuts for peace.
>
> Under each heading, write down what each of these means and the effect it had in Germany, to create a set of revision notes.

Chapter 3, Key Question 3: How far was Hitler's foreign policy to blame for the outbreak of war in Europe in 1939?

Figure 3.2: A German wall chart from 1935. Charts like this were used in 'racial theory' lessons to show what the Nazis considered to be superior and inferior characteristics

> CAMBRIDGE IGCSE™ AND O LEVEL HISTORY OPTION B: COURSEBOOK

> ### ACTIVITY 3.1
>
> a Sum up the three aims of Hitler's foreign policy in the 1930s using just three words for each aim. Then draw a picture to represent each of the aims.
>
> b Find a partner and share your summaries and pictures. Discuss why Hitler developed those specific aims and not others, such as invading Italy or Spain.
>
> c Hitler's foreign policy aims were closely linked to the Nazis' views on race. If Hitler's plans for *Lebensraum* were successful, which areas of Europe would form part of his new *Reich*? What might happen to the groups living in these areas when the Nazis invaded? Discuss your ideas as a class.

Key points

Long-term consequences of the Treaty of Versailles

- The bitter legacy of the treaty lasted through the 1920s and 1930s. It stirred nationalist feelings that many politicians used to gain popularity, including Hitler.
- The treaty separated millions of Germans from their homeland, and they became minorities in new countries like Poland. These groups campaigned to re-join Germany.
- Britain and France took different views about the implementation of the treaty.
- Hitler and the Nazis made it a key policy to overturn the Treaty of Versailles.
- Hitler's other aims included looking for living space (*Lebensraum*) and creating a unified empire (*Reich*) of German-speaking people.

3.2 What were the consequences of the failures of the League of Nations in the 1930s?

You have already studied the impact of the League of Nations, the organisation set up after the end of the First World War. The League's failures in the 1930s had a significant effect on Hitler's plans for Germany. Italy, under its own dictator Benito Mussolini, was similarly affected.

KEY FIGURE

Benito Mussolini (1883–1945)

Mussolini was Italy's prime minister from 1922 to 1943. As a fascist dictator, he was a close ally of Hitler during the Second World War. Mussolini wanted to restore the grandeur of the Roman Empire by increasing Italy's overseas empire and the fascist sphere of influence. When war started in 1939, Mussolini tried to match Germany's initial successes but could never match Germany's military resources. Mussolini was replaced as prime minister in 1943. However, he served as the head of the Italian Social Republic until he was captured and executed by Italian partisans in 1945.

Chapter 3, Key Question 3: How far was Hitler's foreign policy to blame for the outbreak of war in Europe in 1939?

Figure 3.3: Lord Robert Cecil (see Chapter 2) speaking at the Women's International League before the Disarmament Conference in Geneva

The Disarmament Conference

Disarmament was a feature of the treaties that ended the First World War, but it was only the losers of the war who were made to disarm. The League of Nations organised a conference to meet in Geneva between 1932 and 1934 to discuss broader plans for disarmament. However, it failed to reduce the levels of weapons in land, sea and air. France was willing to disarm, but only if Britain and the USA guaranteed they would too. Neither was willing to give such a guarantee.

Hitler's plan was for **rearmament**, not disarmament. He argued that France was not serious about disarmament and the Germans left the conference and withdrew from the League of Nations in 1933.

The failure to achieve anything substantial at the Conference damaged the League's international reputation. Countries including Germany, Italy and Japan were already rearming.

Manchuria

In 1931, the Japanese invasion of Manchuria was the first time the League of Nations faced a challenge from a great power. If the League had met the challenge and the Japanese had been stopped this would have been a **deterrent** to other Great Powers such as Germany and Italy. However, with the world looking on, the League's failure to stop the Japanese showed Japan as well as Hitler and Mussolini that the League was incapable of stopping an aggressive country from making territorial gains. As Japan rejected the findings of the Lytton Report (see Chapter 2), it withdrew from the League of Nations.

> **KEY TERMS**
>
> **rearmament:** increasing the number of weapons and personnel in the armed forces in order to become a strong military power again
>
> **deterrent:** an action that puts off (deters) a country from being aggressive towards others

Abyssinia

Both Hitler and Mussolini were delighted at the outcome in the Far East. The League could not take effective action and it was proving impossible to put international interests ahead of national interests. This meant that further aggressive behaviour from Italy was extremely likely, and that Hitler would soon be furthering his policy of destroying the Treaty of Versailles. The Italian conquest of Abyssinia in 1935 (see Chapter 2) was humiliating for the League because the Great Powers – France and Britain – were shown to be playing a double game. They supported the application of sanctions while at the same time negotiated behind the back of the League with the aggressor, Italy, in the form of the Hoare-Laval Pact.

As time went on, it was harder and harder for Britain and France to keep Italy on their side and detached from Hitler's Germany. Italy withdrew from the League in 1937. Mussolini visited Berlin in September 1937. In November of the same year, Italy signed the Anti-Comintern Pact with Germany and Japan to present a united front against Soviet communism – an ideology all three countries hated.

What were the consequences of the League's failure?

The League's three main failures in the 1930s were covered in newspapers all over the world. The organisation's flaws had been exposed. Collective security through the League was finished. This humiliating result gave Hitler confidence, and he realised that the League would not be able to stop a European war. What would Britain and France do now? Public opinion in both countries was against rearmament, as ordinary citizens had more faith in the League than politicians did.

> ### THINK LIKE A HISTORIAN
>
> A good reputation is hard to build and easy to destroy. In these days of instant news and social media, failures are often very public. It can be difficult to rebuild a reputation once it is damaged. How was the League of Nations' reputation damaged by 1934? How did people know about it? What could have been done at the time to rebuild its reputation?
>
> What examples can you think of in recent times where large organisations or international bodies have found their reputations damaged? How did it happen? Was it their own fault or was another group acting against them? How did the facts of the case become public? Was the organisation able to rebuild its reputation? If so, how?

> ### FOCUS TASK 3.2
>
> Discuss the following questions in pairs. Make notes of your answers.
>
> a Which of the three failures of the League in the 1930s did most to undermine its authority?
>
> b Which of the three failures of the League did most damage to the reputation of Britain and France as its defenders?
>
> c What do you think smaller powers made of the League's failures? What changes in the League do you think they would like to have seen to make it more favourable to them?

Chapter 3, Key Question 3: How far was Hitler's foreign policy to blame for the outbreak of war in Europe in 1939?

Key points
The failures of the League of Nations

- Nationalism and militarism were on the rise in Germany, Italy and Japan during the 1930s. These developments made war likely in Europe and Asia.
- The League experienced three key failures in the 1930s: the Disarmament Conference, the Manchurian crisis and the war in Abyssinia. All three weakened the League's reputation and undermined its authority.
- The confidence of dictators such as Hitler and Mussolini grew as they realised that the League of Nations could not prevent war in Europe.

3.3 Was the policy of appeasement justified?

In the mid-1930s, Britain and France decided on a new policy to deal with Germany: **appeasement**. Since the end of the Second World War, the policy of appeasement and its supporters have been criticised for not opposing Hitler. Hitler's confidence grew as he made successes against the appeasers and made new demands. However, the policy of appeasement was developed by intelligent leaders, and it made sense to them and many ordinary people at the time. This was largely because of a series of aggressive actions that Hitler took from 1935 onwards, which led other nations to try to find ways to stop the situation from getting worse.

> **KEY TERM**
>
> **appeasement:** agreeing to some or all of the opposing side's demands in order to prevent further disagreement

TIMELINE OF HITLER'S ACTIONS, 1935–39

January 1935	A plebiscite is held in Saarland and, influenced by the Nazis, people vote overwhelmingly to join Germany.
March 1935	Hitler publicly announces his intentions to rearm Germany and start conscription.
March 1936	The Rhineland is remilitarised.
October 1936	Italy and Germany sign the Rome–Berlin Axis.
November 1937	Germany and Japan sign the Anti-Comintern Pact.
March 1938	Germany achieves *Anschluss* with Austria.
September 1938	The Sudetenland is transferred from Czechoslovakia to Germany. The Munich Agreement is signed.
March 1939	Germany invades Prague, the capital of Czechoslovakia.
March 1939	Hitler makes claims to Danzig and the Polish Corridor.
September 1939	Germany invades Poland.

Rearmament, 1935

In 1935, Hitler announced German rearmament and introduced conscription, which was prohibited under the Treaty of Versailles. In fact, rearmament had been happening secretly for a few years (see Figure 3.4). Hitler told the world that his actions were defensive, and that Germany was not a threat to international peace.

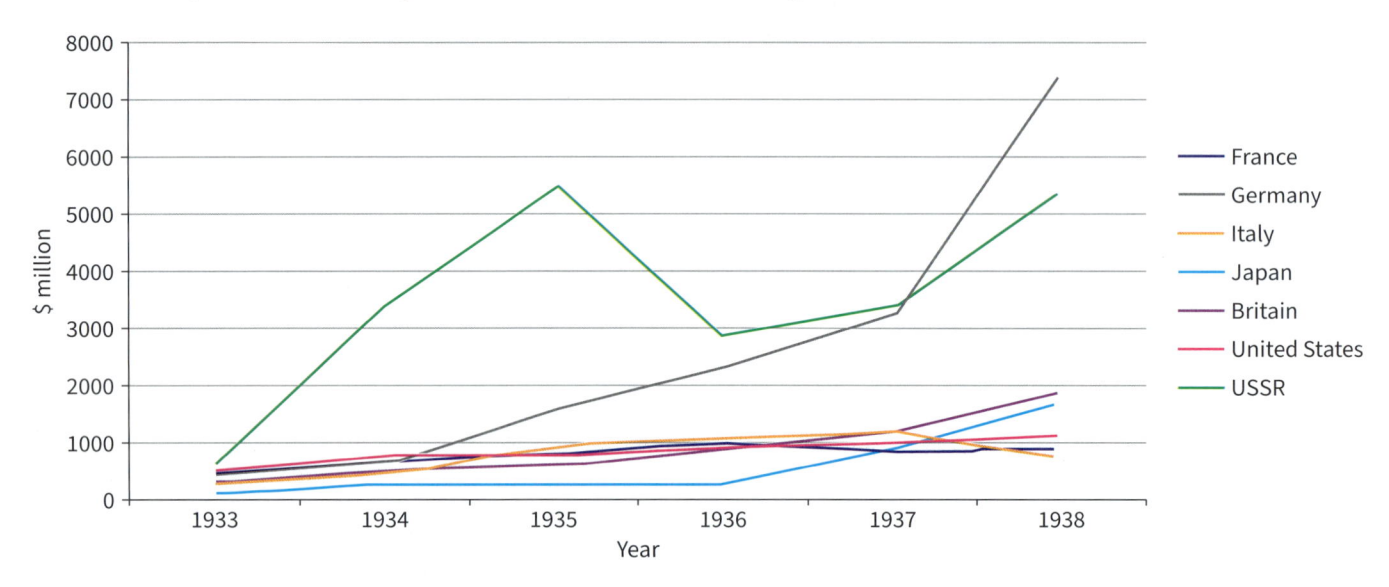

Figure 3.4: A graph showing German and international comparisons of defence spending from 1933 to 1938

FOCUS TASK 3.3

In pairs, look at the graph in Figure 3.4. Make notes on the increases of German expenditure compared with other Great Powers following Hitler's appointment as chancellor in January 1933. Consider the following questions.

a   Why did German defence spending increase suddenly after 1934?

b   What trend can you see in Britain's spending on defence?

c   What hindered the British government from spending more on rearming their country?

As a class, discuss whether or not this graph provides evidence that Hitler was to blame for the war in Europe.

Chapter 3, Key Question 3: How far was Hitler's foreign policy to blame for the outbreak of war in Europe in 1939?

The Saar plebiscite, 1935

The Saar region had been taken from Germany by the Treaty of Versailles and administered by the League of Nations for a period of 15 years. The year 1935 marked the end of the League's control and the timing of a plebiscite – a vote by Saarlanders to decide whether to become part of France, retain their separate status under the League, or re-join Germany.

The result of the plebiscite was very important because the Saar contained coalfields, factories and railway stations. Nazi supporters living in the Saar fought a fierce campaign to re-join Germany. Opponents were intimidated and there was violence. However, League observers confirmed that the voting was fair and free. In January 1935, 90.3% voted to return the Saar to Germany, 9% wanted to retain their status under the League and 0.4% to become part of France. On 1 March, the Saar officially re-joined Germany and stage one of Hitler's plan to unify all Germans was complete.

The result was a triumph for the Nazi regime. It gave Hitler the moral authority to push on with his demands for unification with Austria and the Germans in Sudetenland. The result also made it difficult for democratic governments to oppose Hitler's claims elsewhere, which may explain why they later adopted the policy of appeasement as he pushed his claims.

> **THINK LIKE A HISTORIAN**
>
> *Reich* is the German word for 'empire'. In English, we refer to Hitler's Germany as the 'Third Reich', which is a half translation of *Dritte Reich* ('Third Empire'). The German expression was created to show that Nazi rule followed two earlier German empires, but at the time it mainly called itself the *Deutsches Reich* ('German Empire'), just as it had done earlier under both an emperor and as a republic.
>
> Do you know what your country's name means and how it got that name? Does it refer to the type of political system (e.g. 'Republic'). Is the name represented on the national flag? Has your country always had this name or has it changed over time? If so, why? Do some research if you do not know. If you have lived part of your life in a different country, research that, too.

The Rhineland, 1936

In 1936, Hitler focused his attention on the Rhineland (see Figure 3.5). This was still part of Germany, but it had been demilitarised by the Treaty of Versailles and occupied by foreign troops for 15 years.

In March 1936, 22 000 German troops marched into the Rhineland. Was this the first step to a planned war or was it an opportunity that Hitler took for himself and for Germany? Hitler predicted that neither France nor Britain would do anything, and he was right. The French and British leaders recognised that the Rhineland was really part of Germany and neither wanted to risk a war. Once German troops were established in the Rhineland, Hitler made promises of continued peace, and even offered France and Britain a non-aggression pact.

Most German generals opposed the move into the Rhineland. They feared that the French would defeat their half-trained, inadequately equipped army within hours. But the French public was worried about provoking another war, and the French government feared that the German forces were stronger than they were in reality. In England, the public was indifferent to the German occupation of the Rhineland, making it difficult for any British leaders who wanted to stop Germany. Once again, appeasement seemed the best policy.

Figure 3.5: A map showing the position of the Rhineland; the area was demilitarised after the Treaty of Versailles

SOURCES 3D & 3E

The 48 hours after the march were the most nerve-racking in my life. If the French troops had [challenged] us we would have had to withdraw with our tails between our legs.

Source 3D: Hitler commenting on the remilitarisation of the Rhineland, after the event

Hitler has got away with it! France is not marching. Instead, it is appealing to the League of Nations. Oh, the stupidity of the French. I learnt today that the German troops were under strict orders to beat a hasty retreat if the French army opposed them in any way.

Source 3E: William Shirer, a US journalist working in Berlin in 1936, commenting on the remilitarisation of the Rhineland

SOURCE ANALYSIS 3.3

Read Sources 3D and 3E.

a What do these sources suggest would have happened if the French had challenged the German troops?

b Based on your understanding of Source 3D, what lessons might Hitler have learnt from the Rhineland that shaped his later foreign policy decisions?

Chapter 3, Key Question 3: How far was Hitler's foreign policy to blame for the outbreak of war in Europe in 1939?

> **THINKING SKILLS**
>
> Re-read the information about the remilitarisation of the Rhineland. Choose one of the following people. Write a diary entry describing your thoughts and emotions about the event, explaining why you feel as you do:
>
> - a German soldier marching into the Rhineland
> - a French woman living in the Rhineland
> - a British tourist visiting the Rhineland
> - a German journalist reporting on the event.

The Rome–Berlin Axis and the Anti-Comintern Pact, 1936–37

The division of Europe's Great Powers had taken shape by early 1937. Britain was once again allied with France as Germany and Italy grew closer. In part this was because Italy had fallen out of favour with the other European countries after its invasion of Abyssinia (see Chapter 2). By this time, Germany and Italy shared a common ideology, as both were ruled as fascist dictatorships. The alliance was sealed by the signing of the Rome–Berlin Axis in October 1936. This committed both countries to following a common foreign policy. From this time on, Germany and its partners in military aggression would be known as the Axis Powers.

In November 1936, Germany and Japan signed the Anti-Comintern Pact, an agreement that focused on opposing the spread of communism. Japan was looking for allies who would be willing to support it if it was attacked by the communist Soviet Union, and the pact included a secret clause that required both countries to help each other if either of them was attacked by the Soviet Union. Italy joined the Pact a year later, and Hungary and Spain added their signatures in 1939.

Anschluss with Austria, 1938

The Treaty of Versailles banned the union of Germany and Austria. However, as most Austrians spoke German, this decision ran against the principle of national self-determination, as outlined in President Wilson's Fourteen Points (see Chapter 1). The word *Anschluss* means both 'union' and '**annexation**'. When it occurred in 1938, Hitler called his invasion of Austria a union, to bring Austria's seven million German-speaking people into one German *Reich*. However, his opponents called it an annexation – a forced takeover.

The *Anschluss* was a striking example of Hitler's ability to combine clear aims with patient preparation and then seizing an opportunity when it arose. To begin with, Hitler regularly spoke about creating a 'Third Reich' unifying all Germans, including the Austrian people. Hitler was also patient. After being warned off taking over Austria by Mussolini in 1934, he waited for four years until the time was right to try again. During this period, the Austrian Nazis undermined the government from within and Mussolini decided to give Hitler whatever he wanted in Austria.

> **KEY TERM**
>
> **annexation:** possession of a country or region, usually by force or without permission

From gradual takeover to invasion

The timing of the *Anschluss* was not of Hitler's choosing, but he seized the opportunity when it arose. Chancellor Kurt Schuschnigg of Austria wanted his country to remain independent. He had tried to limit Austrian Nazis from encouraging union with Germany. In response, Hitler made a series of demands that would turn Austria into a German-controlled state. On 9 March 1938, Schuschnigg tried to retake the initiative from Hitler by calling a referendum that asked Austrians to vote for a 'free and German, independent and social, Christian and united Austria'. When news of the planned referendum reached Hitler, he demanded Schuschnigg's resignation and changed his policy of 'gradual absorption' to 'immediate invasion'. He had originally planned to replace Schuschnigg with Arthur Seyss-Inquart, a leading Austrian Nazi, and take control gradually. But as the situation changed, Hitler quickly decided to incorporate Austria into the *Reich* by force.

The *Anschluss* was over in days and most Austrians welcomed it. To legitimise his takeover, Hitler organised a plebiscite in early April to prove to the world that the *Anschluss* was what the Austrian people wanted. They voted by a large majority to join the Third Reich.

Hitler had used his army beyond Germany's frontiers for the very first time. He was immensely popular in Germany because he had expanded German territory as well as increasing the population and resources of the Third Reich. The **Führer's** confidence in his abilities and the perceived weakness of Germany's opponents reached new heights.

> **KEY TERM**
>
> **Führer:** a German word meaning 'leader' or 'guide'. The title is usually associated with Adolf Hitler

Figure 3.6: A map of Europe in April 1938, just after Hitler's annexation of Austria

Chapter 3, Key Question 3: How far was Hitler's foreign policy to blame for the outbreak of war in Europe in 1939?

FOCUS TASK 3.4

The key question asks you to judge how far Hitler's foreign policies were to blame for the Second World War in Europe. How would you answer this based on what you have learnt so far? In small groups, discuss the question.

- First consider events in the Saar, the Rhineland and Austria. What do they suggest about the causes of the Second World War?

- Now add the Spanish Civil War, the Rome–Berlin Axis and the Anti-Comintern Pact into the discussion. Do they complicate the question? Why, or why not?

In your groups, agree a judgement based on 'how far' Hitler's foreign policies were to blame for the war: fully, mostly, partly, a little or not at all.

Share your judgements as a class and record how many groups chose each judgement. When you have completed this chapter, come back to this question and discuss whether you have changed your mind and would reach a different conclusion.

ACTIVITY 3.2

a   In pairs, discuss the following questions. Make notes of your ideas.

- Why was Austria part of Hitler's plan for a Third Reich?
- Why did Hitler not want Kurt Schuschnigg to hold a referendum?
- Did Hitler plan the *Anschluss* or did he just seize an opportunity?

b   Join up with another pair and work together to create a storyboard of the events of the *Anschluss* using pictures and words. Display your finished storyboard and take feedback from other groups. Have you missed out any key events? Have you told the story of the *Anschluss* clearly and in a logical order?

SOURCES 3G & 3H

Source 3G: A photo taken at the time of the *Anschluss* in March 1938. Here, Austrian girls welcome some of the first German soldiers to reach Vienna, the capital of Austria

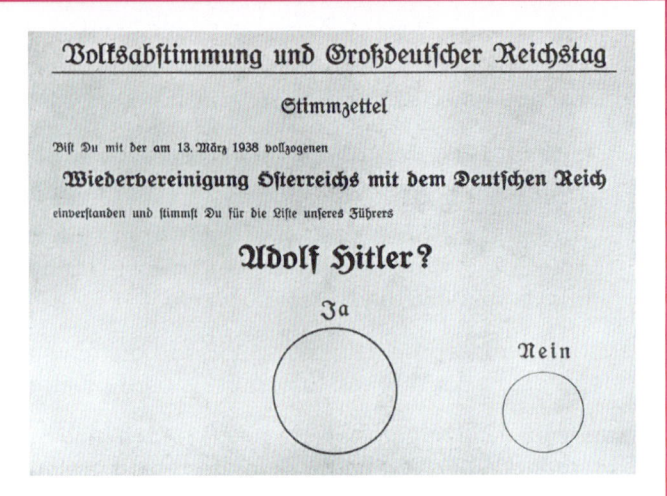

Source 3H: A voting ballot slip from 10 April 1938. The text says: 'Do you agree with the reunification of Austria with the German *Reich* that was enacted on 13 March 1938, and do you vote for the party of our leader Adolf Hitler?' The large circle is labelled 'Yes', the smaller 'No'

SOURCE ANALYSIS 3.5

Study Sources 3G and 3H.

a   What links these two sources?

b   Do you think that the response to the *Anschluss* in Source 3G was the same for all Austrians? Explain your answer.

c   What can you see in Source 3H that suggests the plebiscite was not a fair process? Do you think a fairer process could have changed the result of the plebiscite?

REVISION TIP

Storyboards like the one you created in Activity 3.2 can be useful revision tools. Try creating one to help you remember the sequence of German actions, dates and locations in the 1930s. Start with words and pictures to show the first few that you have read about in this section: Saar, Rhineland and Austria. As you get closer to 1939, add further boxes to your storyboard to tell the whole story.

The Spanish Civil War, 1936–39

The Spanish Civil War was a conflict that reflected the ideological divide that existed in Europe in the 1930s: fascism versus communism, liberal democracy versus dictatorship. General Francisco Franco led the Nationalist rebels against the Republican government in Spain.

Hitler and his Italian counterpart Mussolini saw the fighting in Spain as an ideal opportunity to test out military equipment that had only seen action on the training ground. Both countries gave support to the Nationalists against the democratically elected, left-leaning Republican government.

When war broke out in 1936, Hitler immediately sent aid to Franco's forces. German aid amounted to $215 million by the time the conflict ended in 1939. Between late July and early October 1936, the Germans transported 13 523 troops and 270 100 kilograms of war supplies from north Africa to Andalusia in southern Spain. These African soldiers proved decisive in Franco's victory over the Republicans. Italy's involvement was also important for the Nationalists. Mussolini sent 80 000 men to support Franco. Italian supplies included 1800 cannons, 3400 machine guns and 157 tanks.

Figure 3.7: Republican fighters defending an unidentified road against Nationalist forces during the Spanish Civil War

At the same time, the communist USSR helped the Republican government. Britain and France stayed out of the conflict, fearing that it might spill over beyond Spain's borders to the rest of Europe. They placed an ban on war supplies and volunteers going to Spain. It worried the Soviet leader Joseph Stalin that neither Britain nor France provided help and made him wonder if they could be trusted if it came to a war with Germany.

The Spanish Civil War was important in Hitler's plans for the rest of Europe. He was keen to gain access to resources from Spain for his own weapons industry. The dive-bombing attacks that the *Luftwaffe* ('German air force') inflicted on Spanish towns such as Guernica were useful practice for Hitler's air force (see Figure 3.8). In time, dive-bombing developed into the strategy called *Blitzkrieg* ('lightning attack') that was widely used in the Second World War. The Nationalist victory in 1939 increased Hitler's confidence about the impact of his rearmament programme for German military forces. While the Spanish Civil War was continuing, Hitler was able to achieve further success in Austria and Czechoslovakia, without starting a war. The Spanish conflict did not become a wider European war, and this suited Hitler who knew Germany was not yet ready for such a huge fight.

Figure 3.8: The Spanish city of Guernica after the German *Luftwaffe* had finished its attack using dive-bombing techniques, May 1937

Chapter 3, Key Question 3: How far was Hitler's foreign policy to blame for the outbreak of war in Europe in 1939?

SOURCE 3F

Source 3F: A Republican propaganda poster from the Spanish Civil War. The title translates as 'What are you doing to stop this?'

SOURCE ANALYSIS 3.4

Study Source 3F.

a What does the map in the background show?

b What do the two hands holding daggers represent? How do you know?

c The cap on the map was a symbol used by republican revolutionaries. What do the chains around it suggest?

d What do you think is the overall purpose of the poster and who is the target audience?

How did Britain and France react?

By the mid-1930s it was clear that Hitler was trying to destroy the Versailles peace settlement. But what could other countries do about it? The League of Nations' failure to keep the international peace meant that they had to find another way to stop German aggression. The problem with that was that public and political opinion in both Britain and France were still against pursuing a policy that risked war. Both countries were still suffering from the economic effects of the Depression (see Chapter 2), and they also wanted to keep their empires safe. Britain and France both had colonies in the Far East and were worried that Japan's wish for new territory might result in a war on two fronts. Both countries hoped to avoid such a war by making reasonable concessions to German grievances. So, the policy of appeasement developed. It was largely driven by British prime minister Neville Chamberlain, but the French also adopted this approach.

> ### KEY FIGURE
>
> #### Neville Chamberlain (1869–1940)
>
> Chamberlain came to politics late. He was first elected as a member of parliament in 1918 and became a member of several Conservative governments. By 1935, Chamberlain was persuaded of the need for rearmament, recognising that the English Channel by itself was no defence against enemy planes. He became prime minister in May 1937 and his name will always be linked with the policy of appeasement that he adopted. When war began in September 1939, Chamberlain stayed on as prime minister, but after a disastrous military campaign in Norway, he was forced to resign.

Hitler's actions in influencing the Saar plebiscite and remilitarising the Rhineland had caused concern in Britain and especially France. However, Austria was far enough away for the German *Anschluss* to seem less problematic at first. Britain and France protested to Hitler but realised that there was little they could do without Italy's help, and Italy had allied with Germany through the Rome–Berlin Axis. Appeasing Hitler in the case of Austria did keep peace in Europe, but it also boosted his confidence.

SOURCE 3I

Source 3I: A British cartoon by David Low, published in 1938 after the *Anschluss*. Britain is shown at the end carrying a basket representing the British Empire. The quote reads: 'Why should we take a stand about someone pushing someone else when it's all so far away . . .'

SOURCE ANALYSIS 3.6

Study Source 3I.

a   Is the cartoonist critical of the *Anschluss* or of Britain's response to it?

b   Why does Low call his cartoon 'Increasing Pressure'?

Chapter 3, Key Question 3: How far was Hitler's foreign policy to blame for the outbreak of war in Europe in 1939?

Both Britain and France had already begun a more serious programme of rearmament. However, they knew it would take time to fully rearm and be ready for a major war, so appeasement seemed the best approach in the meantime. The policy faced its toughest test in September 1938, when Hitler set his sights on Czechoslovakia.

ACTIVITY 3.3

In pairs, create a 'What if . . . ?' graphic organiser based on the 'What if' questions below. It could be a spider diagram / flow chart / infographic poster. Use colours and images to help distinguish and organise your ideas.

Discuss each question first and make notes of all your ideas and responses. Afterwards, go through your notes and pick out the strongest ideas to record in your graphic organiser.

What if . . .

- . . . the British government had disregarded public opinion and challenged Hitler with increased armaments and the threat of war?
- . . . both the British and French governments had joined forces and stationed troops on the border with Germany along with a significant number of planes?
- . . . the League of Nations had put in place strong sanctions to punish Germany for its aggression?

THINKING SKILLS

Work in groups of four. Consider the situation in Europe in 1937. Germany and Italy are rearming. There are weak states neighbouring these two countries. The League of Nations seems unable to control aggression. In your groups, discuss what you would have done to:

- keep the two aggressors apart
- handle Hitler's demands in relation to the Treaty of Versailles
- prepare for war in ways that do not increase the risk of war.

The crisis over Czechoslovakia, 1938

Austria was incorporated into Hitler's *Reich*, but he still wanted to appear reasonable in his demands. Was it not reasonable to want the 3.5 million Germans living in the Sudetenland to join the *Reich*? After all, it was next to Germany (see Figure 3.9) and the Sudeten Germans claimed that they suffered discrimination at the hands of the Czech government in the capital, Prague.

Hitler had other reasons to dislike Czechoslovakia. The country was very new because it had been created in 1919 as part of the Paris Peace Settlement. To keep its frontiers secure, the Czech government had made alliances with both France and the Soviet Union. In addition, Czechoslovakia was a democracy – something Hitler hated just as much as the Treaty of Versailles. So, how did Hitler approach the Sudetenland, given his aim to unite all Germans?

Figure 3.9: A map showing the position of the Sudetenland, part of Czechoslovakia in 1938

Unrest in the Sudetenland, 1938

Until late May 1938, Hitler had no immediate plan for attacking Czechoslovakia. On 28 March, Hitler told Konrad Henlein, the leader of the Sudeten Germans, to make demands for **home rule** for the Sudeten Germans. Of course this would be unacceptable to the Czech leader, Edvard Beneš, and his government because it would break up the country. Hitler was surprised to learn that the Czechs had partially mobilised their army in response to rumours of an imminent German attack. The rumours were untrue, but instead of denying them Hitler was now determined to 'smash Czechoslovakia'. However, he knew he needed to be careful, to avoid world opinion turning against him. So, throughout the summer of 1938, Hitler continued to encourage the Sudeten Germans to campaign for home rule. By early September, he had secretly finalised his plans for action against the Czechs.

On 12 September, Hitler made a speech bitterly attacking the government of Czechoslovakia. He claimed that the Czechs discriminated against the Sudeten Germans, and that they had forced 600 000 Germans from their homes. His words caused an uprising in the Sudetenland. Believing that war was coming, Neville Chamberlain flew to meet Hitler at Berchtesgaden, the Führer's mountain retreat

> **KEY TERM**
>
> **home rule:** a political arrangement in which a part of a country governs itself independently of the central government of a country

in Bavaria, on 15 September. There, Hitler emphasised his wish for friendship and cooperation between Britain and Germany, but he also threatened war if the issue of the Sudeten Germans was not resolved. Chamberlain, the appeaser, said he was ready to agree to the peaceful handover of the Sudetenland to Germany if the French and Czech governments also agreed.

At a second meeting on 22 September, Chamberlain reported to Hitler that he had secured approval from all three governments. However, Hitler now made additional demands. He wanted the Sudetenland to be occupied by German troops immediately. Chamberlain was horrified at Hitler's change of mind. At their previous meeting there had been no mention of troops or an invasion. Chamberlain returned to London to prepare Britain for war. The British navy and the French army were told to mobilise.

KEY FIGURE

Edvard Beneš (1884–1948)

Beneš was born in what was then the Austro-Hungarian Empire. When the country of Czechoslovakia was created after the First World War, Beneš was its first foreign minister. In 1935, he became president. Beneš opposed Germany's claim to the Sudetenland in 1938 but had to accept the Munich Agreement or face war with Germany. He resigned soon after. The following month he went to England, where he established a Czech government-in-exile. After the war, Beneš returned to Czechoslovakia and became president again in June 1946. Bad health prevented Beneš from opposing the gradual takeover of Czechoslovakia by the USSR after the war. He died in September 1948.

The Munich Agreement, 1938

Hitler realised he was on the edge of a war with Britain and France that he was not quite ready for. So, he agreed to Chamberlain's and Mussolini's suggestion of an international conference to be held in Munich. Chamberlain, the French prime minister Daladier, Mussolini and Hitler met on 29 September 1938 (see Figure 3.10). They agreed the following points.

- The Sudetenland would be handed over to Germany over a ten-day period.
- In any part of the Sudetenland where the population was mixed, plebiscites would be held to decide what would happen.
- The four leaders would guarantee the remaining part of Czechoslovakia after Polish and Hungarian claims had been satisfied.

When Beneš was presented with the Munich Agreement, he had little choice but to agree. If not, the Czech army would face stronger German forces in a war that it would lose.

After the Munich Agreement had been signed, Chamberlain asked Hitler to sign a second document that promised both men would do everything they could to promote peace in Europe and to resolve any differences by peaceful means. With Hitler's signature and his own on this 'piece of paper', Chamberlain returned to London believing he had saved Europe from war.

Figure 3.10: Chamberlain, Daladier, Hitler and Mussolini (left to right) at the meeting to sign the Munich Agreement

SOURCE 3J

Source 3J: A cartoon published in the British magazine *Punch* in October 1938, showing Prime Minister Neville Chamberlain rolling the world towards peace during the Czech crisis.

SOURCE ANALYSIS 3.7

Study Source 3J.

a What does this cartoon suggest about Chamberlain's role in keeping the peace during the Czech crisis of 1938?

b How far is this an accurate picture of the policy of appeasement?

c What features or words would you add to this cartoon (and its caption) to ensure it reflects the leaders and appeasement accurately?

Chapter 3, Key Question 3: How far was Hitler's foreign policy to blame for the outbreak of war in Europe in 1939?

> **FOCUS TASK 3.5**
>
> a   In pairs, copy and complete this table to compare the *Anschluss* with Austria and the crisis in Czechoslovakia. How did nations apply the policy of appeasement to German actions? What was the result? Use the information in this section and research using any other resources available. When you have finished, compare your table with another pair's. Add anything to yours that you may have missed out.
>
> | Austria, March 1938 | Czechoslovakia, September 1938 |
> |---|---|
> | Similarities ||
> | Differences ||
>
> b   In your groups of four, discuss the following questions.
>
> - Do your completed tables suggest that appeasement was working?
> - How might the appeasement policy have been changed to make it more effective?
> - Does the chart provide evidence that appeasement was justified?

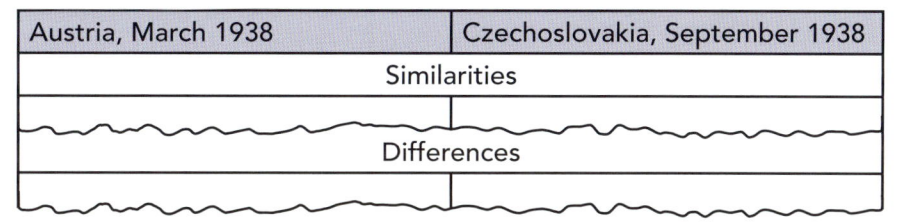

Was the Munich Agreement justified?

The Munich Agreement caused controversy in 1938 and it has done so ever since. Some arguments for and against applying the policy of appeasement are outlined in Figure 3.11.

For appeasement	Against appeasement
Although rearmament had started, Britain was not ready to fight a war in September 1938 and Chamberlain knew this. Britain needed more time to rearm.	If war had broken out against Germany, Britain and France might have been supported by the USSR.
The Sudetenland was populated by Germans and so a war in 1938 would have been against the principle of national self-determination.	If war had started in September 1938, Britain and France would have the backing of the 36 divisions of the Czech army fighting behind their strong defences on the frontier.
The British Empire was not united behind Britain in wanting to fight a war in 1938. South Africa and Canada had indicated that they were not willing to support a war in Europe.	Munich came to be seen as the worst example of the policy of appeasement and the USSR no longer trusted Britain or France.
Britain's air defences were not ready and an attack by the *Luftwaffe* could have meant an immediate defeat for Britain.	Britain and France, two Great Powers, had abandoned a small power, Czechoslovakia, to its fate.
Hitler claimed to be helping Britain and France by standing up to communism and said that they should be more concerned about the Soviet Union than Germany.	Hitler had proved by his earlier actions that his claims could not be trusted.
If war broke out, it was unlikely that the USA would be persuaded to join, so European nations would have had to fight without the strong backing of the USA.	Germany was clearly becoming the dominant power in Europe, and appeasement was not preventing this – war was inevitable.

Figure 3.11: A table showing arguments for and against appeasement

SOURCE 3K

Source 3K: A cartoon by David Low, drawn after the Munich Agreement was signed at the end of September 1938

SOURCE ANALYSIS 3.8

Study Source 3K.

a What do you think Chamberlain might have said about this cartoon?

b What might Hitler might have said about the cartoon? Explain your answer.

FOCUS TASK 3.6

Neville Chamberlain called the Munich Agreement 'peace with honour'.

The future prime minister of Britain Winston Churchill said: 'We have suffered a total and unmitigated defeat. You will find that in a period of time Czechoslovakia will be engulfed in the Nazi regime.'

a Do you think the policy of appeasement was justified? Plan a short essay in which you explore this key question, considering both sides of the argument. Structure your plan in the following way, making notes in each section.

- Introduction: Whether appeasement was justified or not depends on who you ask. Consider what a historian might say, or a British person who lived at the same time as Chamberlain, or a German adviser to Hitler.
- Paragraph 1: Arguments in favour of justifying appeasement plus any weaknesses or qualifications.
- Paragraph 2: Arguments against justifying appeasement plus any weaknesses or qualifications.
- Conclusion: On balance, where do you place your judgement on the spectrum of opinion?

b Share your essay plan with a partner. Give each other feedback, then improve your essay plan.

Chapter 3, Key Question 3: How far was Hitler's foreign policy to blame for the outbreak of war in Europe in 1939?

The invasion of Czechoslovakia, March 1939

For six months, the Munich Agreement held. Then, on the morning of 15 March 1939, German troops entered Prague and the remaining areas of Czechoslovakia. They seized Czech reserves of gold and hard currency. The Germans also took over all the weapon factories and mines that would now provide crucial raw materials for their armament plans. They also picked up a substantial haul of weapons: nearly 500 tanks and nearly 1600 aircraft.

The impact of the German invasion

Besides the fact that it broke the Munich Agreement, the invasion of Czechoslovakia stood out from previous aggressive actions. Having repeatedly stated that he was only interested in unifying Germans into one *Reich*, Hitler had now conquered seven million Czech people. His territorial ambitions had been exposed.

British and French public opinion changed significantly after the invasion. Chamberlain realised that the Munich Agreement had meant nothing to Hitler and declared that the German leader was attempting 'to dominate the world by force'.

The invasion of Czechoslovakia marked the end of appeasement. It proved that Hitler had been lying at Munich and could not be trusted. Chamberlain announced that Britain would defend Poland if it was attacked by Germany, and France made the same guarantee. For Germany, the takeover of Czechoslovakia strengthened Hitler's hold on Central Europe and helped his preparations for war. The large Czech army was no longer a threat. Airfields that could have been used to attack German cities and the Czech weapons industry were in German hands.

Figure 3.12: Czech citizens watch as German troops drive through Prague after the invasion of March 1939

> THINKING SKILLS

Look at the photograph in Figure 3.12 of the people in Prague watching the Germans invade their city. What range of emotions can you see on their faces? What thoughts might lie behind those emotions? Imagine you are in that crowd. What is it like? Write down your responses to these questions.

- What can you see happening?
- What sounds can you hear?
- How do you feel, watching your country being taken over by another? Fear? Anger? Acceptance?
- What happened ten minutes after the last Germans passed by you?

3.4 How important was the Nazi–Soviet Pact?

After Munich in September 1938, most people thought that appeasement was over. In February 1939, Chamberlain publicly guaranteed to defend French security. France and Britain began joint military planning. In March, they offered security guarantees to Poland, Romania and Greece. Rearmament increased.

British and French officials still hoped to keep the peace with Germany, but Hitler now wanted war. In April 1939, he abandoned the Anglo-German naval agreement of 1935 and signed a ten-year agreement with Italy known as the Pact of Steel, which reinforced the Rome–Berlin Axis. Hitler's foreign minister, Joachim von Ribbentrop, assured the Führer that Britain and France were bluffing, and had no intention of guaranteeing the security of other European nations, particularly Poland. Dismissing the signs that Britain and France really did mean war, Hitler turned to the Soviet Union.

Relations with the USSR

Of all the consequences of the Munich Agreement, few were as important as the damage it caused to the relationship between the USSR and Britain and France. Stalin had not been invited to the meeting at Munich and was not part of the agreement. Stalin concluded that he could not trust the western powers. He needed to make his own deal with Germany.

Hitler had already planned his next move against Poland, and it was vital that this would not meet with Soviet opposition. Stalin wanted to ensure that his own frontier was secure. After just one day of negotiations, on 23 August 1939, the two countries signed the Nazi–Soviet Pact (see Figure 3.13).

Part of the pact was a non-aggression treaty lasting ten years. The pact contained guarantees of economic cooperation and a promise that neither country would make agreements with other nations. The pact also included **secret protocols** which divided the territories that lay between Germany and the Soviet Union into spheres of influence. The western half of Poland was Germany's. The rest of Poland plus Latvia, Estonia and Lithuania fell into the Soviet sphere. Stalin regained some territory the USSR had lost at the end of the First World War, but also gained some time that he desperately needed to prepare his military.

> KEY TERM
>
> **secret protocol:** an addition to a formal agreement that is not made public

Chapter 3, Key Question 3: How far was Hitler's foreign policy to blame for the outbreak of war in Europe in 1939?

Figure 3.13: The signing of the Nazi–Soviet Pact in August 1939; Stalin and the German foreign minister, Ribbentrop, look on

The consequences of the pact

Some historians believe that if Britain, France and the USSR had allied against Hitler in 1939, war might have been prevented because Hitler would not have wanted to fight on two fronts. However, a lack of trust prevented this alliance forming. British and French leaders suspected that Stalin was secretly supporting communist groups in other countries. At the same time, Stalin suspected that the British and French really wanted a European war in which the Nazis and the communists would destroy each another.

For both Hitler and Stalin, the pact was a deal of convenience rather than a genuine friendship. Stalin did not trust Hitler any more than he trusted France and Britain. However, he was pleased at the chance to gain land in eastern Poland.

By 1939, British, French and Soviet leaders all knew that war with Germany was inevitable. Their tactic now was to put it off for as long as possible to allow them time to prepare. But Hitler was quick to move to the next phase. On 1 September, Germany invaded Poland.

ACTIVITY 3.4

Look at this quotation from historian A.J.P. Taylor:

It is difficult to see what other course the Soviet Union could have followed.

a   In pairs, discuss the following idea and decide whether or not you agree with Taylor that Stalin had no choice but to sign the Nazi–Soviet Pact.

Stalin had choices in August 1939. Instead of signing the Pact with Hitler, he could have:

- not signed any agreement with anyone
- signed an agreement with Britain and France
- signed an agreement with Poland.

> **CONTINUED**
>
> b Find another pair who have come to a different conclusion than you. Have a debate in which you each have two minutes to present your arguments to each other. Have you changed your mind after the debate? Take a class poll and see how many people think that Stalin had no choice, and how many feel he could have pursued other options.

> **FOCUS TASK 3.7**
>
> a On your own, summarise the Nazi–Soviet Pact, including the secret protocols. Make notes to answer these questions.
>
> - What would Hitler gain from the pact?
> - What would Stalin gain from the pact?
> - Why did Britain and France not trust Stalin?
> - Why did Stalin not trust Britain and France?
> - Was the pact of little importance / some importance / great importance? Give two reasons for your choice.
> - Was it the fault of the western powers that Stalin decided a pact with Hitler was his only possible course of action?
>
> b *Britain and France were to blame for the Second World War. It was their fault that a strong alliance was not built to oppose Hitler.*
>
> Discuss this statement in groups of four. Record your key points and then explain them to the class.

3.5 Why did Britain and France declare war on Germany in September 1939?

In March 1939, Germany bullied Lithuania into handing over the disputed territory of Memel to Germany. This was to be Hitler's last seizure of land before the start of the Second World War. The seizure of Memel, and the German occupation of Czechoslovakia the same month, increased pressure on Poland to give in to Hitler's demands. The Polish city of Danzig had been declared a free city in the Treaty of Versailles, but now Germany wanted it back. Hitler also demanded land links through Poland to East Prussia. The implications were clear: Poland was next on Hitler's list. On 3 April 1939, he secretly issued orders to begin preparing for war. Five months later, on 1 September, German forces invaded Poland.

Chapter 3, Key Question 3: How far was Hitler's foreign policy to blame for the outbreak of war in Europe in 1939?

The guarantee for Poland

Britain and France had to honour their agreement to come to Poland's defence. If they did not, they would lose their status as Great Powers. They would have to accept the destruction of the existing international system based on diplomacy and instead accept the new world order based on the principle of 'might makes right'. It was in the interests of both Britain and France to fight.

The declaration of war

On 3 September 1939, Chamberlain made a radio announcement (see Figure 3.14): 'This morning the British ambassador in Berlin handed the German government a final note, that unless we heard by 11 o'clock that they were prepared to withdraw at once from Poland, then a state of war would exist between us. I have to tell you now that no such undertaking has been received, and that, consequently, this country is at war with Germany.' France did the same a few hours later.

Hitler had wanted war but had hoped to choose both his opponents and the timing of the conflict. In September 1939, he believed that France and Britain were still following appeasement, so it came as a surprise to find that he was now at war with both Britain and France (see the map in Figure 3.15).

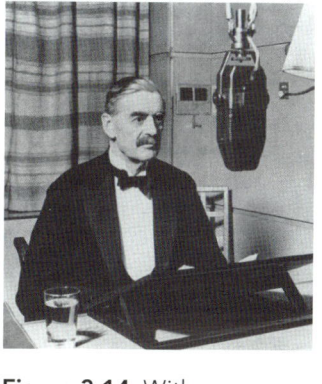

Figure 3.14: With appeasement in pieces, Chamberlain spoke to the nation from Downing Street on 3 September 1939

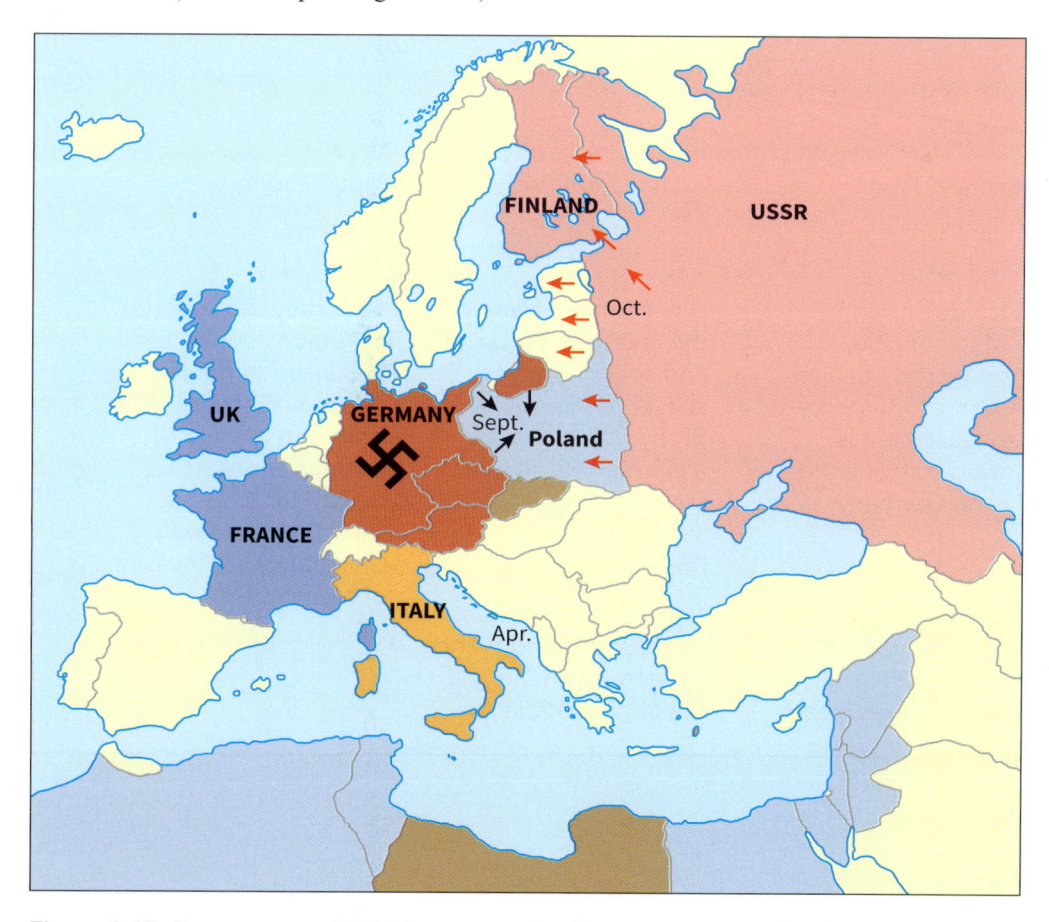

Figure 3.15: Europe at war, 1939. You can see the German expansion leading to the outbreak of war in September; once Germany attacked Poland from the west, the Soviet Union attacked it from the east

135

ACTIVITY 3.5

Hitler did not really believe that Britain and France would honour their agreement to come to Poland's defence. What might have happened if he had been right?

a   In pairs, create a flow diagram to show the process of events. Start with Britain and France's guarantee to Poland. Then add a box for the German invasion of Poland. Now work out alternative actions for Britain and France that do not involve declaring war on Germany.

b   Present your flow diagram to another pair and discuss the similarities and differences. Come to an agreement on any differences and then give a group presentation to the class.

FOCUS TASK 3.8

The 1930s is a complicated period. To help you explore all the different events and their consequences, copy the diagram below onto a large sheet of paper. Using your knowledge from this chapter, add examples.

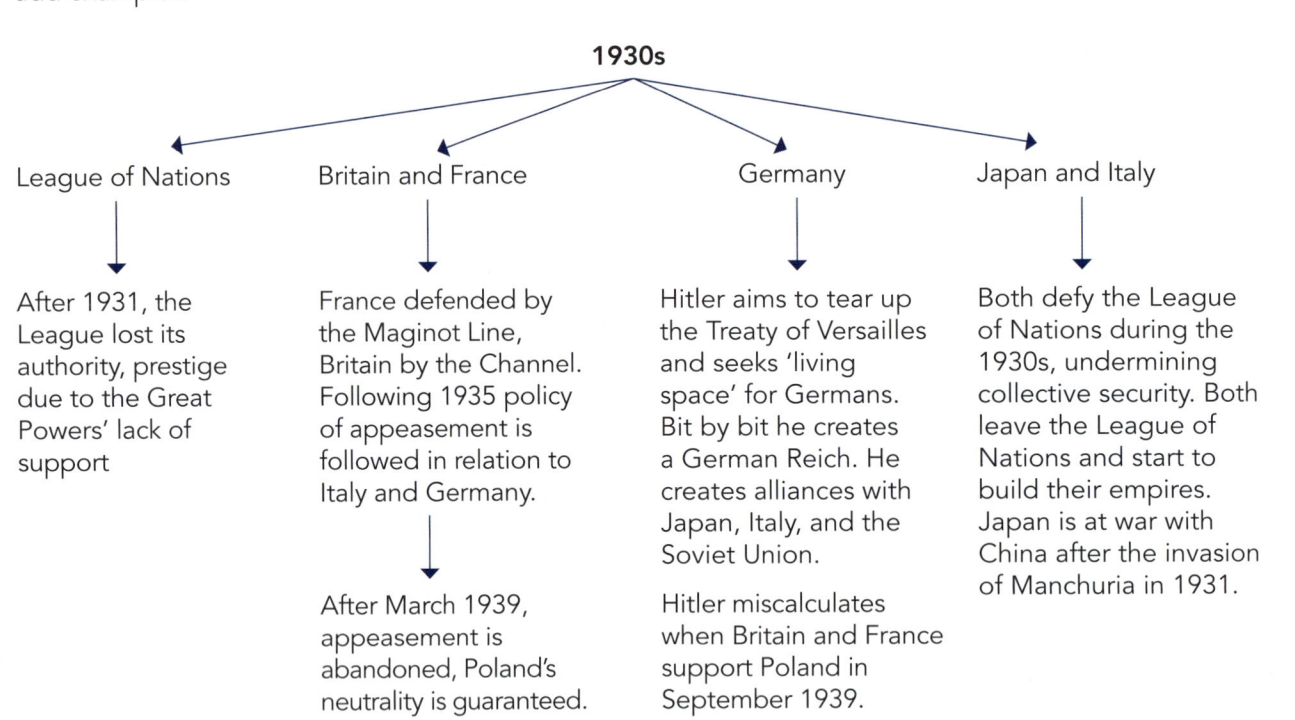

1930s

- **League of Nations**
  - After 1931, the League lost its authority, prestige due to the Great Powers' lack of support

- **Britain and France**
  - France defended by the Maginot Line, Britain by the Channel. Following 1935 policy of appeasement is followed in relation to Italy and Germany.
  - After March 1939, appeasement is abandoned, Poland's neutrality is guaranteed.

- **Germany**
  - Hitler aims to tear up the Treaty of Versailles and seeks 'living space' for Germans. Bit by bit he creates a German Reich. He creates alliances with Japan, Italy, and the Soviet Union.
  - Hitler miscalculates when Britain and France support Poland in September 1939.

- **Japan and Italy**
  - Both defy the League of Nations during the 1930s, undermining collective security. Both leave the League of Nations and start to build their empires. Japan is at war with China after the invasion of Manchuria in 1931.

Chapter 3, Key Question 3: How far was Hitler's foreign policy to blame for the outbreak of war in Europe in 1939?

FOCUS TASK 3.9

a On a piece of A4 paper, draw the diagram below. Now colour in the centre box to make it stand out. Your task is to make the centre box 'happen' by drawing arrows between any of the other boxes, but the final arrow must target the centre box. The only rule is that when you draw an arrow between two boxes, the first box must help explain the second box. You can draw as many arrows as you please but you must stick to this rule.

- The growth of nationalism and militarism in countries ruled by dictators
- The impact of the Great Depression
- Hitler's policy and actions during the 1930s
- . . . declared war on Germany in September 1939
- The failures of the League of Nations
- The policy of appeasement
- The Nazi–Soviet Pact
- The long-term effects of the treaty of Versailles, 1919

b In pairs, use the diagram to work out the most significant causes. Take a small piece of card and cover up each of the boxes in turn. Ask: 'Would the war have started if factor X [covered up] had not been present?' If the answer is 'no', then the factor is of some importance. If the answer is 'yes', the war would still have happened in some way or other, then the factor is of less importance. Put a star (*) next to any factors you identify as more important. Use your findings to help you decide how much blame lies with Hitler and his foreign policies in the 1930s.

SUMMARY

- Hitler's foreign policy in the 1930s was guided by his desire to overturn the Treaty of Versailles, find *Lebensraum* ('living space') for the German people and unify all Germans in one *Reich* ('empire').
- The Treaty of Versailles was supposed to be implemented by the League of Nations, but Britain wanted a softer approach than France and this caused disagreements.

> CAMBRIDGE IGCSE™ AND O LEVEL HISTORY OPTION B: COURSEBOOK

CONTINUED

- The League of Nations was not able to prevent conflicts in the 1930s, and this undermined its influence and importance.
- Britain and France wanted to keep Germany and Italy apart during the 1930s but failed to do so. Their next step was to follow a policy of appeasement.
- Appeasement was based on listening to Hitler's demands, discussing a reasonable solution with him and implementing it.
- The Munich Agreement in September 1938 marked a turning point in appeasement. France, Britain, and Italy agreed to hand over the Czech Sudetenland to Hitler.
- In March 1939, Hitler seized the rest of Czechoslovakia.
- Poland's neutrality was safeguarded by France and Britain in March 1939.
- Hitler did not think the promise was sincere. He invaded Poland on 1 September 1939 and Britain and France declared war on 3 September.

KEY SKILLS EXERCISES

Knowledge and understanding

1. Hitler was a powerful dictator. What made him so popular?
2. What were Hitler's foreign policy aims?
3. Why was *Lebensraum* so important to Hitler?

Application

4. Why did Hitler look for *Lebensraum* in the east rather than the west?
5. Why did Hitler remilitarise the Rhineland as his first major action in foreign policy?
6. Why did Britain and France think it was better to appease Hitler than to challenge him?
7. Why did Hitler risk war with Britain and France in September 1939 when Germany invaded Poland?

Analysis

8. Analyse the links between Hitler's three main foreign policy aims.
9. Analyse the reasons for the order of Hitler's foreign policy successes: Rhineland, Austria, Czechoslovakia and Poland.
10. Analyse the role of the Treaty of Versailles in making another world war inevitable in the 1930s.
11. Analyse the key attitudes of the Soviet Union towards the West and vice versa and how they changed during the 1930s.

Evaluation

12. Evaluate the importance of the policy of appeasement in causing the Second World War.
13. Evaluate the importance of public opinion in France and Britain in contributing to the Second World War.
14. Analyse the roles of Adolf Hitler and Benito Mussolini in making the Second World War very likely.
15. Was empire building in Germany and Italy the single most important cause of the Second World War? Explain your answer.

Chapter 3, Key Question 3: How far was Hitler's foreign policy to blame for the outbreak of war in Europe in 1939?

1 This introduction is not targeting the question. Remember to focus on what is being asked, not what you want to write about! This question is specifically asking about 'reasons'. You will need to provide two different reasons, both of which need to be explained and supported by knowledge of the 1930s.

2 After a weak beginning, this answer improves with a good paragraph that addresses one of the reasons for appeasement. The writer has explained the policy without defining it separately and has added relevant and accurate historical knowledge.

3 This introduction to the paragraph echoes the one before and follows a good structure in response to this question.

4 Again, knowledge of the 1930s has been used here to illustrate the policy of appeasement rather than defining it separately as in the first paragraph.

5 Here we have a clear, analytical paragraph focused on the first statement: 'not prepared for conflict'. The writer adds a clear explanation and shows sufficient historical knowledge to support their thinking.

IMPROVE THIS ANSWER

Why did France and Britain follow a policy of appeasement towards Germany in the 1930s?

Sample answer: The policy of appeasement can be defined as managing international problems through negotiation and compromise. This policy was pursued by both Britain and France for several reasons. **1**

The first reason why appeasement was followed is that public opinion in both Britain and France was decidedly against any actions that might start another war like the Great War. Memories of the losses experienced in that conflict made men and women averse to supporting a confrontational foreign policy. In democracies, French and British politicians were sensitive to public opinion and the results of surveys suggested that if they wanted to stay in power, they had to pursue a policy that sought to manage Hitler's claims about the harsh terms within in the Treaty of Versailles. This helps to explain why he was able to invade the Rhineland in 1936 and rearm the soldiers stationed there, without provoking a war against France and Britain. **2**

The second reason for appeasement **3** is that the British and French were not prepared for a conflict and could not rely on the League of Nations to prevent one. During the Depression both governments had cut spending on their military; but this would only work if war could be avoided. Britain and France believed that they did not have the military strength to challenge German aggression. The League had proved that it could not act to stop aggression and when Hitler took Germany out of the League in October 1933, the French and British decided that they could not rely on the League to stop German aggression. Appeasement was seen as the viable alternative to the League. **4** Both Britain and France saw Hitler as a rational leader who had some valid criticisms of the Treaty of Versailles that could be addressed through discussion. A rational leader could negotiate and reach agreement. This was why appeasement was pursued. Germany left the League in 1933 and started to rearm the army, navy and air force, so from the French and British point of view, appeasement was in many ways the League's replacement. **5**

Now write an improved response using this guidance.

CAMBRIDGE IGCSE™ AND O LEVEL HISTORY OPTION B: COURSEBOOK

PRACTICE QUESTIONS

1 Hitler promised Germans that he would tear up the treaty of Versailles.
   a What territorial clauses of the treaty did Hitler want to change? [4]
   b Why did Hitler want to create one German Reich? [6]
   c Which country carried more blame for not stopping Hitler's aggression before September 1939: Britain or the Soviet Union? [10]
   [Total: 20]

2 Why did appeasement fail to stop a war breaking out in Europe in 1939?
   Study the background information and the sources carefully, and then answer **all** parts of the question. You may use any of the sources to help you answer the questions, in addition to those sources which you are told to use. In answering parts a–e you should use your knowledge of the topic to help you interpret and evaluate the sources.
   a How far do sources A and B agree? [8]
   b Study Source C.
      Why was Source C published at this time? Explain your answer using details from the source and your own knowledge. [8]
   c Study Source D.
      How useful is this source in explaining why the policy of appeasement failed in 1939? Explain your answer using details from the source and your own knowledge. [7]
   d Study sources E and F. How far do you trust what Hitler said about Britain in source E, given the evidence in source F?
      Explain your answer using details from the sources and your own knowledge. [8]
   e Study **all** the sources.
      How far do these sources provide convincing evidence that the policy of appeasement was always going to fail in preventing war in Europe in 1939?
      Explain your answer using details from the sources and your own knowledge. [9]
   [Total: 40]

Background information

Appeasement was the policy followed by Britain and France in relation to Hitler's Germany from the mid-1930s. It was a controversial policy at the time, and it is still debated today. The aim of appeasement was to prevent war breaking out by seeking agreements with Hitler over the changes he wanted to make to the Treaty of Versailles. Memories of the First World War were still fresh and public opinion was against rearmament in case that led to war.

However, following the Munich Agreement rearmament began in both France and Britain. In March 1939, Hitler ignored the Munich Agreement and invaded Czechoslovakia. Britain and France immediately promised to guarantee Poland's security.

Source A: A cartoon published in a US newspaper shortly after the Munich Agreement was signed in September 1938

Chapter 3, Key Question 3: How far was Hitler's foreign policy to blame for the outbreak of war in Europe in 1939?

CONTINUED

Source B: A British cartoon by David Low, published in March 1939

Source C: A Soviet cartoon from 1939, showing Hitler's 'war machine' being pointed towards the USSR by two police officers, one French and one British. 'CCCP' is Russian for the USSR

141

> **CONTINUED**
>
> *The German visit was from my point of view a great success, because it achieved its objective, that of creating an atmosphere in which it is possible to discuss with Germany the practical questions involved in a European settlement. Both Hitler and Göring [Commander-in-Chief of the Luftwaffe] said separately, and emphatically, that they had no desire or intention of making war [. . .] Of course, they want to dominate eastern Europe; they want as close a union as possible with Austria as they can get without incorporating her into the Reich.*
>
> **Source D:** Part of a memorandum written by Neville Chamberlain, in November 1937
>
> ---
>
> *The following special reasons make me confident. There is no actual rearmament in England, just propaganda. The construction programme for the navy for 1938 has not yet been fulfilled. Little has been done on land. England will only be able to send a maximum of three divisions to the continent. A little has been done for the Air Force, but it is only a beginning. France lacks men due to the decline in the birth rate. Little has been done for rearmament. The enemy had another hope, that Russia would become our enemy after the conquest of Poland. Our enemies are little worms, I saw them at Munich.*
>
> **Source E:** Part of a speech made by Hitler to his military commanders, 27 August 1939
>
> ---
>
> *Appeasement was far more than a weak [. . .] policy of concession to potential aggressors. It was [. . .] consistent with the main lines of British foreign policy going back to the nineteenth century.*
>
> *'Appeasement' [. . .] meant a policy of adjustment and accommodation of conflicting interests broadly to conform with Britain's unique position in world affairs. It involved no preconceived plan of action, it rested upon a number of political and moral assumptions about the virtue of compromise and peace. It involved using the instruments of British power – trading and financial strength and a wealth of diplomatic experience – to their fullest advantage.*
>
> **Source F:** R.J. Overy, writing in 1987
>
> ---
>
> *Timidity was the main feature of French political leadership. At the critical moments – in March 1936 and September 1938 – leaders steered away from any suggestion of constraining Germany by force. This timidity had three main causes. Firstly, there was the caution of the military chiefs. Early in 1936 before Hitler walked into the Rhineland, Marshal Gamelin thought that France could not fight Germany with any certainty of victory. Secondly, French public opinion was deeply divided and the lack of national unity prevented a forceful response to Hitler's moves. Thirdly, from September 1935 onwards, military and political leaders were convinced that France could not fight Germany unless assured of British help. British help was considered vital for the protection of French shipping and supplies in the Mediterranean.*
>
> **Source G:** British historian Anthony Adamthwaite in 1977

Chapter 3, Key Question 3: How far was Hitler's foreign policy to blame for the outbreak of war in Europe in 1939?

PROJECT

You are going to work in pairs to invent an 'alternative history' of the 1930s, in which the war in Europe was prevented. You should use words and pictures to present your ideas.

Start by looking at the timeline of events in the 1930s at the start of section 3.3. Decide on the point in the timeline that you consider was crucial to saving the peace in Europe.

On a large sheet of paper, describe this crucial moment.

Using pictures, maps and speech bubbles, formulate a specific response either from the League of Nations or from the two great powers, Britain and France. The response must be strong enough to destroy Hitler's confidence and discourage him from further aggression.

Create a wall display of all the alternative histories and visit this 'exhibition'. Did other pairs choose the same or a different crucial moment? Do you agree with their alternative story of what might have happened?

SELF-EVALUATION CHECKLIST

After studying this chapter, complete this table:

You should be able to:	Needs more work	Almost there	Ready to move on
Describe the long-term consequences of the Treaty of Versailles that were exploited by Germany.			
Explain the consequences of the League of Nations' failures in the 1930s, particularly disarmament, Abyssinia, and Manchuria.			
Explain Hitler's main aims: tearing up the Treaty of Versailles, creating *Lebensraum* in the east and establishing a new German *Reich*.			
Explain the steps Hitler took in the 1930s to achieve these aims, including rearmament, remilitarisation, *Anschluss* with Austria and invading Czechoslovakia.			
Understand the policy of appeasement and how it was applied to Hitler at the time.			
Explain why appeasement was a topic of debate at the time and has been since, giving your own judgement on whether it was justified.			
Understand the importance of the Nazi–Soviet Pact in the lead-up to war.			
Explain why Britain and France eventually abandoned the policy of appeasement and declared war on Germany in September 1939.			

> Chapter 4, Key Question 4:

Who was to blame for the Cold War?

FOCUS POINTS

This chapter will help you to answer these questions:

- Why did the US–Soviet alliance begin to break down in 1945?
- How had the USSR gained control of Eastern Europe by 1948?
- How did the United States react to Soviet expansionism?
- What were the consequences of the Berlin Blockade?
- Who was more to blame for starting the Cold War: the United States or the USSR?

Chapter 4, Key Question 4: Who was to blame for the Cold War?

4.0 What is this enquiry about?

In this chapter, you will investigate the deterioration of the wartime alliance between the USA and the USSR. You will see that the problems in the alliance were visible during the war itself. As historians, you will need to evaluate the responsibilities of both countries for post-war hostility, see their actions in context (or in a range of different contexts) and then reach a decision about 'blame'.

Ask yourself:

- Was the USA to blame?
- Was the USSR to blame?
- Were they both to blame?
- Was neither to blame?

Reaching a judgement is an important part of the enquiry, but it is only the last stage. First, you need to collect evidence in order to reach that judgement, but also in order to show how you reached it.

FOCUS TASK 4.1

Copy the table and complete it as you read through the following sections. Record information and evidence in response to each question.

	How did it happen and whose fault was it?	Evidence to support the judgement
Why did the US–Soviet alliance begin to break down in 1945?		
How had the USSR gained control of Eastern Europe by 1948?		
How did the United States react to Soviet expansionism?		
What were the consequences of the Berlin Blockade?		
Who was more to blame for starting the Cold War: the United States or the USSR?		

4.1 Why did the US–Soviet alliance begin to break down in 1945?

What was the Cold War?

The Cold War was a period of intense competition between the USSR and its allies and the USA and its allies. Beginning in the mid-1940s, it lasted until the beginning of the 1990s. It was called a 'cold' war because it did not lead to military conflict between the two sides. Instead, there were **proxy wars** across the globe, in which local conflicts were supported by both **superpowers**. Beyond wars there was rivalry to be the most powerfully armed and the most successful in space exploration: the arms race and the space race. However, although a direct war never broke out, the constant military threat experienced by both sides heightened tension between the USSR and the USA. This was as much of an influence on political decision-making as an actual war.

KEY TERMS

proxy war: a war in which a country does not fight but provides another country or side with war material to show support

superpower: the name given to the USSR and the USA after the Second World War to emphasise their economic, military, political and nuclear strength compared to other countries

145

Figure 4.1: A map showing the military alliances of NATO and the **Warsaw Pact** in Europe in 1955. Away from Europe, the USA and Canada were also NATO members. In 1963, Mongolia asked to join the Warsaw Pact but it was rejected. Albania left the Warsaw Pact in 1968.

> ### KEY TERM
>
> **Warsaw Pact:** a defensive military alliance of Eastern European states, including the USSR, Hungary, Romania, Bulgaria, Albania Czechoslovakia, East Germany and Poland, established as a response to NATO (the North Atlantic Treaty Organization)

ACTIVITY 4.1

a   In pairs, look at the map in Figure 4.1. Talk to each other about each country and find out what you each know about it. Then cover up the map and test your partner's map memory: *Which countries is X next to? What is north of Y?* Uncover the map and learn from your mistakes.

b   Identify the countries on the map that are likely to cause tension between the two superpowers. Explain your choices. Write down your responses and share them with another pair for comment.

Chapter 4, Key Question 4: Who was to blame for the Cold War?

What was the 'Grand Alliance'?

In June 1941, the Germans invaded the USSR. This was part of Hitler's plan to acquire *Lebensraum* in the east. The invasion gave the USSR and Britain a common enemy. When the Japanese bombed the US naval base at Pearl Harbor in December 1941, the USA joined Britain and the USSR in the war, creating the Grand Alliance. The Alliance's objective was to defeat the Axis Powers: Nazi Germany, Italy and Japan.

SOURCE 4A

Source 4A: A Soviet poster produced in 1942 showing the Grand Alliance choking Hitler. At the very top of the poster it says: 'He [Hitler] won't get out of this noose'. The Soviet noose says: 'Alliance between the USSR, Britain and the USA'. The USA and British nooses say 'Agreement' and 'Partnership'.

SOURCE ANALYSIS 4.1

Study Source 4A.

a Which countries made up the Grand Alliance?

b What was the Alliance's key purpose? Who were the Axis Powers?

c What is the message about the Grand Alliance in this source? Use details in the poster to support your answer.

Why did the Alliance begin to break down in 1945?

There were three main reasons for the breakdown of the Alliance:

- ideological differences
- wartime disagreements over Lend–Lease and military strategy
- tensions created by the three wartime and post-war conferences: Tehran, Yalta, and Potsdam.

Ideological differences

The USA and the USSR were very different societies.

- The USA was a capitalist democracy with voting rights and multi-party elections with a free press. Its society and economy were based on a belief in private property.
- The USSR was a communist one-party state, with no opposition and state-controlled press. Its society and economy were planned by the state. Individuals were not allowed to own property.

Leaders in the USA and Britain believed that the USSR wanted to spread communism beyond its borders into central and eastern Europe and into Asia. Soviet leader Joseph Stalin suspected the West of wanting Hitler's army to attack and weaken the Soviet Union. There was little trust between members of the Grand Alliance. It was more of a marriage of convenience, but until the Axis Powers were defeated they had to stick together.

Wartime disagreements

Winning the war against Hitler meant working together. To a large extent the Grand Alliance did so, but there were pressures that eroded its effectiveness.

To help the USSR fight the Nazi invaders, the US government began sending it war supplies. Under a system called Lend–Lease, the USA loaned military equipment for the duration of the war at no charge. By 1945, the USA had sent the USSR supplies valued at nearly $11 billion. About 25% of this was in the form of munitions and 75% consisted of industrial equipment, raw materials and food. Despite this, the Soviet Union did not act like a grateful partner, and this upset the USA.

SOURCE 4B

THE WAY OF A STORK

Source 4B: A US cartoon commenting on the Lend–Lease programme, published in January 1941

SOURCE ANALYSIS 4.2

Study Source 4B.

a How can you tell that the eagle represents the USA?

b What impression of the Lend–Lease scheme does the cartoonist give?

c Make a list of the items that the bird is carrying. What do you think this means?

d Why has the cartoonist drawn the Statue of Liberty in the background?

e Why would Stalin not have wanted Soviet people to see this cartoon?

Chapter 4, Key Question 4: Who was to blame for the Cold War?

Tensions in the Grand Alliance: the Second Front

As early as 1942, Stalin wanted the USA and Britain to invade Western Europe and engage the German army to relieve pressure on the Red Army in the east. It did not happen immediately. US President Franklin D. Roosevelt promised a second front, but it was repeatedly postponed. Instead of an Anglo–American invasion of German-occupied France, Britain and the USA sent troops to North Africa and Italy. They delayed the invasion of Europe itself until June 1944.

SOURCES 4C & 4D

The most important disagreement, however, was over the opening of a Second Front in the West. Although Stalin only grumbled when the invasion was postponed until 1943, he exploded the following year when the invasion was postponed again until June of 1944. In retaliation, Stalin recalled his ambassadors from London and Washington and fears soon arose that the Soviets might seek a separate peace with Germany.

Source 4C: From the website of the US Department of State

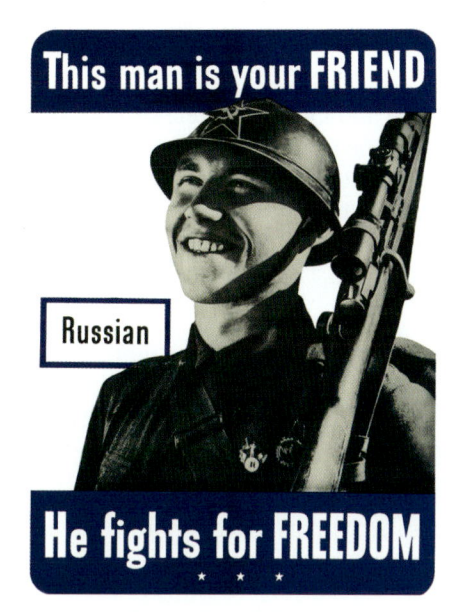

Source 4D: A poster produced by the US government in 1942. It shows a uniformed Soviet soldier.

SOURCE ANALYSIS 4.3

Study sources 4A, 4B, 4C and 4D.

a For each source, write a one-sentence caption that sums up the Grand Alliance relationship.

b Why do Sources 4A, 4B and 4D suggest a different sort of relationship between the Grand Alliance partners from Source 4C? Do the different impressions mean that some of the four sources cannot be trusted for assessing the strength of the Grand Alliance?

c What does Source 4D tell you about the USA and the USSR?

d The Grand Alliance is sometimes called a 'marriage of convenience'. Why?

Key points

The Grand Alliance

- The German invasion of the USSR and the attack on Pearl Harbor threw together the USA, the Soviet Union and Britain into the Grand Alliance.

- It was a marriage of convenience with one unifying aim: to defeat the Axis Powers of Germany, Italy and Japan.

- There were strains in the Grand Alliance because of a lack of trust and because the Soviet Union wanted the USA and Britain to start a second front in Western Europe.

149

Wartime and post-war conferences

By late 1943, as the war was turning in their favour, the leaders of the Grand Alliance began to consider what kind of peace they wanted once Japan, Germany and Italy had been defeated.

The Tehran Conference, 1943

The Big Three (Roosevelt, the British prime minister Winston Churchill and Stalin) met in November 1943. At Tehran, wartime leaders coordinated their military strategies against Germany, Italy and Japan. Stalin got what he wanted – a date (June 1944) for the Anglo–American invasion of German-occupied France. The USSR agreed to launch a major offensive on the Eastern Front. This would divert German troops from northern France.

The important issues of Eastern Europe and Germany were discussed. During these negotiations, Roosevelt secured an assurance from Stalin that **referenda** would be held in the republics of Lithuania Latvia and Estonia to see if they wanted to become part of the USSR. Stalin stressed that he would not agree to any international control over the elections. Roosevelt, Churchill and Stalin also discussed the post-war **partition** of Germany into Allied zones of occupation. They agreed to investigate this further before they made a final decision.

Broader international cooperation was a major part of the negotiations at Tehran. Roosevelt and Stalin privately discussed the make-up of the United Nations. Roosevelt outlined his vision of an organisation led by 'four policemen' (the USA, Britain, China and the USSR) who would have the power to deal immediately with any threat to peace.

Finally, the leaders agreed that, at the end of the war, the USSR could restore its 1921 border with Poland. Poland would be compensated with its western border moving further west at Germany's expense. The new German–Polish border would be the Oder and Neisse rivers.

> **KEY TERMS**
>
> **referendum:** a vote by the people on a single political issue with the result of the vote informing a political decision
>
> **partition:** the division of a country or area into two or more parts

> **REVISION TIP**
>
> One way to remember the order of the conferences is to remind yourself of this Revision 'TYP': **T**ehran, **Y**alta, **P**otsdam. Even if all the dates and details are not at your fingertips, you can use this 'TYP' to get them in the right order!

Figure 4.2: Two maps showing the borders of Poland in 1938 and after its western border with Germany had been moved to the Oder-Neisse rivers

The Yalta Conference, February 1945

The war in Europe was in its final stages when Roosevelt, Stalin and Churchill met at Yalta in February 1945. By this time, the Red Army had occupied most of Central and Eastern Europe. The issues that had emerged at Tehran, especially those regarding Poland, now needed solutions.

The main issue was what to do with Germany when war ended. The agreed policy can be summed up in five D-words:

- demilitarisation (disbanding the armed forces)
- de-Nazification (removing all former Nazis from positions of power)
- democratisation (restoring free elections and a multiparty system)
- de-industrialisation (reducing Germany's heavy industry)
- decentralisation (taking power away from central government).

There were no detailed arrangements about how these might be achieved, but each of the Grand Alliance partners was responsible for carrying them out in their respective German zones, once war was over.

THINKING SKILLS

In a group of three, imagine that you represent the three countries of the Grand Alliance. How will you respond to the five Ds? Take each point in turn and discuss what practical steps could be taken to achieve each one from your country's point of view. Remember that the USSR is a totalitarian state and the Western powers are democracies. Will you agree on what to do? If you cannot agree, what will you do?

Make a note of your points and share these with another group of three. If you cannot agree, record that, too. Ask them to assess your thinking and to give you feedback for improvement.

REFLECTION

Reflect on the Thinking skills activity. How was learning in groups of three different from working in pairs? Did it make agreement harder or easier to reach? Why?

When you joined with another three, what role did you play? Did everyone get a fair chance to explain their view? How was this organised? Did you take turns or did everyone speak whenever they liked? How hard was it to work in a group of six? What did you learn personally from the experience?

Places and problems	Agreements	Remaining tension
Germany	1. Germany (and Berlin) temporarily divided into Soviet, American, British and French occupation zones. 2. Germany to pay $20 billion reparations, 50% to the USSR. 3. The implementation of the five Ds in all four zones after its defeat. War crimes trials for captured Nazis.	The division of Germany was only temporary. A future conference would decide its future. Stalin wanted more reparations from Germany than agreed, because so much of the USSR had been destroyed.
Poland	1. New Soviet–Polish borders would give Poland German territory in the west as compensation for territory in the east surrendered to the USSR. 2. Early elections.	1. The West rejected Soviet demands that Germans now in Poland should be repatriated to Germany. 2. Stalin wanted a Polish government that would be friendly to the Soviet Union. He supported the 'Lublin Poles' (mostly communist) while Roosevelt and Churchill backed the 'London Poles' (non-communist).
Eastern Europe	Early elections would take place in all Eastern European countries liberated from Nazi Germany by the Soviet Red Army.	Stalin wanted governments friendly to the USSR and was worried that free elections would not produce them.
Ending the war	Stalin agreed to join the war against Japan once Germany had been defeated. In return, the USSR would receive South Sakhalin and the Kurile Islands.	Truman was concerned about the USSR gaining influence in the Far East when it was the USA that had done most of the fighting against Japan.
United Nations Organisation (UN)	The creation of the United Nations – with a five-member Security Council – to replace the League of Nations at the end of the war.	Stalin wanted all Soviet republics to have seats in the proposed UN's General Assembly, but the USA and Britain only agreed to three.

Figure 4.3: A table showing the agreements made at the Yalta Conference and the issues that remained unresolved

> **KEY TERMS**
>
> **repatriate:** to send or bring someone back to the country that they came from
>
> **Security Council:** a small group of countries that has responsibility for peacekeeping within the United Nations

Chapter 4, Key Question 4: Who was to blame for the Cold War?

SOURCES 4E, 4F & 4G

Source 4E: A cartoon called 'Trouble with some of the pieces', showing Stalin, Roosevelt and Churchill assembling a jigsaw puzzle of Europe at Yalta in 1945

It was not a question of what we would let the Russians do, but what we could get the Russians to do.

Source 4F: Future Secretary of State James Byrnes, commenting on the Yalta Conference

To this day, many of Roosevelt's most vehement detractors accuse him of 'handing over' Eastern Europe and Northeast Asia to the Soviet Union at Yalta despite the fact that the Soviets did make many substantial concessions.

Source 4G: Office of the Historian, USA Department of State (an official US government website)

SOURCE ANALYSIS 4.4

Study Sources 4E, 4F and 4G.

a What clues does the cartoonist in Source 4E give you to help identify each of the three leaders?

b What is the key message of the cartoon?

c To what extent is the message in Source 4E supported by evidence from Sources 4F and 4G?

FOCUS TASK 4.2

There were 11 million Soviet soldiers in Central and Eastern Europe at the end of the war. In pairs, look back at the table in Figure 4.3 about the Yalta Conference, then look at Sources 4E, 4F and 4G again. Create a chart like the one below. Write down the areas of disagreement and the reasons they occurred. In the third column, give each disagreement a mark out of 5 for the strain it put on the Grand Alliance, where 1 is a small strain and 5 is a significant strain.

Compare your completed charts with another pair. Discuss where you put different marks and why that was.

Areas of disagreement at Yalta	Why did these occur?	Mark 1–5

> CAMBRIDGE IGCSE™ AND O LEVEL HISTORY OPTION B: COURSEBOOK

> KEY FIGURE
>
> **Joseph Stalin (1878–1953)**
>
> Stalin led the Soviet Union between 1922 and 1953. His reputation is very mixed. Some still revere him as the leader who industrialised the Soviet Union and helped it to catch up with the West. He was a victorious leader in the Second World War and he cemented the USSR's position as a world power. Others see him as a brutal dictator who deliberately starved his people, carried out forced deportations and executed hundreds of thousands in the Great Purge. He created a totalitarian society in which opposition to his rule was not tolerated. At the end of the war in 1945, the USSR was one of two superpowers (the USA was the other).

What changed between February and July 1945?

Roosevelt died in April 1945 and was replaced by his vice president, Harry S. Truman. Truman had little experience of foreign affairs, but took a stronger attitude towards Stalin and the USSR's security fears in Eastern Europe. In April, Truman met with the Soviet foreign minister, Vyacheslav Molotov, and lectured him on the importance of sticking to agreements. In May 1945, just three days after Germany's surrender, Truman abruptly ended the Lend–Lease scheme to the USSR. Ships that had already left for the Soviet Union were recalled to port. As a result, relations deteriorated still further by the time the Allies met at Potsdam in July 1945.

In Britain, Clement Attlee, who had been deputy prime minister in a wartime coalition government, replaced Churchill as prime minister after a general election in July.

> KEY FIGURE
>
> **Harry S. Truman (1884–1972)**
>
> Truman grew up on his family's farm. He fought in the First World War, after which he opened a shop. In 1933, he was elected as senator for Missouri and was chosen as Roosevelt's running mate in the 1944 election. When Roosevelt died in April 1945, the job of leadership passed to Truman as vice president. He is remembered as the president who authorised the use of atomic weapons against Japan to end the Second World War. After the war, Truman helped to found the United Nations, issued the Truman Doctrine to contain communism, and passed the $13 billion Marshall Plan to rebuild Europe.

The Potsdam Conference, 1945

At the Potsdam Conference in July and August 1945, the Allies were represented by Truman, Stalin and Attlee. With Germany beaten and Japan on the verge of defeat, the USA took a tougher approach towards the USSR. Leaders reached some agreement on future plans, but tension remained.

Chapter 4, Key Question 4: Who was to blame for the Cold War?

The future treatment of Germany was discussed in detail. To ensure Germany's demilitarisation and disarmament, the Allies decided to abolish the following.

- The SS: this was a paramilitary group under Adolf Hitler and the Nazi Party in Nazi Germany, and later throughout German-occupied Europe during the Second World War. Its main job was to carry out surveillance and maintain security usually by terrorising people.
- The SA: also known as the Stormtroopers, these men wore brown uniforms and helped Adolf Hitler gain power in 1933. Its main purpose was to provide security for Nazi rallies and assemblies, and to break up the meetings of opposing political parties.
- The Gestapo: the secret police of Nazi Germany and, later, of Nazi-occupied Europe. Its role was to investigate crimes against the Nazi Party such as treason. The Gestapo was above the law and could use any method to implement orders from the Nazi leadership.
- Air, land and naval forces.

To ensure Germany's democratisation, the Allies felt it was essential to get rid of the Nazi Party. They planned to prevent all Nazi activity and to prepare for the reconstruction of German political life in a democratic state.

Places and problems	Agreements	Remaining tension
Germany	1. Division of the country and the capital, Berlin, into four zones. 2. Payment of reparations confirmed, but amount was reduced and industrial goods had to come from each power's own zone. The USSR had to provide agricultural goods from its zone in return for industrial goods from the three western zones. 3. Decisions on the 'Five Ds' and war crimes trials were confirmed.	1. The USSR was only given limited reparations. 2. Disagreements about de-Nazification led to each zone implementing this separately. The USSR was worried that former Nazis could return to power in the western zones. 3. The West wanted a quick economic recovery for Germany, but Stalin wanted to keep Germany weak. 4. Stalin was concerned about the impact of the capitalist western zones on the eastern zone.
Poland	Stalin agreed to let more 'London Poles' (non-communists) join the 'Lublin Poles' government (mostly communist) already in place.	Although Stalin agreed to allow more 'London Poles' to join the existing government, Truman's request for free elections in Poland was turned down.
Eastern Europe	1. The USSR would take land from Germany, Romania and Czechoslovakia. The three Baltic republics (Latvia, Lithuania and Estonia) would become part of the USSR. 2. Germans living in Poland, Hungary and Czechoslovakia would be moved to Germany.	The USA was concerned about growing Soviet control in the eastern European countries of Poland, Hungary, Romania, Bulgaria and Czechoslovakia.

(Continued)

Places and problems	Agreements	Remaining tension
The war	Following Germany's surrender in May 1945, the USSR had been preparing to attack Japan, as agreed at Yalta. Truman informed Stalin that the USA had developed a new and powerful weapon, the atomic bomb.	1. Truman decided to use the new atomic bombs on Japan, partly to keep the USSR out of the Pacific War. 2. Truman refused to allow the USSR a role in the post-war occupation of Japan. 3. Truman refused to share atomic secrets with the USSR. Stalin immediately ordered the Soviet atomic weapon programme to be accelerated, so starting the nuclear arms race.
United Nations	1. The UN was formally created. 2. The USA, the USSR, Britain, France, and China would be the five permanent members of the Security Council, each with a veto.	As the Cold War developed, both East and West increasingly used their power of veto to block or delay UN actions that did not suit them.

Figure 4.4: The agreements made at the Potsdam Conference and the issues that remained unresolved

Issues causing tension in the Grand Alliance

Germany had used Poland as an invasion route into Russia/USSR in 1914 and 1941. Stalin believed it was vital that the USSR should be able to control Poland (and other eastern European states) after the Second World War, or at least ensure that a friendly government ruled it. Serious differences remained about how Poland should be governed. Stalin broke his promise of free elections, but Roosevelt and Churchill could do little about it. The Red Army's occupation made intervention impossible without war breaking out again.

At Potsdam, Truman argued that the USSR should take reparations from its zone of Germany. As this was mainly rural and poorer than the industrial western zones, Stalin objected. Eventually, it was agreed that the USSR could also have 25% of the machinery from the three western zones, but only if the USSR sent 60% of the value of these industrial goods to the West in the form of raw materials (especially coal). The Soviets demanded German coal from the western zones, but the Americans wanted it to help in the economic recovery of Western Europe.

Further disagreement occurred because the Soviets were treating their eastern zone of Germany as if it was part of the USSR. German factories were dismantled and moved to the Soviet Union. Stalin wanted to punish the Germans and take their resources. Although some reparations had been delivered, the Soviets were not supplying food in return as agreed. The USA argued that no more reparations should leave their zone until the Soviets exported the food, clothing, timber and machinery that were needed. The Soviets refused. The difficulties in implementing and interpreting the Yalta and Potsdam agreements was a significant cause of the breakdown of the Grand Alliance.

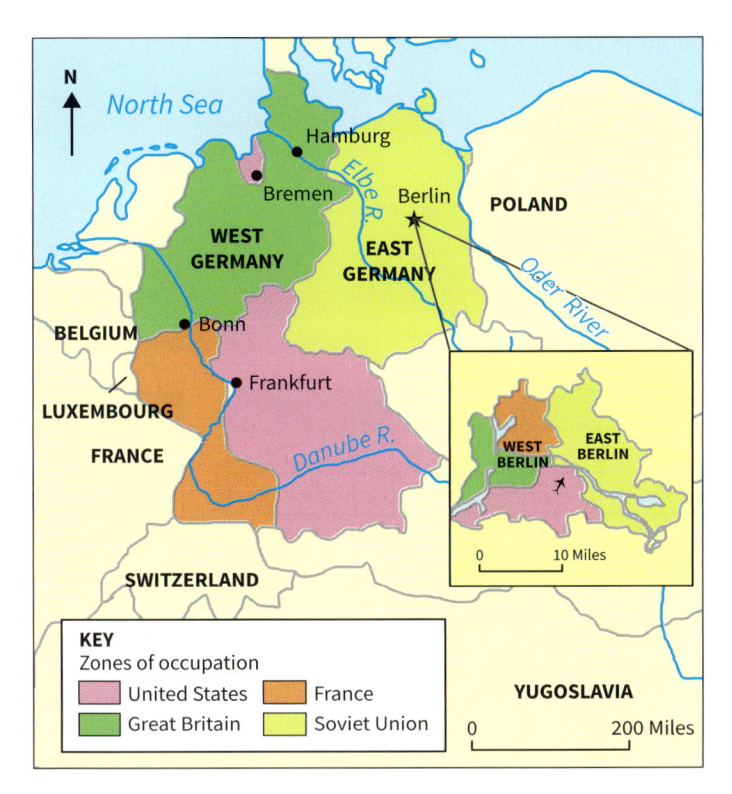

Chapter 4, Key Question 4: Who was to blame for the Cold War?

Figure 4.5: A map showing the division of Germany into four zones of occupation after the Second World War

FOCUS TASK 4.3

In pairs, look back at the table in Figure 4.4 about the Potsdam Conference and the other information in this section. Create a chart like the one below. Write down the areas of disagreement and the reason they occurred. In the third column, give each disagreement a mark out of 5 for the strain it put on the Grand Alliance, where 1 is a small strain and 5 is a significant strain.

Compare your completed charts with another pair. Discuss where you put different marks and why.

Areas of disagreement at Potsdam	Why did these occur?	Mark 1–5

What was the Soviet attitude to peace-making?

Stalin's foreign policy was shaped by the devastation that the USSR had suffered. He had to make sure that his country would not be invaded again. Millions of Soviet troops marched westwards, pushing back the retreating German army. Stalin wanted to take advantage of the military situation in Europe to strengthen Soviet influence and prevent another invasion from the West. He also believed that the USSR should receive reparations that matched its losses.

The devastation that the Second World War caused in the USSR included:

- the death of about 30 million soldiers and civilians
- the destruction of 25 million homes
- the destruction of 31 000 factories
- the destruction of 84 000 schools
- 10.5 million people who were made refugees
- the killing of 17 million cattle
- the destruction of 100 000 state farms.

	1940	1942	1944	1945
Bread (millions of tonnes)	19.0	10.8	9.0	9.9
Meat (thousands of metric tonnes)	1285	607.5	464.3	561.9
Butter (thousands of metric tonnes)	205.2	100	95.4	105.3
Clothing items (millions)	183	54	47	50
Pairs of shoes (millions)	211	52.7	67.4	66.1

Figure 4.6: A table comparing output by the Soviet economy and the impact of the war

THINKING SKILLS

Imagine that you have been instructed by Stalin to write a letter to President Truman to get him to understand the damage done to the USSR during the war. Choose the six most important items of data in the bullet list and the table. Write a short letter to Truman, being as persuasive as you can. Include the six statistics you have chosen.

ACTIVITY 4.2

Look at the facts and statistics in Figure 4.6 and in this section as a whole. Why do you think it was so hard for the people and government of the USA to understand Stalin's point of view in the peace-making process?

What was the US attitude towards peace-making?

Roosevelt, Stalin and Churchill shared certain objectives. They all wanted to limit the power of Germany and prevent another war. They wanted cooperation to continue in peacetime. They wanted a world organisation for maintaining peace to replace the League of Nations. The United Nations was set up in New York towards the end of 1945.

However, Roosevelt wanted to break up empires and 'spheres of influence'. He believed that all states should have the right to self-determination (see Chapter 1). In addition, he hoped that democracy would flourish so people could enjoy free elections and free speech. For Truman, the lesson of the policy of appeasing Hitler in the 1930s was that democracies had to stand up to dictators. His approach was called **containment**: Soviet influence and power must be 'contained' by the USA and its allies. The spread of communism had to be opposed.

Truman and the atomic bomb

Although the Allies reached agreement on several difficult issues, this progress was undermined in August 1945 when the USA exploded the world's first atomic bombs on the cities of Hiroshima and Nagasaki in Japan. This weapon was a new threat to the Soviets. Truman saw the atomic bomb as a way of ending the war against Japan without Soviet assistance. This would prevent any Soviet demands for influence in Asia.

KEY TERM

containment: the name given to the USA's policy aimed at preventing the spread of communism after the Second World War. The word was first used in a 1947 article by US diplomat George Kennan, and soon after it was adopted by President Harry Truman

Chapter 4, Key Question 4: Who was to blame for the Cold War?

SOURCES 4H & 4I

"WHY CAN'T WE WORK TOGETHER IN MUTUAL TRUST & CONFIDENCE?"

Source 4H: A British cartoon published in November 1945, showing President Truman asking the question of Attlee and Stalin

Source 4I: A photograph showing the destruction caused by the atomic bomb dropped on Hiroshima on 6 August 1945. A second nuclear bomb was dropped on Nagasaki on 9 August. The first bomb killed 66 000 and injured 69 000; the second killed 39 000 and injured 25 000. These are estimates only.

> CAMBRIDGE IGCSE™ AND O LEVEL HISTORY OPTION B: COURSEBOOK

> **THINKING SKILLS**
>
> The dropping of the atomic bombs on Japan was a momentous decision. Imagine you worked in the White House in 1945. President Truman asks you for advice on what he should do. What would you have said to him? Which side of the debate would you be on? Why? What are your two strongest arguments? Which would be your weakest two arguments? Explain why.
>
> Once the president made the decision to drop the bombs, how would you have reacted? Do you think your attitude would change after you had seen photographs and film of the two devastated cities?

Key points

The breakdown of the Grand Alliance

- By late 1943, the Grand Alliance was winning the war. Three conferences were held to make plans for peace.
- At Tehran (1943) and Yalta (February 1945), Stalin (USSR) met with Roosevelt (USA) and Churchill (Britain).
- By Potsdam in July 1945, Truman had replaced Roosevelt and Atlee had replaced Churchill.
- Issues that were discussed included the future United Nations, the boundaries for Poland, reparations for the USSR and the division of Germany and Eastern Europe.
- The dropping of the atomic bomb on Hiroshima and Nagasaki in August 1945 ended the war, but complicated relations between the USA and the USSR, which had not yet developed its own atomic bomb.

4.2 How had the USSR gained control of Eastern Europe by 1948?

When Germany surrendered in 1945, there were 11 million Red Army soldiers in Eastern Europe. They had driven the Germans out of Poland, Romania, Hungary, Czechoslovakia and Bulgaria. When the war ended, many Soviet soldiers stayed where they were.

Stalin's motives for expanding into Eastern Europe were mixed. Ideology played a role. The USSR was the world's first and leading communist country, and Stalin wanted to see its expansion. Soviet security also played a part. Russia/USSR had been invaded three times in the 20th century, so Stalin wanted a buffer zone between the West and his own country.

Stalin did not achieve control over Eastern Europe immediately. In different countries he took different actions and moved at different speeds. In general, there were two phases.

- Throughout 1944–47 Stalin and his advisers worked with local politicians to set up coalition governments. Here, local communists served alongside politicians from other parties.
- In 1948–49, 'people's republics' emerged. These were one-party communist dictatorships under Moscow's control.

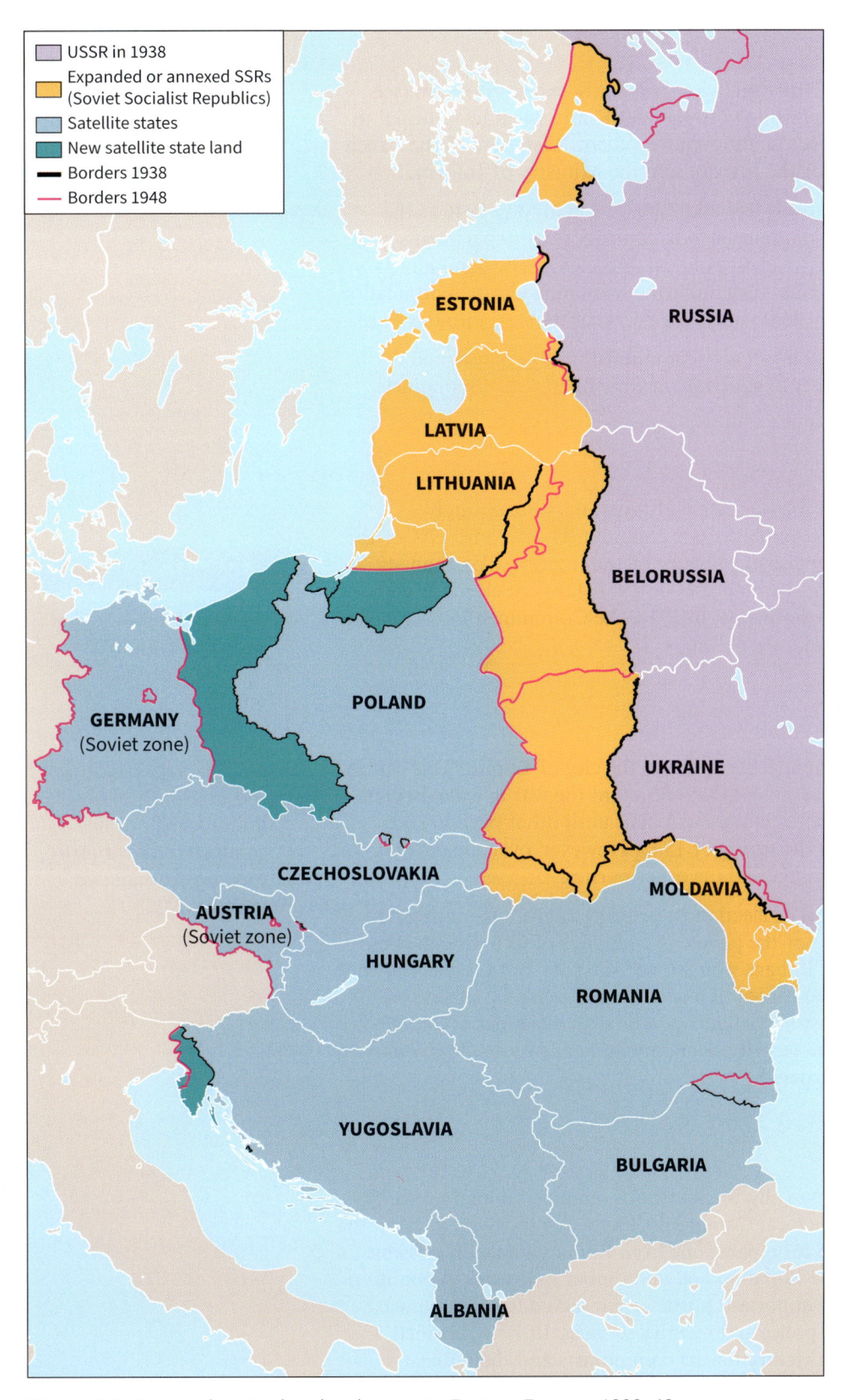

Chapter 4, Key Question 4: Who was to blame for the Cold War?

■	USSR in 1938
■	Expanded or annexed SSRs (Soviet Socialist Republics)
■	Satellite states
■	New satellite state land
—	Borders 1938
—	Borders 1948

Figure 4.7: A map showing border changes in Eastern Europe, 1938–48

161

Czechoslovakia

Edvard Beneš had been president of the Czech government in exile in London (see Chapter 3). He signed a treaty of friendship with the USSR and when he returned to Prague it was with a Moscow-approved coalition government. Members of the Czech Communist Party ran the Ministry of the Interior and the Ministry of Information.

The communists emerged from a relatively free and fair election in May 1946 as the largest party, with 31% of the vote. Communists took control of key departments such as law and order, which enabled them to arrest political opponents. The communists were popular in Czechoslovakia partly because they drove the remaining German population out of the country (many had already fled) and allowed Czechs to move into these areas.

To force new elections in February 1948, all non-communist ministers resigned. New elections were blocked and places in government were filled with communists.

Hungary

Hungary had been a German ally in the war. Most Hungarians were strongly anti-communist. In the election of November 1945, communists won only 17% of the vote. They were given one government post: Ministry of the Interior. Communists used the secret police to **persecute** non-communists. In 1947, falsified elections gave communists control of a coalition government. In 1948, the Communist Party merged with the Social Democratic Party and took power.

Poland

In Poland, the USSR created a national government in the city of Lublin. This was in opposition to the London Polish government that had spent the war in exile. Britain and the USA would not recognise the Lublin government until other parties were represented in it, which happened in the spring of 1945. However, over the next two years, the communists gradually marginalised the other parties.

Elections were held in January 1947. The election was rigged to give the impression that the government had the backing of the people. An alliance of left-wing parties, including the communists, were said to have won 80% of the vote, but there is evidence that the real figure was less than 50%. A coalition government made up of several parties ruled Poland. The Communist Party had 5 positions in a cabinet of 24, but they included important roles in charge of security, economy and education. Opposition politicians were arrested or even murdered.

Romania

Romania was another wartime German ally. Soviet troops remained in place once the Germans had been pushed back. The local Communist Party was relatively weak at the end of the war. The USSR's demand for reparations from Romania made it possible for Soviet Union to control shipping and Romania's oil and timber industries. A coalition government was formed in 1945 and important posts were reserved for communists. There was a gradual takeover of the police and security services. In 1946, falsified elections produced an overwhelming victory for the communists and their allies. **Show trials** were used to eliminate political opponents. In December 1947, King Michael was forced to abdicate.

> **KEY TERMS**
>
> **persecution:** hostility and ill treatment of certain groups in society
>
> **show trial:** a trial held in public with the intention of influencing public opinion rather than making sure justice is served

Chapter 4, Key Question 4: Who was to blame for the Cold War?

Bulgaria

In Bulgaria, communists had been a respectable political party before the war. In September 1944, a coalition containing communists was formed. Gradually, this government was purged of anti-communist rivals. In September 1946, the monarchy was abolished and 11 year old King Simeon II was sent into exile. In 1947, a new constitution was implemented that destroyed any opposition to the communists.

Yugoslavia

Yugoslavia was not part of the Soviet empire. Josip Broz (known as Tito) was a communist, but he led the liberation of his country from the Nazis. Tito's Popular Front held an election in November 1945 in which it received 96% of the vote. Tito formally deposed King Peter and proclaimed the Republic of Yugoslavia on 31 January 1946. Stalin was tempted to invade Yugoslavia once Tito showed he was not going to be controlled from Moscow. However, he decided against it because of Tito's great popularity. Yugoslavia remained an independent communist country throughout the Cold War.

Iran

Although Stalin established a secure sphere of influence in the **Soviet Bloc** by the end of 1948, he was not successful everywhere. In 1946, he broke an agreement with the British to leave oil-rich Iran six months after the end of the war. It was only after pressure from the USA and the **United Nations Security Council** that Soviet troops left.

Turkey

In Turkey, Stalin demanded a naval base for the USSR on the Dardanelles, a narrow strait linking the Black Sea and the Mediterranean. The USA responded by sending naval ships. When Stalin found out that the USA and the British were supporting Turkey, he backed down and gradually withdrew some of the troops that had been deployed near the Soviet–Turkish border in 1946.

KEY TERMS

Soviet Bloc: the group of Eastern European states that were aligned with the USSR, taking their political direction from Moscow (also sometimes called the Communist Bloc or the Eastern Bloc)

United Nations Security Council: the main decision-making body of the UN for military and security matters with 15 members – five permanent (the USA, Britain, China, France and Russia) and ten temporary, each permanent member has the power of veto, meaning members can block any decision or action from being taken

SOURCE 4J

Source 4J: A British cartoon from March 1946 showing Winston Churchill, the British wartime prime minister, taking a look at developments in Eastern Europe behind the Iron Curtain

SOURCE ANALYSIS 4.5

Look at Source 4J.

a What does the cartoon show? What does it mean?

b Look back at Figure 4.1. What was it about Yugoslavia's geographical position that may have helped it stay outside the Soviet empire?

> CAMBRIDGE IGCSE™ AND O LEVEL HISTORY OPTION B: COURSEBOOK

> **FOCUS TASK 4.4**
>
> a In pairs, copy and complete this table about Soviet motives and actions in Eastern Europe and US reactions to them. Add to the last column when you have read Section 4.3. Join up with another pair and compare your tables. Add anything you have missed.
>
> | Country | Soviet motives | Soviet actions | US reactions |
> |---------|----------------|----------------|--------------|
> | | | | |
> | | | | |
> | | | | |
> | | | | |
>
> b In your groups of four, discuss which of these words best describes the way that Stalin gained control of Eastern Europe by 1948 and which countries they apply to. Justify your choices.
>
> - violence
> - threats
> - democratic elections
> - popular support
> - illegal and undemocratic methods
> - propaganda
> - cautious and careful

4.3 How did the United States react to Soviet expansionism?

The Grand Alliance leaders never met again after Potsdam (see Section 4.1). To discuss the details of the four zones of occupation and reparations, their foreign ministers met later in 1945. The Grand Alliance had not yet broken up, but agreements about the future of Europe were proving increasingly difficult to make. Germany had no government yet and so a final peace treaty was never signed.

In February 1946, the US **diplomat** George Kennan sent a telegram to President Truman outlining what he believed Stalin wanted in Eastern Europe. He wrote that the USSR and Stalin were fearful of the outside world, and that Stalin was determined to spread communism. However, he believed that the USA was stronger than the USSR, and that communism could be 'contained'. The tougher policy Truman could have followed in Eastern Europe was called 'rollback' because it would have rolled back communism towards the USSR. Truman rejected the policy because it would have involved using force to overthrow one or more governments in Eastern Europe. Truman had no desire to start another war, this time against the USSR. However, the president was determined to contain communism so it would not spread any further west. He did this by pouring money into anti-communist parties in Italy. In the 1948 elections, $10 million was spent in this way.

Truman's advisers had read Kennan's Long Telegram and took the messages on board. Just a few weeks later, in March 1946, Churchill was invited by Truman to make a speech. This became known as the 'Iron Curtain' speech.

> **KEY TERM**
>
> **diplomat:** an official whose job is to represent one country in another, and who usually works in an embassy

Chapter 4, Key Question 4: Who was to blame for the Cold War?

SOURCES 4K, 4L & 4M

Source 4K: The front page of *The New York Times*, 2 August 1945

There isn't a doubt in my mind that Russia intends an invasion of Turkey and the seizure of the Black Sea Straits to the Mediterranean. Unless Russia is faced with an iron fist and strong language another war is in the making. Only one language do they understand – how many divisions (soldiers) have you? I'm tired of babying the Soviets.

Source 4L: President Truman criticises his Secretary of State James Byrnes for being too trusting of Stalin, December 1945

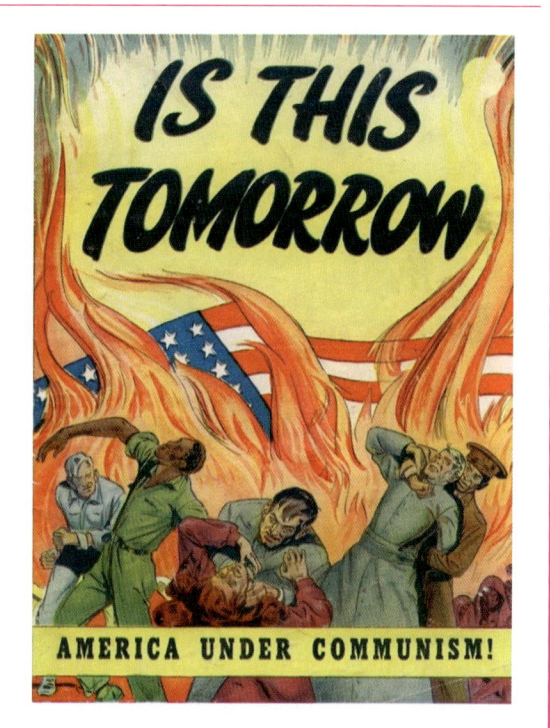

Source 4M: An American poster published in 1947

SOURCE ANALYSIS 4.6

a Study Sources 4K and 4L. What do they tell you about US attitudes towards the USSR?

b Think back to Stalin's takeover of Eastern Europe. Does the poster in Source 4M exaggerate what happens when communists rule a country?

> SOURCE 4N

A shadow has fallen upon the scenes so lately lighted by the allied victory. Nobody knows what Soviet Russia and its communist international organisation intends to do in the immediate future.

From Stettin in the Baltic to Trieste in the Adriatic, an iron curtain has descended across the continent. Behind that line lie all the capitals of the ancient states of Central and Eastern Europe – Warsaw, Berlin, Prague, Vienna, Budapest, Belgrade, Bucharest and Sofia . . . all are subject in one form or another, not only to Soviet influence but to a high measure of control from Moscow.

The Communist parties, which were very small in all these Eastern European countries, have been raised to pre-eminence and power far beyond their numbers and are seeking everywhere to obtain totalitarian control. Police governments are prevailing in nearly every case, and so far, except in Czechoslovakia, there is no true democracy.

Source 4N: Part of Churchill's 'Iron Curtain' speech made at Fulton, Missouri in March 1946

> **SOURCE ANALYSIS 4.7**
>
> Study Source 4N. Both Churchill's speech and Kennan's Long Telegram became famous and they were certainly read in Moscow. Put together, what do you think was the reaction of the Soviet leadership? Which statements would have upset them the most? Why?

Figure 4.8: Soviet and US soldiers meeting at the River Elbe in May 1945 as the two countries' armies, advancing from west and east, meet in the middle of Europe

The end of the Grand Alliance and the start of the Cold War

The USSR refused to withdraw from Iran six months after the end of the Second World War. Truman applied pressure and disguised military threat, and eventually forced Stalin to move his soldiers out of Iran. Truman's 'iron fist' approach seemed to be supported by an analysis of intelligence data. In September 1945, the **Clifford-Elsey Report** concluded that the Soviet Union was targeting Greece and Turkey to gain access to the Mediterranean Sea.

> **KEY TERM**
>
> **The Clifford-Elsey Report:** a report written by two of President Truman's top security advisers. In it, the advisers made suggestions about 'containing' communism.

Chapter 4, Key Question 4: Who was to blame for the Cold War?

In 1946, it seemed to Britain and the USA that communism was on the march everywhere. In France and Italy, communist parties were popular and likely to do well in elections. In Greece, a civil war was raging with the British supporting the monarchists and Yugoslav leader Tito supporting the communists. Stalin kept the USSR out of the Greek conflict. One reason for this was that he had agreed that Greece would be part of the Western Allies' sphere of influence. He also wanted the fighting in Europe to be over.

In February 1947, an urgent telegram arrived for the US president: the British government could no longer afford to intervene in Greece and Turkey to provide military and economic support. It would withdraw its troops. Truman and his advisers were concerned that Greece would fall to communism unless something was done quickly. On 12 March 1947, Truman addressed Congress. His speech signalled a turning point in US foreign policy and set the scene for the next four decades of Cold War conflict. This became known as the Truman Doctrine.

SOURCES 4O & 4P

At the present moment in world history, nearly every nation must choose between alternative ways of life. The choice is too often not a free one. One way of life is based on the will of the majority and is distinguished by free institutions, guarantees of individual liberty, freedom of speech and religion and freedom from political oppression. The second way of life is based upon the will of the minority forcibly imposed on the majority. It relies upon terror and oppression, a controlled press and radio, fixed elections and the suppression of personal freedoms. I believe it must be the policy of the United States to support free peoples who are resisting subjugation by armed minorities or by outside pressures. [. . .] The seeds of totalitarian regimes are nurtured by misery and want. They grow in the evil soil of poverty and strife. [. . .] The free peoples of the world look to us for support in maintaining their freedoms.

Source 4O: An extract from Truman's speech to Congress, 12 March 1947

Source 4P: A US cartoon showing Stalin's reaction to news of the Truman Doctrine

SOURCE ANALYSIS 4.8

a Look back at Figure 4.1. What does it add to your understanding of Congress accepting the Truman Doctrine and voting for financial aid to Greece and Turkey?

b Look at Source 4O. Why did President Truman not name the Soviet Union in his speech?

c Source 4P suggests that Stalin did not like President Truman's Doctrine. Why has the cartoonist put Truman's statement in a pipe? What reasons would Stalin have for disliking the Doctrine?

> ### ACTIVITY 4.3
>
> In pairs, create a diagram or graphic organiser to represent the Truman Doctrine, recording everything you know about it and how it might affect the USA and other countries. Make sure you include the world in your graphic, since Truman's commitment was global. Show on your infographic the places where Truman had already intervened: France and Italy. Now add Greece and Turkey.
>
> Display your diagrams or infographics around the classroom, and review and respond to each other's work.

Congress voted for $400 million in aid to be sent to Greece and Turkey without delay. Under the Truman Doctrine, the USA reversed the attitude it had adopted when Congress refused to back President Wilson and join the League of Nations. Now, the country had an open-ended commitment to fight communism anywhere in the world.

The Marshall Plan

Having introduced a new policy, the president now needed the economic resources to back it up. These were announced by Secretary of State George Marshall in June 1947. The European Recovery Programme, or 'Marshall Plan' as it is almost always called, was intended to help Europe recover economically and so prevent the growth of communism. It was designed to minimise trade barriers. A total of $13.3 billion was invested in Europe between 1948 and 1953. The Plan was offered to all European countries – capitalist and communist alike. The USSR felt that the aid should not be offered to Germany, as this would break the Potsdam agreement of July 1945. Suspicious of the USA's motives, the USSR refused to take part and instructed its allies in the Soviet bloc to refuse as well.

> ### ACTIVITY 4.4
>
> In pairs, storyboard a short film that shows the Soviet intentions in Europe and beyond and what the US government did about it. Include in the storyboard the reaction of the Soviet leadership.
>
> When you have completed your storyboard, share it with another pair for assessment. They should write their feedback on sticky notes to put on the storyboard and you should then improve it based on this feedback. Display your final storyboards in the classroom and invite further comments for improvement.

How did the USSR react?

The Truman Doctrine upset Stalin, but he was more concerned by the Marshall Plan. It could damage Soviet interests. If any Eastern European country accepted the invitation, their economy would be tied to that of the USA. In turn, this would undermine Soviet control and economic ties. Stalin could not allow this to happen.

Chapter 4, Key Question 4: Who was to blame for the Cold War?

In response to the Marshall Plan, Stalin organised a meeting of Communist Party leaders in September 1947. At this conference, leaders were left in no doubt about the threat to communism created by the Plan. Their response was to create Cominform (Communist Information Bureau). The purpose of Cominform was to coordinate actions between the various communist parties under Soviet direction.

SOURCES 4Q & 4R

Source 4Q: A cartoon illustrating attitudes towards the Marshall Plan in 1948

Source 4R: A British cartoon published in Punch magazine on 18 June 1947

SOURCE ANALYSIS 4.9

Study Sources 4Q and 4R.

a Using details from Source 4Q, describe what the cartoon is depicting and what its message is. Does it seem to you to offer a fair and balanced comment?

b To what developments is the cartoon in Source 4R referring? Is the cartoon an accurate representation of those developments?

> **THINKING SKILLS**

The Truman Doctrine and the Marshall Plan represented important changes in US foreign policy compared with the 1920s and 1930s, when the USA was not even prepared to join the League of Nations.

If you had lived in the USA during this period, what fears hopes and expectations might you have of the new global role that Truman outlined in his speech if you were:

- a soldier
- a civilian.

If you lived in Britain or France during this period, what hopes, fears, and expectations might you have of the president and the USA?

FOCUS TASK 4.5

In pairs, draw a timeline from January 1945 to December 1948 in the middle of a sheet of paper. Give it a title: 'The End of the Grand Alliance'. On the left, mark the timeline 'Containment' and on the right, 'Soviet reaction'. Mark on each side the relevant agreements, policies and events that contributed to the end of the Grand Alliance and marked Soviet expansion during this period.

Look at your completed timeline. Discuss in your pairs whether you think that there was no chance of saving the Grand Alliance right from the start or whether there was a turning point that marked when it could no longer be saved. Give three reasons for your choice and then put forward your arguments to the class.

Key points

US reactions to Soviet expansionism

- After the Potsdam Conference and the dropping of nuclear bombs on Japan, relations in the Grand Alliance were fragile.

- Kennan's Long Telegram in February 1946, immediately followed by Churchill's Iron Curtain speech in March, showed the split in the Grand Alliance and in the geography of Europe.

- Although the Red Army occupied most of Central and Eastern Europe, Truman was determined to contain the spread of communism so it did not affect Western Europe, but he could not 'roll back' the red tide.

- Money was spent by the US on anti-communist political parties in both Italy and France to sway election results.

- The Truman Doctrine in March 1947 and the Marshall Plan of 1948 were key turning points in US foreign policy because the Doctrine was global in its reach and the Plan was open to all of Europe.

4.4 What were the consequences of the Berlin Blockade?

The Grand Alliance was finally broken by the developments in 1947. A Cold War had broken out in full public view.

What to do with Germany?

The question of what to do with Germany split the Grand Alliance, although they broadly agreed the following.

- The country would be divided into four zones, each administered by an ally – France, UK, USA and USSR. A conference would then agree Germany's future shape and nature.
- Berlin, the capital, would also be divided into four zones.
- The Soviet Union could take reparations from Germany.
- Poland's border would be moved to the west to the Oder-Neisse rivers.
- The Grand Alliance agreed to de-Nazify, demilitarise and democratise Germany.
- Governing Germany would be the job of the Allied Control Council. This would decide matters that affected the whole country.

Meetings did take place to discuss in greater detail the future of Germany, including the London Conference between September and October 1945. However, each time the foreign ministers met, there were more disagreements, and few joint decisions were made. This was because each side took a different approach to Germany.

Aims of Britain, France and the USA	Aims of the USSR
The western governments remembered the lessons from the end of the First World War: a humiliating and punitive peace treaty would only create resentment and lead to the wish for revenge.	The USSR remembered the invasions in 1914 and 1941. Germany was defeated but it would soon recover and pose a future threat to Soviet security. It had to be punished and weakened economically so that it would not have the resources to start another war.
The German economy was vital for the whole of Europe, and the USA saw it as a good market for American goods. Therefore, it was important that it recovered and the USA could help by giving it Marshall Aid.	Germany had to be stripped of its industrial resources and the equipment taken back to the Soviet Union to help its economy rebuild itself. Reparations amounting to $20 billion were to be taken by, or given to, the Soviet Union.

Figure 4.9: A table showing the contrasting views and aims of the Western Allies and the USSR

The Grand Alliance splits apart, 1947–48

In January 1947, Britain and the USA created a single economic unit called the Bizone (or 'Bizonia') out of their respective German zones. The French added their zone a year later to create Trizone. Stalin was worried that the western powers were no longer interested in agreeing on the future for the whole of Germany.

The Moscow Conference, attended by the foreign ministers, met many times in 1947 but they could reach no agreements. In March that year, the three western powers agreed to unite their zones politically into one government. The USA said that Marshall Aid would be available to the western zones of Germany. Stalin reacted by stopping and searching all freight shipments into West Berlin.

In June 1948, the western powers introduced a new currency for use in all four German zones. The Soviets refused to allow the new currency in their eastern zone.

The Berlin Blockade and the Berlin airlift

Stalin reacted to the new currency by cutting off West Berlin by water, road and rail. Then he turned off the gas and electricity. He hoped to force the western powers out so he could bring the entire city under Soviet rule. Stalin's advisers told him that West Berliners and the western powers would surrender after four to six weeks because they could not survive without essentials like fuel and food.

The West thought carefully about how to respond. Only a year earlier, President Truman had revealed the Truman Doctrine. Doing nothing for Berliners would mean the policy was an empty gesture. However, if he tried to use force to open the roads and railways, this might provoke a military response.

Britain, the USA and France jointly agreed not to give in. Instead, they said they could supply West Berliners with provisions from the air. Over the next 11 months, the three airports in West Berlin had regular landings by aircraft full of coal, food and fuel for the isolated citizens. Children who fell ill were flown out of the city so they could receive medical help in the West. By 1949, planes were landing every 90 seconds in a constant queue of airlifted supplies. In all, 277 000 flights fed the city. Although the airlift appeared to be an entirely unselfish act, it is worth noting West Berlin was a nest of **espionage** and intelligence-gathering. Losing such a wonderful window on East Germany would limit opportunities for spying and reduce the impact of western propaganda broadcasts by radio.

> **KEY TERM**
>
> **espionage:** the government practice of using spies to obtain intelligence on political and military developments in foreign countries

THINKING SKILLS

Imagine Stalin has asked you to draw up a list of advantages and disadvantages for the USSR when it cuts off West Berlin from road and rail access, gas, electricity and water. Consider what you know of western attitudes and Soviet attitudes in this early stage of the Cold War. Write a response to Stalin, based on the following points.

Advantages:

- What will the Soviet Union get out of this action?
- Why will the West not be expecting this?
- Why will the West not respond militarily to the situation in West Berlin?
- Estimates vary but most advisers think West Berliners will last six weeks at most before giving up.
- If successful, it will enhance Stalin's role as the leader of international communism.

Disadvantages:

- We do not know what the West will do. What *could* they do?
- World opinion will see this as justifying the Truman Doctrine and Marshall Plan.
- How sure are Stalin's advisers about the resilience of the West Berliners?

Chapter 4, Key Question 4: Who was to blame for the Cold War?

What could Stalin do? His advisers had misjudged the West. Six weeks came and went, and still West Berlin survived. Stalin dared not shoot down any plane for fear of provoking a military response. Instead, the Soviets tried to block radio signals. This had little effect. In the end, Stalin lifted the blockade in May 1949.

SOURCES 4S & 4T

Source 4S: A British cartoon from 1948 showing the Berlin Airlift and Stalin

Source 4T: A photo of supplies of flour being unloaded by West Berliners during the Berlin Blockade

SOURCE ANALYSIS 4.10

Study Sources 4S and 4T.

a   Why didn't Stalin issue orders to shoot down planes like this before they reached West Berlin?

b   Is Source 4S a pro-western cartoon or a pro-Soviet one? Use details to explain your answer.

The Berlin Blockade transformed the West's public perception of Berlin. It was no longer seen as a supporter of Nazism, but rather a symbol of freedom and democracy. From now on the city had to be protected whatever the cost.

The blockade was over, but it had signalled the end of the Grand Alliance. The division of Europe was now complete and the Iron Curtain was in place. It lasted for over 40 years.

The formation of NATO

Politicians in Western Europe were worried that Stalin would continue to look for weaknesses to exploit in Western Europe and to follow his expansionist policies. So, in April 1949, Western European governments asked the USA for a military commitment to Europe. Truman agreed to join and lead the North Atlantic Treaty Organization (NATO). This was a significant change in US foreign policy, showing the genuine fear of the USSR and of communism that existed in the USA and in Western Europe.

Along with the USA, 11 other countries became members of NATO: Britain, France, Canada, Italy, Denmark, Iceland, Norway, Portugal, Belgium, Holland and Luxembourg. This new organisation had one main purpose: an armed attack against one or more of them would be considered an attack on all. This was 'collective security' – something that the League of Nations had tried and failed to establish.

Once NATO was in place, the western powers stopped waiting for the Soviets to agree on the future of Germany. Instead, in May 1949, the formal unification of the western zones took place. The Trizone became the Federal Republic of Germany (West Germany). A new constitution was agreed and national elections were held in August 1949. Konrad Adenauer, leader of the right-wing Christian Democrats, became the first chancellor of West Germany. Although responsibility for the internal development of the Federal Republic of Germany was now in Adenauer's hands, the country's foreign policy was still controlled by the western powers until 1951.

> **KEY FIGURE**
>
> **Konrad Adenauer (1949–1963)**
>
> Adenauer was West Germany's chancellor between 1949 and 1963. He was a skilful politician who firmly believed in capitalism and liberal democracy. He refused to recognise East Germany as a proper country. Early on, he switched priorities from denazification to recovery. He created close relations with France, the USA and Britain. He promoted European unity. He also took his country into NATO and oversaw the re-establishment of military and intelligence services in 1955–56. He ensured that democracy in West Germany took firm root and that its people experienced economic prosperity – sometimes called an 'economic miracle' given the swathes of the country that had been devastated.

West Berlin was not part of West Germany so British, French and US soldiers remained there to defend the city from an attack.

The Soviets reacted quickly to the creation of West Germany. In October 1949, the new German Democratic Republic (East Germany) was announced. East Berlin was part of East Germany and became the country's capital. All government responsibilities were in the hands of the communist Socialist Unity Party created in 1946 by the forced merger of the Social Democratic Party and the German Communist Party in the Soviet Zone.

Although the USSR did not immediately create a military alliance to oppose NATO, it did tighten its control over its satellite states. In January 1949, the Council for Mutual Economic Assistance (COMECON) was created to coordinate the development of the national economies of each of the Soviet Bloc countries. Each of the east European economies would develop along similar lines to that of the Soviet Union.

Chapter 4, Key Question 4: Who was to blame for the Cold War?

In August 1949, the Soviet Union successfully tested its first atomic bomb. Now, the USA no longer had a monopoly on atomic weapons. The nuclear arms race had begun and would continue throughout the Cold War.

The Berlin Blockade was the first Cold War crisis. Both sides had survived without any military force being used. Now that each side possessed nuclear weapons, both sides had to take great care not to provoke the enemy into using them. In this sense, although the blockade was a crisis, it actually stabilised the superpower relationship.

In May 1955, French, British and US soldiers that had occupied West Germany since 1945 withdrew. Soon after, West Germany joined NATO on the condition that it would have no biological, chemical or atomic weapons.

The Warsaw Pact

The response from the Soviet Bloc to these developments in Western Europe was to create a central command for their armed forces. On 14 May 1955, eight communist countries agreed to unify their armed forces in the Warsaw Pact. The principle of collective security behind NATO was now in place for Eastern Europe.

The Warsaw Pact central command was dominated by the Soviet Union. The commander-in-chief was always a Soviet army officer. The same can be said of the deputy and the three branches of the armed forces: army, navy and air force. These military developments further increased the USSR's control of Eastern Europe.

FOCUS TASK 4.6

a   Work in pairs. On six pieces of paper, write one consequence of the Berlin Blockade. Discuss each of the consequences and decide on an order of importance for international peace. Move the pieces of paper around until you have a ranking you agree on, with the most important at the top. Make sure you can justify your rankings. Team up with another pair and discuss each other's rankings. See if you can reach a common list.

b   In your groups of four, discuss this question: *Fear is the key to understanding the Berlin Blockade and its failure. Do you agree with this explanation of the Blockade?* As a four, share your thinking with the class and invite their comments.

THINK LIKE A HISTORIAN

To varying degrees, Germany and Japan were devastated during the Second World War. However, in the years that followed, both countries' economies made quick recoveries and were soon challenging the economies of the winners: the USA, Britain and the USSR.

Thinking about the world of work, why was it easier for the Germans and the Japanese to start rebuilding their economies from scratch rather than build on what was already in place? Consider the following: **trade unions**, the location of industries, establishing new businesses with new technology, ports, infrastructure like roads and railways, and rebuilding cities. What new jobs would exist that didn't before the war?

KEY TERM

trade union: an organisation for workers, who work together to try to achieve common goals, such as increased wages or improved conditions

4.5 Who was more to blame for starting the Cold War: the United States or the USSR?

At the start of this chapter, you read about two different views of the Cold War: one blamed the Cold War on the USSR, the other on the USA. In this section, you will have the opportunity to make a final judgement. You might decide that both superpowers were to blame or that one was more to blame than the other. Whatever your judgement, you will need to back it up with evidence.

In what ways was the USSR to blame for the Cold War?

Argument 1: Communism was an ideology that was naturally expansionist. The USSR's view of the future was that communism could not coexist with capitalism; one or the other had to be eliminated. From the West's point of view, it looked as if Stalin intended to impose communism on as many countries as possible. This made them suspicious.

Argument 2: The USSR ended the Second World War having suffered much more than any other country. Its losses were unimaginable: 27 million dead. It had every right to make demands in Eastern Europe, but it did not help its Allies to understand the situation from the Soviet standpoint. This was Stalin's fault. He was used to issuing orders rather than discussing attitudes, feelings and perceptions.

Argument 3: Before the war, the USSR did not join with other countries to make a Popular Front to fight Hitler. From Stalin's point of view this distrust of the West had not been changed by the experience of being part of the Grand Alliance. Stalin just did not trust anyone or any country.

Evidence

Stalin did not stick to the Yalta agreement. Between February and July 1945, when the Potsdam conference took place, communist governments were installed in Poland and Romania. By the end of 1949, communists controlled all of Eastern Europe.

Stalin did not appreciate the importance that Truman and Churchill placed on free elections for the liberated countries. Democracy was not important in Stalin's peace-making. He wanted Soviet-friendly governments bordering the USSR.

The creation of COMECON made sure that each country within the Soviet Bloc followed the same economic model as the Soviet Union. Cominform and COMECON were set up to coordinate communist governments and industries. This was seen as a threat by the USA, as it excluded the West.

The Berlin Blockade was provocative and angered the USA, which saw it as a threat to freedom.

> **REVISION TIP**
>
> Timelines are a good way to recall and revise key events and to assess causes and consequences. Go back to the timeline you created in Focus task 4.5 and extend it to include the Berlin Blockade and the events that followed. Use it for revisions to see the connections between the events that led to the Cold War in the post-war period.

Chapter 4, Key Question 4: Who was to blame for the Cold War?

Figure 4.10: Left to right: Churchill, Truman and Stalin at the Yalta Conference in 1945

Stalin's personality

The personality of the Soviet leader was a significant factor in bringing about the Cold War. He was obsessed with his country's security and defence, and was paranoid about his own safety. He could not allow liberated countries to be anti-Soviet and so he ruled out free elections.

How can Stalin's role in the Cold War be defended?

The role of the USSR and of Stalin in particular can be defended using the following evidence.

Some historians argue that the West did not fully appreciate the USSR's security concerns at the end of the war. Russia had been invaded three times in 50 years (in 1914, 1918 and 1941). Furthermore, Stalin believed that the West's policy of appeasement in the 1930s was a deliberate plan to enable Nazi Germany to expand eastwards rather than westwards.

Stalin's suspicions of the West were confirmed by examples of wartime secrecy. The USA had not shared the atomic bomb with its Grand Alliance partner. In addition, Britain and the USA had refused to open a second front to relieve the pressure on the Red Army fighting the Germans in the east until June 1944.

> CAMBRIDGE IGCSE™ AND O LEVEL HISTORY OPTION B: COURSEBOOK

> **SOURCE 4U**
>
> *The foreign policy of the USA is characterized by a striving for world supremacy.*
>
> *The real meaning of the many statements by President Truman and others is that the United States has the right to lead the world. All the forces of American diplomacy – the army, the air force, the navy, industry and science – are enlisted in the service of this policy. [They have established] a system of naval and air bases stretching far beyond the boundaries of the United States, through the arms race and through the creation of ever newer types of weapons.*
>
> **Source 4U:** Part of the 'Novikov Telegram' sent by the Soviet Ambassador to the USA, Nikolai Novikov, 27 September 1946

> **SOURCE ANALYSIS 4.11**
>
> Read Source 4U. What evidence can you find in it that could be used to *defend* Stalin from the charge that he was to blame for starting the Cold War?

In what ways was the USA to blame for the Cold War?

Argument 1: '**Dollar Imperialism**' was the motive for USA involvement in Europe.

The economy in the USA had recovered from the Great Depression during the Second World War. In fact, it did more than recover, it doubled in size. President Truman and his advisers were worried that, once peace arrived and the US military forces came home, there would be another economic slump. To stop this, the USA needed to have a European market for the goods it was producing.

Argument 2: President Truman did not trust the Soviets' words or deeds. Even after Hiroshima and Nagasaki, Truman did not feel he could share the secrets of the atomic bomb with Stalin and the Soviets.

Truman had been confrontational with the USSR after Roosevelt died in April 1945 and this soured Soviet–US relations. He believed having and using the atomic bomb would make it easier to impose his will on the Soviet Union. This is one of the reasons he ordered the bombs to be dropped on Japan. The Truman Doctrine and Marshall Plan were seen by the USSR as provocative and designed to isolate the USSR.

> **KEY TERM**
>
> **Dollar Imperialism:** American actions designed to build influence and economic power using their resources and their influence to extend markets for selling American goods and products

Evidence

The Marshall Plan was really designed to ensure the recovery of a capitalist, free-market Europe so that Europeans could buy American goods.

The creation of Bizonia and then Trizonia was a clear breach of the Potsdam agreement and was an attempt to introduce capitalism across the whole of Germany.

The airlift to circumvent the Berlin Blockade was seen as confrontational by the Soviets.

How can the role of the USA be defended?

The role of the USA and of President Truman in particular can be defended using the following evidence.

Stalin's dismissive attitude towards the 'London Poles' illustrated his wish to break the wartime agreements. The Truman Doctrine was a defensive and not an offensive reaction to the developments in Greece and Turkey. West European governments were invited and welcomed the Marshall Plan. They had a choice and made it freely to join the European Recovery Programme. This was in sharp contrast to Stalin's takeover of Eastern Europe by 1948 using force.

Chapter 4, Key Question 4: Who was to blame for the Cold War?

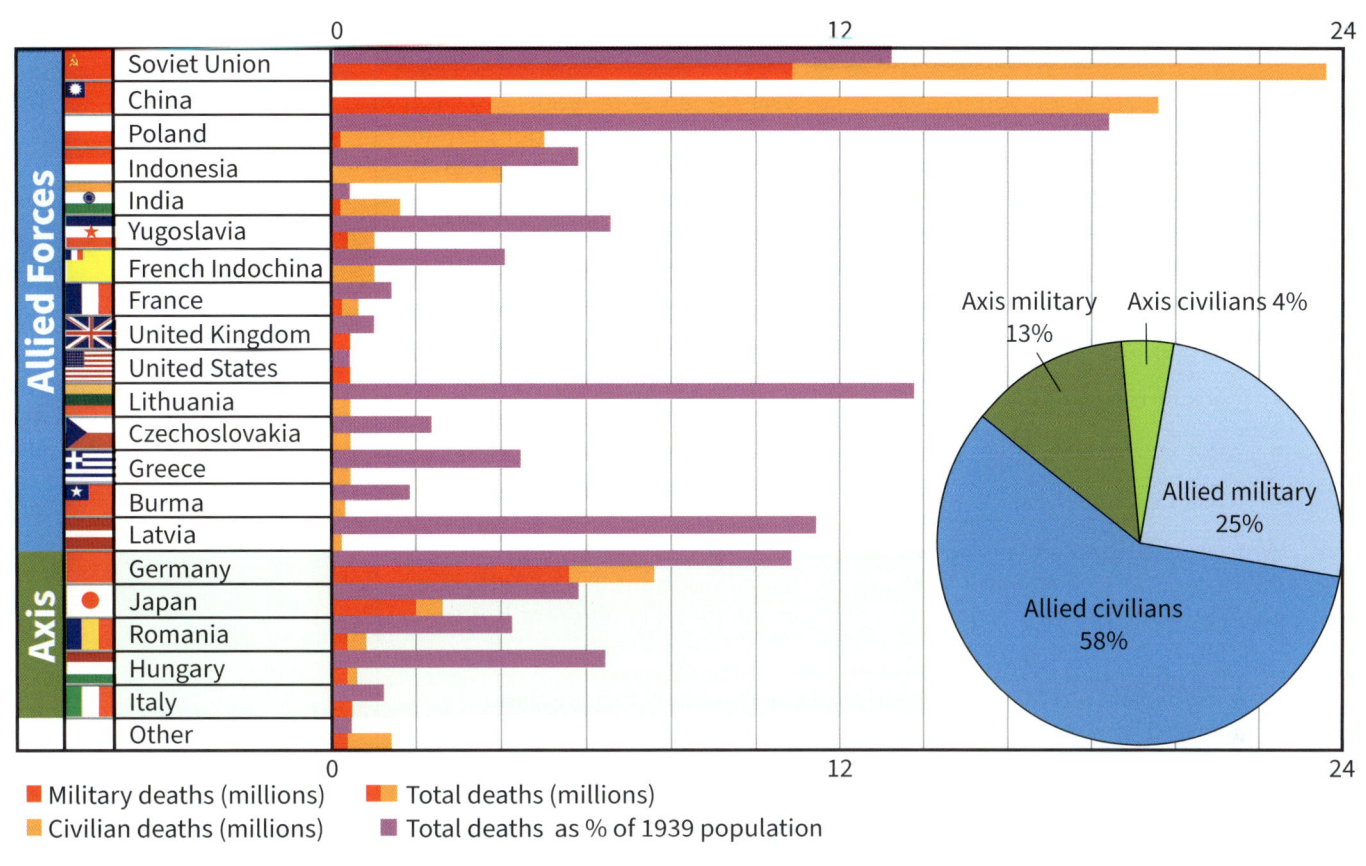

Figure 4.11: A graph showing comparisons of deaths by country during the Second World War

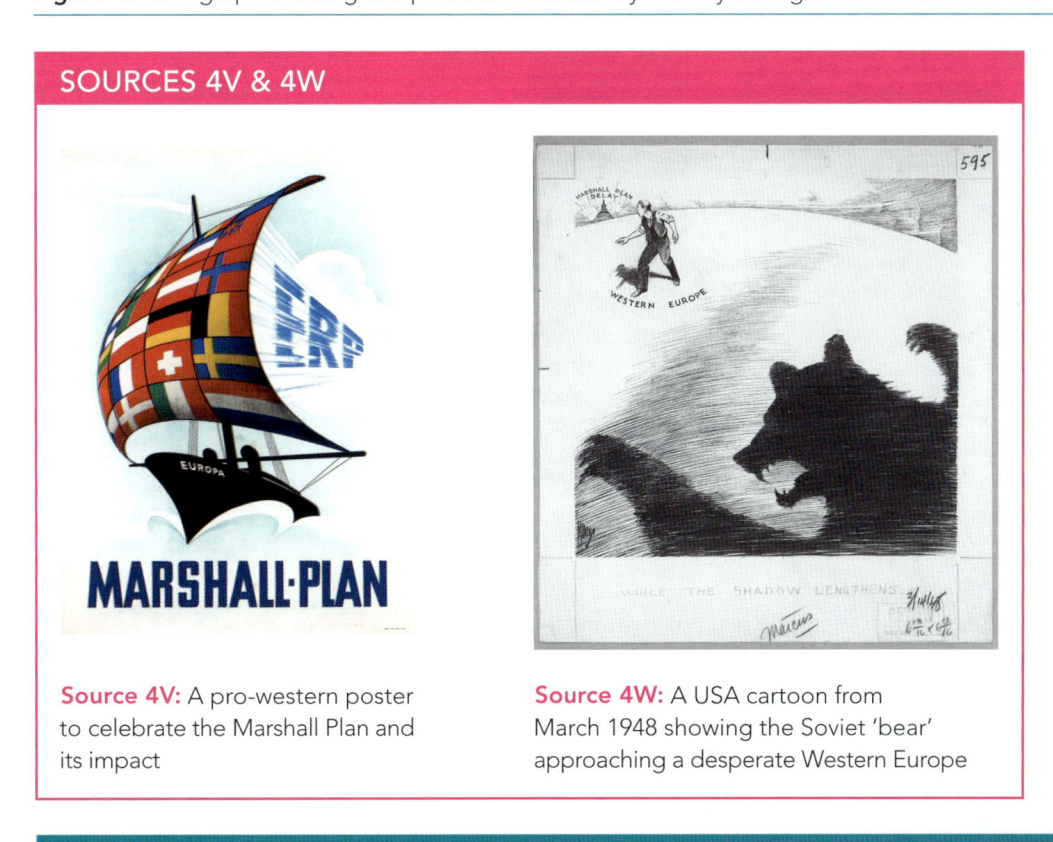

- Military deaths (millions)
- Civilian deaths (millions)
- Total deaths (millions)
- Total deaths as % of 1939 population

SOURCES 4V & 4W

Source 4V: A pro-western poster to celebrate the Marshall Plan and its impact

Source 4W: A USA cartoon from March 1948 showing the Soviet 'bear' approaching a desperate Western Europe

SOURCE ANALYSIS 4.12

Study Sources 4V and 4W. What evidence can you find in them that could be used to defend Truman from the charge that he was to blame for starting the Cold War?

179

> CAMBRIDGE IGCSE™ AND O LEVEL HISTORY OPTION B: COURSEBOOK

FOCUS TASK 4.7

a   In pairs, discuss when you think the Cold War began. After your discussion, write a short paragraph explaining your choice. If your partner disagrees with you, summarise their opinion and why you disagree with it.

b   Next, discuss why the Cold War broke out. Put this list of causes in order of significance:

- ideological differences
- incompatible objectives in Europe after the end of the war
- lack of trust on both sides
- atomic weapons
- disagreements over the future of Germany.

Write a paragraph explaining why you chose that order, drawing attention to the causes you think are the most important. If you and your partner reach different conclusions and put the items in different orders, summarise their opinion and explain why you disagree with it.

c   Now look again at your prioritised list of causes. Does this help you decide who is more to blame? Discuss tour ideas.

SUMMARY

- The Cold War lasted approximately 45 years. It came after the Second World War when the two superpowers were the only Great Powers left, with Britain and France, Japan and Germany all severely weakened.
- From 1941 to 1945, the USA and USSR were partners with Britain in the Grand Alliance. Although all three partners agreed on some broad aspects of the peace, they disagreed about the details.
- Despite several conferences, the Cold War broke out because of the conflicting objectives and priorities of the USA and the USSR.
- The different approaches to post-war Germany in the four zones illustrate the split in the Grand Alliance.
- Trust no longer existed after the Berlin Blockade of 1948–49.
- The Grand Alliance shattered. Instead of partnership, cooperation and open discussion, there was hostility, mistrust and espionage.

KEY SKILLS EXERCISES

Knowledge and understanding

1   Why were the USA and the USSR both superpowers, but Britain was not?
2   Why did the USSR need Lend–Lease so badly?
3   Why did the capitalist USA mistrust the communist USSR?
4   Why did the history of the USSR shape its mistrust of the USA?

Chapter 4, Key Question 4: Who was to blame for the Cold War?

> **CONTINUED**

Application

5   Why could the USA and the USSR not trust each other completely?
6   Why did Stalin want to develop a security buffer between the USSR and Eastern Europe?
7   Why did Truman take a different approach to peace-making than Roosevelt?
8   Why was it vital for Western Europe to have the USA as a partner in NATO?

Analysis

9   Analyse why the Grand Alliance fell apart by 1947.
10 Analyse the reasons why Stalin told the leaders of eastern European countries not to take part in the Marshall Plan.
11 Analyse why it was so important for the West that Berlin survived the blockade.
12 Analyse the key differences between the perceptions of the USA towards the USSR and vice versa.

Evaluation

13 Evaluate the importance of ideology in causing the Cold War.
14 Would the Cold War have been prevented if President Roosevelt had lived longer?
15 To what extent was the Cold War inevitable following the end of the Second World War?
16 Stalin was a brutal dictator and was responsible for millions of deaths in the Soviet Union. So, why did the British and the Americans sit down and negotiate with him?

---

1 This is not a helpful introduction because it does not target the question precisely. Although the knowledge is accurate, it is not strictly relevant because there is nothing to explain why Britain, the USA and the USSR found it so hard to agree.

2 Although accurate knowledge is being shown, the writer has not faced the question directly. They are describing what happened rather than why disagreements happened.

3 This is a strong opening sentence that responds precisely to the question. It sets up the rest of the paragraph with a clear structure.

IMPROVE THIS ANSWER

Why did the Grand Alliance find it hard to agree on the future of post-war Germany?

Sample answer: At the end of the Second World War the Grand Alliance had beaten Germany. During the war there had been several conferences and the future of Germany was discussed many times. **1** The Grand Alliance did agree on dividing the country into four and the capital, Berlin, into four but this arrangement was supposed to be provisional and not permanent. There were to be further discussions in the months that followed the end of the war in Germany, May 1945. **2**

Disagreement about the future of Germany happened for two main reasons: attitudes towards Germany and suspicions of motives on all sides of the Grand Alliance. **3** Britain and the USA wanted a defeated Germany to be treated very differently from the Treaty of Versailles in 1919. In that treaty, Germany was punished for starting the war in 1914; but the British and Americans did not want to repeat what they believed was a 'mistake' after the Great War. They argued that Germany must be rehabilitated into a whole, democratic country. The Soviet view was very different. Stalin wanted to punish Germany. He thought that unless that happened, another war would

> CAMBRIDGE IGCSE™ AND O LEVEL HISTORY OPTION B: COURSEBOOK

CONTINUED

erupt. So, Stalin argued for high reparations, friendly governments in the countries on its doorstep, and complete disarmament. Only these actions could ensure a peaceful post-war Europe in years to come. **4**

The second reason for disagreements was that Stalin was negotiating from a position of strength; the British and Americans were not. As Hitler committed suicide in April 1945, there were 11 million Red Army soldiers on the ground because they had played a key role in liberating European countries from Nazi control. This dominance in Central and Eastern Europe worried Churchill and Roosevelt. They suspected that their wartime ally, Stalin, wanted to create a peacetime Soviet empire – not by the ballot box but by force – and this included the Soviet zone of Germany. With a large Soviet army on the ground, British and American suspicions multiplied as time went on and caused disagreements with Stalin. Suspicion and mistrust on all sides resulted in a divided Germany and the Iron Curtain. **5**

Now write an improved response using this guidance.

4 In this paragraph the point is clear, and the explanation is good. However, the historical knowledge is thin. This could be improved if the writer had made mention of the Yalta Conference in February 1945. Further knowledge could be used to support the analysis of the Soviet attitude towards Germany.

5 This paragraph contains a clear point, relevant analysis and shows some relevant historical knowledge. This could be developed. For example, Churchill and Roosevelt's concerns about Stalin's ambitions for Germany were underlined when they rejected Stalin's proposal that all the Germans living within the 'new' borders of Poland should be repatriated to the 'new' Germany.

PRACTICE QUESTIONS

1. During the Second World War civilians suffered a lot.
   a. What hardships did civilians experience? [4]
   b. Why was the Allies' consolidation of victory in Germany so difficult to achieve? [6]
   c. The contribution of the United States was the main reason why the Allies defeated the Axis powers. Is this a fair judgement? [10]

   [Total: 20]

PROJECT

You are going to work in pairs to research, write and present two different accounts of the events after the Second World War that led to the Cold War. One account will be from a Soviet perspective and the other will be from a US perspective.

Each account should be 400 words long. Both accounts should start in 1943 and end in 1947.

First, decide how you will split the work. You might choose to research and write one account each, then swap and check each other's writing. Or you might decide to work together to research and write both accounts.

Use the information in this chapter and any other resources you have available to find out as much as you can about events that took place in both spheres of influence after the Second World War. Try to find images, maps, graphics and statistics to support your accounts.

When you have finished, present your accounts to the class. Read one account each. Explain how both accounts are justified.

Chapter 4, Key Question 4: Who was to blame for the Cold War?

SELF-EVALUATION CHECKLIST

After studying this chapter, complete this table:

You should be able to:	Needs more work	Almost there	Ready to move on
explain why the USA, the USSR and Britain formed the Grand Alliance against the Axis Powers of Germany, Italy and Japan			
explain why there were strains in the Grand Alliance during the war			
understand that after the victory in 1945, both the USSR and the USA misunderstood the views and security needs of the other			
describe how the borders of Poland changed and why Germany was divided into four zones controlled by the Allied Powers			
explain why the USSR succeeded in holding on to the territories in Central and Eastern Europe taken during the defeat of Germany			
show why the USA was determined to 'contain' the USSR and communism			
describe why Eastern Europe would be regarded as a Soviet victory, but the Berlin Blockade and airlift were a US and Allied victory			
explain why the Marshall Plan was offered to all of Europe but only Western Europe took up the plan			
make a judgement on who was more to blame for starting the Cold War, giving reasons.			

> Chapter 5, Key Question 5:

How effectively did the United States contain the spread of communism?

FOCUS POINTS

This chapter will be explored through case studies of the following:

- The United States and events in Korea, 1950–53
- The United States and events in Cuba, 1959–62
- American involvement in Vietnam, 1955–75

Chapter 5, Key Question 5: How effectively did the United States contain the spread of communism?

5.0 What is this enquiry about?

When Lenin's Bolshevik party came to power in Russia in 1917 the international community was not happy. The USA was one of several powers that sent troops to fight in the Russian Civil War (1918–21), hoping to destroy the new communist regime. This failed, and no US president would accept the communist government in Moscow until Franklin D. Roosevelt in 1933. The need to unite to fight fascism during the Second World War meant that the two powers became allies in 1941. This was a temporary alliance. Events after 1945 showed that the relationship between the world's two remaining superpowers could not stay friendly.

From 1950 to 1973 there were many tests of the policy of containment (see Chapter 4), but three examples stand out: the Korean War, the Cuban Missile Crisis and the war in Vietnam. In this chapter, you will analyse the results of the USA's involvement in these three events and reach a judgement about the success of the policy of containment. After studying these three examples, you will need to return to the key question: How effectively did the United States contain the spread of communism?

To reach a judgement you will need to:

- understand the cause and effect of each event
- evaluate US policy and strategy – what was the USA trying to achieve and how close did it come to success?
- assess whether the threat of communism had increased or decreased after a quarter of a century of containment.

5.1 The United States and events in Korea, 1950–53

Background to a crisis

In January 1950, President Harry S. Truman ordered a review of the USA's foreign policy in response to increasing levels of threat that had developed throughout 1948–49. Several incidents had raised concerns about the global spread of communisms:

- 1948: Czechoslovakia was taken over by a communist government.
- 1948–49: the Berlin Blockade brought the two superpowers close to conflict.
- 1949: communists finally won the Chinese Civil War under Mao Zedong.
- 1949: the USSR produced a nuclear weapon, at least three years in advance of US estimates.

The Chinese Revolution of 1949 was a significant event because it meant the Cold War had spread from Europe to Asia. Communists under Mao Zedong defeated the US-backed Nationalists led by Chiang Kai-Shek. This came at the end of an intense civil war that had begun in 1945, in which Chiang received significant support from US President Truman. However, his forces were poorly led, and corrupt commanders even sold their weapons to Mao's men. The victory raised fears in the USA, as China was a member of the United Nations Security Council. It increased the possibility of communism spreading in Asia. Communist forces were also fighting for control of Indochina and the Philippines.

> CAMBRIDGE IGCSE™ AND O LEVEL HISTORY OPTION B: COURSEBOOK

> KEY FIGURE
>
> ### Mao Zedong (1893–1976)
>
> Mao Zedong was born into a peasant family in central China. He co-founded the Chinese Communist Party (CCP) in 1921. For the next 28 years, he led the CCP through struggles against the Nationalists and the Japanese. This included the Long March of 1934, where he led his supporters on a 9700 kilometre journey to escape Nationalists. After coming to power in 1949, he completely reshaped Chinese society, often with disastrous consequences. Famine caused by the Great Leap Forward (1958–62) killed at least 20 million people, but some historians think it is far higher. However, Mao did set the basis for China to become a superpower.

The result of Truman's investigation was National Security Council report 68 (or 'NSC 68'), which outlined four options.

1. Continue with the USA's existing policies.
2. Fight a preventative war to block Soviet expansion.
3. Withdraw behind the shield of 'fortress USA' and do nothing about the expansion of communism around the world.
4. Start a programme of massive rearmament to surpass the forces available to communism.

Truman chose the fourth option. US armed forces had been in a bad state since 1945, but now they were to be expanded. Containment was to be put forcefully into practice. This remained US policy until the end of the Vietnam War.

What caused the Korean War?

From 1910 to 1945, Korea had been ruled as a colony by Japan. Young Koreans were taught at school in the Japanese language, and all political opposition was banned. Koreans were used as conscripts as Japan fought wars from 1937 to 1945. When the war ended, Korea was freed from Japanese control by Soviet troops in the North and US troops in the South. As in Germany, the country was divided and ruled by occupying forces. The dividing line was the 38th parallel.

> ### THINKING SKILLS
>
> The National Security Council (NSC) was founded in 1947. Its role was to assist the US State Department and the president in making decisions about foreign policy. In groups, put yourselves in the position of Truman's NSC advisers. Write answers to the following questions.
>
> - Which of the developments in 1948–49 posed the greatest threat to US security? Which posed the least threat? Give reasons for your selections.
> - Which of the four options presented to Truman in NSC 68 would you recommend? Give reasons for your decision.
>
> Present your ideas to other groups and listen to theirs. After hearing their opinions have you changed your mind about any of your own choices? Make changes to your answers if necessary.

Chapter 5, Key Question 5: How effectively did the United States contain the spread of communism?

Figure 5.1: A map of the Korean peninsula, showing the 38th parallel, which divided North Korea from South Korea. Note how close both capitals, Pyongyang and Seoul, are to the border. Note also how small the area of Pusan is, to which the South retreated, and how bold MacArthur's counterattack on Inchon was.

Korean communists in the North were led by Kim Il-Sung. During the Second World War, he had been in Moscow where he was trained for leadership by Joseph Stalin. In the South, the USA appointed anti-communists led by Syngman Rhee as the new government. All foreign troops withdrew in 1949 after agreement was reached in the UN. However, fighting soon broke out between northern and southern forces along the border.

SOURCE 5A

Source 5A: A statue of Kim Il-Sung in Pyongyang, North Korea

ACTIVITY 5.1

In pairs, look at the map in Figure 5.1.

a   Identify three challenges posed by containing communism in this region.

b   Consider solutions to these challenges. In your pairs, note down how you would organise a military campaign to contain communism in the Korean peninsula. What forces would you need?

c   On what basis could you make a judgement about the success or failure of US policy in the Korean War?

SOURCE ANALYSIS 5.1

Study Source 5A.

a   What do you notice about the statue in this photograph?

b   Why do you think the statue was presented in this way? What impression does it give of Kim Il-Sung as a leader?

187

Kim Il-Sung was keen to reunite Korea under his leadership, but he knew that conquering the South would require outside assistance. He approached Stalin in early 1949, but his proposal for an invasion was rejected as the Berlin Blockade was still going on. A year later, however, Stalin's mood was different. The development of nuclear weapons and the Chinese Revolution in October 1949 made an invasion of South Korea much easier. Stalin gave Kim Il-Sung his support and on 25 June 1950 North Korea launched a full-scale invasion of the South.

It was a huge force: 200 000 troops, 10 000 of whom had been specially trained in the USSR. Another 40 000 had gained experience fighting in the Chinese Civil War of 1945–49. These soldiers were also supplied with Soviet weapons, such as T-34 tanks. Southern forces were ill-equipped, poorly trained and there were no more than 100 000 of them. They were soon retreating as North Korean forces marched across the 38th parallel. The capital city, Seoul, was quickly taken, and all Korea was occupied except for Pusan in the far south (see Figure 5.1).

SOURCE 5B

BELIEVE IT OR KNOUT

Source 5B: A *Punch* cartoon published in June 1950

SOURCE ANALYSIS 5.2

Study Source 5B.

a Which leader is the teacher supposed to be?

b What is the message of the cartoon?

c Cartoonists often use irony to make a point. Look up the word 'irony' and discuss it with a partner. In what ways could this cartoon be considered to be ironic?

Chapter 5, Key Question 5: How effectively did the United States contain the spread of communism?

US reactions to the invasion of South Korea

Although the invasion came as a surprise, the USA had been watching events in the Korean peninsula closely. The US authorities' experience of directly running South Korea from 1945 to 1948 had not been easy. Rhee was elected president in 1948, but the South was deeply divided politically and he ruled as a dictator. In April 1950, he performed badly in elections due to corruption in his government. While the USA had been happy to withdraw its forces from 1948 to 1949, these changing events in Asia made the USA reconsider giving strong support to Rhee as the best hope for containment.

A second reason for US interest in Asia was linked the Chinese Revolution of October 1949. Mao was now in power in China, but the USA refused to accept this. The USA continued to recognise Chiang Kai-Shek as the rightful leader. Chiang lost the civil war and escaped to Taiwan in 1949. In January 1950, the USSR refused to attend the United Nations Security Council because the USA would not accept Mao's government. It was still refusing to attend Security Council meetings in June when North Korea invaded South Korea. This gave the Americans a unique opportunity to use the UN to establish a coalition of powers against the spread of communism.

President Truman appealed to the UN to come to Rhee's aid. The response was surprisingly quick. On 27 June, it ordered member nations to support the South. Truman sent US forces from Japan, led by the Second World War general Douglas MacArthur. Another 14 countries contributed to the UN army and five countries sent medical support. This was the first time that the UN had gathered an international army, and the organisation was determined to show that it was stronger and more capable than its predecessor, the League of Nations (see Chapter 2).

SOURCE 5C

Korea is a small country, thousands of miles away, but what is happening there is important to every American.

On Sunday, June 25th, Communist forces attacked the Republic of Korea.

This attack has made it clear, beyond all doubt, that the international Communist movement is willing to use armed invasion to conquer independent nations. An act of aggression such as this creates a very real danger to the security of all free nations.

The attack upon Korea was an outright breach of the peace and a violation of the Charter of the United Nations. By their actions in Korea, Communist leaders have demonstrated their contempt for the basic moral principles on which the United Nations is founded. This is a direct challenge to the efforts of the free nations to build the kind of world in which men can live in freedom and peace.

This challenge has been presented squarely. We must meet it squarely.

Source 5C: Truman's televised speech on 19 July 1950

SOURCE ANALYSIS 5.3

Read Source 5C.

a Was Truman right in claiming that events in Korea were 'important to every American'?

b This speech was shown on television. How do you think ordinary Americans would have reacted to it?

> CAMBRIDGE IGCSE™ AND O LEVEL HISTORY OPTION B: COURSEBOOK

> **FOCUS TASK 5.1**
>
> Consider the motives for US involvement in Korea. Summarise the two key reasons described on the previous page. Which of the two factors do you think was more significant for the USA entering the war: events in Korea or events in China? Write a 100-word position paper explaining which events were more significant and why. Make sure you compare the two factors in your paper.
>
> When you have completed your 100 words, swap papers, read each other's work and then discuss your answers. Did you choose the same events and give similar reasons? If you disagree with your partner on any points, explain why.

> **KEY FIGURE**
>
> **Douglas MacArthur (1880–1964)**
>
> MacArthur was one of the most famous, and controversial, American generals of the 20th century. Born into a military family, he graduated top of his class at West Point and served with distinction in the First World War. He courted controversy in 1932 when he crushed a demonstration of World War 1 veterans called the 'Bonus Army' in Washington, D.C. He was a key figure in the Second World War, especially in the 'island-hopping' campaign in the Pacific. After the war, he was military governor of Japan and was recalled to service to lead the Korean campaign. His sacking by Truman came as a shock to the American public, especially as he was one of the very few generals to be awarded the five-star rank. His was known for his significant ego. President Eisenhower, who also held five-star rank as a Second World War general, said 'MacArthur could never see a sun, or even a moon for that matter, in the heavens, as long as he was the sun.'

The course of the war, 1950–53

The events of any war can often seem confusing, so it helps to break them down into clear phases.

Phase One: liberating the South

The early success of the northern forces resulted in Rhee's army being surrounded in Pusan. Even the US troops that had landed early had not been able to prevent this. They were told they would be back in Japan within six weeks and not to pack much equipment. Instead, they found themselves in a heavy battle. MacArthur's response was to launch a bold landing by sea further north. He hoped this would allow him to cut off the northern army. In September, MacArthur landed his forces at Inchon in the west of the peninsula. This was difficult, as there was a concrete sea wall there and conditions were dangerous for landing the boats. Despite this, MacArthur managed to get his forces on land and defeated the communist troops. By early October, US troops had retaken Seoul and reached the 38th parallel.

> **FOCUS TASK 5.2**
>
> From what you have learnt about MacArthur's attack in Phase One, do you think President Truman's aims would have been satisfied by the end of this stage? On your own, write out Truman's aims as you understand them. Then add one sentence to each aim to say whether it was met. In pairs, discuss your responses and explain your decisions.

Chapter 5, Key Question 5: How effectively did the United States contain the spread of communism?

Figure 5.2: General MacArthur talks to US troops at a communications post in Korea, September 1950

Phase Two: 'rollback' – the UN invasion of the North

Communist forces had been driven out of the South, which meant that containment had been achieved. However, MacArthur was keen to move beyond the 38th parallel and go even further, rolling back communism in China as well as Korea. He saw it as an opportunity not only to prevent the spread of communism but perhaps to actually eradicate it from Asia.

President Truman was less enthusiastic about this plan. However, when he arrived in Korea to meet MacArthur it was clear which man was in control. Despite China's warning that it would take action if anyone invaded North Korea, MacArthur sent his forces across the border and pushed onwards throughout late October. He did so without telling the president his plans. In November, China responded by sending 500 000 troops across the Yalu River, which marks the border with North Korea.

> **THINKING SKILLS**
>
> If you had to decide what the USA should have done after Phase One, would you have taken MacArthur's approach, or would you have hesitated to move further north, like Truman? Write some brief notes, explaining your choice.

Phase Three: the Chinese counterattack

It was at this point that UN forces began to struggle. The Chinese were less well armed but there were more of them. The cold conditions caused guns to jam and stop working, which removed any advantage the UN soldiers had in terms of equipment. China also had aerial support from Russian MiG-15s, which were faster than US planes, could fly higher and had better firepower. By the end of November, MacArthur's men had suffered heavy casualties and were in retreat. In January 1951, Chinese forces recaptured Seoul.

As this battle continued, Truman was asked repeatedly whether he would agree to the use of nuclear weapons. He had authorised their use against Japan in 1945, so would he do so again? He refused to rule it out completely, which upset his UN allies. The British prime minister, Clement Attlee, flew to Washington, D.C. in December 1950 to reinforce his opposition to the use of nuclear weapons. Accepting international concerns, Truman stated he would not take this step.

Phase Four: stalemate and peace talks

A UN **counterattack** in spring 1951 stopped the Chinese forces at the 38th parallel. As the original plan had been to liberate South Korea up to this line, Truman considered peace talks. It was clear that MacArthur disagreed, and he publicly criticised the president. Truman sacked the general – a very unpopular move in the eyes of the US public. Under the new commander, General Ridgeway, US strategy switched to defence. A Chinese offensive was successfully fought back, and heavy casualties were inflicted.

In July 1951, the two sides sat down to discuss peace terms. The main disagreement was the issue of prisoners of war (POWs). There had been a great deal of movement of troops up and down the Korean peninsula, and large numbers of soldiers had been captured on both sides. Approximately 130 000 communist soldiers were being held in the South, and they had been given the option to remain there. Half of them accepted. In the North, conditions were terrible. Half the US POWs died in the winter of 1950–51.

The Chinese took over the running of POW camps to improve conditions but also to **indoctrinate** UN soldiers. Eventually, in September 1953, there was an exchange of 77 000 communist fighters for 12 700 UN troops (known as Operation Big Switch).

> **KEY TERMS**
>
> **counterattack:** an attack designed to stop an attack by an enemy
>
> **indoctrinate:** to make someone believe a set of values or principles without questioning them

Chapter 5, Key Question 5: How effectively did the United States contain the spread of communism?

SOURCE 5D

Source 5D: A cartoon from June 1950. It shows President Truman and the United Nations rushing to take part in the Korean War in support of South Korea. Both are flying over the grave of the League of Nations.

SOURCE ANALYSIS 5.4

Study Source 5D.

a Why has the cartoonist drawn President Truman running?

b How does this cartoon convey the differences between the League of Nations and the United Nations in their attitudes towards peacekeeping?

c This cartoon was created in June 1950. How do you think the same cartoonist would have drawn Truman a year later?

The end of the war

As peace talks continued throughout 1952–53, there seemed to be no end to the war. Truman had decided not to stand for re-election in 1952, and his replacement as president in January 1953 was Dwight D. Eisenhower, a Second World War general. Eisenhower promised to end the Korean War. Two months after Eisenhower took office, Stalin died and, after a power struggle in the USSR, Nikita Khrushchev became Soviet leader.

With new leaders in place, the chances of agreeing peace improved. The UN helped to arrange a **ceasefire** on 27 July 1953, which was accepted by all sides, except Syngman Rhee. International involvement in the fighting ended, but there has never been a peace treaty between North and South, so technically the war is not yet over. In fact, the 38th parallel remains the most heavily militarised place on Earth.

KEY TERM

ceasefire: an agreement between two armies to stop fighting in order to allow discussions to take place

> CAMBRIDGE IGCSE™ AND O LEVEL HISTORY OPTION B: COURSEBOOK

> **THINK LIKE A HISTORIAN**
>
> Unlike Truman, Eisenhower had been a military hero in the Second World War before he became president. Some people (especially at the time Eisenhower was elected) feel that military experience is important for a president because the job involves many decisions about conflict and power. However, others think that this is not healthy, and that the military should not have too much influence in politics.
>
> What experience and skills do you think a president should have today? Should they be a lawyer? A general? A teacher? A businessperson? Should they be very successful, or should they be an ordinary person? How might this affect their approach to the job and therefore you as an ordinary citizen? Why?

The most tragic consequence of the war was the horrific loss of life. Seoul and Pyongyang were both extensively damaged and civilian casualties reached 3 million – around 10% of the total population. Other losses by country were:

- North Korea: 406 000 combat deaths
- South Korea: 217 000 combat deaths
- China: 500 000 combat deaths
- USA: 36 914 combat deaths and illness, with another 7800 still unaccounted for
- UN: 3000–4000 deaths, including 686 British losses, with 1102 missing in action (the highest number of coalition forces after the USA).

Weapons such as **napalm** had catastrophic human and ecological results. Chinese casualties were high, but arguably Mao was the main victor for two reasons. Firstly, the war helped him to secure his power in China. Secondly, it ended a period of more than a century of Chinese defeats at the hands of western powers.

> **KEY TERM**
>
> **napalm:** a petrol-based chemical weapon that sticks to its target and burns at a very high temperature. It is often used to clear forests, preventing the enemy from having a place to hide, but when it comes into contact with skin it causes terrible burns

SOURCE 5E

Source 5E: The Korean War memorial in Washington, D.C.

> **SOURCE ANALYSIS 5.5**
>
> Study Source 5E.
>
> a The Korean War memorial is very different from other war memorials that have been built. Why do you think it has been made this way?
>
> b Do you think it is an effective way to help people remember the war?

Chapter 5, Key Question 5: How effectively did the United States contain the spread of communism?

FOCUS TASK 5.3

The USA spent $67 billion on the war and, in addition to combat deaths, over 100 000 soldiers were injured.

a   Were these costs justified in order to contain communism? Find three facts in this section to support your answer.

b   In pairs, question each other about your ideas and arguments. Do you agree with each other's assessment? If not, why not?

THINKING SKILLS

Look back at Truman's decision not to use nuclear weapons in Phase Three. Take some time to think about that moment in the war, then write responses to the following questions.

- If you were Truman at that time, would you have used nuclear weapons?
- Imagine you are Truman several years after the war ended and you are thinking about its outcome. Do you think you would regret any of your decisions?

ACTIVITY 5.2

The Korean War is often called the 'forgotten war'. Work in pairs to investigate why this was. Complete the following tasks.

a   List three reasons why the war could be considered a failure for the USA. Find evidence from this section to support each reason. Join up with another pair and give each other feedback on your reasons and evidence. If the other pair has noted a reason or evidence you had not identified, add it to your list.

b   In your groups of four, discuss the following question: *Who came out of the war with more damage to their reputation: Truman or MacArthur?* Present your conclusions to the class.

Key points

The Korean War

- The Korean War was fought between 1950 and 1953, but a peace treaty has never been signed between North Korea and South Korea.
- The North invaded the South with the aim of uniting the whole peninsula under communism.
- President Truman saw this as a chance to 'contain' communism, which meant stopping it from spreading.
- This was the first conflict where the UN sent in a military force.
- After initial success, UN forces were pushed back when China became involved.
- The war ended where it began, but military and civilian casualties were substantial.

5.2 The United States and events in Cuba, 1959–62

Khrushchev and Eisenhower got on better than Stalin and Truman had when they met in 1955 – the first meeting between Soviet and US leaders since 1945. However, the arms race and spy networks developed to such a point that neither side could trust the other. Major incidents only worsened the relationship between the two. The U2 incident (see 'Causes of the Missile Crisis') showed the extent of spying, while the Berlin Wall became an icon of the Cold War (see Chapter 6).

Technology played an important role in increasing tension. In 1957, the USSR put the first satellite (called Sputnik) into space, and also developed long-range nuclear missiles called Inter-Continental Ballistic Missiles (**ICBMs**). In 1959, the USA developed Polaris missiles, which could be launched from submarines. The basic theory of the arms and technology race was **Mutually Assured Destruction (MAD)**. This was the idea that neither side would start a nuclear war because launching weapons would destroy both sides. This did not comfort civilians around the world.

The USA's reaction to the Cuban Revolution, 1959–61

In 1898, the USA defeated Spain in a short war that gave the Americans effective control over Cuba. After this, US businesses took over trade on the island and owned much of the land and natural wealth, particularly the valuable sugar and oil industries. From 1933, they supported the corrupt dictator Fulgencio Batista, but he was overthrown by Fidel Castro in 1959. Castro came to power along with colleagues including his brother Raul and the famous revolutionary Ernesto 'Che' Guevara. Castro's followers were a mixture of communists and Cuban nationalists, but they were all strongly against US influence on their island.

> **KEY TERMS**
>
> **ICBM:** Inter-Continental Ballistic Missile, a long-range missile that can travel from one continent to another carrying a nuclear warhead
>
> **Mutually Assured Destruction (MAD):** a concept put forward by US Secretary of Defense Robert McNamara in 1962, based on the idea that as the USA had around 25 000 nuclear weapons and the USSR roughly half that, neither country would risk war as it would inevitably lead to widespread death and destruction

> **KEY FIGURE**
>
> **Fidel Castro (1926–2016)**
>
> Castro was the son of a wealthy farmer and studied law before becoming a full-time revolutionary. He greatly admired the legendary Cuban nationalist José Martí but had also read Karl Marx. His rise to power involved one of the great **guerrilla war** campaigns of the 20th century. His 300 men defeated 10 000 regular soldiers in the Sierra Maestra mountains. Castro led the Cuban Revolution and ruled Cuba for almost half a century.

> **KEY TERM**
>
> **guerrilla war:** a war fought not in open battle but using small attacks to try to destroy an enemy's confidence. Guerrilla techniques include blowing up supplies and laying traps to cause injuries

Chapter 5, Key Question 5: How effectively did the United States contain the spread of communism?

This revolution was a problem for Washington because of Cuba's strategic and economic significance. Castro let the USA keep its base at Guantanamo Bay, and guaranteed the safety of Americans in Cuba. However, he wanted to show Cuba's new freedom from US control so, in 1960, he signed a trade agreement with Moscow and received weapons as well. This led to a series of measures that went back and forth between the two sides.

- Castro took control of $1 billion of US investments in Cuba, including oil refineries. He nationalised these assets, meaning they now belonged to Cuba.
- Eisenhower started a trade embargo, which included sugar – Cuba's most valuable export. The USSR agreed to buy sugar from Cuba to save its economy.
- The USA announced it would not buy oil from Cuba. Again, the USSR bought the oil instead, even though it was inconvenient to send Soviet ships to the capital of Cuba, Havana.

Castro had never been a member of the Cuban Communist Party. However, when he met Khrushchev at the United Nations in 1960, they greeted each other like old friends, and Castro referred to himself as a 'good Marxist-Leninist'.

The US Central Intelligence Agency (**CIA**)'s response to these events was to train a group of 1400 Cuban exiles with the intention of invading the island and overthrowing Castro. They mistakenly believed that he was unpopular and poorly armed.

In April 1961, the Cuban exiles landed at the Bay of Pigs, where they were easily defeated. Castro had 20 000 soldiers supported by Soviet tanks. By this time, Eisenhower had been replaced by President John F. Kennedy, and the defeat was hugely embarrassing for the new president. When he met Khrushchev at the Vienna Summit in June 1961, the relationship between the two superpowers was worse than ever.

KEY TERM

CIA: Central Intelligence Agency, founded in 1947 by the National Security Act with the aim of collecting, evaluating and sharing intelligence about national security

SOURCE 5F

Source 5F: Castro's soldiers celebrate their victory at the Bay of Pigs in April 1961. They are sitting in a boat captured from the CIA-trained invaders.

SOURCE ANALYSIS 5.6

Look at the men in the photograph in Source 5F.

a What are the main differences you notice between these guerilla fighters and other soldiers?

b In which conditions would these fighters be more effective than regular soldiers and why?

197

> CAMBRIDGE IGCSE™ AND O LEVEL HISTORY OPTION B: COURSEBOOK

> **FOCUS TASK 5.4**
>
> a Select facts from this section to create a flow diagram showing the main developments in Cuba from 1959 to 1961.
>
> b Swap flow diagrams with a partner. Give feedback to each other about your diagrams and consider ways in which you can improve them.

Causes of the Missile Crisis

Khrushchev decided to introduce nuclear weapons to Cuba in the summer of 1962. As part of NATO, the USA had put nuclear weapons in Italy and Turkey. This was a deliberate move. These countries were close to the USSR so the response time would be limited if a missile was launched. Khrushchev wanted to respond by placing nuclear missiles on Cuba, just 145 kilometres from the USA's eastern coast. Over that summer, Che Guevara and Raul Castro met with Soviet leaders to arrange for the shipment and installation of the missiles.

In September 1962, President Kennedy warned the USSR that he would do whatever it took to stop the USSR placing nuclear weapons on Cuba. Khrushchev promised that this would not happen. On 14 October, a U2 spy plane flew over Cuba and took pictures of missile **silos**. Two days later, Kennedy was shown the proof that Khrushchev had lied.

> **KEY TERM**
>
> **silo:** an underground space in which missiles are stored

Figure 5.3: A map showing the range of medium-range and intermediate-range nuclear missiles if launched from Cuba at the United States

Chapter 5, Key Question 5: How effectively did the United States contain the spread of communism?

Kennedy's options

Kennedy had five realistic options.

1. Do not react: the USA had more nuclear weapons and the Turkish site gave it the same advantage. MAD meant that nothing essentially had changed. However, this would be seen as a sign of weakness after the Bay of Pigs.
2. Air attacks on military targets: the aerial destruction of all the missile silos. However, Soviet engineers would be killed and if one silo remained it could still be used to counterattack.
3. Invasion by the US army: this would remove the missiles, and communism, completely. However, a similar Soviet response (for example, in Berlin) might be expected.
4. Use diplomacy: the UN could provide a forum for discussions, but Khrushchev still denied that the missiles existed. Again, it might look like weakness.
5. Blockade: it could prevent warheads arriving and avoid war. However, it might cause a similar Soviet response, such as a repeat of the Berlin Blockade. Also, some missiles were already in Cuba and could be working within a week.

Kennedy chose a blockade (publicly called a 'quarantine' to make it sound healthy and less like an act of aggression), as this was felt to be a balance between appearing to be weak and using violence. This option was still not guaranteed to work.

> **THINKING SKILLS**
>
> Which option would you have taken if you were in Kennedy's position? Why? Write a brief position paper (200 words maximum) stating which option you consider to be best and why. Make sure you say why the other positions are flawed.

The week of crisis

After the Bay of Pigs embarrassment, Kennedy was reluctant to rely on his military chiefs, so he formed a special team called **Ex-Comm** to advise him. He knew that 20 Soviet ships carrying nuclear missiles were on their way to Cuba.

THE CUBAN MISSILE CRISIS, 1962

22 October	The USA informed Britain about the discovery of the missile silos. Kennedy broke the news in a TV address to the nation.
22 October	Kennedy ordered a naval blockade of Cuba. Khrushchev publicly denied that there were missiles on Cuba.
23 October	Khrushchev sent a letter stating that Soviet ships would attempt to sail through the USA blockade.
25 October	There was a clash in the UN between Adlai Stevenson and Valerian Zorin (see Figure 5.4). The USA provided photographic evidence of the missile sites (see Figure 5.4).

(Continued)

> **KEY TERM**
>
> **Ex-Comm:** the Executive Committee of the National Security Council (NSC) – this included members of the NSC, but Kennedy also invited significant non-military figures: his brother Robert Kennedy (the Attorney-General); Theodore Sorensen (White House Counsel); Truman's Secretary of State Dean Acheson; and former ambassador to the USSR Tommy Thompson, who knew Khrushchev personally

THE CUBAN MISSILE CRISIS, 1962

26 October	Soviet ships carrying warheads turned back before the USA blockade. However, some missiles and warheads made it to Cuba before the blockade was in place. The USA threatened an invasion. Castro called for a nuclear strike from the USSR.
26 October	Khrushchev's first offer was made in a letter to Kennedy. He said the missiles would be withdrawn if the USA promised not to invade Cuba. This was the first Soviet admission that missiles actually existed on Cuba.
27 October	A U2 spy plane was shot down over Cuba and the pilot was killed. Kennedy was encouraged to start an invasion, but he delayed. Khrushchev made a second offer in another letter to Kennedy. He demanded that the USA remove missiles from Turkey in exchange for removal of the Cuban missiles. Kennedy responded to Khrushchev's first offer, but ignored the second. Robert Kennedy met with USSR ambassador Anatoly Dobrynin. There would be no official deal, but the USA would guarantee not to invade Cuba again and to remove Turkish missiles in the near future. The USSR could not reveal that this was done in exchange for the removal of Cuban missiles.
28 October	Khrushchev accepted these terms, ending the crisis.

THINK LIKE A HISTORIAN

Ex-Comm was an important group for Kennedy, as he needed people that he could trust. If you were a leader and had to deal with a crisis, who would you seek advice from, and why? What would be important to you in bringing in people who could help you?

REVISION TIP

History is not about dates, but knowing the order of events is important so you know why one thing leads to another. It also helps you to describe *how* things happened. The timeline of the Cuban Missile Crisis is the shortest period of time you will study in this course. Summarise the events on flashcards, without dates. Instead, put the date on the back of each card. Practise putting the events in the right order, then turn them over to see if you got it right.

Chapter 5, Key Question 5: How effectively did the United States contain the spread of communism?

> **ACTIVITY 5.3**
>
> a Look at the timeline of events in the Cuban Missile Crisis. Identify the moment / event that you think was the turning point.
>
> b In pairs, compare your ideas. Justify to each other why you think the event you chose was the most important. Does your partner change your mind about your own choice?
>
> c As a class, count up how many people have chosen particular events. Listen to some other pairs justifying their choices. Have they chosen different events, or given different reasons?
>
> d Write a paragraph to explain your final choice of turning point, justifying your decision.

> **REFLECTION**
>
> In Activity 5.3, you had to make a decision about a turning point. This means you had to identify a key moment when the course of the overall event suddenly changed. How did you reach that decision? When you discussed it with your partner, had they chosen a different event? Was their logic different from yours? Did their decision change the way you thought about yours? How did the class discussion affect your thinking?
>
> It is important to consider why we see some historical events as more important than others. Remember the thought process you went through in this activity when you next have to consider turning points in a series of important events.

Figure 5.4: The battle at the UN between the US ambassador Adlai Stevenson and Soviet ambassador Valerian Zorin on 25 October 1962. Stevenson humiliated Zorin by producing pictures taken from planes flying over the missile sites, proving that the Soviets had been lying.

> **FOCUS TASK 5.5**
>
> Look at Figure 5.4. It shows the moment when the USA provided evidence to the world that the USSR had been lying about the missile sites.
>
> What effect did this revelation have on the development of the crisis? What do you think the reaction would have been in Moscow? How would Khrushchev have reacted?

The consequences for the three leaders

In the end, Khrushchev backed down, although he later claimed it was a triumph for him personally, and for Cuba. Others in Moscow did not share this view and he was replaced by Leonid Brezhnev in 1964. Kennedy managed to resist his military advisers, who called for air strikes and invasion, but took a huge risk in doing so. The final settlement terms looked much better for him, but in reality the USA had a less powerful position than before the crisis. Castro was still in power and the USA lost its Turkish missile sites. However, to US and world opinion, Kennedy had successfully stood up to Khrushchev and saved everyone from a nuclear war.

The crisis began over Cuba, but Castro was not involved in negotiations to end it. On 26 October, he told Khrushchev to launch a nuclear attack, so it is perhaps unsurprising that he was kept out of decision-making after that. The deal to end the crisis came as a complete surprise to him. He was extremely angry, and it took some time to repair relations between Cuba and the USSR.

SOURCE 5G

Source 5G: A US cartoon showing Kennedy and Khrushchev during the Cuban Missile Crisis, 1962

SOURCE ANALYSIS 5.7

Study Source 5G.

a What is the main message of the cartoon?

b How does the cartoonist communicate this message?

Chapter 5, Key Question 5: How effectively did the United States contain the spread of communism?

> **FOCUS TASK 5.6**
>
> Think about Castro's role in the Cuban Missile Crisis. Write a paragraph addressing the following questions.
>
> a   What role did Castro play in the outbreak and the development of the crisis?
>
> b   How important was his role?
>
> c   Did he gain anything from the outcome?

The aftermath of the crisis

The Cuban Missile Crisis was the closest that the two superpowers ever came to a nuclear war. A hotline was set up between the White House and the Kremlin to improve communications in the event of a future crisis. In August 1963, they signed the Nuclear Test Ban Treaty, each side promising not to test any more nuclear weapons. This did not reduce existing nuclear stockpiles, but it did stop the arms race. Khrushchev did not survive much longer in power, but Castro did. He only stepped down as Cuba's leader in 2008 and was succeeded by his brother Raul. Kennedy was assassinated in November 1963 and was succeeded by his vice president, Lyndon B. Johnson.

Key points

Crises in Cuba

- The Cuban Revolution of 1959 caused problems for the USA because Castro overthrew the US-supported government.

- The USA failed to remove Castro from power after the disastrous Bay of Pigs invasion in 1961.

- Cuba is very close to Florida in the USA. This proximity made Cuba an attractive partner for the USSR.

- Khrushchev decided to send nuclear missiles to Cuba, but publicly denied that he was doing so.

- When the USA discovered his plan, it led to a crisis that lasted about a week and brought the world to the brink of nuclear war.

- Kennedy chose a 'quarantine' option rather than an air strike or military invasion, and eventually the USSR backed down.

- The USA had to give up its missile bases near the USSR, but Kennedy was widely felt to have handled the crisis better than Khrushchev.

CAMBRIDGE IGCSE™ AND O LEVEL HISTORY OPTION B: COURSEBOOK

5.3 American involvement in Vietnam, 1955–75

Background: the French war in Vietnam

From the 1860s, France controlled the colony of Indo-China, which comprised Vietnam, Cambodia and Laos. After France was defeated by Nazi Germany in 1940, it lost control of Indo-China to Japan. At the end of the war, the communist leader Ho Chi Minh announced that Vietnam was independent. However, the French regained control, which soon led to war. From 1946 to 1954, French losses reached 72 000, which was actually more than the USA later lost. The Chinese Revolution of 1949 made things worse, as Mao supplied arms to the North Vietnamese forces, the **Viet Minh**.

SOURCE 5H

Source 5H: The Vietnam War Memorial in Washington, D.C. It lists the names of all the US soldiers killed in action.

KEY TERMS

Viet Minh and Viet Cong: names given by western politicians and journalists to Vietnamese communist forces. Viet Minh (for the northern communists) is a contraction of 'Vietnamese' and 'Ho Chi Minh', and Viet Cong (for the southern communists) is a contraction of a Vietnamese expression for 'Vietnamese communists'

SOURCE ANALYSIS 5.8

Look at Source 5H. If Korea is the forgotten war, then Vietnam is one of the most well-known conflicts, but a painful one for Americans to recall. Compare and contrast this memorial to the Korean War Memorial in Source 5E. Which do you think is more effective and why?

KEY FIGURE

Ho Chi Minh (1890–1969)

Born Nguyen That Thanh in 1890, Ho Chi Minh travelled widely and helped to establish the French Communist Party. He also trained in Moscow and China, and formed the Viet Minh in 1941 to fight the Japanese. It was at this point that he changed his name to Ho Chi Minh, which means 'bringer of light'. He led the fight against the French from 1946 and was made President of North Vietnam in 1954. Ho supported the **Viet Cong** in their fight against the Americans until his death in 1969. When the Viet Cong captured Saigon, they renamed it Ho Chi Minh City.

Chapter 5, Key Question 5: How effectively did the United States contain the spread of communism?

Figure 5.5: Ho Chi Minh's body was preserved and publicly displayed after his death in 1969, adding to his cult of personality

Despite being given $2.6 billion in aid by the USA between 1950 and 1954, the French were unsuccessful in Vietnam. They withdrew after a heavy defeat at Dien Bien Phu in March 1954. They had controlled the towns, but Ho Chi Minh's guerrilla forces controlled the north and the countryside. Peace was signed through the 1954 Geneva Agreements. The main points set out in the peace treaty were that:

- Indo-China would be divided into four parts: North and South Vietnam, Laos and Cambodia
- North Vietnam was divided from the South at the 17 °N line of latitude; Northern forces were to withdraw from the South
- all foreign troops would withdraw from Indo-China
- elections would be held in 1956
- an international commission would ensure that the settlement was kept.

Several nations, including the USSR, China and Britain, signed the agreements, but the USA refused. In 1956, US president Eisenhower persuaded the South Vietnamese president, Ngo Dinh Diem, not to hold elections because evidence suggested that the communists would win.

THINKING SKILLS

Look at the list of terms of the Geneva Agreements. Eisenhower refused to sign them. Would you have done the same? From a US perspective, write a sentence in response to each bullet point, explaining your position.

> CAMBRIDGE IGCSE™ AND O LEVEL HISTORY OPTION B: COURSEBOOK

> KEY FIGURE
>
> **Ngo Dinh Diem (1901–63)**
>
> Diem came from a noble family and served as a minister to Emperor Bao Dai of Vietnam. He overthrew the emperor in 1954, and worked with the USA. However, Diem was a strict **autocrat** and gave powerful jobs to members of his family. He was extremely corrupt, promoted Christianity over Buddhism and often rejected US advice. He was removed by his own generals and murdered in a coup in 1963.

Reasons for US involvement in Vietnam

Civil war broke out, and in 1960 the National Liberation Front (known as the Viet Cong) was created in South Vietnam. This group was a mixture of anti-government forces, including Buddhists, patriots and communists. They used guerrilla tactics, operating from a complex network of tunnels and well-equipped underground bases that included hospitals. Even if US troops found an entrance, many were booby-trapped so they struggled to get through. The Viet Cong's war against Diem's government was successful. In part this was due to the fact that the Viet Cong received supplies through the Ho Chi Minh Trail. This ran through neighbouring Laos and Cambodia and allowed for weapons and supplies to be secretly brought south from North Vietnam and China.

> KEY TERM
>
> **autocrat:** a ruler who rules alone, has supreme authority and demands complete obedience from their subjects

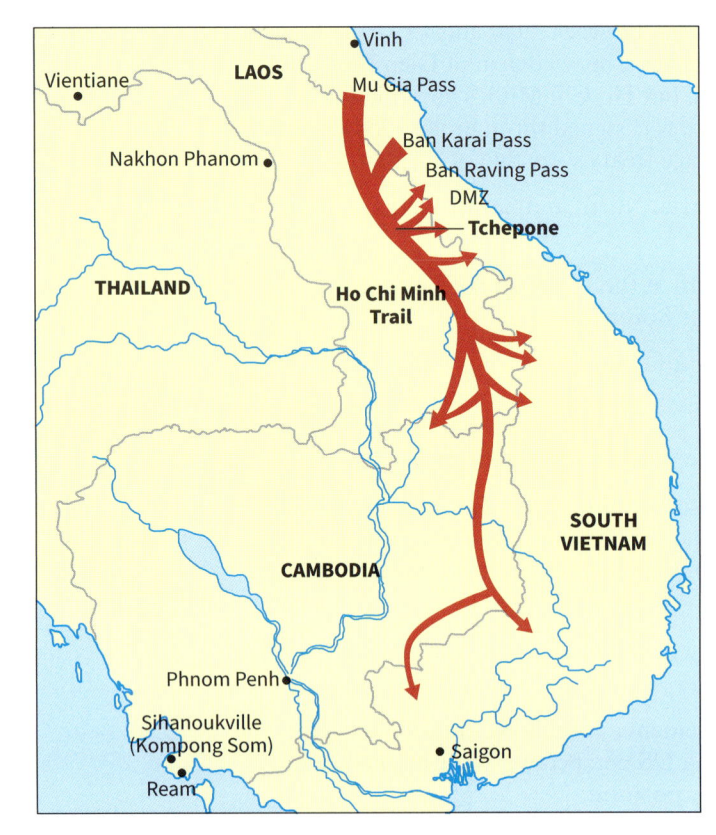

Figure 5.6: This map shows the route of the Ho Chi Minh Trail, which the North used to send Viet Cong fighters and supplies to support them into the South

Chapter 5, Key Question 5: How effectively did the United States contain the spread of communism?

> **FOCUS TASK 5.7**
>
> Look at Figure 5.6 and then use the internet to find out more about the Ho Chi Minh Trail.
>
> a   Select five key facts that demonstrate its significance in the USA's withdrawal from the war.
>
> b   In small groups, share your five facts and give each other feedback. Do you agree with each other's choices?
>
> c   Together, come up with a final list of the five facts you all agree are the most significant.

Kennedy's first foreign policy action on becoming president in 1961 was in Laos, where the communist group Pathet Lao was trying to overthrow the monarchy. The Viet Minh and the Pathet Lao had worked together to fight the French. Eisenhower told Kennedy that the country was like 'cork in the bottle': once it popped, the whole region could fall to communism. Therefore, the CIA trained an anti-communist force and supplies were flown in from Thailand. Aerial bombing began and continued heavily until 1975.

In South Vietnam, 16 000 military advisers were sent to help Diem. However, in 1963, Buddhist protests against the government began. Kennedy was tired of Diem, especially after an embarrassing defeat at Ap Bac. In November 1963, the CIA helped to stage an internal coup that ended in the bloody execution of Diem and his advisers. Kennedy himself was assassinated later that month.

Figure 5.7: A Buddhist monk protesting at Diem's religious policies in 1963. He was sitting in the lotus position in the central square in Saigon as he burned to death. Diem was a strict Catholic and refused to let anyone celebrate Buddha's birthday.

> CAMBRIDGE IGCSE™ AND O LEVEL HISTORY OPTION B: COURSEBOOK

> **REVISION TIP**
>
> Create a table in which you list the names of all the national leaders mentioned in this chapter, such as Ngo Dinh Diem, Fidel Castro and Syngman Rhee, and their role in the events you read about. It is easy to fall into the trap of focusing only on the leaders of the superpowers, but it is important that you know what other leaders stood for and the parts they played.

Johnson and increasing US involvement

Lyndon B. Johnson – a firm believer in the **Domino Theory** – became president on Kennedy's death. The next presidential election was due in November 1964, so Johnson was also under pressure to be seen being tough on communism. In August, before the election, he was given the opportunity to expand US involvement in the war through the Gulf of Tonkin incident, when a US warship was alleged to have come under North Vietnamese fire. Congress gave the president permission to send more military power to Vietnam.

> **KEY TERM**
>
> **Domino Theory:** the theory that if one country fell to communism, so would its neighbours, and their neighbours in turn, like a row of dominoes

> **SOURCE ANALYSIS 5.9**
>
> Study Source 5I. What does this poster suggest about the war that the USA was involved in and the people it was fighting against?

SOURCE 5I

Source 5I: A poster published in 1963

208

Chapter 5, Key Question 5: How effectively did the United States contain the spread of communism?

US tactics

In 1965, the Viet Cong attacked a US base at Pleiku. US bombing grew heavier through Operation Rolling Thunder. The Viet Cong were still being supplied by the USSR and China through the port of Haiphong and then through the Ho Chi Minh Trail. The USA was afraid to bomb the port for fear of hitting Soviet ships. General Westmoreland advised Johnson to send ground troops and the president reluctantly agreed.

The USA was now involved in a total war. Its tactics for victory were as follows.

- Heavy use of bombing from planes to destroy Viet Cong strongholds. Chemical weapons such as napalm and **Agent Orange** were used to destroy trees and jungle, useful hiding places for the enemy.
- 'Search and destroy' missions. Combat units would go out into the countryside to locate Viet Cong weapons stores, bases and fighters. They would punish any villages helping the enemy.

The year 1968 was an important one in the war. Despite the US government claiming that victory was close, the North Vietnamese Army became more heavily involved. The Tet Offensive (launched on Tet, the Vietnamese New Year) saw Viet Cong troops almost capture the US embassy in Saigon. Although it failed, the battle showed that Westmoreland's claim that the Viet Cong were close to defeat was inaccurate. Anti-war protests in the USA increased after this.

> **KEY TERM**
>
> **Agent Orange:** a chemical weapon used by the Americans to destroy crops and forests to make it harder for the Viet Cong to feed themselves, and to hide. However, it also had horrific side effects on people's physical health

Figure 5.8: Children fleeing the village of Trang Bang after a napalm bombing in 1972. The little girl running naked in the photograph here is Phan Thi Kim Phúc, who was nine years old at the time.

> **THINKING SKILLS**
>
> The photograph in Figure 5.8 shows the effects of napalm. The children are running away from a bombed village and Phan Thi Kim Phúc's clothes have been burned off. Imagine you are an American seeing this image in a newspaper at the time. What would your reaction be? What, if anything, would you do?

The My Lai massacre

One main reason for increased anti-war sentiment in the USA was the incident that became known as the My Lai Massacre. In March 1968, a company of US soldiers was sent on a search and destroy mission to the small village of My Lai. They killed 374 men, women and children, plus their livestock, and burned down the village. No Viet Cong were found. The horror only ended when US helicopter pilot Hugh Thompson landed and threatened to shoot the soldiers. The incident was kept secret for a year, but when it became public an investigation was launched. Of the 14 men charged, only the commanding officer, Lieutenant William Calley, was found guilty. He was sentenced to life in prison for this war crime but received a presidential pardon in 1974.

Figure 5.9: A US marine setting fire to a house in My Lai during the infamous massacre in 1968

Nixon's war

The consequence of this dramatic year was that Johnson announced in 1968 that he would not seek re-election. The new president, Richard Nixon, promised to end the war but did not want to withdraw in a humiliating way. His policy of **Vietnamisation** reduced US troop numbers significantly. In 1970, Nixon extended the aerial bombing into Cambodia. He did this without telling Congress, which increased public criticism when it was discovered. During nationwide protests, four students were killed at Kent State University by the Ohio National Guard. Many felt that the war was now being fought not just in Vietnam, but in the USA itself. By 1972, even some war veterans were protesting against Nixon's policies, throwing away their medals. Nixon also replaced the Cambodian ruler with the corrupt and deeply unpopular Lon Nol.

> **KEY TERM**
>
> **Vietnamisation:** a policy based on reducing US troops in Vietnam and encouraging the South Vietnamese Army (ARVN) to do more of the fighting

Chapter 5, Key Question 5: How effectively did the United States contain the spread of communism?

Figure 5.10: The aftermath of the Kent State University protests in May 1970, during which four students were shot dead

ACTIVITY 5.4

In May 1970, a protest against Nixon's expansion of the war into Cambodia took place at Kent State University (see Figure 5.10). The governor of Ohio sent in the National Guard, which opened fire on the protestors. Four students were shot dead. A later investigation called the use of arms 'unnecessary, unwarranted and inexcusable'. Over 500 universities were shut down afterwards as protests grew.

a   Research the anti-war movement in the USA by finding two useful websites.

b   Make notes on why you found the websites useful, and what you learnt from them.

c   Write a 150-word article from the perspective of a university student newspaper. What would you say about the war in Vietnam, and what would you urge your readers to do?

REFLECTION

Research is a key skill for a historian, and it involves looking at articles, books and websites. Online resources can be easy to find, but difficult to assess in terms of their suitability and accuracy. Discuss with a partner the qualities you look for in a good website. How do you decide which ones to use? What makes one website more effective for research than another?

Figure 5.11: Boxer Muhammad Ali (born Cassius Clay) in 1966, pointing to a newspaper headline about anti-war protests

> ### ACTIVITY 5.5
>
> Look at the picture of the boxer Muhammad Ali in Figure 5.11. Ali was a strong critic of the war in Vietnam. Use the internet or any other resources available to research his actions in this period. What did he do and how significant was his opposition in shaping public opinion? Create a factual summary, around one page long, of Ali's involvement in the politics of the anti-Vietnam protests.

Led by Nixon's National Security Adviser, Henry Kissinger, peace talks made progress in 1972. To force the North's hand, the USA launched the heaviest aerial bombardments yet: Operation Linebacker I and II. Nixon also secretly made a promise to the South that the USA would support it if it was invaded again by the North. Again, Congress was not told this.

In January 1973, a peace treaty was signed and US troops began withdrawing from Vietnam. The South would have to look after itself, especially as Nixon was forced to resign in 1974 over his involvement in the Watergate scandal. The North invaded the South in March 1974 and won a decisive victory in April 1975. When the North Vietnamese seized the capital, Saigon, they entered the US embassy, forcing helicopters to evacuate staff. It was a deeply humiliating moment for the USA and marked the country's total defeat in Vietnam. Cambodia and Laos fell to communism the same month.

Chapter 5, Key Question 5: How effectively did the United States contain the spread of communism?

Figure 5.12: South Vietnamese people fleeing from Saigon with the help of the US military, April 1975

> **REVISION TIP**
>
> You have read about US presidents Truman, Eisenhower, Kennedy, Johnson and Nixon in this chapter. Make sure you know about each president. For example, when were they in office? What big decisions did they make? In what circumstances did they leave office? Most importantly, how well did they contain communism? Create a table recording key information about and policies of each president.

Effects of the Vietnam War

Below are just some of the consequences of the war.

- South Vietnam lost 2.5 million civilians.
- 300 000 citizens of South Vietnam were tortured in 're-education camps' after the war.
- The Viet Cong included children, women and the elderly in their ranks. This meant it was very hard for US forces to know who was actively involved in the war, and who were simply civilians.

213

- North Vietnam lost 650 000 soldiers and the Viet Cong lost 1 million.
- The USA lost 58 220 men.
- Around 1.5 million people escaped Vietnam in boats in 1975–90, heading for Hong Kong and Australia.
- Vietnam's economy was destroyed by bombing. Use of chemical weapons massively increased cancer rates and led to babies being deformed at birth.
- Many US soldiers became drug addicts. By 1971, four times more men were treated for drug addiction than wounds from fighting.
- Congress passed the War Powers Act (1973) to restrict the president's ability to send troops abroad.
- Communism in Cambodia under Pol Pot led to mass murder during 1975–79 in which more than 2 million people were killed, almost one-third of the population.

> **FOCUS TASK 5.8**
>
> Use the bullet points outlining the effects of the war (here and on the previous page) to create a spider diagram including information about each of these states:
>
> - USA
> - North Vietnam
> - South Vietnam
> - Cambodia
> - Laos.
>
> As well as the consequences of the war, add information about the key leaders and events that caused them.

Why did the USA lose the war?

There are two main reasons for the USA's defeat in Vietnam. They both contributed significantly to the withdrawal of troops in 1973, although historians disagree which cause was more significant.

Military factors

The Viet Cong were well organised and difficult to identify. The Ho Chi Minh Trail kept them supplied and they dressed like villagers and farmers, so they looked like civilians. They had also been fighting the Japanese and the French with the same guerrilla tactics so they were very experienced, unlike US soldiers who fought for one year then returned home. This meant that ordinary soldiers did not build up much experience. Modern technology was of little use in Vietnam and was probably counter-productive as it cost the USA political support.

Domestic factors

The public was increasingly against the war and as propaganda was so important in the Cold War, the USA could not afford to be seen to be killing innocent civilians. Protests like the one at Kent State University divided the nation. Presidents Johnson and Nixon became figures of hate. Both left office with their reputation in ruins. As early as 1966, more than the half the US public disapproved of the conflict. No president could keep on fighting when the media was showing the horrific nature of the war through TV, photographs and articles.

What about containment?

A third factor in the American withdrawal was that Vietnam became less strategically important as the Domino Theory was proved to be incorrect. Cambodia and Laos fell to communism, but Thailand and the Philippines did not. In the late 1960s the USSR and China argued, and there was even the possibility of war between them. Nixon's policy of *détente* (meaning 'relaxation') improved relations with the USSR and China so whatever happened in Vietnam seemed to have less disastrous consequences than might have been imagined in the 1960s.

Chapter 5, Key Question 5: How effectively did the United States contain the spread of communism?

Key points

The Vietnam War

- The first fighting in Vietnam after the Second World War involved the French, who had held the territory as a colony.
- The 1964 Gulf of Tonkin incident expanded US involvement in Vietnam, as part of the strategy to prevent the spread of communism through 'Domino Theory'.
- Despite their significant technological superiority, the USA struggled to win the war against the Viet Cong and Viet Minh, who knew the territory better and used guerrilla tactics effectively.
- As US casualties mounted, so too did domestic opposition to the war.
- President Nixon promised to end the war but did so by extending the aerial bombing campaign to neighbouring countries.
- The US eventually left Vietnam in 1973 and the communist forces achieved a total victory over South Vietnam in 1975.

SUMMARY

- The Korean War was the first Cold War conflict outside of Europe.
- The war lasted for three years and was the first test of the USA's new policy of containment.
- The war ended after three years of brutal fighting and was a stalemate. North and South Korea remain divided to this day as a consequence.
- The Cuban Revolution of 1959 gave the USA a new challenge, as it had a close ally of the USSR right next to their shores.
- The Bay of Pigs was a failed attempt by President John F. Kennedy to deal with the problem of Fidel Castro's new government.
- The Cold War nearly became a 'hot war' when the USSR tried to place missiles in Cuba, but they backed down after an intense diplomatic crisis.
- The USA feared the spread of communism because of its belief in the Domino Theory, and this led to its support of President Diem in South Vietnam.
- After the Gulf of Tonkin incident, the USA sent more of its own troops to fight.
- The Viet Minh and Viet Cong used guerrilla tactics and the Ho Chi Minh trail meant they were always well supplied with weapons and equipment.
- Nixon withdrew US forces in 1973 and South Vietnam fell to communism in 1975.

> CAMBRIDGE IGCSE™ AND O LEVEL HISTORY OPTION B: COURSEBOOK

KEY SKILLS EXERCISES

Knowledge and understanding
1. How did NSC 68 lead to US involvement in the Korean War?
2. What was the Cuban Revolution and why did it cause problems for the USA?
3. What happened in the Gulf of Tonkin incident?
4. How did the My Lai massacre and the Tet Offensive undermine support for the Vietnam war?

Application
5. Why is the Korean War known as the 'forgotten war'?
6. What evidence could the USSR use to justify its decision to place nuclear weapons in Cuba?
7. Why was Kennedy seen as the victor in the global media over Cuba, and was this justified?
8. Did the USA win the military conflict in Vietnam, but lose the media war?

Analysis
9. Analyse **one** reason why America faced a threat from communism in each of the three examples (Korea, Cuba, Vietnam).
10. Analyse **three** reasons from any of the case studies to show why America either succeeded or failed to contain communism.
11. Analyse the leadership qualities shown by Truman, Kennedy and Johnson.

Evaluation
12. Evaluate the success of the UN's military intervention in the Korean peninsula.
13. Cuba was perhaps the closest the world came to a nuclear war between two superpowers. Evaluate the level of risk that the USA and the USSR took during the crisis. How close did it come to a being a nuclear conflict?
14. Discuss the reasons for opposition to the Vietnam War, and evaluate the role these factors played in US withdrawal.

IMPROVE THIS ANSWER

'The main reason for America's withdrawal from Vietnam was due to military failure.' How far do you agree with this statement? Explain your answer.

Sample answer: America withdrew from Vietnam in 1973 after almost a decade of struggling to win the war. **1** President Nixon withdrew his forces there after it became clear that the USA could not completely defeat the VietCong (supported by the Viet Minh) and would eventually lose the war. However, domestic pressure and protests were also a significant factor. The war was very unpopular and it could be argued that this was more important in Nixon's decision to end involvement in the war. **2**

1 This is a good opening sentence as it shows both a clear focus on the question and also provides accurate knowledge to show the context.

2 This introduction provides alternative explanations and that gives a balanced approach and shows that both sides have been considered.

Chapter 5, Key Question 5: How effectively did the United States contain the spread of communism?

3 This has some good evidence but the selection could be better. For example, the Tet Offensive would be a very good example to use to support the argument being made.

4 This section arguably strays away from the argument about domestic opposition and becomes more about military factors again. It would be better if the answer had focused on protests at Kent State University, for example, than use of chemical weapons. Always choose the most relevant evidence to support your answer.

5 This conclusion is effective because it gives a clear answer to the question and justifies it. The answer given is consistent with the argument developed earlier.

CONTINUED

Given that America was a military superpower it was surprising that they had failed to defeat their Vietnamese opponents. This was widely perceived as a failure, and the number of casualties was very high at over 50,000. The Vietnamese used guerrilla tactics to harrass US forces and cause injuries (for example, from booby-traps) which meant units had to struggle through the countryside carrying wounded men. The VietCong didn't wear uniforms and so were very hard to identify, and many old people and children helped with passing on information or hiding weapons. **3** America lost the war because they didn't really know who they were fighting, and that meant it was impossible to end the conflict with military force. That was why Nixon decided to withdraw his forces in 1973.

However, the war was extremely unpopular in America and both President Johnson and President Nixon were heavily criticised. Johnson even stepped down in 1968 rather than run again for the presidency over his handling of the war. Mass protests continued in the 1960s and 1970s and many young men, like Muhammad Ali, dodged the draft. America had enjoyed a major success against the USSR over the Cuban Missile Crisis but their role in Vietnam, especially using chemical weapons like Agent Orange, had invited global criticism. Nixon had promised 'Vietnamisation', meaning more South Vietnamese forces taking action rather than American, but what he actually did was extend the war into Cambodia. **4** Overall Nixon had lost popular support for the war and this was a significant reason why he withdrew his forces from Vietnam.

On balance, the main reason for American withdrawal was due to military failure. This was because from 1964 to 1973 they had failed to achieve success and so domestic unpopularity increased as time went on. Had a military success been possible then Nixon might have carried on, but it was clear that this wasn't possible and so that was the main reason. **5**

Now write an improved response using this guidance.

PRACTICE QUESTIONS

1 The Cuban Missile Crisis of 1962 came very close to becoming a direct conflict between the USA and the USSR.

   a Describe the Cuban Revolution. [4]

   b Why was there a crisis over Cuba in 1962? [6]

   c How far did Khrushchev achieve his objectives over Cuba in 1962? Explain your answer. [10]

   [Total: 20]

2 a Study Source A.

   What is the cartoonist's message? Explain your answer using details of the source and your knowledge. [8]

SHAKING THE OLIVE BRANCH

Source A: A US cartoon from 1966 during the bombing campaign of Operation Rolling Thunder in Vietnam. 'LBJ' were the initials of President Lyndon Baines Johnson

   b Study Source B.

   Are you surprised by this source? Explain your answer using details of the source and your knowledge. [8]

   The Associated Press had reported last Friday that General MacArthur discussed the campaign with Major General John B. Coulter and remarked, with a smile: 'You tell the boys that when they get to the Yalu (River) they are going home. I want to make good on my statement that they are going to eat Christmas dinner at home.'

   Source B: General MacArthur's 'Home by Christmas' statement, 28 November 1950

   [Total: 16]

Chapter 5, Key Question 5: How effectively did the United States contain the spread of communism?

PROJECT

Work in groups of three. Each group member chooses Korea, Cuba, or Vietnam. For your chosen case study, develop a set of revision notes recording all the key information about the event. Check that you include:

- the main events in chronological order
- the key individuals
- important concepts that affected decisions and actions.

Try to keep these notes short. There is a lot of information, so focus on the most important basics to begin with. When you have completed your notes come back together in your group of three and share them with each other.

Use your combined notes to discuss and then create a five-minute presentation for the class based on this question: *Which president was most successful in containing communism: Truman, Eisenhower, Kennedy, Johnson or Nixon?*

Develop a visual presentation and make sure that you provide a judgement for each president. Consider:

- How successful were they?
- What were their failures?
- Should they have chosen other options at key moments?

Deliver your presentation to the class. Leave time at the end for questions, and be prepared to defend your decisions.

SELF-EVALUATION CHECKLIST

After studying this chapter, complete this table:

You should be able to:	Needs more work	Almost there	Ready to move on
understand the causes of the Korean War, 1950–53			
describe the events of the war from 1950 to 1953			
evaluate the success of the US policy of containment in Korea			
understand the causes of the Cuban Missile Crisis of 1962			
describe the events of the Cuban Missile Crisis and analyse its results			
understand the causes of US involvement in Vietnam			
describe the military events of the war			
explain the reasons for domestic opposition to the war in America			
evaluate the overall success of containment in the three case studies.			

> Chapter 6, Key Question 6:

How secure was the USSR's control over Eastern Europe, 1948–c.1989?

FOCUS POINTS

This chapter will help you to answer these questions:

- Why was there opposition to Soviet control in Hungary in 1956 and Czechoslovakia in 1968, and how did the USSR react to this opposition?
- How similar were events in Hungary in 1956 and in Czechoslovakia in 1968?
- Why was the Berlin Wall built in 1961?
- What was the significance of Solidarity in Poland for the decline of Soviet influence in Eastern Europe?
- How far was Gorbachev personally responsible for the collapse of Soviet control over Eastern Europe?

6.0 What is this enquiry about?

This enquiry looks at what happened in Eastern Europe after Stalin had established a buffer zone up to 1949. It is important to remember that all the states within this buffer zone had suffered greatly under Nazi occupation. Some communist leaders had escaped because they knew they would be executed if they were found by the Nazis. They spent the war in Moscow and knew Stalin personally. He therefore wanted them to be in power after the war ended in 1945.

Hitler's forces were defeated by two key groups. The first were local **partisans**. These resistance movements often included communists, such as Josef Tito's group in Yugoslavia. The second group was the USSR's Red Army, which played a decisive role.

To understand the events between 1949 and 1989 covered in this enquiry, you should keep in mind differing perspectives.

- Many communists believed that government from Moscow offered the best source of protection after the horrors of the Nazi occupation. There was also widespread gratitude towards the Soviets.

- Others on the left believed that their country should be fully independent, without taking orders from the USSR. They found inspiration in Yugoslavia's leader, Josef Tito.

- A third group wanted to ally with the USA and the West.

Soviet power seemed too strong to be challenged successfully. This belief was reinforced by events in Budapest in 1956 and Prague in 1968. You will also learn about Berlin, arguably the most important city in the whole Cold War. Why was Berlin so politically and strategically important? Finally, if Soviet power was so strong then why did it collapse so suddenly in the late 1980s? Was Poland the main cause of this collapse? Was one man – Mikhail Gorbachev – mainly responsible for the end of communist rule in Eastern Europe?

> **KEY TERM**
>
> **partisans:** armed groups formed to fight against an enemy that is controlling a country

KEY FIGURE

Josef Tito (1892–1980)

Josef Tito was born Josef Broz in what is now Croatia. He led partisan resistance to the Nazis. Tito was a communist, but he believed in being independent. He resisted Stalin's demands and formed a non-aligned movement in the Cold War with Nehru of India and Nasser of Egypt. This group of nations refused to side with either the USA or the USSR. Tito ruled Yugoslavia until his death in 1980.

Chapter 6, Key Question 6: How secure was the USSR's control over Eastern Europe, 1948–c.1989?

SOURCE 6A

Source 6A: Josef Tito, leader of Yugoslavia, in May 1970

SOURCE ANALYSIS 6.1

Study Source 6A.

a What impression do you get of Tito from this photograph?

b How did Tito's public image differ from Stalin's?

EASTERN BLOC MEMBERS
- Satellite states
- USSR-aligned until 1948
- USSR-aligned until 1960

Figure 6.1: A map of Eastern Europe in 1949

ACTIVITY 6.1

The term 'geopolitics' refers to the impact that geography has on international politics. Working in small groups, analyse the map in Figure 6.1, which shows the Soviet buffer zone in Eastern Europe.

a In your groups, discuss the following questions. Consider issues such as the position of the countries and the length of their borders.

- What areas might be considered a weakness in the buffer zone?
- Which sections do you think were most important to overall security?

b Make a list of all the countries and write one sentence on each that shows why they were important for Stalin to control.

> CAMBRIDGE IGCSE™ AND O LEVEL HISTORY OPTION B: COURSEBOOK

> **KEY FIGURE**
>
> **Imre Nagy (1896–1958)**
>
> Nagy participated in the 1917 Bolshevik Revolution in Russia, and was involved in the brief Soviet republic in Hungary in 1919. Forced to leave Hungary, he lived in the USSR from 1930 to 1944. However, unlike Rákosi he was not a Stalinist, and he wanted **reform**. He was arrested for his actions in 1956, and secretly executed for treason in 1958. Nagy was buried in an unmarked grave, which was only discovered in 1989. When he was given a proper burial, 100 000 people attended his funeral.

> **KEY TERM**
>
> **reform:** the desire to make changes to the political system and the way it works

6.1 Why was there opposition to Soviet control in Hungary in 1956 and Czechoslovakia in 1968, and how did the USSR react to this opposition?

The situation in Hungary

There were several reasons why Hungary was resistant to Soviet control in 1945. It was a strongly religious nation, and the Catholic Church was very powerful. Hungary had also been a joint partner in the Austro-Hungarian Empire from 1867 to 1918. Hungarians were nationalistic and preferred to be the rulers, not the ruled.

The Red Army occupied Hungary in the Second World War, but the Communist Party lost the election of 1945. Stalin rigged elections in 1947 to ensure that he controlled the government. His main ally in Hungary was Mátyás Rákosi. Rákosi was a communist who spent the Second World War in the USSR. He now led the government and persecuted all opposition ruthlessly. For example, in 1949 he imprisoned the head of the Hungarian Catholic Church, Cardinal Mindszenty. He also executed the foreign minister, László Rajk, in 1949. Although he was a communist, Rajk was critical of Stalin's attempts to control Hungary. In Rákosi's show trials, modelled on those of Stalin in the 1930s, around 100 000 Hungarians were sent to labour camps.

Rákosi's position was weakened when Stalin died in 1953. That year, anti-communist demonstrations in East Berlin were crushed by the police and the army. The USSR also withdrew troops from Austria, which had been stationed there since the end of the Second World War. Many people saw this as a sign that communism was being relaxed in Europe.

Rákosi lost his position as prime minister to fellow communist Imre Nagy. A power struggle began because Rákosi remained general secretary of the Hungarian Communist Party, while Nagy was prime minister. It seemed that Rákosi had won when he managed to remove Nagy from office in 1955.

Causes of opposition in 1956

While this power struggle was taking place in the capital of Hungary, Budapest, a similar one was going on in Moscow. After Stalin died in 1953, Nikita Khrushchev competed with other powerful figures for control of the government. By early 1956, it was clear that Khrushchev had won. He made a famous speech against Stalin in February of that year, in which he criticised the dictator's rule and admitted that mistakes had been made. Having Khrushchev in power in the USSR created a problem for all the Stalinist governments in Eastern Europe. Would they be able to continue as they had before?

KEY TERM

Politburo: the main government group in a communist country, which makes all the important decisions

KEY FIGURE

Nikita Khrushchev (1894–1971)

Khrushchev joined the Bolsheviks in 1918 and was loyal to Stalin in the 1930s. He joined the **Politburo** in 1939 and was a leading figure during the war. He managed to win control of the Communist Party after a long power struggle following Stalin's death. He led the USSR during a critical period in the Cold War before being removed from power in 1964. He was the only Soviet leader to die during the Cold War and not be buried at the Kremlin.

REVISION TIP

Organising information is a key skill. Keep a file with the names of all the key people you learn about during your studies. For each one, add a single sentence saying who they are and refer to this as you read through the information. It will help you to recall information on the leading individuals.

Khrushchev's attack on Stalin was so fierce that some people fainted in shock. Such disloyalty would have been punishable by death in Stalin's era, but now that Stalin was dead Khrushchev was announcing a change in direction. Although initially secret, Khrushchev deliberately allowed his speech to become public. There was an uprising in Poznán in Poland, in which 100 people died. Khrushchev considered using force to restore order, but eventually he decided to reach a deal with the Poles. As long as they stayed in the Warsaw Pact, he would allow more moderate communists to run the government. This brought the reformer Władysław Gomułka to power and calmed the situation in Poland.

Hungarian students demonstrated in sympathy with the protestors in Poland. As events gathered momentum, Rákosi was removed in July 1956. His replacement was another Stalinist, Ernő Gerő. Gerő was unable to control a campaign within the Hungarian Communist Party to correct the errors of the purges in 1949. There was a state funeral for Rajk on 6 October, which became a public demonstration. Up to 200 000 people took to the streets of Budapest to protest against almost a decade of Stalinist control by Moscow. Three weeks later, students rioted and tore down a statue of Stalin (see Source 6C). The police tried to restore order, but Hungarian soldiers took the side of the protestors. The situation became critical.

SOURCES 6B & 6C

Source 6B: A 15 year old Hungarian girl armed with a machine gun, 1956

Source 6C: Revolutionaries dismantling the statue of Stalin, October 1956

SOURCE ANALYSIS 6.2

Study Sources 6B and 6C. What can you infer from these pictures about the nature of Hungarian resistance to the USSR?

ACTIVITY 6.2

Imagine you are a news reader for Radio Free Europe. Write a script of maximum 100 words to describe the scenes you can see in Sources 6B and 6C. Think about what your audience would want to know and the language you need to use.

Khrushchev surrounded Budapest with Soviet soldiers, but he seemed to prefer a peaceful solution. He allowed Nagy to become prime minister and pass some reforms. Nagy promised free speech, democratic elections and the release of political prisoners such as Cardinal Mindszenty. However, unlike the situation in Poland, Hungarians were not pacified by these gains. Encouraged by broadcasts coming from **Radio Free Europe**, based in Munich, they continued the fight. These broadcasts gave the impression that western powers, especially the USA, would come to help.

Nagy had to decide whether to stay loyal to Moscow or back calls for more reform. On 1 November he took a fateful step. He announced that Hungary would leave the Warsaw Pact and asked the United Nations for help.

> **KEY TERM**
>
> **Radio Free Europe:** a radio station established in 1950 to provide radio broadcasts for people living in communist countries in Eastern Europe. It was funded by the US Congress, broadcast in fifteen different languages and reached tens of millions of people

SOURCE 6D

The Government of the Hungarian People's Republic has received trustworthy reports of the entrance of new Soviet military units into Hungary. The president of the Council of Ministers [. . .] objected to the entrance of new military units into Hungary. He demanded the immediate and fast withdrawal of the Soviet units. He announced to the Soviet ambassador that the Hungarian government was withdrawing from the Warsaw Pact, simultaneously declaring Hungary's neutrality, and that it was turning to the United Nations and asking the four Great Powers to help protect its neutrality.

Source 6D: An extract from a telegram issued by Imre Nagy to all foreign embassies in Hungary on 1 November 1956

THINKING SKILLS

Read Source 6D. Consider the source from the perspective of the United Nations and NATO.

- Why might this telegram cause them difficulty?
- How might they react to it?
- How do you think they *should* have reacted to it?
- How would you have reacted to it?

The Soviet response

This went too far for Khrushchev. At dawn on 4 November, he sent in 200 000 men and 4000 tanks. Fighting in Budapest lasted for a week. It is impossible to know the death total for certain, but the USSR lost around 700 soldiers and Hungarian death estimates range from 3000 to 30 000. Although the world was shocked, it was distracted by events in Egypt, where the UK and France were involved in the Suez Crisis, which was a major international crisis that also involved Israel. The promise of aid on Radio Free Europe proved false and Nagy was removed from power. He was replaced by Janos Kadar, who ruled the country for the next three decades.

Figure 6.2: Soviet tanks on the streets of Budapest, October 1956

SOURCE 6E

This fight is the fight for freedom by the Hungarian people against the Russian intervention, and it is possible that I shall only be able to stay at my post for one or two hours. The whole world will see how the Russian armed forces, contrary to all treaties and conventions, are crushing the resistance of the Hungarian people. They will also see how they are kidnapping the prime minister of a country, which is a member of the United Nations, taking him from the capital, and therefore it cannot be doubted at all that this is the most brutal form of intervention.

Source 6E: Nagy's final radio broadcast to the Hungarian people, 4 November 1956. A few hours later he was arrested.

SOURCE ANALYSIS 6.3

Read Source 6E. Do you think Nagy knew that he was going to fail when he made this statement? Select three short phrases from the source that support your answer.

FOCUS TASK 6.1

Why was there opposition to Soviet rule in Hungary? Create a table in which you list three different reasons. Against each reason, list specific evidence to support it from the information you have read in this section.

Swap tables with a partner, and compare and discuss your ideas. Did you come up with the same ideas? If not, justify your choices. Using both of your lists, discuss and agree which was the main reason and why.

Chapter 6, Key Question 6: How secure was the USSR's control over Eastern Europe, 1948–c.1989?

Key points

Resistance to Soviet rule in Hungary

- After the Second World War, Hungary was controlled by the USSR.
- When Stalin died in 1953, Nikita Khrushchev became leader of the USSR.
- Khrushchev's 'secret speech' led to calls for reform in Eastern Europe, and widespread protests against Soviet control in Hungary.
- Imre Nagy tried to take Hungary out of the Warsaw Pact, which led to Khrushchev sending in troops to restore Soviet control.

The situation in Czechoslovakia

Czechoslovakia was a new nation, created out of the Austro-Hungarian Empire in 1919. It was economically the strongest of the Eastern European countries, as it had well-developed industries and had prospered between 1919 and 1939. However, it was weakened by the Munich Treaty of 1938, when Hitler gained the Sudetenland from Czechoslovakia (see Chapter 3). Germany then invaded and captured Prague in 1939. The Czech people felt that they had been abandoned by the western powers, and this helped to create a strong communist underground movement in the country. After the war, communists nearly won a majority in the elections of 1946. Although not in power, they were given control of the police and the army after pressure on the new government from Moscow.

However, communists struggled to maintain popularity. Czechoslovakia was hit by the harsh economic conditions of the winter of 1946–47. When new elections were due to be held in 1948, Stalin ordered a complete government takeover by force. Two weeks later, the foreign minister, Jan Masaryk, died in mysterious circumstances when he fell from a window. Prime Minister Klement Gottwald – a strong ally of Moscow – blamed the West for Masaryk's alleged suicide. He introduced a Soviet-style constitution and banned all forms of political opposition.

Masaryk's death encouraged the US Congress to support the Marshall Plan (see Chapter 4). The US government realised that if Czechoslovakia could fall under communist control, then so might all other major European states. Stalin denied the Czech government Marshall Aid, which caused resentment over the loss of independence.

> ### REFLECTION
>
> Working individually and working with a partner are both effective ways to learn, but they are different experiences. Which do you prefer and why? Think about the reasons you identified by yourself for opposition to Soviet rule in Hungary and the ones your partner had. If there was a difference in your thinking, what was it and why? For the reason you had to agree as the main one, how did you reach that decision? Learning how to work collaboratively is an important skill in school and in later life. Think about how you can get more out of working with someone else.

KEY FIGURE

Jan Masaryk (1886–1948)

Jan Masaryk was the son of Czechoslovakia's founder, Tomas Masaryk. He became a politician and served as foreign minister of Czechoslovakia from 1940 until his death in 1948. He was a popular liberal and the only non-communist in the Czech government. He was under huge pressure at the time of his death, but there were many unusual aspects of his apparent suicide. For example, the doctor who examined his body died two weeks later, again as the result of an apparent suicide.

THINK LIKE A HISTORIAN

History is full of mysteries. It is often impossible for historians to be certain what really happened in certain cases, such as Masaryk's death or the Reichstag Fire (see Chapter 7). Evidence might point towards a conclusion, but it is only indirect (or 'circumstantial').

How much evidence do you think we need in order to be certain about what happened? How can we know that something is true or not? Think about legal cases today. To win a case, lawyers have to *prove* that something did or did not happen 'beyond a reasonable doubt'. If you were a lawyer presenting Masaryk's case to court today, do you think you would be able to prove what happened beyond a reasonable doubt?

ACTIVITY 6.3

Given what you know about the consequences of Masaryk's death, do you think it was ordered by the Soviets? Or did he really die by suicide? Have a class discussion on this issue. At the end, take a vote on which explanation seems most likely.

Causes of opposition to Soviet Rule

Despite these issues there was little disturbance in Czechoslovakia. Poland, Hungary and East Germany had all shown their discontent from 1953 to 1956 in the period after Stalin died, but Czech protests were more restrained. The poet and playwright Václav Havel wrote anti-totalitarian plays in the 1960s and was twice imprisoned for his outspoken political views. Attitudes hardened in the mid-1960s because the economy was clearly failing. Housing was poor, wages were low, and attempts at reform by the government all failed.

Complaints against the government became more prominent in 1966. Reformist groups wanted change, but they were careful to learn the lessons of the Hungarian uprising of 1956. Their aim was not to end communism, but to relax it. Student protests were held throughout 1967, demanding that Communist Party leader Antonín Novotný (leader since Gottwald's death in 1953) be removed from power. In January 1968, Novotný was replaced as First Secretary of the Communist Party by the reformer Alexander Dubček.

Chapter 6, Key Question 6: How secure was the USSR's control over Eastern Europe, 1948–c.1989?

> **FOCUS TASK 6.2**
>
> In pairs, discuss the following questions.
>
> - What similarities do you notice between the situations in Czechoslovakia and Hungary?
>
> - Why was it difficult for Moscow to establish support for communism in the two countries?
>
> On your own, write one paragraph in answer to each question. Swap your writing with your partner and give each other feedback. Note two 'what went well' (WWW) points and one 'even better if' (EBI) point. Swap back and revise your paragraphs to improve them based on the feedback.

Prague Spring, 1968

In April 1968, Dubček introduced a number of reforms, starting a period known as the Prague Spring. He described his policies as 'socialism with a human face'. Dubček hoped to show that socialist (in this context, communist) policies could be more about human needs than power politics.

By this time, the leader of the USSR was Leonid Brezhnev, who had replaced Khrushchev in 1964. Dubček tried to make it clear that he did not intend to end communism or leave the Warsaw Pact. However, his reforms were extensive, and included the following.

- Freedom of speech was permitted; newspapers could criticise the government.
- Czechoslovaks were allowed to travel abroad to visit countries beyond the Iron Curtain.
- Businesses could run themselves, rather than being told what to produce by the government.
- Workers' councils could be formed, like trade unions.
- A new parliament was to be freely elected.

Brezhnev's reaction was predictably negative. In July 1968, senior Soviet leaders visited Prague and warned Dubček about the possible consequences of his reforms. Military preparations were being made, just as they had been in 1956 over Hungary.

The Soviet invasion and its consequences

Much like Nagy, Dubček was emboldened by domestic support for his reforms. He turned to Romania (led by Nicolai Ceauşescu) and Yugoslavia (led by Tito). Both men were willing to stand up to Moscow, and Dubček hoped that they could unite against Brezhnev, but he had miscalculated. In August, Brezhnev carried out his threat and sent in 200 000 troops and 2000 tanks to capture Prague. There was far less violence than in Budapest in 1956, although 72 protestors were killed. The Czech government was overthrown. Dubček was arrested, but was not executed. He returned to politics in 1989 when communist rule collapsed in Czechoslovakia.

There were two main domestic consequences:

- An estimated 150 000 people managed to escape Czechoslovakia into Austria and Germany during the Soviet invasion, as security temporarily collapsed on the border.
- A lone protest was made by a student called Jan Palach. He died after setting fire to himself in Wenceslas Square.

Externally there were two main consequences:

- The Chinese were furious with Brezhnev. They had disapproved of the Hungarian invasion of 1956, and this made the relationship between Russia and Beijing even worse. Shots were exchanged along the Chinese–Soviet border and the following years saw tension increase almost to the point of war.
- The crushing of the Prague Spring gave rise to the Brezhnev Doctrine, which stated that Moscow had the right to interfere with military force if any country in Eastern Europe attempted to abandon communism. When this doctrine was eventually abandoned by Mikhail Gorbachev it was a critical factor in the end of the Cold War.

Figure 6.3: Residents of Prague surround tanks in the streets during the invasion, August 1968

Chapter 6, Key Question 6: How secure was the USSR's control over Eastern Europe, 1948–c.1989?

SOURCE 6F

"She Might Have Invaded Russia"

Source 6F: A cartoon from September 1968 by Herblock of the *Washington Post* showing Brezhnev (right) crushing the Prague Spring

SOURCE ANALYSIS 6.4

Study Source 6F.

a What is the message of this cartoon?

b How does the cartoonist convey this message?

Key points

- Like Hungary, Czechoslovakia had been independent before the Second World War.
- After the war, Stalin established control and prevented Czechoslovakia from having support from the USA.
- Czechoslovakia did not react as strongly as the rest of Eastern Europe when Khrushchev came to power after Stalin's death.
- The 1968 Prague Spring was an attempt to introduce moderate reforms.
- Even this was unacceptable to the new Soviet leader, Leonid Brezhnev, who used force to crush opposition in Czechoslovakia.

6.2 How similar were events in Hungary in 1956 and in Czechoslovakia in 1968?

Historians often take two different examples and study them side by side to identify similarities and differences. This is called a comparative analysis. In this topic, you will do a comparative analysis of events in Hungary and Czechoslovakia. Before reading on, look at Focus task 6.3.

> ### FOCUS TASK 6.3
>
> Create a table like this.
>
> | | Similarities between 1956 and 1968 | Differences between 1956 and 1968 |
> |---|---|---|
> | Causes | | |
> | Events | | |
> | Consequences | | |
>
> Write down one example in each box to show similarities and differences between the Hungarian uprising and the Prague Spring in their causes, main events and their consequences. You can keep the reasons brief but base them on what you have read so far. When you have finished, read on to see if your reasons match the ones discussed in the text that follows.

Similarities in causes

In both cases there was a battle to control the government between leaders who were close to Moscow and leaders who were sympathetic to public opinion. In Hungary this was between Rákosi and Nagy. In Czechoslovakia, it was between Gottwald and Masaryk in 1948, and then in 1967–68 between Novotný and Dubček.

Both countries had reasons to resent direct control by Moscow. Hungary was very religious and nationalistic. Czechoslovakia had a strong economy and a developed sense of capitalism.

Differences in causes

Hungary was a reaction to events in the USSR (the death of Stalin) and in Poland. What began as a sympathy protest for Polish people developed into demands for their own freedom. In Prague, the causes were economic weakness and poor standards of living, rather than events elsewhere.

The two events were separated by 12 years. Hungarian people still thought that they could leave the Warsaw Pact (and communism) once Stalin died. The Czech people knew in 1968 that this was not possible, so their aims were less radical. They also knew there would be no outside support because of US involvement in Vietnam (see Chapter 5).

Similarities in events

In both cases, there was an alliance of reform-minded communists and those who were more nationalistic. Both groups agreed that their country should have more freedom from Moscow. Also, students were central to the protests in both Budapest and Prague.

The USSR allowed the situation to develop up to a point, then used lethal force to crush opposition. Khrushchev and Brezhnev were alike in that they could not allow a breach in the buffer zone, so they used violent methods to assert Moscow's authority.

Figure 6.4: Student protesters in Prague, handing out literature encouraging rebellion against Soviet rule, September 1968

Differences in events

The Prague Spring was perhaps less of a threat than Nagy's reforms. Dubček never intended to leave the Warsaw Pact. Nagy, on the other hand, would have left the Warsaw Pact and appealed to the United Nations.

The Hungarians believed that they would win outside support because of broadcasts on Radio Free Europe. This meant that there was far more violence and a higher number of deaths in Hungary than in Czechoslovakia.

Similarities in consequences

In each case, the events led to a strengthening of Moscow's control over the buffer zone, while the authority of the West was weakened. The USA failed to support Hungary in 1956 in part because of the Suez Crisis and they failed to support the Czechoslovaks in 1968 due to Vietnam. (Fear of starting a third world war was also an issue, of course.) The consequence of this was that opponents of communism knew they would have to do things for themselves in the future.

Both countries had to wait until the late 1980s before they could show opposition to communism again.

Differences in consequences

The number of deaths in Budapest was far higher than in Prague. The consequences for the leaders were also different: Nagy was executed; Dubček was not.

Interestingly, Brezhnev used Warsaw Pact forces in Prague whereas Khrushchev used Soviet forces in Budapest. Moscow was aware in the late 1960s that it had to show a united Eastern European stance against opposition.

> **REVISION TIP**
>
> The comparative analysis method you have used here works well for other aspects of the Cold War. Try using it for learning about the wars in Korea and Vietnam in Chapter 5.

> **FOCUS TASK 6.4**
>
> Look back at your table from Focus task 6.3.
>
> a Were your similarities and differences the same as in the text?
>
> b Now that you have finished reading about the two events, which do you think are stronger, the similarities or the differences? Write a paragraph explaining your answer.
>
> c Have a class discussion about your findings to secure your understanding of these two events, their similarities and their differences.

> **SOURCE 6G**
>
> *I must say, I am convinced that you must share some of the blame for your present situation.*
>
> **Source 6G:** An extract from an open letter written by Václav Havel to Alexander Dubček, August 1969

> **SOURCE ANALYSIS 6.5**
>
> Read the short extract in Source 6G.
>
> a Is Havel's analysis fair? Why, or why not?
>
> b Could the same be said for Nagy in Hungary? Explain your answer.

> **THINK LIKE A HISTORIAN**
>
> Something that many people have to do as part of their job is a risk assessment. This involves making a list of all the possible risks that you might face in planning an activity or an event, and then thinking of ways you can reduce those risks.
>
> Think about the events of 1956 and 1968 from the USA's perspective. What might their risk assessment look like, in terms of getting involved in defending the people of Hungary and Czechoslovakia? What might the consequences of taking greater action have been in each case?

6.3 Why was the Berlin Wall built in 1961?

The Berlin Blockade of 1948–49 escalated tensions in Europe (see Chapter 4). However, when Eisenhower became US president in 1953, he took a more relaxed attitude to Berlin than Truman had. On a visit to Britain in 1956, Khrushchev told the media: 'You do not like communism. We do not like capitalism. There is only one way out – peaceful co-existence.'

Eisenhower was hopeful of working with Khrushchev to decrease Cold War rivalry if they could find a solution over Berlin. However, events in the late 1950s meant that tension actually increased.

Inter-Continental Ballistic Missiles

Events in Hungary in 1956 showed Khrushchev's brutal side. The Soviet leader was volatile and unpredictable, and the West had no idea how to handle him. At a meeting of the United Nations in 1960 he famously interrupted a speech by the British prime minister, Harold Macmillan, several times by slamming his fists on the table. A week later Khrushchev insulted the Philippine delegate by allegedly taking off his shoe and hammering the desk with it. His erratic behaviour was particularly worrying because of the development of Inter-Continental Ballistic Missiles (ICBMs) in the arms race. These rockets had first been developed by the USSR in 1958 to carry explosives, including nuclear explosives. The USA followed in 1959, and in 1962 the USA developed the sophisticated Minuteman missiles, which were capable of crossing continents. With the development of these weapons, any political crisis could have more serious military effects than perhaps was the case in the late 1940s.

Figure 6.5: One of the USA's ICBMs on display at a theme park, being viewed by a group of high school students, May 1959

The situation in East Germany

East Germany's population had fallen to 17 million by 1961. It was the only Eastern European country to have a decreasing population. Approximately 2.8 million people had escaped from the communist world by going to West Berlin up to 1961, as there was no physical separation of the zones, including many skilled workers and intellectuals. This exodus was harming the East German economy and costing the USSR money. So, Khrushchev made finding a solution a priority.

Eisenhower did not want to find himself in the same situation as Truman, where a crisis over Berlin could escalate into a major war. In November 1958, Khrushchev demanded that foreign military powers withdraw from Berlin within six months. Eisenhower responded with a different proposal. He suggested that Berlin should be controlled by the United Nations and that both sides should withdraw.

While this would reduce the possibility of conflict, it did not solve the Soviet problem of emigration to the West through Berlin. Yet Khrushchev was still keen to discuss Eisenhower's idea. He became the first Soviet leader to visit the USA when he arrived for a tour in September 1959. The trip was a great success, and the two men agreed to meet again for talks in Paris in 1960.

The U2 incident

The KGB (the Soviet international spy agency) was aware of U2 flights over the USSR. These specialist spy planes, developed for the CIA, could reach heights of 70 000 feet and their cameras could get a clear image of a piece of ground that was only 76 cm wide. The USSR could detect the planes on radar but could not shoot them down as they were too high up. However, in May 1960, new Soviet S-75 anti-aircraft defences damaged a U2 plane. The pilot, Gary Powers, parachuted to the ground and was captured.

At first, Eisenhower denied that the plane had been spying. The official line was that it was a weather plane that had gone off-track. Khrushchev paraded the pilot on Soviet television, exposing the lie. Eisenhower admitted the truth but refused to apologise. In response, Khrushchev cancelled his summit meeting with Eisenhower.

Eisenhower had served his second term as president and John F. Kennedy won the election in 1960. He promised to take a tougher line with Moscow.

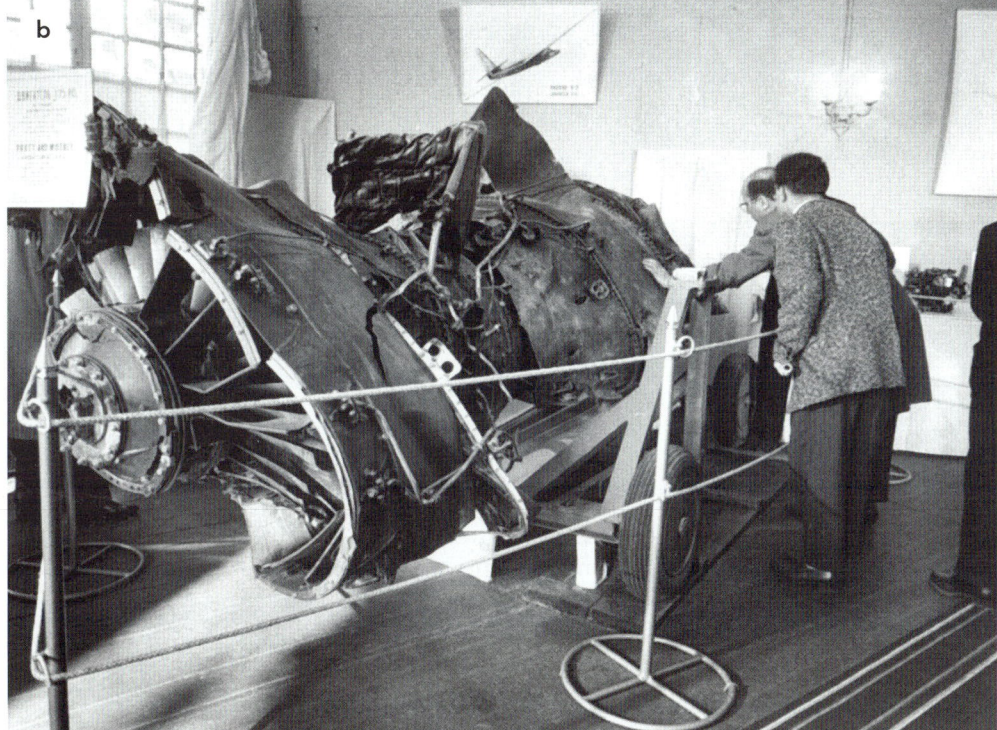

Chapter 6, Key Question 6: How secure was the USSR's control over Eastern Europe, 1948–c.1989?

Figure 6.6 a–b A U2 spy plane, and the wreckage of the U2 shot down over the USSR in May 1960; the US government claimed it was a weather plane

THINKING SKILLS

Read the information about the U2 incident again and look at the two pictures on this page.

- If you were in Eisenhower's position, how would you have handled the incident?
- Now consider the same situation from Khrushchev's position.
- How would you feel, and how would you respond?

FOCUS TASK 6.5

Who was more to blame for the breakdown of relations from 1958 to 1961, the USA or the USSR? Create a table or other graphic organiser to record points attributing blame to each side, with reasons and justifications. Decide who you have more evidence against. In pairs, discuss your findings. Do you agree with each other? Why, or why not? After your discussion, add or change your graphic organiser if you want to. Then write a short paragraph summarising your findings.

Kennedy and Khrushchev: the Vienna summit, 1961

The relationship between Kennedy and Khrushchev was more like the situation had been in the early days of the Cold War. The two men were due to meet for the first time at the Vienna summit in June 1961. Just before this meeting, the CIA failed in an attempted invasion of Cuba to overthrow Fidel Castro's government (see Chapter 5). The same month, the Soviets had another major propaganda victory when Yuri Gagarin became the first man in space.

Vienna marked one of the lowest points in the US–Soviet relationship. Khrushchev attacked Kennedy over Berlin. He banged his fist on the table and shouted: 'I want peace but if you want war that is your problem!' Kennedy responded: 'It will be a cold winter.' Straight after the meeting Kennedy increased US military spending by $3.25 billion.

On 25 July, Kennedy addressed the people of the USA in a televised speech. He warned: 'We seek peace but we shall not surrender.' With so much tension and fear over Berlin, the movement of people to the west of the city became a stampede. Over a thousand people each day **defected** through West Berlin.

> **KEY TERM**
>
> **defect:** to leave a country, region or political party, often to join an opposing one

Building the Berlin Wall

Khrushchev chaired a meeting of Warsaw Pact leaders in Moscow, including East Germany's communist leader, Walter Ulbricht. Ulbricht was instructed to build a wall around West Berlin (keeping its citizens penned in), but not to cut off western access to the city. Overnight on Sunday 13 August 1961, workers began putting up barbed wire and concrete pillars as Soviet tanks stood close by. By the time the news reached Washington, the city was already physically separated.

Many West Berliners had been out in the East that night, at clubs or restaurants, or visiting family. They were forbidden to return home, and found themselves stranded in East Berlin. Many tried to swim across the river or even jump from buildings to get back to West Berlin. Three days later, the barbed wire was replaced with a concrete wall 1.8 metres high. West Berliners could visit the East if they had a special visa. There were seven checkpoints at which they could cross. East Berliners could visit the West with special permission too, but they could only pass at the point where the US and Soviet zones met: Checkpoint Charlie.

The Wall ran for 166 kilometres around the perimeter of West Berlin. It separated families, and even the underground rail network was shut down. The sewers were blocked and booby-trapped to stop people from escaping through them. Over time, the Berlin Wall became more heavily fortified. There were electric fences, guard towers with **snipers**, **landmines** and many other features. The Soviets called it the 'Anti-Fascist Defence Wall' because it was supposedly protecting them from future German or western aggression.

> **KEY TERMS**
>
> **sniper:** someone who shoots at people from a hidden position
>
> **landmine:** a bomb on or under the ground, which explodes when someone steps on it or when a vehicle drives over it

Chapter 6, Key Question 6: How secure was the USSR's control over Eastern Europe, 1948–c.1989?

Figure 6.7: Workers constructing the concrete block Berlin Wall, November 1961

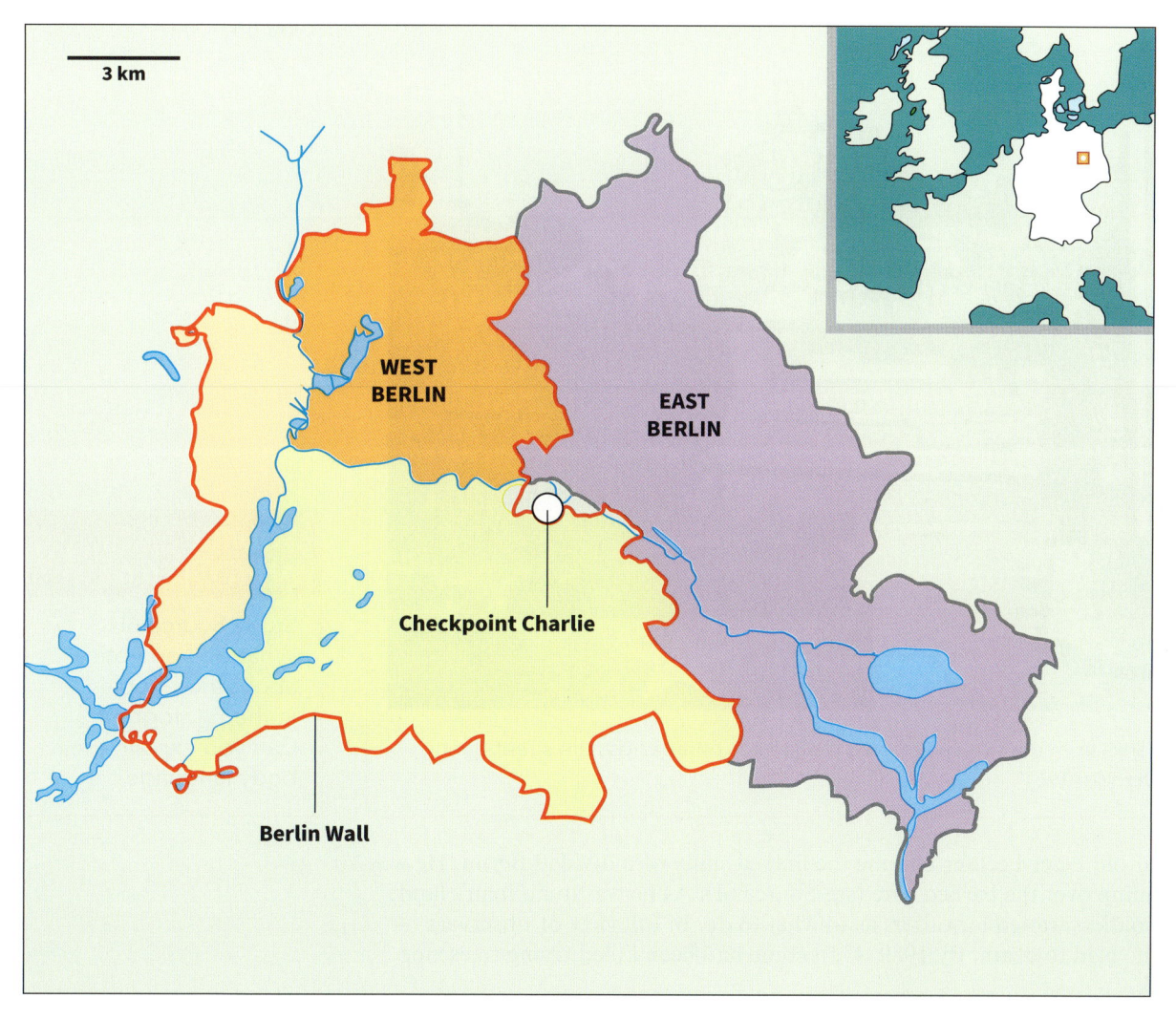

Figure 6.8: A map showing the location and extent of the Berlin Wall when it was completed

The US response and the crisis of October

Despite pressure from the mayor of West Berlin, Willy Brandt, Kennedy did not act. The Soviets had not completely cut off the city (as they had in 1948) and no clear act of aggression had taken place. The president did reappoint the main figure of the airlift, General Clay, and sent 1500 US troops along the Autobahn from West Germany to increase the garrison. The Soviets did not stop them. In public, Kennedy spoke in support of West Berliners but in private he was not willing to risk war.

However, a crisis erupted in October 1961 after a trivial incident. A US official and his wife were denied entry to East Berlin, where they were due to see a play. General Clay was outraged and sent tanks to Checkpoint Charlie. Soon, Soviet tanks appeared as well. A short distance separated them, with guns pointed at one another for 16 hours. At the height of the crisis, Kennedy managed to send word to Khrushchev that he would withdraw if the Soviets did. They agreed and the crisis passed, but the world had come close to war over Berlin again.

SOURCE 6H

Source 6H: Tanks from the two superpowers face each other across the street during the crisis of October 1961

In 1962, 18 year old Peter Fechter became the first casualty of a divided Berlin. He was shot trying to jump over the barbed wire (see Source 6I). As he was in no man's land, East German soldiers waited for orders as to what to do. In full view of observers on both sides, he bled to death. By 1989, 171 people had been killed trying to escape across the Wall.

THINKING SKILLS

On the internet, search for a video called 'Walled In: The Inner German Border' by Die Welt (DW) English. Consider the impact that the Wall had on the daily lives of Berliners. Imagine you were one of the people in East Berlin who had been separated from your family in West Berlin. What impact would the Berlin Wall have on your life? What would you do?

SOURCE ANALYSIS 6.6

Study Source 6H. What do you notice about the people in the photograph? Can you explain their body language?

Chapter 6, Key Question 6: How secure was the USSR's control over Eastern Europe, 1948–c.1989?

SOURCES 6I & 6J

Source 6I: Peter Fechter's body in no man's land, 17 August 1962

Source 6J: East German border guard Hans Conrad Schumann spontaneously jumped the fence on 15 August 1961 – the day before construction began on the Wall

SOURCE ANALYSIS 6.7

Study Sources 6I and 6J. How might the USSR explain these incidents? Relate your answer to the Soviet name for the Berlin Wall: the 'Anti-Fascist Defence Wall'.

243

> CAMBRIDGE IGCSE™ AND O LEVEL HISTORY OPTION B: COURSEBOOK

ACTIVITY 6.4

a Look back at the information about the Berlin Blockade in Chapter 4. Now review what you have learnt about the building of the Berlin Wall and compare the two events. Construct a knowledge organiser to record your thoughts about which incident was more serious and why.

b Using your notes, have a class debate about the two incidents. Consider these questions.

- Who was the aggressor on each occasion?
- Which leader out of Stalin, Truman, Eisenhower, Khrushchev and Kennedy handled the situation over Berlin most effectively?
- Now think about the rest of the world. Would non-aligned countries have been more sympathetic to the USA or the USSR?

REFLECTION

It is easy to confuse the Berlin Blockade and the Berlin Wall. We often have misconceptions about things in any subject, and history is the same. When you find things confusing, what steps do you take to address misconceptions? How do you organise information so that it is clear and makes sense to you?

FOCUS TASK 6.6

The word 'causation' refers to the causes of events. These are often broken down into short term and long term. Short-term causes are the events that happened immediately before, and longer-term causes are the factors that happened further back (usually many years before).

In pairs, identify and describe two short-term and two long-term causes of the building of the Berlin Wall. Join up with another pair and compare your thoughts. Justify your ideas.

6.4 What was the significance of Solidarity in Poland for the decline of Soviet influence in Eastern Europe?

Poland was a problem for the USSR. It was the largest country in the buffer zone, with a population of 26 million when Stalin died. Around 95% of the country was Catholic, so they resisted the communist idea that religion was a myth. Protests in 1956 brought Władysław Gomułka to power, and he ruled until 1970. However, the economy was not growing. In 1970, Gomułka was replaced by Edvard Gierek after protests about rising bread prices. The population had risen to 35 million by 1979, so huge financial assistance was needed. The USSR gave $3 billion per year to keep the Polish economy working.

In summer 1980, there was a large strike in Gdansk, again over food prices. During the strike, 45 people were killed by soldiers. Gierek was removed and replaced by Stanisław Kania. However, wages remained low, food was in short supply and unrest was growing.

As Brezhnev entered his final years, the Soviet state was becoming increasingly corrupt. Its main focus for foreign policy was Afghanistan. Soviet troops invaded Afghanistan in 1979 and stayed for a decade.

Chapter 6, Key Question 6: How secure was the USSR's control over Eastern Europe, 1948–c.1989?

> **SOURCE 6K**
>
> *Stalin, Khrushchev and Brezhnev are travelling in a train. The train breaks down.*
>
> *'Fix it!' orders Stalin.*
>
> *They repair it but still the train doesn't move.*
>
> *'Shoot everyone!' orders Stalin. They shoot everyone but still the train doesn't budge.*
>
> *Stalin dies.*
>
> *'Rehabilitate everyone!' orders Khrushchev.*
>
> *They are rehabilitated, but still the train won't go. Khrushchev is removed.*
>
> *'Close the curtains,' orders Brezhnev, 'and pretend we're moving!'*
>
> **Source 6K:** A Russian joke about the different Soviet leaders

> **SOURCE ANALYSIS 6.8**
>
> Read Source 6K. What can you infer from this source about the leadership styles of Stalin, Khrushchev and Brezhnev?

Solidarity (*Solidarnosc*), 1980–89

The situation in Poland was more complicated for Moscow to control than it had been in Hungary or Czechoslovakia. There were four main reasons for this.

- In 1956 and 1968, the solution had been to change the leaders. In Poland, Gomułka and Gierek had been replaced, yet problems continued.
- The Soviet economy was also struggling in the 1980s, a problem worsened by the cost of the war in Afghanistan.
- In 1978, the Archbishop of Krakow, Karol Wojtyłłam, was elected Pope John Paul II, the first Polish pope. He visited Poland in 1979 to emotional scenes. Around 2 million people lined the streets of Warsaw to welcome him.
- In 1980, Ronald Reagan was elected president of the USA. He was far more aggressive towards communism than his predecessors and raised hopes in Eastern Europe that he might do more than previous presidents.

> **SOURCE 6L**
>
> **Source 6L:** Pope John Paul II being greeted by the Polish people in Krakow, during his tour of Poland in 1979

> **SOURCE ANALYSIS 6.9**
>
> Study Source 6L.
>
> a What does this image tell you about Pope John Paul II?
>
> b What impression might this photograph have made on the leaders of the USSR?

> ## FOCUS TASK 6.7
>
> Do some further research on how the Polish Pope John Paul II's popularity undermined Soviet authority in Eastern Europe. Write a paragraph summarising what you have discovered. In your paragraph, consider the extent to which he was responsible for the eventual collapse of communism.
>
> Exchange your paragraph with a partner and give each other feedback on what you have written. Then improve your answer based on your partner's feedback.

Following the strikes in the summer, a new trade union called Solidarity was formed in Gdansk by a local electrician called Lech Wałęsa. It soon had 9 million members. The government banned Solidarity, but the Polish Supreme Court declared in November 1980 that it was a legal organisation. The government had to come to an agreement with Solidarity. Trade unions and the strikes were permitted, as well as increases in pay and pensions. This was an amazing victory for Polish workers.

> ## KEY FIGURE
>
> ### Lech Wałęsa (b. 1943)
>
> Wałęsa worked as a mechanic, then as an electrician. He became active in the trade union movement in the 1970s and was targeted by the government because of this. He led the Gdansk shipyard strike in 1980 and won greater rights for workers. He was awarded the Nobel Peace Prize in 1983, and continued to protest against communist rule. He was a proud Catholic and won support from Pope John Paul II. When communism collapsed, Wałęsa became president of Poland, and served from 1990 to 1995 in this role.

Over the winter, Brezhnev considered sending in troops as he had done in Prague in 1968. However, instead he decided to remove Kania and appoint a military ruler who could break Solidarity's power: General Jaruzelski. In 1981, Jaruzelski declared **martial law** and took serious action against strikes. In one incident, a mine in Upper Silesia was flooded by riot police. The miners on strike were below ground so they all drowned. Jaruzelski also imprisoned Wałęsa and the other leaders of Solidarity. None of these measures broke the movement. Wałęsa was released under pressure from the public.

In 1984, the government faced a significant crisis over a priest called Jerzy Popiełuszko, who had links to Solidarity. He had been beaten to death in jail by police. Around 250 000 people attended his funeral. In 1988, a nationwide campaign of strikes paralysed Poland's economy.

Jaruzelski had failed to get popular support for his economic reforms and now the mood across Europe was changing. Free elections were finally held in Poland in June 1989. Solidarity won 99 out of 100 seats in the Senate. Jaruzelski was forced to bring them into his government. One year later, with communist regimes collapsing across Eastern Europe, Lech Wałęsa was elected as president of Poland.

> ## KEY TERM
>
> **martial law:** the control of a city or country by the military rather than by its usual leaders

Chapter 6, Key Question 6: How secure was the USSR's control over Eastern Europe, 1948–c.1989?

Figure 6.9: Thousands of Polish people gather to show support for Wałęsa and Solidarity during the 1990 election

ACTIVITY 6.5

Work in groups of three. Research and write a news report about the problems developing in Poland in the 1980s. In your script, you should:

- set out the key facts using the information in this chapter
- include Wałęsa, Jaruzelski and Pope John Paul II, plus any other people you think are important
- select at least three key facts from the text to inform your story.

If possible, film your report, with one of your group as the main news presenter, one as a reporter based in Poland and another as a reporter based in Moscow. The final report should be no more than two minutes long.

Share your news reports with the class and give each other feedback.

Why did Solidarity succeed?

When analysing the reasons for Solidarity's success, you can organise the information into two categories: internal factors and external factors.

Internal factors:

- The cost of living was too high, especially food prices, and aid from the USSR prevented the economy from growing as there was no incentive to try new methods.

- Lech Wałęsa proved to be a formidable opponent for Jaruzelski, and Pope John Paul II was a hero in Poland. Many Poles attribute the collapse of communism to the power of Catholicism.

- The extent of support for Solidarity and its organisation were vital. Events in Hungary and Czechoslovakia were quite uncoordinated in comparison. With 9 million members – a quarter of the population – the government could not arrest everyone involved.

External factors:

- The Polish people received strong backing from US president Ronald Reagan and British prime minister Margaret Thatcher. She visited a shipyard in Gdansk in 1988 during the strike campaign.

- Solidarity was seen in a similar light to other great freedom movements of the period. The main one was the African National Congress (ANC) in South Africa, which fought against racism and injustice, and was led by Nelson Mandela, who spent 27 years in jail fighting for his beliefs. Mandela was one of the most famous political leaders in the world, and he and Wałęsa were often mentioned in the same context by the media.

- The USSR had a crisis of leadership in the early 1980s. Brezhnev died in 1982 and was followed by two leaders in quick succession. Yuri Andropov died in 1984 and Konstantin Chernenko died in 1985. There was no question of Moscow sending in the military to impose order, especially with soldiers committed in Afghanistan from 1979 to 1989.

ACTIVITY 6.6

a Using the internal and external factors listed, create a mind map showing the relationship between all the reasons for Solidarity's success. In pairs, compare your mind maps and then decide whether you need to add any new information to yours.

b Which do you think was more important: the internal or external factors?

c Research Lech Wałęsa online and make some notes about him. Was he more influential in Poland than Pope John Paul II? Give reasons for your answer.

FOCUS TASK 6.8

Why did Solidarity in Poland prove more difficult for the USSR to contain than events in Hungary in 1956 or Czechoslovakia in 1968? Discuss your ideas in small groups. Make a note of your ideas and the reasons different group members give.

6.5 How far was Gorbachev personally responsible for the collapse of Soviet control over Eastern Europe?

The Soviet Union experienced economic problems in the 1970s and 1980s. Corruption became a serious issue under Brezhnev. The old system of planning economic growth under five-year plans was heavily criticised. It prevented new methods and innovation at a time when the wider world was seeing huge changes with the development of microchip technology. These pressures had to be dealt with by new leader, Mikhail Gorbachev, who came to power in 1985, marking the start of a period of significant change. Gorbachev's reforms were designed to modernise and improve communism,

Chapter 6, Key Question 6: How secure was the USSR's control over Eastern Europe, 1948–c.1989?

but in fact communism collapsed by 1991. Was it Gorbachev's fault, or was the situation already past the point of saving?

KEY FIGURE

Mikhail Gorbachev 1931–2022

Gorbachev was born into a peasant family in a village in the Caucasus. His first job was as an assistant to a combine harvester operator, but he studied law in Moscow and was a youth leader in the Communist Party. He was the youngest member of the main decision-making body, the Politburo, when he joined in 1980. He took over as leader in 1985 and introduced significant changes in a bid to modernise the USSR and save communism. He won the Nobel Peace Prize in 1990, but lost power in 1991. When he ran for election as president, he came seventh and won only 0.5% of the vote. His wife Raisa was a significant figure in this period too.

SOURCE 6M

Source 6M: Mikhail Gorbachev meeting workers in Moscow, 1985

SOURCE ANALYSIS 6.10

Look at Source 6M. What does this photograph suggest about Gorbachev's leadership style compared to previous Soviet leaders such as Stalin and Brezhnev?

Gorbachev's reforms

Two major reforms were introduced by Gorbachev.

- *Perestroika* – this means 'restructuring'. The aim was to breathe life into the economy and encourage new ideas. Workers could set up their own businesses from 1986 as central planning was abolished.

- *Glasnost* – this means 'openness'. This allowed greater freedom of speech and an end to punishing critics of the government. In 1986, the prominent critic Andrei Sakharov, a famous physicist, was released from prison. An elected parliament called the Congress of People's Deputies was also introduced.

249

These reforms had a huge impact on Soviet life. Criticism poured out and party leaders at all levels were challenged for their corruption and incompetence.

Gorbachev also changed the USSR's foreign policy. He met Reagan and Thatcher at summits in Geneva in 1985 and Reykjavik in 1986. These meetings focused on reducing weapons stockpiles and ending the war in Afghanistan. In 1987, the Intermediate Nuclear Forces (INF) Treaty was signed, which led to 2692 missiles being destroyed by 1991. However, the most crucial step for Eastern Europe was Gorbachev's speech to the United Nations in December 1988 (see Source 6N). He announced massive cuts in Soviet weapons and forces stationed in Eastern Europe, signalling the end of the Brezhnev Doctrine.

SOURCE 6N

The relations between the Soviet Union and the United States of America have a history of five and a half decades. As the world changed, so did the nature, role and place of those relations in world politics. For too long a time they developed along the lines of confrontation and sometimes animosity – either overt or covert. But in the last few years the entire world could breathe a sigh of relief thanks to the changes for the better in the substance and the atmosphere of the relationship between Moscow and Washington.

Source 6N: An extract from Gorbachev's speech to the United Nations, 7 December 1988

SOURCE ANALYSIS 6.11

Read Source 6N.

a What do you think Gorbachev meant when he said that relations between the USSR and the USA 'developed along the lines of confrontation and sometimes animosity – either overt or covert'?

b Do you think Stalin and Truman would agree with what Gorbachev says in this source? Explain your thinking.

FOCUS TASK 6.9

Why did relations improve between Moscow and Washington in the 1980s? Make a list of reasons and put them in order of importance. Now discuss them in a group. After you have reviewed each other's lists, rewrite yours, adding in new factors, and making a new order of importance.

Consequences in Eastern Europe

At a meeting with Eastern European leaders in March 1989, Gorbachev confirmed that he was abandoning the Brezhnev Doctrine. This meant that Eastern European states would have to find their own solutions for dealing with domestic opposition. As with Khrushchev's 'secret speech' in 1956, expectations had been raised and soon there were challenges. Hungary opened its borders to allow free movement into Austria, breaching the Iron Curtain, and Solidarity won the Polish elections. The most striking protest was the 'Baltic Chain', formed on 'Black Ribbon Day' on 23 August 1989, an international day of protest against human rights violations in the USSR. The cities of Tallinn, Riga and Vilnius were linked together by a 675 kilometre human chain of 2 million people. It was a clear challenge to Soviet authority.

Chapter 6, Key Question 6: How secure was the USSR's control over Eastern Europe, 1948–c.1989?

SOURCE 6O

Source 6O: The Baltic Chain, an example of non-violent protest, August 1989

> **SOURCE ANALYSIS 6.12**
>
> Compare the Baltic Chain protest shown in Source 6O to those in Hungary in 1956 (Sources 6B and 6C). Why was the non-violent protest more effective as a means of criticising the USSR?

The moment that symbolised the end of the Cold War took place in Berlin. The East German communist leader, Erich Honecker, was removed in October 1989. Reforms were being considered by the new leader Egon Krenz, such as allowing East Germans to emigrate permanently.

In a day of confusion on 9 November, a press conference was held where an official suddenly announced that Berliners could move across the checkpoints without a passport or permit. He had misread the document he had been given, and the consequence was enormous. That night, 2 million Berliners flooded the checkpoints and crossed the divide. Bemused soldiers watched as they started to pull the wall down. Twenty-eight years of separation ended overnight.

Demonstrations in Czechoslovakia that month brought about a peaceful change known as the 'Velvet Revolution' (or the 'Gentle Revolution'). Václav Havel was elected president in 1990. In Hungary, Kadar had resigned in 1988 and with the border opened to Austria in 1989 the collapse of communism soon followed. A centre-right government was formed in 1990.

The role of Ronald Reagan

Events seemed to accelerate after 1985 when Gorbachev came to power. However, there were longer-term causes that can be attributed to Ronald Reagan.

Reagan ended the period of relaxed relations with Moscow (known as *détente*). The US boycotted the Moscow Olympics in 1980. In retaliation, the Soviets boycotted the Los Angeles Olympics in 1984. Reagan called the Soviet Union the 'evil empire' in a speech in 1983.

He believed the Cold War could be won by increasing weapons spending beyond the limits that the Soviets could afford. From 1981 to 1986, he increased the USA's defence spending from $179 billion to $370 billion. Part of this was the ambitious Strategic Defence Initiative (SDI). SDI would have created satellites to shoot down ICBMs in flight. The media called it the 'Star Wars' programme because it sounded like science fiction, and many people have doubted whether it was even possible. If it was, it would have made all Soviet ICBMs obsolete. The USSR did not have the money to keep pace with this.

Reagan's approach towards the USSR has been described by some historians as a 'Second Cold War', as the relationship with the Soviets deteriorated so suddenly and sharply. At the end of 1983, a Korean passenger jet was shot down by Soviet planes when it accidentally entered their air space. US criticism was so hostile that some in Moscow thought they might launch a nuclear attack. Relations had not been this tense since 1962.

Figure 6.10: Gorbachev and Reagan at the Geneva Summit in 1985

When Gorbachev came to power, Reagan maintained his attitude but was persuaded by Thatcher to talk to the new Soviet leader. Reagan opened up the question of Berlin by visiting the city in June 1987. He gave a speech in which he issued a dramatic challenge to Gorbachev (see Source 6Q).

THINK LIKE A HISTORIAN

Historians often look at how events are interpreted – that is, the different arguments that people put forward when explaining or justifying actions and events. There is no right or wrong interpretation, just different ways of viewing things. For example, Reagan's supporters claim that he ended the Cold War by defeating the USSR in the arms race. His critics say he risked a second Cold War.

Test this approach yourself by thinking of at least two ways of interpreting a situation each time you come across a disagreement. It could be from watching a news programme, or seeing friends disagree over something. Think about the benefits of being able to interpret any situation from more than one perspective. How does it change the way you view the world?

Chapter 6, Key Question 6: How secure was the USSR's control over Eastern Europe, 1948–c.1989?

SOURCE 6P

I am cautiously optimistic. I like Mr Gorbachev. We can do business together. We both believe in our own political systems. He firmly believes in his; I firmly believe in mine. We are never going to change one another. So that is not in doubt, but we have two great interests in common: that we should both do everything we can to see that war never starts again [. . .] And secondly, I think we both believe that they are the more likely to succeed if we can build up confidence in one another and trust in one another.

Source 6P: Margaret Thatcher in a TV interview in 1984. She met Gorbachev just before he came to power

SOURCE ANALYSIS 6.13

Read Sources 6P and 6Q. Thatcher and Reagan were close allies. Does Reagan's statement in 6Q show that Thatcher was not being genuine in her message in 6P?

SOURCE 6Q

There is one sign the Soviets can make that would be unmistakable, that would advance dramatically the cause of freedom and peace. General Secretary Gorbachev, if you seek peace, if you seek prosperity for the Soviet Union and Eastern Europe, if you seek liberalisation: Come here to this gate! Mr Gorbachev, open this gate! Mr Gorbachev, tear down this wall!

Source 6Q: Ronald Reagan's speech in Berlin, 12 June 1987

ACTIVITY 6.7

Read Source 6P and then research Margaret Thatcher's role in the Cold War online. Compare and contrast her views with those of Reagan and Gorbachev. How significant was she in ending the Cold War? Work in pairs to write a 100-word answer to this question and be ready to share your answer with the class.

FOCUS TASK 6.10

Who do you think had a greater impact on ending communism in Eastern Europe: Gorbachev or Reagan? Write a paragraph on each leader, giving evidence as to why they were responsible. Swap your paragraphs with a partner, and give each other feedback about what you have written. Together, reach a decision on who had the more significant impact and why. Then, write a final paragraph to your essay.

Communism collapsed across Eastern Europe in 1990. The effects spread inside Russia too, where communism ended in December 1991 as the USSR disintegrated into the separate republics that made up the union. Gorbachev's reputation inside and outside Russia could scarcely be different. In the West, he was a peacemaker unlike any other Soviet leader. In the East, he was the man who destroyed communism and lost the Cold War.

> CAMBRIDGE IGCSE™ AND O LEVEL HISTORY OPTION B: COURSEBOOK

SUMMARY

- Protests against Soviet dominance in Hungary in 1956 and Czechoslovakia in 1968 were both ruthlessly crushed by Moscow.
- Hungarian demands were more radical and were motivated by the belief that foreign help was coming.
- Czech demands, despite being more modest, were also too dangerous to be considered.
- The Berlin Wall was built as a reaction to growing tensions in the 1950s and early 1960s. It remained until 1989.
- The Solidarity movement in Poland was different from the events of 1956 and 1968 in Hungary and Czechoslovakia because it was more widespread and had greater international support.
- When Mikhail Gorbachev became leader of the USSR, he planned a reformed, more humane and responsive communism, taking over the government of the Warsaw Pact countries, but his intentions were not realised.
- When not enforced by military power, Soviet control of East Germany, Hungary, Czechoslovakia and Poland collapsed, and without that control the communist governments quickly fell from power.

KEY SKILLS EXERCISES

Knowledge and understanding

1. What is a buffer zone?
2. How was opposition to Soviet control demonstrated in Hungary?
3. How did Brezhnev react to the Prague Spring?
4. What was Solidarity?

Application

5. Why do you think the USSR never used force to capture West Berlin, despite using this approach in Budapest and Prague?
6. Why was Poland more difficult to use force in?
7. Why do you think Gorbachev took a different approach to the previous Soviet leaders? Give **three** reasons.

Analysis

8. Analyse the reasons for the thaw in relations between the USA and the USSR. Did it come more from the Soviet side or from the USA?
9. Analyse the role played by other leaders, for example from Pope John Paul II or Margaret Thatcher in the thaw in Cold War relations.
10. Analyse the role played by technology in changing the decisions that leaders had to make.

Evaluation

11. Evaluate the significance of Radio Free Europe in inspiring Hungarian rebels to stand up to Khrushchev.
12. Evaluate the importance of the Berlin Wall as a symbol of the Cold War.
13. Evaluate the role played by Solidarity in bringing the Cold War to an end.

Chapter 6, Key Question 6: How secure was the USSR's control over Eastern Europe, 1948–c.1989?

IMPROVE THIS ANSWER

To what extent was Gorbachev responsible for the end of the Cold War?

Sample answer: Mikhail Gorbachev became leader of the Soviet Union in 1985. He was determined to change things so he introduced new policies which were very important. He ended the Cold War by bringing peace and although he lost power and communism collapsed he was a very good leader and he deserves a lot of respect for what he did. **1**

One of the reasons he ended the Cold War was Perestroika. This means 'reform' in Russian. This was because he thought the Soviet Union was falling behind America and it needed to change its political system to make up the difference. He changed the Brezhnev Doctrine and that meant that there was more freedom in Eastern Europe, which led to people wanting to leave communism. This happened in Berlin and that was a big reason why the Cold War ended. **2**

Another reason why Gorbachev ended the Cold War was because of Glasnost. This was his idea and Glasnost means 'openness'. Gorbachev spoke to workers and he allowed people to have their own ideas and express themselves as they wished. This was unlike other Soviet leaders like Stalin. Because of this, people started to criticise communism and they wanted to leave it, so by 1991 people in the USSR wanted to change their system. This ended the Cold War because Russia was no longer communist. **3**

These reasons mean that Gorbachev was a major reason why the Cold War ended. **4** He came up with Perestroika and Glasnost and that meant that everyone wanted to end communism, which ended the Cold War. This is why he was the most important factor and was responsible for ending the Cold War. **5**

Now write an improved response using this guidance.

---

1 Can you see the problem? The answer only looks at Gorbachev, and not a different reason. It will need to introduce a second reason otherwise it will not be a balanced argument.

2 This is accurate and makes a reasonable argument, and includes some good evidence like the Brezhnev Doctrine.

3 Sadly the answer is still only about Gorbachev, and this is just an extension of the same argument rather than a counter argument. What else could have been offered as an explanation for the end of the Cold War?

4 This tries to answer the question but it hasn't acknowledged that 'to what extent' is the command term.

5 The essay finishes with a one-sided argument, so the full question hasn't been answered. Can you write a better conclusion that would address the full range of arguments, keeping in mind 'to what extent'?

CAMBRIDGE IGCSE™ AND O LEVEL HISTORY OPTION B: COURSEBOOK

> **PRACTICE QUESTIONS**
>
> 1 The USSR tried to extend its control over Eastern Europe during the Cold War.
>   a Describe the main events in Berlin in 1961. [4]
>   b Why was there opposition to communist control in Poland? [6]
>   c How far was Ronald Reagan responsible for the end of the Cold War? Explain your answer. [10]
>   [Total: 20]
>
> 2 Study Sources A and B.
>   How far do these two sources agree? Explain your answer using details of the sources and your own knowledge. [8]
>
> *We shall not yield to violence. We shall not be deprived of union freedoms. We shall never agree with sending people to prison for their convictions. The gates of prisons must be thrown open and persons sentenced for defending union and civic rights must be set free. [. . .] The defence of our rights and our dignity, as well as efforts never to let ourselves to be overcome by the feeling of hatred – this is the road we have chosen.*
>
> **Source A:** Lech Wałęsa's speech on receiving the Nobel Peace Prize, November 1983
>
> *[The USSR], one of the richest countries in the world, endowed with immense overall potential, was already sliding downwards. Our society was declining, both economically and intellectually.*
>
> *And yet, to a casual observer the country seemed to present a picture of relative well-being, stability, and order. The misinformed society under the spell of propaganda was hardly aware of what was going on and what the immediate future had in store for it. The slightest manifestations of protest were suppressed.*
>
> **Source B:** Mikhail Gorbachev's speech on receiving the Nobel Peace Prize, June 1991
>
> [Total: 8]

Chapter 6, Key Question 6: How secure was the USSR's control over Eastern Europe, 1948–c.1989?

PROJECT

You are going to work in groups of four to research Soviet control of Eastern Europe. You will create a shared research document and you will present your findings to the class as a group.

Step 1: Each group member must choose one place from this list.

- Hungary
- Czechoslovakia
- Berlin
- Poland

Create a shared document that you can all work on, so that you each have the information created by the other group members.

Step 2: Make a list of three reasons why each of the places was a security problem for the Soviet Union, and the challenges that Moscow might have to contend with. Think about political reasons economic reasons and other factors like size of population.

For your research, use this chapter and any other books you have in your school library, or websites and articles that you find useful. Make sure you include the reference at the end of your section. This means adding the title and author of a book you have used, or the URL of a website you have used.

When you have finished the text, try to add graphics, images, diagrams and headings to improve the presentation of the document.

Step 3: Create a shared group presentation. Each group member should add one slide for each of the three reasons you have identified. Choose one visual source for each slide and be prepared to analyse it in front of the class.

Step 4: Present to the class. When other groups are presenting, make notes on any information they have included that adds to your understanding of the topic.

SELF-EVALUATION CHECKLIST

After studying this chapter, complete this table:

You should be able to:	Needs more work	Almost there	Ready to move on
understand why there was opposition to Soviet rule in Hungary in 1956			
understand why there was opposition to Soviet rule in Czechoslovakia in 1968			
explain why the USSR reacted the way it did to the events of 1956 and 1968			
compare and contrast the causes and consequences of 1956 and 1968			
explain why the Berlin Wall was built in 1961			
understand the significance of Solidarity in Poland in the 1980s			
evaluate the role played by Mikhail Gorbachev in the collapse of Soviet control over Eastern Europe			
assess the contributions made by other leaders, such as Walesa, Reagan, Thatcher and Pope John Paul II, in the collapse of Soviet control over Eastern Europe.			

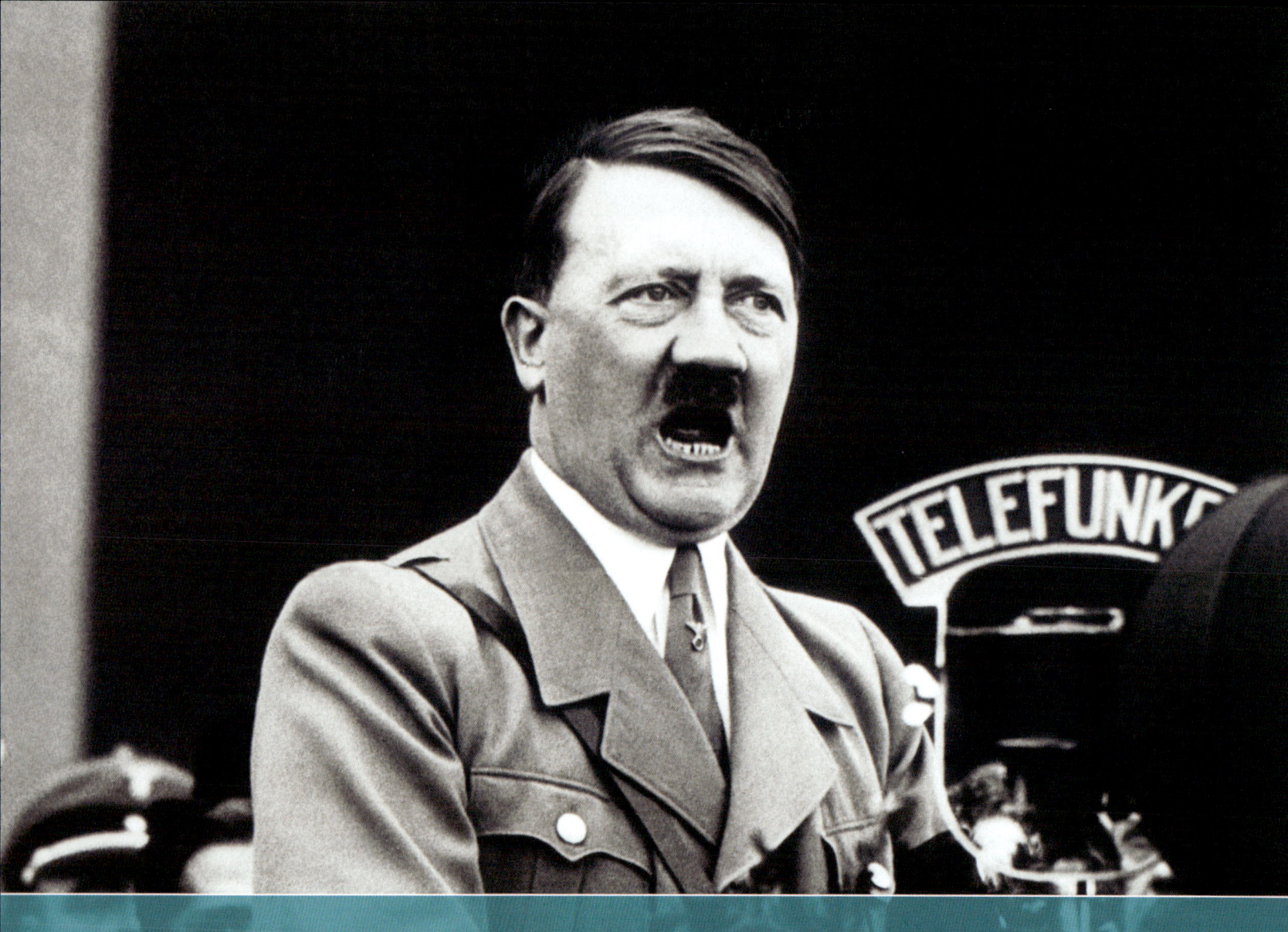

Chapter 7:
Germany, 1918–45

FOCUS POINTS

This chapter will help you to answer these questions:

- Was the Weimar Republic doomed from the start?
- Why was Hitler able to dominate Germany by 1934?
- How effectively did the Nazis control Germany, 1933–45?
- What was it like to live in Nazi Germany?

Chapter 7: Germany, 1918–45

7.0 What is this Depth study about?

This chapter covers the period in German history from the Revolution of 1918 through to the end of the Second World War. Germany was a well-developed and educated society – one of the most advanced in the world – yet it failed in its democratic experiment. The result was a dictatorship led by Adolf Hitler. The first half of this chapter deals with the Weimar Republic, the reasons for its failure and the rise of the Nazis. The second half looks at life in the Third Reich, exploring how Hitler maintained control and the consequences of his rule for all groups in society.

7.1 Was the Weimar Republic doomed from the start?

> **FOCUS POINTS**
>
> This topic will help you to answer these questions:
> - How did Germany emerge from defeat at the end of the First World War?
> - What was the impact of the Treaty of Versailles on the Republic?
> - To what extent did the Republic recover after 1923?
> - What were the achievements of the Weimar period?

How did Germany emerge from defeat at the end of the First World War?

The Revolution of 1918 and the establishment of the Republic

Towards the end of 1918, Germany was losing the First World War. The army was retreating in disorder, attacked by British, French and US troops. Kaiser Wilhelm II ordered the German navy to attack the Allies. Considering it a suicide mission, the sailors based at Kiel mutinied on 9 November. The German Revolution had begun.

Told clearly by the head of the War Office, General Groener, that he could no longer rely on the army, the kaiser abdicated. He handed power to his chancellor. In turn, the chancellor passed power to the leader of the largest party in the Reichstag, Friedrich Ebert of the Social Democrats (SPD). Ebert knew that he needed the support of the army if he was to maintain control. He approached Groener and they agreed the secret Ebert–Groener Pact. The army would support the new government and the government would support the army. Both sides wanted to avoid revolution.

On 11 November, Ebert's colleague Matthias Erzberger signed the Armistice with the Allied Powers. The conditions laid down by the French were strict. The German army had to leave France and abandon all its heavy weapons. An armistice is meant to be a ceasefire, but this was a surrender.

The Weimar constitution

In January 1919, Germany adopted a new constitution. The new political system this established was called the Weimar Republic, after the town of Weimar where the constitution was signed. With the end of the Kaiser's militaristic rule, democratic institutions were strengthened and the country became a republic. Some of the key features of the constitution are outlined below.

- Democracy: Everyone over the age of 20 could vote. Political parties were represented in a parliament called the Reichstag. Voting in elections was by **proportional representation**.

- Rights: Every German citizen had freedom of speech, freedom of religion and equality before the law.

- Chancellor: The chancellor appointed ministers and they ran the government on a daily basis. The support of the Reichstag was needed, so normally the leader of the largest party was made chancellor.

- President: The president was the head of state, head of the protector of the constitution. They could appoint and dismiss the chancellor. In a crisis, the president could allow the chancellor to use **Article 48** to pass an emergency **decree**.

- Regions: Germany was made up of 17 individual states called *Länder* that had power over, for example, police and education.

- Justice: The president appointed judges. Anyone who tried to overthrow the new system could be charged with treason.

Many people thought the new constitution was the most democratic in the world. The emphasis on democracy and individual rights seemed to be exactly what US President Woodrow Wilson had demanded in 1918 as part of the peace treaties. The Germans had played their part in removing the kaiser so they expected Wilson to honour the terms of his Fourteen Points, which suggested minimal punishment for Germany (see Chapter 1).

> **KEY TERMS**
>
> **proportional representation:** a voting system in which the proportion of assembly seats won by parties closely resembles the proportion of the votes cast in the election
>
> **Article 48:** the clause in the constitution that allowed the government to rule using emergency powers in a crisis
>
> **decree:** an official statement that something must happen

ACTIVITY 7.1

Look at the list of the main features of the Weimar constitution.

a   In pairs, make a list of the democratic strengths of the new constitution. Try to think of at least three strengths.

b   Join up with another pair and compare your lists of strengths. Discuss which of the strengths was most important for Germany democracy.

c   Now, debate what the weaknesses of the constitution are. If a German political party was opposed to democracy, how might they challenge the new constitution?

What was the impact of the Treaty of Versailles on the Republic?

The Versailles Settlement and German reactions to it

In May 1919, the German government was given the provisional peace terms and told that there would be no negotiation. Wilson's promises had not been kept.

Not only was Germany to be heavily punished, it also had to admit responsibility for starting the war. The German people were shocked, and the government resigned in protest. However, the Germans had no option but to accept. They were faced with the threat of mutiny, revolution, economic collapse, a continuing blockade and invasion. The Treaty of Versailles was signed on 28 June 1919.

> ### THINK LIKE A HISTORIAN
>
> The French military commander Ferdinand Foch said of the Treaty of Versailles: 'This is not a treaty, it is an armistice for 20 years.' How do you think people would have reacted to this prediction in Britain, France and Germany?
>
> Predictions are often made about the future, and people who work in the stock market or in new business ventures ('start-ups') have to guess what the future will hold. Yet the British politician Edmund Burke once said that 'you can never plan the future by the past'. Do you agree? Can we know what is likely to happen next based on our knowledge of the past and the present?

Four common phrases summarised popular opinion from 1919.

- Many ex-soldiers felt that the army had been betrayed by corrupt politicians in October and November 1918. They had not actually lost the war on the battlefield and were still in France when the Armistice was signed. This became known as the 'stab in the back' (*Dolchstoss*).
- The politicians who had signed the Armistice in November 1918 were labelled the 'November criminals'.
- The Treaty of Versailles was referred to as a 'Diktat' (a dictated peace).
- Wilson's peacekeeping body, the League of Nations, was called 'the League of Victors', as it was believed to exist only to keep Germany weak.

> ### THINKING SKILLS
>
> Look back at the terms of the Treaty of Versailles in Chapter 1. How you might have reacted to them if you were a:
>
> - German teenager
> - German soldier returning from the Western Front
> - middle-aged German woman
> - German business owner
> - German pensioner?
>
> Write a sentence for each person.

SOURCE 7A

Source 7A: A German cartoon from 1942 depicting the 'stab in the back' theory

> **SOURCE ANALYSIS 7.1**
>
> Look at Source 7A. What message is the cartoonist trying to communicate? Look at the symbols and consider the imagery that has been used to help you interpret the cartoon.

Left-wing political developments: three failed uprisings

In January 1919, the Spartacist Party, led by Rosa Luxemburg and Karl Liebknecht, seized government buildings in a bid for power. Ebert called on the army and the Freikorps, small private military groups often made up of ex-soldiers, to help crush the uprising. Liebknecht and Luxemburg were arrested, and both were violently beaten and shot. The first attempt at a communist revolution failed and the Ebert–Groener Pact had passed its first test of loyalty.

In February 1919, the leader of the large southern German state Bavaria, Kurt Eisner, was killed. Communists seized power in March, so Ebert again turned to the army. By May 1919 order had been restored and around 600 communists killed.

The third attempt at a communist uprising occurred in 1920 in the Ruhr valley. Workers formed the Ruhr Army, which gained 50 000 members. They were defeated by the army and the Freikorps, with at least 1000 workers and 250 soldiers and policemen killed.

Despite considerable support, communists failed to seize power. Even so, they continued to cause trouble in the form of strikes and demonstrations up to 1923.

Figure 7.1: Government troops advancing in the streets of Berlin during the communist Spartacist uprising, January 1919

Right-wing political developments: uprising and assassinations

The Freikorps supported the government in 1918 and 1919 because many former soldiers hated communists and blamed them for the 1918 defeat. Once the threat of revolution seemed over, Ebert ordered them to disband.

One Freikorps leader, General Lüttwitz, refused and joined forces with the leader of the patriotic Fatherland Party, Wolfgang Kapp. With 12 000 Freikorps, they marched on Berlin in an event known as the Kapp Putsch. This time the Ebert–Groener pact failed. The army, willing to shoot communists and strikers, refused to fire. Kapp was made chancellor of a new militaristic government but it had little popular support. Berlin workers opposed to Kapp organised a general strike. All public services, such as electricity and water, stopped working. The putsch collapsed after only four days and Kapp fled to Sweden, never to return.

As Hitler found out in 1923, many judges sympathised with the right wing. Only one person involved in the Kapp Putsch was actually sent to prison. Freikorps men formed a secret society called Organisation Consul, which assassinated government officials. By 1923, Organisation Consul had killed 354 politicians. There were only 28 convictions for these murders, with one being given the death penalty.

Two of the most notorious assassinations were those of Matthias Erzberger (1921) and Walther Rathenau (1922). Erzberger had signed the Armistice in 1918. Rathenau was the foreign secretary and had been involved in the Versailles negotiations. The Freikorps hated him because he was Jewish. Approximately 700 000 people protested in Berlin after his death on 24 June, and he was given a state funeral in the Reichstag. Until Hitler came to power, 24 June was a day of public commemoration for opponents of anti-Semitism.

FOCUS TASK 7.1

At the end of the war, Germany was divided into three broad groups of political opinion. They are summarised in Figure 7.2. How did each grouping react to:

- the Treaty of Versailles
- the new constitution?

Copy the table and add two more rows to record the reactions of each group.

	Left	Centre left and centre right	Right
Beliefs	An equal society based on communism. They were inspired by Lenin's Bolsheviks in Russia who achieved a revolution in 1917.	Democracy and the new constitution. They wanted reform and democracy, not revolution.	Return of the monarchy, protection of private property, defeat of communism, strong government, rebuilt German prosperity and power.
Supporters	The working classes and the poor. They were represented by the Spartacists (later the Communist Party or KPD).	Working and middle classes. Included Social Democrats, Centre and various liberal and conservative parties.	Conservatives, nationalists, monarchists, big business, the army and the Freikorps, people who had lost their savings in high inflation or their job during high unemployment.
•			
•			

Figure 7.2: A table showing German political factions in 1919

ACTIVITY 7.2

Review the five uprisings that took place in the early years of the republic.

a   Make a knowledge organiser using this structure and add in the key information from the text.

Uprising	Key events and dates	Key figures	Key facts	Outcome
Spartacists				
Bavaria				
Ruhr valley				
Kapp Putsch				
Organisation Consul				

b   In groups, discuss each event. Rank them in order of the seriousness of the threat to the Weimar government. Can you agree on what the order of danger was?

c   Now consider why they all failed. Are there any common themes that you can identify?

The French occupation of the Ruhr, 1923

In April 1921, the Reparations Committee set up by the Allies reported on the damages the Germans had to pay for the First World War. The amount announced was $33 billion. Germans were shocked and angry. In 1922, the government announced that it could not afford to pay the next instalment. Ebert tried to get concessions, but the French were not interested. When the payment deadline had passed in January 1923, French and Belgian troops entered the Ruhr valley to seize goods (mainly coal) in place of the payments.

The German government ordered a policy of passive resistance, not fighting with the French and Belgians but not cooperating either. However, with no foreign support coming, Germans in the Ruhr started to challenge the occupation forces. French soldiers killed approximately 100 protesters and expelled another 100 000 from the region.

Hyperinflation

The government turned to a radical solution. It owed money, so it decided to print more banknotes. The debt was so high that huge amounts had to be printed. This worked in the short term, paying off more than $1 billion of debt, although only within Germany as the Allies refused to accept German currency. However, over time, this led to high levels of inflation and hyperinflation.

Many people benefited, as they were now easily able to pay off mortgages and loans. But many others lost out. Workers' wages did not rise as quickly as prices, and those with savings found that they were now worthless. Older people who lived off a fixed monthly pension were sent into poverty. Huge piles of banknotes were needed to buy simple things.

Figure 7.3: An automotive factory in the Ruhr region being dismantled during the occupation of 1923

Date	Value of $1 in German marks
1914	4.2
1919	8.9
1920	14.0
1921	64.9
1922	191.8
January 1923	17,792
July 1923	353,412
September 1923	98,860,000
November 1923	200,000,000,000

Figure 7.4: A table showing the impact of hyperinflation

Gustav Stresemann became chancellor in August 1923 and ended the campaign of passive resistance. He resumed reparations payments and abolished the worthless currency. The French and Belgian soldiers withdrew from the Ruhr. Despite these successes, Stresemann was unpopular for giving in to the French. He resigned as chancellor in November but became foreign minister in the new government.

KEY FIGURE

Gustav Stresemann (1878–1929)

Stresemann was a politician and an economist. He was first elected in 1907 and proved his patriotism during the war. Right-wing and pro-Freikorps after the war, the wave of political assassinations persuaded him that moderation was needed. He went on to become Weimar Germany's most influential politician, serving as chancellor and then foreign secretary. He shared the Nobel Peace Prize in 1926 with the French foreign minister Aristide Briand. His death in 1929 left Germany without a strong leader to oppose Hitler.

FOCUS TASK 7.2

Many of Germany's problems were a result of the Treaty of Versailles, but not all of them. Some were a result of domestic political struggles. Draw up two bullet-point lists to summarise what you have learnt so far about Germany in the years immediately after the First World War.

- Problems caused by the Treaty of Versailles.
- Problems caused by German political developments.

Evaluate each list. Which side was more problematic? Decide for yourself if Germany's problems mainly resulted from Versailles or if they came from divisions within the country. Then join up with a partner and give each other feedback on your ideas.

To what extent did the Republic recover after 1923?

Foreign policy and economic achievements

Stresemann's new role as foreign minister allowed him to rebuild relations with the other European nations. French action over the Ruhr was widely seen as extreme, while Stresemann had compromised. This created the chance of discussing Germany's future with other governments.

In 1923, Stresemann had destroyed the old currency by claiming back all banknotes in circulation and burning them. In its place he introduced a new temporary form of money called the Rentenmark. Later in 1924 this was replaced with the Reichsmark, which solved Germany's cash problems.

In 1924, he negotiated the Dawes Plan with a group appointed by the Reparations Committee. Germany would only pay an instalment of reparations when it could afford to, and the occupation of the Ruhr would be ended. US banks loaned Germany 800 million Reichsmarks, which helped to restart economic growth. By 1928, German industry was back to the level it had been at in 1914.

In 1929, another agreement was reached over reparations. Once again, the USA was involved. Reparations would be cut further and more loans were to be given. By the time the plan came into action Stresemann had died and the US economy had collapsed because of the Wall Street Crash. However, by 1929, Germany had been largely rehabilitated into the international community.

In the election of 1924, political parties that supported the Republic won only 52% of the seats in the Reichstag. Opponents of the system won 39.4%. Yet by 1928, this had changed as support rose to 72.8% and opposition fell to 13.3%.

Cultural achievements

It was clear that German society was going through a significant period of cultural change in the 1920s. Before the war, German society was very conservative. Young people and, in particular, women were not encouraged to socialise by themselves. After the war, these groups embraced a new way of living and seemed determined to leave the past behind – including all the unhappiness and suffering of the war era. That caused tensions with the older generation, who saw such open and free behaviour as shocking and disrespectful. Berlin was at the heart of this change. A vibrant nightlife emerged, characterised by night clubs and cabarets. American music, especially jazz, became popular.

Art saw some of the most profound changes. Movements like Dadaism brought striking new forms of painting that captured the spirit of the age. Artists like Hannah Höch, George Grosz and Otto Dix became famous, as their work showed the contrast between the old and new ways of living. Bauhaus was also a significant movement, as this emphasised new forms of architecture. The Bauhaus School of Art and Architecture was founded by Walther Gropius in 1919 and produced artists such as Wassily Kandinsky and Paul Klee. It is notable that one of Hitler's first acts as chancellor in 1933 was to close the Bauhaus school – the Nazis were not at all in favour of modern art.

Figure 7.5: The 1st International Dada Fair in Berlin, 1920. Many of the leading artists of the movement, such as George Grosz and Hannah Höch, are in the picture.

SOURCES 7B & 7C

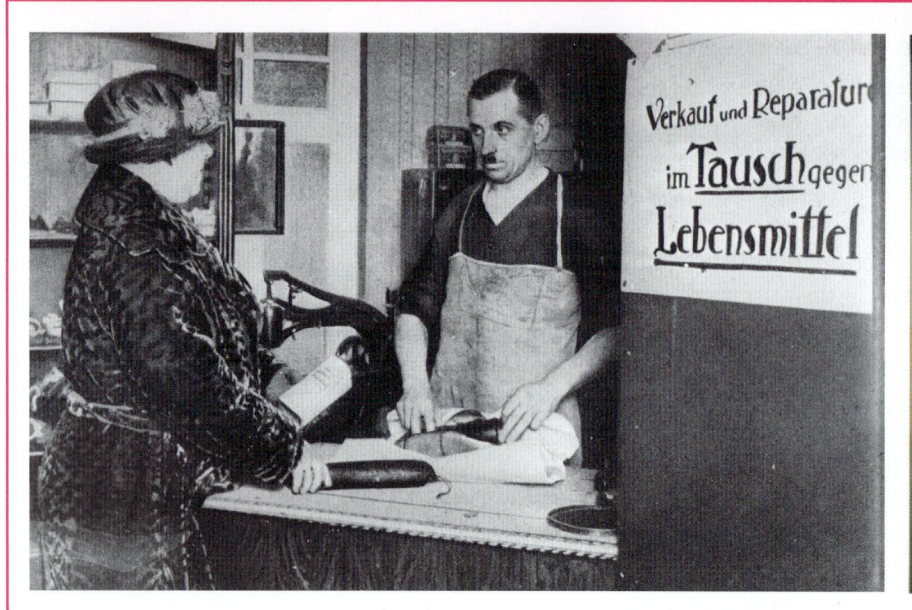

Source 7B: A photograph of a woman paying for her shoes to be repaired not with money but by bartering a sausage, c. 1923. The notice on the wall announces in German 'Sales and repairs in exchange for food'.

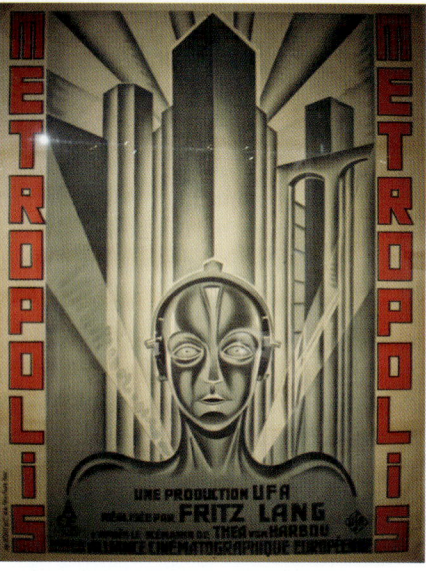

Source 7C: A poster for the film *Metropolis* by Fritz Lang (1927). The film showed how futuristic thinking had replaced the classical culture of the Kaiser's period. It popularised science fiction in world cinema.

Cinema became popular, with Marlene Dietrich emerging as Germany's first film star. She went on to Hollywood in 1930 and became the highest paid actress in the USA. Science fiction became popular (see Source 7C). The German film industry was one of the most innovative and successful in the world, and the power of the 'silver screen' to captivate audiences was not lost on the Nazis. Hitler was an avid film watcher, and Joseph Goebbels would make cinema a central feature of Nazi propaganda.

However, beneath the surface, problems remained. The economic recovery was based on US support, and while Stresemann had reduced reparations, he had not changed the terms of the Treaty of Versailles. In fact, he had agreed to some of its harshest clauses, such as the demilitarisation of the Rhineland.

Another worrying event was the death of Friedrich Ebert in 1925, one year before a presidential election was due. The centre-left Ebert was replaced with the right-wing Paul von Hindenburg as the new president.

SOURCE ANALYSIS 7.2

Compare sources 7B and 7C. Which do you think is a better reflection of life in Germany between 1919 and 1929? Was it more a period of collapse, or a 'golden age'? Explain your thinking.

Key points
The Weimar Republic

- The Weimar Republic began as Germany lost the First World War.
- It had a constitution that was very democratic.
- It faced challenges in the immediate aftermath of the war from extremists on both the left and right wings of German politics.
- In 1923 it faced its greatest crisis when the French occupied the Ruhr valley and when the economy collapsed as a result of hyperinflation.
- It recovered from 1924 and entered a period of political and economic stability, with many cultural achievements.

7.2 Why was Hitler able to dominate Germany by 1934?

> **FOCUS POINTS**
>
> This topic will help you to answer these questions:
>
> - What did the Nazi Party stand for in the 1920s?
> - Why did the Nazis have little success before 1930?
> - Why was Hitler able to become chancellor by 1933?
> - How did Hitler consolidate his power in 1933–34?

What did the Nazi Party stand for in the 1920s?

In January 1919, Anton Drexler, a railway worker in Munich in Bavaria, founded the German Workers Party (DAP). It had at most 40 members and held meetings in beer cellars around the city. In September 1919, a 30 year old army corporal named Adolf Hitler attended a DAP meeting. He worked for the army as an **informant** on the new political parties. Drexler was impressed and invited him to join the party. Hitler was put in charge of propaganda. In 1921, he successfully challenged Drexler for the leadership.

Nazi ideas and methods

Hitler made significant changes to the DAP in 1920–22.

1. He changed its name to the National Socialist German Workers Party (NSDAP – or 'Nazi Party' for short) to attract more supporters.
2. He helped to write the party's 25-Point Programme, which opposed the Treaty of Versailles, stated that only 'pure' Germans, not Jewish people, could be German citizens, and opposed large-scale capitalism.
3. He introduced the swastika as the party's symbol.

KEY FIGURE

Paul von Hindenburg (1847–1934)

Born in Prussia, Paul von Hindenburg served in wars against Austria and France. He was promoted to Field Marshall before his retirement in 1911. Recalled to service in 1914, he led the German army alongside Ludendorff until 1918. A monarchist, he became president in 1925, and he was re-elected in 1932. He despised Hitler, but eventually found it impossible not to appoint him chancellor. Hindenburg's death in 1934 removed the last obstacle to Hitler's total authority.

KEY TERM

informant: someone who finds information and gives it to another person or organisation

4 He set up the *Stürm Abteilung* (SA) as the party's **paramilitary** wing (also known as the Brownshirts because of their uniform).
5 He bought a newspaper called the *Völkischer Beobachter* to spread Nazi Party ideas and propaganda.
6 He introduced the Hitler salute ('Heil Hitler!').

> ### SOURCE 7D
>
> Only a member of the race can be a citizen. A member of the race can only be one who is of German blood, without consideration of creed. Consequently no Jew can be a member of the race.
>
> **Source 7D:** An extract from the NSDAP's 25-Point Programme, published in 1920

> ### FOCUS TASK 7.3
>
> In pairs, organise Hitler's reforms into a spider diagram. Indicate links between the six reforms, showing how they would relate to each other. For example, points four and six would link together in the militaristic nature of the NSDAP. You need to agree on the layout and the links, so discuss your ideas and make a draft diagram first. Think about how you can improve it before deciding on the final version.

> ### KEY TERM
>
> **paramilitary:** describing a group that is organised like an army, but is unofficial and often illegal

> ### SOURCE ANALYSIS 7.3
>
> Study source 7D and review the knowledge organiser you made in Activity 7.2. Which groups in society would agree with this statement and why?

Why did the Nazis have little success before 1930?

The Munich Putsch, 1923

By 1923, the Nazis had 20 000 members, mostly in Bavaria. Using the trouble that the government had caused with hyperinflation as justification, Hitler decided to seize power. To succeed, he needed the support of the Bavarian state government, led by Gustav von Kahr, and the army, led by General Otto von Lossow. His plan was to lead a march on Berlin, where the army would help to overthrow the Weimar Republic.

On 8 November 1923, Kahr gave a speech in a Munich beer hall. Hitler entered the room, fired a gun in the air and announced that a 'national revolution' had begun. Men from the SA surrounded the building. However, Kahr and Lossow were not convinced, even when General Ludendorff appeared in support. After some time waiting, Ludendorff persuaded Hitler to let the men go home and put off the march. On the morning of 9 November, 2000 Nazis marched towards the city centre. Kahr and Lossow had alerted the police and army, who were waiting. The police opened fire, killing 16 Nazis. The leaders were arrested.

Hitler's trial and sentence

Hitler went on trial for the putsch in February 1924. His speeches were widely reported and the trial made him famous outside Bavaria for the first time. In the 1924 elections, Nazis won 32 seats in the Reichstag with 6.5% of the national vote.

Figure 7.6: Members of the *Stürm Abteilung* (SA), during the Munich Putsch, 1923

FOCUS TASK 7.4

Look again at your knowledge organiser from Activity 7.2. Make brief notes from this section about the Munich Putsch, and then compare that event to the other challenges to the Weimar government. What similarities and differences do you notice about the Munich Putsch? How serious was it compared to the other events? Be prepared to share your ideas in a class discussion about the significance of the Munich Putsch.

Hitler was found guilty of high treason. He could have been executed for this, but the right-wing judge gave him a sentence of just five years in prison. He served nine months. Ludendorff was released. Hitler used his time in Landsberg Prison to write his book *Mein Kampf* ('My Struggle'), which set out his political beliefs.

SOURCE 7E

For, gentlemen, it is not you who pronounce judgement upon us, it is the external Court of History which will make its pronouncement upon the charge which is brought against us. The verdict that you will pass I know. But that Court will not ask of us, 'Did you commit high treason or did you not?' That Court will judge us as Germans who wanted the best for their people and their fatherland, who wished to fight and to die. You may pronounce us guilty a thousand times, but the Goddess who presides over the Eternal Court of History will with a smile tear in pieces the charge of the Public Prosecutor and the verdict of this court. For she acquits us.

Source 7E: The conclusion to Hitler's trial speech

SOURCE ANALYSIS 7.4

Evaluate Source 7E. How might this speech have been received by the public in 1924? Think about the political context after the events of 1919–24.

Changing methods: the legal strategy

Hitler was released in December 1924. While he was in prison the NSDAP had fallen into disarray. He reorganised the party and announced a new strategy. Violent revolution had failed, so the Nazis would instead campaign in elections to become the most popular party in Germany.

Hitler divided Germany into different regions, called *Gaue*. Each *Gau* would have a leader, a *Gauleiter*, who was responsible for winning support and spreading the party message. Hitler also founded several new organisations to appeal to different social groups:

- the Hitler Youth
- the Nazi Teachers' Association
- the Order of German Women
- the Union of Nazi Lawyers.

From 1925 to 1928, the number of Nazi Party members increased from 27 000 to 108 000.

In 1926, Hitler set out the idea of the *Führerprinzip* ('leader principle'), which made his own authority unquestionable. This was important, as some members argued for more left-wing policies that appealed to workers instead of racist right-wing policies. This left-wing group was led by two brothers, Gregor and Otto Strasser.

SOURCE 7F

[. . .] we shall have to hold our noses and enter the Reichstag against the Catholic and Marxist deputies. If outvoting them takes longer than outshooting them, at least the result will be guaranteed by their own constitution.

Source 7F: Hitler's justification of his new strategy

SOURCE ANALYSIS 7.5

Read Source 7F. What did Hitler mean by this statement?

The work of the SA and SS

The SA had been formed in 1920 as a unit to protect Nazi speakers at meetings. Under Ernst Röhm's leadership, it grew quickly and was heavily involved in the street-fighting of 1920–23. After the Munich Putsch, Röhm left for Bolivia, so Hitler re-established the SA in 1925.

Approximately half of its members were unemployed young men, to whom membership offered a purpose, a uniform and hot meals. The Party also had SA hostels where they could stay. From 1927, there was an annual rally at Nuremberg, which was useful for propaganda. The filmmaker Leni Riefenstahl made a famous documentary on the 1934 rally called *The Triumph of the Will*.

In 1925, Hitler created his own personal bodyguard, the *Schutzstaffel* ('protection squad', SS). This was led by Heinrich Himmler from 1929. This group later became the most significant organisation in the Nazi state.

The campaign against the Young Plan

Despite the changes, the Nazis won 12 out of 491 seats in the Reichstag in the 1928 elections, only 2.6% of the national vote. This was significantly less than in 1924, when they won 32 seats. The Nazis needed more publicity, and respectability.

Figure 7.7: SA men marching in 1933

Chapter 7: Germany, 1918–45

An opportunity arose in 1929 over the Young Plan. This followed on the Dawes Plan, and reduced reparations payments, spreading them over 59 years. However, nationalists felt that agreeing to it meant accepting reparations and the acceptance of war guilt that this implied. A national campaign against the Young Plan was launched by the wealthy young Alfred Hugenburg, leader of the German National People's Party (DNVP). The Nazis took part in the campaign, and successfully won the publicity and respectability that would be crucial to their success in the 1930s. Hugenburg's party lost many votes to the Nazis after 1930, and he joined Hitler's cabinet in 1933.

KEY TERM

cabinet: a small group of the most important people in a government, who advise the leader

SOURCE 7G

![Simplicissimus magazine cover, München, 10. April 1932, 37. Jahrgang Nr. 2. "Die Sieghaften" by E. Schilling. Shows Hitler giving a Nazi salute and Hugenberg adjusting his pince-nez, both riding horses. Caption: „Man sieht es ihnen eigentlich gar nicht an, daß sie eine Niederlage erlitten haben." — „Sie wissen es ja auch noch nicht, sie lesen doch bloß ihre eigenen Blätter."]

Source 7G: A German magazine cover from 1932, showing Hitler alongside Hugenberg

SOURCE ANALYSIS 7.6

Study Source 7G. What impression is the artist trying to give of the following:

- Hitler
- Hugenberg
- their relationship?

THINKING SKILLS

Imagine you are a member of the SA. You were involved in the Munich Putsch of 1923. How would you react to Hitler's new strategy from 1924 onwards? Would you continue to support the party? Write a diary extract from after the 1928 elections explaining your thoughts and feelings about the direction the party is heading under Hitler's leadership.

273

> **FOCUS TASK 7.5**
>
> Look back at the changes to the Nazi Party between Hitler's release from prison in 1924 and 1929. Why did the Nazis make few gains in this period? Brainstorm this question in groups and identify three reasons why Hitler's legal strategy failed to make a significant impact in the 1920s. In your groups, put together a presentation about these changes and show:
>
> - why Hitler failed to win many followers in this period
> - why this period was not necessarily one characterised by failure.
>
> Make your presentation to another group and take their questions and feedback.

Leading Nazis

Hitler was supported by several key people, including the following.

- Ernst Röhm: a First World War captain and leader of the SA. He was arrested in the Munich Putsch but released.
- Joseph Goebbels: head of propaganda and a deputy in the Reichstag. He edited a Nazi newspaper called *Der Angriff* ('The Attack') and was made *Gauleiter* of Berlin.
- Hermann Göring: a First World War pilot who was also involved in the Munich Putsch. He was a deputy in the Reichstag and helped Hitler make important contacts in business circles.
- Heinrich Himmler: head of the SS from 1929. He took part in the Munich Putsch and assisted with party propaganda. His influence grew after Hitler came to power.

> **ACTIVITY 7.3**
>
> In groups of four, choose one of the leading Nazis each. Create a one-page fact sheet on your leader, selecting information to create a profile of each man. Research them online or using any other resources available and find information to cover:
>
> - biographical details (e.g. full name, date and place of birth)
> - career before joining the Nazi Party
> - role in the party
> - useful facts about them
> - how and when they died.
>
> Share your fact sheets with the group so that you all have a copy. Present your findings to each other, giving your thoughts about what your figure contributed to Hitler's rise to power. Give each other feedback on your fact sheets and presentations.

> **REFLECTION**
>
> Reflect on how you approached Activity 7.3 and how well you think it went. Assess your ideas and contribution using the following questions.
>
> - How difficult did you find the research task?
> - What did you learn from other members of the group during the research process?
> - How might you improve the selection and presentation of information in your fact sheet?
> - If you had to do this task again, what changes would you make to your research methods?
> - How well would you be able to recall the information in the fact sheets you made in your groups?

Why was Hitler able to become chancellor by 1933?

The impact of the Depression on Germany

Germany's economic recovery was built on borrowing from US banks. When the US stock market crashed in October 1929, the banks lending money to Germany needed it back. The effects were disastrous. In 1931, a major Austrian bank, Kreditanstaldt, collapsed. This affected German banks, so the crisis deepened. Unemployment increased significantly. In 1929, 1.4 million Germans were out of work. By 1933, this had increased to 6 million.

Hitler's message in the 1920s was that Germany should not take money from the USA. It now looked like he had been right all along. In the election of 1930, the Nazis made their first big breakthrough, winning 107 seats – second only to the SPD.

Several key methods were used to exploit the widespread feelings of distress.

- Propaganda: Goebbels used cinema and radio to spread the Nazi message. It was carefully crafted to appeal to specific groups. Posters were designed with simple but effective slogans that emphasised Hitler as the man who would save Germany.

- Speeches: Hitler was a very persuasive speaker and seemed to express the anger and frustration that so many Germans felt. By 1933, 6000 Party members had been trained to deliver messages that would appeal to their audience. In the countryside, they would talk about problems facing farmers. In the city, they would talk about unemployment. Nazi policies were flexible, so many Germans could find something that appealed to them.

- Political violence: Röhm returned from Bolivia in 1930 to lead the SA and expanded their numbers dramatically. By the end of 1932 they had 425 000 men – over four times the size of the army. They frequently beat up communists and disrupted Communist Party (KPD) meetings. In the summer of 1932, 82 people died in street fighting in Berlin.

The success of these methods is reflected in the increase in votes for the Nazis after the Wall Street Crash in 1929 (see Figure 7.8). However, the KDP (the communists) also increased up to November 1932. Like the Nazis, they wanted to end the Weimar Republic. The SPD were the largest party that supported democracy. In the last three elections, half of the German public backed the two parties that wanted to end Weimar democracy.

Date	Nazi % of the vote	Nazi seats in the Reichstag	SPD seats	KPD seats
May 1928	2.6	12	153	54
September 1930	18.3	107	143	77
July 1932	37.3	230	133	89
November 1932	33.1	196	121	100
March 1933	43.9	288	120	81

Figure 7.8: A table showing the increase in votes for the Nazi Party, 1928–33

Weimar chancellors, 1930–33

The man in charge when the Wall Street Crash first hit Germany was SPD leader Herman Müller. He led a coalition government that disagreed over how to tackle the Depression. Müller resigned as chancellor in 1930 and died the following year. Although the SPD was the largest party in the Reichstag, it lacked clear leadership after this.

The 1932 presidential elections

Hitler decided to challenge Hindenburg in the 1932 presidential election. Goebbels organised an election campaign in which Hitler flew around Germany to address crowds in different cities on the same day.

No candidate won the required 50% of the vote, so a second round was staged with the three most successful candidates: Hindenburg, Hitler and the communist leader Ernst Thälmann.

	Hindenburg	Hitler	Thälmann
% of votes	53	36.8	10.2
Number of votes	19.4 million	13.4 million	3.7 million

Figure 7.9: A table showing the results of the 1932 presidential election run-off

> **REVISION TIP**
>
> The percentage of votes and number of seats are excellent evidence to use in answers about Hitler's rise to power. Practise recalling these statistics with a partner so you can show your detailed knowledge in a written answer.

FOCUS TASK 7.6

On a large sheet of paper, create a timeline or a flow diagram showing what happened in Germany in 1932 and 1933. Include all the main events and the key people involved in them. In pairs, share and compare your diagrams. Has your partner included anything you have missed out? Add anything you feel is useful to your timeline or flow diagram.

How did Hitler become chancellor?

In the election of July 1932, the Nazis won 230 seats and overtook the SPD to become the largest party. Hindenburg still refused to make Hitler chancellor, but six months later he was persuaded to change his mind. Why? The answer lies in political deals that were made out of the public eye.

Franz von Papen was not a popular choice as chancellor in 1932. He had less Reichstag support than Müller or Heinrich Brüning, and he resigned from the Centre Party (which distrusted him) shortly after being appointed chancellor. Schleicher soon realised that von Papen lacked authority. Hindenburg agreed to sack von Papen and make Schleicher chancellor instead.

Name	Background	Time as chancellor	Policies
Heinrich Brüning	Leader of the Centre Party	March 1930–May 1932	Cut government spending and increased taxes. This decreased Germany's debt but was unpopular: people called him the 'hunger chancellor'. He ruled using Article 48 as he had little support in the Reichstag. He used this to ban the SA.
Franz von Papen	Centre Party aristocrat and an officer and diplomat in the First World War	June–November 1932	Right-wing and a Hindenburg adviser. He tried to bring the Nazis into his government and lifted the ban on the SA. The KPD and the Nazis voted together to bring down his government.
Kurt von Schleicher	General and political adviser to Hindenburg	November 1932–January 1933	Undermined Brüning. Although defence minister under von Papen, he decided Germany needed a strong man to deal with the crisis. Thought he could split and use the Nazis.

Figure 7.10: The chancellors before Hitler in the 1930s

Schleicher's plan was to split the Nazis. He knew that some Nazi members preferred the left-wing Strasser brothers to Hitler, so he offered Gregor Strasser the role of vice chancellor. The Nazis had lost votes in the election of November 1932, so Hitler's methods did not seem to be working. The election campaigns of 1932 also left them short of money. Strasser wanted to take the job, openly questioning Hitler's authority.

At a meeting of the Nazi leadership in December 1932, Hitler made an emotional appeal for support. He attacked Strasser's disloyalty and won the backing of the *Gauleiters*. It was a significant moment. The Strassers resigned from the party and Schleicher's plan failed.

Von Papen now saw an opportunity to gain revenge on Schleicher. He went to Hindenburg with a plan that Hitler should be made chancellor, but in a government that had few Nazi ministers. Von Papen would be vice chancellor and there would be many conservative ministers to limit Hitler's power. Either Hitler would do well and the financial crisis would end, so Hindenburg could take the credit for appointing him, or, Hitler would do badly and the crisis would get worse, causing Nazi support to collapse.

This seemed a win-win situation. Fearing an uprising by either the Nazis or the KPD, appointing Hitler as chancellor seemed to be the least dangerous option. Hindenburg invited him to form a government on 30 January 1933, just nine years after he was jailed for treason.

Figure 7.11: A photograph of Hitler and Hindenburg taken at a parade in March 1933. What do you notice about their body language?

FOCUS TASK 7.7

a   Why did Hitler become chancellor? Select the most important information and organise it into a mind map showing the reasons why Hitler was appointed. Cover these key points:

- the impact of the Depression
- the weakness of Weimar chancellors
- Hitler's leadership
- the role played by other Nazi leaders.

b   In pairs, discuss the four factors in Hitler's rise to power. Was it mainly due to the weaknesses in Germany after the depression, or because of the strengths of the Nazis as a movement?

c   Write an answer to this question: *To what extent was Hitler's appointment as chancellor due to the weaknesses of the Weimar Republic?*

How did Hitler consolidate his power in 1933–34?

When Hitler was appointed chancellor, there were several limitations to his power.

- Hindenburg had the power to sack him.
- He did not control the army.
- There were only three Nazis in a cabinet of 14 ministers: Hitler, Göring and Wilhelm Frick.
- The economy was still weak.
- With 196 of the 584 seats, he lacked a majority in the Reichstag.

Despite these problems, Hitler managed to turn Germany into a dictatorship by the summer of 1934. There were four important steps that destroyed the Weimar Republic and turned Germany into the Third Reich.

Step one: the Reichstag Fire

Hitler's first act as chancellor was to call a new election, hoping to win a majority in the Reichstag. Street-fighting left 69 people dead. Hitler blamed the violence, like Germany's other problems, on the KPD.

On 27 February, a week before the election, the Reichstag burned down. A Dutch communist named Marinus van der Lubbe was found at the scene and confessed. Some historians believe the Nazis were guilty and that van der Lubbe was merely a **scapegoat**. Whatever the real cause, Hitler persuaded Hindenburg to sign the 'Decree For the Protection of People and State' the next day. This limited individual rights and gave the government more power. The leaders of the KPD were arrested, as Hitler claimed they were attempting a revolution.

After the fire, hundreds of the Nazis' opponents were arrested. Hitler won the election with 288 seats. This was not enough to rule without a coalition, and far fewer than the 434 seats needed to change the constitution.

> **KEY TERM**
>
> **scapegoat:** someone who is blamed for something to avoid others taking responsibility

Figure 7.12: Demonstration in New York about the Reichstag Fire

Step two: the Enabling Act

When the Reichstag deputies met in the Kroll Opera House on 23 March, Hitler proposed a measure to grant dictatorial power to the government for the next four years. SA men surrounded the building. He made a speech in an atmosphere of intimidation. The SPD opposed the measure but the banned KPD could not take part. The DNVP supported the Nazis, but Hitler needed a two-thirds majority vote to change the constitution. This left the Catholic Centre Party holding the balance of power. Hitler promised to protect the Catholic Church and Catholic schools to win their support for the Enabling Act. It passed by 444 to 94.

The Enabling Act gave Hitler enormous power. He no longer needed the support of the Reichstag to make laws or decisions. He only needed Hindenburg's backing. Hitler had achieved what he set out to do in 1924.

> **THINKING SKILLS**
>
> For the Enabling Act to pass, Hitler had to gain the support of the Catholic Centre Party. Imagine you are the leader of that party. Write a press release (a statement for the media) explaining why you have decided to support Hitler rather than oppose the Enabling Act. Try to write the statement without considering what you know about events after 1933. Base it on what you know of German history up to the Reichstag Fire.
>
> When you have finished, consider whether you have any sympathy for the Catholic Centre Party leadership. What alternative did they have? Would you have done the same thing or not?

Step three: the Night of the Long Knives

By June 1933, opposition parties had been banned. Trade unions were outlawed in May, and workers were instead represented by the Nazi-led German Labour Front. The only opposition Hitler still had to fear now lay within his own party.

Once in power, radical Nazi members expected action, particularly against Jewish people, the Treaty of Versailles and big business. Hitler knew it was too early to make any bold moves for fear of alarming business leaders and foreign governments.

The SA was not happy with Hitler's caution. It had 2.5 million members by 1934 and Röhm was increasingly outspoken in his criticism. He felt Hitler was too friendly with rich conservatives and had lost touch with ordinary Nazis. Himmler hated Röhm and fed Hitler rumours of his disloyalty. He claimed Röhm was planning a putsch and even forged evidence to prove this.

Hitler made his move on 30 June, which became known as 'the Night of the Long Knives'. The SA were given a holiday so Röhm and his men were staying at a hotel in Bavaria. Hitler travelled there with a group of SS men. Röhm was arrested and executed. An estimated 200 people were killed, including Schleicher, Gregor Strasser and von Kahr. The cabinet issued a decree that said simply: 'The measures taken on 30th June and 1st and 2nd July to suppress the acts of high treason are legal, being necessary for the self-defence of the state.' Hitler had legalised murder by the state.

Step four: the presidency

When Hindenburg died on 2 August 1934, Hitler became president while also remaining chancellor. He was simply the *Führer* ('leader'). This was approved in a country-wide referendum by over 90% of those who voted. Every soldier had to swear an oath of allegiance to Hitler personally: 'I swear by God this holy oath, that I will render to Adolf Hitler, *Führer* of the German Reich and People, Supreme Commander of the Armed Forces, unconditional obedience, and that I am ready, as a brave soldier, to risk my life at any time for this oath.'

The last obstacle to Hitler's complete control of power had been removed.

Key points

Hitler's domination of Germany by 1934

- The Munich Putsch (1923) was Hitler's first attempt to seize power. It ended in failure, as he was sent to prison.
- After his release, he set the Nazi Party on a different course, with the aim of coming to power by legal means.
- He was helped by key figures such as Goebbels, Himmler, Göring and Röhm.
- Despite his changes, the Nazis made little progress in elections until after the Wall Street Crash of 1929, when the German economy faced problems.
- Hitler's rapid rise to popularity was rewarded in 1933 when Hindenburg appointed him as chancellor.
- By 1934, Hitler had turned Germany into a dictatorship, as well as establishing complete control over his own party.

> **FOCUS TASK 7.8**
>
> Get into groups of four. Each group member should take one of the four steps which led to the creation of the Third Reich. You have 60 seconds to argue why your step was the most significant turning point in Hitler's plan to establish a dictatorship.
>
> After hearing each group member speak, each of you should write down which step you think was actually the most important and give a reason why you think this. Share your decisions as a group. Do you all agree?

7.3 How effectively did the Nazis control Germany, 1933–45?

> **FOCUS POINTS**
>
> This topic will help you to answer these questions:
> - How much opposition was there to the Nazi regime?
> - How effectively did the Nazis deal with their political opponents?
> - How did the Nazis use culture and the mass media to control the people?
> - Why did the Nazis persecute many groups in German society?
> - Was Nazi Germany a totalitarian state?

How much opposition was there to the Nazi regime?

The arrest of rival political leaders in 1933 and the economic recovery by 1936 both limited opposition to the Nazi regime. However, Hitler's more radical foreign policies from 1938, and the attacks on Jews, increased some people's concerns about the nature of his government. When the war began in 1939, this opposition became much more evident. Although fear silenced much criticism, secret police reports show that resentment increased among the general public as the war went on.

There were four main categories of opposition to Nazi rule between 1933 and 1945.

Church opposition

The Roman Catholic Bishop of Münster, August von Galen, gave a sermon that condemned the Aktion T-4 programme. This was a **euthanasia** programme in which people with physical or mental disabilities were killed by lethal injection, starvation or gassing. Aktion T-4 started at the beginning of the war and ran officially until August 1941. Around 70 000 people died. Hitler wanted Bishop Galen arrested, but Goebbels warned that he was too popular with the people. Galen was sent to a **concentration camp** in 1944 but survived.

Protestant pastor Dietrich Bonhoffer was a vocal critic of Nazism and was arrested in 1943. He was active in the resistance and helped many Jews to escape Germany. He was executed in April 1945 at Flossenbürg concentration camp.

Youth opposition

Galen's example provided inspiration for the White Rose group in Munich. This was founded in 1942 by Hans and Sophie Scholl, siblings who attended Munich University. With their followers, they distributed leaflets that openly attacked the Nazis. These were smuggled out of Germany, reprinted, and dropped by Allied planes over cities. However, it was not difficult for the authorities to put a stop to the group. The Scholls and their accomplices were arrested, tortured and executed in February 1943.

> ### SOURCE 7H & 7I
>
> *First they came for the Communists*
> *And I did not speak out*
> *Because I was not a Communist*
> *Then they came for the Socialists*
> *And I did not speak out*
> *Because I was not a Socialist*
> *Then they came for the trade unionists*
> *And I did not speak out*
> *Because I was not a trade unionist*
> *Then they came for the Jews*
> *And I did not speak out*
> *Because I was not a Jew*
> *Then they came for me*
> *And there was no one left*
> *To speak out for me.*
>
> **Source 7H:** A poem by Martin Niemöller, a Protestant pastor who opposed the Nazis and spent eight years in concentration camps. He wrote this poem after the war in 1946.
>
> *Somebody, after all, had to make a start. What we wrote and said is also believed by many others. They just don't dare express themselves as we did.*
>
> **Source 7I:** Sophie Scholl, speaking at her trial in 1943

> ### KEY TERMS
>
> **euthanasia:** allowing someone to die, or assisting their death, in order to end their suffering. The Nazis applied this to people with disabilities
>
> **concentration camp:** a prison for political opponents, designed to 'purify' them through hard labour. In the Second World War, Jewish, Roma and Sinti people were also sent to these camps

> ### SOURCE ANALYSIS 7.7
>
> Compare and contrast Sources 7H and 7I. In what ways are their messages similar? In what ways are they different?

Political opposition

The SPD set up an exile group called SOPADE. This was based in Prague until Hitler invaded Czechoslovakia. They tried to report to the outside world what was happening in Germany. Also on the left, the Red Orchestra was a spy network that sent information to the USSR from 1936. Many of their spies were tortured and killed by the **Gestapo**.

A small group of conservatives formed an opposition discussion group about how to run Germany after Hitler was gone. It was led by Helmuth von Moltke. The von Moltke family was famous in Germany for its status in the military. The Gestapo knew this group as the Kreisau Circle and several members were executed in 1944 after the army bomb plot.

Military opposition

Key figures within the army shared Hindenburg's doubts about Hitler. This increased as the war went on, leading to an assassination attempt codenamed Operation Valkyrie. The man chosen to plant the bomb was Colonel Claus von Stauffenberg. He turned against Hitler after witnessing the savagery of the Russian front in 1942. Stauffenberg attended a meeting with Hitler on 20 July 1944. He placed a briefcase bomb on the floor and left the room. However, the bomb was moved just before it went off. Four people were killed, but Hitler's only injury was a damaged eardrum from the explosion. A planned uprising in Berlin failed and 5000 conspirators were executed afterwards.

> ### ACTIVITY 7.4
>
> a Make a spider diagram of the different groups (categories) that opposed Hitler's regime. Evaluate how serious a threat to the Nazi regime each group was. Clearly label your diagram to show the level and nature of threat posed to the Third Reich.
>
> b There were at least 40 assassination attempts on Hitler. Research Georg Elser online and write a brief summary of his plot. What do you think motivated him? What does his story tell us about opposition to Hitler?
>
> c What common themes have you noticed about the nature of opposition to the Nazis? Discuss your ideas in small groups.

> **KEY TERM**
>
> **Gestapo:** Nazi secret police who used cruel methods to oppress opposition to the Nazis

> **REFLECTION**
>
> Reflect on your approach to Activity 7.4. How did you reach a conclusion about the seriousness of the threat that each group posed? What criteria did you base your decision on? How useful do you find producing a diagram compared to writing notes? Organising information is a key skill, so try to find a way of doing this that makes sense to you. How can you lay out information most effectively so that you learn it well?

How effectively did the Nazis deal with their political opponents?

Hitler's consolidation of power is known as *Gleichschaltung*, which means 'coordination'. Germany was now a dictatorship, ruled by one party and one man. There were still limits to Hitler's power but only those willing to risk their lives showed open opposition. Authority was maintained through the police state. There were several levels to this:

- the orpo and Kripo: the regular police
- the Gestapo: the secret police, which dealt with moral and political opposition
- the SA, under Himmler's control after 1934
- the SS, which expanded to take over many aspects of the Nazi regime
- the army.

The most important person in all of this was Heinrich Himmler. In 1936, Himmler was put in charge of all police in Germany. He wielded immense power. His deputy, Reinhard Heydrich, was head of the SD, the party's internal security police and main source of intelligence.

The Gestapo had a network of informers, but they were overwhelmed with information from the public. Neighbours often reported on people they did not like as a way of settling personal rivalries. Anyone found guilty of 'deviant behaviour' could be sent to a concentration camp. The first of these was Dachau, which was opened in March 1933. Goebbels made sure it was heavily publicised so that potential opponents knew what would happen to them.

KEY FIGURES

Heinrich Himmler (1900–45)

Himmler joined the Nazis in 1923. In 1929, Hitler put him in charge of his personal bodyguard, the SS. Himmler built it up from 280 men to 52 000 by 1933. It became the most significant organisation in the Nazi state, and he controlled the whole apparatus of terror. Considered to be the principal architect of the Holocaust, Himmler tried and failed to negotiate a peace deal with the USA in 1945. Hitler sacked him and ordered his arrest just before the end of the war. Himmler died by suicide after being captured in 1945.

Reinhard Heydrich (1904–42)

Heydrich was one of the few Nazis who conformed to the racial ideal of being blond-haired and blue-eyed. He was tipped to be a leader after Hitler. As an SS officer, he was an ally of Himmler and chaired the Wannsee Conference in January 1942, which ordered the Holocaust. He ran the SD (a security branch of the SS), assisted in the Gestapo and oversaw Bohemia and Moravia after the fall of Czechoslovakia. He died in 1942 after an assassination attempt by Czech patriots. In retaliation, the SS murdered the population of an entire town, Lidice.

Economic policy and rearmament

The Depression that followed the Wall Street Crash had plunged Germany into chaos. Yet by 1936, unemployment had been resolved and the economy was recovering. How was this achieved?

In many ways, Hitler was lucky, because the Depression actually peaked in late 1932. He also had Hjaldmar Schacht as his economics minister. Schacht was an experienced banker who had helped Stresemann to end hyperinflation in 1923. His New Plan of 1934 set about creating jobs through public works schemes such as the building of the *Autobahn* (the motorway). Another significant project was the launch of the *Volkswagen* ('people's car'). The government spent a lot of money to create these jobs, but it stimulated industry. In turn, the state received more tax income, as more people were employed.

Chapter 7: Germany, 1918–45

Figure 7.13: Hitler testing out a new Volkswagen Beetle, 1939

Hitler aimed to rebuild the armed forces as part of his plan to destroy the Treaty of Versailles and restore German pride and economic strength after the defeat of the Great War. In 1935, he announced an expansion of the army from 100 000 to 500 000. He also announced that he would build an air force, the *Luftwaffe*, which created new jobs in manufacturing.

By 1936, unemployment was down to pre-1929 levels. That year, Hitler set up the Four-Year Plan Office under Göring. He wanted Germany to be ready for war which meant producing more weapons and materials. Germany was to aim for **autarky**. If Germany had no need of imports then it did not matter who Hitler declared war on. This was now Göring's task. Schacht disagreed, but he lost the argument. He was removed from office in 1937.

Göring was no economist. The Four-Year Plan Office failed to achieve its targets for production. In particular, the Nazis lacked oil and rubber, which were essential war materials. This had serious consequences in the Second World War.

> **KEY TERM**
>
> **autarky:** when a state can provide entirely for itself without needing to trade with anyone else (economic independence)

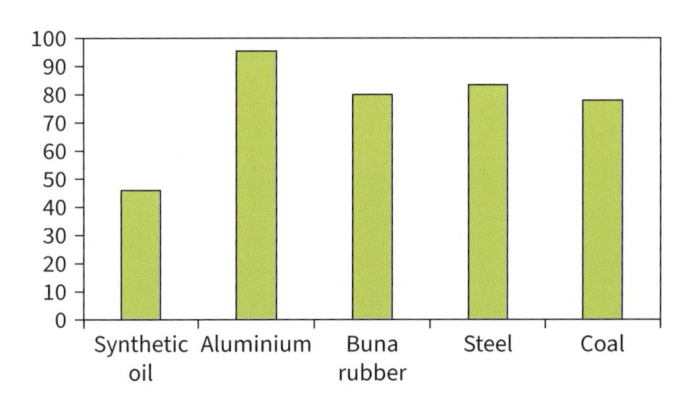

Figure 7.14: A graph showing the percentage of targets met by the Four-Year Plan by 1942

How did the Nazis use culture and the mass media to control the people?

The state controlled the radio, but newspapers were privately owned. The Editors Law of October 1933 made editors responsible for everything published in their newspaper. If a journalist wrote something critical of the Nazis, the editor would be punished. As a result, editors ensured no such articles were published.

In March 1933, the Ministry for Popular Enlightenment and Propaganda was created, with Goebbels in charge. He ensured that all art and entertainment conformed to Nazi values. A cheap radio called the 'People's Receiver' was mass-produced so that more Germans could receive entertainment and propaganda. By 1939, 70% of the population had a radio, the highest level of ownership in the world.

In 1937, Goebbels arranged an exhibition called 'Degenerate Art'. It was intended to educate the public by showing art that was against Nazi values, mainly modern art. It included works by Picasso, Matisse and Van Gogh. More than 4 million people had seen the exhibition by 1940.

Figure 7.15: Hitler and Goebbels touring the exhibition on 'Degenerate Art' in 1937

FOCUS TASK 7.9

a   In pairs, look online for images of Nazi propaganda. Choose one image each. Analyse these examples together. What made them appeal to ordinary Germans? What techniques are being used?

b   Discuss the importance of propaganda in maintaining the Nazis' authority in Germany. Was it more important than other factors, such as the use of terror?

c   After your discussion, write 150–200 words answering the question. Swap writing with your partner and give each other feedback on how the answer could be improved, considering the examples you have both looked at.

> **ACTIVITY 7.5**
>
> a   Hold a class debate about the reasons why Hitler was able to maintain power in the period from 1933 to 1939. In particular, debate these reasons:
>
> - Goebbels' propaganda
> - Himmler's police state
> - Schacht's economic policies.
>
> As a class, decide on the relative importance of each factor.
>
> b   Following the debate, write a paragraph for each bullet point, giving your own evaluation on how important each factor was. Write a conclusion showing which was most significant and why. Write one sentence giving your argument, and a second sentence justifying that argument.

Why did the Nazis persecute many groups in German society?

There were two main reasons for the persecution of particular groups in society.

- **Ideological reasons:** The 25-Point Programme of 1920 and *Mein Kampf* showed hostility to Jewish people, foreigners, communists and anyone who was believed to be against the national interest. Nazi notions of racial purity (the study of eugenics) meant they discriminated against people with mental or physical disabilities.
- **Political:** Hitler never won a majority of the vote in an election. Even in March 1933, with KPD leaders under arrest and the SA intimidating all opposition parties, the Nazis won 43.9%. This meant that 56.1% of Germans voted for other parties even after Hitler became chancellor. He knew that he either had to win over the doubters or intimidate them.

Persecution of religious groups

The moral principles of some religious groups led them to challenge the Nazis. Church leaders also offered a rival influence for Germans. Churches could not simply be shut down, like the KPD, but they could be neutralised. In July 1933, the vice chancellor, von Papen, signed a concordat with the Catholic Church, which guaranteed that its freedoms, rights and property would be protected.

To gain the support of Protestants, a new organisation called the German Christians was created, led by a *Reich* bishop. This aimed to blend Christian and Nazi principles but had little success. In 1934, Martin Niemöller (see Source 7H) and Dietrich Bonhoffer set up the Confessing Church for non-Nazi ministers. It gained the support of 7000 of Germany's 17 000 pastors. In response, priests and pastors were arrested, church schools were closed and funds were confiscated. Niemöller was sent to a concentration camp in 1937 and remained there until 1945.

> **KEY TERMS**
>
> **eugenics:** the theory that it is possible to improve humans by only allowing particular people to produce children
>
> **concordat:** an agreement between the Catholic Church and a government

Persecution of homosexual people

In June 1935, the Nazis changed the criminal code to make homosexuality illegal. As many as 100 000 men were imprisoned under this law, and up to 15 000 were sent to concentration camps. Gay men were made to wear a pink triangle, and many were forced to undergo castration operations. Some were subjected to medical experiments by Nazi scientists who thought they could 'cure' homosexuality.

The Nazis did not make it illegal for women to be gay, but women's organisations were shut down. In the 1920s there were many successful lesbian associations and clubs, especially in cities like Frankfurt, Hamburg and Berlin. The most famous clubs in Berlin were the Violetta Women's Club (*Damenklub Violetta*) and Monbijou Women's clubs (*Damenklub Monbijou*).

Persecution of Jewish people

There were only 503 000 Jewish people in Germany in 1933, which was less than 1% of the population. This did not stop the Nazis seeing them as a threat, but Hitler realised he had to be careful. His first priority was to revise the Treaty of Versailles, which meant making a good impression with foreign nations.

There was little official action against Jewish people in the early years. A one-day boycott of Jewish shops was held on 1 April 1933, but this was mainly to please the SA and had little impact. In 1935, the Nuremberg Laws explained who was considered a Jew and who was considered a German. Jews were not allowed to be citizens of the *Reich* and were forbidden from marrying or having sexual relations with a German.

Figure 7.16: SA officers enforcing the boycott of Jewish shops in 1933; the poster tells Germans not to buy from Jewish people

The 1936 Olympic Games were held in Berlin, so again Hitler and Goebbels put aside their anti-Semitism to show the world how advanced and peaceful Germany was. Many Jewish people, having emigrated in 1933, returned to Germany because it appeared that the Nazis were not as bad as they had feared.

However, in 1938 things suddenly became much worse. Hitler forced *Anschluss* ('union') with Austria (see Chapter 3). Jewish people in Vienna were treated very badly. Heydrich's assistant Adolf Eichmann deported thousands of Jews. On 7 November that year, a Jewish German called Herschel Grynszpan went into the German embassy in Paris and shot a minor official called Ernst vom Rath. Grynszpan's parents were Polish Jews and had been deported from Germany against their will in October, along with 17 000 others.

Goebbels persuaded Hitler that the time was right for a mass action against the Jews in Germany. Dressed in plain clothes, SS men were ordered to attack Jewish homes, shops and synagogues. At least 100 people were killed in the violence. This became known as *Kristallnacht*: the 'Night of Broken Glass'.

Jewish people were blamed for these events and the fines that were issued reached one billion marks. From this time on, Jews were heavily persecuted. Jewish businesses were confiscated and children were excluded from schools and universities. Much worse was to come when Germany descended into war.

Figure 7.17: A Jewish synagogue in Frankfurt on fire during *Kristallnacht*, 1938

REVISION TIP

The website of United States Holocaust Memorial Museum in Washington, D.C. is useful for revising all aspects of the Nazi regime. You will find supporting articles on the website for much of the content for this chapter. You can find it by typing USHMM into a search engine.

Persecution of minority ethnic groups

Roma people can trace their origin to modern-day India and Pakistan. There are many different groups, including Sinti, Kalderashi and Lalleri. The Sinti traditionally lived on German-speaking lands. The Nazis believed that the Roma people were racially inferior so they too were persecuted during the 1930s, and increasingly after 1939. The number of Roma people in pre-war Europe is not known exactly, but estimates are over 1 million. Of these, up to 500 000 died in the Holocaust.

The black population of Weimar Germany stood at 24 000. Under the Nazis, black people were constantly harassed. They were forced into unemployment and not allowed to go to university. A sterilisation programme of interracial children began in 1937. Many teenagers were forced to undergo painful procedures and were ordered not to have sexual relations with Germans.

Figure 7.18: The England football team played Germany in Berlin in 1938, and gave the Nazi salute before kick-off

> **THINKING SKILLS**
>
> Look at the photograph of the football team on this page. Imagine you are one of the England team and have been told that you have to give the Nazi salute or you will not be allowed to play. How would you react? What would you say? Remember it is 1938, and the events of the Second World War have yet to take place.

Was Nazi Germany a totalitarian state?

A totalitarian state is one in which the government has total power over all individuals and institutions. Two US historians have identified six key features of such a state:

1 an official ideology
2 a single-party state, led by one person
3 total control of the military
4 total control of media and communication
5 a police state that uses terror to suppress opposition
6 total control of the economy.

> ### ACTIVITY 7.6
>
> a   Look at the six criteria listed. How far do they apply to the Third Reich? For each one, select at least three pieces of evidence that argue for or against it applying to Germany.
>
> b   Make brief notes indicating how you would answer the question: *How effectively did the Nazis control Germany, 1933–45?*
>
> In pairs, share and compare your ideas to both of these tasks.

Key points

Nazi oppression

- There was a significant amount of opposition to the Nazis, from political groups, and church and youth groups.
- To deal with opposition, the Nazis created an elaborate police state, with concentration camps and the Gestapo as key features.
- Mass media was used very effectively, mainly by Goebbels, to create a favourable impression of Hitler and the Nazi state.
- The Nazis believed in racist theories that led to persecution of ethnic minority groups, as well as social groups.

7.4 What was it like to live in Nazi Germany?

> **FOCUS POINTS**
>
> This topic will help you to answer these questions:
> - How did young people react to the Nazi regime?
> - How successful were Nazi policies towards women and the family?
> - Did most people in Germany benefit from Nazi rule?
> - How did the coming of war change life in Nazi Germany?

How did young people react to the Nazi regime?

The NSDAP was keen to indoctrinate young people with Nazi principles to secure Germany's future. Jewish and politically suspect teachers were removed. The curriculum was changed. Subjects such as biology were used to emphasise German racial superiority. Teachers went on Nazi ideology courses.

Outside school, indoctrination continued. For boys there was the Hitler Youth, led by Baldur von Schirach. They went camping, sang songs and did athletics, which was meant to prepare boys for the army. By 1938, it had 7.1 million members. In 1939, membership was made compulsory. Girls went to the League of German Maidens where they learnt cooking and domestic skills. The result of this was that children were brought up to be loyal to Hitler and the nation above all else. Some children even informed on their parents to the Gestapo if they said something that contradicted what they had been taught in school or the Hitler Youth.

However, some young people formed opposition groups. One of the most famous of these was the Edelweiss Pirates. They listened to American jazz ('black music', which the Nazis accused of being racially inferior) and dressed in their own style. They attacked the Hitler Youth and caused so much concern that 12 Pirates were publicly hanged in Cologne in 1944 as a warning to others.

SOURCES 7J, 7K & 7L

Indoctrination was daily and systematic. Jazz, modern art and comic strips were considered degenerate and forbidden. I could easily imagine Donald Duck, Mickey Mouse, or Superman and their likes dutifully arrested by the Gestapo to serve in some hard labour squad. [. . .] We had special classes building model airplanes, to make us future pilots in the Luftwaffe, of course.

Source 7J: An extract from *Tomi: A Childhood Under the Nazis*, the autobiography of the artist Tomi Ungerer, 1998

Source 7K: An Edelweiss Pirate group

Source 7L: The executions of 12 members of the Edelweiss Pirates in Cologne, November 1944

SOURCE ANALYSIS 7.8

Study Sources 7J, 7K and 7L.

a What Nazi ideologies is this source trying to teach young people in school?

b What can you infer from each source about youth opposition to the Nazis?

c Which source is most useful as evidence of youth culture in Nazi Germany? Explain your answer.

KEY TERM

indoctrination: the process of repeating an idea or belief until they accept it without question

How successful were Nazi policies towards women and the family?

The First World War and the Weimar era saw huge changes for German women. They worked in factories and could vote under the Weimar constitution. Young women used the freedom of the 1920s to go to clubs and socialise. The Nazis were appalled by this trend. Many older women were also unimpressed by the younger generation, and they worried more about family stability and employment for their husbands. Initially, such women tended to vote for conservative parties and backed Hindenburg instead of Hitler for the presidency in 1932. It was only by the July 1932 election that large numbers of women had shifted their support to the NSDAP.

Kinder, Küche, Kirche

Nazi policies towards women were summed up in the slogan '*Kinder, Küche, Kirche*' ('children, kitchen, church'). Women could only have specialist jobs that men should not do, such as being a midwife. Only 10% of university places were available for women. As political parties and trade unions had been banned, women had no way of protesting against these policies.

Young women were encouraged to marry German men of pure blood and have as many children as possible. The Honour Cross of the German Mother was awarded for having several children: bronze for four, silver for six and gold for eight. In 1936, the SS went a step further and established the *Lebensborn* programme, where officers would have children with unmarried women who were deemed racially pure. There was no obligation to act as a responsible father and the women were given financial support to raise the child.

Did most people in Germany benefit from Nazi rule?

One of the key reasons why the Nazis were able to win support was through establishing economic stability. This meant higher levels of employment and higher standards of living (see Section 7.3). Many German people were financially better off under Nazi rule than they had been in the early years after the First World War. However, not everyone benefited from life under the Nazis. Many groups were subjected to terrible persecution.

Policy towards workers

The Nazis distrusted the workers, most of whom had voted for the SPD and KPD. The 'Strength Through Joy' programme was established with two key aims.

- To win workers' support by providing leisure and holiday activities they might not otherwise be able to afford, such as skiing or theatre trips.
- To fill workers' spare time with activities, limiting their ability to think about politics, thereby reducing opposition.

By 1936, there were 30 million workers enlisted in the programme, but there was little evidence that it converted the working class. Both internal SD reports and SOPADE sources reveal that workers were happy to accept the free holidays but did not necessarily adopt Nazi ideology.

SOURCE 7M

His words had power. He was emotional. He was sentimental, he was never intellectual [. . .] The lonely bachelor, the non-smoker, the crusading teetotaller – the glorious fighter for Germany's honour who had gone to prison for his convictions. It was a richly emotional picture for the women to gaze on.

Source 7M: Katherine Thomas was a British visitor to Germany and published a book on German women in 1943. She wrote this extract after hearing Hitler speak in public.

SOURCE ANALYSIS 7.9

Read Source 7M. What does it tell us about the nature of Hitler's appeal to women in Germany?

How did the coming of war change life in Nazi Germany?

War economy

In the first two years of the Second World War, campaigns went well for the Nazis and there was little disruption to life on the home front. Food rationing, introduced in 1939, was not too severe. However, as autarky failed, more restrictions were put in place. With the 1941 invasion of the USSR, Germany began to struggle so the transition was made to **total war**. The economy was completely focused on the war, and by 1944 61% of the workforce was in war-related employment.

The biggest problem was producing weapons. The Four-Year Plan failed to produce the amount of equipment that the *Wehrmacht* (army) needed. In 1942, Hitler appointed Albert Speer as Minister of Armaments. Despite his inexperience – he was Hitler's personal architect with no background in industry – he reorganised German industry and by 1944 there was a 300% increase in production. Even this was not enough. In the vital year of 1944 Germany could only produce 40% of the tanks and 25% of the planes that the USA, USSR and Britain together could.

> **KEY TERM**
>
> **total war:** a war that uses the full economic and military capacity of a nation. Every person is involved in the war effort in some way

German women in the war

Things changed for women in the Second World War. As 12.5 million German men served in the armed forces, women were needed to perform war-related work. This was mainly in weapons factories and on farms. However, many brave women joined the resistance, including Minna Cammens, Maria Terwiel and Gertrud Staewen. These women used Nazi stereotyping to escape questioning by pretending they were supporters or pretending to be pregnant. At the same time, many women suffered for opposing Nazism. A female-only concentration camp was set up at Moringen in November 1933. The largest of the female camps was established at Ravensbrück in 1938, where an estimated 50 000 women died.

The impact of the war on Jewish people

On 1 September 1939, the Wehrmacht invaded Poland. Now 3 million additional Jews were living in German-occupied territory. This presented its own problems. Jews were banned from working or living freely, so the *Reich* had to provide for them. The first **ghetto** was set up in Poland in October 1939. By the end of the war, there were more than 1000 of these areas. The largest was the Warsaw ghetto, which held over 400 000 people.

The June 1941 invasion of the Soviet Union further increased the number of Jews under Nazi control. German intentions in this invasion were clear. Just behind the *Wehrmacht* were four *Einsatzgruppen* ('action groups'), which totalled around 3000 men. Their orders were to murder Jewish people and throw their bodies in mass graves. By the end of the year they had killed 700 000 people. The war with the USSR was draining money and troops. Staffing the ghettos was costly. Killing Jews was the solution chosen. The SS were the driving force behind this. However, by the end of 1941 there were concerns about the efficiency of the operation. A new method was required.

> **KEY TERM**
>
> **ghetto:** an area in which a specific ethnic group (usually Jewish) is forced by law or threat of violence to live

The Wannsee Conference and the Final Solution

On 20 January 1942, a meeting was held in Wannsee, just outside Berlin. It was run by Heydrich and arranged by his deputy Eichmann. This planned the 'Final Solution of the Jewish question'. Heads of government departments, the SS and the *Wehrmacht* were ordered to focus on killing all Europe's Jews. Special camps had been built where Jews would be murdered using Zyklon B (hydrogen cyanide) and their bodies cremated.

What the Nazis termed the Final Solution later came to be known as the Holocaust. Approximately 6 million people were killed. Around half of the victims died in the peak period of murder, from spring 1942 to February 1943. By 1944, the war against the USSR was failing so this gradually brought an end to the Holocaust by spring 1945.

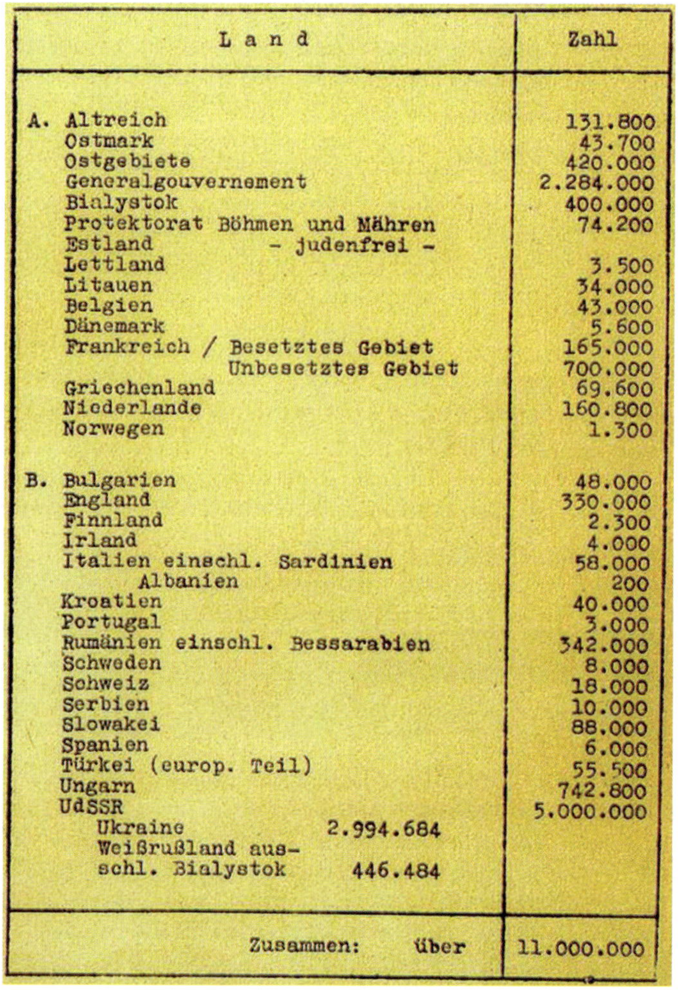

Land	Zahl
A. Altreich	131.800
Ostmark	43.700
Ostgebiete	420.000
Generalgouvernement	2.284.000
Bialystok	400.000
Protektorat Böhmen und Mähren	74.200
Estland - judenfrei -	
Lettland	3.500
Litauen	34.000
Belgien	43.000
Dänemark	5.600
Frankreich / Besetztes Gebiet	165.000
Unbesetztes Gebiet	700.000
Griechenland	69.600
Niederlande	160.800
Norwegen	1.300
B. Bulgarien	48.000
England	330.000
Finnland	2.300
Irland	4.000
Italien einschl. Sardinien	58.000
Albanien	200
Kroatien	40.000
Portugal	3.000
Rumänien einschl. Bessarabien	342.000
Schweden	8.000
Schweiz	18.000
Serbien	10.000
Slowakei	88.000
Spanien	6.000
Türkei (europ. Teil)	55.500
Ungarn	742.800
UdSSR	5.000.000
Ukraine 2.994.684	
Weißrußland ausschl. Bialystok 446.484	
Zusammen: über	11.000.000

Figure 7.19: A document from the Wannsee Conference showing the Nazi estimates on the Jewish populations in each country

Camp	Estimated no. of victims
Auschwitz	1 100 000
Treblinka	925 000
Belzec	434 500
Majdanek	130 000
Chełmno	172 000
Sobibor	167 000

Figure 7.20: A table showing the estimated number of victims of the German death camps (*Source: United States Holocaust Memorial Museum*)

Country	No. of victims
Poland	2 900 000
Ukraine	900 000
Hungary	450 000
Romania	270 000
Belarus	245 000
Lithuania	220 000
Germany	130 000
Russia	107 000
Holland	106 000
France	90 000

Figure 7.21: A table showing the countries with the highest number of Holocaust victims

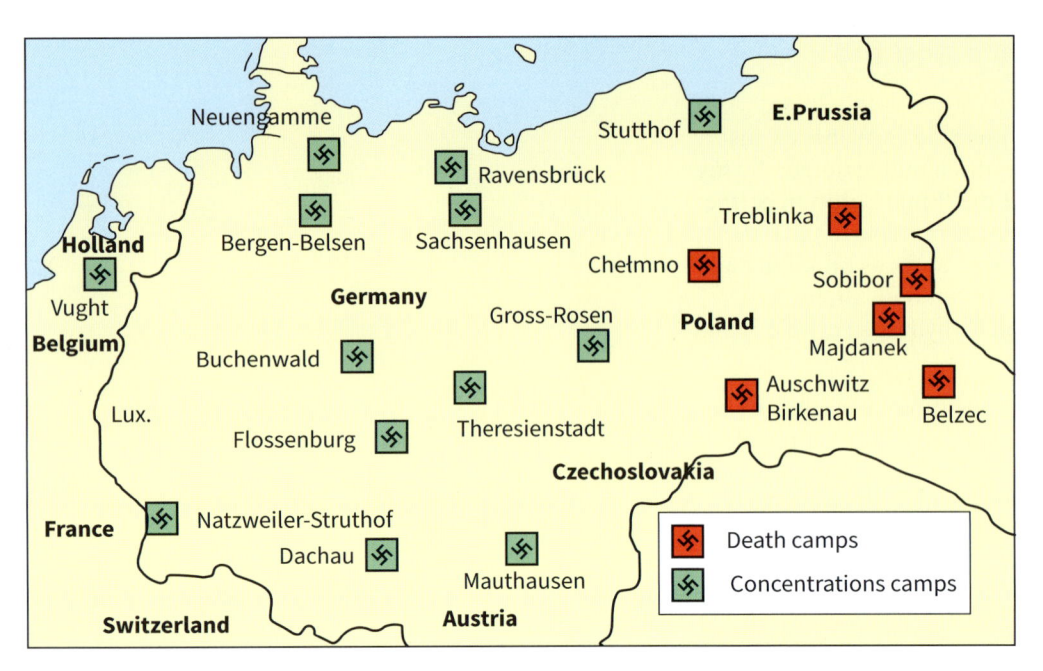

Figure 7.22: A map showing the location of the six death camps that accounted for more than half of all Holocaust victims. Concentration camps were for hard labour and were intended to contribute to the war economy. The death camps were specifically to murder people.

Key points

Life in Nazi Germany

- Many young people were indoctrinated by the Nazi education system which imposed ideological values on them.
- The Nazis had a traditional view of women, which reduced education and employment opportunities in favour of having children and remaining at home.
- Many people did benefit from Nazi policies, particularly due to the economic recovery.
- The war transformed life in Germany, especially as the tide turned against Hitler.
- The war gave the Nazis the opportunity to carry out their most horrific policies, like the Aktion T-4 programme and the Holocaust.

FOCUS TASK 7.10

Make some notes on the main factors that affected life for ordinary people in Germany in the second half of the 1930s. In pairs, use your notes to discuss life for different groups under the Nazis. Try to think of one word or phrase that sums up how each of the following people might feel about the Nazi regime:

- a Jewish businessman
- a Catholic church leader
- a gay man
- a young married woman
- an elderly Roma man
- a member of the Hitler Youth
- a working-class member of the workers' Strength Through Joy programme.

Join up with another pair and share and compare your ideas.

SUMMARY

- The Weimar Republic had a problematic start but recovered and enjoyed some prosperity from 1924 to 1929.
- Hitler established a political movement in the 1920s that made little progress before 1929 but thereafter was more popular than any other German party.
- The Nazis maintained control over Germany after 1933 through use of the police state, heavy propaganda and the benefits of a stronger economy.
- Anyone who opposed the Nazis was suppressed or executed as they operated a police state.
- The Nazis formed an idea of the perfect Aryan 'race' and began persecuting those who did not fit this ideal.
- German society was divided between those the regime favoured and those who were persecuted. Some benefited and many others suffered.
- Young people were indoctrinated into Nazi ideology through groups such as Hitler Youth and women were encouraged to marry.
- Groups such as Jewish and Roma people suffered persecution, particularly after war broke out.

KEY SKILLS EXERCISES

Knowledge and understanding

1. Name three forms of left-wing opposition to the Weimar Republic, and three forms of right-wing opposition.
2. What changes did Hitler make to the Nazi Party when he became leader?
3. Define the term 'totalitarianism'.

Application

4. How did the changes that Hitler made after 1924 benefit the Nazi Party after the Wall Street Crash?
5. Why did Hindenburg oppose Hitler, and why did he change his stance?
6. Suggest two reasons, other than Hitler's leadership, why the Nazis were a popular party in Germany by 1933.

Analysis

7. Analyse two reasons why opposition groups failed to successfully challenge the Nazis before the Second World War.
8. Analyse the roles played by Goebbels and Himmler in running the Nazi state.
9. Analyse the impact of the Second World War on the people of Germany.

Evaluation

10. Evaluate the policies put in place by the Nazis in the 1930s that discriminated against the Jews.
11. Evaluate the role played by other religious groups in both supporting and challenging Nazi policies.
12. Evaluate the reasons for the Holocaust. Did Hitler work towards a grand plan, or was anti-Semitism driven more by the SS?

IMPROVE THIS ANSWER

Why did Hitler become Chancellor in 1933?

Sample answer: Hitler became Chancellor because he was leader of the largest party in Germany. **1** The Nazis weren't popular before the Wall Street Crash and the Great Depression began in 1929, so he was never able to become leader of Germany before that. However, after this many workers in Germany became unemployed and by 1933 this had reached 6 million people. **2** Hitler promised to fix the problems and heal the economy, and many voters listened to this. The other parties had either failed to fix the problems, like the Social Democrats, or they were too radical, like the KPD. **3** Hitler ran a very good campaign and used new methods like cinema advertising and flying around Germany by plane, so he appeared to be a much more modern leader. Although Hindenburg didn't like Hitler, he tried lots of ways to keep him out of power. These didn't work and in the end he had to appoint him as Chancellor because he had won a majority of the votes in Germany so was the most popular leader. **4**

Now write an improved response using this guidance.

1 A good reason is identified, so we have one factor.

2 This is accurate and provides some good evidence.

3 Perhaps, but the Nazis were also very radical – Hitler had been in jail for trying to overthrow the government, so this point is a little weak.

4 There is a factual error here, as Hitler never won a majority of the vote in Germany. Also the answer only really develops one factor and doesn't offer a second clear reason. You can see this in the structure, because it is only one paragraph rather than two. Make sure you have two reasons at least and give each one a separate paragraph.

PRACTICE QUESTIONS

1 Hitler became chancellor of Germany in 1933.
   a What happened in the Munich Putsch? [4]
   b Why did the Wall Street Crash make the Nazis more popular? [6]
   c 'The main reason for Hitler's rise to power was the weakness of the Weimar government.' How far do you agree with this statement? Explain your answer. [10]
   [Total: 20]

2 a Write an account of opposition to the Nazis. [15]
   b Discuss the impact of the Holocaust on minorities in Germany. [25]
   [Total: 40]

Chapter 7: Germany, 1918–45

PROJECT

You are going to work in pairs to create a set of revision cards covering the key information in this chapter. You will create ten cards for each of the following topics.

- The impact of Versailles on Germany
- Uprisings against the Weimar Republic 1919–33
- Successes of the Weimar Republic 1924–29
- The early years of the Nazi Party 1919 to 1929
- Hitler's rise to power 1930 to 1933
- Hitler's consolidation of power 1933–34
- Opposition to the Nazi regime
- The Nazi police state
- The use of propaganda and media
- The persecution of opposition and minorities
- Young people and women in Germany
- People who benefited from Nazi rule
- Germany in the Second World War
- Leading Nazis

Start with the first topic and find the relevant section in this chapter. In your pairs, write a list of questions that you think encapsulate the key information you need to know from this section.

When you have a list, decide between you on the ten questions that you think are the most important. Write each question on one side of a piece of card.

Between you decide on a clear, concise answer to each of your ten questions. You can use this book, the internet and any other resources available to you to come up with the answers. Write the answers clearly on the back of each card.

Then move on to the next topic and repeat the process until you have a set of ten cards for each topic.

Practise asking and answering the questions in your pairs. You could swap cards with another pair and see whether they asked the same questions in the same way and if they gave the same answers.

SELF-EVALUATION CHECKLIST

After studying this chapter, complete this table:

You should be able to:	Needs more work	Almost there	Ready to move on
understand the political and economic problems Germany faced after the First World War			
assess the impact that the Treaty of Versailles had on Germany up to 1923			
explain why Germany recovered after 1923 and describe the main achievements of this period			
identify the key features of the Nazi Party under Hitler's leadership from 1920 to 1933			
explain why Hitler came to power in January 1933			
explain how Hitler turned Germany from a democracy into a dictatorship from 1933 to 1934			
describe the various opposition groups to Nazi rule, and evaluate their impact			
understand why the Nazi state was so ruthless at dealing with opposition and minority groups			
assess the role that propaganda played in maintaining power for Hitler			
understand what is meant by a totalitarian state, and assess whether this applies to Germany under the Nazis			
describe how young people and women were treated under the Nazis, and how they reacted			
explain why some people benefited from Hitler's policies in the 1930s			
evaluate the effects of the Second World War on Germany society.			

> Chapter 8:
Russia, 1905–41

FOCUS POINTS

This chapter will help you to answer these questions:

- Why did the Tsarist regime collapse in 1917?
- How did the Bolsheviks gain power, and how did they consolidate their rule?
- How did Stalin gain and hold on to power?
- What was the impact of Stalin's economic policies?

8.0 What is this Depth study about?

In 1913, the Russian Empire covered one-sixth of the world's land surface. That year the tsar, Nicholas II, celebrated the 300th anniversary of his family's reign. The Russian monarchy seemed very secure. However, five years later, Russia had been transformed by two revolutions. In 1917, the Provisional Government ruled for a few months, before communists seized power in November. The communist government was led by Vladimir Lenin until his death in 1924, then Joseph Stalin rose to power by 1929.

Despite these dramatic changes, many features of life in Russia remained the same. Society was still mostly rural. Many people in Russia described the economy as 'backward' because it had been left behind by the Industrial Revolution that swept the rest of Europe in the 1800s. Stalin ruled as a dictator, but in the years before 1941, the Union of Soviet Socialist Republics (USSR) was modernised, affecting the lives of millions of people.

After such a long period of stability, what caused Russia to have two revolutions in 1917? What were the consequences of these revolutions, and how were people's lives altered as a result?

Figure 8.1: A photograph of Tsar Nicholas II, taken in 1913, when the Romanov family were celebrating 300 years on the Russian throne. Nicholas II became tsar, age 26, after his father, Tsar Alexander III, died in 1894. Nicholas is surrounded by his four daughters, his wife Alexandra (center back) and his only son, Alexei (second from the right).

KEY FIGURE

Nicholas II (1868–1917)

Nicholas II became tsar in 1894 aged 26. He did not feel well prepared for political leadership but he was committed to **autocracy**, believing it was the best form of government for Russia. He was devoted to his wife, Alexandra, and to his children but was easily influenced and took advice from his wife and her favoured advisers. Nicholas believed that he needed to know the business of government in great detail, and often interfered in the work of his ministers. However, he did not really understand the extent of the social, political and economic changes that Russia needed. Nicholas lost the support of his government and his generals after 1915 and was forced to abdicate in March 1917. He and his family were shot by the Bolsheviks in July 1918, at a key point in the Russian Civil War.

KEY TERM

autocracy: a system of government in which one leader, often a monarch, has absolute power

Chapter 8: Russia, 1905–41

8.1 Why did the Tsarist regime collapse in 1917?

> **FOCUS POINTS**
>
> This topic will help you to answer these questions:
> - How well did the Tsarist regime deal with the difficulties of ruling Russia up to 1914?
> - How did the tsar survive the 1905 Revolution?
> - How far was the tsar weakened by the First World War?
> - Why was the revolution of March 1917 successful?

Figure 8.2: A map showing Russia's natural landscape, main cities and industrial centres before 1914

How well did the Tsarist regime deal with the difficulties of ruling Russia up to 1914?

The Russian Empire

In 1914, the Russian Empire appeared strong, but its size slowed communications and its long borders exposed it to attack. Only 44% of Russia's population were ethnic Russians. Most Russians followed the Russian Orthodox Christian faith. The government, based in the capital, St Petersburg, was dominated by Russians, who tried to unite the empire through a process known as **Russification**. These policies were extremely unpopular, and many national minorities wanted greater independence. Persecution of Jewish people was particularly harsh, and the government even encouraged **pogroms**.

> **KEY TERMS**
>
> **Russification:** the official policy of forcing non-Russians to accept the Russian language and Russian rules in schools and in local government
>
> **pogroms:** riots or semi-organised violence directed against Jewish people and their property

Tsarist government

Tsar Nicholas II was the head of an outdated system of government. He was the supreme ruler, holding all power and authority. He was a caring family man, but he was not an effective monarch and there was little coordination of policymaking. Unlike many other countries at the time, Russia had no political opposition and no elections, because there was no parliament.

Nicholas often took advice from his wife, Alexandra, in his dedication to maintaining the Tsarist regime. The tsarina was German by birth, and she did not speak Russian fluently. She was so shy that the royal couple avoided hosting social events, and they lacked support from the **aristocracy**, which made up 1.5% of the population but owned 25% of the land and held a lot of power.

> **KEY TERM**
>
> **aristocracy:** a class of people who hold high social rank

SOURCES 8A, 8B & 8C

The Emperor of all the Russias is an autocratic and unlimited monarch. God commands that his supreme power be obeyed out of conscience as well as fear.

Source 8A: An extract from Russia's Fundamental Laws of Tsarism

I am not prepared to be a tsar. I never wanted to become one. I know nothing of the business of ruling.

Source 8B: A comment from Nicholas II on the death of his father

Source 8C: The crest of the Russian monarchy and state in the time of Nicholas II. The double-headed eagle symbolised Russia's geographical position, looking to east and west at the same time. It also represented Tsarism's history and its intention to remain into the future.

SOURCE ANALYSIS 8.1

Study Sources 8A, 8B and 8C.

a   What does each of the following phrases from Source 8A mean?

- 'Emperor of all the Russias'
- 'autocratic and unlimited monarch'
- 'God commands that his supreme power be obeyed'
- 'obeyed out of conscience as well as fear'.

b   How might the Fundamental Laws protect Nicholas, even if he was not an effective ruler?

c   Compare and interpret these three sources. What can you learn from them about the reasons why Nicholas II found ruling Russia difficult?

Chapter 8: Russia, 1905–41

> **ACTIVITY 8.1**
>
> Nicholas II kept a diary in which he detailed his daily activities, as well as his thoughts and feelings. Imagine you are the tsar. Write a diary entry in which you explain how well you feel you are suited to the role. Consider:
>
> - how you think Nicholas II's family life might have affected his ability to rule Russia
> - how Nicholas's own personality might have caused difficulties with ruling Russia.
>
> Share some examples of your diary entries as a class and discuss what characteristics come across from them. How might this have set the Russian up for disaster?

The Tsarist system was supported by a huge **bureaucracy** across the country. Generally, the system was corrupt and inefficient. Government officials were usually members of the aristocracy, but some officials who controlled local government organisations (*zemstvo*) were reforming members of the **liberal intelligentsia**.

Russia's population and social structure

The peasantry

In 1900, around 80% of Russia's population were peasants, or **serfs**. Before 1861, peasants were the property of the landowners. Even after the serfs were freed in 1861, Russia's peasants had to pay for their land in 49 annual payments. This was a huge debt for many of them. The majority of peasants lived in village **communes**. Although there were some successful peasant farmers (*kulaks*), most continued to live on farms that were too small to produce enough food, and they suffered from land hunger.

Figure 8.3: A Russian cartoon from 1901 criticising the 'social pyramid'. From the top, the images and labels show: the royal family (we reign over you); the aristocracy (we rule you); the Church (we fool you); the army (we shoot at you); capitalists (we eat for you); workers (we work for you); peasants

KEY TERMS

bureaucracy: a system for managing a country or organisation operated by a large number of officials who follow the rules very carefully

liberal intelligentsia: a group of educated people (doctors, lawyers, teachers, writers and other professionals) who were active in political leadership. They became frustrated at the 'backwardness' of tsarism

serfs: peasants who were forced to work for a landowner. Serfdom was common in Europe in the Middle Ages, but Russia's system lasted longer than in most other places

commune: a community of people who live together and share property, resources and labour

kulaks: wealthier peasants (the word '*kulak*' means 'fist' or 'tight-fisted': mean with money)

Figure 8.4: A Russian peasant village, c.1900

Industry and industrial workers

The Russian government made no plans for modernisation until the 1890s, when Sergei Witte, the Minister of Finance, began a series of reforms, including the construction of the 6000-kilometre Trans-Siberian Railway. Industrial production increased by 6–8% every five years after 1885 – the fastest growth rate in the world.

Russia's working class caused the government concern. Many peasants moved to cities such as Moscow and St Petersburg in search of work. However, sanitation was poor and disease was common. Workers endured 12-hour factory shifts in unsafe conditions. They received low wages and paid high taxes. Workers' rights were not legally protected, and trade unions and strikes were illegal. These problems caused dissatisfaction, especially among socialists, and the government had to use soldiers to end strikes 522 times in 1902.

Year	Coal	Pig iron	Oil	Grain
1870	0.6	0.3	0.1	0
1890	5.4	0.8	3.5	32.6
1910	24.3	2.6	8.5	67.1

Figure 8.5: A table showing annual industrial and agricultural production in Russia (million tonnes)

Opposition to Tsarism

The government's harsh response often turned industrial strikes into political protests, and Russia's revolutionary parties grew at this time. Although they were all influenced by the theories of Karl Marx, they disagreed on how best to end Tsarism.

> ### KEY FIGURE
>
> #### Karl Marx (1818–83)
>
> Marx was born in the German state of Prussia, but he was forced to leave in 1849 because of his radical writings about society, economics, politics and power. In his most famous books, *The Communist Manifesto* and *Das Kapital*, Marx argued that human history is dominated by conflict between different social classes. According to Marx's theory, the middle classes (the bourgeoisie) would win control of the means of production from the monarchy and aristocracy, and this would lead to capitalism. Marx predicted that the working classes (the proletariat) would work in return for wages under capitalism, but only until they grew frustrated with their lack of political power, at which time they would seize control in a socialist revolution.

The Socialist Revolutionaries

The Socialist Revolutionaries wanted to destroy Tsarism and give all land to the peasants. Socialist Revolutionaries believed that violence was the most efficient way to achieve political change, and their terrorist section assassinated government officials. They had support from peasants and urban workers.

The Social Democrats

The Social Democrats wanted to destroy Tsarism and give power to the proletariat. They aimed to encourage revolution among urban workers, but they disagreed about how best to do this. In 1903, there was a major disagreement and the party split. The two new groups – Bolsheviks and Mensheviks – were rivals, although their members knew each other well.

- The Bolsheviks (which means 'the majority') believed that a small group comprising only radical revolutionaries could inspire the working classes to revolution through writing newspapers, books and leaflets. They were led by Vladimir Lenin.
- The Mensheviks (the name means 'the minority', even though their numbers were larger than the Bolsheviks) believed that the party should welcome anyone. They did not believe that the working classes could be rushed into revolution, preferring to wait for the right moment.

Government control

The government's response to political problems was almost always to repress rather than to reform. Opposition parties were illegal, and political **dissenters** were executed or sent into exile in Siberia or abroad. The government's methods of control were generally very effective.

- The Okhrana was formed to combat anti-government activity. It used techniques such as spying, opening mail, bugging rooms and tapping telephone lines.
- Laws gave police and local governors emergency powers to arrest and imprison suspects, to close down and fine newspapers, to shut down local parliaments, and to control what was published.
- The army was regularly used to control the population, especially the peasantry.
- Since the government lacked a network of state control in many areas, it relied heavily upon the Russian Orthodox Church. The Church used its spiritual authority to teach the Russian people that obedience to the tsar was their duty.

> **KEY TERM**
>
> **dissenter:** someone who strongly and publicly disagrees with something, especially a political position

FOCUS TASK 8.1

a In pairs, discuss how the tsar could use each of the four methods described above to keep different kinds of people under control. Make notes of your ideas.

b In your pairs, copy and complete the following table to summarise the problems Nicholas II faced in ruling Russia before 1905. When you have completed it, join up with another pair and compare your tables. Add any notes to your table that you may have missed out.

	The empire	Tsarism and Nicholas II's style of government	Population	Economy	Opposition to Tsarism
Non-urgent problems					
Urgent problems					

c Which of Russia's difficulties were unavoidable, which were created by the government, and which were worsened by the Russian government? Draw up three lists with your partner.

THINKING SKILLS

Imagine you are Sergei Witte, head of the tsar's Committee of Ministers, in 1904. Using the table of problems you created in Focus task 8.1, what would you advise Nicholas II was the most serious problem? Write the tsar a letter, asking for a meeting to discuss this problem and explaining to him why it deserves his attention.

How did the tsar survive the 1905 Revolution?

Why did a revolution break out in 1905?

The long-term causes of the 1905 Revolution had been building for many years.

- Workers were angry about long working hours, low pay, unsafe working conditions and poor living conditions. They also wanted more political power (see Source 8D).
- Peasants were angry about poverty, land hunger, high taxes and debt.
- National minorities wanted greater independence and an end to Russification.
- The middle classes wanted an elected government, as well as more civil and political rights.
- Revolutionaries wanted a complete overthrow of the tsarist regime.

In the medium term, in 1903 and 1904 the government made several serious errors. Firstly, as a **concession** to middle-class demands, censorship was relaxed. Secondly, in February 1904, as a result of a dispute over influence in the Far East, the Japanese attacked the Russian base at Port Arthur. The following Russo–Japanese War saw a series of disastrous defeats for Russia, on sea and land. The humiliation of these defeats, the economic effects of the war, and the stories of official incompetence that appeared during the conflict, were all very damaging for the government. Finally, the government failed to stop the middle classes discussing their proposed reforms of the Tsarist system openly in November 1904.

In the short term, a large strike developed in St Petersburg over the sacking of four workers. All the conditions for the 1905 Revolution were present, but the spark was Bloody Sunday. On 22 January 1905, 200 000 protesters marched through St Petersburg to the Winter Palace, the home of the tsar, to deliver a petition to him. They were led by a priest, Father Gapon, a double agent working for the police.

KEY TERM

concession: something that is allowed or given up, often in order to end a disagreement

SOURCE ANALYSIS 8.2

Look at the petition delivered by Father Gapon on Bloody Sunday in Source 8D.

a What are the complaints listed in it?

b What are the protesters' demands?

c How would you describe the tone of the petition?

d Are you surprised by the content or the tone of the petition? Explain your ideas.

e Which do you think would have been more concerning to the tsar: the content, or the tone of the petition? Explain your answer.

SOURCE 8D

Sovereign! We, workers and inhabitants of the city of St. Petersburg, our wives, children and helpless old parents, have come to you, Sovereign, to seek justice and protection. We are treated like slaves who must suffer a bitter fate and keep silent. And we have suffered, but we only get pushed deeper and deeper into an abyss of misery, ignorance and lack of rights.

Our first request was that our employers discuss our needs together with us. But they refused to do this on the grounds that the law does not provide us with such a right. Also unlawful were our other requests: to reduce the working day to eight hours; for them to set wages together with us and by agreement with us; to examine our disputes with lower-level factory administrators; to increase the wages of unskilled workers and women to one ruble per day; to abolish overtime work; to provide medical care attentively and without insult; to build shops so that it is possible to work there and not face death from the awful drafts, rain and snow.

Sovereign, this is what we face and this is the reason that we have gathered before the walls of your palace. Do not refuse to come to the aid of your people. Tear down the wall that separates you from your people and let it rule the country together with you.

Source 8D: Extract from the petition carried by protesters on Bloody Sunday, 1905

The protesters never delivered their message to the tsar, who was not even at the Winter Palace that day. Instead, they were met by soldiers who opened fire, killing 200 people and wounding another 800. News of the killings damaged the tsar's reputation and caused further protests.

SOURCE 8E

Source 8E: *Zhupel* (Bugbear) of Revolution, a revolutionary cartoon by Boris Kustodiev, 1905

SOURCE ANALYSIS 8.3

Study Source 8E.

a What aspect of life in Russia before 1905 does the skeleton symbolise?

b The colour red is used in four different ways in this image. Identify the four different uses. What do you think each use represents?

c What message does the cartoonist intend to convey?

d This cartoon was published in one of many newspapers and magazines that started in Russia during 1905. What message would the publication of this cartoon send to readers, considering the way the Tsarist regime had kept Russia under control before 1905?

EVENTS OF 1905

January	Bloody Sunday 400 000 workers are on strike by the end of January.
February	Grand Duke Sergei is killed by a Social Revolutionary assassin. Students at Moscow University protest so the government closes all universities. A new Interior Minister, Alexander Bulygin, is appointed. Peasants begin stealing from landowners' land. The army is used 2700 times to put down peasant uprisings before October 1905.
June	Rotten meat on the battleship *Prince Potemkin* causes a rebellion. The rebels are shot by the captain, so the crew mutinies and sails to Odessa, which is in the middle of a general strike. There, people help the sailors. Troops sent in to break up the crowds kill 2000 people. The mutiny does not spread but is a major embarrassment for the government. National minorities demand change. In Poland there are more strikes than in the rest of the Russian Empire combined. Georgia declares its independence.
August	The tsar issues a manifesto on the creation of a state **Duma**. This plan is rejected by revolutionaries for being too weak.
October	A general strike develops. Transport stops, lights go out, telephone lines go dead, shops close, food is hard to find, robberies and lootings increase, and the Moscow water system fails. As state censorship begins to fail, newspapers critical of the government are launched. The St Petersburg **Soviet** is created. It has the same powers as the government; organising the strikers, publishing a newspaper (*Izvestiia*), establishing a private army and distributing food.

> **KEY TERMS**
>
> **Duma:** the Russian name for a parliament
>
> **Soviet:** the Russian word for 'council'. The name for an elected group at several different social levels in the USSR

FOCUS TASK 8.2

Study the timeline of the 1905 Revolution. It shows how workers, peasants, the armed forces, national minorities, political parties and the tsar himself reacted in 1905. On your own, create a table that outlines the following information for each group or person.

- What motivated them?
- What evidence is there that the revolutionary opposition groups influenced this group?
- In which of the events did this group pose the most serious threat to Tsarism?

Compare your completed table with a partner's and discuss any similarities and differences in the information you have included.

> KEY FIGURE

Leon Trotsky (1879–1940)

Lev Davidovich Bronstein (Trotsky) joined the Mensheviks, and was a leading figure in the St Petersburg Soviet. Exiled after 1905, he returned to Russia after March 1917 and joined the Bolsheviks. He became head of the Petrograd Soviet and led the Bolshevik Revolution. As Commissar for Foreign Affairs, he negotiated the Brest-Litovsk treaty, and as Commissar for War, he built up the Red Army. He was sidelined after Lenin's death, expelled from the party in 1927 and then exiled. He criticised Stalin from exile and was murdered in Mexico on Stalin's orders in 1940.

How did the tsar regain control in the short-term?

Nicholas's response to the revolutionary events was very effective. In August 1905, Sergei Witte ended the Russo–Japanese war, which reduced pressure on the government. In October 1905, Nicholas issued the October Manifesto (see Source 8F), granting some civil freedoms. This satisfied many liberals, conservatives and moderate socialists.

Peter Stolypin was appointed prime minister in 1906. He sent the army into the countryside with orders to show no mercy. Around 15 000 peasants were executed by hanging. The hangman's noose became known as 'Stolypin's necktie'. Another 45 000 were deported. The rebellion in the countryside ended.

In December, the government acted against revolutionaries. Troops arrested the St Petersburg Soviet. A Bolshevik armed uprising in Moscow was crushed. By 1917, all leading revolutionaries were dead, in exile in Siberia or in hiding abroad.

> **SOURCE 8F**
>
> *On the improvement of order in the state*
>
> *The disturbances and unrest in St Petersburg, Moscow and in many other parts of our Empire have filled Our heart with great sorrow. The disturbances could give rise to national instability and present a threat to the unity of Our State. The oath which We took as Tsar compels Us to use all Our strength, intelligence and power to put a speedy end to this unrest. The relevant authorities have been ordered to take measures to deal with outbreaks of disorder and to protect people.*
>
> *Fundamental civil freedoms will be granted to the population, including real personal inviolability, freedom of conscience, speech, assembly and association.*
>
> *Participation in the Duma will be granted to those classes of the population which are at present deprived of voting powers, and this will lead to the development of a universal franchise.*
>
> *It is established as an unshakeable rule that no law can come into force without its approval by the State Duma and representatives of the people will be given the opportunity to take real part in the supervision of the legality of government bodies.*
>
> **Source 8F:** An extract from the October Manifesto, 1905

> **SOURCE ANALYSIS 8.4**
>
> Read Source 8F.
>
> a What concessions did Nicholas II grant? Write a list.
>
> b Why do you think the tsar granted these concessions? Does he appear to want to address the problems raised by the protesters? Explain your answer.
>
> c Look back at your notes on the Bloody Sunday petition. How effectively did these concessions deal with the concerns of the people who began the protests in January 1905? Explain your answer.

Key points

How was control restored?

- Nicholas II restored control after the 1905 Revolution using a mixture of force and concessions.
- Force was used against the revolutionaries in the major cities and against the peasant uprisings across the empire.
- Although the revolution was over by the end of 1905, the restoration of political control took longer.
- Concessions were used to win the loyalty of the liberals and some of the peasantry between 1906 and 1914.

FOCUS TASK 8.3

Consider how Nicholas II was able to survive the 1905 Revolution. Work in pairs. Copy and complete the following table using the information in this section and using research from any other sources you have available.

Factors explaining Nicholas's survival	When was this factor important?	Who did this satisfy / pacify?	How effective was this factor in restoring calm?
Peace with Japan			
October and November Manifestos			
Use of repression			
Acting against revolutionary leaders			
Loyalty of the army			
Lack of unity among opposition			

How did government change after 1905?

By April 1906, the government was back in control. The tsar issued the Fundamental Laws. These restated the principles of Tsarism and revised some of the promises in the October Manifesto. Voting laws were designed so that the elections would put pro-tsarist representatives in power.

The Dumas, 1906–14

Many deputies in the first Duma were optimistic about the prospects for democratic government in Russia, but they quickly realised that Tsar Nicholas had no intention of allowing them real power. There were four Dumas before 1914. The first two were very critical of Nicholas, and the Tsar dissolved the Duma both times. After electoral law changes, the third Duma was much less critical, and Nicholas tolerated it from November 1907 until 1912. However, it had no significant power, and gradually came to oppose the government. It was a similar story with the fourth Duma.

Figure 8.6: Tsar Nicholas speaking at the opening of the first Duma, 1906

Government policies in the countryside

Stolypin tried to win the support of the peasants by offering incentives for them to buy farms or move to farms in Siberia. By 1914, almost 2 million peasants had left communes. Peasants owned half of Russia's land and agricultural productivity was increasing. Harvests were good for five years in a row, and peasant violence was declining. However, most farms were still small and inefficient, and conditions remained poor for the peasant class.

Industry and the workers

Stolypin increased industrial output and planned education programmes and regulations on factory work. Despite this, production remained lower than Britain, Germany and the USA, and workers' conditions were still poor. There were increasing numbers of workers, and more of them were literate and politicised. In one strike in the Lena goldfields in Siberia in April 1912, soldiers killed 270 workers and injured many more.

	Number of strikes	Number of strikes classified as 'political'
1911	466	24
1912	2032	1300
1913	2404	1034
1914 (Jan–Jul)	3534	2401

Figure 8.7: Strikes in Russia between 1911 and 1914

The middle class and the nobility

Modern methods led to increased industrial production, which meant more wealth for the middle classes. However, Stolypin was assassinated in 1911, which pleased landowners and industrialists who were concerned that his reforms were going too far. Nicholas II had decided to sack him anyway, but many of the middle class were frustrated by the tsar's tendency to appoint incompetent ministers.

> **REFLECTION**
>
> Which of the following statements do you most closely agree with?
>
> - Tsarism was as strong as ever in July 1914.
> - Tsarism looked strong but was weak in reality in July 1914.
> - Tsarism was weak; revolution was near in July 1914.
>
> How did you come to your decision? What process did you follow to reach conclusions? Discuss your ideas with a partner and consider the similarities in your approaches to this question.

How far was the tsar weakened by the First World War?

In July 1914, Russia mobilised its army to support its ally Serbia. The outbreak of war caused an outburst of patriotism. The Duma passed a vote of loyalty to Nicholas, and the tsar changed the name of the capital from St Petersburg to Petrograd, because it sounded more Russian. This optimism did not last long.

The military impact of the war

Russia's army of 1.4 million men was the largest in Europe in 1914, but Russia's military campaign was disastrous. Defeats at the Battles of Tannenberg and Masurian Lakes were especially heavy. During 1915, the Russian army was forced to retreat nearly 1000 kilometres into Russia and 2 million men were lost. A major offensive was launched in 1916, but after supply problems the Russians were forced to retreat again.

The Russian army's leadership was incompetent from the start. Supply shortages in the early months of the war meant that thousands of Russian soldiers were sent into battle with no boots or weapons. After Nicholas II took personal command of the army in August 1915, military defeats reflected very badly on the tsar.

The economic impact of the war

Government spending rose from 4 million roubles a year to 30 million. However, government income fell because the war reduced foreign trade, and because Nicholas II tried to ban vodka (30% of government income came from alcohol tax). The government printed more money, but this caused inflation. Between July 1914 and early 1917, average wages increased by 100%, but prices rose faster. In Petrograd, the price of milk increased by 150% between August 1914 and late 1916, butter by 830%, and meat by 900%.

The social impact

Millions of people were directly affected by the fighting, and the conscription of 13 million peasants into the army caused labour shortages in the countryside. Throughout 1914 and 1915, thousands of Russian army officers were killed. These were almost all the sons of aristocratic families, which caused great anger.

The government took horses to be used by the army. This affected agricultural production, and shortages of goods such as sugar, paraffin and matches also angered the peasants. As a result of the war, peasant soldiers became much more influential. The government had armed millions of dissatisfied people. Especially in Petrograd, where the garrison was in the centre of the city, soldiers became increasingly aware of the political situation.

The political impact of the war

The Duma began criticising the government's handling of the war. It formed the 'Progressive Bloc' and requested political reform in 1915. Tsarina Alexandra ran the government while Nicholas was away with the army. There were many rumours about her. She was accused of being a German spy and of having an affair with Gregory Rasputin, a drunken traveller who claimed to be a priest. The Russian nobles disliked Rasputin, but Alexandra trusted him because she believed he could treat her son, who suffered from the bleeding disease haemophilia. However, the most damaging rumour about Alexandra was that Rasputin was giving her political advice. Several aristocrats became so concerned about Rasputin's influence that they murdered him in December 1916.

Figure 8.8: A cartoon showing Rasputin, Nicholas and Alexandra

> **THINK LIKE A HISTORIAN**
>
> What modern examples are there of famous people whose reputations have been negatively affected by rumour or exaggeration in popular media? Why do people enjoy gossip or rumours about famous people's private lives? How much harm do you think it can do? When you read articles or social media posts about people in the public eye, do you believe them, or do you question whether they are true or exaggerated?

Why was the revolution of March 1917 successful?

The March 1917 Revolution began as a series of peaceful protests on the streets of Petrograd, and it ended with the tsar's abdication. The people who began protesting in early March 1917 would never have imagined that two weeks later the tsar would be gone, with political power in the hands of some Duma deputies.

EVENTS OF MARCH 1917

7 March	Workers in Petrograd's largest factory go on strike over bread shortages, low wages, poor working conditions and rising prices.
8 March	Strikers and those celebrating International Women's Day mingle on the streets. Around 250 000 people participate in peaceful demonstrations.
9 March	Strikes spread and factories come to a standstill. Rumours about bread shortages cause some violence, but protesters remain generally peaceful.
10 March	The tsar, who is still at the front, orders the Petrograd garrison to use force to stop the protesters.
11 March	Some soldiers ignore orders to shoot at demonstrators and begin to support the crowds. Other troops open fire and kill 50 protesters. Duma ministers send a message to Nicholas, saying 'the situation is serious [...] the capital is in a state of anarchy' and demand that a new government be formed. Nicholas replies that this is not true, that the army must be used to end the disturbances, and that the Duma be suspended.
12 March	Up to 170 000 soldiers ignore orders to fire at protesters. Soldiers and strikers seize weapons, open the prisons and gather those who are loyal to the tsar. The government resigns. Duma members form a Provisional Government. At the same time, in the same building, workers and soldiers elect their own representatives, and form the Petrograd Soviet of Workers', Sailors' and Soldiers' Deputies.
13 March	Almost all Petrograd soldiers join the revolution. The Provisional Government assumes control and orders the arrest of tsarist ministers. Nicholas decides to return to Petrograd.
14 March	The revolution spreads to Moscow and the Kronstadt naval base outside Petrograd. Nicholas's train is stopped by railway workers and soldiers. Nicholas's generals advise him to abdicate.
15 March	The Provisional Government gains control, with conditional support from the Soviet. The tsar abdicates.

SOURCES 8G & 8H

Source 8G: Protesters in Petrograd on International Women's Day, 8 March 1917

Source 8H: Children looking at the head of a destroyed statue of Tsar Alexander III after the March Revolution

SOURCE ANALYSIS 8.5

Study and interpret Sources 8G and 8H. Write a news report for a foreign newspaper in which you describe the nature of the protests on 8 March 1917.

8.2 How did the Bolsheviks gain power, and how did they consolidate their rule?

> **FOCUS POINTS**
>
> This topic will help you to answer these questions:
>
> - How effectively did the Provisional Government rule Russia in 1917?
> - Why were the Bolsheviks able to seize power in November 1917?
> - Why did the Bolsheviks win the Civil War?
> - To what extent was the New Economic Policy a success?

How effectively did the Provisional Government rule Russia in 1917?

The Provisional Government was made up of Duma members. The most important were:

- prime minister Prince Lvov
- foreign minister Paul Miliukov
- justice minister Alexander Kerensky.

The March Revolution created an atmosphere of goodwill, and the Provisional Government had the support of many people. However, it faced some significant problems. These were partly due to the fact that the social and economic demands of most ordinary Russians had not changed. In addition, the Provisional Government had never been elected, but had appointed itself. Could it really rule Russia effectively?

The main problems the Provisional Government faced, plus its policies and their consequences, are outlined in the following table.

Despite these problems, the Provisional Government introduced some significant political reforms.

- The Okhrana was abolished.
- Political prisoners were released.
- Press censorship was abolished.
- The police were replaced by a people's militia.
- Independent judges and trial by jury were introduced.
- Capital punishment and exile were abolished.
- All men and women over the age of 20 were given the vote.
- Discrimination on the grounds of class, religion, race, gender or belief was made illegal.

However, by September 1917, the parties in the Provisional Government – the liberals, the Mensheviks and the Socialist Revolutionaries – had become discredited. As the Bolsheviks became more powerful, the Provisional Government made several serious mistakes.

Problems in summer 1917	Policies	Consequences of policies
The Petrograd Soviet The Soviet had 3000 members. It was elected by soldiers, sailors and workers, and it had their support. Through delegates it controlled railways, postal and telegraph communications systems, factories and the armed forces. The Soviet published Order No. 1 on 1 March 1917, which gave it control over the army.	Kerensky (who was also a member of the Soviet) negotiated on behalf of the Provisional Government. The Soviet would support the Provisional Government if it granted reforms. These included an amnesty for prisoners, civil liberties, the end of official discrimination and granting workers' rights to join unions and to strike. The Provisional Government also agreed not to send Petrograd soldiers to fight on the front line.	The Provisional Government and the Soviet cooperated for several months. This was known as 'Dual Power'. The Provisional Government was relieved that the Soviet did not make more radical demands and was grateful that the Soviet brought the army under control. Many moderates in the Soviet had no desire for more radical change.
The First World War Most members of the Provisional Government wanted to continue fighting. But while some hoped to make territorial gains if the Allies won, the moderates only wanted to fight to protect Russian territory.	In June 1917, the Provisional Government ordered a new offensive. For three days things went well, then the attack fell apart. Soldiers shot their officers, and up to 2 million Russian soldiers deserted.	The army started disintegrating. Many ordinary soldiers turned to the Bolsheviks for solutions.
The land problem By summer 1917 the countryside was in revolt. There was no one there to stop peasants from seizing landlords' property. Violence increased.	The Provisional Government wanted land in Russia to be redistributed fairly, but it also wanted to ensure this was done in an organised way.	The Provisional Government encouraged the peasants to wait for national elections and a Constituent Assembly, so that the land redistribution process could be supervised. The peasants ignored them and the land seizures continued.
The demands of national minorities National minority groups demanded more power as soon as Nicholas II abdicated, but the Provisional Government could not agree on how to respond.	When Ukraine demanded self-government, socialists in the Provisional Government were prepared to grant it.	Liberals feared that the Russian Empire was about to break up. Prince Lvov resigned, leaving Kerensky to become prime minister.
Economic problems Food shortages, inflation, high prices and supply problems were still causing a great deal of hardship in the cities. As conditions worsened, more strikes broke out.	The Provisional Government promised to double the amount it paid peasants for grain, but the supply did not improve. Liberals in the government supported the capitalists, while socialists supported the workers, but neither had plans for how to improve things.	Factory committees became more powerful and began to take control to keep the factories working. Workers were dissatisfied with the Provisional Government. One million people took part in strikes in Russia in September 1917, and many of them turned to the Bolsheviks.

> **KEY TERM**
>
> **amnesty:** an official pardon for crimes committed

> **THINKING SKILLS**
>
> Think about the problems that the Provisional Government faced in the summer of 1917. If you were a government adviser, which of the problems would you say was the most serious, and why? Write a short paragraph.
>
> Write one sentence on behalf of each of the following groups to explain to the government why its policies are unpopular from your point of view:
>
> - peasants
> - workers
> - soldiers and sailors
> - aristocracy
> - capitalists
> - national minorities.

Why were the Bolsheviks able to seize power in November 1917?

In March 1917, the Bolsheviks were a small Marxist revolutionary party with only around 10 000 members. Almost all their leaders were in exile or abroad. They did not participate in the March Revolution, but by April 1917, leading Bolsheviks, including Lenin, Trotsky and Stalin, were back in Petrograd.

> **KEY FIGURE**
>
> ### Vladimir Lenin (1870–1924)
>
> Vladimir Ilyich Ulyanov (Lenin) became involved in radical politics after his older brother was executed by the tsarist regime for belonging to a revolutionary group. Lenin emerged as leader of the Bolshevik faction after the split of the Social Democrats. He started working against the Provisional Government in April 1917. He persuaded the Bolsheviks that a revolution was possible and, with Trotsky, led the November Revolution. Lenin created the first communist regime, leading it through the Russian Civil War. He was the first leader of the Soviet Union, but he died in 1924, after a series of strokes.

In April 1917, the German government paid for Lenin to return to Petrograd, hoping he would cause trouble and force Russia to pull out of the war. Lenin's policies at the time were different from other parties and were immediately popular.

'All Power to the Soviets'

- The Bolsheviks would stop cooperating with the Provisional Government and other parties.
- The Soviets should seize power in the name of the working class at once.

'Peace, Land and Bread'

- An immediate end to the war.
- Give the peasants the right to take landlords' land.
- Workers and peasants should control the food supplies.

As the Provisional Government became less effective, the Bolsheviks won majorities in the Petrograd Soviet, the Moscow council elections, the key Petrograd Vyborg district and the Kronstadt naval base. Trotsky (who had been a Menshevik but joined the Bolsheviks after Lenin's return) was also elected head of the Petrograd Soviet in September. They had over 250 000 supporters by October 1917, with strong support among soldiers, sailors and workers.

Two events helped the Bolsheviks to realise the time was right for them to seize control: the 'July Days' and the Kornilov Affair.

The 'July Days', July 1917

Bolsheviks led protests against the Provisional Government. Troops loyal to the government opened fire on protesters, and they all fled. The Provisional Government issued arrest warrants for leading Bolsheviks and captured Trotsky. Lenin escaped to Finland in disguise. He stayed in hiding until it was safe to return.

Figure 8.9: Protesters flee after troops open fire during the 'July Days'

The Kornilov Affair, September 1917

In August, Prime Minister Kerensky appointed General Kornilov to lead the army. Kornilov agreed to send soldiers to defend Petrograd, but Kerensky worried that the army would overthrow the Provisional Government. As Kornilov's men approached, Kerensky panicked. He requested support from the Soviet and the Bolsheviks, as they really controlled the military, and he gave amnesty to those who had been imprisoned. Around 25 000 Bolsheviks volunteered to defend Petrograd and they were armed by the government. Kornilov and his men were captured, but Kerensky and the Provisional Government were discredited. In contrast the Bolsheviks were seen as defenders of the revolution. They won majorities in elections to Soviets all over Russia.

The November Revolution

Lenin wrote to leading Bolsheviks from his hiding place in Finland. He announced that the time was right for revolution, but key Bolsheviks like Lev Kamenev, Grigory Zinoviev and even Trotsky remained unconvinced. Two weeks later, Lenin was back in Petrograd, where he persuaded his colleagues to organise the revolution.

There were several reasons both for the Provisional Government's failure and the Bolsheviks' success.

Reasons for the failure of the Provisional Government are as follows.

- It was weakened by its temporary nature and the existence of the Soviet.
- Its policies made it increasingly unpopular.
- Kerensky made several mistakes in the summer of 1917.
- It lost the support of key groups and was defenceless by November 1917.

THE NOVEMBER REVOLUTION

2 November	The Soviet sets up a Military Revolutionary Committee (MRC). Trotsky is one of its leaders. Petrograd garrisons come under MRC control.
5 November	Kerensky shuts down Bolshevik newspapers. Lenin argues that Kerensky is starting a counter-revolution.
6 November	Lenin orders the arrest of the Provisional Government. At dawn, Trotsky orders Bolsheviks to take control of Petrograd's bridges and railway stations.
7 November	The Bolsheviks control Petrograd, but the Provisional Government remains inside the Winter Palace. Kerensky escapes in a car stolen from the US embassy. That night, the battleship *Aurora* fires its shot, the Bolsheviks storm the Winter Palace and members of the Provisional Government are arrested.

FOCUS TASK 8.4

a   In pairs, discuss the following questions.

- Why were the Bolsheviks successful in securing their power?
- Why did the 'July Days' help Bolsheviks to realise that the time was right for an uprising?

b   Now look at the list of reasons for the Provisional Government's failure and the Bolsheviks' success. In your pairs, write down one example as evidence for each reason. Then rank the reasons in order of importance. Join up with another pair and compare your lists. Have you ranked them in the same order? If not, why do you think that is? Justify your decisions and agree a final ranking.

Reasons for the success of the Bolsheviks are listed here.

- Their policies made them different from the other parties and won them support.
- They were led by determined, charismatic and skilful leaders such as Lenin and Trotsky.
- They were lucky on several occasions.
- They gained control of key institutions such as the Moscow and Petrograd Soviets.

> **REFLECTION**
>
> Think about the way you approached Focus task 8.4. Share your final answers with a partner. How did you make your decisions about judging success and failure? Did your partner take the same approach? After discussing, would either of you change your ideas or take a different approach to similar questions next time?

Why did the Bolsheviks win the Civil War?

Lenin created a new government, which issued several decrees:

- Decree on Land: peasants could seize any land previously belonging to the tsar, the Church and aristocracy.
- Decree on Peace: Russia asked Germany for an armistice in the war.
- A maximum eight-hour day for workers, 48-hour week.
- Social insurance (old age, unemployment, sickness benefits) was introduced.
- Non-Bolshevik press was banned.
- Rights of self-government for all parts of the Russian Empire introduced.
- Workers' control of factories introduced.
- Equal rights to property ownership.
- Democratisation of the army – officers were to be elected, soldiers' soviets assumed control of the army, and ranks, saluting and decorations were abolished.
- Banks were nationalised.
- Cheka (secret police) was set up.
- Marriage and divorce became civil matters, equal rights for women wanting a divorce.

> **ACTIVITY 8.2**
>
> a   Look back at the timeline of the November Revolution. Using the timeline and any other knowledge you have, create a table to record evidence of how important Lenin was and how important Trotsky was to compare the two leaders.
>
> b   In your opinion, which Bolshevik leader was more important? Write a paragraph explaining your ideas.
>
> c   Split the class into two groups: those of you who felt Lenin was more important and those who thought Trotsky was. Hold a class debate to argue your ideas.

> **ACTIVITY 8.3**
>
> a   Study the list of the Bolsheviks' early decrees. In small groups, put together a presentation outlining the measures the Bolsheviks took to please their traditional supporters. Consider what they did for:
>
> - workers
> - soldiers and sailors
> - peasants.
>
> b   Explain which decrees might make Russia fairer and more democratic, and which suggested that Russia might become less free and fair.
>
> c   Present your ideas to the class. Allow time for people to ask questions and give you feedback at the end.

The Constituent Assembly

Many Bolshevik ideas were very popular, but in 1917 and 1918 Lenin's government also took steps that angered some of the Russian people. Lenin had promised to allow elections for the Constituent Assembly to go ahead, hoping for a Bolshevik majority. However, when the results came in, the Bolsheviks were shocked.

Party	% of votes	Seats
Socialist Revolutionaries	41.0	380
Bolsheviks	23.5	168
Kadets	4.8	17
Mensheviks	3.0	18
Others	31.5	120

Figure 8.10: A table showing the results of the Constituent Assembly elections, December 1917

The Constituent Assembly first met for the first and only time on 18 January, and it refused to support Lenin's proposals. The following day, Lenin sent soldiers to close down the Assembly. From this point on, Lenin ruled by decree or used Bolshevik control in the Congress of Soviets to pass his laws. Lenin admitted that he was establishing a dictatorship, but he said it was a dictatorship of the proletariat.

> **THINKING SKILLS**
>
> If you were a Bolshevik member of the Constituent Assembly, would you agree with Lenin's decision to close it down after just one meeting? How would you feel about the dissolution of the Constituent Assembly if you were Social Revolutionary or a Menshevik?

The Treaty of Brest-Litovsk, March 1918

Lenin had promised an immediate end to the war. When peace talks began in December 1917, Trotsky intended to extend negotiations until a communist revolution broke out in Germany. The Germans, frustrated with Trotsky's time-wasting, restarted the war and advanced 240 kilometres into Russia in five days. A treaty was signed at Brest-Litovsk in March. By the terms of the treaty, Russia had to pay reparations of 300 million gold roubles. It also lost:

- 60 million people (34% of the population)
- 32% of its agricultural land
- 54% of its industry
- 89% of its coal mines
- 26% of its railways.

The treaty showed Lenin's willingness to make sacrifices in order to achieve his aims. Many Russians were horrified by the treaty's harshness. A Socialist Revolutionary tried to kill Lenin in August 1918 and by the end of the year, a civil war had broken out.

Figure 8.11: A map showing Russian losses by the terms of the Treaty of Brest-Litovsk

What happened in the Russian Civil War?

The Russian Civil War lasted from summer 1918 until spring 1921. It was actually several small wars, fought by 20 different armies. The Bolsheviks (the Red Army, or Reds) fought various forces.

- The Whites: This was a very broad group, including anti-Bolshevik socialists, liberals, tsarists and nationalists. Few wanted Tsarism, some wanted the Constituent Assembly recalled, but all wanted to beat the Bolsheviks. Otherwise, they had little in common.
- The Greens: These were peasant armies who fought to defend their own areas.
- Foreign armies, including the Czech Legion: A unit of Czech nationalists who had been fighting the Austrians on the Eastern Front. They fought against the Bolsheviks as they travelled to the Western Front.

As Commissar for War, Trotsky was in charge of the Red Army. He turned it into a force of 3.5 million men by the end of 1920. He did this by employing former imperial army officers and threatening to take their families hostage to ensure their loyalty. He also attached Political Commissars to each unit, to ensure loyalty. Trotsky reintroduced ranks, saluting and strict discipline, including the death penalty for cowardice. Finally, he did not interfere in military decisions, but used his War Train to travel to where fighting was heaviest to inspire his men.

Figure 8.12: An armoured train, like the one Trotsky used in the Civil War

War Communism

The Bolshevik government introduced 'War Communism'. These were harsh measures to regain control, including:

- government control of all industries
- strict worker discipline, including execution for strikers
- food rationing
- outlawing private trade
- forcing peasants to hand over grain and publicly hanging anyone who resisted (this policy, and poor harvests in 1920–21, led to a famine that killed an estimated 7 million people)
- the 'Red Terror' – the Cheka arrested or executed people suspected of being the Reds' enemies and in July 1918, the royal family were shot.

There were three phases of fighting.

- **June–November 1918:** The Reds fought Green armies and the Czech Legion. Two Socialist Revolutionary uprisings occurred, but the Whites defeated them.

- **November 1918–December 1920:** Several White and foreign armies threatened the Reds.

    Admiral Kolchak's White army was defeated by the Reds at the end of 1919.

    General Denikin's White army got within 320 km of Moscow and almost defeated Stalin's army at Tsaritsyn but was beaten in 1920.

    General Yudenich's White army attacked Petrograd through Estonia in October 1919 but was beaten by the Reds.

    British forces were sent to Murmansk, the French fleet was sent to the Black Sea, Japanese forces captured Vladivostok and US troops were sent to watch the Japanese. These foreign armies did little fighting and had all withdrawn by 1920.

    The Poles attacked Russia in 1919-1920 and captured Kiev. The Reds pushed them back to Warsaw, but Poland gained large areas of territory in the 1921 Treaty of Riga.

- **August 1920–December 1921:** For over a year the Reds prevented outbreaks of violence all over the country.

    Peasants attacked Reds in the Tambov region in late 1920. A 100 000-strong Red army was sent to crush the rebels in 1921.

    In February 1921, sailors in the Kronstadt naval base rose up in protest at the Bolsheviks' harsh methods, and at War Communism in particular. Kronstadt sailors had been at the head of the November Revolution and now they made a series of demands for political freedom. It took 50 000 Red Guards two weeks to defeat the uprising. Over 2000 were killed or executed and almost 5000 injured.

> **KEY TERM**
>
> **Kronstadt:** a region of the city of St. Petersburg, famous for its large naval base

Key points

The Russian Civil War

- The Russian Civil War was really several different conflicts, all fought against the Bolsheviks (Reds) at the same time.

- It began in mid-1918 and was largely over by the end of 1921.
- The Reds defended the central part of Russia, including Moscow and other major cities.
- Their opponents were anti-Bolshevik groups, including forces from foreign interventionist forces, who fought on different fronts and with different aims.

Figure 8.13: A map showing the progress of the Russian Civil War

SOURCE 8I

Source 8I: A Soviet poster from 1920, which glorifies the role of the Kronstadt sailors

SOURCE ANALYSIS 8.6

Study Source 8I. What messages about the Bolsheviks does this poster convey?

FOCUS TASK 8.5

In pairs, review the information in this section. Consider how the Kronstadt Rebellion was an important turning point in the revolution. Copy the following table and work together to fill in the gaps.

	Red strengths	Opposition weaknesses
Geography	The Bolsheviks controlled the centre of western Russia, including Moscow and Petrograd. This gave them control of most of the railway system, industry, weapons and supplies, and the densely populated areas.	Opposition armies were separated by hundreds of miles, which made co-ordination impossible. The areas they held were thinly populated so recruitment was hard. They had little industry and poor transport links.
Strength		The opposition armies were small and poorly resourced. They received little assistance from the Russian peasants, who did not want to lose their land.
Leadership		White generals treated their armies with disgust. Many White soldiers deserted.
Unity		The opposition were never united. They had no common aims and did not cooperate.
Propaganda	The Bolsheviks used propaganda very effectively. They used posters, films, loudspeakers and trains travelled around the country producing new material for local areas to keep morale high.	Opposition forces did not use propaganda to win support. Bolshevik propaganda about what would happen if the Whites won hurt the opposition forces.
Foreign help	Foreign help for the Whites allowed the Reds to portray themselves as the patriots.	

To what extent was the New Economic Policy a success?

The failures of War Communism and the Kronstadt uprising forced Lenin to rethink. At the Communist Party Congress in March 1921, he announced the New Economic Policy (NEP). This involved:

- state ownership of heavy industry, transport and banking
- an end to seizing grain–instead the state took 50% of a peasant's grain, and peasants could sell the rest for profit
- allowing private businesses – people could produce goods and sell them.

Rationing was reduced so people had to buy food, but they had more income and there was more food available.

Lenin stated that the NEP was not a defeat, but a tactical retreat. There was still opposition from inside the party, but the NEP was popular because the economy began to recover.

Why did Lenin introduce the NEP?

By 1923, 75% of all trade was in private hands, and traders called 'Nepmen' supplied all kinds of goods. They were harassed by the Cheka (now renamed the GPU). Peasants did well under the NEP, but urban workers struggled. Unemployment rose, wages remained generally low and working conditions did not improve. Many people wondered whether Lenin had abandoned the idea of creating a workers' paradise.

	1921	1922	1923	1924	1925
Grain harvest (million tonnes)	34	46	51	47	70
Coal (million tonnes)	8	9	12	15	16
Electricity (million kWhs)	520	775	1146	1562	2925
Steel (thousand tonnes)	166	356	643	1034	1937

Figure 8.14: A table showing recovery under the New Economic Policy, 1921–25

> **REVISION TIP**
>
> When revising, it is helpful to begin by identifying the main events in the topic. You can do this by constructing a timeline. Most main events will also have some smaller steps. For example the main event of the 1905 Revolution is the overall name given to a number of events over the course of almost a year. Make sure you know the details about the key stages or smaller events in each case. For each of the events on your timeline, revise 3–5 causes and 3–5 consequences.

> **FOCUS TASK 8.6**
>
> Study the list of factors that explain the Bolsheviks' success in securing their control. Work in groups and divide up the list between you. Write a speech to convince your classmates that your factor was the most important. Listen to the other speeches and see if you agree with their reasoning.
>
> - Lenin's government early decrees
> - The leadership of Lenin and Trotsky
> - The crushing of opposition by the Cheka
> - The defeat of enemies in the Russian Civil War
> - War Communism
> - The New Economic Policy
> - The Treaty of Brest-Litovsk
> - Support from the people and optimism about the future

8.3 How did Stalin gain and hold on to power?

> **FOCUS POINTS**
>
> This topic will help you to answer these questions:
>
> - Why did Stalin, and not Trotsky, emerge as Lenin's successor?
> - Why did Stalin launch the Purges?
> - What methods did Stalin use to control the Soviet Union?
> - How complete was Stalin's control over the Soviet Union by 1941?

Figure 8.15: Lenin and Stalin, shortly before Lenin's death in January 1924

Why did Stalin, and not Trotsky, emerge as Lenin's successor?

Lenin had led the Bolshevik party to success in revolution and war. However, throughout 1922 and 1923, he suffered a series of strokes that left him paralysed and unable to speak. He died in January 1924.

There were several challengers for the leadership, but none had enough support to take over. Lenin had written about each of the leading Bolsheviks, but this was not common knowledge. With hindsight, we can see that there were two strong candidates for the leadership.

	Joseph Stalin	Leon Trotsky
Background	Stalin was born in Georgia. He attended Christian school but became interested in Marxism and was expelled from school for reading banned literature. His revolutionary alias 'Stalin' meant 'man of steel'.	Leon Trotsky was born in Ukraine. He became interested in revolutionary politics and became a writer. He spent time in prison, where he adopted the name of one of his jailers as his alias, and in exile abroad.
Personal qualities	He was cold, cunning and ruthless.	He was independent, arrogant, highly intelligent and a brilliant speaker. He could be disrespectful to colleagues.
Career in the Communist Party	He joined the Bolshevik Party when it was founded in 1898. He was involved in hijackings, extortion and murder. His dedication impressed Lenin. He was editor of the party newspaper, *Pravda*, in 1917, but did not play a leading role in the October Revolution.	He met Lenin in 1902 but sided with the Mensheviks until 1917, when he joined the Bolsheviks. He planned the October Revolution, was a leading member of the Party's Central Committee and was Commissar for War.
Support base	Stalin was General Secretary of the Party, so he controlled invitations to party congresses, where the Central Committee was chosen and major policies were discussed. He could remove Trotsky's supporters or transfer them to minor positions. He organised Lenin's funeral in 1924.	Trotsky's support base was the Red Army, where he was very popular after the Civil War. He was also popular with younger party members and students.
What did Lenin write in his 'Political Testament'?	'Comrade Stalin, having become Secretary-General, has unlimited authority concentrated in his hands, and I am not sure whether he will always be capable of using that authority with sufficient caution.' 'Stalin is too rude and this is intolerable in a Secretary-General. I suggest that comrades think about a way of removing Stalin from that post and appointing another man [who is] more tolerant, more loyal, more polite and more considerate.'	'Comrade Trotsky [. . .] is distinguished not only by outstanding ability. He is personally perhaps the most capable man in the present Central Committee, but he has displayed excessive self-assurance and shown excessive preoccupation with the purely administrative side of the work.' 'He should not be blamed for not being a member of the party before 1917.'

KEY FIGURE

Joseph Stalin (1878–1953)

Stalin was the son of a cobbler. He sided with the Bolshevik faction after the Social Democrats split in 1903. He was arrested and exiled numerous times before 1917 and was appointed Commissar for Nationalities in the first Bolshevik government, and also a member of the Politburo. He served without distinction in the Russian Civil War but was appointed General Secretary of the Communist Party in 1922. He became rivals for power with Leon Trotsky, Lev Kamenev, Grigory Zinoviev and Nikolai Bukharin after Lenin's death in 1924, but defeated them all and was securely in control by 1928.

THE LEADERSHIP STRUGGLE WAS DECIDED BY EVENTS BETWEEN 1924 AND 1929.	
January 1924	Stalin is a coffin-bearer and makes a speech at Lenin's funeral. He implies that he was Lenin's closest friend. Stalin allegedly lies to Trotsky, who was recovering from illness, about the date of the funeral, and Trotsky's absence seems very disrespectful.
April 1924	Stalin creates a 'Cult of Lenin', changes Petrograd's name to Leningrad and publishes a book on Lenin, all implying that he was a close colleague. He also recruits 1 million young, uneducated urban workers into the party. They like Stalin's style, believing that Trotsky is too intellectual.
May 1924	The Central Committee, including Trotsky, votes to keep Lenin's 'Political Testament' secret at the 13th Party Congress because it criticises them. During the Congress, Trotsky attacks Stalin. Stalin sides with Lev Kamenev and Grigory Zinoviev, two leading Bolsheviks and allies of Lenin, and their supporters outvote Trotsky.
December 1925	Zinoviev and Kamenev attack Trotsky before the 14th Party Congress, and Trotsky hits back. Stalin lets his rivals discredit each other. At the Congress, Zinoviev and Kamenev criticise the NEP and call for rapid industrialisation. Stalin's supporters outvote them easily.
1926 and 1927	Zinoviev, Kamenev and Trotsky form the United Opposition. They demand an end to the NEP and rapid industrialisation. Stalin and Nikolai Bukharin argue in favour of the NEP. Stalin controls the programme for the 15th Party Congress, and the United Opposition are not allowed to present their ideas. Desperately, they appeal directly to Moscow workers and are expelled from the party for acting illegally.
1928	Stalin criticises the NEP, using the arguments of the United Opposition. Stalin's supporters vote Bukharin and his supporters out of the Politburo. Stalin's position is now secure.

Trotsky believed that the USSR should pursue a policy of 'Permanent Revolution'. Russia should help communists abroad, because bringing about revolutions worldwide would strengthen the USSR. Stalin instead proposed a policy of 'Socialism in One Country'. This meant strengthening communism and creating a Soviet workers' paradise that was superior to the capitalist west. Stalin's ideas were much more popular.

> **FOCUS TASK 8.7**
>
> a In pairs, discuss the following questions.
>   - What advantages did Stalin have in the leadership struggle?
>   - How might Stalin's colleagues have stopped him from becoming leader of the USSR?
>
> b Why did Stalin win the leadership struggle? In your pairs, write one sentence about each of the following, giving examples:
>   - Stalin's policies were more popular
>   - Trotsky made several mistakes
>   - Stalin was fortunate on several occasions
>   - Stalin controlled the Party
>   - Stalin's personal characteristics
>   - Trotsky's personal characteristics and background
>   - in-fighting between other party member
>   - other factors.

Why did Stalin launch the Purges?

By 1933 the Communist Party was extremely unpopular. The Soviet state always used force to achieve its aims, but in the period 1934–38 up to 18 million people were imprisoned. In addition, perhaps 1.5 million people were executed by the NKVD, as the GPU was now known. This is known as 'The Purges' or 'The Terror'. Victims were arrested, usually at night. They were then given either long, high-profile trials known as 'show trials', or secret and very brief trials. After the trial, they were executed immediately or sent to a prison camp.

Historians have suggested many reasons for the Purges:

- to destroy opposition and terrify the population
- to destroy potential leadership rivals
- this was the Bolsheviks' usual response when dealing with enemies
- to remove anyone disloyal to USSR in the face of the growing threat from Nazi Germany
- to find scapegoats for economic failures
- to deflect hostility away from the government
- to provide slave labour for huge logging, gold-mining and canal building projects.

The Purges began after December 1934, after the assassination of Sergei Kirov, the party leader in Leningrad. The state's reaction was to begin a series of arrests to try to prevent opposition. Many people believe that Stalin was responsible for Kirov's murder, because Kirov won more votes than Stalin at the 17th Party Congress, and some people at the time wanted Kirov to be made party leader. Within two years, other leading party members were also dead.

Figure 8.16: Workers voting to demand the execution of Trotsky supporters accused of spying during a show trial, 1937

> **THINKING SKILLS**
>
> Imagine you witnessed the Purges at first-hand. Many Soviet citizens were victims of the Purges, but many also played a role as well. Study the photograph of workers at a Soviet factory voting in favour of a resolution demanding the execution of so-called Trotskyist spies. How would you react to being asked to support such a resolution?

The victims of the Purges

Several groups found themselves victims of the Purges.

- The Party (1934–38): One million people were arrested in connection with Kirov's murder. Most of the senior party leaders were arrested and executed. Zinoviev and Kamenev (1936) and Bukharin (1938) were given show trials before their executions. They were forced to admit to ridiculous charges, and false evidence was provided. Trotsky was murdered by an NKVD agent in Mexico in 1940. Around 500 000 lower-ranking party members were also arrested.

- The Secret Police: Over 3000 NKVD members were purged. The NKVD chief, Yagoda, was given a show trial and executed. His replacement, Yezhov, was also executed in 1939. He was replaced by Beria, who survived the Purges.

- Anti-Soviet spies (1937): Several politicians were accused of spying for Nazi Germany.

- The army (1937): Three out of five marshals in the Red Army, 14 of 16 army commanders, 60 of 67 corps commanders and 35 000 officers were all tried for treason and executed. Only one senior Soviet Air Force commander survived the Purges.

- The people: Colleagues, friends and family of those arrested were also likely to be targeted. One in 18 of the Soviet population was arrested during the Purges.

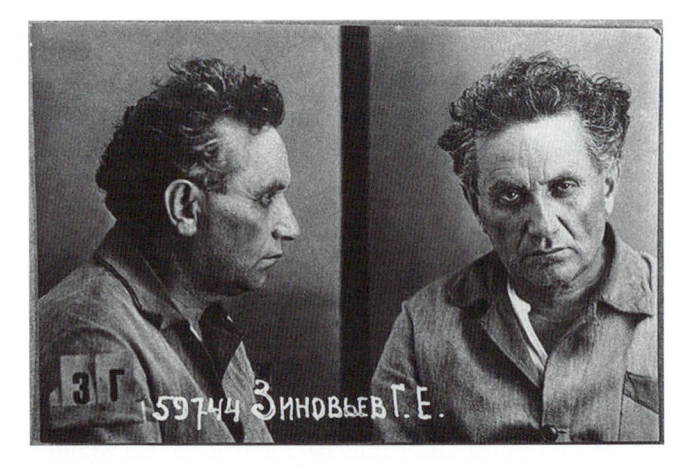

Figure 8.17: Zinoviev's NKVD file photo, taken shortly before he was shot

Chapter 8: Russia, 1905–41

> ### ACTIVITY 8.4
>
> a In small groups, research one of the show trials. Create a storyboard to explain what happened. Present your story board to the class and describe the events of the show trial.
>
> b When you have all finished your presentations, discuss the similarities between the trials. What seem to be their typical features?

Key points

The Purges

- The Purges were an act of brutal repression carried out by Stalin against various individuals and groups perceived as enemies.
- The Communist Party had always purged itself of 'undesirable' members by expelling people from the party, but Stalin used arrest, imprisonment and execution as well.
- Historians generally agree that the Great Purge began with the show trials of 1936 and ended in 1938 when Stalin removed Yezhov as head of the NKVD.

What methods did Stalin use to control the Soviet Union?

Stalin's control of the USSR was not dependent only upon forcing people to obey.

The 1936 Constitution

Every citizen over 18 had a vote, and people enjoyed freedom of the press, religion and organisation. They were also guaranteed employment. However, in practice the Constitution restricted rights and ensured that only communist candidates could stand in elections. While the Soviet Constitution appeared to signal the creation of a democratic state, the reality of life in the USSR did not match what the Constitution promised.

The personality cult and propaganda

The Cult of Lenin appeared everywhere, in newspapers, statues and the cinema. It was designed to encourage the Russian people to imitate Lenin's commitment to the revolution. A second cult was dedicated to Stalin. As early as 1925 the town of Tsaritsyn was renamed Stalingrad. Stalin was portrayed as the saviour of socialism in propaganda. By 1941, Stalin dominated the USSR physically as well as politically. He was presented as Lenin's heir and the only person who could interpret party ideology, with a god-like status. There was genuine enthusiasm for Stalin in the 1930s.

Rewriting history

Another significant aspect of the cult was the reinterpretation of history. *The History of the All-Union Communist Party* or *Short Course* was published in 1938. This exaggerated Stalin's role in the revolution and the Civil War, while other Bolsheviks were given only minor roles. Photos were altered, and old heroes of the USSR were removed from history.

Supervision of art and culture

Government control over news, art and culture ensured that the Soviet people were exposed to a very narrow range of views. Leading newspapers were used for propaganda, highlighting the state's achievements. Radio stations were controlled by the government. Cinema became a popular form of entertainment in the 1930s, and propaganda trains with travelling cinemas took film into rural areas. Towns built huge new cinemas. After 1934, Socialist Realism meant that all art films, books, theatre and music had to be straightforward, optimistic, easily understood and feature realistic but idealised heroes who performed fantastic tasks.

Religion

The Bolsheviks intended to make Russia a non-religious state. The teaching of religion was banned, hundreds of churches were destroyed or shut down and religious schools were closed. However, despite this suppression, the Bolsheviks did not succeed in destroying religion.

How complete was Stalin's control over the Soviet Union by 1941?

By 1941, Stalin undoubtedly had great control over the Soviet Union and his dictatorship might even be called totalitarian. It seems likely that he wanted control over every aspect of every citizen's life, but in fact he was limited by several factors.

- Personal limits: no single person could have controlled everything in an empire as large as USSR.

- Political limits: members of the Politburo opposed Stalin in 1930s. For example, in 1932, when Stalin wanted to execute Ryutin, the Politburo refused and he was sentenced to 10 years in a labour camp instead. This was a rare act of defiance, and in fact Ryutin was re-tried and executed within those 10 years.

- Political limits: The bureaucracy could block policies. Telling political jokes was always popular in the USSR. Thousands were imprisoned for this in the 1930s, but the popularity of these jokes proves that Stalin was unable to control people's feelings and what they said to their friends and family.

> ### FOCUS TASK 8.8
>
> a   Look back over the previous pages. Make two lists:
>
> - evidence that Stalin's control over the population was complete or very nearly complete
>
> - evidence that Stalin was not in complete control of the population.
>
> b   Some historians have argued that Stalin's was a totalitarian regime because it had total control. Do you agree? Make notes of your ideas and then discuss them with a partner.

8.4 What was the impact of Stalin's economic policies?

> **FOCUS POINTS**
>
> This topic will help you to answer these questions:
> - Why did Stalin introduce the Five-Year Plans?
> - Why did Stalin introduce collectivisation?
> - How successful were Stalin's economic changes?
> - How were the Soviet people affected by these changes?

Why did Stalin introduce the Five-Year Plans?

Stalin's economic policies aimed to industrialise and modernise the USSR as quickly as possible. He wanted to do this for several reasons, including increasing the USSR's military strength, making the country self-sufficient, increasing food supplies, creating a socialist society and improving living standards. He hoped all this would secure his own position.

At the 15th Party Congress in 1927, Stalin ended the NEP and announced the First Five-Year Plan. There would be three Five-Year Plans before 1941. They were all centrally planned, which meant that:

- government planning agencies like GOSPLAN set overall targets
- government departments allocated targets to different regions
- local bosses set targets for each factory
- factory managers set targets for workers.

The First Five-Year Plan, 1928–32

The first plan emphasised heavy industry. The labour force doubled to 23 million by 1932, and production increased dramatically. This plan was supposed to lay the foundations for future development, so 1500 factories and many cities were built from nothing. For example, in 1929 there were only 25 people living at Magnitogorsk, but by 1932, when a huge iron and steel works had been built, the population had risen to 250 000.

The Second Five Year Plan, 1933–37

Heavy industry was also the priority in the Second Five-Year Plan. However, new industries were created, and there was greater emphasis on rail links, including Moscow's spectacular underground rail system. Big projects included the Dnieprostroi hydroelectric dam. The USSR became almost self-sufficient in machine-making. Food rationing ended and families had more money to spare.

> **THINKING SKILLS**
>
> In 1931, Stalin said:
>
> *We are fifty or a hundred years behind the advanced countries. We must make good this distance in ten years. Either we do it, or they will crush us.*
>
> Imagine you were a Soviet worker in 1931. How would you respond to a speech like this? How would you feel about the language Stalin uses here?

Figure 8.18: Building the vast iron and steel works at Magnitogorsk in the 1930s

Figure 8.19: The Dnieprostroi hydroelectric dam. This was the largest dam in Europe when it was built. It was destroyed by the Germans in 1943.

The Third Five-Year Plan, 1938–41

The Third Five-Year Plan was supposed to deliver more consumer goods. However, when the Second World War began in 1939, the government ordered a further focus on heavy industry. Machinery and engineering increased, but steel, oil and consumer goods did not. The Purges and the change of priorities caused chaos.

The Five-Year Plans caused huge problems for the Soviet government. There were shortages of vital supplies, and production was held back by unskilled and unreliable workers. The government took several measures to deal with this, including:

- bonuses and incentives, such as better housing or clothes encouraged workers to stay in their jobs
- higher wages for skilled workers
- wages in line with how much an individual produced, to increase productivity
- encouraging workers to break production records; propaganda encouraged workers to compete to produce more
- offering training and education to workers
- fines for workers who failed to follow the rules; causing damage or leaving without permission could lead to a prison sentence
- using slave labour on the most dangerous projects; around 300 000 prisoners worked on the Baltic-White Sea Canal, and 25 000 died.

Why did Stalin introduce collectivisation?

In 1928, the USSR was short of grain by around 2 million tonnes. The state could not get the peasants to hand over the grain they had harvested. Soviet industry was extremely backward. For example, there were still an estimated 5 million wooden ploughs in use. Stalin's solution was **collectivisation**. Peasants would combine their individual farms to create large collective farms, known as *kolkhoz*. All their possessions, from tools to animals, were collectivised. Peasants would also share their labour, live communally and share any profits.

The government claimed that this was a more efficient way of farming. It supplied fertilisers and Machine and Tractor Stations (MTS), and expertise and labour could be shared. It argued that greater agricultural efficiency would release people for industrialisation so collectivisation would help to achieve the Five-Year Plans targets. Collectivisation also meant that the state would be able to collect the grain it needed more easily and the surplus could be sold abroad.

The Soviet authorities felt that collectivisation was the socialist way to farm. It would teach the peasants how to live and work communally. Rich peasants (*kulaks*) were blamed for hoarding grain. Stalin imagined that richer peasants wanted to destroy the Communist state. Collectivisation offered the opportunity to attack the *kulaks*.

The logic of collectivisation

Kolkhozes were supposed to have many benefits for peasants. They had schools, libraries and hospitals attached to them. They ran technical lectures on modern farming techniques.

To begin with, collectivisation was voluntary. However, few peasants volunteered to join collectives so the state began using force. In December 1929, Stalin announced that the *kulaks* would be stopped. An army of 25 000 (The 'Twenty-five Thousanders') urban workers was sent to find *kulaks* and persuade poorer peasants to join the collectives. Each region was given a quota of *kulaks* to find. Usually these were ordinary peasants who were better farmers.

> **KEY TERM**
>
> **collectivisation:** organising all of a country's production and industry so that it is owned and managed by the government

SOURCE 8J

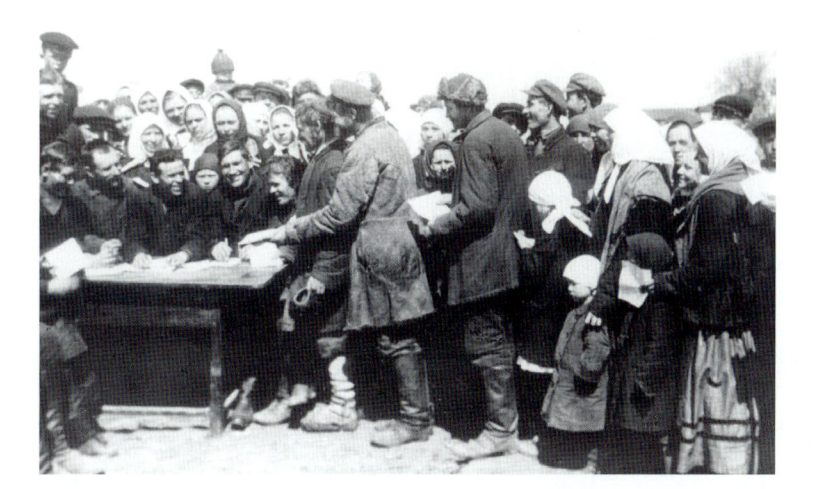

Source 8J: Peasants signing up for a collective farm in 1932

> **SOURCE ANALYSIS 8.7**
>
> Photographs like Source 8J were printed in Soviet media in the 1930s.
>
> a Why do you think photographs like this were used by the state?
>
> b How useful is this photograph as evidence of the success of collectivisation by 1932?

Kulaks were divided into three categories: counter-revolutionaries (to be shot or sent to labour camps); active opponents of collectivisation (to be deported elsewhere in the USSR); and those expelled from their own land. Up to 10 million were deported or sent to prison camps after 1930.

Some peasants fought back, and many destroyed their property or killed themselves or their livestock. At the end of 1934, the government announced that 70% of households had been collectivised, and this figure had risen to 93% by 1937. The effects on agriculture were disastrous.

Key points
Collectivisation

- Collectivisation was a process of massive change to the way food was grown in USSR.
- It was introduced by Lenin as an option for peasants, but Stalin made it compulsory, and he used force to speed up the movement of peasants from individual household farms into huge collective farms.
- Between 1928 and 1939 agriculture was transformed, with disastrous consequences for the rural population.

FOCUS TASK 8.9

Write three paragraphs summarising the reasons for and effect of collectivisation in the 1930s. Consider the following questions.

- How was collectivisation supposed to aid the Five-Year Plans?
- Why did Stalin use force to get peasants to join collective farms?
- Why did Stalin's economic policies make the party unpopular by 1934?

When you have finished your paragraphs, swap with a partner and assess each other's work. Give feedback in the form of three 'what went well' (WWW) points and two 'even better if' (EBI) points. Then improve your paragraphs using the feedback your partner has given you.

How successful were Stalin's economic changes?

Industrialisation

As Figure 8.20 shows, the Five-Year Plans achieved some significant increases in industrial production. However, there were also major problems with the Five-Year Plans, and some historians claim that the production figures were not accurate. Factory managers were under huge pressure, and there was widespread corruption.

	1928	1932	1936	1940
Electricity (m kWhs)	5	14	33	48
Coal (million tonnes)	32	58	115	151
Oil (million tonnes)	11	19	25	28

(Continued)

Chapter 8: Russia, 1905–41

	1928	1932	1936	1940
Pig iron (million tonnes)	3	6	13	14
Steel (million tonnes)	4	5	11	12
Locomotives	478	828	1566	1220

Figure 8.20: A table showing output figures for Soviet industry during the Five-Year Plans

SOURCE 8K

What are the results of the five-year plan in four years in the sphere of industry?

Have we achieved victories in this sphere?

Yes, we have. We did not have an iron and steel industry, the basis for the industrialisation of the country. Now we have one.

We did not have a tractor industry. Now we have one.

We did not have a real and big industry for the production of modern agricultural machinery. Now we have one.

We did not have an aircraft industry. Now we have one.

In output of electric power we were last on the list. Now we rank among the first.

In output of oil products and coal we were last on the list. Now we rank among the first.

And we have not only created these new great industries, but have created them on a scale and in dimensions that eclipse the scale and dimensions of European industry.

Source 8K: Stalin, speaking about the results of the First Five-Year Plan in 1933

SOURCE ANALYSIS 8.8

Read Source 8K.

a Compare Stalin's claims with the table in Figure 8.20. To what extent are his assessments of the results of Soviet industrialisation accurate?

b How far can we trust official statements about economic progress like Stalin's?

Collectivisation

Collectivisation was a disaster for the USSR. Grain harvests dropped below 1928 levels for five of the following seven years. Stalin refused to believe there was not enough grain. He believed the *kulaks* were hiding it. He ordered that all grain found was to be confiscated, with catastrophic results. Peasants could not plant crops the following year, and they did not have enough food for their animals, so 10 million horses died in five years. In Ukraine, collectivisation caused a famine that killed between 3 million and 7 million people in 1932–34.

	1928	1929	1930	1931	1932	1933	1934	1935
Grain harvest (million tonnes)	67	65	76	63	63	62	61	68
State procurement of grain (million tonnes)	10	15	20	21	17	21		
Grain export (million tonnes)	0	0	4	5	2	2		
Cattle (million)	64	61	47	43	36	35	38	45
Pigs (million)	26	20	14	14	12	12	17	23
Sheep and goats (million)	147	147	109	78	52	50	52	61

Figure 8.21: A table showing the results of collectivisation

> CAMBRIDGE IGCSE™ AND O LEVEL HISTORY OPTION B: COURSEBOOK

> **FOCUS TASK 8.10**
>
> a   In pairs, look back at the information in this section and create a table to record the successes and failures of Stalin's economic policies.
>
> b   Join up with another pair, in your groups use your completed tables to inform a discussion on how successful you think Stalin's economic policies were. Make sure you give reasons and evidence for your ideas.

How were the Soviet people affected by these changes?

For most people in the USSR, Stalin's economic policies had both positive and negative effects.

Workers

Many workers supported the Five-Year Plans. Urban workers made up 33% of the population by 1939. Some benefited from better education opportunities. Exceeding targets brought rewards like higher pay, and better conditions and housing. Because of overcrowding, shortages and poor facilities, living standards fell for most people. Average incomes fell by about 50% after 1928. Fresh foods, luxury goods, housing, shoes and clothing were not available.

Women

Stalin's social policies had a significant impact on women. The revolution had promised liberation, but most women still maintained their traditional roles. In addition, Collectivisation left women to do much of the work in the countryside, and the Five-Year Plans saw the female workforce increase by 10 million after 1928. Most domestic labour was still done by women, despite the promises of equality. However, women did gain higher education opportunities and 40% of engineering students were women by 1940. *Crèches* were set up to provide childcare. Free health care and paid holidays were offered to encourage women to go to work.

The government became so concerned about some of the negative effects of its social policies that it restated traditional values. Marriage was made more important and divorce made more expensive. Awards and tax reductions were given to 'mother-heroines' who had ten or more children. Abortion was made illegal after 1933.

Youth

Education policies had significant results. In 1930, universal primary education for four years was introduced. Numbers in secondary education increased from 1.8 million in 1926 to 12 million by 1938. In 1913, around 78% of the population were illiterate, but by 1934 it was just 8%.

However, communism could not be taught from books. It was taught through a young person's wider life through membership of a youth organisation, the Komsomol. This meant many people joined the Communist Party as children. Members were organised in brigades and had their own banners, flags, uniforms and songs. There was a wide range of activities, including demonstrations, editing newspapers, voluntary work, plays and concerts.

Figure 8.22: A poster advertising the Komsomol, 1932

THINK LIKE A HISTORIAN

What political youth organisations do you know of today? Do you think these kinds of organisation are good or bad? Why? If you had been a young person in the USSR, would you have joined the Komsomol? What do you think were the advantages and disadvantages of membership?

National minorities

Despite being Georgian, Stalin had no sympathy with the non-Russian regions of the USSR. His policies were very similar to the tsars' Russification policies. Non-Russian national identities were suppressed. Russian became the official language of all the Soviet republics and was taught in schools. In the 1930s, whole populations, including Poles, Finns, Chechens, Inguish and Koreans, were deported from their homes because Stalin did not trust them. They became second-class citizens in the areas they were moved to. In Ukraine, the effects of Collectivisation were especially severe, and Ukrainian nationalism was crushed. In Ukraine, the famine that resulted from Collectivisation is known as the *Holodomor*, and some historians argue that it was a deliberate act (rather than an accidental tragedy) and describe it as a 'terror-famine'.

SUMMARY

- The tsarist government was backward and inefficient, and it experienced many difficulties in ruling Russia before 1905.
- Nicholas II survived the 1905 Revolution because of the weakness of his opponents, and because the army remained loyal to him, but the First World War fatally weakened the tsarist regime.
- The revolution in March 1917 enjoyed huge popular support, but the role of the army was vital.
- The Provisional Government faced significant difficulties but made some very important mistakes.
- Organisation, ruthlessness and military power enabled the Bolsheviks to seize power in November 1917.
- The Bolsheviks won the Civil War in Russia because of the divisions among their opponents, geographical advantages and Trotsky's leadership.
- The New Economic Policy was a success in the short-term, but it caused significant political problems for the Bolsheviks, who could not agree on how and when to end it, or what to replace it with.
- Stalin's scheming and Trotsky's mistakes combined to ensure that Stalin won the leadership struggle after Lenin died.
- Stalin launched the Purges to rid the USSR of all those he considered enemies, regardless of their actual guilt.
- Stalin used a mixture of repression, rewards and propaganda in order to control the USSR, but even he could not control every aspect of life in the Soviet Union.
- Stalin's Five-Year Plans were intended to modernise Soviet industry, and collectivisation was intended to revolutionise the countryside.
- Stalin's economic policies brought huge changes, production increases in industry and catastrophe in agriculture.
- All aspects of Soviet society were affected by Stalin's policies, with positive and negative effects for most.

REVISION TIP

When revising topics that stretch over long periods or over significant periods of change, it is helpful to understand how things changed and how things continued the same. Decide the key start and end dates, and the key categories for comparison, and then collate your notes under the headings 'Changes' and 'Continuities'.

KEY SKILLS EXERCISES

Knowledge and understanding

1. Give **two** ways in which Russia was modernising by 1905.
2. How did the First World War create new problems for Nicholas II?
3. Identify the main groups who played a significant role in bring about the abdication of the tsar in March 1917.

Application

4. Why was Tsar Nicholas II forced to abdicate in March 1917?
5. How did the Soviet government's policies change after the Russian Civil War?
6. Suggest **one** way life changed during Stalin's period in power for each of the following groups: women, children, peasants, national minorities.

Chapter 8: Russia, 1905–41

CONTINUED

Analysis

7   'Russia was not modernising fast enough by 1905.' To what extent do you agree?

8   Analyse **two** of the reasons Russia was a difficult country to govern before 1905.

9   'The Bolsheviks were successful in November 1917 because of the failures of the Provisional Government.' How far do you agree with this statement?

Evaluation

10   Evaluate the extent to which Stalin's rule was a complete disaster for the Soviet people.

11   Discuss the reasons for opposition to Lenin's government in 1918.

12   Evaluate the importance of the First World War in causing the collapse of Tsarism. If Russia had not been involved in the war, do you think that a revolution would still have happened in Russia?

---

1 This sentence answers the question directly, but it only provides the points on one side of the argument.

2 The answer provides some specific details and some reasoning that connects the main point, made in the first sentence, and the rest of the paragraph.

3 This example is good because it includes some specific, accurate facts, and supports the points made in the previous sentences.

4 This is another instance that includes some specific factual evidence.

5 This sentence repeats the key idea made in the first sentence to round off this side of the argument.

6 This sentence provides the arguments against the key points made in the first paragraph.

7 Here, the answer provides some specific evidence.

IMPROVE THIS ANSWER

> 'Tsarism was doomed to collapse before the First World War.' How far do you agree with this statement? Explain your answer.

Sample answer: While it is not accurate to suggest that Tsarism was 'doomed', it was certainly at risk of collapse before the outbreak of the First World War. **1** Tsar Nicholas II's autocratic regime was out of date in that it relied on a system of personal loyalty to the Tsar, but it was severely weakened by 1914 because the Tsar and his family had become unpopular with the Russian aristocracy. **2** The Tsarist system was built on the economic foundation of peasant agriculture, which was backward and inefficient, and was vulnerable to harvest failures (which happened once very three years, on average). **3** The health of Tsarism was threatened by opposition from different groups in Russian society. Although not all peasants supported the Socialist Revolutionaries and not all urban workers joined the Social Democrats, many members of the liberal intelligentsia resented their lack of political influence. **4** These weaknesses and threats meant that Tsarism was in a precarious position before the First World War. **5**

Despite its weaknesses before 1914, Tsarism was growing stronger in some ways. **6** The October Manifesto of 1905 reformed Tsarism to a degree and created the Duma (parliament) system. **7** Nicholas II did not weaken Tsarism by allowing the Dumas, but he did satisfy some members of the intelligentsia and satisfy their demands for democracy. Russia was modernizing and industrializing faster than

> CAMBRIDGE IGCSE™ AND O LEVEL HISTORY OPTION B: COURSEBOOK

CONTINUED

any other country in the world before 1914, with an average economic growth rate of 6–8% per year. **8** Russia's economy was not as modern as some countries' but it was not collapsing before 1914. It is true that Tsar Nicholas II was unpopular with many of his subjects, and the Tsarist regime was shaken by the 1905 Revolution, but Nicholas had survived. **9** The army, the Okhrana and the government were all still loyal to the Tsar and this was not likely to change before World War One broke out.

Overall, it is clear that Tsarism was still strong in 1914. Although Tsar Nicholas II was personally weak, and Tsarism suffered from numerous long-term weaknesses, **10** Tsarism was slowly being strengthened in the years before 1914. While the seeds for collapse were already sown before World War One, Tsarism was certainly not doomed.

Now write an improved response using this guidance.

> **8** This sentence provides some very detailed evidence in support.
>
> **9** Here, the key points on one side of the argument are summarised.
>
> **10** The points on the other side of the argument are outlined here, with an indication of which side of the argument is stronger.

PRACTICE QUESTIONS

1. Lenin and the Bolsheviks faced many difficulties when they tried to seize power and consolidate their control.
   a. Describe the Kornilov Affair. [4]
   b. Why did Lenin introduce the New Economic Policy? [6]
   c. 'Lenin's leadership was the main reason why the Bolsheviks were able to consolidate their control by 1922.' How far do you agree with this statement? [10]

   [Total: 20]

2. a. Write an account of Tsar Nicholas II's restoration of control after the 1905 Revolution. [15]
   b. Discuss the importance of the Russo–Japanese War in causing the 1905 Revolution. [25]

   [Total: 40]

PROJECT

You are going to work in pairs to write a dialogue between two people debating the changes that took place in Russia between 1905 and 1941.

First, come up with a list of things that changed in Russia/USSR in this period and things that stayed the same (continuities), using a table like this. Decide how you will do this research. You may decide that one of you will investigate changes and one continuities, or you may choose to work together on both lists.

Chapter 8: Russia, 1905–41

> **CONTINUED**
>
> Some examples have been given to start you off. Add to the table, using the information in this chapter, your own knowledge and independent research online or using any other resources you have available. Try to add at least five more rows.
>
> | Changes | Continuities |
> | --- | --- |
> | Tsarism was replaced with communism. | Both Tsarism and Communism were very harsh systems of political control. |
> | Peasants lost their individual land and were forced to join collective farms. | Russian agriculture remained very backward and inefficient. |
>
> When you are happy with your table, rank both lists in order of importance.
>
> Now work together to write your dialogue. One person should be a strong supporter of the communist regime, who marvels at the changes brought about since 1905. The other should be more sceptical about the changes. The focus of the discussion should be the extent to which things really changed.
>
> You could begin by taking on one role each and improvising a conversation. Then note down what worked well and develop the dialogue to improve the parts that didn't.
>
> Make sure the conversation covers all the points in your table and refers to their relative significance.
>
> When you have finished, get together in groups of six and perform your dialogues to each other.

SELF-EVALUATION CHECKLIST

After studying this chapter, complete this table:

You should be able to:	Needs more work	Almost there	Ready to move on
identify the main features of the tsarist state and Russian society in the years before 1914			
understand the reasons for the 1905 revolution and why Tsarism did not collapse in 1905			
describe the impact of the First World War and evaluate why there was a revolution that led to the end of Tsarism in 1917			
evaluate the effectiveness of the Provisional Government after March 1917			
understand why the Bolsheviks were able to seize power in November 1917 and how they consolidated control			
explain why the Bolsheviks fought and won a civil war			
explain why Stalin, not Trotsky, emerged as the leader of the USSR			
describe the nature of Stalin's leadership and the methods he used to control the country			
evaluate how complete Stalin's political control had become by 1941			
explain why Stalin launched major economic modernisation programmes after 1928			
identify the main features of the Five-Year Plans and collectivisation			
evaluate the effects of Stalin's policies on the economy and the Soviet people.			

Chapter 9:
The United States, 1919–41

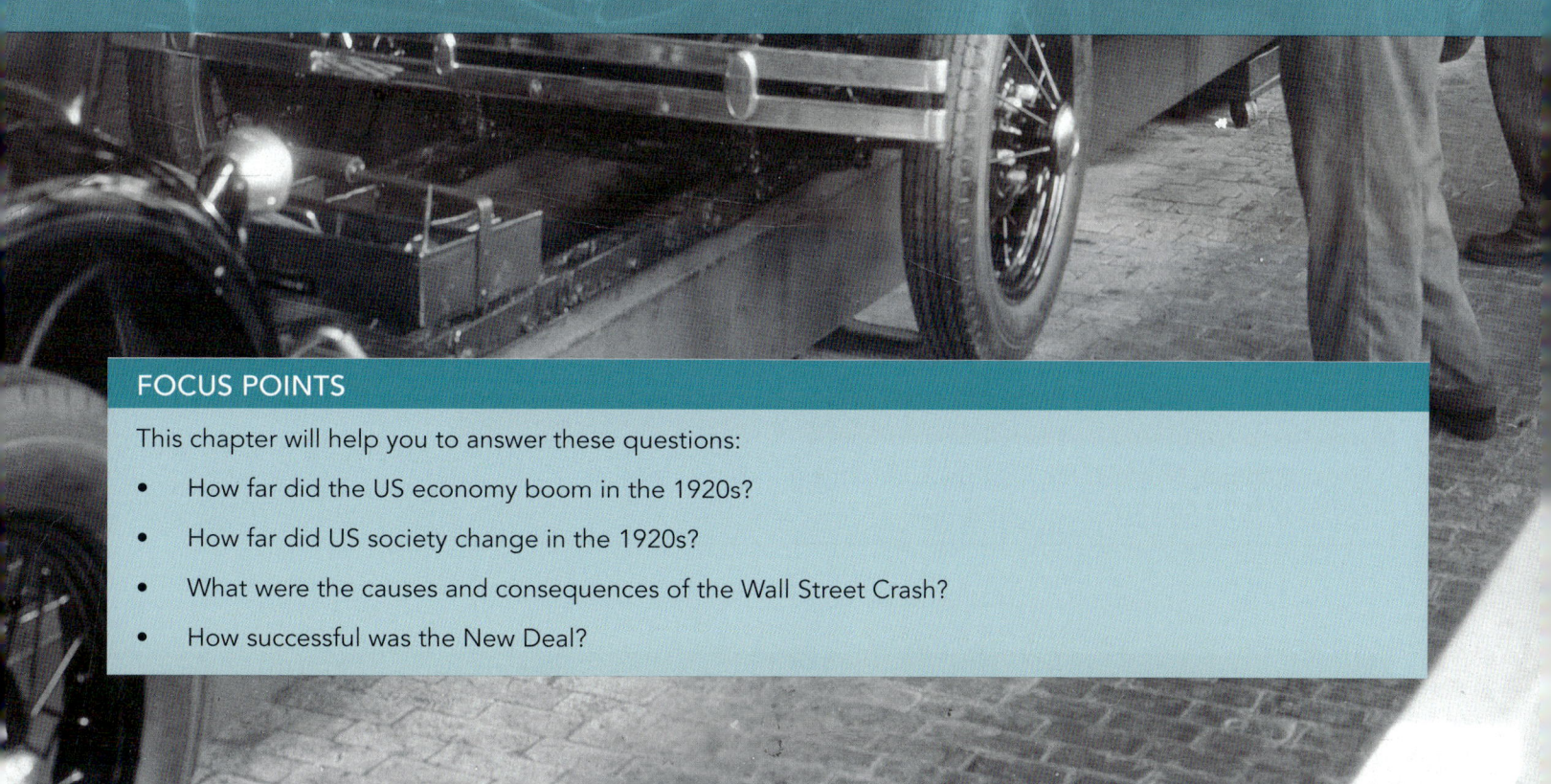

FOCUS POINTS

This chapter will help you to answer these questions:
- How far did the US economy boom in the 1920s?
- How far did US society change in the 1920s?
- What were the causes and consequences of the Wall Street Crash?
- How successful was the New Deal?

9.0 What is this Depth study about?

This chapter looks at developments in the USA from the end of the First World War to its entry into the Second World War. You will learn about the reasons for the economic prosperity of the 1920s and how this affected different groups of people. Following the 'boom' years came the Depression and the Wall Street Crash. You will be studying their causes and the impact they had. Lastly, you will learn about President Roosevelt and his 'New Deal' for the American people, which was an attempt to resolve the country's difficulties.

9.1 How far did the US economy boom in the 1920s?

> **FOCUS POINTS**
>
> This topic will help you to answer these questions:
>
> - On what factors was the economic boom based?
> - Why did some industries prosper while others did not?
> - Why did agriculture not share in the prosperity?
> - Did all Americans benefit from the boom?

On what factors was the economic boom based?

The end of the First World War in November 1918 left the USA in a strong position. Its losses were relatively small and there was no damage to its own land. In fact, the US economy benefited in several ways. Its European allies bought food and goods from US farms and factories. The Allies also received almost $10 billion in loans from US banks during and immediately after the war. The US expanded into new overseas markets as its competitors struggled to recover from the war.

The 1920s saw a continuous economic boom. The annual **Gross National Product** rose by 40% between 1922 and 1929, and many Americans enjoyed a better standard of living than anywhere in the world. A huge range of consumer goods was available, made using new technology and mass-production methods. It seemed that US economic progress was unstoppable.

> **KEY TERM**
>
> **Gross National Product:** the total value of all the goods and services produced by a country

Chapter 9: The United States, 1919–41

Figure 9.1: A well-stocked shop in America in the 1920s – evidence of the 1920s economic boom

Figure 9.2: The 1920s boom in car sales and production was a key indicator of improved standard of living for many people in the USA

ACTIVITY 9.1

In pairs, look at the two photographs on this page. Describe to each other what you can see in each one. What features of these photographs suggests that the 1920s was a boom period for many people in the USA? Which parts of the economy seem to be prospering? After your pair discussions, come together as a class and share your ideas.

The economic boom of the 1920s can be seen in the following data.

- In many US industries, **real wages** rose by nearly 25% between 1921 and 1929, while real average weekly earnings for unskilled males rose 8.7% between 1923 and 1929.
- Unemployment fell from 11.9% to 3.2%.
- Output per industrial worker increased by 43%.
- In 1912, 16% of Americans lived in homes with electricity, but by 1927 this had reached 63%.

> **KEY TERMS**
>
> **real wages:** the amount of money that people earn taking account of any inflation and tax changes
>
> **supply and demand:** supply refers to the amount of goods (or food) that are available to buy. Demand refers to how many people want to buy those goods (or food). When supply of a product increases, the price of a product goes down and vice versa

FOCUS TASK 9.1

Look at the data listed above. Copy and complete this table, using the data and any evidence you found in the photographs you explored in Activity 9.1. When you have finished, join up in pairs and compare your tables. Add anything you may have missed to improve your understanding.

Evidence of the boom	Does it affect **supply, demand,** or both?
Unemployment fell	This will increase demand because people will have money in their pockets that they did not have when they were out of work.

CONSUMER DEVICES INVENTED BEFORE 1920

1905 — **Electric iron:** Invented by businessman Earl Richardson in 1905. His design made the iron with more heat in the point.

1907 — **Washing machine:** The first electric washing machine was called the Thor and was produced by Hurley Electric Laundry Equipment Company in 1907. Electric washing machine sales reached 913,000 in the USA in 1928.

1907 — **Vacuum cleaner:** James Spangler invented his 'electric suction-sweeper' – the first practical domestic vacuum cleaner. He sold the rights to it the following year to his relative William Hoover to give him permission to make them.

1908 — **Ford Model T:** These cheap cars could be bought easily and workers could now live in the suburbs and drive into the cities for work.

1913 — **Radio:** Italian inventor Guglielmo Marconi made the first radio broadcast in 1900. In 1913, US engineer Edwin Armstrong invented a special circuit that made long-range radio transmission of voice and music practical.

1913 — **Refrigerator:** The first refrigerator for home use was invented by Fred W. Wolf. In 1923, Frigidaire introduced the first self-contained unit, expanding the market and introducing Americans to domestic refrigerators and freezers for food storage.

Long-term causes of the economic boom

The long-term causes of the economic boom included the following.

- The USA had lots of natural resources such as oil, coal, timber, iron, coal, minerals and land. Its borders were not threatened by other countries.

- Electricity and power stations had been developed in the 1870s and 1880s. By 1929, about 70% of manufacturing activity relied on electricity, compared to roughly 30% in 1914. Mass electrification was ready in the 1920s.

- By 1900, mechanisation in farming was driving the rural population of the USA out of jobs. Many migrated to the cities to take jobs in factories. By 1920, there were many more urban Americans than rural ones.

- Many new consumer items were not invented in the 1920s but years before. It took time to improve designs and the effectiveness of the inventions (see timeline of consumer devices invented before 1920).

Short-term causes of the economic boom

There were also several short-term causes. These explain why the boom happened during the decade of the 1920s.

- Investments: Before the 1920s, not many ordinary people would have bought and sold stocks. Now, however, more people began investing. Some used their savings, while others borrowed money to buy stocks. By the late 1920s, the New York Stock Exchange was trading 6–7 million shares or stocks per day, compared with a pre-war rate of 3–4 million.

- Consumer culture and advertising: With more money, the average American felt confident about buying goods. Newspapers, magazines and radios carried advertisements designed to persuade people to buy modern conveniences. Many adverts targeted women, encouraging them to buy labour-saving devices such as refrigerators, washing machines and vacuum cleaners.

- Buy now pay later: The purchase of these consumer goods was made easier by hire purchase – buying of goods on credit through a series of payments over time. To attract Americans to join these hire purchase schemes, adverts were located by roads, on the radio, in newspapers, magazine catalogues and in cinemas.

SOURCE ANALYSIS 9.1

Study Source 9A.

a   Identify the three products in this advertisement.

b   How does this advertisement make the products appear more attractive to potential purchasers?

c   This advert was placed in a magazine. How can you tell?

d   Why are men not featured in the advert?

SOURCE 9A

Gifts that bring HEALTH CLEANLINESS and LEISURE to the HOME

The ELECTROLUX WATER SOFTENER ensures a constant supply of delightfully soft water which protects your health and beauty, saves your soap and fuel, and lengthens the life of your laundered fabrics.

The ELECTROLUX REFRIGERATOR Refrigeration is the one safe way of keeping food absolutely fresh without the aid of preservatives or canning. The Electrolux Refrigerator is the only one in the world which operates continuously—without mechanism, without vibration and in *absolute silence*—by gas, electricity or paraffin

The ELECTROLUX CLEANER is not only a most efficient carpet cleaner—its exceptionally powerful suction searches the angles of the stairs, under low-built furniture, in the folds of the curtains and recesses of upholstery without complicated changing of parts. As it cleans the Electrolux purifies the air you breathe.

There are Electrolux models for every home obtainable at terms convenient for every income.

WHEN you give a woman an Electrolux Suction Cleaner you are not only giving her the means of keeping the home clean, you are presenting her with extra hours of leisure every day —all the year through— and for many years, too. And the home which also possesses the Electrolux Refrigerator and the Electrolux Water Softener is completely equipped with the finest appliances which domestic science has yet produced for ensuring wholesome food and clean, soft water.

ELECTROLUX LTD

MAKERS OF THE WORLD'S HIGHEST QUALITY DOMESTIC REFRIGERATORS, SUCTION CLEANERS, WATER SOFTENERS AND FLOOR POLISHERS
HEAD OFFICE 153-155 REGENT STREET, LONDON W.1
WORKS: LUTON, BEDFORDSHIRE
28 Branches and 506 Distributors throughout Great Britain.

Please Post this Coupon NOW

I am interested in your...................
.... and shall be glad if you will send me descriptive brochure and inform me of the name of your nearest Distributor, where, without any obligation on my part, I can test your claims for myself.

Name...................
Address...................
(H. & G.)...................

Source 9A: A UK advertisement for three products that were mass-produced in the mid-1920s

SOURCE 9B

Consumer item	Percentage of homes in 1920 that owned one	Percentage of homes in 1930 that owned one.
Radio sets	0	40
Vacuum cleaners	9	30
Washing machines	8	24

Source 9B: The growth of mass consumption in US households, 1920–30

SOURCE ANALYSIS 9.2

Look at Source 9B.

a   How useful is this table for studying the economic boom of the 1920s? What does it *not* tell you about the boom?

b   What other evidence would you need to understand how far American people benefited from the increased production of manufactured goods?

Republican government policy

The federal government helped to stimulate the boom. There were three Republican presidents from 1921 to 1933, and they all followed a *laissez-faire* policy that reduced taxes and left businesses to make their own decisions. In particular, President Herbert Hoover (1929–33) called for 'rugged individualism', believing that people should succeed through their own talents and work. The tax cuts for workers left them with more money to spend.

Governments departed from the *laissez-faire* policy on one issue. The 1922 Fordney-McCumber Act raised tariffs to their highest ever level and allowed the government to increase them annually. This made imports more expensive, protecting US industries from foreign competition.

Mass production and standardisation

Car-maker Henry Ford was the founder of the Ford Motor Company. He mass produced his vehicles so that they could be offered to consumers at a low price. He did this by introducing the assembly line, which involved dividing the process of making a car among many workers, each of whom performed one specific task repeatedly. Ford introduced standardisation of car models to make it quicker and easier to build them – for example, his Model T car was only available in black. By 1929, Americans owned 23 million cars.

The car industry created a demand for rubber for tyres, glass for windscreens, and other materials. Garages were built to provide petrol, servicing and repairs. Motels and restaurants were built to meet the needs of travellers on long journeys. On the edge of cities, suburbs expanded, as people could travel further to their workplace. As a result, rural areas were less isolated from large towns and cities.

> **KEY TERM**
>
> *laissez-faire*: a French term meaning 'leave alone' – a policy of minimising government involvement especially in the economy

Figure 9.3: An assembly line in one of Henry Ford's car factories in the 1920s, showing how cars were constructed in stages with one person doing one specific job

> ### FOCUS TASK 9.2
>
> - New consumer goods were made that saved time and made life easier.
> - The USA had plenty of raw materials that were necessary for energy and manufacturing.
> - Wages increased and this meant that Americans had more spending power.
> - Cars gave Americans the freedom to get away from the cities and yet travel to work. They also stimulated a range of other industries such as glass and rubber.
> - Hire-purchase agreements made it possible to buy now and pay later.
> - **. . . so the US economy boomed during the 1920s and people prospered.**
> - The advertising industry encouraged Americans to demand an improved quality of life and involvement in leisure activities.
> - Mass production of certain goods made it possible to reduce prices for consumers.
> - Electricity in cities brought light and heating to American homes and power to factories.
> - In the 1920s, Republican governments adopted a policy of *laissez-faire*. Taxes were cut and imports were made more expensive.

Chapter 9: The United States, 1919–41

> **CONTINUED**
>
> **a** Copy the diagram onto a large sheet of paper. Connect the statements by drawing arrows showing how one statement explains another. When you have drawn the arrows write on them what the link is. You can draw as many arrows as you like. The final two arrows should point to the **centre bubble**.
>
> **b** Write a short paragraph explaining and justifying the links you have created.
>
> **c** Using a small piece of card, cover up each statement and ask yourself: *If this factor was absent in the 1920s, would the boom have taken place?* If the answer is 'yes' then this factor is less significant than others. If the answer is 'no' then this is a significant factor. Draw a second box around each significant factor to identify the more important causes of the economic boom.

> **REFLECTION**
>
> How challenging did you find Focus task 9.2? List any difficulties that you had and share your top three with a partner. Listen to your partner's list. Is there any overlap between the two? Discuss in pairs how you could do the task in a different way to make it more successful.

Why did some industries prosper while others did not?

New industries in the 1920s

The car industry was a success story and stimulated growth in related industries, such as road-building. The US road network had doubled in length by 1930. Other new industries included commercial flying. This was an attractive leisure activity in the 1920s because of the development of larger and more comfortable aeroplanes. Aviator Charles Lindbergh became the first person to fly solo across the Atlantic in 1927, making flying seem glamorous. Bessie Coleman also contributed substantially to popularising flying for leisure.

> **KEY FIGURE**
>
> **Bessie Coleman (1892–1926)**
>
> Coleman was the first African-American female pilot. Coleman liked to perform for crowds in her hometown in Texas. Because Texas was **segregated** at the time, the organisers wanted two separate entrances: one for African-Americans and one for white people. Coleman refused to perform unless there was only one gate for everyone. Only 34 years old when she died, Coleman's last flight was on a plane that was poorly maintained and a mechanic's wrench was found to have jammed the controls.

> **KEY TERM**
>
> **segregation:** the separation of black people and white people in many areas of public life, such as education and public transport

The construction industry enjoyed a period of growth because big business needed new office buildings. New building materials and techniques meant that tall buildings known as skyscrapers were possible. These became a familiar part of the urban landscape. At 319 metres, the Chrysler Building in New York was the tallest in the world when completed in 1930. The following year the Empire State Building surpassed it at 381 metres.

Figure 9.4: Construction work on a skyscraper in the 1920s, showing workmen on the scaffolding high above the city streets

The decline of traditional industries

Some older industries suffered from overproduction and under-consumption. The coal industry did not enjoy a boom because it was producing too much coal, and demand for it declined as oil, gas and electricity became more popular.

Railways struggled to compete with the increase in road traffic and the expansion of the road network. Rail still transported goods for industry, but road transport was becoming increasingly important.

Shipbuilding also declined due to reduced demand. After the end of the war in 1918, US shipbuilders had empty order books.

The textile industry faced several challenges. For example, women in the 1920s preferred shorter dresses that required less material than pre-war designs. The introduction of cheap synthetic fibres, such as nylon and rayon, could be made in factories requiring fewer workers. This was a threat to traditional textiles industries such as cotton.

FOCUS TASK 9.3

a On your own, create a chart to show the performance of US industries in the 1920s. List the industries, and note how they performed in the 1920s and the reasons for their performances. Link these to ideas of supply and demand.

Name of industry	Performance: boom / stable / decline	Reasons for performance

b Colour code the industries that were new in the 1920s. Explain their success.

c Now compare your chart with a partner. Sort out any differences together.

d Together, decode the three main reasons why some US industries performed better than others in the 1920s.

Why did agriculture not share in the prosperity?

Agriculture experienced a boom during the war. However, as European farmers began to recover, prices for US farm produce fell. Wheat dropped from $183 a **bushel** in 1920 to 38 cents in 1929. Farmers who had taken out loans to increase the size of their farm and buy tractors and combine harvesters could not repay the banks. By 1924, 600 000 farmers were bankrupt and over 1 million farm workers had left the land in search of other jobs.

KEY TERM

bushel: a dry measure of 8 gallons, which is about 36 litres

SOURCE 9C

Nearly everything was done on credit [. . .] the small farmers back at that time [. . .] They all had to borrow money every year to make a profit. So, if they had a bad crop year, a lot of them, that's the way they lost their farms. The bad times back there, was 1920 and you just can't imagine the number of people then that was big men the year before who had lost everything they had.

Source 9C: Clay East, who ran a petrol station in a rural community in Arkansas, recalls the problems faced by tenant farmers in the 1920s

SOURCE ANALYSIS 9.3

Read Source 9C.

a What does the phrase 'big men' mean?

b How useful is this source for identifying the causes of problems facing farmers in the USA in the 1920s?

c Clay East was not a farmer. He ran a petrol station. Does this make his evidence less valuable? If so, why?

d What other kinds of sources would be useful for investigating agriculture at this time?

Demand for cotton and wool declined because artificial fibres became increasingly popular. Fewer farm animals were needed as the car industry boomed, so reducing the demand for animal foodstuffs such as hay and oats.

Rural communities lagged behind the towns. In 1930, more than 90% of farms were still not connected to the electricity network.

Less than half the US population lived in the countryside in the 1920s and so the effects of the farming crisis were severe and affected many people. However, there were some exceptions. Large-scale wheat farmers in the Midwest, and fruit growers in California and Florida, continued to prosper.

> ### FOCUS TASK 9.4
>
> In pairs write two paragraphs, one entitled Great War Farming boom, the other entitled Post-war Farming bust. Use all the boxes to write the two paragraphs but ensure that you include explanations of why the arrow from one box explains the next box.
>
> in wartime → high demand for food → high prices → farmers borrowed money → bought land and machinery → prosperity
>
> post-war → demand for food fell → farmers went bankrupt → prices collapsed → labourers laid off → poverty

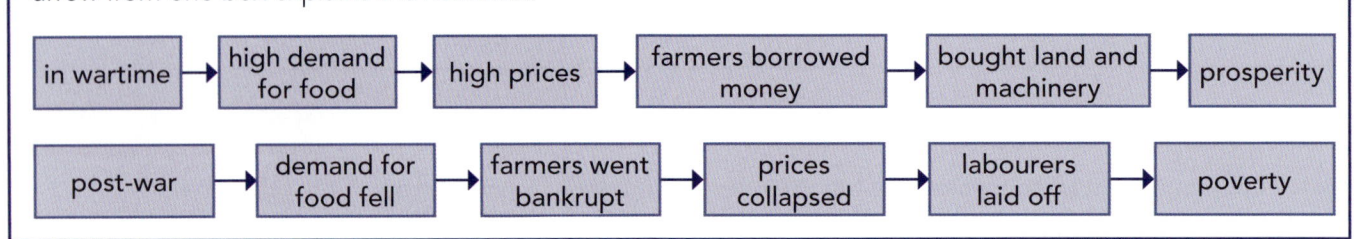

Did all Americans benefit from the boom?

The US remained an unequal society in the boom years. For example, while farm workers' wages were falling, skilled factory workers' pay rose. Across the country, people in the more agricultural South benefited less than those in the industrialised North.

Unskilled and casual workers, and the 2 million unemployed, were unable to purchase the goods available to better off Americans. For them, life was a matter of survival, not participation in the consumer boom.

Workers in older industries faced unemployment or wages that failed to keep up with the cost of living. Coal miners' standard of living dropped. By 1929, their wages had fallen to a third of the national average. Textile industry employers, faced with rising competition, employed cheaper female or child labour to reduce costs.

Farmers and farm workers were badly affected by the agricultural collapse of the 1920s. Bankruptcy turned some farmers into tenants on their own land. Others moved to industrial cities or to California, where fruit farms were creating employment. **Share-croppers** rented farmland. When prices of farm produce fell, they struggled to pay the rent. They were often **evicted** from their homes so were both unemployed and homeless.

Black Americans formed a disproportionate part of the country's poor. In cities such as New York and Chicago, they tended to be confined to poorly paid employment. They often lived in overcrowded conditions in segregated areas known as ghettoes. Many farm workers in the South were black, and one million of them lost their jobs in the 1920s.

> **KEY TERMS**
>
> **share-cropper:** a farmer who rents land and who gives part of their crop as rent
>
> **evict:** to force someone to leave a place, usually because they have not paid the rent they owe for land or property

	1919	1930
Average farm worker	$13.50	$7.50
Skilled factory worker	$22.30	$28.60

Figure 9.5: Changing average weekly pay of farm and factory workers, 1919–30

Weaknesses in the economy by the late 1920s

The boom did not happen for all Americans or in all parts of the economy. Certain weaknesses also meant that the boom was not destined to last, including:

- uneven distribution of wealth
- problems in farming
- problems in relation to trade with other countries
- speculation on the stock market and the lack of regulation.

> ### FOCUS TASK 9.5
>
> On your own, sort the following groups of people into those who benefited from the economic boom of the 1920s and those who did not:
>
> - coal miners
> - car-factory workers
> - cotton textile workers
> - small farmers
> - California fruit growers
> - southern black farm workers
> - department store employees.
>
> Make a chart with two columns to show your findings, and for each group outline the reasons why they either did well or did not do well in the 1920s. Share your findings with a partner and check each other's table.

Key points

The economic boom of the 1920s

- The boom in the US economy improved the standard of living for many Americans: improved wages allowed workers to buy consumer goods.
- Not all industries and not all Americans benefited from the boom. Traditional industries (like coal) suffered but new industries (like car making) did much better.
- Agriculture was unaffected by the boom. Many farm owners lost their farms and farm workers left the land and migrated to northern cities to work.

- The Republican-led federal government believed that it was not the job of the government to interfere in people's lives or intervene in the economy. This policy is called 'laissez-faire'.
- The value of companies on the Wall Street stock exchange climbed upwards, out of control and without regulation.

9.2 How far did US society change in the 1920s?

> **FOCUS POINTS**
>
> This topic will help you to answer these questions:
>
> - What were the 'Roaring Twenties'?
> - How widespread was intolerance in US society?
> - Why was Prohibition introduced, and then later repealed?
> - How far did the roles of women change during the 1920s?

What were the 'Roaring Twenties'?

The prosperity created by the economic boom of the 1920s led to major changes in US society. There were new opportunities for entertainment. Women enjoyed greater freedom. However, there was also a strong reaction against the social changes, often from older and more conservative people. Life changed much less in the countryside than in the cities.

> **KEY TERM**
>
> **speakeasy:** an illegal bar that sold alcoholic drinks

Social and cultural change

Jazz music was one of the key attractions of night clubs and **speakeasies** throughout the 1920s. Band leaders such as Duke Ellington and Louis Armstrong brought jazz to the cultural mainstream in the USA. Songwriters and composers such as George Gershwin and Al Jolson helped to make jazz 'respectable' to its critics. Jolson, in particular, popularised jazz; here was a famous white man singing jazz and the blues. Bessie Smith was the most popular and highest paid singer of the time, singing about racism, poverty and female sexuality. In a country made up of people from diverse cultures and backgrounds, jazz helped to create a national identity.

Figure 9.6: Bessie Smith performing with her jazz band c.1924

Chapter 9: The United States, 1919–41

Figure 9.7: One of the most popular night clubs was the Cotton Club in Harlem, New York

Silent films and talkies

The 1920s was also the golden age of cinema and the rise of Hollywood. To begin with, films were silent. A pianist or an orchestra would play music to accompany events on the screen. From 1927, with the success of Al Jolson's *The Jazz Singer*, 'talkies' appeared, in which the actors's voices could be heard. 'Picture palaces' like the New York Roxy seated 4000 people. Attendance soared, from 50 million a week in 1920 to 90 million by 1930. Films created a new popular culture with common speech, dress, behaviour and heroes. Sadly, Hollywood did its share of reinforcing racial stereotypes of minority groups.

Radio across America

In the 1920s, radio became the new source of news and entertainment for people in both the countryside and the cities. Radio sales rocketed from $60 million in 1922 to $426 million in 1929. Even people in remote rural areas could listen to entertainment such as musical variety shows and comedies, as well as news and sporting events. This helped to create a sense of common culture in the USA, particularly in relation to baseball and American football, which people followed keenly on the radio.

Spectator sports

With a booming economy, many workers had more leisure time. New and bigger sport stadiums and gymnasiums were built. The spread of radio made it easier for fans to keep up with their favourite teams.

Baseball was considered the national pastime. More people went to baseball games, followed baseball and played baseball for fun than any other sport. The most famous athlete of the 1920s was baseball star George Herman 'Babe' Ruth, the right fielder for the New York Yankees.

Figure 9.8: Baseball star Babe Ruth, who hit more home runs than any player had before

> ### ACTIVITY 9.2
>
> a   In pairs, copy and complete the table to show how changes in entertainments affected US society in the 1920s. Use the information in this section and do some further research using the internet and any other resources available to you.
>
> | Entertainment | Information | Impact |
> |---|---|---|
> | Music | | |
> | Film | | |
> | Radio | | |
> | Sport | | |

> **CONTINUED**
>
> b Join up with another pair, and compare and add to your tables if necessary. In your groups of four, discuss which of the items you placed in the first column was:
>
> - more important to rural Americans than those in the cities and town
> - more important for black Americans than white Americans
> - most important in bringing together diverse communities and creating a sense of national community.

How widespread was intolerance in US society?

The 1920s were a time when several minority groups faced intolerance, discrimination and persecution.

Immigrants

The US had been founded on the idea of immigration. The inscription on the Statue of Liberty in New York harbour famously welcomes the world's 'huddled masses' to a new life of freedom and opportunity. However, immigrants became less welcome in the early 20th century for several reasons.

A growing number of immigrants came from Eastern Europe or Asia. Most were illiterate and unskilled. Many people feared that these immigrants would not 'fit in' to society because their racial and cultural background was different from that of established American citizens and well-established immigrant communities. Working-class Americans feared competition for jobs at a time when employment opportunities were threatened by mechanisation in industry.

Congress responded to these fears by introducing legal quotas for immigrants in 1921. The quotas were intended to reduce the number of people coming from Eastern Europe. The quota was reduced from 3% to 2% in 1924, and in 1929 a further measure restricted the number of immigrants to 150 000 a year.

Total population	106 million
White	94 million
Black	10.5 million
Native American	0.2 million
Asian	0.1 million
Hispanic	1.2 million

Figure 9.9: A table showing the population of the USA in 1920

FOCUS TASK 9.6

It can be difficult to measure how widespread intolerance was because the answer cannot be reduced to statistics.

Create a table like the one below. As you read through this section, fill in the table with name of the group and examples of intolerance or tolerance they experienced in the 1920s. Also consider the USA's overall demographics from the table in Figure 9.9 to help you make a judgement about 'how widespread' intolerance was.

Group	Experience of intolerance / tolerance
Immigrants	

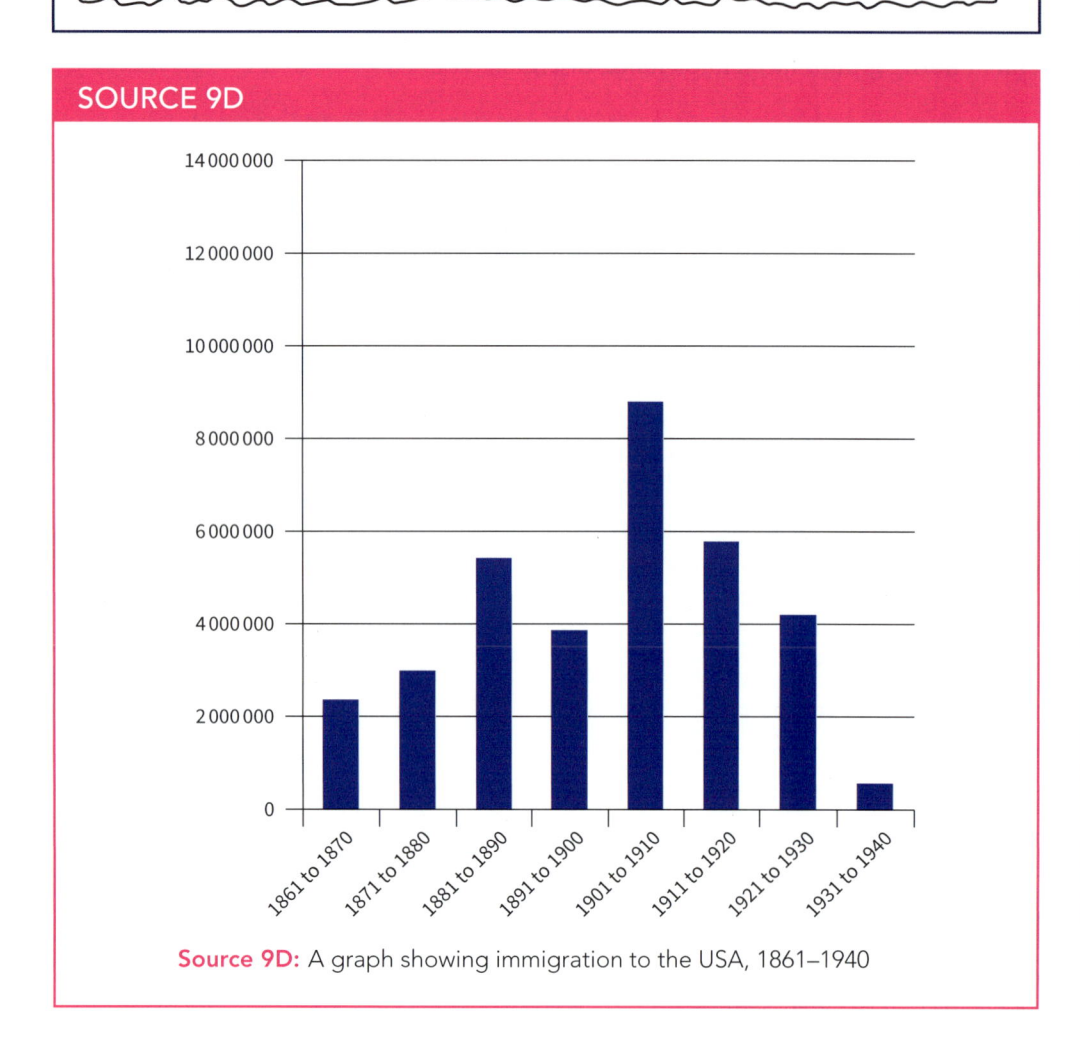

SOURCE 9D

Source 9D: A graph showing immigration to the USA, 1861–1940

SOURCE ANALYSIS 9.4

Study Source 9D.

a What does this graph suggest about the impact of the new immigration laws in the USA in the 1920s?

b Why would many US workers be pleased to see this evidence of the impact of the new immigration laws?

c Why would business owners be unhappy that the flow of immigrants from Europe had slowed down?

The 'Red Scare'

The 'Red Scare' is a label used to describe the period 1919–20. 'Red' refers to communism but not all those involved in causing the Red Scare were communists. A fear of immigrants was part of the Red Scare. After the Russian Revolution of 1917, many people in the West connected extreme political ideas such as communism with the arrival of immigrants from Eastern Europe. In the USA, fears grew after a series of bomb attacks were blamed on **anarchists**. These included an attack on the home of the government's chief law officer, Attorney General Mitchell Palmer, in 1919. Palmer decided to remove what he called 'foreign-born subversives' from the USA. In all, about 6000 suspected anarchists and some communists were arrested in the Palmer raids. The Red Scare was used as an excuse for illegal searches, seizures and unwarranted arrests by the police.

The vulnerability of immigrants was highlighted by the Sacco and Vanzetti case. This was a notorious criminal trial in 1921, in which two Italian anarchists, Nicola Sacco and Bartolomeo Vanzetti, were accused of murder during an armed robbery. The case was a controversial one, with unclear evidence and significant differences in the stories given by witnesses. They were found guilty, and both were executed in 1927. Although the case revealed widespread prejudice against foreigners, there was also considerable support for the men's appeals and many felt that they were victims of a **miscarriage of justice**.

> **KEY TERMS**
>
> **anarchist:** someone who believes in getting rid of government
>
> **miscarriage of justice:** when someone is punished by the law courts for a crime they have not committed

Discrimination against black Americans

In 1920, 10.5 million black Americans were living in the USA—75% of whom lived and worked in the South. Although the American Civil War (1861–65) had ended the practice of enslaving black people, many southern states found ways to limit their freedoms. The Jim Crow laws enforced segregation to keep black people and white people apart. In practice, this meant separate churches, hospitals, schools, parks and other public places. Within the legal system, black Americans could not serve on juries. In some states, literacy tests or other qualifications were imposed to make it more difficult for black people to register to vote.

From 1910 onwards the 'Great Migration' saw a million southern black people move to northern cities like New York, Detroit and Chicago in the hope of finding employment and better treatment. Even though there was no formal segregation in the North, newcomers still experienced discrimination in employment and some elements of segregation in schools and public housing.

Figure 9.10: A separate area for black people at a baseball game in 1922

The Ku Klux Klan

The popularity of the **Ku Klux Klan (KKK)** revived in the early years of the 20th century. Many new members believed that black people were taking their jobs. Some white Americans were angered by the rising crime and violence in the cities and blamed black people for it. The KKK also targeted Catholics, Jews and foreign-born minorities who they claimed were anti-American.

Black Americans were threatened, kidnapped, beaten and murdered. By 1925, the Klan had an estimated 2 million members and enjoyed the private support of a number of politicians, judges and senior policemen in some southern states. One Klan leader, David Stephenson, declared, 'I am the law in Indiana.' The police authorities often ignored **lynchings** carried out by white people, including Klan members. They also failed to investigate many instances of violence against black people.

> **KEY TERMS**
>
> **Ku Klux Klan:** a white supremacist organisation founded in the South after the Civil War. In its revived form in the early 20th century, the KKK's official policy was to terrorise black people, Catholics, Jews, immigrants, communists and anarchists
>
> **lynching:** an illegal execution carried out by a mob, not by judicial process, often on black men
>
> **race riot:** a public, often violent, fight caused by racial anger or hatred

Figure 9.11: Ku Klux Klan officers in their robes and hoods, initiating a new member (seen kneeling) into their secret rituals, 1925

Race riots

In 1919, **race riots** took place in 23 cities. It did not take much to set off the violence because racial tensions and injustices were simmering. In July 1919, a young black man called Eugene Williams unintentionally wandered onto a public beach on Lake Michigan, Chicago, that was segregated for white people. Williams was attacked and drowned. Five days of rioting followed in which 38 people died – 23 of them black. Many more were injured, and a thousand black families were made homeless.

Two years later, worse violence occurred in the city of Tulsa, Oklahoma. A young black woman was arrested for allegedly assaulting a white girl in a lift. A fictitious newspaper report of the incident sparked violence. About 300 black people died in the Tulsa race riot, and a thousand homes and businesses belonging to black people were burned down. For many Americans, both black and white, it seemed that black people had no civil rights at all.

Chapter 9: The United States, 1919–41

Figure 9.12: A black man being beaten by white men during the Chicago race riots; he later died of his injuries

> ### ACTIVITY 9.3
>
> a Work in small groups. Find out a bit more about the Ku Klux Klan in the 1920s. Using your research and the information in this section, create a graphic organiser such as a mind map to record what you have discovered. Put 'KKK' in the middle of the page, and then around it put what you have discovered about membership of the Klan, its aims, its tactics and why it succeeded in persecuting different groups.
>
> b In 1925, Klan membership was about 2 million, but it had many more supporters than this. How does this add to your understanding of how widespread intolerance was in the USA in the 1920s? Discuss your ideas in small groups. Try to explain why the Ku Klux Klan had such a fearsome reputation.

Religious intolerance

White Protestant Americans had long viewed Roman Catholics with suspicion. They believed that the Catholic Church was undemocratic and therefore un-American. Protestants also claimed that separate Catholic schools prevented young people from becoming loyal American citizens. In 1921, a member of the KKK assassinated a priest, Father James Coyle, in Birmingham, Alabama. In 1922, the state of Oregon passed a law that tried to ban Catholic schools, although this law was later struck down by the Supreme Court. Intolerance against Catholics simmered under the surface of life in the USA in the 1920s.

SOURCE 9E

Source 9E: An illustration from a book published in 1928 by the Protestant bishop Alma Bridewell White

SOURCE ANALYSIS 9.5

Study Source 9E.

a What or who is 'Rome'? Why is it shown grasping at the USA?

b What is the purpose of this illustration?

c Do you think the book that this illustration appeared in was pro- or anti-Ku Klux Klan? Explain your thinking.

d Does the figure holding the club labelled 'The Ballot' convince you that they are a force for democracy? Why or why not?

Another feature of religious intolerance during this period was the attempt by Christian **fundamentalists** to ban the teaching of the **theory of evolution**. They argued that God created the world in six days. In 1925, the so-called 'Monkey Trial' took place in Dayton, Tennessee. A teacher named John Scopes taught his students the theory of evolution deliberately, so that a case could be brought against him which he felt would bring the issue to public attention. The court eventually ruled against Scopes, but the trial exposed the weaknesses of his opponents' arguments.

THINKING SKILLS

Do a bit more research on the Scopes 'Monkey Trial'. Imagine you are a newspaper reporter in court, watching the conclusion of the trial. Write two brief accounts describing the outcome.

- Write one as if you strongly believed that the theory of evolution was wrong and should not be taught in schools.
- Write the second from the point of view of someone who believes in the science of the theory of evolution and feels that the judgement in the trial is a miscarriage of justice.

KEY TERMS

fundamentalists: someone who believes in traditional forms of a religion or who strictly believes what is written in a holy book such as the Christian Bible

theory of evolution: the theory of biologist Charles Darwin in the 19th century, that life on Earth developed over millions of years, and that humans and apes are descended from a common ancestor

> **FOCUS TASK 9.7**
>
> You should now have completed the table you started in Focus task 9.6, collecting evidence about intolerance in the USA.
>
> In pairs, use your table to test the accuracy of this statement: 'Intolerance was part of everyday life in US society in the 1920s.' Take account of ethnicity, race and religion. Plan a written response, looking at all sides of the argument and eventually reaching a conclusion.

Why was Prohibition introduced, and then later repealed?

After the First World War, anti-drink campaigners gained support in Congress and the 18th Amendment to the US Constitution was passed in 1919. This banned the 'manufacture, sale or transportation of intoxicating liquors'. The Volstead Act of 1920 was designed to enforce the 18th Amendment. The Act defined 'intoxicating liquors' as anything containing more than 5% alcohol.

What were the effects of Prohibition?

Legal breweries and distilleries quickly closed, and alcohol consumption dropped. However, continuing demand led to many illegal stills being set up. These produced poor-quality whisky that was nicknamed 'moonshine', which caused an increase in alcohol-related deaths. Previously law-abiding American citizens now bought alcohol in illegal bars known as speakeasies, which charged high prices. Illegal traders known as bootleggers did very well. The USA's lengthy land and sea borders meant it was almost impossible to prevent the smuggling of alcohol.

Organised criminal gangs fought for control of the now illegal drink trade. The city of Chicago became notorious for its gang warfare during Prohibition, where Al Capone led one of the most famous gangs. With too few government agents to enforce the law, and widespread corruption among police, local politicians and officials, the gangsters thrived. In this way, Prohibition unintentionally damaged people's health, turned law-abiding citizens into law breakers, and caused corruption and violence in many US cities.

Why did Prohibition come to an end in 1933?

The Volstead Act proved impossible to enforce. A committee set up by Herbert Hoover in 1929 concluded that Prohibition was not working. The government was fighting a losing battle, and the rule of law was being undermined. After the start of the Depression and the election of Franklin Roosevelt as president, the 18th Amendment was repealed. The government hoped that making alcohol legal again would create jobs, stimulate economic recovery and create a legal industry that could be taxed and regulated.

> **KEY FIGURE**
>
> **Al Capone (1899–1947)**
>
> Capone was a gang leader who gained control of the illegal drink trade in Chicago. He dominated the city's political scene through bribery and election fixing. In the 1929 St Valentine's Day Massacre, his gang killed seven members of a rival group in a Chicago garage. Capone was eventually prosecuted and imprisoned not for his gangster activities, which were difficult to prove, but for income tax evasion.

How far did the roles of women change during the 1920s?

Greater political rights?
Before the First World War, women in the USA could vote in some state elections, but not in federal ones. In 1920, the 19th Amendment to the Constitution gave women equal voting rights with men. The first time women could vote in a federal election was the 1920 presidential election. However, women's organisations were concerned that only about 26% of eligible women voted. These new voters supported President Harding in about the same proportion as male voters did so. In fact, the hard-fought right to vote made no significant difference at the start of the decade.

More independent lifestyles
In the 1920s, a new kind of young urban woman emerged: the 'flapper'. Flappers wore fashionably short skirts without the restrictive undergarments of the pre-war era. They cut their hair short. They smoked and drank in public, socialised openly with men and enjoyed greater personal freedom.

Women in rural areas did not usually enjoy the same access to education or careers as urban women. Their lives remained hard, governed by the rhythm of the seasons on a farm and dependent first on fathers, and then on husbands. They could not get credit independently of their husbands and had no legal protection against domestic abuse. Access to contraception was improving, with campaigner Margaret Sanger establishing the first birth-control clinic in 1923, but was still limited in availability and efficiency, and still controversial. Married women were still responsible for domestic life including childcare.

Working women
The proportion of women in the workforce did rise in the 1920s, but only from 20.4% to 22%. Women were generally paid less than men, and employment usually occurred in areas traditionally seen as 'female', such as teaching, clerical work, domestic service, nursing, the garment trades and librarianship. Even at this time, the traditional division of labour was the norm in the USA: a husband working for wages outside the home, a wife working without wages within it.

Figure 9.13: A 'flapper' striking a pose that would have been considered daring in the 1920s

REVISION TIP
There is a lot to remember about the Roaring Twenties, particularly about the social changes. Create a mind map for each of the following topics:
- women
- black Americans
- entertainment
- radio and the media.

For each topic, use two colours to highlight changes that were short-lived and changes that lasted longer.

FOCUS TASK 9.8

a   In pairs, copy and complete this table to help you analyse the changes experienced by women.

Group of women	What were their social and economic lives like?	Changes in the 1920s
Rural women		
Urban women		
Professional women		
All women		

b   Do you agree that the overall position of women in US society did not improve significantly in the 1920s? Discuss this in your pairs.

Key points
Social changes in the 1920s

- Different groups in different parts of the USA experienced the boom of the 1920s in a variety of ways.
- Many black Americans migrated to the north in search of jobs and freedom from racism.
- The KKK was a powerful white organisation that made unprovoked attacks on black Americans and their property.
- Immigrant unskilled workers in the cities faced intolerance because of their background and lack of skills.
- The film-making industry centred on Hollywood grew and provided entertainment for millions, especially after the 'talkies' were introduced. Racist stereotypes appeared in film and radio.
- Prohibition temporarily shut down the production and sale of alcohol across the USA. This gave rise to a gang culture as rival gangs fought to control the trade in illegal alcohol. Prohibition was eventually ended because it was too difficult to enforce.
- The lives of women in rural areas hardly changed at all. In cities there were more job opportunities and more entertainment.

9.3 What were the causes and consequences of the Wall Street Crash?

FOCUS POINTS

This topic will help you to answer these questions:

- How far was speculation responsible for the Wall Street Crash?
- What impact did the Crash have on the economy?
- What were the social consequences of the Crash?
- Why did Roosevelt win the election of 1932?

How far was speculation responsible for the Wall Street Crash?

During the boom years of the 1920s, some people made money by buying stocks and shares in US companies and then selling them for a profit, when prices rose. This practice is known as speculation. It relied on companies continuing to perform well so that the value of shares would keep rising. This was until October 1929 when the Wall Street Crash occurred and, almost overnight, the value of shares collapsed, leaving many investors and banks facing huge losses.

Wall Street in New York is where the stock market is based. In the 1920s, when its activities were not regulated by government, growing numbers of ordinary people bought shares in the hope of making money. Many borrowed money to do so. When share prices rose, they could sell their shares, repay the loan and still make a profit. By 1929, 3 million Americans owned shares. More people bought shares, pushing share prices beyond their real value. Too little attention was paid to the actual performance of the companies themselves, and too much to the performance of their shares on the stock market. In addition, the rising stock market was based on shareholders' confidence.

With the value of shares rising even when the demand for goods had started to fall, US companies were extremely overvalued. In the autumn of 1929, some investors, who could see dangers ahead, became worried enough to begin selling shares. As prices fell, investors panicked. On 'Black Thursday', 24 October, almost 13 million shares were sold in one day. On 29 October, more than 16 million shares were traded. There were too many sellers and too few buyers. The value of the shares collapsed, causing both banks, businesses and individuals to lose their money.

Figure 9.14: Crowds gather outside the New York Stock Exchange at the time of the 1929 Wall Street Crash

Chapter 9: The United States, 1919–41

Key points

The Wall Street Crash

- The economic boom lasted until mid-1928 in many industries.
- A lack of government regulation and the over-valuation of companies on the stock market led to a rapid increase in share-buying. Around 9000 banks and around 3 million private citizens bought shares.
- Companies were overvalued because of speculation.
- The slow initial drop in stock prices caused by the selling of these shares in early and mid October had a knock-on effect. Banks, companies and private speculators began the rush to sell shares.
- This caused a sudden collapse in the market, with too many people wanting to sell and not enough people wanting to buy.

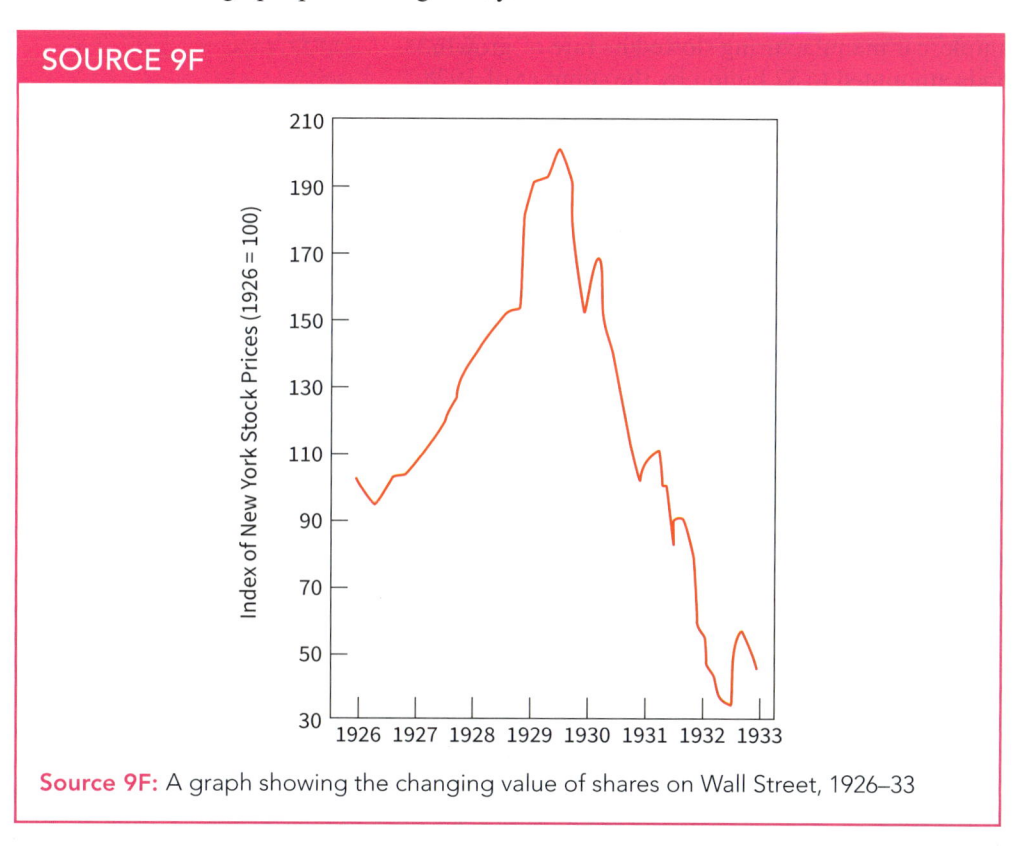

SOURCE 9F

Source 9F: A graph showing the changing value of shares on Wall Street, 1926–33

SOURCE ANALYSIS 9.6

Study Source 9F. What can you learn from this graph about the background to the Wall Street Crash?

ACTIVITY 9.4

a   Divide your class into two even groups. Each group should debate one of the following questions.

- 'Without the booming economy in the US in the 1920s, the Wall Street Crash would not have happened.' To what extent do you agree with this judgement?

- 'Greed and more greed.' It was speculation and nothing but speculation that caused the Crash of October 1929. Do you agree?

> CONTINUED
>
> b   Before you start, choose two people as scribes to take notes of everyone's ideas. Nominate one person as the chairperson, who is responsible for keeping the debate on track and making sure everyone gets a chance to speak. By the end of your discussion, you should have reached an agreement.
>
> c   Use your discussion and the notes you have made to present your judgement to the other half of the class. Make sure you explain your thinking clearly and explain how you resolved any disagreements.

Did the Wall Street Crash cause the Depression?

The Wall Street Crash did not cause the Great Depression, but it did make it worse. Farming had been in a depression since the start of the 1920s. Now industries started to share some pain, too. For example, car manufacturing slowed its rate of growth in 1925. Stockpiles of unsold goods amounted to $2 billion by the summer of 1928. This drop in demand was starting to happen in more industries in late 1928 and 1929.

What impact did the Crash have on the economy?

Financial effects of the Crash

The financial effects of the Crash were immediate. Millions of shares became worthless. Investors who had bought stocks with borrowed money were bankrupted because they could not pay back their loans.

The American people no longer trusted Wall Street and investment in general. Businesses found it difficult to secure loans for investment in new projects. Business uncertainty affected job security. As American workers faced uncertainty, they were reluctant to buy consumer goods. The decline in demand continued to spiral downwards.

Economic effects of the Crash

The economic effects were equally serious. The decline in stock prices caused bankruptcies and bank failures. There were 25 000 banks in the USA in 1929, but the majority of them operated without any financial support should they fail. It was not unusual for banks to fail, but disaster struck in the last two months of 1930 when 600 banks collapsed, bringing the total for that year to 1352.

Seeing the banks in trouble, people lost confidence and queued to withdraw their money. By 1933, more than 4000 banks had gone out of business. A vicious cycle developed.

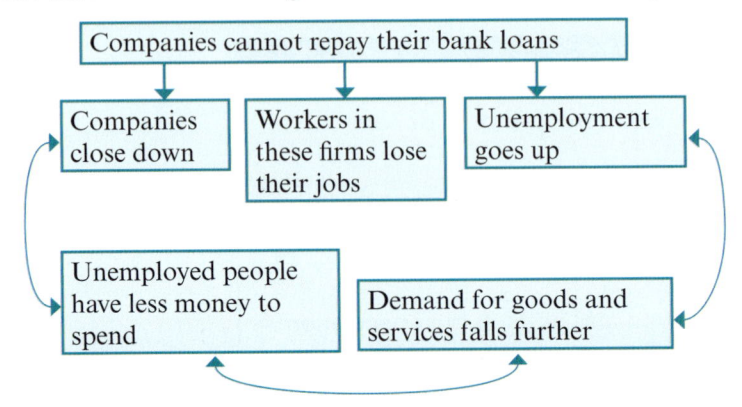

```
Companies cannot repay their bank loans
    ↓              ↓                ↓
Companies    Workers in      Unemployment
close down   these firms     goes up
             lose their jobs
    ↓                              ↓
Unemployed people          Demand for goods and
have less money to         services falls further
spend
```

Unemployment reached 4.3 million (almost 9% of the workforce) in 1930. By 1932 it had rocketed to 12 million (almost 24% of the workforce). Those who found a job usually had to work for lower wages, making the fall in demand worse.

In 1930, the government introduced the Smoot-Hawley tariff, which was higher than previous **import tariffs**. Other countries did the same for US imports, causing world trade to shrink, further damaging US industry.

This was the Great Depression: what started in the USA soon spread to Europe.

> **KEY TERM**
>
> **import tariffs:** taxes on goods imported into a country

> **THINK LIKE A HISTORIAN**
>
> Today, we live in a global economy that influences all our lives. Research your country's role within the global economy. What does it export? What does it import? Is there a trade balance or imbalance between exports and imports? Who do you trade with? Why? How does your school or life at home reflect these international links?
>
> What jobs and career opportunities are there in this sector of your country's economy? What essential and desirable skills and knowledge do you need?

> **REVISION TIP**
>
> When revising historical events such as the Wall Street Crash or the Great Depression, remember that different groups in society experienced them in different ways. For example, a banker or professional in the city might argue that the Depression started in 1929. A poor farmer or coal miner or cotton textile worker would argue that it began well before 1929. Practise writing answers that identify specific groups that did or did not suffer.

What were the social consequences of the Crash?

The effects of the Wall Street Crash and Depression in the cities

Unemployment rose steadily until, by 1933, almost a quarter of the workforce was jobless. The industrial areas of the North and West, where entire factories closed, were worst hit. It was almost impossible to find another job in these areas.

One consequence of unemployment was homelessness as householders became unable to meet mortgage or rent payments. Many slept on the streets or resorted to travelling in search of work. In 1932, an estimated 2 million **hobos** risked their lives by hitching rides on long-distance trains. Several hundred thousand people built shanty towns of wood and cardboard on the edges of cities. These were known as 'Hoovervilles' in mockery of Herbert Hoover, president at the time of the Wall Street Crash. These were unhealthy places without running water and sewage systems.

The Depression affected family life. It discouraged people from marrying and having children. Marriages fell from 1.23 million in 1929 to 982 000 in 1932. The suicide rate went up from 14 per 100 000 people to 17 between 1929 and 1932.

The social problems of the Depression were worsened because there was no **welfare state** provided by the federal government. Instead, individual towns and cities ran

> **KEY TERMS**
>
> **hobos:** homeless, unemployed people travelling across the country in search of work
>
> **welfare state:** a government-run system of national assistance to tackle poverty or unemployment

limited programmes of assistance. Churches and charities provided soup kitchens to provide basic meals. In some cases, unemployed people joined together to help themselves. Sometimes farmers allowed them to collect food that could not be sold. Desperate people begged or stole simply to survive.

Figure 9.15: A family in a Hooverville in Ohio, 1938

SOURCE 9G

Jesse Jackson, the self-declared mayor of Hooverville, was one of the men who had a strong distaste for organized charity. [. . .] Jackson and his friends rounded up whatever they could find and began to create shelters. Seattle city officials were not thrilled about this new development. In an [. . .] attempt to disband these shantytowns and unemployed 'jungles', city officials burned down the entire community, giving the men only seven days' eviction notice. [. . .] Hooverville residents, for their part, were not put off by the city's attempt to disband them. They simply dug deeper embankments for their homes and re-established the community.

Source 9G: An extract from an account of a Hooverville settlement in Seattle, Washington State, in the north-western USA

SOURCE ANALYSIS 9.7

Read Source 9G.

a What does the source tell you about the attitudes of the unemployed in Seattle towards the Great Depression?

b Why do you think the officials did not want a Hooverville outside Seattle?

c How could you find out if this example from Seattle was typical across the USA?

The Depression in rural USA

The Depression worsened an already bad situation for farmers in the USA. Low prices fell further, sometimes making it pointless for farmers to even harvest their crops. In Oregon, farmers killed thousands of sheep because the price the sheep would fetch at market would not cover the cost of transporting them there.

In Kansas, Oklahoma, Texas, New Mexico and Colorado, farmers faced an additional challenge. Soil erosion and dust storms ruined thousands of farmers, and many sold and left. They moved to the west coast in search of work, but they rarely found it. Locals often viewed them suspiciously. The newcomers usually had to work for low wages, living in temporary camps.

SOURCE 9H

Source 9H: A still from the film adaptation of John Steinbeck's 1939 novel *The Grapes of Wrath*

SOURCE ANALYSIS 9.8

Look at Source 9H. Steinbeck's novel is set in the USA during the Depression. It tells the story of a farming family that moves from Oklahoma to California in search of work like picking fruit.

a   Can you trust a novel like *The Grapes of Wrath* as evidence of the impact of the Great Depression on rural America? By definition, a novel is fiction. What other sources could you use with 9H to make it more reliable?

b   What message does the image in Source 9H give us? How valuable is the image in finding out about rural conditions during the Depression?

> CAMBRIDGE IGCSE™ AND O LEVEL HISTORY OPTION B: COURSEBOOK

> **THINK LIKE A HISTORIAN**
>
> Migration stories are regularly reported in the news today. Find a current migration story and read about it. It might be about a group of people or an individual. Base your research on the following questions.
>
> - Why are these migrants on the move?
> - Where did they live and where do they want to move to? Why?
> - How has the media reported on this migration?
> - Is their journey in progress or has it reached an end? If so, is it the end they hoped for? Or have their expectations been dashed?
>
> When you have finished your research, consider what circumstances surrounding migration are like those 100 years ago and what factors are different.

> **REFLECTION**
>
> Reflect on the research you did for the 'Think like a historian' feature. What approach did you take? How did you choose a story to investigate? How did you research and record the information? Did anything surprise you? What would you do next time to improve your research practice?

Did all Americans face hardship?

Although they were affected by the Wall Street Crash, the rich tended to suffer less than the rest of society. Some had not invested everything in stocks and shares but had kept a proportion of their wealth in gold and property, which kept their value. Some bought the property of less fortunate people quite cheaply. This made the rich even richer. Nevertheless, many Americans experienced a social and economic crisis in the early 1930s.

> **ACTIVITY 9.5**
>
> a In pairs, choose one group in US society in the late 1920s and 1930s and research their experiences of the Depression in greater depth. Choose from: rural, urban, women, men, black, white, North, South, rich, poor, or a combination.
>
> b Present your findings to the class using IT, maps, graphs and primary sources. Structure your presentation to answer these questions:
>   - How badly did the Depression hit this group?
>   - What options or choices did they have?
>   - Whatever they chose to do, did it make any significant difference to their lives? Why, or why not?

Key points

Social consequences of the Crash

- Almost everyone in the USA suffered from the Depression. The loss of work put strain on individuals, relationships and families.
- Homelessness was one consequence that many suffered. They did what they could to create shelter in so-called 'Hoovervilles'.

382

- Farmers left the land and headed west to California where they hoped to find work.
- Many Americans relied on charity and handouts to survive because there was no significant welfare provision or safety net.

Why did Roosevelt win the election of 1932?

Franklin Delano Roosevelt (FDR), the Democratic Party's candidate, defeated the sitting president, Republican Herbert Hoover, in the November 1932 election.

Roosevelt took over the government when the Depression was at its worst. He was popular because he offered a message of hope at a time of great crisis. By contrast, his predecessor seemed to have no answers to the misery of his fellow Americans.

Figure 9.16: Roosevelt (right) greeting his defeated predecessor, Herbert Hoover, on the day he took over as president, March 1933

> **KEY FIGURE**
>
> **Herbert Hoover (1874–1964)**
>
> Hoover was a skilled administrator. He organised the distribution of food to people in Europe affected by the fighting in the First World War. After serving as secretary of commerce in the Republican administrations of the 1920s, he was elected president in 1929. He believed that American individualism was not a call for selfishness. Rather, it meant looking out for others and the community as a whole. For Hoover, individualism meant service to others.

Hoover's policies

Hoover believed that hard work was the key to continued prosperity. This was an appealing message while the boom lasted, but after the Wall Street Crash, people wanted positive action from the government.

Hoover appeared complacent about the problems of people badly affected by the Depression. In the first year of the Depression, he insisted that the good times would return if government maintained its traditional *laissez-faire* approach. Individual states and charities could relieve poverty, not the federal government. Hoover did start a Farm Board to help farmers by buying up surplus food.

His Reconstruction Finance Corporation, created in 1932, provided $2 billion in loans to businesses. His government financed public works schemes, including the Boulder Dam on the Colorado River. This was completed after he had left office and was later renamed the Hoover Dam. Yet these measures were not nearly enough to deal with the scale of the problems that the US economy faced – 13 million were out of work by 1933.

As a result, Hoover seemed not to care about the plight of many ordinary Americans. 'In Hoover we trusted, now we are busted' was one well-known farmers' protest slogan. He was criticised for his handling of the 'Bonus Marchers.' In 1924, 20,000 army veterans from the Great War had been promised an extra payment by Congress that would be distributed in 1945. In the summer of 1932, some of them travelled to Washington to call for the money to be paid early because they were desperate. They set up camp on the edges of the city with their families.

Many went home after the Senate did not pass the Bonus Bill. The remaining Bonus Army occupied government buildings. After police were ordered to evict them, a riot started, and two bonus marchers were shot dead. The sight of the police and the army clearing out unarmed citizens with force outraged many Americans. Even though Hoover had not given the orders to burn the camp, he was blamed for this military operation, and it damaged his reputation even more.

Hoover's health began to suffer. Visitors to the White House noticed a man who had aged prematurely. In the election on 8 November 1932, Hoover won only six states.

What did Roosevelt offer?

At the Democratic Party convention in the summer of 1932, nominee Franklin D. Roosevelt impressed many people with one promise: 'I pledge you, I pledge myself to a new deal for the American people.' The contrast with Hoover could not have been clearer. Roosevelt spoke with confidence and energy. Hoover looked exhausted and had nothing new to offer the American voters.

Throughout his election campaign, Roosevelt highlighted Hoover's failures. He toured the USA by plane and train, attracting large crowds with the campaign song 'Happy Days Are Here Again'. Roosevelt gave 27 major speeches compared with Hoover's ten. Roosevelt stated clearly that he would repeal Prohibition, whereas Hoover's ideas on the subject were vague. Americans blamed Hoover for the Great Depression and the deaths of veterans on the Bonus March. In contrast, Roosevelt offered both hope to poor people and reassurance to the many middle-class Americans who feared that without urgent action, the country might slide into revolution.

On 8 November 1932, FDR won with the support of 23 million people, equivalent to 57% of the vote, and won all except 6 of the 48 states of the USA.

Key points

Hoover and Roosevelt

- Roosevelt did not have detailed policies, but he had the advantage over Hoover because he had not presided over the Great Depression since 1928.
- Roosevelt used the radio effectively, Hoover did not.
- Roosevelt promised all Americans a 'New Deal'. It was a memorable catch phrase that summed up his fresh approach to America's many problems. Hoover had nothing new to offer.

KEY FIGURE

Franklin Delano Roosevelt (1882–1945)

Roosevelt came from a privileged background and was noted for his charm as well as his skill as a politician. He served as Assistant Secretary of the Navy under President Wilson. Just before he turned 40, he caught polio. From that point on, he was unable to walk unaided. Roosevelt was a man of great determination and ambition. In 1928 he was elected governor of New York State and in 1933 became the US's first disabled president.

> **FOCUS TASK 9.9**
>
> a In pairs, create two election leaflets for the 1932 election: one for Roosevelt and one for Hoover. Set out their policies and reasons why the American people should vote for them.
>
> b Share your leaflets with another pair and work with your own partner to assess the other pair's leaflets. Improve your own leaflets to respond to the feedback if necessary.
>
> c As a group of four, use the leaflets as a starting point for a discussion on why Roosevelt won the election of 1932.

9.4 How successful was the New Deal?

> **FOCUS POINTS**
>
> This topic will help you to answer these questions:
>
> - What was the New Deal as introduced in 1933?
> - How far did the character of the New Deal change after 1933?
> - Why did the New Deal encounter opposition?
> - Why did unemployment persist despite the New Deal?
> - Did the fact that the New Deal did not solve unemployment mean that it was a failure?

What was the New Deal as introduced in 1933?

The New Deal was not a detailed set of proposals when Roosevelt was elected. His policies evolved over time, reflecting his election statement that what the country needed was 'bold, persistent experimentation'. Historians divide the Roosevelt era into a 'First New Deal' in 1933, followed by a second one in 1935. Roosevelt's first year in office was a period of intense government activity, focused on reviving the economy, getting people working again and stopping them from losing their homes and farms. Its purpose was summed up in the 'three Rs': relief, recovery and reform.

Roosevelt's inaugural speech, March 1933

The speech Roosevelt gave at his **inauguration** is one of his most famous. Words would not fix the USA's problems, but it was important to generate some optimism. He succeeded, telling his audience that 'the only thing we have to fear is fear itself'. Roosevelt broadcast a series of radio addresses, known as 'Fireside Chats' because of their informal style. In these, he explained his policies and encouraged people to look to a rosier future. Radio was relatively new, and Roosevelt was the first president to use it effectively to communicate with the American people.

> **KEY TERM**
>
> **inauguration:** the formal public ceremony at which a new president takes the oath of office and officially takes on the role

> CAMBRIDGE IGCSE™ AND O LEVEL HISTORY OPTION B: COURSEBOOK

SOURCE 9I

I know that the American people will understand this [. . .] I do not deny that we may make mistakes of procedure as we carry out the New Deal. I have no expectation of making a hit every time I come to bat. What I seek is the highest possible batting average, not only for myself but for the team.

Source 9I: An extract from Roosevelt's second 'Fireside Chat', 7 May 1933

SOURCE ANALYSIS 9.9

Read Source 9I.

a   What was the purpose of President Roosevelt's radio broadcast?

b   How effective do you think the extract from Roosevelt's broadcast is? Look at the use of language and the tone of the passage. Consider the mood of the people listening to Roosevelt at a time of great national uncertainty.

c   What might President Hoover say in response to FDR's comments in this fireside chat?

d   This is part of a radio broadcast. How would a President have 'talked' to the nation before the invention of radio?

THINKING SKILLS

Imagine you lived in the USA in the early 1930s. You have been suffering the effects of the Great Depression for more than two years, you are unemployed and struggling to provide for your family. Write a diary entry explaining your thoughts and feelings about the election of Roosevelt as president. Do you feel confident he will turn things around? If so, why? If not, why not?

'The Hundred Days'

Roosevelt persuaded Congress to give him emergency powers to tackle the most immediate problems in his first hundred days in office. The first task was to restore confidence in the banking system. Roosevelt closed the banks temporarily, and only allowed those banks that the government had certified as reliable and properly run to reopen. He encouraged people to start saving money in the banks once again. Next came the Glass-Steagal Act, which introduced government regulation of Wall Street and protected ordinary people from having their savings wiped out by the reckless investment decisions of the banks. Another decision was the ending of Prohibition. This stopped the gangs bootlegging and provided the government with a new source of tax revenue.

The alphabet agencies

Roosevelt set up several government bodies known by their initial letters, called the 'alphabet agencies'. Their aim was to promote economic recovery and provide assistance to the most vulnerable groups in US society. This dramatically extended the role of the federal government in people's lives. It brought relief to millions of people but provoked opposition from conservatives, who saw it as undue interference in the workings of the market and the lives of individuals. Another criticism was that the New Deal was not planned in detail, and some agencies overlapped with others in their activities.

The alphabet agencies were important in three main areas.

Area 1: Helping the poor and unemployed

- Civilian Conservation Corps (CCC): provided men aged 18–25 with work on conservation projects such as planting trees to prevent soil erosion. More than 2 million men had taken part in this work by the time the US entered the Second World War. It developed useful practical skills and gave participants a sense of purpose.

- Federal Emergency Relief Administration (FERA): provided assistance for the poor in the form of financial grants to state governments.
- Civil Works Administration (CWA): provided employment for 4 million people for a short-term period in 1933–34. Its job-creation schemes varied from road-building to sweeping leaves.
- Public Works Administration (PWA): sponsored building projects, such as the construction of dams and bridges.
- Home Owners' Loan Corporation (HOLC): supplied loans to people unable to pay their mortgages and in danger of losing their homes.

Area 2: Promoting industrial recovery

- National Recovery Administration (NRA): set up by the National Industrial Recovery Act (NIRA). It aimed to restart industrial production by setting fair prices for goods, while raising workers' wages and improving conditions in the workplace. Companies taking part signed codes of practice, and in return were issued with a 'Blue Eagle' logo to show that they were good employers. This encouraged Americans to buy from them. Over 5000 industries had decided to participate by September 1933 and the Blue Eagle became famous.

Area 3: Helping farmers

- Farm Credit Administration (FCA): provided low-interest loans to farmers.
- Agricultural Adjustment Act (AAA): rewarded farmers for cutting production levels. Many were angry to see animals slaughtered and crops ploughed back into the ground, but farm incomes doubled during 1933–39. It did not help farm labourers and share-croppers, as many of them had been replaced by machinery.
- Tennessee Valley Authority (TVA): covered an area of the South 80,000 square miles in size, including parts of seven states from Mississippi to Virginia. The region was prone to flooding and soil erosion, and there were high levels of poverty and unemployment. Tree planting helped to prevent soil from being washed away. The building of government-funded dams created jobs, controlled the flow of rivers and generated electricity, which helped to modernise the area's economy. This helped both agriculture and industry, and is generally regarded as one of the New Deal's outstanding successes.

FOCUS TASK 9.10

a Copy and complete the following table to record the changes that Roosevelt implemented on taking office and what impact they had.

Policy	Aim	Relief, reform, or recovery?	Impact: success / failure / mixed

b In pairs, use your completed tables to discuss this question: *How far did the First New Deal in 1933 achieve the aims of bringing about economic recovery and relieving poverty?* Reach a judgement, then join with another pair and compare your ideas.

Key points
The First New Deal, 1933

- FDR focused on select key areas for his 'first' New Deal: helping the poor and the unemployed, promoting industrial recovery and helping farmers.
- He did not promise complete success but stressed that he was experimenting to find out what worked for Americans.
- Alphabet Agencies were the means by which FDR delivered his New Deal.
- Some conservatives did not like the 'experiments' because they thought there was too much interference in the economy and in society, which they believed was not the government's role.

How far did the character of the New Deal change after 1933?

In 1935, the Supreme Court ruled that the NRA and the AAA were illegal because the federal government had no right to interfere in states's affairs. Roosevelt had to consider how to secure re-election in 1936, and he was under pressure from radical critics who wanted more done. The Second New Deal brought a change of emphasis, focusing on longer-term plans for social justice and welfare, and establishing workers' rights. There were several major initiatives in 1935.

Works Progress Administration (WPA)

The WPA was a new initiative to tackle unemployment through major building projects. Examples included the San Francisco Bay Bridge and New York's La Guardia airport. It also supported the work of artists and writers, helping to improve the quality of life in many communities as well as giving work to more than 8 million people. It avoided the shame attached to receiving financial handouts by putting people to work in return for money.

National Labour Relations Act (NLRA)

The NLRA upheld the right of workers to form and join trade unions, and to engage in **collective bargaining**. It also set up the National Labour Relations Board to protect workers who were victimised by employers.

> **KEY TERM**
>
> **collective bargaining:** negotiations between trade unions and employers on wages and conditions of work

Social Security Act (SSA)

The SSA signalled a big shift away from individuals making their own preparations for old age and other hazards of life. It created the first pensions for the elderly, together with benefits for orphans and victims of industrial accidents. It also set up a national system of insurance against unemployment. Although the payments were small, it marked a very important development in the relationship between government and citizens.

Resettlement Administration (RA) and Farm Security Administration (FSA)

The RA helped farm workers and share-croppers move to better land. In 1937 it was replaced by the FSA, which gave loans to help these people buy their own land. However, its effects on the position of the poorest people in rural areas were limited.

SOURCE 9J

Source 9J: A cartoon showing Roosevelt as a doctor, visiting 'Uncle Sam' (the symbol of the US), depicted as his patient, 6 May 1935

SOURCE ANALYSIS 9.10

Look at Source 9J.

a What message is the cartoonist sending about the way Roosevelt approached the USA's problems?

b Is the message positive or negative? Explain your choice by referring to the source.

Key points

The Second New Deal, 1935–36

- The Supreme Court struck down the AAA and NRA legislation because it interfered in state matters.
- Roosevelt focused his second new deal on workers's rights and longer-term plans for social justice: the NLRA.
- The SSA was a radical departure and established pension rights for all and insurance against unemployment.

Why did the New Deal encounter opposition?

Opposition from the right

The New Deal faced opposition from conservatives who felt that it undermined the idea of 'rugged individualism' and excessively extended the power of the federal government. Opponents included some in the Republican Party and many business leaders. More conservative members of the Democratic Party in the South also did not support the New Deal. These more traditional Americans believed in self-help, and many of them accused Roosevelt of promoting socialist or even communist ideas.

Although Roosevelt faced hostility from the political right, it was never sufficiently well-organised to be a serious challenge to his position as president. The Republicans were divided about the New Deal, and moderate members of the party did not oppose it completely. The party's candidate for the presidency in the 1936 election, Alf Landon, found it hard to develop a distinctive policy position in opposition to Roosevelt.

Opposition from rich Americans and business owners

To fund some of the changes in the first New Deal, President Roosevelt increased taxes on the rich. Given his wealthy family background, many people felt that he was betraying his own class and argued that the New Deal schemes were a waste of money. However, Roosevelt argued that a few were making sacrifices for the many.

Business leaders felt that Roosevelt's policies increased the power of trade unions and interfered with the right of business leaders to run their companies. The business community opposed other changes, too, claiming that policies and relief proposals went too far and cost too much. In the second New Deal, business owners were angered that workers' rights were expanded. Press owner William Randolph Hearst, referred to FDR as 'Stalin Delano Roosevelt'.

Opposition from the left

On the left were those radicals who felt that the New Deal had not done enough to cure unemployment and poverty. Three individuals wanted to go further than Roosevelt in redistributing wealth to the poor: Huey Long, Dr Francis Townsend and Father Charles Coughlin.

Long, Townsend and Coughlin appealed in different ways to different sections of the public, and they may have indirectly influenced Roosevelt to adopt more radical policies in the Second New Deal. However, like Roosevelt's right-wing critics, they were not able to unite to oppose him. The three men's supporters came together in 1936, to form the Union Party, but their candidate, William Lemke, won only 2% of the vote in the presidential election.

Roosevelt won another term in the White House in 1936, with over 27 million votes, because victims of the Depression were grateful for what he had done to help them or decided he should finish the work he had started. Roosevelt's victory was also due to the weaknesses of the Republican Party. For most voters, they offered little to tempt them away from FDR, even if his New Deal produced mixed results. It was an indication of the ineffectiveness of the Republicans that they lost three consecutive elections in 1932, 1936 and 1940. They could not find a candidate to match Roosevelt.

KEY FIGURE

Huey Long (1893–1935)

Huey Long served as senator for Louisiana. He was a Democrat who initially supported the New Deal but called for more radical action from 1934. His 'Share the Wealth' campaign called for higher taxation of the rich to fund welfare reforms. Long was a persuasive speaker and his movement was popular, attracting 8 million supporters. FDR's supporters feared him as a possible presidential candidate in the 1936 election, but he was assassinated in September 1935.

> **KEY FIGURES**
>
> ### Dr Francis Townsend (1867–1960)
>
> Dr Francis Townsend, pictured in about 1930, was a retired doctor who campaigned for government pensions of $200 a month for all citizens aged over 60. Recipients would be obliged to spend the money to stimulate the economy. The plan would have also freed up jobs for younger workers. Townsend secured 20 million signatures on a petition to Congress promoting his ideas.
>
> ### Father Charles Coughlin (1891–1979)
>
> Like Long, Father Charles Coughlin turned against the New Deal after initially supporting it. The 'radio priest' used his broadcasts to call for increased workers' rights and state control of industry. He was particularly popular in the industrial North and Mid-West, and had an audience of 30 million by 1936. He lost influence after he started expressing admiration of European fascism.

Opposition from the Supreme Court

Roosevelt faced difficulties with the Supreme Court because most of its members had been appointed by earlier Republican administrations. Supreme Court justices hold their position for life.

In two key legal cases, the Supreme Court ruled that Roosevelt had exceeded his presidential powers. One was the 1935 'Sick Chicken Case'. The Schechter poultry firm was prosecuted under the National Industrial Recovery Act (NIRA) for selling chickens that were dangerous for humans to eat. The company appealed to the Supreme Court, which decided that the NIRA was unconstitutional because the federal government did not have powers to regulate businesses. In the 1936 *US v Butler* case, the Supreme Court ruled against the Agricultural Adjustment Act. The Court said that it was the responsibility of individual state governments, not the Federal government, to support farmers.

Roosevelt was frustrated and declared in 1937 that he would impose a retirement age of 70 on Supreme Court justices. He wanted to appoint younger judges who would support his policies. This plan to 'pack' the Court appeared arrogant and unconstitutional. Roosevelt lost some public support and met opposition in Congress. A few thought he was becoming a dictator like Stalin, Hitler, or Mussolini.

Although Roosevelt did not get his way, some judges took voluntary retirement and their successors were more cautious in their attitude towards New Deal measures. They accepted both the National Labour Relations Act and the Social Security Act.

> **REVISION TIP**
>
> Historians are divided about the success of the New Deal. It is important that you consider some of the arguments that have been put forward on both sides. Then you should make your own assessment of what FDR achieved.

> CAMBRIDGE IGCSE™ AND O LEVEL HISTORY OPTION B: COURSEBOOK

SOURCE 9K

Do We Want A Ventriloquist Act In The Supreme Court?

"YES, YES, WE ALL VOTE YES!"

PACKED COURT

Source 9K: A cartoon from 14 February 1937, on the subject of Roosevelt's plan to pack the Supreme Court. The figure on the left is Uncle Sam, symbol of the USA

SOURCE ANALYSIS 9.11

Study Source 9K.

a What view of Roosevelt do you think the cartoonist taking?

b Do you agree with this view? Explain your answer.

Why did unemployment persist despite the New Deal?

Unemployment in the US persisted through the 1930s. At its peak in 1933 (12 million), it fell to 8 million and even increased in 1937–8 to reach 11 million. Why was this? Consumer demand remained below the levels reached in the twenties, and the construction industry was only a quarter of that in the boom years. Persistent unemployment affected workers in the 'old industries': cotton textiles, iron and steel, timber and wood, and construction. Even those who had jobs found it difficult to stay in work. FDR's relief programmes helped these Americans to survive but overall the New Deal did not succeed in providing enough jobs to stimulate a sturdy recovery and a significant decline in unemployment. In addition, the labour force grew by 16% during the 1930s and those 'new' workers alone would need a further 8 million jobs, so this made unemployment even worse than it was. FDR must take some blame, too. In 1937, he saw that there were signs of economic improvement so he halved all the WPA jobs – unemployment shot up. Finally, there was little dialogue between FDR's government and the business community to improve employment.

Did the fact that the New Deal did not solve unemployment mean that it was a failure?

The case for the New Deal

Some historians argue that the New Deal played a crucial role in lifting the USA out of the Depression. According to this argument, Roosevelt's actions in his first hundred days saved the banking system from collapse and he stopped the slide of businesses into bankruptcy.

The New Deal saved the most vulnerable members of society from starvation, homelessness, and gave jobs and hope to millions. It was much better than the limited approach of Hoover.

The greatest successes of the New Deal included the regeneration of the Tennessee Valley, the major building projects of the Public Works Administration and the employment created by the Works Progress Administration. The Second New Deal improved workers' rights and created a basic welfare state with the Social Security Act. Under FDR the better roads, bridges, water and sewage systems made a big difference to American lives.

Roosevelt saved the USA from turning fascist or communist. The USA entered the Second World War in good shape, with morale high.

The case against the New Deal

The New Deal's critics point out that although unemployment initially fell, it was not cured. In 1937, concerned about government debt, Roosevelt cut public spending and there followed another slowdown in economic activity. Unemployment, which had remained consistently high at 7.7 million, rose to almost 11 million in 1938. The government then resumed spending on public works schemes and unemployment began to fall back again.

According to this argument, it was preparation for the Second World War, not the New Deal, that was the most important cause of continued economic recovery.

The lives of certain groups improved only a little. Women benefited less than men since most of the jobs created by the New Deal were in traditionally male occupations, involving manual labour. Women continued to be paid less than men on average. Some states ignored their responsibility to provide welfare payments to women, by disqualifying those unmarried women with children, for example. Black Americans did not gain significantly from the New Deal. Roosevelt was too scared of a negative reaction from southern white people in his party to tackle the continuing segregation of black people.

Some critics argue that Roosevelt delayed economic recovery by over-regulating industry and allowing the growth of powerful trade unions. Free-market capitalism, left alone, would have ended the slump. Instead, Roosevelt was the creator of a too-powerful government, which discouraged people from relying on their own efforts and initiative.

	1928	1933	1939
Gross National Product ($ billion)	100	55	85
Value of consumer goods purchased ($ billion)	80	45	65
Unemployment (millions)	2.0	12.8	9.4

Figure 9.17: A table containing some indicators of US economic performance, 1928–39

FOCUS TASK 9.11

In pairs, look at the table in Figure 9.17 and the evidence in this section. Discuss the following question: *Overall, do you consider the New Deal to have been at best only a partial success?* After your pair discussion, share your ideas as a whole class.

> CAMBRIDGE IGCSE™ AND O LEVEL HISTORY OPTION B: COURSEBOOK

THINK LIKE A HISTORIAN

Work and careers change over time. Make a list of the technologies that helped Americans to do their work in the 1920s. Then make a list of technologies that help people to do their work today. Compare the two.

What jobs did Americans do in the 1920s? One hundred years later, which of the jobs still exist and which have disappeared. Write down three reasons why jobs are still the same and three reasons why jobs have gone.

SUMMARY

- The USA experienced an economic boom in the 1920s, but not all industries, and not all American people, gained from it. Agriculture was stuck in depression throughout the 1920s and much of the 1930s.
- Between 1919 and 1941, the USA was a divided society, with extremes of wealth and conflicts over race, culture and politics.
- Social changes in this period lasted, film making in Hollywood, sports like baseball, jazz and votes for women in federal elections.
- Intolerance was widespread in the USA, particularly affecting black Americans, who were targeted by groups such as the Ku Klux Klan.
- The weak foundations of the economic boom were exposed by the Wall Street Crash of 1929 and the following Depression.
- Roosevelt's New Deal tackled some of the economic and social problems without solving unemployment and bringing about complete recovery from the Depression.

KEY SKILLS EXERCISES

Knowledge and understanding
1. Explain the link between demand and supply.
2. What causes prices to go up and what causes them to fall?
3. How did mass production help the economic boom of the 1920s?

Application
4. Why was advertising such an important part of the boom?
5. Why did the Republican governments of the 1920s not intervene in the US economy?
6. Was it just chance that so many new inventions arrived in shops within a few years of each other?
7. Why was it that car making stimulated other parts of the economy?

Analysis
8. Analyse **three** reasons for the strength of the booming economy in the 1920s.
9. Analyse why some successes in the 1920s continued beyond the decade.
10. Analyse the role of the banks in the 1920s. How much of the boom was their lending power?
11. Analyse the key differences between those industries that prospered in the boom and those that did not.

Evaluation
12. Evaluate the importance of 'rugged individualism' in making the boom so successful.
13. Would the Great Depression have happened without the Wall Street Crash?
14. Did the New Deal save capitalism in the US?
15. Why did the 1930s in the USA not see more radical ideas take root and flourish?

394

Chapter 9: The United States, 1919–41

1 This answer begins very well. Without separately defining HP, the writer uses a clear example to illustrate what HP meant to ordinary Americans.

2 The answer ties HP agreements to the increase in real wages to show the connections between different features of the boom. It keeps a sharp focus on the question.

3 The response provides plenty of examples of the link between spending power, HP and increased wages. It could be improved further if it identified which groups of Americans would benefit most from HP.

4 This second paragraph still retains the focus on HP and the boom, but links it to the advertising industry. Perhaps the writer could discuss why women were targeted in taking out HP agreements for domestic consumer items.

5 The focus of the response is widened to include American consumerism as a new feature of American culture, including shopping in department stores and buying stocks and shares at a discount. The comment at the very end needs a little more development to ensure it is connected to the idea of HP.

IMPROVE THIS ANSWER

Why was the use of hire purchase agreements important for the growth of the American economy in the 1920s?

Sample answer: Hire purchase agreements (HP) were an important factor in stimulating the 1920s boom because it enabled ordinary Americans to buy consumer items like cars and spread the cost over time. Otherwise, buying a Model T Ford would be too expensive to buy all at once for many Americans; it cost about $260. The increase in demand that HP agreements stimulated was a crucial part of the boom years. **1** Although average real wages increased by 25% during the 1920s, the addition of HP agreements meant that spending power of the American consumer was even stronger. **2** And it wasn't just the car industry that benefitted. Other expensive items could also be bought using HP: fridges, washing machines and hoovers. **3**

HP agreements widened the ownership of the new consumer items that were available to most Americans during the 1920s. Advertising and HP worked together to stimulate demand. **4** Adverts for HP were placed in cinemas, in catalogues, in magazines and on the radio. Even if you had never thought about it, HP agreements were part of the new mainstream culture of consumerism. In many ways, advertising and HP bound American society together so that people felt they belonged; they were part of something and lived in the richest country in the world. While real wages were increasing, HP agreements enabled ordinary Americans to buy several things at the same time and not wait until they could afford the full price of them all. It is no surprise that the number of department stores rocketed, showing off what was available and what could be bought on credit. If you had money to spare after buying your Ford, you could always invest in Wall Street stocks and shares by buying 'on the margin'. **5**

Now write an improved response using this guidance.

PRACTICE QUESTIONS

1   The Wall Street Crash of 1929 was followed by a prolonged economic depression in the USA.
    a   What happened in the Wall Street Crash? [4]
    b   Why was the Great Depression in the USA so severe? [6]
    c   'The main reason why Franklin Roosevelt won the 1932 presidential election was that President Hoover's policies had failed to end the Depression.' How far do you agree with this statement? Explain your answer. [10]
    [Total: 20]

2   a   Write an account of the economic changes for industrial workers in the 1920s. [15]
    b   Discuss the impact of film and media on US society. [25]
    [Total: 40]

PROJECT

You are going to work in pairs to create posters that summarise events of the 1920s and 1930s in the USA.

Get two large pieces of paper. Title them '1920s: Boom' and '1930s: Bust'.

Using the information in this chapter and any other resources you have available, create two posters summarising the events of each decade. Use speech bubbles, images, words and statistics to encapsulate the events in an imaginative way.

As a class, create an exhibition of all your posters. Put sticky notes next to each poster. As you walk around viewing the posters, write comments on the sticky notes, and place them on the posters to comment on what they have done well and how they could be improved. Be polite and constructive.

SELF-EVALUATION CHECKLIST

After studying this chapter, complete this table:

You should be able to:	Needs more work	Almost there	Ready to move on
explain why the 1920s saw an economic boom in the USA and how far the benefits of this prosperity were felt across society			
describe how US society changed in the 1920s			
describe how intolerance manifested itself in US society in the 1920s, including against immigrants and black people			
explain the causes of the Wall Street Crash, and the impact of the crash on the US economy and society from 1929			
describe Hoover's and Roosevelt's responses to the Great Depression			
explain the policies involved in the First and Second New Deals			
evaluate how far Roosevelt was successful in dealing with the problems of the US economy.			

Preparing for assessment

FOCUS POINTS

In this chapter you will learn how to:
- differentiate between the assessment papers
- identify and prepare for different question types
- understand the different key skills you will need to demonstrate.

The information in this section is based on the Cambridge International syllabus. You should always refer to the appropriate syllabus document for the year of examination to confirm the details and for more information. The syllabusdocument is available on the Cambridge International website at www.cambridgeinternational.org.

12.1 Developing and practising key skills

There are three sets of key skills that you will need to develop and then demonstrate to show your understanding of what you have learnt. In the syllabus, these skills are called 'assessment objectives' (AOs):

AO1: An ability to recall, select, organise and deploy knowledge of the syllabus content.

AO2: An ability to construct historical explanations using an understanding of:
- cause and consequence, change and continuity, similarity and difference
- the motives, emotions, intentions and beliefs of people in the past.

AO3: An ability to understand, interpret, evaluate and use a range of sources as evidence, in their historical context.

This chapter will show you how you can demonstrate these skills.

12.2 The structure of the assessment

For Cambridge O Level History, you will have to complete two assessment components, the Structured question paper and the Document question paper. Paper 1, the Structured question paper will test both the Core Content and the Depth Studies. Paper 2, the Document question paper will test only the Core Content.

For Cambridge IGCSE History, you will have to complete three out of the four assessment components. The Structured question paper and the Document question paper are compulsory. For the third part, your school will opt to do either the coursework (Component 3) or the Alternative to coursework paper.

The following table shows the content of the three papers and the coursework.

Assessment	Core Content	Depth Study
Paper 1: structured questions	Yes	Yes
Paper 2: document questions	Yes	No
Component 3: coursework (Cambridge IGCSE only)	No	Yes
Paper 4: alternative to coursework (Cambridge IGCSE only)	No	Yes

Structured question paper

In this paper, you will need to answer three structured questions, each of which has three parts. Two of these questions will be on Core content and one question will be on the Depth study you have learnt about.

> **REVISION TIP**
>
> Always make sure you check the time allocated and work out how long to spend on each question. Remember that as well as writing the answer, you will also need to factor in time to read the questions carefully, choose those you will answer and plan your answers. It is a good idea to practise these skills using past papers which will help you to feel more prepared for your assessment.

Document question paper

This paper gives you the opportunity to demonstrate your skills in analysing and using sources. This makes it different from the other papers for two reasons.

- You are given sources and questions that test your ability to analyse texts and pictures, as well as applying your own knowledge.
- The number of sources and the marks for each part of the question may vary. You will need to think carefully about how long to spend analysing the sources and how much time you need to write an answer to each part of the question.

Coursework

If your school is following this option, you will produce one piece of extended writing based on a Depth study. Coursework is marked by your teacher and externally moderated. The coursework assignment can be based on one of the depth studies in the syllabus or on a Depth study devised by your own teachers.

Your completed coursework assignment can be up to a maximum of 2000 words long and it should focus on assessing the significance of one aspect of your chosen depth study. For example:

- Assess the significance of the use of terror in Nazi Germany.
- Assess the significance of Trotsky for the Bolsheviks in the period 1917 to 1924.

Your teacher can give general guidance, but coursework must be your own learning, and you must acknowledge the source of any materials you quote.

Coursework will provide an opportunity for you to demonstrate key skills: the ability to recall, select, organise and deploy factual knowledge; and the ability to construct a supported explanation. It is important to ensure that everything you write is clearly focused on the question. Make sure you know the topic well, so that you support your argument and conclusion with accurate, relevant evidence.

Alternative to coursework paper

It consists of structured essay questions on the depth studies. Each depth study from the syllabus will have a choice of two questions, and you should choose **one** of them to answer.

12.3 Short answer and extended response questions

In the Structured question paper, all questions are essay-style and divided into three parts: **a**, **b** and **c**.

Look at this sample answer (written by the author) to a sample Structured question.

In the 1920s, the USA experienced an economic boom.

a **Describe the main economic policies of the Republican governments in the 1920s.**

b **Why was Henry Ford successful as a businessman?**

c **'Almost all Americans enjoyed a rising standard of living in the 1920s.' How far do you agree with this statement? Explain your answer.**

a *The Republican governments believed in laissez-faire, which meant leaving businesses alone to make profits. They helped firms by cutting taxes, which meant that people had more money to spend on the goods that they made. Businesses also had less money taken away from them in taxes.*

A second policy was the use of tariffs (taxes on imported goods), which made American goods cheaper to buy than foreign products. This protected American industries and helped them to grow. An example was the 1922 Fordney-McCumber tariff.

Comment: This is a good answer. It makes two major points and develops them, without becoming too long.

b *Henry Ford made a fortune out of car manufacturing. The most important reason why he was successful was his introduction of the assembly line method, which made mass production possible. This involved the body of the car being passed on a conveyor belt to different workers, who each carried out a particular task such as fixing the doors or wheels on. The importance of this was that it sped up the work and therefore cut the costs of production. Another reason for Ford's success was the standardisation of parts. His factories made cars to a standard specification. For example, he famously said that his customers could have any colour car they liked as long as it was black. Again, this kept the costs down. Ford believed that it was better to sell a large number of cars cheaply than a smaller number of more expensive cars. His best known car, the Model T Ford, became affordable to ordinary Americans as its price fell from almost $1000 to under $300 between 1908 and 1927.*

Comment: This answer identifies two reasons for Ford's success – assembly line production and standardisation – and explains why they were important. Ford's beliefs about what made for successful business practice are noted. There is an appropriate level of detail.

c *The USA was a very unequal society, in which opportunities to make money varied greatly across the country. The people who benefited most were those who owned or worked in newer industries such as car manufacture, electricity generation, or the new department stores which sold all kinds of consumer goods. The successful industries were linked together. For example, as businesses expanded, they needed larger office premises. This meant that there were many job opportunities for those who worked in the construction industry, building the new skyscrapers in the business districts of New York. These workers, and those employed in factories which were making consumer goods which people wanted to*

Preparing for assessment

buy, found that their wages increased and so they in turn could buy goods and perhaps shares on the stock exchange.

On the other hand, people who worked in older industries such as coal and textiles, which were facing competition and declining demand in the 1920s, found that their standard of living dropped. Their wages were cut as their employers made losses, and some lost their jobs. New immigrants, who usually had to take the poorest paid jobs, were affected particularly badly. Small farmers and farm workers also suffered, as agriculture was experiencing a slump long before the Wall Street Crash of 1929. Banks took over the farms of those who could not pay their mortgages, forcing them to look for work elsewhere. The most vulnerable were the share-croppers in the South, many of whom were black. They rented land and paid their landlords a proportion of what they produced, so when prices of farm produce fell they were unable to pay.

On balance it is not true to argue that almost all Americans were better off in the 1920s. Nearly half the population lived in the countryside, where the conditions were worst. For example, 90% of farms were still not connected to the electricity grid in 1930. However, until the Great Depression and the Wall Street Crash, which wiped out fortunes on a devastating scale, life was good for many millions of people.

Comment: This is a good answer because it gives equal weight to both sides of the argument and provides a developed, fully supported explanation. The closing paragraph reaches a conclusion, explaining how far the learner agrees with the statement in the question.

12.4 Source-based questions

The Document question paper requires you to answer **one** question on **one** prescribed topic from the Core content. The question has **five parts**, a–e, and you should answer all parts. These questions require you to analyse and use sources that are provided.

Reading and preparing the sources

Under pressure of time, it can be difficult to spot everything you need to in the sources. This is why you should try to read them twice, as the second time you will notice things that you did not see straight away. You can use highlighters to annotate the question paper, to highlight the key parts of a source if that helps you pick out the relevant details. However, you cannot use highlighters on your answer script.

It may also help to label each source with the question number it relates to. This will help you to think about the exact skills you need to respond to the source. For example, if a question asks what the message of Source C is, write 'message' next to the source. This will also stop you writing about the wrong source in relation to a question.

> **REVISION TIP**
>
> Keep in mind three letters: **ATQ**. **A**nswer **T**he **Q**uestion! You should never just describe the sources or write vague answers. You must provide an answer to exactly what you have been asked. If the question is about the message of the source, say 'the *message* of the source is . . .'. If the question asks *why* the source was published, say 'this source was published because . . .'.

Reading and answering the questions

Double-check that you are writing about the correct source (or sources) before beginning each question. Also, make sure that you pay close attention to the key words in the question so that you answer appropriately.

For example, is the question asking you to answer based solely on the source provided or are you being asked to apply your knowledge to this as well?

Different styles of questions

When studying sources, you will come across a variety of questions. For example:

- What is the message of a source?
- How far does one source support another source?
- Does one source prove that another source is lying?
- Why was this source produced when it was?
- How far do all the sources support a particular argument?
- We can group these questions into the following types.

Interpretation

This means understanding what the source is saying. Interpretation questions might ask you about the *message* of the source. For instance: *What is the author, artist, or photographer trying to say?*

It may help to think about *who* created the source and *when*. Then think about who the source is aimed at – its target *audience*. Asking yourself these questions can help you to clearly interpret a source.

Purpose

Some questions ask *why* a source was produced. Sources do not just appear by themselves – someone has to make, draw, or write them. Therefore, think about who made the source and why. Use any details you are given about the source, such as the author, date and perhaps events that have just taken place. These are all important to evaluate and consider in your answer. You should arrive at a conclusion about what the author intended when they created the source. What was their purpose? What were they trying to achieve?

Comparison

Questions that focus on two sources are often comparison questions. This means you need to pick out similarities and differences. When responding to a comparison question, you may find it helpful to write two paragraphs, one that looks at the ways in which the sources agree and one that looks at the ways in which they disagree. Then just answer the question to finish off.

Pay close attention to the wording of a question, for example: *How far do these sources disagree?* This sounds as if you only have to show how the sources disagree, but the wording at the start is *How far . . .* This means you need to consider their similarity too. The same applies if the question asks about how far they agree – think about the

> **REVISION TIP**
>
> Do not just write a source is biased. All sources are biased in one way or another. There are no 'neutral' sources. However, just because a source is biased does not mean that historians cannot use it. Instead, you could consider a source's strengths and weaknesses and study the source in the context in which it was made, along with *other* sources about the same event, person, or question.

ways they agree and disagree to reach your answer. You might find it helpful to respond with a phrase like 'to a large extent, the sources . . .' or 'to a small extent, the sources . . .'. Starting your answer in this way can help you to keep your response focused on exactly what is being asked.

Evaluation

Some questions will require you demonstrate your evaluation skills. Evaluation questions might ask:

- How useful is the source?
- How reliable is the source?

Remember that *all* sources are useful for some enquiry or question, it is just a matter of what they can be used for. At the same time, no sources are flawless. Carefully consider the question and first ask yourself what *aspects* of the source help you to answer it. Then think about limitations of the source. What is not ideal about the source? What other sources would you want so you can better understand the issue identified in the question?

If a question asks about reliability, evaluate the source based on its merits. In what ways might the author be credible? Is there any reason to doubt the accuracy of what they present in the source? A different way of thinking about reliability is to ask, *How trustworthy is the source*, or *How far can the source be trusted?* Your own historical knowledge alongside other sources will help you to respond to these questions.

Testing a hypothesis

Questions that ask you to judge how far sources support a particular argument are likely to require a fuller response. Remember to use all the sources to evaluate a particular argument. You might want to prepare your answer by creating a simple table with two columns: 'Agree with **hypothesis**' and 'Disagree with hypothesis'.

Go through all the sources and decide, based on the issue in the question, if they agree or disagree. You might end up with something like this:

> **KEY TERM**
>
> **hypothesis:** a statement or argument about an event or person in the past

Agree	Disagree
B	A
D	C
E	F
G	H
I	

Once you have identified which sources support and which sources challenge the hypothesis, you can start writing. Make sure that you explain how each source either supports or challenges the hypothesis. Make this absolutely clear: for example, you could start sentences with 'Source 12A supports the statement *because* . . .'. This will help to keep you focused on answering the question rather than simply describing the source.

Make sure that you address each source separately and that you *explain* how each source supports or disagrees with the hypothesis.

CAMBRIDGE IGCSE™ AND O LEVEL HISTORY OPTION B: COURSEBOOK

Types of sources

There are two basic types of sources: textual and visual.

Text sources

These are written sources, such as part of a modern history book, a diary, a speech, a letter, or an official document. Each type of source is slightly different, so think about why this might be. One obvious reason is that they are written for a different audience, so their purpose will be different. A diary is for personal reflection, a letter is to another person, an official document might just be for others in the government, and a speech is for a very wide audience. Think about the intended audience when preparing your responses.

Visual sources

Visual sources might take the form of political cartoons, photographs and posters. Cartoonists use a variety of techniques: symbolism, stereotypes, humour and signposting. Signposting means inserting text to help the reader understand the meaning. Always pay attention to the text in a cartoon – it is there for a reason. Learners often find photographs very hard, especially as they believe that the camera does not lie. Think about this: the photographer has chosen to take a picture at a specific moment, looking at a particular thing. These are both decisions that might be because they want to convey a message. This means that when you consider photographs as evidence, you also need to consider their strengths and weaknesses, and sometimes they can be misleading. The camera may not lie, but the photographer can mislead.

Answer the source analysis questions below, then look at the guidance to see if you are on the right track.

SOURCES 12A & 12B

Source 12A: The England football team giving the Hitler salute before a match in Berlin in 1938

Source 12B: A *Washington Post* cartoon from 1965 about increasing US involve-ment in Vietnam. The title is 'the ascent into the unknown'.

404

Preparing for assessment

> ### SOURCE 12C
>
> *From Stettin in the Baltic to Trieste in the Adriatic, an iron curtain has descended across the Continent. Behind that line lie all the capitals of the ancient states of Central and Eastern Europe. Warsaw, Berlin, Prague, Vienna, Budapest, Belgrade, Bucharest and Sofia, all these famous cities and the populations around them lie in what I must call the Soviet sphere, and all are subject in one form or another, not only to Soviet influence but to a very high and, in many cases, increasing measure of control from Moscow.*
>
> **Source 12C:** An extract from a speech by Winston Churchill, 5 March 1946, in Fulton, Missouri, USA. President Truman was in the audience when the speech was given.

SOURCE ANALYSIS 12.1

Look at Sources 12A, 12B and 12C.

a Are you surprised by Source 12A? Explain your answer.

b What is the message of the cartoon in Source 12B?

c Why was the speech in Source 12C given in 1946?

Guidance

Source 12A

With 'surprise' questions, think about what is unusual about the source and then try to find an explanation. In this case it's quite easy: we would not expect the English football team to be giving a Hitler salute. This seems the complete opposite to what British people believed, and, of course, Hitler was the enemy in the Second World War. This makes it very 'surprising'. However, if we know the context then we can explain why this is not too surprising. First, it is in Berlin, the capital of Germany, so the team would be under pressure to show respect for their hosts. Second, it was in May 1938 before the war began and the British government was still pursuing a policy of appeasement. If the official government policy was to work with Hitler to achieve peace then we can understand why the English football team made this salute. If they had not saluted it might have damaged Anglo-German relations, which the British prime minister, Neville Chamberlain, very much wanted to avoid.

Source 12B

This cartoon is full of symbolism. The soldier represents all American servicemen, and the 'ascent into the unknown' means he has no idea what lies ahead. This is made all the more difficult by the smoke up the staircase (representing Vietnam), which makes it hard to see where the danger lies. The cartoon was drawn by an American cartoonist in 1965 just a year after President Johnson got Congress to agree to send ground troops into Vietnam after the Gulf of Tonkin incident. Clearly, the cartoonist feels this is unwise and will possibly lead to disaster.

Source 12C

This speech was given in the US in 1946 by Winston Churchill. Remember, Churchill was not prime minister at this time as he lost the election of 1945. The speech tells us about his fear of the 'increasing measure of control from Moscow' in Eastern Europe.

> **REVISION TIP**
>
> You can quote from the sources, but make your quotations short (1–6 words). Avoid copying out whole chunks of the source. Focus on strong language and key evidence. Look at the way quotations are used in the guidance on Source 12C and follow this style.

He calls this the 'iron curtain'. His audience is American and includes President Truman, so he is trying to influence American policy in the hope that the President might act against Stalin, the leader of the Soviet Union. By this point, Stalin had control of most of Eastern Europe and even the countries outside the 'Soviet sphere' such as Czechoslovakia were under threat. Therefore, this speech was made because relations had broken down since Yalta and Potsdam and Churchill wanted the US to make a stand against the USSR to prevent the permanent loss of 'the capitals of the ancient states' to the outside world.

12.5 Structured essay questions

In the Alternative to Coursework paper, you will be asked structured essay questions about the depth studies. These essay questions have two parts: **a** and **b**. Typically, in part **a**, you will be asked to write an account of something, and in part **b**, you will be asked to discuss the impact, importance, or contribution of something. The focus of part **b** will be an event, a person, or a change within a depth study topic.

For part **a**, make sure you have a plan for your account that addresses the question in a logical and coherent way. Focus on the *main* events or developments. Use your knowledge carefully. Remember: answer the question.

You should spend more time on part **b** as more marks are available for this part. The command word 'discuss' means that should write about the factor that appears in the question and assess it in relation to other factors that are *not* mentioned. One way to plan your answer for part **b** might be to:

- explain the stated factor and relate it to the question focus (two paragraphs)

- explain other factors that are not in the question but are relevant to it: include a judgement about their relative importance / significance to the factor stated in the question

- conclude with a clear judgement that directly addresses the question by pulling together in one paragraph all the factors you have discussed.

> **TIP**
>
> Before starting to write your part **b** answer, always make a brief plan. Your answer needs to demonstrate your ability to select relevant evidence, and to produce a coherent argument, not just to recall facts.

Look at the sample question part b on Depth study D: The First World War, 1914–18 and the sample answer (written by the author).

b **Discuss the importance of the USA's entry into the First World War in bringing about the defeat of Germany.**

b The United States made an important contribution to Allied victory in the First World War for several reasons. After joining the war in April 1917, it was able to provide Britain and France with additional manpower and economic resources. It entered the war when the Allies were facing major challenges and morale was low. US involvement provided psychological as well as material support.

The most obvious contribution made by US was the arrival of large numbers of new, fresh troops. The US rapidly expanded its army until, by the end of the war, it had over 2 million troops in France. The US entered the war at a critical time for the Allies, when there was good reason to believe that Germany had a chance of winning. Thousands of tons of merchant shipping had been sunk by German U-boats in the Atlantic. Russia dropped out of the war after the Bolshevik Revolution and in March 1918 signed the Treaty of Brest-Litovsk with Germany. This freed up tens of thousands of German troops, who were transferred to take part in the Ludendorff offensive on the Western Front, where they met with strong initial success. The arrival of large numbers of American troops therefore came just at the right moment, when Britain and France were badly in need of reinforcements.

The US forces, under General John Pershing, made a crucial contribution to victory in the 'Hundred Days' campaign in the summer and autumn of 1918. In September, they made a decisive assault in the Meuse-Argonne region, cutting off important German supply routes. One of the reasons why the German leaders asked for peace talks was that they knew that increasing numbers of Americans would continue to arrive, making it pointless to continue fighting.

The US also had huge industrial strength which could be brought to bear. It produced three times as much steel as Germany and Austria-Hungary combined. The US had a population of 90 million and large amounts of natural resources, making it a formidable opponent in a war which had become a slogging match between rival economies. It had provided Britain and France with loans before April 1917 and this aid was continued.

However, the US contribution should not be exaggerated. The US was slow to mobilise its manpower and its great numbers did not begin to make a decisive difference until the summer of 1918. Full US involvement was hindered by disputes between Pershing and his French and British counterparts. He insisted on the Americans fighting as an 'associated power', largely independent of the allied armies.

Other factors were important in bringing about allied victory. The British and French had significantly improved their fighting methods by 1918. They no longer launched costly frontal attacks, after prolonged artillery bombardments which failed to disrupt the enemy defences. They had learnt more flexible tactics and become more accurate in directing artillery fire, using the 'creeping barrage' to cover infantry assaults. US troops were not battle-hardened as the British and French were, and they had to learn on the job. They also used large amounts of allied equipment, including French tanks and artillery.

It is also important to note that Germany was more exhausted than Britain and France by mid-1918. It was struggling to replace lost manpower and was not in a position to stage another large-scale assault after the Ludendorff offensive fizzled out. The British naval blockade was starving Germany of food and vital raw materials, imposing an unbearable strain on its economy.

Overall, the US made a vital contribution to the outcome of the war. Although Britain and France successfully repelled the Ludendorff offensive, there is a question mark as to whether, on their own, they could have launched a new campaign to dislodge the Germans from the ground they already held. The arrival of US forces was certainly not the only reason for the victory but it was one of the most important, because it provided the Allies with vital support and boosted their morale at a critical stage.

Guidance: A good answer should demonstrate the range of skills you have developed:

- accurate, relevant knowledge used to support the answer and the conclusion
- a good understanding of the stated factor in the question and other key factors that are relevant to the question
- a well-argued and supported conclusion
- writing that is precise and to the point, as part of an answer which is well structured, balanced and focused.

Comment: This is an excellent answer. There is a clear structure, with an introduction which immediately gets straight to the argument and the stated factor, showing that the learner has a clear focus. The stated factor (the contribution of the United States) is fully discussed along with range of other relevant factors. This answer includes accurate contextual knowledge that is used to support the argument. Finally, there is a well-reasoned conclusion which draws the arguments together in a satisfying way.

Glossary

*Asterisked glossaries entries can be found in the two chapters which are available as part of your digital resource on Cambridge GO.

abdicate: to give up the throne or the responsibility of leading a country

agency: an organisation that acts on behalf of other organisations. In the League of Nations, different agencies focused on specific issues under the authority of the Council

Agent Orange: a chemical weapon used by the Americans to destroy crops and forests to make it harder for the Viet Cong to feed themselves, and to hide. However, it also had horrific side effects on people's physical health

air raid: an attack by enemy aircraft, usually dropping bombs*

alliance: a group of two or more countries that agree to support each other if they are attacked by another country

Allied Powers: the name given to the alliance of France, Britain and Russia at the start of the First World War. Japan (1914), Italy (1915), and the USA (1917) later joined the Allied Powers

amnesty: an official pardon for crimes committed

anarchist: someone who believes in getting rid of government

annexation: possession of a country or region, usually by force or without permission

anti-Semitism: hostility towards or prejudice against Jewish people

appeasement: agreeing to some or all of the opposing side's demands in order to prevent further disagreement

arbitration: a method of resolving a dispute peacefully using an independent, neutral authority that listens to evidence like a judge and then issues a ruling

aristocracy: a class of people who hold high social rank

armaments: military equipment and weapons

armistice: a formal agreement between countries at war to stop fighting for a period of time to allow peace talks to take place

Article 48: the clause in the constitution that allowed the government to rule using emergency powers in a crisis

artillery: large guns that fire shells great distances that, upon landing, explode causing death and destruction

Aryan: belonging to a group of white people with pale hair and blue eyes, believed by the Nazis to be better than other groups

autarky: when a state can provide entirely for itself without needing to trade with anyone else (economic independence)

autocracy: a system of government in which one leader, often a monarch, has absolute power

autocrat: a ruler who rules alone, has supreme authority and demands complete obedience from their subjects

autonomy: the right of a country or region to be independent and to govern itself

barricade: a line or pile of objects often put together quickly to form a barrier to stop people getting past*

bayonet: a long, sharp blade fixed to a rifle*

beachhead: an area of beach defended but then taken by the invader and made secure so it can be used to launch further attacks inland

bilateral: involving two countries or sides*

biplanes: a type of aircraft with two sets of wings, one above the other*

Blitz: the night time bombing of London and other cities in Britain by the Luftwaffe*

blockade: a form of economic warfare where one country attempts to prevent goods being imported to its rival. The Royal Navy's blockade in the First World War also ensured that German ships could not get out of port

Bolshevik: another word for communist – someone who believes in creating a classless society where everyone is equal

boycott: to refuse to take part in something as a way of expressing disapproval

budget deficit: when a country's expenditure is more than its income; the deficit is the difference between the two amounts

buffer zone: a neutral area that separates two other areas that might come into conflict

409

bureaucracy: a system for managing a country or organisation operated by a large number of officials who follow the rules very carefully

bushel: a dry measure of 8 gallons, which is about 36 litres

cabinet: a small group of the most important people in a government, who advise the leader

capitalism: an economic and social system in which property is privately owned, the role of the state is small and people enjoy freedom of expression and religion, and have a choice of political parties to elect as the government

cavalry: soldiers who fought mounted on horses*

ceasefire: an agreement between two armies to stop fighting in order to allow discussions to take place

Central Powers: the name given to the German and Austro-Hungarian empires at the beginning of the First World War. The Ottoman Empire joined the Central Powers later in 1914 and the Kingdom of Bulgaria joined in 1915

CIA: Central Intelligence Agency, founded in 1947 by the National Security Act with the aim of collecting, evaluating and sharing intelligence about national security

civil war: a war in one country between two or more sides from within that country

coalition: a government made up of two or more different parties, often established when no single party wins a majority of votes

collective bargaining: negotiations between trade unions and employers on wages and conditions of work

collectivisation: organising all of a country's production and industry so that it is owned and managed by the government

colony: a country or region under the political rule of a more powerful country that is often far away

Comintern: a Soviet-led organisation designed to promote communist ideology in countries outside the Soviet Union

commission: a committee made up of officials who investigate an issue or dispute and then produce a report that reaches conclusions and makes recommendations

commune: a community of people who live together and share property, resources and labour

communism: an economic and social system in which property and economic activity are controlled by the state. In communist countries, religion is banned and the media is censored, and everyone works for the state

communist state: in theory, a society that is based on the principles of equality and common ownership of property

concentration camp: a prison for political opponents, designed to 'purify' them through hard labour. In the Second World War, Jewish, Roma and Sinti people were also sent to these camps

concession: something that is allowed or given up, often in order to end a disagreement

concordat: an agreement between the Catholic Church and a government

Conference of Ambassadors: a diplomatic organisation established at the Paris Peace Conference, and based in Paris, to supervise the completion of issues that were resolved by the peace treaties

conscientious objector: someone who refuses to serve in the armed forces for moral or religious reasons

conscription: the act of forcing people by law to join the armed forces

constitution: the main set of laws by which a country is governed; the constitution sets out the powers of the government and the rights and freedom of the individual

containment: the name given to the USA's policy aimed at preventing the spread of communism after the Second World War. The word was first used in a 1947 article by US diplomat George Kennan, and soon after it was adopted by President Harry Truman

convention: an informal agreement between leaders and politicians on a matter than involves them all

convoy: a group of ships that travel together for protection*

corps: the main subdivision of an army*

counterattack: an attack designed to stop an attack by an enemy

coup: an attempt to seize political power by force rather than through democratic means

court martial: a trial in a military court for members of the armed forces*

covenant: a formal and binding set of rules for an organisation

credit: the ability to buy goods but to defer payment until an agreed date in the future

creeping barrage: a line of artillery fire advancing ahead of attacking infantry, usually at a rate of 50 metres per minute*

Glossary

decree: an official statement that something must happen

defect: to leave a country, region or political party, often to join an opposing one

delegation: a group of people who officially represent a country or organisation at meetings or conferences

demilitarised: describing an area of land in which no soldiers and no weapons are permitted

democracy: a country in which people vote freely for the political party they want to govern them

Democrat and Republican: members of the two main opposing political parties in the USA

desertion: leaving the armed forces without permission

deterrent: an action that puts off (deters) a country from being aggressive towards others

dictatorship: a system of government in which one person controls a country without holding elections and without being restrained by a parliament, maintaining power using the army and police

diktat: a treaty or other agreement that has not been negotiated with a defeated country but imposed without any discussion with it

diplomacy: the management of relationships between countries

diplomat: an official whose job is to represent one country in another, and who usually works in an embassy

disarmament: the process of destroying some or all weapons and armed forces that could be used in fighting a war

dissenter: someone who strongly and publicly disagrees with something, especially a political position

Dollar Imperialism: American actions designed to build influence and economic power using their resources and their influence to extend markets for selling American goods and products

Domestic policy: matters that relate to the home country

Domino Theory: the theory that if one country fell to communism, so would its neighbours, and their neighbours in turn, like a row of dominoes

duma: the Russian name for a parliament

dynasty: a series of rulers who are all from the same family

Einsatzgruppen: mobile killing units that murdered Jews and other Soviet citizens during the German invasion of the USSR*

embargo: a partial or complete end to trade with a country (an example of a trade sanction)*

embargo: a government ban on the trade of certain key exports to another country

empire: an area of territory usually comprising more than one country, ruled by a single monarch or government

epidemic: an infectious disease that has spread over a wide area, affecting thousands of people

espionage: the government practice of using spies to obtain intelligence on political and military developments in foreign countries

eugenics: the theory that it is possible to improve humans by only allowing particular people to produce children

euthanasia: allowing someone to die, or assisting their death, in order to end their suffering. The Nazis applied this to people with disabilities

evict: to force someone to leave a place, usually because they have not paid the rent they owe for land or property

Ex-Comm: the Executive Committee of the National Security Council (NSC) – this included members of the NSC, but Kennedy also invited significant non-military figures: his brother Robert Kennedy (the Attorney-General); Theodore Sorensen (White House Counsel); Truman's Secretary of State Dean Acheson; and former ambassador to the USSR Tommy Thompson, who knew Khrushchev personally

exemption: special permission not to do something

exile: when an individual, group or government is forced out of their own country and lives in or operates from a different country

exploitation: the act of using someone unfairly to your own advantage, e.g. people may be exploited in the workplace by being overworked and underpaid

fascist: someone who follows fascism, an extreme right-wing political system based on a single powerful leader with no political opposition, state control and extreme pride in country and race

foreign policy: government attitudes and action towards countries that lie outside the borders of the home country

führer: a German word meaning 'leader' or 'guide'. The title is usually associated with Adolf Hitler

fundamentalist: someone who believes in traditional forms of a religion or who strictly believes what is written in a holy book such as the Christian Bible

gangrene: a medical condition caused by loss of blood supply, especially to parts of the body farthest from the heart (e.g., toes), which leads the flesh there to die*

gas grenade: a small, handheld weapon, designed to be thrown at an enemy, which releases a poisonous gas

Gestapo: Nazi secret police who used cruel methods to oppress opposition to the Nazis

ghetto: an area in which a specific ethnic group (usually Jewish) is forced by law or threat of violence to live

Global North: includes the wealthiest and most industrialised countries mostly located in the northern hemisphere

Global South: includes the areas of Latin America, Asia, Africa and Oceania; most of them are less economically developed

Great Powers: countries that have considerable military, diplomatic and economic power, and influence

Greater Asian Co-Prosperity Sphere: the development of a group of Asian states led by Japan, which was to be self-sufficient in resources and food and be free from Western influence; the concept is sometimes shortened to GEACPS*

Gross National Product: the total value of all the goods and services produced by a country

guerrilla war: a war fought not in open battle but using small attacks to try to destroy an enemy's confidence. Guerrilla techniques include blowing up supplies and laying traps to cause injuries

High Command: a group of the most senior officers in a country's armed forces, which oversees all military decisions

hobos: homeless, unemployed people travelling across the country in search of work

home rule: a political arrangement in which a part of a country governs itself independently of the central government of a country

humanitarian: relating to actions aimed at improving peoples' lives and reducing suffering

hyperinflation: inflation that occurs at a very rapid rate without control

hypothesis: a statement or argument about an event or person in the past

ICBM: Inter-Continental Ballistic Missile, a long-range missile that can travel from one continent to another carrying a nuclear warhead

ideology: a particular set of ideas and beliefs, especially ones on which a political system, party or organisation are based

import tariffs: taxes on goods imported into a country

import: to buy or bring in goods from another country

inauguration: the formal public ceremony at which a new president takes the oath of office and officially takes on the role

indoctrinate: to make someone believe a set of values or principles without questioning them

indoctrination: the process of repeating an idea or belief until they accept it without question

infantry: soldiers that fight and march on foot*

inflation: an increase in prices and an accompanying drop in the purchasing value of money

informant: someone who finds information and gives it to another person or organisation

Judaism: a world religion that was developed among ancient Hebrews in the 6th century BCE*

kaiser: the German name for an emperor or king

Ku Klux Klan: a white supremacist organisation founded in the South after the Civil War. In its revived form in the early 20th century, the KKK's official policy was to terrorise black people, Catholics, Jews, immigrants, communists and anarchists

Kronstadt: a region of the city of St. Petersburg, famous for its large naval base

kulaks: wealthier peasants (the word '*kulak*' means 'fist' or 'tight-fisted': mean with money)

laissez-faire: a French term meaning 'leave alone' – a policy of minimising government involvement especially in the economy

landmine: a bomb on or under the ground, which explodes when someone steps on it or when a vehicle drives over it

latrines: field toilets*

Lebensraum: the idea that a successful country needs extra land in which to settle its people. In Hitler's thinking this was the area east of Germany in Poland and the Soviet Union

leprosy: a contagious disease that affects the skin and the nervous system

liberal intelligentsia: a group of educated people (doctors, lawyers, teachers, writers and other professionals) who were active in political leadership. They became frustrated at the 'backwardness' of tsarism

lynching: an illegal execution carried out by a mob, not by judicial process, often on black men

412

Glossary

mandate: a legal responsibility for the development of an area or country following the dissolution of the German Empire

martial law: the control of a city or country by the military rather than by its usual leaders

merchant ship: a ship used for trade rather than military purposes*

militarism: the belief that a country should maintain a strong army, navy and air force and be prepared to use them aggressively to defend or promote national interests. Militarism also suggests the glorification of military ideals such as duty, order, loyalty and obedience

minesweeper: a ship used to discover if mines are present under water and to remove them*

minority group: a recognisable group of people whose religion, language, culture or ethnicity is different from that of most people (the majority) in a country or region

miscarriage of justice: when someone is punished by the law courts for a crime they have not committed

mobilisation: all the actions taken by governments and their military services (army, navy, etc.), including gathering weapons, equipment, and human resources, to prepare for war

monarchy: a country that is ruled by a king, queen, emperor, or tsar

munitions: this includes both ammunition such as bullets and shells, as well as weapons like guns, revolvers and rifles

mustard gas: a weapon used during the First World War, which causes large blisters on exposed skin and lungs

mutiny: an occasion when a group of people, especially sailors or soldiers, refuses to obey orders or attempts to seize control from senior officers

Mutually Assured Destruction (MAD): a concept put forward by US Secretary of Defense Robert McNamara in 1962, based on the idea that as the USA had around 25 000 nuclear weapons and the USSR roughly half that, neither country would risk war as it would inevitably lead to widespread death and destruction

napalm: a petrol-based chemical weapon that sticks to its target and burns at a very high temperature. It is often used to clear forests, preventing the enemy from having a place to hide, but when it comes into contact with skin it causes terrible burns

nationalism: a great love for and pride in your own country and a desire for its political independence (if it does not already have it) as well as a belief that the interests of that nation and its people should be promoted above all others

naval supremacy: having a greater number of battleships than other countries

neutrality pact: an agreement between two or more countries stating that they will not join a war against the other

non-combatant: someone, especially in the armed forces, who does not fight, such as doctors or religious ministers

pacifist: someone who believes that war is wrong and that conflicts should be resolved peacefully

pact: a written agreement between two or more countries to act together in a particular way

paramilitary: describing a group that is organised like an army, but is unofficial and often illegal

partisans: armed groups formed to fight against an enemy that is controlling a country

partition: the division of a country or area into two or more parts

passive resistance: showing in a peaceful way that you oppose something, rather than using violence

patriotism: loving your own country more than any other, and having a great pride in it

peace treaties: documents signed by the countries involved in a war, formally ending the conflict and agreeing on the terms of peace. This might include changing national boundaries, the payment of reparations (resources such as money or coal), and actions to avoid a future conflict

persecution: hostility and ill treatment of certain groups in society

plebiscite: a popular vote open to the entire electorate of a country or region on a specific issue

plenary session: a part of a meeting or conference that everyone attends

pogroms: riots or semi-organised violence directed against Jewish people and their property

Politburo: the main government group in a communist country, which makes all the important decisions

precedent: an action or situation that has already happened that can be used as a reason why a similar action or decision can be taken or made

propaganda: information, ideas, opinions or images that show one side of an argument and which are designed to influence public opinion on a matter

proportional representation: a voting system in which the proportion of assembly seats won by parties closely resembles the proportion of the votes cast in the election

proxy war: a war in which a country does not fight but provides another country or side with war material to show support

punitive: intended as a punishment

puppet ruler: someone given the title of a ruler but who has no real power and is actually controlled by another person or group, such as the military

putsch: an attempt to take power from the government, usually by a small number of armed citizens or soldiers

quota: a strict quantity of goods that may be exported or imported under government control

race riot: a public, often violent, fight caused by racial anger or hatred

Radio Free Europe: a radio station established in 1950 to provide radio broadcasts for people living in communist countries in Eastern Europe. It was funded by the US Congress, broadcast in fifteen different languages and reached tens of millions of people

ratify: to officially vote on and accept a treaty

real wages: the amount of money that people earn taking account of any inflation and tax changes

rearmament: increasing the number of weapons and personnel in the armed forces in order to become a strong military power again

reconnaissance: the process of obtaining information about enemy forces or positions by using aircraft or sending small groups of soldiers*

referendum: a vote by the people on a single political issue with the result of the vote informing a political decision

reform: the desire to make changes to the political system and the way it works

regulation: a rule or a set of rules for organisations that affect parts of the economy

reparations: payment for harm, loss or damage caused, often made by countries defeated in war to the countries that won

Reichstag: The German parliament during the first half of the 20th century

repatriate: to send or bring someone back to the country that they came from

republic: a country that does not have a king or queen but which is usually governed by a president along with officials elected by the people

reserve troops: soldiers who do not serve in the regular army but who can be called on to do military service when needed*

resettlement: the process of helping someone to move to another place to live

right-wing: describing people or groups, often strong nationalists, whose political beliefs are based on an ordered society that values tradition and discipline. They usually oppose socialism and communism, believing that social inequality is natural and desirable, and because both pose a threat to private property

Russification: the official policy of forcing non-Russians to accept the Russian language and Russian rules in schools and in local government

sanctions: penalties or punishments imposed by an official body such as a court of law, intended to affect the country's decision-makers so they change their policies. A typical sanction in international relations is a ban on trade

sanitation: the systems for taking dirty water and other waste products away from buildings in order to protect people's health

scapegoat: someone who is blamed for something to avoid others taking responsibility

scuttle: to deliberately sink a ship. In wartime, navies may do this so that the enemy cannot capture a vessel and begin to use it themselves

secret protocol: an addition to a formal agreement that is not made public

Security Council: a small group of countries that has responsibility for peacekeeping within the United Nations

segregation: the separation of black people and white people in many areas of public life, such as education and public transport

self-determination: the right of an ethnic group to their own independent country instead of living in a country dominated by a different ethnic group

serfs: peasants who were forced to work for a landowner. Serfdom was common in Europe in the Middle Ages, but Russia's system lasted longer than in most other places

share-cropper: a farmer who rents land and who gives part of their crop as rent

shell shock: a term used in the First World War to describe the symptoms of stress, exhaustion, confusion and psychological trauma caused by trench warfare*

show trial: a trial held in public with the intention of influencing public opinion rather than making sure justice is served

Glossary

siege warfare: a tactic in which an armed force surrounds and blockades a town or fortified area in the hope of capturing it

silo: an underground space in which missiles are stored

skirmish: a short, unplanned period of fighting

Slavs: a number of ethnic groups of people in eastern and south-eastern Europe. Slavs and their languages (Russian, Polish, Czech, Serbian) are related, and many (though not all) of them belong historically to the Orthodox Christian churches

sniper: someone who shoots at people from a hidden position

socialist: a believer in socialism, a social and economic system in which wealth and the means of producing and distributing goods are shared and cooperatively managed

sovereignty: the power of a country to control its own government

Soviet: the Russian word for 'council'. The name for an elected group at several different social levels in the USSR

Soviet Bloc: the group of Eastern European states that were aligned with the USSR, taking their political direction from Moscow (also sometimes called the Communist Bloc or the Eastern Bloc)

speakeasy: an illegal bar that sold alcoholic drinks

stalemate: a situation in which neither side in a war can take decisive action to break the deadlock

stockpile: the gathering and storing of a large collection of weapons, including nuclear weapons after 1945

strike: a sudden military attack

successor states: a new, smaller country created after a larger country has been broken up, usually after a conflict

summit: a formal meeting between government leaders from two or more countries

superpower: the name given to the USSR and the USA after the Second World War to emphasise their economic, military, political and nuclear strength compared to other countries

supply and demand: supply refers to the amount of goods (or food) that are available to buy. Demand refers to how many people want to buy those goods (or food). When supply of a product increases, the price of a product goes down and vice versa

tariff: a tax imposed by a government that has to be paid on imports or exports

The Clifford-Elsey Report: a report written by two of President Truman's top security advisers. In it, the advisers made suggestions about 'containing' communism.

theory of evolution: the theory of biologist Charles Darwin in the 19th century, that life on Earth developed over millions of years, and that humans and apes are descended from a common ancestor

total war: a war that uses the full economic and military capacity of a nation. Every person is involved in the war effort in some way

totalitarianism: a political system in which those in power have complete control and allow no opposition

trade union: an organisation for workers, who work together to try to achieve common goals, such as increased wages or improved conditions

trafficking: buying or selling goods or people illegally

trench: a narrow, deep hole or ditch dug into the ground where soldiers hide while attacking an enemy

tribunal: a special court or group of people chosen to examine a particular type of problem

tsar: a Russian emperor

turning point: an event in a war that marks a distinct change of direction of a trend that was taking place up to that point*

ultimatum: a warning or threat that if someone does not do a particular thing, something bad will happen to them

United Nations: an international organisation founded in 1945 to promote development, peace and human rights, replacing the League of Nations

United Nations Security Council: the main decisionmaking body of the UN for military and security matters with 15 members – five permanent (the USA, Britain, China, France and Russia) and ten temporary, each permanent member has the power of veto, meaning members can block any decision or action from being taken

USSR: Union of Soviet Socialist Republics (also known as the Soviet Union), a communist state that spanned parts of Europe and Asia from 1922 to 1991

veto: an official power or right or refuse to allow something

Viet Minh and Viet Cong: names given by western politicians and journalists to Vietnamese communist forces. Viet Minh (for the northern communists) is a contraction of 'Vietnamese' and 'Ho Chi Minh', and Viet Cong (for the southern communists) is a contraction of a Vietnamese expression for 'Vietnamese communists'

Vietnamisation: a policy based on reducing US troops in Vietnam and encouraging the South Vietnamese Army (ARVN) to do more of the fighting

war of attrition: a military strategy where evenly balanced sides try to wear each other down gradually, hoping that the toll on the enemy, especially in terms of casualties, will be heavier than the cost to themselves. The aim is to exhaust the enemy rather than capturing land*

Warsaw Pact: a defensive military alliance of Eastern European states, including the USSR, Hungary, Romania, Bulgaria, Albania Czechoslovakia, East Germany and Poland, established as a response to NATO (the North Atlantic Treaty Organization)*

Wehrmacht: the combined armed forces of the Third Reich: the *Heer* (army), the *Luftwaffe* (air force) and the *Kriegsmarine* (navy)*

welfare state: a government-run system of national assistance to tackle poverty or unemployment

Zeppelins: a large airship, containing gas to make it lighter than air, and with an engine*

> Acknowledgements

The authors and publishers acknowledge the following sources of copyright material and are grateful for the permissions granted. While every effort has been made, it has not always been possible to identify the sources of all the material used, or to trace all copyright holders. If any omissions are brought to our notice, we will be happy to include the appropriate acknowledgements on reprinting.

Thanks to the following for permission to reproduce images:

Cover image: Fred Morley/GI

Introduction Part 1: Nick Lee/GI; Oli Scarff/GI; STF/GI; Prisma by Dukas/GI; **Introduction Part 2:** Print Collector/GI; Popperfoto/GI; Bettmann/GI; General Photographic Agency/GI; Library of Congress/GI; Mirrorpix/GI; Universal History Archive/GI; Popperfoto/GI; IWM/GI; UniversalImagesGroup/GI; Booblgum/GI; **Chapter 1:** Bettmann/GI; Hulton Deutsch/GI; Stock Montage/GI; Bettmann/GI; Front cover cartoon by SEM, in 'La Baionnette', 13 March 1919/Mary Evans Picture Library; A cartoon of Georges Clemenceau taken from a German newspaper in 1919; Hulton Deutsch/GI; UniversalImagesGroup/GI; Ullsteinbild/TopFoto; Sueddeutsche Zeitung Photo/Alamy; Historical Picture Archive/GI; Ullstein bild Dtl/GI; Bettmann/GI(×2); Cartoon by Will Dyson in 'The Daily Herald'/Mary Evans Picture Library; Chronicle/Alamy; Mondadori Portfolio/GI; Interim Archives/GI; **Chapter 2:** Hulton Archive/GI; Bettmann/GI; Hulton Archive/GI; Central Press/GI; Brandstaetter images/GI; Heritage Images/GI; Keystone-France/GI; Hulton Deutsch/GI; Buyenlarge/GI; FLHC 37/Alamy; Bettmann/GI; Granger-Historical Picture Archive/Alamy; Universal History Archive/GI; Fototeca Storica Nazionale/GI; Fototeca Gilardi/Bridgeman Images; David Low, Self-Portrait, Evening Standard, 15 Feb 1935, Solo Syndication/Associated Newspapers Ltd, British Cartoon Archive; Hulton Deutsch/GI; **Chapter 3:** Bettmann/GI; Galerie Bilderwelt/GI; Keystone/GI; David Low cartoon about the Munich Agreement; Hulton Deutsch/GI; Photo 12/GI; Bettmann/GI; Topical Press Agency/GI; STF/GI; Universal History Archive/GI; Library of Congress/GI; Ullstein bild Dtl./GI; Past Pix/GI; Hulton Deutsch/GI; David Low, Increasing Pressure, Evening Standard, 18 Feb 1938, Solo Syndication/Associated Newspapers Ltd, British Cartoon Archive; Davies/GI; Historical/GI; Heritage Image Partnership Ltd/Alamy; David Low, Stepping Stones to Glory, 1936, Evening Standard. Solo Syndication/Associated Newspapers Ltd, British Cartoon Archive; Culture Club/GI; Hulton Deutsch/GI; Fox Photos/GI; Topham Picturepoint/TopFoto; A poster showing a German view of the Treaty of Versailles" taken from Alpha history website; David Low, The End, A Cartoon History of Our Times, 1939, Solo Syndication/Associated Newspapers Ltd, British Cartoon Archive; Bettmann/GI; **Chapter 4:** Popperfoto/GI; Everett Collection/Bridgeman Images; The Way of a Stork/Leslie illingsworth/Reproduced with permission of Punch Ltd., www.punch.co.uk; Pictures from History/Bridgeman Images; Photo 12/Alamy; Bettmann/GI(×2); David Low, Why can't we work together in mutual trust & confidence?, Evening Standard, 30 Nov 1945, Solo Syndication/Associated Newspapers Ltd, British Cartoon Archive; Universal History Archive/GI; Patrice Cartier. All rights reserved 2023/Bridgeman Images; Granger-Historical Picture Archive/Alamy(×2); UniversalImagesGroup/GI; Hulton Archive/GI; The Marshall Tree/EH Shepard/Reproduced with permission of Punch Ltd; Rival Buses/EH Sheperd/Reproduced with permission of Punch Ltd; The Bird Watcher/EH Sheperd/Reproduced with permission of Punch Ltd; Bettmann/GI; Ullstein bild/GI; Historical/GI; Archivio GBB/Alamy; Marcus, Edwin, Artist. While the Shadow Lengthens. 1948. Image. Retrieved from the Library of Congress, https://www.loc.gov/item/acd1996005659/PP/, by permission of the Marcus Family; Bettmann/GI; **Chapter 5:** Bettmann/GI; AFP/GI; ImageBroker/Alamy; Believe it or Knout/Leslie illingworth/Reproduced with permission of Punch Ltd; Fotosearch/GI; Bettmann/GI; David Low, History Doesn't Repeat Itself, Daily Herald, 30 Jun 1950. Solo Syndication/Associated Newspapers Ltd, British Cartoon Archive; The Washington Post/GI; Lois Herman/GI; Keystone/GI; Bettmann/GI; A 1962 Herblock Cartoon, The Herb Block Foundation; Barry Winiker/GI; Bettmann/GI; AFP/GI; Bettmann/GI(×2); David Pollack/GI; Bettmann/GI; Pictures from History/GI; John Filo/GI; Bettmann/GI; Dirck Halstead/GI; Mirrorpix/GI; Bettmann/GI; Interim Archives/GI; **Chapter 6:** Lingxiao Xie/GI; Bettmann/GI; New York Daily News Archive/GI; Bettmann/GI(×2); Keystone/GI(×2); Sovfoto/GI; Bettmann/GI; AFP/GI; A 1968 Herblock Cartoon, The Herb Block Foundation; Hulton Deutsch/GI; Hulton Archive/GI; John Bryson/GI; Carl Mydans/GI; Popperfoto/GI; Keystone-France/GI; Ullstein bild/

GI; Asar Studios/Alamy; Bettmann/GI; Marc Deville/GI; Bernard Bisson/GI; Gysembergh Benoit/GI; Sovfoto/GI; Alfredas Pliadis/Alamy; Bettmann/GI; Stringer/GI; **Chapter 7:** Bettmann/GI; Akg-images/Alamy; Central Press/GI; Hulton Deutsch/GI; Ullstein bild Dtl./GI; Adoc-photos/GI; Three Lions/GI; Album/Alamy; Historical/GI; Photo 12/GI; Ullstein bild Dtl./GI; Interfoto/Alamy; Bettmann/GI; Keystone-France/GI; Historical/GI(×2); Ullstein bild Dtl./GI(×2); Hulton Deutsch/GI; Pictures from History/GI; Print Collector/GI; Universal History Archive/GI; Chronicle/Alamy; Interfoto/Alamy; Bettmann/GI; **Chapter 8:** Brandstaetter images/GI; Hulton Archive/GI; Laski Diffusion/GI; lbusca/GI; Photo 12/GI; Universal History Archive/GI; Bettmann/GI; Heritage Image Partnership Ltd/Alamy; Underwood Archives/GI; Heritage Images/GI; Dorling Kindersley/GI; UniversalImagesGroup/GI; ITAR-TASS News Agency/Alamy; UniversalImagesGroup/GI; Universal History Archive/GI; Interfoto/Alamy; Bettmann/GI; Laski Diffusion/GI; Bettmann/GI; Sovfoto/GI; Universal History Archive/GI(×2); Bettmann/GI; Sovfoto/GI; Heritage Images/GI; Alexander Alland, Jr/GI; **Chapter 9:** Ullstein bild Dtl/GI; Photo 12/GI; Puttnam/GI; Chronicle/Alamy; Ullstein bild Dtl/GI; George Rinhart/GI; Hulton Archive/GI; JP Jazz Archive/GI; Michael Ochs Archives/GI; New York Daily News Archive/GI; Bettmann/GI; Jack Benton/GI; Chicago History Museum/GI; Archive PL/Alamy; Bettmann/GI; Camerique/GI; Photo 12/GI(×2); 20th Century Fox/GI; Brandstaetter images/GI; General Photographic Agency/GI; Hulton Archive/GI; MPI/GI; Fotosearch/GI; Pictorial Parade/GI; Fotosearch/GI(×2); Roger Viollet/GI; **Chapter 10 (online only):** Print Collector/GI(×2); Mirrorpix/GI; Pen and Sword Books/GI(×2); Hulton Deutsch/GI; Hulton Archive/GI; Historical Picture Archive/GI; Everett Collection Historical/Alamy; Universal History Archive/GI; IWM/GI(×2); Ullstein bild Dtl/GI; Universal History Archive/GI; Swim ink 2 llc/GI; Print Collector/GI; Interfoto/Alamy; Bettmann/GI; Lordprice Collection/Alamy; Swim ink 2 llc/GI; Hulton Archive/GI; Hulton Deutsch/GI; Bettmann/GI; Granger 25 Chapel St. Suite 605 Brooklyn, Reproduced with permission of Granger Collection; Paul Thompson/GI; **Chapter 11 (online only):** Historical/GI; Print Collector/GI; Bettmann/GI; Universal History Archive/GI; John Frost Newspapers/Alamy; IWM/GI; Hulton Deutsch/GI; Hulton Archive/GI; Sovfoto/GI; Historical/GI; Pictures from History/GI; Universal History Archive/GI; Historical/GI; Mondadori Portfolio/GI; Popperfoto/GI; Daily Herald Archive/GI; Mirrorpix/GI; Bettmann/GI; Central Press/GI; Ullstein bild Dtl/GI; Universal History Archive/GI; STF/GI; Bettmann/GI; Hulton Deutsch/GI; Universal History Archive/GI; Historical/GI; Fotosearch/GI; Universal History Archive/GI; Interim Archives/GI; **Preparing for Assessment:** Heritage Images/GI; Print Collector/GI; A 1965 Herblock Cartoon,
The Herb Block Foundation.

Key GI = Getty Images.

Index

*Asterisked index entries can be found in the two chapters which are available as part of your digital resource on Cambridge GO.

25-Point Programme, 1920 269, 287

abdication 10, 24, 162, 259, 317, 36 (CH10)*
Abyssinia crisis, 1935–36 89, 92–5, 112
Adenauer, Konrad 174
advertising 355–7
Afghanistan, Soviet invasion, 1979 244, 245, 250
Africa, First World War 18, 21–23 (CH10)*
African National Congress (ANC) 248
agency 85
Agent Orange 209
Agricultural Adjustment Act (AAA) 387, 388
agriculture
    alphabet agencies 387
    collectivisation 341–2, 343–4
    Depression of the 1930s 381–2
    economy boom of the 1920s 355, 361–2
    Farm Security Administration 388
    industrialisation and growth 6
    mechanisation in farming 355
    social consequences of Wall Street Crash 379–80
air raids/aircraft 11 (CH10)*
    see also aviation
AK (Home Army), Poland 33 (CH11)*
Aktion T-4 program 282
Åland Islands crisis, 1920–21 78–9
alcohol
    Prohibition Era 373, 386
    speakeasy bar 364
Alexander III (Tsar) 318
Alexandra (wife of Nicholas II) 304, 316
alliances 10
    see also individual alliances...
Allied Powers/Allies
    advance through Italy 37–38 (CH11)*
    Armistice, 1918 39–45 (CH10)*
    atomic bombs 158–60
    bombing of German cities 29–31 (CH11)*
    consolidation of power in Germany and Japan 43–46 (CH11)*
    definitions 16
    economy boom of the 1920s 352
    First World War becoming a global conflict 18
    and Japanese collaboration, First World War 23–25 (CH10)*
    map of Europe 1914 11
    Normandy invasion 36 (CH11)*, 39 (CH11)*
    Potsdam Conference 154–7, 176
    victory over Axis Powers/Central Powers 37–46 (CH11)*
    victory over Japan 40–43 (CH11)*

Weimar Republic 259, 265
    see also First World War; individual countries...; Second World War
alphabet agencies 386–7
American Civil War (1861–65) 369
amnesty 320
anarchists 369
ANC (African National Congress) 248
Andropov, Yuri 248
Anglo–German naval agreement of 1935 132
annexation 117, 19 (CH11)*
    Anschluss ('union') 41, 117–20, 124, 289
Anschluss ('union'), 1938 41, 117–20, 124, 289
Anti-Comintern Pact 95, 112, 117
'Anti-Fascist Defence Wall' see Berlin Wall
anti-Semitism 107
    see also Aryan race; eugenics
anti-Soviet spies 336
ANZAC (Australian and New Zealand Army Corps) 24 (CH10)*, 33 (CH10)*, 34 (CH10)*, 42 (CH10)*
appeasement 113–32, 135
Arab Revolt and the First World War 25–27 (CH10)*
Arabic (US liner) 31 (CH10)*
aristocracy 304
armaments 32
armistice 10, 60, 259, 261
    of 1918 33, 39–45 (CH10)*
    Dolchstoss ('stab in the back') 53, 261, 262
army see military
art
    'Degenerate Art' exhibition 286
    Joseph Stalin's control over the USSR 338
artillery 18
Aryan race 108, 109
Asian immigrants in the US 367
Asia-Pacific
    Second World War, 1939–c. 1945 2 (CH11)*, 19–26 (CH11)*
    see also China; Japan; Korea; Vietnam
assassinations
    attempted killing of Hitler 283
    Franz Ferdinand (Archduke) and his wife, Sophie 9–10, 12, 13
    Weimar Republic 263–4
Assembly (League of Nations) 71–2
assembly line workers 357, 358
Atlantic Wall bombardments 39 (CH11)*
atomic bombs 7, 158–60, 175, 177, 178, 41–42 (CH11)*
    see also Inter-Continental Ballistic Missiles
Attlee, Clement 154–7, 159, 192
    see also Potsdam Conference
Auschwitz concentration camp 35 (CH11)*
Australian and New Zealand Army Corps (ANZAC) 24 (CH10)*, 33 (CH10)*, 34 (CH10)*, 42 (CH10)*
Austria
    Anschluss ('union') 41, 117–20, 124
    Vienna Summit 1961 197, 240

Austro-Hungarian Empire 30, 224, 2 (CH10)*, 35–36 (CH10)*
    First World War breakout 10–11, 12, 13
autarkies 285
authority, Japanese forces 32 (CH11)*
Autobahn 242, 284
autocrats 206
automotive industry 265, 284, 285, 353, 357, 16 (CH11)*
autonomy 78
aviation 13–14 (CH11)*
    air raids 11 (CH10)*
    Berlin Airlift 172–3
    biplanes 11 (CH10)*
    Blitz attacks/Blitzkrieg 122, 2 (CH11)*, 13 (CH11)*, 26 (CH11)*, 27 (CH11)*
    RAF (Britain) 13–14 (CH11)*
    Zeppelin raids 20, 21, 11 (CH10)*
    see also Luftwaffe
aviation industry 359
Axis Powers
    Allied Powers' victory 37–46 (CH11)*
    Hitler's defeat at Stalingrad 18 (CH11)*
    Rome–Berlin Axis/Anti-Comintern Pact 95, 104, 112, 117, 124, 132
    see also First World War; individual countries...; Nazi Germany; Second World War

Baden, Max of (Prince) 42 (CH10)*, 43 (CH10)*, 44 (CH10)*
Badoglio, Pietro (General) 38 (CH11)*
Balfour Declaration, 1917 26 (CH10)*
'Baltic Chain' protest, 1989 250, 251
bankruptcy 362
    see also Great Depression of the 1930s
barricades 5 (CH10)*
baseball 366, 369
Batista, Fulgencio 196
Battle of Britain, 1940 12–13 (CH11)*
Battle of the Bulge, 1944–45 39 (CH11)*
Battle of Crimea, 1941 15 (CH11)*
Battle of Dunkirk, 1940 4–7 (CH11)*
Battle of Guadalcanal, 1942–43 40 (CH11)*
Battle of Jutland, 1916 29 (CH10)*, 30 (CH10)*
Battle of the Marne 6 (CH10)*
Battle of the Marne, 1914 13
Battle of Masurian Lakes, 1914 35 (CH10)*
Battle of Midway, 1942 20 (CH11)*, 25–26 (CH11)*
Battle of Moscow, 1941–42 16 (CH11)*
Battle of Neuve Chapelle 20 (CH10)*
Battle of Okinawa, 1945 41 (CH11)*
Battle of Passchendaele, 1917 22
Battle of Rostov, 1941 15 (CH11)*
Battle of the Somme, 1916 13 (CH10)*, 15–17 (CH10)*, 18 (CH10)*
Battle of the Somme, 1918 41 (CH11)*
Battle of Stalingrad, 1941 16–18 (CH11)*
Battle of Tanga, 1914 22 (CH10)*
Battle of Tannenberg, 1914 35 (CH10)*
Battle of Verdun, 1916 15 (CH10)*, 18 (CH10)*

419

Battle of Ypres, 1914–18 6 (CH10)*, 12 (CH10)*, 20 (CH10)*
Bauhaus School of Art and Architecture 267
Bavarian Republic, Munich Putsch 52
Bay of the Pigs, April 1961 197
bayonets 9 (CH10)*
beachheads 39 (CH11)*
Beer Hall (Munich) Putsch, 1923 52, 56, 270–1
Belgium
    Battle of Ypres 6 (CH10)*, 12 (CH10)*, 20 (CH10)*
    NATO formation 174
    occupation of the Ruhr 55, 56, 265, 266
    Schlieffen Plan 5 (CH10)*
Beneš, Edvard 126, 127, 162
Berlin Airlift 172–3
Berlin Blockade, 1948–49 171–5, 176, 178, 236
Berlin Wall
    collapse of the Soviet Union 248–53
    construction, 1961 236–44
bilateral talks 75
biplanes 11 (CH10)*
Bizone/Bizonia (economic unit) 171, 178
Black Americans
    Cotton Club, Harlem, New York 365
    Ku Klux Klan 370
    poverty 362
    race riots 370–1
    segregation 359, 369
black gold (oil) 4–5, 93, 355
black populations of Weimar Germany 290
'Black Ribbon Day' international day of protest, 23 Aug 1989 250, 251
'Black Thursday', 1929 376
Blitzkrieg ('lightning war') 122, 2 (CH11)*, 13 (CH11)*, 26 (CH11)*, 27 (CH11)*
blockades 15, 22, 24, 199, 31 (CH10)*
    Berlin Blockade 48, 171–5, 176, 178, 236
Bloody Easter on the Ruhr 55, 56
Bolsheviks 22
    Arab Revolt 27 (CH10)*
    Civil War 323–30, 337
    defeat of Russia on the Eastern Front 36(CH10)*
    November Revolution 323–4, 36 (CH10)*
    power following Revolution of March 1917 319–31
    Russian Revolution, 1905 312
    seizing power in November, 1917 321–4
    Socialist opposition to Tsarism 307
    suppression of religion 338
    Treaty of Brest-Litovsk 23
    see also Red Army
bombings
    Atlantic Wall bombardments 39 (CH11)*
    atomic bombs 7, 158–60, 175, 177, 178, 41–42 (CH11)*
    Blitzkrieg ('lightning war') 122, 2 (CH11)*, 13 (CH11)*, 26 (CH11)*, 27 (CH11)*
    Cuban Missile Crisis 196, 198–203, 238, 239
    ICBMs 196, 237, 252
    trenches 99 (CH11)*
    Zeppelin raids 20, 21, 11 (CH10)*
    see also Luftwaffe
Bonhoffer, Dietrich 282, 287
Bonus Bill/March 384
bootlegging see Prohibition Era
Boulder Dam/Hoover Dam 384
boycotts 72, 251, 288

Brandt, Willy 242
Brezhnev, Leonid 2, 235, 236
    Brezhnev Doctrine 232
    Prague Spring 231, 233
    Solidarity (Solidarnosc) 244, 246, 248
Britain
    appeasement 112, 113, 123–4
    Arab Revolt and the First World War 25–27 (CH10)*
    Armistice, 1918 33, 39–45 (CH10)*
    Battle of Dunkirk 4–7 (CH11)*
    Berlin Blockade 171–5
    Blitzkrieg 13 (CH11)*, 26 (CH11)*, 27 (CH11)*
    civilian bombings 26 (CH11)*, 27–31 (CH11)*
    Council of Four 38
    declaring war on Germany 134–7
    Empire and the Western Front 18–20 (CH10)*
    female workforce, First World War 21
    Gallipoli campaign 33 (CH10)*
    invasion of Poland 3 (CH11)*
    Japanese collaboration 23–25 (CH10)*
    League of Nations 75
    life in Nazi Germany 294
    NATO formation 174
    Nazi–Soviet Pact 131, 132–4, 2 (CH11)*
    RAF 13–14 (CH11)*
    reactions to First World War breakout 14
    Rhineland, 1936 115, 116
    Rome–Berlin Axis/Anti-Comintern Pact 95, 104, 112, 117, 124, 132
    Royal Navy 28–29 (CH10)*, 30 (CH10)*, 34 (CH10)*, 4–7 (CH11)*, 11 (CH11)*
    Schlieffen Plan 5 (CH10)*
    Spanish Civil War 121
    Tehran Conference 150
    Treaty of Versailles 31–8, 46–7, 106
    victory of Allied Powers/Allies in First World War 22, 37–46 (CH11)*
    war at sea 28–29 (CH10)*, 30 (CH10)*, 31 (CH10)*, 4–7 (CH11)*, 11 (CH11)*
    Zeppelin raids 20, 21, 11 (CH10)*
    see also individual British leaders...
British Expeditionary Force (BEF) 5–6 (CH10)*, 4 (CH11)*
British Special Operations Unit 36 (CH10)*
'Britons: Lord Kitchener Wants You' recruitment poster 16 (CH10)*
Brüning, Heinrich 277
Brusilov, Alexei (General) 36 (CH10)*
Buddhism 207
budget deficit(s) 55
buffer zones 46, 222, 223, 235, 244–8
Bukharin, Nikolai 333, 334, 336
Bulgaria 81–2, 163
bureaucracy 305
bushels 361
buy now pay later 355
Byrnes, James 165

cabinets 273
Calley, William (Lieutenant) 210
Cambodia 210, 212, 214
Cammens, Nina 294
Canada 146, 174, 20 (CH10)*, 42 (CH10)*
Canadian Expeditionary Force (CEF) 20 (CH10)*
capitalism 75, 393
Capone, Al 373

carbon dioxide 6
Castro, Fidel 196, 197, 202
Catholicism
    Centre Party 280
    concordat agreements 287
    cultural genocide of Nazi Germany 33 (CH11)*
    Hungary and Soviet control, 1956 224, 227
    intolerance in the US 371
    opposition to the Nazi regime 282
    see also Church
cavalry 6 (CH10)*
CCC (Civilian Conservation Corps) 386
ceasefire(s) 193
Cecil, Robert (Lord) 79, 111
Central Intelligence Agency (CIA) 197, 206–7, 210, 238
Central Powers
    account of collapse 45 (CH10)*
    definitions 16
    Europe 1914 11
    First World War becoming a global conflict 18
    loss to Allies/Allied Powers 22, 37–46 (CH11)*
    Treaty of Brest-Litovsk 23
    see also Axis Powers
CFCs (chlorofluorocarbons) 6
Chamberlain, Neville 124
    appeasement 135
    Czech crisis 127–8
    Germany's invasion of Poland 3 (CH11)*
    Munich Agreement 127, 128
    Nazi–Soviet Pact 131, 132–4, 2 (CH11)*
chancellors 56–7, 118, 260, 266, 267, 268, 275–8
'Che' Guevara, Ernersto 196
Checkpoint Charlie 240, 242
Cheka (Russian secret police) 324, 328, 331, 335, 336
Chernenko, Konstantin 248
Chiang Kai-Shek 90, 91
Chicago
    organised crime 373
    race riots 371
child labour 84–5, 86
China
    Asia-Pacific in the Second World War 19–20 (CH11)*
    détente 214
    First World War becoming a global conflict 18
    Hungarian and Czech invasion by the USSR 232
    Korean War 191–2, 194
    Lytton Report 91
    Revolution, October 1949 188
    Tehran Conference 150
    Treaty of Versailles 47
Chinese Communist Party (CCP) 186
chlorine gas 12 (CH10)*
chlorofluorocarbons (CFCs) 6
Christianity
    fundamentalism 372
    missionaries in China 19 (CH11)*
    see also Catholicism; Church; Protestantism
Chrysler Building, New York 360
Church
    concordat agreements 287
    cultural genocide of Nazi Germany 33 (CH11)*

Index

government control in Russia 308
Hungary and Soviet control 224, 227
opposition to the Nazi regime 282
Russian Empire 303
Solidarity (*Solidarnosc*) 245
Wall Street Crash 379–80
Churchill, Winston
    attitude to peace-making 158
    biography 3 (CH11)*
    Gallipoli campaign 32 (CH10)*, 34 (CH10)*
    'Grand Alliance' 150, 151, 153, 154, 156, 177
    'Iron Curtain' speech 164
    Tehran Conference 150
    USSR's control over Eastern Europe 163
    Yalta Conference 151, 153, 177
    see also Potsdam Conference;
        Second World War
CIA (Central Intelligence Agency) 197, 206–7, 210, 238
cinema 268, 365
civil war(s) 75
    Russia (1918–1921) 185, 323–30, 337
    USA (1861–65) 369
Civil Works Administration (CWA) 387
Civilian Conservation Corps (CCC) 386
civilian populations 286–7, 291–6, 37–39 (CH10)*, 26–37 (CH11)*
    living in Nazi Germany 286–7, 291–6
    victims of The Purges, Russia 336
    see also peasantry; workers
Clay, Lucius D. (General) 242
Clemenceau, Georges 31–8, 46
coal industry 355, 360, 362
coalitions 54
    see also individual coalitions...
Cold War (1945–89) 2, 144–83
    Berlin Wall construction 236–44
    break down of US–Soviet alliance, 1945 145–60
    collapse of the Soviet Union 248–53
    consequences of the Berlin Blockade 171–5
    definitions 145–6
    USA's response to Soviet expansionism 164–70
    USSR's control over Eastern Europe 160–4
    who to blame 144, 176–80
    see also Union of Soviet Socialist Republics
Coleman, Bessie 359
collective bargaining 388
collective security 72, 174
collectivisation 341–2, 343–4, 345
colonies 18, 203–6, 21–23 (CH10)*
    see also Empire
Comintern 95, 112, 117
commission(s) 38, 60
    for Refugees 83
communes 305
communism
    Adolf Hitler becoming chancellor 278
    Bolsheviks 22
    containment by the USA 158, 186–220, 251
    Cuba and communism 196–203
    Depression in Germany, 1929–33 275–6
    Enabling Act 280
    League of Nations 75
    occupation of Japan 46 (CH11)*
    people's republics 160, 227
    persecution of peoples by the Nazis 287
    'Red Scare', 1919–20 369

Reichstag fire 279
Soviet Comintern 95
Vietnam War 203–15
War Communism, Russia 328
Weimar Republic 262, 263
worker policies of the Nazi Party 293
see also individual communist states...; Union of Soviet Socialist Republics
Communist state(s) 2
concentration camps 282, 284, 295–6, 33 (CH11)*, 34–35 (CH11)*
concessions 309
concordat agreements 287
Conference of Ambassadors 79
Confessing Church for non-Nazi ministers 287
conscientious objector(s) 14, 19–20
conscription 19–20
Constituent Assembly elections, Russia 324
constitutions
    1936, Russia 337
    equal voting rights 374
    Treaty of Versailles 49
    Weimar Republic 260
construction industry 360
consumer culture and advertising 354, 355–7
containment policy 158, 186–220
    détente ('relaxation') 214, 251
convention(s) 84
    see also individual conventions...
convoy systems, maritime warfare 31–32 (CH10)*
Corfu Incident, 1923 79–81
corps 4 (CH10)*
cost of war, Treaty of Versailles 28
Cotton Club, Harlem, New York 365
cotton industry 359, 362
Coughlin, Charles (Father) 390, 391
Council of Four 38
Council (League of Nations) 71–2
Council for Mutual Economic Assistance (COMECON) 174, 176
counterattacks 192
countryside *see* rural life
coup(s) 52
    see also individual coups...
court martial 40 (CH11)*
covenant(s) 47, 69–70
Coyle, James (Priest) 371
credit definition 72
creeping barrage(s) 20 (CH10)*
Crowdy, Rachel 84
Cuba and communism 196–203
Cuban Missile Crisis 196
    aftermath 203
    causes 198–203
    U2 spy planes 196, 198, 200, 238, 239
cultural impacts
    advertising 355–6
    genocide of Nazi Germany 33 (CH11)*
    Joseph Stalin's control over the USSR 338
    Weimar Republic 267–8
Cundall, Charles 7 (CH11)*
CWA *see* Civil Works Administration
Czech Communist Party 230
Czech Legion (Russian Civil War) 327
Czechoslovakia
    crisis of 1938 125–7
    invasion, March 1939 131–2
    Soviet control, 1968 224, 229–33, 234–6
    under USSR control 162

Dachau concentration camp 284
Dadaism 267
Daladier, Édouard (Prime Minister) 127, 128
Damenklub Monbijou (Monbijou Women's clubs) 288
Damenklub Violetta (Violetta Women's Club) 288
Danzig (Polish city) 134
DAP (German Workers Party) 269–70
Darwin, Charles 372
Dawes Plan, 1924 57, 267, 273
D-Day 39 (CH11)*
death camps (concentration camps) 282, 284, 295–6, 33 (CH11)*, 34–35 (CH11)*
'Decree For the Protection of People and State' 279
decree(s) 260, 279
defect(s) 240
deforestation 6
'Degenerate Art' exhibition 286
delegation(s)
    League of Nations 75–6
    Treaty of Versailles 31–8, 45, 46, 47, 75–6
demilitarisation 39, 41, 116
democracy/democratisation 28, 260, 43 (CH11)*
Democratic Party 32, 390, 391
    see also Social Democratic Party
demonstrations 48
    see also protest; strikes
denazification 43–44 (CH11)*
Denikin, Anton (General) 328
Denmark and Nato formation 174
Depression of the 1930s
    definitions 87–9
    ILO 85
    League of Nations 87–100
    and Nazi Germany 275–6, 284–5
    New Deal 390, 392–3
    social consequences 379–83
    Wall Street Crash 275–6, 284, 375–85
desertion 24
détente ('relaxation') 214, 251
deterrents 111
dictatorships 92
    see also communism; individual dictatorships...
Dietrich, Marlene 268
diktat ('dictated peace') 40, 261
diplomacy 61
diplomats 164
disarmament 34, 111
Disarmament Conference (League of Nations) 111
dissenters 308
Dix, Otto 267
Dnieprostroi hydroelectric dam 339, 340
DNVP (German National People's Party) 273, 280
Dolchstoss ('stab in the back') 53, 261, 262
Dollar Imperialism 178
domestic factors, USA's loss of Vietnam War 214
domestic policy 95
Domino Theory 208
Dowding, Hugh (Chief Marshal) 12 (CH11)*, 13 (CH11)*
Dreadnought-class battleships 29 (CH10)*, 30 (CH10)*
Dresden bombings 29 (CH11)*, 30 (CH11)*
Drexler, Anton 269–70
Dubček, Alexander 230, 231–2, 236

421

Duma parliament 311, 312, 314, 315, 316, 317, 319
dynasties 10
Dzerzhinsky tractor plant 16 (CH11)*

East Africa (colony) 21 (CH10)*, 22 (CH10)*
East Germany 174
   see also Berlin Wall
Eastern Europe
   Berlin Blockade 171–5, 176, 178, 236
   diplomacy between February and July, 1945 164
   Tehran Conference 150
   US immigrants 367, 369
   USSR's control over, 1948–c.1989 221–57
   Yalta Conference 151–3
   see also Berlin Wall
Eastern Front 35–37 (CH10)*
   Allied Powers' advance through Italy 37 (CH11)*
   breakout of the First World War 13
   defeat of Russia 36 (CH10)*
   'Easterners' and Gallipoli campaign 32–34 (CH10)*
   events on 35–36 (CH10)*
   Tehran Conference 150
   Treaty of Brest-Litovsk 23
Ebert, Friedrich 24, 259, 261, 262, 263, 265, 268, 44 (CH10)*
Ebert–Groener Pact 259, 262, 263
economic impacts/economies
   Bizone/Trizone 171, 174, 178
   Gross National Product 352
   Joseph Stalin 339–45
   life in Nazi Germany 294
   Malaya and Japanese forces 32 (CH11)*
   Nazi regime 284–5, 294
   sanctions, League of Nations 72
   Treaty of Versailles 36–7, 54–7
   tsarism and First World War 316
   Wall Street Crash 275–6, 284, 375–85
   Weimar Republic 267
   see also Great Depression of the 1930s
economy boom of the 1920s 352–64
   agriculture 361–2
   long-term causes 355
   new industries 359–60
   short-term causes 355–7
   weakness in the economy 363
Edelweiss Pirates 291, 292
Editors Law, 1933 286
Eichmann, Adolf 289, 295–6
Einsatzgruppen ('action groups') 294, 14 (CH11)*, 34 (CH11)*
Eisenhower, Dwight D.
   Berlin Wall construction 236–7, 238
   and Cuban communism 197
   end of Korean War 193
   U2 spy planes 238
embargoes 93, 20 (CH11)*
Empire State Building, New York 360
Empire(s)
   and Arab Revolt 25–27 (CH10)*
   Austro-Hungarian Empire 10–11, 12, 13, 30, 224, 2 (CH10)*, 35–36 (CH10)*
   definition 6
   fall and rise of 6–7
   Germany and its colonies 42–4
   map of Europe 1914 30

Ottoman Empire 16, 18, 26, 28, 30, 25–27 (CH10)*, 32–34 (CH10)*
   Reich 108, 115, 117, 131, 287, 288, 294, 3 (CH11)*
   Russian 303
   successor states 45, 106
   Western Front in the First World War 18–23 (CH10)*
   see also individual empires...; *Reich*
employment
   women in the 1920s 374
   see also unemployment
Enabling Act, 1933 280
energy consumption
   between 1820 and 2000 5
   see also natural resources
Enterprise (USS) 25 (CH11)*
epidemics 28
equal voting rights 374
Erzberger, Matthias 53, 263
espionage 172
   anti-Soviet spies 336
   Red Orchestra spy networks 283
   U2 spy planes 196, 198, 200, 238, 239
eugenics 287
   see also Aryan Race
Europe
   African colonies and the First World War 21–23 (CH10)*
   and empire 6–7
   empires broken up by 1918 30
   European Recovery Program 178
   First World War becoming a global conflict 18
   The Hague Conference, 1899 8
   immigrants and US intolerance 369
   see also First World War; *individual countries...*; Second World War
euthanasia 282
evacuations and the Blitz attacks 27–29 (CH11)*
evictions 362
evolution, theory 372
Ex-Comm 199
exemption(s) 19
exile 28
exploitation 83
extermination camps (concentration camps) 282, 284, 295–6, 33 (CH11)*, 34–35 (CH11)*

family
   and Nazi policy 293
   see also civilian populations; women
Farm Credit Administration (FCA) 387
Farm Security Administration (FSA) 388
farmers *see* agriculture
fascism 92, 185
   see also Nazi Germany
Fechter, Peter 242, 243
Federal Emergency Relief Administration (FERA) 387
Federal Republic of Germany *see* West Germany
Ferdinand, Franz 2 (CH10)*
Final Solution 289, 294, 295–6, 33–35 (CH11)*
financial effects
   Wall Street Crash 1929 378
   see also economic impacts/economies
Finland 78–9
First Battle of Ypres 6 (CH10)*, 20 (CH10)*
First Five Year Plan, 1928–32 339

First World War, 1914–18 2, 7–8, 9–26, 1–49 (CH10)*
   aftermath with France 25–6
   aftermath with Germany 24, 259–60
   Armistice, 1918 39–45 (CH10)*
   breakout 10–11, 12, 13–15
   civilian populations 37–39 (CH10)*
   conscription/conscientious objectors 19–20
   expansion to global conflict 18
   extent of 18–27 (CH10)*
   female pacifism 15
   female workforce 21
   fighting the war 15–16
   Gallipoli campaign 32–34 (CH10)*
   Home Front 20–2
   new methods of warfare 10–14 (CH10)*
   and oil 4
   other fronts 3–18 (CH10)*, 28–39 (CH10)*
   propaganda 22
   stalemate 18, 1–18 (CH10)*
   technology of the War Machine 17
   as a total war 20
   Treaty of Brest-Litovsk 23
   trenches 6 (CH10)*, 7–10 (CH10)*
   US economy boom of the 1920s 352
   victory of the Allied Powers 22
   war at sea 28–32 (CH10)*
   who died 16, 17
   see also individual participating countries...
Five Year Plan, Russia 339–340 344
'flappers' (women in the 1920s) 374
Flossenbürg concentration camp 282
Foch, Ferdinand (Marshal) 60, 261, 40 (CH10)*, 42 (CH10)*
food supplies/shortages
   blockades 22, 24, 48, 172, 31 (CH10)*
   collectivisation 341–2, 343–4, 345
   Gallipoli campaign 34 (CH10)*
   Kiel Mutiny 44 (CH10)*
   Malaya and Japanese forces 32 (CH11)*
   Revolution, Germany 1918 43 (CH10)*, 44 (CH10)*
   Solidarity (*Solidarnosc*) 244
   tensions in the 'Grand Alliance' 156
   USA and the Depression of the 1930s 88, 379–80
Ford Motor Company (Henry Ford) 354, 357
foreign policy
   Adolf Hitler 103–43
      aims 108–10
      Allies declare war 134–7
      appeasement 113–32
      League of Nations 110–13
      Nazi–Soviet Pact 131, 132–4, 2 (CH11)*
      Treaty of Versailles 106–10
   League of Nations 95, 110–13
   Weimar Republic 267
'four policeman' (USA, Britain, China and the USSR) 150
Fourteen Points (Wilson) 32–3, 117
Four-Year Plan Office, Nazi Germany 285
France
   advance on Paris by the Nazis 41 (CH10)*, 42 (CH10)*
   appeasement 112, 113, 123–4
   Arab Revolt 27 (CH10)*
   Armistice, 1918 39–45 (CH10)*
   Battle of Dunkirk 4–7 (CH11)*
   Battle of Verdun, 1916 15 (CH10)*

Index

Berlin Blockade 171–5
Council of Four 38
Dawes Plan 57
declaring war on Germany 134–7
end of First World War 25–6
invasion of Poland 3 (CH11)*, 4 (CH11)*
League of Nations 75
Marshal Foch 60, 261, 40 (CH10)*, 42 (CH10)*
Munich Agreement 127, 128
NATO formation 174
Nazi–Soviet Pact 131, 132–4, 2 (CH11)*
occupation of the 55, 56, 265, 266
Paris Peace Conference/Conference of Ambassadors 38, 79, 238
reactions to First World War breakout 14
resistance movements against Nazis 36–37 (CH11)*
Rhineland, 1936 115
Rome–Berlin Axis/Anti-Comintern Pact 95, 104, 112, 117, 124, 132
Spanish Civil War 121
surrender to Nazi forces 8 (CH11)*
Treaty of Versailles 31–8, 46
Treaty of Versailles, long-term consequences 106
Vichy France 9–10 (CH11)*, 20 (CH11)*
Vietnam War 203–6
Western Front 19
see also Battle of the Somme
Franco, Francisco (General) 121
Frank, Hans 32 (CH11)*
Franz Ferdinand (Archduke) and his wife, Sophie 9–10, 12, 13
free-markets see capitalism
Freikorps 263
French, John (General) 5 (CH10)*
FSA (Farm Security Administration) 388
führer ('leader') 118, 280–1
see also Hitler
Führerprinzip ('leader principles') 272
fundamentalists 372

Gallipoli campaign 25–26 (CH10)*, 32–34 (CH10)*
gangrene 8 (CH10)*
gas attacks
  Agent Orange in Vietnam 209
  chlorine gas 12 (CH10)*
  First World War 10, 93, 12 (CH10)*, 14 (CH10)*
  grenades 10
  mustard gas 93, 12 (CH10)*
  phosgene gas 12 (CH10)*
  Second Battle of Ypres 12 (CH10)*
  Zyklon B 295, 35 (CH10)*
gas, natural 5
gasoline (petrol) 4
  see also napalm
Gassed (Sargent) 14 (CH10)*
Gaue (regions)/Gauleiter (leader) 272, 277
Gdansk
  Solidarity (Solidarnosc) 244–8
  strikes over food prices, 1980 244
Geddes, Eric 36
Geneva Conference 91, 93, 111, 205, 250
'Gentle Revolution' 251
George, David Lloyd 31 (CH10)*, 34 (CH10)*
German Communist Party 174

German Democratic Republic (East Germany) 174
  see also Berlin Wall
German East Africa (colony) 21 (CH10)*, 22 (CH10)*
German National People's Party (DNVP) 273, 280
German Workers Party (DAP) 269–70
Germany
  African colonies and the First World War 21 (CH10)*, 22 (CH10)*
  Allied consolidation of victory 43–44 (CH11)*
  Armistice, 1918 33, 39–45 (CH10)*
  attempts at conquering Britain 11–13 (CH11)*
  Berlin Blockade 171–5, 176, 178, 236
  Berlin Wall 236–44, 248–53
  colonies 42–4
  Czechoslovakia invasion 131–2
  and David Lloyd George 36
  division after Second World War 157
  empire by 1918 30
  end of First World War 24
  High Seas Fleet 29 (CH10)*, 30 (CH10)*
  League of Nations 75
  loss to Allied Powers 22
  New Plan of 1934 284
  and oil 5
  Potsdam Conference 154–7, 176, 178
  reactions to First World War breakout 14
  Revolution, October 1918 43–45 (CH10)*
  Rome–Berlin Axis/Anti-Comintern Pact 95, 104, 112, 117, 124, 132
  success of 1918 offensive 40–43 (CH10)*
  technology of the First World War 17
  Treaty of Brest-Litovsk 23, 325, 326
  Treaty of Versailles 36, 42–4, 48–58, 106, 107
  Tripartite Agreement 20 (CH11)*
  U-boats 31 (CH10)*
  war at sea 31 (CH10)*
  'War Guilt' 40
  Zeppelin raids 20, 21, 11 (CH10)*
  see also First World War; Hitler; Nazi Germany; Second World War
Gerő, Ernő 225
Gestapo 283
ghettoes 294, 33 (CH11)*
Gierek, Edvard 244, 245
Glasnost reforms 249
Glass-Steagal Act 386
Gleichschaltung ('coordination') 283–4
Global North 3
  see also individual countries...
Global South 3
  see also individual countries...
global warming 6
Goebbels, Joseph 268, 274, 284, 286, 289
Goering, Hermann 44 (CH11)*
golden age of cinema 365
Gomułka, Władysław 225, 244, 245
Gorbachev, Mikhail 222, 248–53
Göring, Herman 274, 285
Gorky automotive plant 16 (CH11)*
Gottwald, Klement 229, 234
GPU (formerly the Cheka) 324, 328, 331, 335, 336
'Grand Alliance'
  Berlin Blockade 171–5
  break down in 1945 147–56

break down of in 1945 148
definitions 147
issues causing tension 156–7
Second Front 149
start of Cold War 166–8
Tehran Conference 150
US response to Soviet expansionism 164
wartime and post-war conferences 150–6
Yalta Conference 151–3, 177
see also Britain; Union of Soviet Socialist Republics; United States
Grand Fleet (British) 29 (CH10)*
The Grapes of Wrath (Steinbeck) 381
Great Depression of the 1930s 85, 87–100, 275–6, 284, 375–85, 390, 392–3
Great Powers 7, 10
  breakout of the First World War 10–11, 12, 13–15
  Rome–Berlin Axis/Anti-Comintern Pact 95, 104, 112, 117, 124, 132
  see also Allied Powers/Allies; Central Powers; individual countries...
Great War see First World War
Greater Asian Co-Prosperity 21 (CH11)*
Greece
  Corfu Incident 79–81
  Greek-Bulgarian confrontation 81–2
Green Army (Russian Civil War) 327
grenades 10
Grey, Sir Edward 13
Groener, Karl Eduard Wilhelm (General) 259
Gropius, Walther 267
Gross National Product 352
Grosz, George 267
growth
  impacts of 6
  see also economic impacts/economies
Grynszpan, Herschel 289
Guam, US bases attacked by Japan 24 (CH11)*
guerilla war
  Cuba 196
  see also Vietnam War
Guernica and attacks by the Luftwaffe 122
Gulf of Tonkin incident 208

The Hague Conference 8, 15
Haig, Sir Douglas (Field Marshal) 10 (CH10)*, 13 (CH10)*, 15 (CH10)*, 16 (CH10)*, 17 (CH10)*
Hamilton, Sir Ian 33 (CH10)*, 34 (CH10)*
Havel, Václav 230, 251
Health Organization 84
Henlein, Konrad 126
Heydrich, Reinhard 284, 289
Hideki Tojo 20 (CH11)*
High Command 12
High Seas Fleet (Germany) 29 (CH10)*, 30 (CH10)*
Himmler, Heinrich 274, 280, 283–4
Hindenburg Line 16 (CH10)*, 41 (CH10)*, 42 (CH10)*
Hirohito (Emperor) 45 (CH11)*
Hiroshima
  atomic bombs 158–60, 178, 41–42 (CH11)*
  visit by Emperor Hirohito, 1947 45 (CH11)*
Hitler, Adolf
  attempted assassination 283
  becoming chancellor 275–8
  biography 107

423

collapse of Germany, 1945 39–40 (CH11)*
consolidating power in 1933–34 279–81
D-Day 39 (CH11)*
death by suicide 40 (CH11)*
'Degenerate Art' exhibition 286
domination of Germany by 1934 269–81
foreign policy 103–43
    aims 108–10
    Allies declare war 134–7
    appeasement 113–32
    League of Nations 110–13
    Nazi–Soviet Pact 131, 132–4, 2 (CH11)*
    Treaty of Versailles 106–10
'Grand Alliance' 147, 148
Hans Frank 32 (CH11)*
invasion of Abyssinia 89, 92–5, 112
invasion of the Soviet Union 14–19 (CH11)*
kaiser's abdication, First World War 10
Mein Kampf ('My Struggle') 107, 271, 287
Munich (Beer Hall) Putsch 52, 56, 270–1
Munich Treaty and Sudetenland 229
presidential elections 276
Soviet control over Eastern Europe 222
trial and sentence following Munich Putsch 270–1
US attitude towards peace-making 158
Volkswagen ('people's car') 284, 285
Weimar Republic 263, 267
Young Plan 272–5
see also Second World War
Hitler Youth 291
Ho Chi Minh 203–4, 205
Ho Chi Minh Trail 206, 209, 214
Hoare-Laval Pact 93, 112
hobos 379
Hobsbawn, Eric 61
Höch, Hannah 267
Holland and NATO formation 174
Hollywood 365
    see also cinema
Holocaust *see* Final Solution
Holodomor (famine) 345
Home Front, First World War 20–2
Home Owners' Loan Corporation (HOLC) 387
home rule 126
homelessness 362, 379, 382
    see also Great Depression of the 1930s; poverty; unemployment
homosexuality 288
Honecker, Erich 251
Hong Kong, US bases attacked by Japan 24 (CH11)*
Honour Cross of the German Mother 293
Hoover Dam 384
Hoover, Herbert 357, 383–4
Hornet (USS) 25 (CH11)*
Hugenburg, Alfred 273
humanitarianism 73, 83–7
'The Hundred Days' of Roosevelt 386
Hungary
    Communist Party 225
    under USSR control 162, 224–9
    see also Austro-Hungarian Empire
Husain-McMahon agreement, 1915 26 (CH10)*
hydroelectric dams 339, 340, 384
hydrogen cyanide (Zyklon B) 295, 35 (CH11)*
hyperinflation 56–7, 265–6

ICBMs (Inter-Continental Ballistic Missiles) 196, 237, 252
Iceland
    NATO formation 174
    Reykjavik summit, 1986 250
ideologies 8, 147–8, 287
ILO (International Labour Organization) 84–5
immigration, intolerance in US society 367–73
imports 5
    tariffs 379
IMTFE (International Military Tribunal for the Far East) 46 (CH11)*
inauguration 385–6
independence of women in the 1920s 374
Indian troops of the British Empire 20 (CH10)*
Indochina 203–6, 20 (CH11)*
indoctrination 192, 291, 292
    see also propaganda
industrial recovery
    New Deal 391
        alphabet agencies 387
industrialisation
    impacts of 6
    Joseph Stalin 342–3
industry and industrial workers
    Russia's social structure 306
    see also individual industries...; workers
infantry 10 (CH10)*
inflation 55, 56–7, 265–6
informants 269
Inter-Continental Ballistic Missiles (ICBMs) 196, 237, 252
Intermediate Nuclear Forces (INF) 250
International Labour Organization (ILO) 84–5
International Military Tribunal for the Far East (IMTFE) 46 (CH11)*
intolerance in the US 367–73
    Black Americans 369
    immigration 367–8
    Ku Klux Klan 370
    race riots 370–1
    'Red Scare' 369
    religious 371–3
invasion of the Ruhr (1922–1923) 55, 56, 265, 266
investments 355
Iran under USSR control 163
Iron Curtain 163, 164, 173, 250
iron industry 339, 340, 355
'island hopping' ('leapfrogging') 41 (CH11)*
Isoroku Yamamoto (Admiral) 20 (CH11)*, 21 (CH11)*, 25 (CH11)*
Italy
    Allied Powers' advance through 37–38 (CH11)*
    Arab Revolt 27 (CH10)*
    Corfu incident 79–81
    Council of Four 38
    invasion of Abyssinia 89, 92–5, 112
    League of Nations 75, 79–81, 89, 92–5, 96
    NATO formation 174
    Spanish Civil War 121
    Treaty of London 29, 47
    Treaty of Versailles 47
    Tripartite Agreement 20 (CH11)*
    see also Mussolini

Jackson, Jesse 380
Japan
    Allied victory in the First World War 23–25 (CH10)*

atomic bombs 158–60, 178
Communist Party 46 (CH11)*
deterioration of US relationships 19–20 (CH11)*
First World War becoming a global conflict 18
invasion of Manchuria 111
Korean War 186, 189–90
League of Nations 75
Manchurian crisis 89–92, 111
occupation by Allied Powers 43 (CH11)*, 45–46 (CH11)*
Rome–Berlin Axis/Anti-Comintern Pact 95, 104, 112, 117, 124, 132
Russo–Japanese War 309
Second World War 19–20*
    and Allied victory 40–43 (CH11)*
    control of its impacts 32 (CH11)*
    initial stages 24–25 (CH11)*
    Pearl Harbor 20 (CH11)*, 21–23 (CH11)*
    resistance movements 37 (CH11)*
Treaty of Versailles 47
Tripartite Agreement 20 (CH11)*
Jaruzelski, Wojciech (General) 246
jazz clubs 364
The Jazz Singer (Jolson) 365
Jellicoe (Admiral) 29 (CH10)*, 30 (CH10)*
Jewish communities 282, 287, 288–9
    anti-Semitism 107, 108, 34 (CH11)*
    Final Solution 294, 295–6, 33–35 (CH11)*
    Wannsee Conference 295–6
    war and life in Nazi Germany 294
John Paul II (Pope) 245
Johnson, Lyndon B. 208, 209, 214
Jolson, Al 365
journalism 95
    see also newspapers
Judaism 14 (CH11)*
Judenrat 34 (CH11)*
    see also anti-Semitism
'July Days' (1917), Russia 322
justices 260
    see also Supreme Court

kaiser (emperor/king) 10
    see also abdication; individual rulers...
Kamenev, Lev 323, 333, 334, 336
Kandinski, Wassily 267
Kania, Stanisław 244, 246
Kapp Putsch, 1920 52, 263
Kapp, Wolfgang 263
Kemal, Mustafa 33 (CH10)*
Kennan, George 164
Kennedy, John F.
    Bay of the Pigs 197
    crisis of October, 1961 242
    Cuban Missile Crisis 196, 198–203, 238, 239
    U2 spy planes 238
    Vienna Summit 197, 240
    Vietnam War 206–7
Kennedy, Robert 199, 200
Kent State University protest 210, 211
Kerensky, Alexander (justice minister) 319, 322
Khrushchev, Nikita 225
    Berlin Wall construction 236–7, 238, 240
    Cuban Missile Crisis 196, 198–203, 238, 239
    end of Korean War 193
    'secret speech of 1956 229, 250

Index

Soviet control of Czechoslovakia 235
Soviet control of Hungary 225, 227, 235
U2 spy planes 238
Vienna Summit 197, 240
Kiel mutiny, Germany 1918 259, 44 (CH10)*
Kim Il-Sung 187, 188
'*Kinder, Küche, Kirche*' ('children, kitchen, church') 293
Kirov, Sergei 335, 336
Kissinger, Henry 212
Kitchener (Lord) 16 (CH10)*, 33 (CH10)*
Klee, Paul 267
Kolchak (Admiral) 328
kolkhozes (farms) 341
Komsomol women 344, 345
Korea
   annexation 19 (CH11)*
   passenger jet shot down by Soviets 252
Korean War, 1950–53 185–95
   background 185–6
   causes 186–8
   course of 190–3
   end of 193–5
   US reaction to 189–90
Kornilov Affair, September 1917 322
KPD political party
   Adolf Hitler becoming chancellor 278
   Allied consolidation of victory 43 (CH11)*
   Depression in Germany, 1929–33 275–6
   Enabling Act 280
   persecution of peoples by the Nazis 287
   Reichstag fire 279
   worker policies of the Nazi Party 293
Kreditanstaldt (Austrian bank) 275
Kreisau Circle 283
Krenz, Egon 251
Kriegsmachine (navy) 29 (CH10)*, 30 (CH10)*
   see also Wehrmacht
Kristallnacht ('Night of Broken Glass') 289
Kronstadt naval base and sailors 322, 328, 330
Ku Klux Klan 370, 371, 372
kulaks (rich peasants) 305, 341–2, 343–4

laissez-faire policy 357, 383
Lancashire fusiliers 8 (CH10)*
Länder (regions) 260
landmines 240
   see also mines
Landon, Alf 390
Lang, Fritz 268
Laos 212, 214
Laos during the Vietnam War 206–7
latrines 8 (CH10)*
Lawrence, T.E. ('Lawrence of Arabia') 27 (CH10)*
League of Nations 45, 67–100
   aims 69
   Åland Islands crisis 78–9
   Commission for Refugees 83
   Corfu Incident 79–81
   covenant(s) 69–70
   delegations 75–6
   Depression of the 1930s 87–100
   failure of collective security 72
   failures in the 1930s 110–13
   financial issues 73
   Greek-Bulgarian confrontation 81–2
   humanitarian work 83–7
   ILO 84–5

Korean War 193
   membership and failure 71–6
   organisational issues 71, 73
   peacekeeping in the 1920s 77–82
   self-determination 34
   Slavery Commission 86–7
   Vilna crisis 77
   weaknesses 71, 72
   Weimar Republic 261
Lebensborn programme 293
Lebensraum ('living space') 107, 108, 147, 3 (CH11)*, 14 (CH11)*
left-wing politics
   Weimar Republic 262, 263
   see also Democratic Party
Lemke, William 390
Lend–Lease programme 147, 148, 154, 40 (CH11)*
Lenin, Vladimir 321
   Civil War 324, 325
   Constituent Assembly elections 325
   'July Days' 322
   leadership struggle between Stalin and Trotsky 332–5
   New Economic Policy 331
   November Revolution 323–4
   Treaty of Brest-Litovsk 23, 325
leprosy 84
liberal intelligentsia 305
Liebknecht, Karl 262
Liège, Belgium 5 (CH10)*
life expectancy across the 20th century 3
Lindbergh, Charles 359
Lithuania, Memel Territory 134
Lloyd George, David 31–8, 46
Lon Nol (Cambodian ruler) 210
London
   Blitzkrieg ('lightning war') 122, 2 (CH11)*, 13 (CH11)*, 26 (CH11)*, 27 (CH11)*
   treaty 29, 47
   Zeppelin raids 20, 21, 11 (CH10)*
Long, Huey 390
Los Angeles Olympics, 1980 251
Low, David 124, 130, 141
Ludendorff Offensive 41 (CH10)*
Luftwaffe 122, 285
   Battle of Britain, 1940 13–14 (CH11)*
   Battle of Dunkirk 4 (CH11)*
   Battle of Stalingrad 16 (CH11)*, 17 (CH11)*
   Operation Sea Lion 11 (CH11)*
   see also Blitzkrieg; Wehrmacht
Lusitania (passenger liner) 31 (CH10)*
Luxembourg and NATO formation 174
Luxemburg, Rosa 262, 263
Lvov, Prince (prime minister) 319
lynching 370
Lytton Report 91

MacArthur, Douglas (General) 189, 190, 191–2, 40 (CH11)*, 45 (CH11)*, 46 (CH11)*
machine guns 10 (CH10)*
Macmillan, Harold 237
Macmillan, Margaret 61
McNamara, Robert 196
MAD (Mutually Assured Destruction) 196
Maginot Line 3 (CH11)*
Magnitogorsk iron and steel works 339, 340
Malaya, US bases attacked by Japan 24 (CH11)*

Malaya and Japanese forces 24 (CH11)*, 32 (CH11)*
Malayan People's Anti-Japanese Army (MPAJA) 37 (CH11)*
Manchuria invasion by Japan 111
Manchurian crisis, 1931 89–92
mandates 42
Mao Zedong 90, 185, 186
maritime warfare
   Admiral Isoroku Yamamoto 20 (CH11)*, 21 (CH11)*, 25 (CH11)*
   High Seas Fleet (Germany) 29 (CH10)*, 30 (CH10)*
   Kriegsmachine 29 (CH10)*, 30 (CH10)*
   Kronstadt naval base and sailors 322, 328, 330
   Lend–Lease programme 164
   naval supremacy 36
   Pearl Harbor 20 (CH11)*, 21–23 (CH11)*
   Royal Navy (Britain) 28–29 (CH10)*, 30 (CH10)*, 34 (CH10)*, 4–7 (CH11)*, 11 (CH11)*
   submarines and U-boats 31 (CH10)*
Marshall Plan 168–9, 178, 179, 229
martial law 246
Marx, Karl 307
Masaryk, Jan 229, 230, 234
mass media
   Nazi regime 286–7
   see also propaganda
Masurian Lakes, First Battle of 35 (CH10)*
mechanisation in farming 355
Medina, Saudi Arabia 27 (CH10)*
Mein Kampf ('My Struggle') 107, 271, 287
Memel Territory, dispute with Lithuania 134
Mensheviks 307
merchant ships 31 (CH10)*
Metropolis (Lang) 268
Michael (King) 162
middle classes of Russian Revolution, 1905 315
Middle East 4
militarism 104
military
   Freikorps 263
   opposition to the Nazi regime 283
   reductions of power 40
   sanctions, League of Nations 72
   Tsarism and First World War 315
   USA's loss of Vietnam War 214
   veterans and US government 384
   victims of The Purges, Russia 336
   see also individual conflicts...
Miliukov, Paul (foreign minister) 319
Mindszenty (Cardinal) 224, 227
minerals/natural resources 355
miners
   standard of living 362
   strikes, Solidarity (*Solidarnosc*) 246
mines 240, 31 (CH10)*
   minesweepers 32 (CH10)*
Ministry for Popular Enlightenment and Propaganda 286
minority groups 289–90
   Asian immigrants in the US 367
   Black Americans and US intolerance 359, 362, 365, 369, 370–1
   black populations of Weimar Germany 290
   Final Solution 289, 294, 295–6, 33–35 (CH11)*

intolerance in the US 367–73
Jewish communities 282, 287, 288–9, 294, 295–6, 33–35 (CH11)*
Roma people 289, 35 (CH11)*
Treaty of Versailles, long-term consequences 106
Vilna and The League of Nations 77
Minuteman missiles 237
'Miracle of Dunkirk' 5 (CH11)*
miscarriage(s) of justice 369
Missile Crisis, Cuban 196, 198–203, 238, 239
mobilisation 11, 13
monarchies 2
Monbijou Women's clubs 288
'Monkey Trial', Dayton, Tennessee 372
moral disapproval (League of Nations) 72
Moscow Conference , 1947 172
Moscow Olympics, 1980 251
MPAJA (Malayan People's Anti-Japanese Army) 37 (CH11)*
Muhammad Ali (born Cassius Clay) 212
Müller, Herman 276, 277
Munich Agreement, 1938 127–30, 132, 141, 229
Munich (Beer Hall) Putsch, 1923 52, 56, 270–1
munitions 21
Mussolini, Benito
    Allied Powers' advance through Italy 37–38 (CH11)*
    Anschluss ('union') 41, 117–20, 124
    biography 110
    invasion of Abyssinia 89, 92–3, 94, 95, 112
    Japanese invasion of Manchuria 111
    League of Nations 89, 92–5, 96
    Munich Agreement 128
    photo of leader with officers 105
    Spanish Civil War 121
mustard gas 93, 12 (CH10)*
mutinies 22, 24, 259, 44 (CH10)*
Mutually Assured Destruction (MAD) 196
My Lai Massacre 210

Nagasaki atomic bomb 7, 158–60, 178, 41–42 (CH11)*
Nagy, Imre 224, 227, 234, 235, 236
Namibia (formerly South West Africa) 21 (CH10)*, 22–23 (CH10)*
Nansen, Fridtjof 83
napalm 194, 209
National Industrial Recovery Act (NIRA) 387, 391
National Labour Relations Act (NLRA) 388, 391
national minorities, effects of Joseph Stalin's economic policy 345
National Recovery Administration (NRA) 387, 388
National Security Council (NSC) 186, 199
National Socialist German Workers Party (NSDAP) 269, 270, 271, 293
    see also Nazi Germany
nationalism 8, 91
    Ku Klux Klan 370, 371, 372
    Spanish Civil War 121–3
    see also Nazi Germany
NATO (North Atlantic Treaty Organization) 146, 174–5
natural gas 5
natural resources 355
    see also oil industry

naval warfare
    supremacy 36
    see also maritime warfare
Nazi Germany, 1918–45 258–300
    Allied consolidation of power 43–44 (CH11)*
    Anschluss ('union') 41, 117–20, 124
    anti-Semitism 107, 108
    Armistice, 1918 33, 39–45 (CH10)*
    and civilian populations in Europe 32–35 (CH11)*
    collapse, 1945 39–40 (CH11)*
    concentration camps 282, 284, 295–6, 33 (CH11)*, 34–35 (CH11)*
    control of Germany, 1933–45 281–91
    denazification by Allied Powers 43–44 (CH11)*
    Final Solution 289, 294, 295–6, 33–35 (CH11)*
    Gestapo 283
    living in 291–6
    main leaders of the 1920s 274
    Munich Agreement 127–30, 132, 141, 229
    Nazi–Soviet Pact 131, 132–4, 2 (CH11)*
    Normandy invasion 36 (CH11)*, 39 (CH11)*
    Nuremberg Trials 43 (CH11)*, 44 (CH11)*
    opposition to 281–5
    persecution of peoples 287–90
    policy of the 1920s 269–70
    Potsdam Conference 154–7
    The Purges, Russia 336
    recovery from First World War 259–60
    resistance movements in Europe 36–37 (CH11)*
    Schutzstaffel – 'protection squad' (SS) 272, 280, 283, 289, 293, 294, 295
    Soviet control over Eastern Europe 222
    Stürm Abteilung (SA) 269–70, 271, 272, 280, 283, 287, 288
    success before 1930 270–2
    Treaty of Versailles 260–6
    Weimar Republic 259–69
    see also Hitler; Wehrmacht
Nazi–Soviet Pact 131, 132–4, 2 (CH11)*
Neutrality Pact 20 (CH11)*
New Deal (Roosevelt) 385–93
    First New Deal 385–8
    opposition to 389–92
    Second New Deal after 1933 388–9
New Economic Policy (NEP), Russia 331, 339
New Plan of 1934, Germany 284
new world order 28
New York Roxy (picture house) 365
New York Stock Exchange 376
New Zealand (ANZAC) 24 (CH10)*, 33 (CH10)*, 34 (CH10)*, 42 (CH10)*
newspapers
    anti-Vietnam War message 212
    Munich Agreement 141
    Nazi propaganda 286
    Treaty of Versailles 35, 50, 59
    see also propaganda
Ngo Dinh Diem 205, 206, 207
Nicholas II (Tsar) 302, 304, 305
    Eastern Front 36 (CH10)*
    and First World War 315–16
    Russian Revolution, 1905 309–15
Niemöller, Martin 287

Night of the Long Knives 280
NIRA (National Industrial Recovery Act) 387, 391
Nixon, Richard 210–13, 214
    détente ('relaxation') 214, 251
NKVD (formerly the GPU) 324, 328, 331, 335, 336
NLRA (National Labour Relations Act) 388, 391
no man's land 242, 243, 9 (CH10)*
nobility/rich society 315, 390
    tsars 2, 302, 304, 305, 309–16, 318, 36 (CH10)*
    see also individual kings;
non-combatant 19
Normandy invasion, 1944 36 (CH11)*, 39 (CH11)*
North Atlantic Treaty Organization (NATO) 146, 174–5
    see also individual countries...
Norway and NATO formation 174
'November criminals' 261
November Revolution, Russia 1917 323
Novotný, Antonin 230
NRA (National Recovery Administration) 387, 388
NSC (National Security Council) 186, 199
NSDAP see National Socialist German Workers Party
Nuremberg Trials 43 (CH11)*, 44 (CH11)*

October Manifesto, 1905 312, 314
oil industry 4–5, 93, 355
Okhrana
    abolishment 319
    government control 308
Oklahoma race riots 370–1
Olympic Games 251, 289
Omaha beach, Normandy 39 (CH11)*
Operation Bagration 40 (CH11)*
Operation Barbarossa 14–15 (CH11)*, 19 (CH11)*
Operation Dynamo 4 (CH11)*, 5 (CH11)*
Operation Linebacker I and II 212
Operation Michael 41 (CH10)*, 42 (CH10)*
Operation Overlord 39 (CH11)*
Operation Rolling Thunder 209
Operation Sea Lion, 1940 11–12 (CH11)*
opposition(s)
    Politburo and Stalin 338
    Red Army and Hungarian control 224
    to Nazi Germany 281–5
    to New Deal (Roosevelt) 389–92
    to Tsarism 307
    see also protest; Revolution; strikes
organised crime 373
Orthodox Faith, Russian Empire 303, 308
Ottoman Empire 16, 18, 26, 28, 30
    Arab Revolt 25–27 (CH10)*
    Gallipoli campaign 32–34 (CH10)*

pacifism 13, 15
Pact of Steel 132
pact(s) 93
    Pact of Steel 132
    see also individual pacts...
Palach, Jan 232
Palestine Campaign, 1917–18 27 (CH10)*
paramilitaries 270

Index

Paris
    Nazi invasion 41 (CH10)*, 42 (CH10)*
    summit 38, 79, 238
    see also Treaty of Versailles
partisans 222
partition(s) 150
passive resistance 56
passports 83
Patch, Harry 2
patriotism 13
peacekeeping/peace-making 7–8
    diplomacy 61
    Korean War 192
    League of Nations 77–82, 97, 98
    Soviet attitude to Cold War 157–8
    treaties 28
    United Nations 98
    US attitude to Cold War 158–60
    Vietnam War 212
    Weimar Republic 261
    see also individual treaties and conferences...
Pearl Harbor 20 (CH11)*, 21–23 (CH11)*
peasantry
    collectivisation 341–2
    countryside government policy 314
    execution of Martemyan Ryutin 338
    kulaks (rich peasants) 305, 341–2, 343–4
    Russia's social structure 305, 306
    War Communism, Russia 328
people's republics 160, 227
Percival, Arthur (General) 25 (CH11)*
Perestroika reforms 249
'Permanent Revolution' policy, Russia 334
persecution 162
Pershing, John J. (General) 40 (CH10)*
personality cult and propaganda
    (Joseph Stalin) 337
Pétain, Philippe (Marshal) 15 (CH11)*,
    16 (CH10)*, 9–10 (CH11)*
Petrograd, Russia 316, 317–18, 322, 323
petrol 4
Phan Thi Kim Phúc 209
Philippines 214, 237, 19 (CH11)*, 24 (CH11)*
phoney war (Second World War) 448*
phosgene gas 12 (CH10)*
picture houses (cinema) 268, 365
'picture palaces' 365
plebiscites 40, 115, 124, 127
Pleiku (US base) 209
plenary sessions 38
Poland 162, 2 (CH11)*, 3 (CH11)*, 32 (CH11)*,
    33–35 (CH11)*
    Auschwitz concentration camp 35 (CH11)*
    civilian populations under Nazi rule 294,
        32 (CH11)*, 33–35 (CH11)*
    decline of Soviet influence in Eastern Europe
        244–8
    government installed by the USSR 176
    'Grand Alliance' 156
    invasion by Germany 134–7, 3 (CH11)*
    Prague Spring 231, 232, 233, 234, 235, 236
    Solidarity (Solidarnosc) 244–8
    Tehran Conference 150
    Warsaw ghettoes 33 (CH11)*
    Warsaw Pact 146, 175, 225, 227, 231, 234,
        235, 236
    Yalta Conference 151
Politburo 225, 338

political impacts/parties
    assassinations 9–10, 12, 13, 263–4, 283
    execution of Martemyan Ryutin 338
    government control in Russia 308
    left-wing politics/Weimar Republic 262, 263
    murders in Germany 53
    opposition to the Nazi regime 283–5
    persecution of peoples by the Nazis 287
    right-wing politics/Weimar Republic 263–4
    Treaty of Versailles on Germany 52–4
    tsarism and First World War 316
    Tsarist government 304–5
    victims of The Purges, Russia 336
    violence due to Depression in Germany 275
    Weimar Republic 54, 262, 263–4
    see also individual political parties and
        figures...
Pope John Paul II 245
Popiełuszko, Jerzy 246
Portugal and NATO formation 174
post-war conferences see wartime and post-war
    conferences
Potsdam Conference, 1945 154–7, 176, 178
poverty
    alphabet agencies 386–7
    Black Americans 362
    hobos 379
    homelessness 362, 379, 382
    unemployment 362, 379, 386–7, 392–3
    see also Great Depression of the 1930s;
        peasantry
Powers, Gary 238
Poznán, Poland uprising, 1956 225
Prague Spring, 1968 231, 232, 233, 234, 235, 236
precedent(s) 78
presidency
    Adolf Hitler 280–1
    elections, Germany 1932 276
    Roosevelt's inauguration 385–6
    Weimar Republic 260
    see also individual presidents...
Princip, Gavrilo 10–11, 12, 13
prison camps and POWs 17, 192, 17 (CH11)*
Prohibition Era 373, 386
propaganda 22, 105, 268, 275, 286, 337
proportional representation 260
protest
    against Antonin Novotný 230
    against Vietnam War 210, 211, 212
    collapse of the Soviet Union 250
    'July Days', July 1917, Russia 322
    Kiel Mutiny and the German Revolution
        44 (CH10)*
    Prague Spring 231, 232, 233, 235
    Reichstag fire 279
    Russian Revolution, 1905 309–15
    self-immolations 207, 232
    Solidarity (Solidarnosc) 244–8
    see also Revolution; strikes
Protestantism
    intolerance in the US 371, 372
    and Nazi persecutions 287
    opposition to Nazi regime 282
Provisional Government of Russia 319–21, 322,
    323
proxy wars 145
Public Works Administration (PWA) 387
punitive definition 33
puppet rulers 90

'The Purges', Russia 335–7
putsch 52, 56, 263, 270–1
Pyongyang, North Korea 187, 194

Q ships 31 (CH10)*
'quarantine' (blockades) 199
quotas 32

RA see Resettlement Administration
race riots 370–1
racial stereotypes 365
    see also stereotypes
'racial theory' lessons 107, 108, 109
radio
    Nazi propaganda 286
    'Roaring Twenties' 366
    US economic boom 354
    see also propaganda
Radio Free Europe 227
RAF (Royal Air Force) 13–14 (CH11)*
railway industry 360
Rajchman, Ludwig 84
Rajk, László 224, 225
Rákosi, Mátyás 224, 225, 234
Rasputin, Gregory 316
Rathenau, Walther 53, 263
ratify definition 33
rationing see food supplies/shortages
Reagan, Ronald
    collapse of the Soviet Union 250, 251
    détente ('relaxation') 251
    'Second Cold War' 252
    Solidarity (Solidarnosc), Poland,
        1980–89 245
real wages 354
rearmament 111, 114, 284–5
reconnaissance 20 (CH11)*
Reconstruction Finance Corporation (Herbert
    Hoover) 384
recruitment 22, 16 (CH10)*, 19 (CH10)*
Red Army
    advance from the east, Second
        World War 40 (CH11)*
    Allied Powers' advance through Italy
        37 (CH11)*
    Battle of Stalingrad 16–18 (CH11)*
    Civil War 324, 327, 328
    control over Eastern Europe 156, 160,
        222, 224
    D-Day 40 (CH11)*
    victims of The Purges 336
    victory at Stalingrad 18 (CH11)*
    War Communism 328
Red Orchestra spy networks 283
'Red Scare', 1919–20 369
'Red Terror' 328
referenda 150
reforms
    collapse of the USSR 248–50, 251
    occupation of Japan 46 (CH11)*
    Prague Spring 231, 232, 233, 234, 235, 236
    Solidarity (Solidarnosc), Poland, 1980–89 246
    see also protest; Revolution; strikes
Refugees, Commission for 83
regions/Länder 260
regulation(s) 84
    see also individual regulations...
Reich ('empire') 108, 115, 117, 131, 287, 288,
    294, 3 (CH11)*

see also Nazi Germany
Reichstag 60, 259, 276, 277
Reichstag fire 279
religion
    intolerance in the US 371–3
    Joseph Stalin's control over the USSR 338
    Judaism 14 (CH11)*
    persecution of peoples by the Nazis 287
    see also Catholicism; Church; Jewish communities; Protestantism
reparations 23, 40, 57, 265–6, 273
Reparations Commission for Germany (Treaty of Versailles) 60
Reparations Committee, 1921 265
Reparations Committee, 1924 267
repatriation 152
Republican Party
    definitions 32
    laissez-faire policy 357, 383
    opposition to New Deal 389–90
    Spanish Civil War 121–3
    Woodrow Wilson 32
republics 10
    see also individual republics...
reserve troops 6 (CH10)*
resettlement 83
Resettlement Administration (RA) 388
resistance movements
    Second World War, 1939–c. 1945 33 (CH11)*, 35–37 (CH11)*
    see also opposition
Revolt, Arab, First World War 25–27 (CH10)*
Revolution
    establishment of Weimar Republic, 1918 259
    Germany, October 1918 43–45 (CH10)*
    November Revolution, Russia 323–4, 36 (CH10)*
    'Permanent Revolution', Russia 334
    Russia, 1905 309–15
    Russia, March 1917 317–18
rewriting history, Joseph Stalin 337
Reykjavik summit, 1986 250
Rhee, Syngman 187, 189, 190, 193
Rhenish Republic 56
Rhineland 39, 46, 124
    1936 115–17
rich society 315, 390
    see also nobility/rich society
rights 260
    voting rights 374
right-wing politics 52
    Weimar Republic 263–4
    see also Republican Party
riots *see* protest; strikes
'Roaring Twenties' 364–7
Röhm, Ernst 274, 275, 280
'rollback' 164, 191–2
Roma people 289, 35 (CH11)*
    see also Final Solution
Romania 162, 176
Rome–Berlin Axis, 1936 104, 117, 124, 132
Roosevelt, Franklin Delano 383–93
    attitude to peace-making 158
    death and replacement 154
    'Grand Alliance' 150, 151, 153, 154, 156
    inauguration 385–6
    New Deal 385–93
    Pearl Harbor 22–23 (CH11)*
    Russian Civil War 185

Second Front ('Grand Alliance') 149
    Tehran Conference 150
    Yalta Conference 151, 153
Roxy (New York picture house) 365
Royal Air Force (RAF) 13–14 (CH11)*
Royal Navy (Britain) 28–29 (CH10)*, 34 (CH10)*, 4–7 (CH11)*, 11 (CH11)*
Ruhr, invasion of (1922–23) 55, 56, 265, 266
rural life
    after 1905 Russian Revolution 314
    USA and the Great Depression 381–2
Russia
    1905–41 301–50
        Civil War 185, 323–30
        Joseph Stalin 339–45
        Tsarist regime collapse, 1917 303–18
    Eastern Front 35–36 (CH10)*
    empire by 1918 30
    German views of Slavs 108
    government control 308
    population and social structure 1914–17 305–6
    Revolution, 1905 309–15
    Revolution of March 1917 317–18
    Russification 303, 345
    Russo–Japanese War 309
    Schlieffen Plan 3–6 (CH10)*
    Spring Offensive, 1918 36 (CH10)*
    Treaty of Brest-Litovsk 23, 325, 326
    Treaty of Versailles 47
    see also Cold War; individual Russian leaders...; Union of Soviet Socialist Republics
Russification 303, 345
Russo–Japanese War 309
Ruth, Babe 366
Ryutin, Martemyan 338

Saar plebiscite, 1935 115, 124
Saarland 40
Sacco, Nicola 369
Saigon
    evacuation 213
    self-immolation of Thic Quang Duc 207
    US embassy 209
St Petersburg strikes, Russia, 1905 309
Samsonov (Russian Commander) 35 (CH10)*
sanctions 72
sanitation 84
Sargent, John Singer 14 (CH10)*
scapegoats 279
Schacht, Hjaldmar 284
Schlieffen Plan 3–6 (CH10)*
    Belgium 5 (CH10)*
    failure 6 (CH10)*
    First Battle of Ypres 6 (CH10)*
    modifications 4 (CH10)*
    role of BEF 5–6 (CH10)*
    trenches 6 (CH10)*
Scholl, Hans & Sophie 282
Schumann, Hans Conrad 243
Schuschnigg, Kurt (Chancellor) 118
Schutzstaffel – 'protection squad' (SS) 272, 280, 283, 289, 293, 294, 295
Scopes, John 372
scuttle definition 46
SD (Nazi security police) 284, 293
sea lanes 25 (CH10)*
    see also maritime warfare

'search and destroy' missions 209, 210
Second Battle of Ypres 12 (CH10)*, 20 (CH10)*
'Second Cold War' 252
Second Five Year Plan 1933–37 339
Second Front ('Grand Alliance') 149
Second World War, 1939–c. 1945 7–8, 2–50 (CH11)*
    Asia-Pacific 1 (CH11)*, 19–26 (CH11)*, 35 (CH11)*, 37 (CH11)*
    deaths by country 179
    declaration of 134–7
    early development 2–19 (CH11)*
    Europe 1 (CH11)*, 2–19 (CH11)*, 26 (CH11)*, 27–31 (CH11)*, 32–37* (CH11)*
    invasion of Poland 134–7, 3 (CH11)*
    life in Nazi Germany 294–6
    New Deal 393
    and oil 5
    see also individual participating countries...
Secret Police 324, 328, 331, 335, 336
secret protocol(s) 132
Secretariat (League of Nations) 71–2
Security Council(s) 152
segregation 359, 369
    ghettoes 294, 33 (CH11)*
Selassie, Haile (Emperor of Abyssinia) 93, 94, 95
self-determination 33, 34
self-immolation as protest 207, 232
Seoul, South Korea 187, 194
Serbia, First World War breakout 10–11, 12, 13
serfs 305
share-croppers 362
shell shock 8 (CH10)*
shipbuilding industry 360
show trials 162
Sicily, invasion of, 1943 38 (CH11)*
siege of Tsingtao, 1914 23 (CH10)*, 24 (CH10)*
siege warfare 18
silos 198
Singapore and Japanese forces 24 (CH11)*, 25 (CH11)*
Sino–Japanese War (1894–95) 19 (CH11)*
Sinti people 35 (CH11)*
    see also Final Solution
skirmishes 92
skyscrapers 360
Slavery Commission 86–7
Slavs 108
Smith, Bessie 364
snipers 240
Social Democratic Party
    chancellors of Germany 276, 277
    Depression in Germany 275, 276
    Enabling Act 280
    formation of NATO 174
    Revolution of 1918 259
    Russian opposition to Tsarism 307
    SOPADE 283, 293
    worker policies of the Nazi Party 293
social impacts
    Depression of the 1930s 379–83
    Treaty of Versailles on Germany 49–52
    tsarism and First World War 316
    US society in the 1920s 364–75
    Wall Street Crash 1929 379–83
Social Security Act (SSA) 388, 391
Socialism/socialists 13
    opposition to Tsarism 307

Index

'Socialism in One Country' policy, Russia 334
Socialist Revolutionaries, Russia 307
Socialist Unity Party of 1946 174
see also individual Socialist countries...
Solidarity (*Solidarnosc*), Poland, 1980–89 244, 245–8
Solomon Islands 40 (CH11)*
SOPADE 293
South West African colonies 22–23 (CH10)*
sovereignty 40
Soviet Bloc 174
see also individual countries...
Soviet Bloc(s) 163
Soviet Union *see* Union of Soviet Socialist Republics
Soviets 311
Spanish Civil War, 1936–39 121–2
Spartacist Party 262, 263
SPD (Social Democrats of Germany) 174, 259, 275, 276, 277, 280, 283, 293
speakeasy bar 364
spectator sports 366, 369
speeches
  Depression in Germany, 1929–33 275
  'Iron Curtain' speech 164
  'secret speech of 1956' 229, 250
Speer, Albert 294
spies *see* espionage
Spring Offensive, 1918 36 (CH10)*
SSA (Social Security Act) 388, 391
Staewen, Gertrud 294
stalemates 18, 192, 3–18 (CH10)*
Stalin, Joseph
  attitude to peace-making 157–8, 159
  Battle of Stalingrad 16–18 (CH11)*
  Berlin Blockade 171–5
  biography 154
  blame for the Cold War 176–8
  collectivisation 341–2
  control over Eastern Europe 160–4, 222, 224, 225, 226
  D-Day 39 (CH11)*
  economic policies 339–45
  Five Year Plans 339–40
  gaining of power 332–8
  'Grand Alliance' 150, 151, 153, 154, 156, 177
  Korean War 187, 188
  leadership struggle with Trotsky 332–5
  Marshall Plan 168–9
  Nazi–Soviet Pact 131, 132–4, 2 (CH11)*
  Potsdam Conference 154–7, 176, 178
  the Purges 335–7
  Soviet advance from the east, Second World War 40 (CH11)*
  Spanish Civil War 121
  Tehran Conference 150
  US response to Soviet expansionism 164, 167
  Yalta Conference 151, 153, 176, 177
standard of living 4
  economy boom of the 1920s 352–64
  see also Great Depression of the 1930s
Statue of Liberty 367
Steel Pact 132
steel works 339, 340
Steinbeck, John 381
stereotyping 294, 365, 14 (CH11)*
Stevenson, Adlai 201

stock market crash 1929 275–6, 284, 375–85
  see also Great Depression of the 1930s
stockpiles 40
Strasser, Gregor (& Otto) 272, 277, 280
Strategic Defence Initiative (SDI) 252
'Strength Through Joy' programme 293
Stresemann, Gustav (Chancellor) 56–7, 266, 267, 268
strikes
  after Russian Revolution, 1905 314–15
  against troop mobilisation 13
  definition 13
  French resistance to Nazi occupation 37 (CH11)*
  German Revolution, 1918 43 (CH10)*, 44 (CH10)*
  hyperinflation in Germany 56
  Solidarity (*Solidarnosc*) 244–8
  Tsarism and St Petersburg 309
Stürm Abteilung (SA) 269–70, 271, 272, 280, 283, 287, 288
  Enabling Act 280
  Night of the Long Knives 280
submarines 31 (CH10)*
successor states 45, 106
Sudetenland 125–7, 229
summits 82
  see also individual summits...
'superpowers' (Great Powers) 7, 145, 242
  see also individual countries...
supply and demand 354
Supreme Court (US) 371, 388, 391–2
Sykes-Picot Agreement, 1916 26 (CH10)*, 27 (CH10)*
synthetics industry 360

'talkies' (cinema) 365
tanks 228, 10 (CH10)*
tariffs 32, 379
technology of the War Machine 17
Tehran Conference, 1943 150
Tellini, Enrico 79
Tennessee Valley Authority (TVA) 387
'The Terror'/The Purges, Russia 335–7
'terror-famine' 345
Terwiel, Maria 294
Tet Offensive 209
textile industry 360, 362
Thailand 214, 24 (CH11)*, 32 (CH11)*
Thälmann, Ernst 276
Thatcher, Margaret 250, 252
theory of evolution 372
Thic Quang Duc 207
Third Five Year Plan, 1939–41 340
Third Reich 115, 117, 118
  see also Nazi Germany
Thompson, Hugh 210
Thompson, Tommy 199
timber industry 355
Tito, Josef 222, 223
Tokyo war crimes trials 46 (CH11)*
total war 20
  see also First World War
totalitarianism 104, 290, 338
  see also dictatorships; fascism
Townsend, Francis 390, 391
tractor plants 16 (CH11)*
trade unions 175, 244–8
  see also workers

trafficking 84
Trang Bang village 209
Treaty of Brest-Litovsk 23, 325, 326
Treaty of London 29, 47
Treaty of Versailles 27–66
  aims and motives 31–8
  Anschluss, 1938 117
  Danzig (Polish city) 134
  delegations 31–8, 45, 46, 47
  demands of the victors 38–47
  impact on Germany up to 1923 48–58
  justification 58–62
  long-term consequences 106–10
  persecution of Jewish communities by the Nazis 288
  public expectation 28
  rearmament, 1935 114
  Rhineland, 1936 116
  Slavery Commission 86
  tearing up of 108
  territorial changes 41
  Weimar Republic 260–6, 268
trenches 10, 6 (CH11)*, 7–10 (CH10)*
trials/tribunals
  conscription/conscientious objectors 19
  court martials 40 (CH11)*
  definitions 19
  IMTFE 46 (CH11)*
  Nuremberg Trials 43 (CH11)*, 44 (CH11)*
  show trials 162
  war crimes 43 (CH11)*, 44 (CH11)*, 46 (CH11)*
Tripartite Agreement 20 (CH11)*
Triple Alliance *see* Central Powers
Triple Entente *see* Allied Powers/Allies
Trizone/Trizonia (economic unit) 171, 174, 178
Trotsky, Leon 312, 322, 325, 327, 332–5
Trotsky supporters and The Purges 336
Truman, Harry S.
  atomic bomb 158–60
  atomic bombs 41–42 (CH11)*
  biography 154
  Cuban Missile Crisis 196
  defense of role in Cold War 178–80
  'Grand Alliance' 154
  Korean War 185, 186, 189–90, 191–2, 193
  Potsdam Conference 154–7, 176, 178
  Truman Doctrine 168, 172
  US response to Soviet expansionism 164, 165, 167
  Yalta Conference 177
Tsarist regime and its collapse, 1917 303–18
tsars 2, 302, 304, 305, 309–16, 318, 36 (CH10)*
Tulsa race riots 370–1
Turkey
  Gallipoli campaign 32–34 (CH10)*
  invasion by Russia 165
  under USSR control 163
  see also Ottoman Empire
turning point(s) 18 (CH11)*, 25–26 (CH10)*
TVA (Tennessee Valley Authority) 387

U2 spy planes 196, 198, 200, 238, 239
U-boats 31 (CH10)*
Ukraine 343, 345
Ulbricht, Walter 24 (CH10)
ultimatums 24 (CH10)*
unemployment
  alphabet agencies 386–7

economy boom of the 1920s 362
hobos 379
and the New Deal 392–3
see also Great Depression of the 1930s
Union of Soviet Socialist Republics (USSR)
    advance from the east, Second World War 40 (CH11)*
    Anti-Comintern Pact 95, 112, 117
    attitude to peace-making 157–8
    becoming a superpower 7
    blame for the Cold War 176–8
    control over Eastern Europe, 1948–c.1989 221–57
        Berlin Wall construction 236–44
        Czechoslovakian situation, 1968 224, 229–33, 234–6
        Hungarian situation, 1956 224–9, 234–6
        Mikhail Gorbachev and collapse of Soviet Union 248–53
        Solidarity in Poland 244–8
    Cuban Missile Crisis 196, 198–203
    D-Day 40 (CH11)*
    definitions 7
    democratisation of Nazi Germany 43 (CH11)*
    denazification of Germany 43–44 (CH11)*
    détente 214, 251
    end of Korean War 193
    gaining control of Eastern Europe 160–4
    invasion by Hitler, 1941 14–19 (CH11)*
    Jewish people in Poland 294
    League of Nations 75
    Moscow Conference 172
    Mutually Assured Destruction 196
    Nazi–Soviet Pact 131, 132–4, 2 (CH11)*
    Neutrality Pact 20 (CH11)*
    Olympic Games boycotts 251
    reaction to the Marshall Plan 168–9
    Spanish Civil War 121
    Treaty of Versailles, long-term consequences 106, 107
    war and life in Nazi Germany 294
    see also individual Soviet leaders...
United Nations Security Council (UNSC) 163, 189
United Nations (UN)
    Berlin Wall and East Germany 238
    collapse of the Soviet Union 250
    Cuban Missile Crisis 201
    ICBMs 237
    Korean War 187, 191–2, 193
    Korean War 191–2
    League of Nations 72
    occupation of Japan 46 (CH11)*
    peacekeeping 98
    Tehran Conference 150
United States
    1919–41 351–96
        economy boom of the 1920s 352–64
        Franklin Delano Roosevelt 383–93
        Prohibition Era 373
        societal change in the 1920s 364–75
        Wall Street Crash 1929 375–85
    Armistice, 1918 39–45 (CH10)*
    atomic bombs on Japan 7, 158–60, 178, 41–42 (CH11)*
    attitude to peace-making 158–60
    Battle of Midway, 1942 20 (CH11)*, 25–26 (CH11)*

Berlin Blockade 171–5
blame for Cold War 178–80
CIA 197, 206–7, 210, 238
containment of communism 184–220
    events in Cuba, 1959–62 196–203
    and Korea, 1950–53 185–95
    Vietnam, 1955–75 203–15
containment policy 158, 186–220, 251
Council of Four 38
crisis of October, 1961 242–4
Cuban Missile Crisis 196–203, 238, 239
Dawes Plan 57
deterioration of Japan relationship 19–20 (CH11)*
entry into the First World War 40 (CH10)*
Great Depression of the 1930s 85, 87–100, 275–6, 284, 375–85, 390, 392–3
ICBMs 237
ILO 85
immigration, 1861–1940 368
intolerance 367–73
    Black Americans 369
    immigration 367–8
    Ku Klux Klan 370
    race riots 370–1
    'Red Scare' 369
    religious 371–3
Japanese offensive, Second World War 24–25 (CH11)*
League of Nations 74, 75
Lend–Lease scheme 147, 148, 154, 40 (CH11)*
life in Nazi Germany 294
Mutually Assured Destruction 196
NATO formation 174
New Deal (Roosevelt) 385–93
Olympic Games boycotts 251
Pearl Harbor 20 (CH11)*, 21–23 (CH11)*
population, 1920 367
Reichstag fire 279
Solidarity (*Solidarnosc*) 245
and Soviet expansionism 164–70
Supreme Court 371, 388, 391–2
Treaty of Versailles 31–8, 45, 107
USSR's control over Eastern Europe 229, 235
victory of Allied Powers 22
war at sea 31 (CH10)*, 32 (CH10)*
Washington, D.C. Vietnam War Memorial 204
Watergate scandal 212
Weimar Republic 268
see also Cold War; *individual US leaders...*
UNSC (United Nations Security Council) 163, 189
Upper Silesia miner's strikes and riots 246
uprisings
    Weimar Republic 262, 263–4
    see also protest; Revolution; strikes

van der Lubbe, Marinus 279
Vanzetti, Bartolomeo 369
'Velvet Revolution' ('Gentle Revolution') 251
Versailles Treaty *see* Treaty of Versailles
veterans and US government 384
vetoes 72
Vichy France 9–10 (CH11)*, 20 (CH11)*
Victor Emmanuel III (Ling) 38 (CH11)*
Vienna Summit 1961 197, 240

Viet Minh and Viet Cong 204, 209, 210, 214
    see also Vietnam War
Vietnam War, 1955–75 203–15
    background 203–6
    effects of 213–14
    loss of the USA 214
    Lyndon B. Johnson 208, 209, 214
    My Lai Massacre 210
    reasons for US involvement 206–8
    Richard Nixon 210–13
    US tactics 209
    Vietnamisation 210
Vilna crisis, 1920 77
Violetta Women's Club 288
Volkswagen ('people's car') 284, 285
Volstead Act (Prohibition) 373
vom Rath, Ernst 289
von Bismark, Otto 14
von Falkenhayn, Erich 15 (CH10)*
von Galen, August 282
von Hindenburg, Paul 268, 276, 277, 278, 279, 280, 283, 293
    biography 269
    and Erich von Ludendorff 41 (CH10)*, 43 (CH10)*
von Kahr, Gustav 270, 280
von Lettow-Vorbeck, Paul (General) 22 (CH10)*
von Lossow, Otto (General) 270
von Ludendorff, Erich (General) 269, 270, 41 (CH10)*, 42 (CH10)*, 43 (CH10)*
von Lüttwitz, Heinrich Freiherr (General) 263
von Moltke, Helmuth 283, 4 (CH10)*, 6 (CH10)*
von Papen, Franz 277, 278, 287
von Rennenkampf, Paul (Russian Commander) 35 (CH10)*
von Ribbentrop, Joachim 132, 133
von Scheer (Admiral) 29 (CH10)*, 30 (CH10)*
von Schleicher, Kurt 277, 278, 280
von Schlieffen, Alfred (Count) 3–6 (CH10)*
von Stauffenberg, Claus (Colonel) 283
voting rights 374

Wake Island 25 (CH11)*
Wałęsa, Lech 246, 247, 248
Wall Street, Glass-Steagal Act 386
Wall Street Crash 1929 275–6, 284, 375–85
    'Black Thursday', 1929 376
    causes/consequences 375–85
    economic effects 378
    financial effects 378
    social consequences 379–83
    speculation 375–9
    see also Great Depression of the 1930s
Wannsee Conference 295–6, 34 (CH11)*
war
    of attrition 7 (CH10)*
    break down of 'Grand Alliance' in 1945 148
    civil wars 75, 185, 323–30, 337, 369
    crimes trials 43 (CH11)*, 44 (CH11)*, 46 (CH11)*
    economy and life in Nazi Germany 294
    new methods, First World War 10–14 (CH10)*
    and peace 7–8
    stalemates 18, 192, 3–18 (CH10)*
    trenches 10, 6 (CH10)*, 7–10 (CH10)*
    War Communism, Russia 328
    'War Guilt' 40, 49
    see also individual conflicts...

Index

War Powers Act 1973 214
Warsaw
    ghettoes 294
    impact of German occupation 33 (CH11)*
Warsaw Pact 146, 175, 225, 227, 231, 234, 235, 236
wartime and post-war conferences 150–6
    see also individual conferences...
wartime treaties 28
    see also individual treaties...
Washington, D.C. Vietnam War Memorial 204
Watergate scandal 212
wealth 4
    nobility/rich society 315, 390
    see also peasantry; poverty
Wehrmacht (army) 294, 2 (CH11)*, 3 (CH11)*
    attempts at conquering Britain 11 (CH11)*
    Battle of Stalingrad, 1941 16–18 (CH11)*
    Blitz attacks 13 (CH11)*, 26 (CH11)*, 27 (CH11)*
    Jewish people in Poland 294
    surrender of France 8 (CH11)*
    Wannsee Conference 295
Weimar chancellors, 1930–33 276
Weimar Republic 52–4, 56, 259–69
    black populations 290
    constitution 260
    establishment and 1918 Revolution 259
    hyperinflation 265–6
    left-wing politics 262
    Munich (Beer Hall) Putsch 52, 56, 270–1
    occupation of the Ruhr 265, 266
    recovery after 1923 267–8
    Treaty of Versailles 260–6
welfare state(s) 379–80
West Germany
    Berlin Blockade 171–5
    see also Berlin Wall
Western Front 25
    breakout of the First World War 13

France, 1917 19
    stalemate 3–18 (CH10)*
White, Alma Bridewell (bishop) 372
White Army (Russian Civil War) 327, 328
White Nationalism 370, 371, 372
    see also Ku Klux Klan
White Rose Group 282
Wilhelm II (Kaiser) 14, 5 (CH10)*, 43 (CH10)*, 44 (CH10)*
Wilhelmshaven mutiny, Germany 1918 44 (CH10)*
Wilson, Woodrow 31–8, 45, 47
    Anschluss 117
    collapse of Central Powers 45 (CH10)*
    entry of the US into First World War 40 (CH10)*
    Fourteen Points 32–3, 117
    Kiel Mutiny and the German Revolution 44 (CH10)*
    war at sea 32 (CH10)*
    Weimar Republic 261
The Withdrawal from Dunkirk, June 1940 (Cundall) 7 (CH11)*
Witte, Sergei 308, 312
Wojtyłłam, Karol (Pope John Paul II) 245
women
    effects of Joseph Stalin's economic policy 344, 345
    life in Nazi Germany 294
    Nazi policies, and family 293
    new industries of the 1920s 359, 360
    pacifism 15
    as part of workforce 21
    race riots in the US 370
    Revolution of March 1917, Russia 317, 318
    roles in the 1920s, USA 374
    voting rights 374
wool industry 362
    see also cotton industry
workers

assembly line workers 357, 358
automotive industry 357, 358
government policy after 1905 Russian Revolution 314–15
industrialisation 6, 342–3
Joseph Stalin's economic policy 344
miners (and protests) 246, 362
policies of the Nazi Party 293
The Purges, Russia 336
Roosevelt's New Deal 388, 391
Russia's social structure 306
social structure in Russia 306
Solidarity (*Solidarnosc*) 244–8
Tsarism and St Petersburg 309
women in the workforce 21
    see also agriculture; strikes
Works Progress Administration (WPA) 388
world population by region, 1900–2000 3

Yalta Conference, February 1945 151–3, 156, 176
Yorktown (carrier) 25 (CH11)*
Young Plan 272–5
youth
    effects of Joseph Stalin's economic policy 344
    and Nazi Germany 282, 291, 292
Ypres, Belgium 17
    see also Battle of Ypres
Yudenich, Nikolai (General) 328
Yugoslavia
    Josef Tito 222, 223
    under USSR control 163

Zeppelin raids 20, 21, 11 (CH10)*
Zimmermann, Arthur 40 (CH10)*
Zinoviev, Gregory 323, 333, 334, 336
Zorin, Valerian 201
Zyklon B 295, 35 (CH11)*